Practical Cryptology and Web Security

Visit the *Practical Cryptology and Web Security* Companion
Website at **www.pearsoned.co.uk/yuen** to find valuable
student learning material including:

- Sample contents
- Source code for program examples from each chapter

Practical Cryptology and Web Security

PK Yuen

PEARSON

Addison
Wesley

Harlow, England • London • New York • Boston • San Francisco • Toronto
Sydney • Tokyo • Singapore • Hong Kong • Seoul • Taipei • New Delhi
Cape Town • Madrid • Mexico City • Amsterdam • Munich • Paris • Milan

Pearson Education Limited

Edinburgh Gate
Harlow
Essex CM20 2JE
England

and Associated Companies throughout the world

Visit us on the World Wide Web at:
www.pearsoned.co.uk

First published 2006

ISBN-13: 978-0-32126-333-9
ISBN-10: 0-32126-333-2

British Library Cataloguing-in-Publication Data
A catalogue record for this book is available from the British Library

Library of Congress Cataloging-in-Publication Data
Yuen, P. K.
    Practical cryptology and Web security / P.K. Yuen.
        p. cm.
    Includes index.
    ISBN 0–321–26333–2 (alk. paper)
    1. Cryptography.   2. Web sites—Security measures.   I. Title.

TK5102.94.Y83 2006
005.8′2—dc22
                                        2005048662

10 9 8 7 6 5 4 3 2 1
10 09 08 07 06

Typeset in 9.5/12pt Palatino by 35

Printed and bound in Great Britain by Biddles Ltd, King's Lynn

The publisher's policy is to use paper manufactured from sustainable forests.

To Arthur and Rody

Contents

Supporting resources

Visit **www.pearsoned.co.uk/yuen** to find valuable online resources:

- Sample contents
- Source code for program examples from each chapter

For more information please contact your local Pearson Education sales representative or visit **www.pearsoned.co.uk/yuen**

Preface

This book is about practical cryptology and security skills on the World Wide Web (Web), providing an instant course and a reference guide for university students, Web designers, young programmers and industry professionals to apply cryptographic techniques directly to applications. There is no encryption/decryption background assumed. By keeping the abstract theory and mathematics of cryptology to a minimum, students or readers with basic level of mathematics and some knowledge of HTML design or programming should be able to finish the book smoothly.

All major encryption algorithms (or ciphers) are systematically covered, and implemented with Web technologies and Web pages, including:

- one-way ciphers: UNIX Crypt, MD5, MD5Crypt and SHA;

- block ciphers: DES, Tri-DES, CAST128, Blowfish, RC6 and AES;

- stream ciphers: OTP, RC4, ISAAC and SEAL2;

- public-key ciphers: Diffie–Hellman, ElGamal, RSA and elliptic curves.

In some cases, coding optimization is also discussed and illustrated with examples. Studying the coding optimization of algorithms such as DES and AES imparts better knowledge of the structure of algorithms and takes the render one step closer to professional implementations and algorithmic designs.

The subject of cryptology relates to attacks as well as to encryption/decryption. Crypto-attacks such as brute-force (Try-Them-All) are also introduced and implemented in an early chapter of the book (Chapter 2), so that security risk can be assessed in terms of the time and computational resources needed to crack a cryptographic system.

The contents and materials of each chapter are application oriented, covering some of the main objectives of cryptology, such as message confidentiality, authentication, data integrity and non-repudiation. From message encryption/decryption, password schemes, HTTP authentications, digital signatures, certificates and secure emails to SSL security, HTTPS secure Web sites and digital contracts (XML digital contracts), over 120 fully working examples are provided; many of them are projects from industries, forming a complete series of security applications on the Internet and World Wide Web.

All examples are presented in cut-and-paste format, which can be reused in your applications. Together with more than 300 illustrations and screenshots, both cryptographic encryption/decryption skills and security on the Web are demonstrated step by step.

Acknowledgements

First, my deepest gratitude is devoted to my friends, colleagues and individuals dedicated for this project. These include David Dillon, Cormac Lucas, Arthur Yuen, Danielle Pacey, Darren Ricks, Tench Wong, Richard Smyth, and Charlie Yuen. Their contributions, hard work, valuable feedback, constructive suggestions, understanding and encouragement were crucial in making this book possible. In particular, I pay tribute to Arthur and Charlie for their involvement in testing my programs and code. Their programming experiences were extremely helpful to me at a critical time during development of this book. Special thanks go to Dan Levin, my colleague and business partner, for his full support of this project.

I greatly appreciate the contributions and professionalism of the editorial team at Pearson Education, including Simon Plumtree, Kate Brewin, Owen Knight, Tim Parker, Tony Clappison, Lionel Browne and Gary Hall for their long hours, efforts and excellent work, which contributed greatly to the quality of this book. It was truly a great joy to work with them.

Publisher's acknowledgements

We are grateful to the following for permission to reproduce copyright material:

Figures 1.03, 2.21, 2.23 and 2.25 are Screenshots taken from the Netscape browser. Netscape Communicator browser window© 2005 Netscape Communications Corporation. Used with permission. Netscape Communications has not authorized, sponsored, endorsed, or approved this publication and is not responsible for its content; Figures 1.04; 2.7 and 10.05 are Screenshots taken from the Opera browser and are used by kind permission of Opera Software ASA; Figure 1.24 is a Screenshot taken from PKZIP software. Copyright © 2003 PKWARE, Inc. and its licensors. All rights reserved. PKZIP is a registered trademark of PKWARE, Inc.; Figures 7.07a and 7.07b are Screenshots taken from Javascript Chaos Engine. Copyright © 2005 Syntropy; Microsoft product screenshots reprinted with permission from Microsoft Corporation.

1

Basic security skills on the World Wide Web

1.1 An introduction to network security

1.1.1 Secure and insecure networks

Before the International Business Machines Corporation (IBM) launched the first version of the *Personal Computer* at the beginning of the 1980s, computers were mainly expensive mainframes and workstations. Not many organizations could afford to own one. Computer networking was a luxury beyond the reach of ordinary people, households or even medium sized companies. Only government and big companies, such as financial institutes, could have a number of them networked together to form a proprietary network. This kind of networking still exists and is very much alive among big organizations such as banks. They use it for centralized database information such as accounts, fund transfer and transactions. The physical links and private data transmission of these networks established an essential secure environment for the operations and business activities. Since all terminals connected to the network are known, users and operations can be traced and logged. Business secrecy and security is achieved. These kinds of network are generally referred to as 'secure' or 'private' networks. For this type of network environment, security is mainly an internal (or human) affair and not a serious problem on a global scale.

Personal computers, the Internet and the World Wide Web opened the floodgates for affordable computer networking and created a new model for companies, big or small, to conduct business online. Twenty-four hours a day and seven days a week, connecting people all over the globe for business is not a problem any more. If you have something to sell, buyers can come to you instantly from all over the world through the Internet. The Internet is, basically, a vast collection of interconnected networks that all use the TCP/IP protocol. This protocol specifies the same structure and data transmission, linking machines and computers together and forming a global and open network.

A document (or Web page) written in HyperText Markup Language (HTML) or Extensible HyperText Markup Language (XHTML) can be displayed by any machine on the Internet equipped with a Web browser such as Microsoft Internet Explorer (IE), Netscape (NS) or Opera. The contents of a Web document (or Web page) can be text, graphics, images, sound and music, movies, games or any combination of these. The entire community on the Internet and all the Web documents is referred as the World Wide Web (or Web). The Web is an ideal place to publicize and exchange information to reach the global network population. More importantly, the Web is an ideal place to conduct business online. All buying, selling and even transactions can be completed within minutes. All of a sudden, we have a global economy reaching every corner of the world. This is the power – bringing people and business together via global networking using the public protocol, HyperText Transport Protocol (HTTP).

However, when the same network configuration, languages and data transmission protocol are used around the world, activity on the Internet operates in an insecure environment. In other words, the security provided by the private network no longer exists. Basically, you don't know who is connecting to your network site. The identity of your customer or supplier is difficult to trace. In general, from a security point of view, the Internet is a place where anybody can be everybody. While countries and international communities are struggling to impose regulations on Internet use, very little trust can be built (legally built) among online businesses. Again, all of a sudden, online frauds are everywhere.

Since Web pages can be read by any computer with a Web browser, orders can be placed by almost anyone. For example, if someone orders goods from your Web site, do you know or trust his/her identity? Do you trust his/her credit card number? Even if you can get the money from the credit card company, how do you know you are not charging someone else illegally?

Similarly, as a customer do you trust the online company when you order something on the Internet you haven't heard of? We have come to an age when even thieves are doing online business!

Even for personal purposes, do you trust your Internet service provider (ISP) to deliver your emails and important messages to your bank and lawyer? How do you know that the instructions to your banker have not been altered? Also, how can your banker identify you from your email? Would you believe it if you are told, 'We are going to offer you a signed digital contract on the Web'? All these issues raise a series of critical security threats for the Internet and Web community. Without proper solutions to these problems, it is hard to see how we can establish trust and accept our responsibility seriously.

In order to address these security issues and offer protection over such an insecure network as the Internet, cryptography (part of cryptology) techniques are required. Cryptography techniques, including encryption and decryption, can provide a protection layer between you and the receiving person (see Figure 1.1).

Fig. 1.1 Security on the Internet and World Wide Web using cryptography

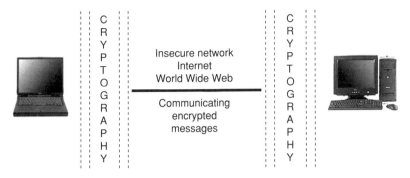

Encryption offers information security so that messages can be transmitted safely over the insecure Internet and Web environment. Only the authorized receiving end can decrypt and obtain the original message. With cryptography, secure networks can be achieved in almost any network environment. In fact, modern cryptography techniques and their applications go far beyond encryption/decryption. They can be used to address and provide solutions to all the security issues mentioned earlier in this section. In order to have a understanding of the subject, let's begin with the meaning and terminology of cryptography.

1.1.2   Digital cryptography on the Web

Cryptography is about information security. Information security has existed for more than 4000 years. In ancient civilizations, such as Egypt, Rome and China, people were fully aware of the importance of data secrecy and security. Important messages were usually disguised from anyone for whom they were not intended. For example, important messages from the king or military orders were often sealed and encrypted with symbolic substitution methods or written with special ink only visible under heat. In ancient Rome, messages from the emperor were sometimes produced shifting characters by 3 from the character table. This coding method is known as 'Caesar coding'. In terms of English, it is equivalent to changing 'A' to 'D' and 'B' to 'E'. In this case, the readable 'SECRET MESSAGE' turns out to be 'VHFUHW PHVVDJH'.

In order to guarantee delivery, the message was accompanied by a trusted messenger and guarded heavily for further protection. These security measures are the ancestors of all the encryptions, or more precisely cryptography, used today. In particular, in modern terms they illustrate the following important aspects related to information security.

- Confidentiality – make the message available only to those intended.

- Data integrity – make sure no alterations can be made.

- Authentication – proof of data and entity identification.

- Non-repudiation – protection against false denial.

These are the primary objectives of cryptography. Cryptography can be considered to be a subject worthy of study as well as providing information secrecy, integrity and identity. In our Internet and Web environment, mathematical formulae and algorithms are used to encrypt and decrypt data (i.e. digital cryptography). Furthermore, in addition to encryption/decryption, the objectives of cryptography also include how to establish trust in the message itself and in the identity of the sender.

It is believed that the systematic study of cryptography before 1960 was largely classified research and development carried out by governments with a rigorous military nature. This is due to the fact that cryptography and its associated knowledge ensured the secrecy and accuracy of information and was vital for many national security services.

Handling both true and false information, in military terms, is generally considered to be 'intelligence'. In many cases, it can determine the result of a battle. It was certainly an important factor in the outcome of the last two world wars and will continue to play an important part in future military affairs and national security activities.

It is not difficult to realize that secret message transmissions, such as the location of a submarine and missile launch sequences, must be heavily guarded by the strongest cryptographic protection using passwords (or digital keys). Messages encrypted by these keys and methods are so secure that if you had a billion computers each performing a billion instructions per second, you would not be able to decrypt them before the end of this universe. This feature is referred to as 'strong cryptography'.

One thing you may not know is that you can benefit from this kind of strong cryptography protection in daily life. Whether for personal or business purposes, you can encrypt your daily emails with strong cryptography by clicking a button. You can also perform identity checking of the sender and identify yourself. The data verification techniques guarantee that no one can alter or modify your message without being traced. In addition to data integrity, this can be used to protect your downloadable software against viruses and alterations. For Web communication, you can establish a secure Web connection with strong cryptography which is transparent to the user. The confidentiality of your Web site and business transactions are protected at a similar level to the military standard.

In order to practice information security or cryptography on the Internet and Web, the first thing you need is a browser with security capabilities. In this book, we have assumed that the following browsers are used:

Fig. 1.2   Internet Explorer Version 6

- Microsoft Internet Explorer version 6 or higher – Figure 1.2;

- Netscape 7 or higher – Figure 1.3;

- Opera 6 or higher – Figure 1.4.

Fig. 1.3   Netscape 7.0

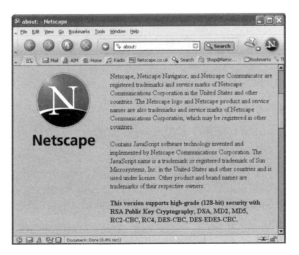

Source: Netscape Communicator browser window © 2005 Netscape Communications Corporation. Used with permission. Netscape Communications has not authorized, sponsored, endorsed, or approved this publication and is not responsible for its content.

Fig. 1.4 Opera Version 6

These browsers are known to have 128-bit cipher (or encryption) strength and are fully capable of accepting, handling and interpreting the following cryptography features:

- 128-bit encryption/decryption;
- security alert;
- digital keys and signatures;
- Certificates from Certificate Authority (CA);
- Secure Sockets Layers (SSL);
- Transport Layer Security (TLS);
- Hypertext Transport Protocol with SSL Security (HTTPS).

Don't worry too much about the security terms and functions at this point. We will cover and use them step by step. With these features, much encryption/decryption, data integrity and identity authentication on the Web can be implemented and put into practical use. Also, by using online encryption/decryption between the browser and the Web site, you can establish a real-time secure connection in the insecure Web environment connecting your online business to Web clients. The established security is so strong that it is comparable to the military standard. That means it is almost impossible for a third party or intruder to break into the Web connection and interfere with the Web dialog between your Web site and clients.

In order to understand how encrypted messages are communicated on the Web environment, a basic understanding of the structure of the Web, or more precisely the browser and server dialog, is necessary.

1.2 The Web browser–server dialog

1.2.1 The structure and configurations of the Web

The Internet can be considered to be a huge number of connections (wire or wireless) connecting computers around the world forming a global network. Computers armed with Internet software are able to communicate with each other. Among all the Internet software, the Web browser, such as Microsoft Internet Explorer, Netscape and Opera, is a clear winner. Many people may even think that Web browsers and their related applications are conquering every corner of the Internet. One of the most important activities of a Web browser is to execute the so-called HyperText Transport Protocol (HTTP) command to request a document (usually an HTML/XHTML file) from another computer on the Internet. For example, when you issue the following command on your browser software

```
http://www.pws-ex.com/abc.html
```

you are requesting the file abc.html from the remote computer on the Internet with address (or URL) www.pws-ex.com. The returned document (usually in HTML format) is displayed in the browser window. If the page you are requesting contains a hyperlink to another computer (or server) and you have activated the link, a request will be sent to the new server. As a result, the browser will display the newly returned document.

The machine requesting documents on the Internet is referred to as the client. The computer on the Internet delivering the HTML/XHTML document is called the server (or HTTP server). In order to deliver HTML/XHTML documents, server software such as Internet Information Services (IIS) or Apache must be running and listening in the server at all times. Figure 1.5 shows a Web operation in action.

One of the major features of the Web is the use of HTML/XHTML documents. This language contains a rich set of formatting elements specifying how a document should be handled and opens up endless possibilities for designers to develop documents to be displayed by browsers. HTML/XHTML documents reside within the Web community and are therefore known as Web pages.

The Web page is one of the central objects and characteristics of this book. Many security measures are implemented as Web pages and put into direct and practical use. However, it is not our intention to provide a full and intensive study of them. In fact, a basic understanding of HTML design and scripting, such as ECMAScript or JavaScript, is assumed. Our goal is to integrate strong protection into the insecure Web environment. For this reason, only those HTML/XHTML elements related to Web security and applications will be introduced.

Now let's consider how Web pages are communicated between browsers and servers.

Fig. 1.5 Web configuration

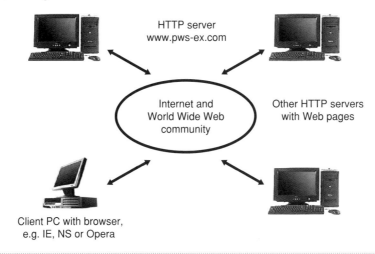

HTTP server
www.pws-ex.com

Internet and
World Wide Web
community

Other HTTP servers
with Web pages

Client PC with browser,
e.g. IE, NS or Opera

1.2.2 Web browser and server dialog

One of the best ways to understand how the Web really works is to examine the actual browser and server dialog. As a simple demonstration example, consider an HTML document ex01-01.htm (all these 'ex' files, and 'lx' files, are presented in distinctive boxes in the book) in the server www.pws-ex.com.

```
Example: ex01-01.htm - A simple page

1:  <html>
2:  <head>
3:      <title>Example: ex01-01.htm</title>
4:  </head>
5:  <body style="font-family:arial;font-size:28pt;text-align:center">
6:    I Know How The Web <br> Works Now
7:  </body>
8:  </html>
```

This is a basic document (or page) written in HTML language and will display a simple message on your browser screen. The building blocks of all HTML documents are the markup language commands (sometimes called Tag names or elements). The HTML language element <html> in line 1 is to ask the browser to start processing an HTML page. After the HTML header, there is a head and a title element. The text between the title tag names (<title>) will be displayed as the title bar of your browser. The element <body> in line 5 sets the beginning of the content of your page. Line 6 is the message you wish to display. Inside the body element <body>, some Cascading Style Sheet (CSS) settings are defined. Basically, CSS is a feature of HTML to provide the formatting style and controls of the document. In this case, the style attributes are:

```
style="font-family:arial;font-size:28pt;text-align:center"
```

This statement gives instructions to the browser to use the Arial font and size 28pt (28 points) to display the message(s) defined in line 6. The CSS value text-align:center is used to align the message at the centre of the browser screen. The line break element <br> used in line 6 will generate a new line on the document.

The forward slash in line 7 indicates the closure of the <body> element. Line 8 denotes the closure of the HTML, and hence ends the page.

HTML is a text-based language so that it can be displayed, printed and edited directly using your favourite editor. If you type this code (without the line numbers) and upload it to the server www.pws-ex.com, you can request the document using the following command on your browser:

```
http://www.pws-ex.com/ex01-01.htm
```

This page will be displayed in your browser window as shown in Figure 1.6.

Fig. 1.6 ex01-01.htm

Again, this book is not an introductory text on HTML or XHTML and we will not go through every aspect of XHTML/HTML and page design. However, Web pages and some knowledge about scripts will be required in order to understand and use this book effectively. Elementary experience with the C/C++ language is helpful but not essential. Let's move on to how the Web really works.

Consider the following HTTP command to request a document.

```
http://www.pws-ex.com/ex01-01.htm
```

This command will send a request to the site www.pws-ex.com (the URL or address of an HTTP server) and ask for the document named ex01-01.htm. A classic message that your browser sends is shown in 1x01-01.txt.

```
Example: 1x01-01.txt

 1: GET /ex01-01.htm HTTP/1.1
 2: Host: www.pws-ex.com
 3: Accept: text/html
 4: Accept: image/gif
    ....
    ....
30: Accept:
31: User-Agent:        ((Your browser software ID))
32: From:              ((Your Email Address ID))
34:    * a blank line *
```

Line 1 indicates which file the client wants and announces that the communication is HTTP version 1.1. Line 2 contains the host (or server) name. This communication relies on a series of Accept keywords in MIME (Multipurpose Internet Mail Extension) format. The text in line 3, text/html, indicates that the browser is expecting an HTML document in return. The text in line 4, image/gif, means that the browser is also happy to accept any image in gif format. The blank line (line 34) at the end identifies the end of the request.

The server is www.pws-ex.com and it will respond with a similar message as shown in 1x01-02.txt.

In line 1, the Web server agrees to use HTTP for communication and the status 200 identifier indicates the successful completion of the whole request. After some HTTP system variables, the statement Content-type: text/html in line 6 is to confirm that the document return will indeed be an HTML document (or page). From this dialog, you can see that the entire HTML page (i.e. ex01-01.htm) is transmitted to the browser after the 'blank line' in line 8. This style and transmission format is specified by the so-called HTTP protocol. The browser will finally be able to interpret this page and display it as shown in Figure 1.6.

```
Example: lx01-02.txt

 1: HTTP/1.1 200 OK
 2: Date: Wednesday, 13-Oct-2004 13:04:12 GMT
 3: Server:    ((Your Server Information))
 4: MIME-version: 1.0
 5: Last-modified: Wednesday, 13-Oct-2004 11:33:16 GMT
 6: Content-type: text/html
 7: Content-length: 195
 8:       * a blank line *
 9: <html>
10: <head>
11:       <title>Example: ex01-01.htm</title>
12: </head>
13: <body style="font-family:arial;font-size:28pt;text-align:center">
14:   I Know How The Web <br /> Works Now
15: </body>
16: </html>
```

This browser–server dialog is important in understanding how the Web behaves and is sometimes referred to as the 'canonical client–server interaction'. It is the foundation for all technologies involving interaction between browser and servers, including security.

1.2.3   My first page with security

From the dialog in lx01-02.txt you can see that the communication is mainly character-based and can be easily read by everyone armed with the same HTTP protocol application. In other words, the raw format of the HTTP protocol is an insecure environment and has no security at all. In this case, you may need to apply your own security measures for data protection. Consider the Web page generated by ex01-02.htm.

```
Example: ex01-02.htm – My first page with security

1: <html>
2: <head>
3:     <title> My First Page With Security: ex01-02.htm</title>
4: </head>
5: <body style="font-family:arial;font-size:28pt;text-align:center">
6:   L Nqrz Krz Wkh Vhfxulwb <br> Rq Wkh Zhe Zrunv Qrz
7: </body>
8: </html>
```

This page is similar to example `ex01-01.htm` except that the message in line 6 is disguised (or encrypted). When this page is requested by the following HTTP command

```
http://www.pws-ex.com/ex01-02.htm
```

the same browser–server process as described above is used. In particular, the server will return the entire Web page to the browser. Since the encrypted message is transmitted back to the browser, you will have a display as shown in Figure 1.7. If the page is hijacked by an intruder through the browser–server dialog, the security of the message is not compromised.

This is a simple example. Basically we have performed a character transformation on the message. It is easy to find out that we have changed 'A' to 'D' and 'B' to 'E'. It is not difficult to work out that the original message is:

```
I Know How The Security <br> On The Web Works Now
```

This encryption is, in fact, the Caesar code mentioned in Section 1.1.2. Sometimes, browser and server generate encrypted messages at run time with an agreed encryption method to increase security. They are transmitted and supported by the browser–server dialog. This example demonstrates one point – provided the encryption method is strong enough, messages can be protected and transmitted via the World Wide Web.

Since most security issues involve scripting and programming on the Web, we need a more disciplined language which is technically compatible with HTML. For this reason, we generally use XHTML as the fundamental language for Web pages.

Fig. 1.7   `ex01-02.htm`

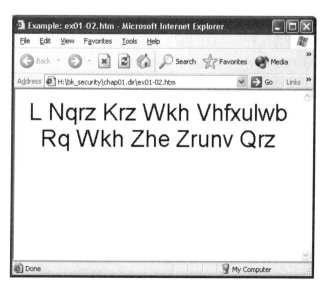

1.2.4 Using HTML and migrating to XHTML

By the time you read this, some of you may already be familiar with XHTML as recommended by the World Wide Web Consortium (W3C). Indeed, by bringing a strict programming style, strong discipline and XML compatibility to HTML pages, XHTML is a more effective environment for dealing with the advancing Web technologies we are facing today, including security and cryptography. Following this standard and W3C's recommendation, Web pages in this book are in XHTML format. Since HTML and XHTML are almost identical from a practical point of view, we generally use .htm as the file extension.

To convert an HTML page into XHTML is not difficult. The first thing you have to do is replace the html element, `<html>`, of an HTML page by the four lines in `1x01-03.txt`.

```
Example: 1x01-03.txt - My first XHTML page with security

1: <?xml version="1.0" encoding="iso-8859-1"?>
2: <!DOCTYPE html PUBLIC "-//W3C//DTD XHTML 1.0 Transitional//EN"
3:    "http://www.w3.org/TR/xhtml1/DTD/xhtml1-transitional.dtd">
4: <html xmlns="http://www.w3.org/1999/xhtml" xml:lang="en"
   lang="en">
```

This is the recommended XHTML header from the W3C authority and we will use it at the top of almost all Web pages in this book.

Line 1 specifies the document as XML version 1.0 with character set as Latin-1/ Western European. In many cases, this is the only requirement for a well-formed XML page. Including this statement will ensure that all XHTML pages are confirmed to XML standard and they are all well-formed XML documents. Lines 2 and 3 define the Document Type Definition (DTD) as xhtml1.0 transitional. Line 4 specifies the `xmlns` (XML name space). This header will make sure that the document will be displayed properly on dedicated XML software.

Since most XHTML pages are practically compatible with HTML, to migrate an HTML page to XHTML is not difficult. In general, you can follow the basic steps below.

1 Replace the HTML header `<html>` with the XHTML header as in `1x01-03.txt`.

2 Use lower case for all elements.

3 All elements should be closed (empty elements such as `<br>` should be replaced by `<br />`). This is why XHTML pages only have elements.

4 All attributes should be quoted (e.g. `height="100" width="130"`).

5 Stop using deprecated HTML elements such as `<font>` and replace with the CSS style.

These simple guidelines will help you to convert from HTML to XHTML structure and lay a strong Web programming foundation. We will use these conventions for Web design and programming throughout this book.

For our first XHTML document, consider `ex01-03.htm`.

```
Example: ex01-03.htm - My first XHTML page

 1: <?xml version="1.0" encoding="iso-8859-1"?>
 2: <!DOCTYPE html PUBLIC "-//W3C//DTD XHTML 1.0 Transitional//EN"
 3:   "http://www.w3.org/TR/xhtml1/DTD/xhtml11-transitional.dtd">
 4: <html xmlns="http://www.w3.org/1999/xhtml" xml:lang="en"
      lang="en">
 5: <head>
 6:      <title> My First XHTML Page: ex01-03.htm</title>
 7: </head>
 8: <body style="font-family:arial;font-size:28pt;text-align:center;
 9:   background:#000088;color:#ffff00">
10:   <br />Practical Web Security<br />
11:   <img alt="pic" src="line1.gif" height="7"
      width="450" /><br /><br />
12:   Message: <br />
13:     Qiix Qi Ex 7tq
14: </body>
15: </html>
```

Lines 1–4 are the XHTML header mentioned in `lx01-03.txt`. As recommended by the W3C authority, CSS is used to set the formatting style (line 8). In this case, we have set the background color as dark blue (`background:#000088`) and text color as yellow (`color:#ffff00`). Since the line break element `<br>` in HTML has no end tag (empty element), `<br />` is used to reflect that we are using the W3C XHTML recommendation. After the main title in line 10, an image element `<img>` is defined in line 11,

```
<img alt="pic" src="line1.gif" height="7" width="450" />
```

This image is a long graphical line with dimensions `height=7` pixels and `width=450` pixels. Since image element `<img>` is an empty element, a forward slash is added at the end. As recommended by the XHTML standard, all image elements should have the `alt` attribute. When the picture is not available for any reason, the text message 'pic' is displayed to prevent confusion. In line 13, an encrypted message is included. A screenshot of this page is shown in Figure 1.8.

Fig. 1.8 My first XHTML page

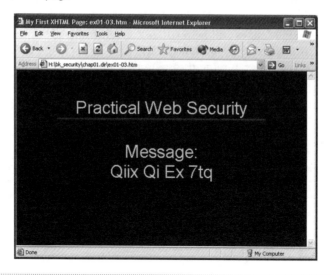

Yes, you are right – the encrypted message is another example of Caesar code with a different forward shifting. By shifting back the character by four, the original message is

```
Meet Me At 3pm
```

From the construction of the browser–server dialog, we know that this entire XHTML page will be returned to the browser. The encrypted message, and hence the security of the page, is preserved on the Web environment and network transmission.

By today's standard, encryptions of this type are very simple and provide no security at all when under attack (see Section 1.5). In fact, with modern cryptography techniques, message encryptions today are far more sophisticated and can discourage the most determined intruder armed with the most powerful computing resources in the world. Despite all the terminologies, the intention of encryption is to manipulate messages with specific purposes. Now, let's consider some basic skills to manipulate messages and maintain security on the Web.

1.3   Web page skills for message manipulation and security

In this section, some practical skills for manipulating messages on the Web are introduced. These skills will be used from time to time throughout this book, forming one of the fundamental building blocks on Web security. We begin with number systems used on the Web. Web pages are constructed to display and perform conversions between decimal, hexadecimal, octal and binary values. As a direct use of these number systems, the American Standard Code for Information Interchange (ASCII) and, more importantly, the Unicode from Unicode Consortium (www.unicode.org) are introduced. With Unicode, numerical representation of any message in any language in the world is possible, and it can be done in an elegant way. In other words, security or message protection can be performed on data that are independent of languages and platforms. As a direct application, an implementation of Caesar code is also presented. In order to perform all these in the Web environment, the more intensive XHTML language and ECMAScript (or JavaScript) are used in this section.

1.3.1   Number systems used on the Web

Basically, a computer is a machine which operates only on numbers. They can only manipulate and understand digital values called binary numbers. Together with binary, three other number systems are popular and used by computer programmers:

- decimal number system (base 10);

- binary number system (base 2);

- octal number system (base 8);

- hexadecimal number system (base 16).

For a simple example, consider the integer 127 represented in the decimal number system. The decimal number system has 10 symbols, one for each digit: 0, 1, 2, 3, 4, 5, 6, 7, 8 and 9. For most of us, the decimal system is the one we use for everyday notation and mathematics.

The binary number system, on the other hand, contains only two digits, namely 0 and 1. For example, the value 3 in the decimal system is equivalent to the value 11 in the binary system,

> 3 (decimal) = 11 (binary) and 255 (decimal) = 11111111 (binary)

Since binary systems can be implemented easily in hardware, they are the ideal choice for computer operation. In fact, all the information inside a computer is stored as binary values. However, a binary number, in general, is much longer than the decimal counterpart and cumbersome to work with. Therefore two other systems, namely octal and hexadecimal, are also popular among programmers and in applications on computer systems.

In the octal number system (base 8), eight symbols ranging from 0 to 7 are used. The hexadecimal number system has base 16 and consists of 16 unique symbols: 0, 1, 2, 3, 4, 5, 6, 7, 8, 9, a, b, c, d, e, and f. For example, hexadecimal f represents the value 15 in decimal and ff is 255 in decimal:

255 (decimal) = 377 (Octal) = ff (hexadecimal)

For practical purposes, we are not going to show you how to perform conversions between these number systems. Instead, we will show you how to display, convert and handle them using Web pages.

As a markup language, pure HTML/XHTML coding provides no facilities for handling number system conversions directly. To perform calculations and use different number systems, ECMAScript (or JavaScript) is needed. Consider ex01-04.htm.

```
Example: ex01-04.htm = Number systems on the Web

 1: <?xml version="1.0" encoding="iso-8859-1"?>
 2: <!DOCTYPE html PUBLIC "-//W3C//DTD XHTML 1.0 Transitional//EN"
 3:    "http://www.w3.org/TR/xhtml1/DTD/xhtml1-transitional.dtd">
 4: <html xmlns="http://www.w3.org/1999/xhtml" xml:lang="en"
    lang="en">
 5: <head>
 6:    <title> Number Systems on the Web - ex01-04.htm</title>
 7: </head>
 8: <body style="font-family:arial;font-size:28pt;text-align:center;
 9:    background:#000088;color:#ffff00">
10:    <br />Number Systems On The Web<br />
11:    <img alt="pic" src="line1.gif" height="7"
       width="550" /><br /><br />
12:    <script>
13:       var deci=255;
14:       var hexSt, octSt, binSt;
15:       hexSt = deci.toString(16);
16:       octSt = deci.toString(8);
17:       binSt = deci.toString(2);
18:       document.write("Hexadecimal(255) = " + hexSt + "<br/>");
19:       document.write("Octal (255) = " + octSt + "<br/>");
20:       document.write("Binary(255) = " + binSt + "<br/>");
21:    </script>
22: </body> </html>
```

With the knowledge of XHTML gained from Section 1.2, lines 1–11 are easy to understand. The interesting part of this page is the script block `<script>` defined in lines 12–21. Statements inside the script block will be interpreted by the browser as ECMAScript. ECMAScript (or ECMA262) is the standard scripting language defined by the European Computer Manufacturers Association (ECMA) to provide programming capabilities on HTML/XHTML pages (see http://www.ecma.ch). ECMAScript is widely used and practically compatible with JavaScript.

Line 13 defines a variable called `deci` with decimal value 255. Line 14 defines three variables `hexSt`, `octSt` and `binSt`. They are used to store the hexadecimal, octal and binary representations of the decimal number `deci`. Consider the statement in line 15:

```
hexSt = deci.toString(16)
```

Since variable `deci` contains the value 255 (base 10), the function `deci.toString(16)` will convert this number into a base 16 number (hexadecimal) and store this hexadecimal value in the variable `hexSt` as a string. After the execution of this statement, the text stored in the variable `hexSt` is 'ff'.

Similarly, the statements in lines 16 and 17 are used to convert the value of `deci` into octal and binary representations respectively.

In ECMAScript, the function `document.write()` is used to output a string to the browser for display. For example, the statement in line 18 will output the following XHTML text to the browser:

```
Hexadecimal(255) = ff <br/>
```

Browsers such as IE, NS or Opera will have no problem in displaying this text on your screen. A screenshot of this page in Internet Explorer is shown in Figure 1.9.

Number systems and ECMAScript are two important subjects in this book. We will use them from time to time in the rest of the book.

1.3.2   The ASCII character set

In order to communicate with people, computers store the characters of a language such as English by assigning a number to each character. For example, one of the classic numerical representations of English letters (character code) is the ASCII character set. ASCII is an 8-bit character set defining alphanumeric characters ranging from 0 to 255. Some of the printable ASCII characters related to the English language are listed in Table 1.1.

The table shows the decimal values for a number of ASCII characters. For example, the exclamation mark '!' has the decimal ASCII value of 33. Character 'A' has the ASCII decimal value of 65. The ASCII value of the character 'k' is 107. That is:

A = ASCII (65)   and   k = ASCII (107)

Fig. 1.9 Number systems on the Web

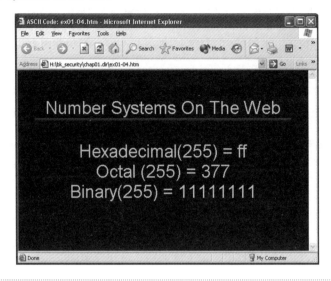

ASCII values can also be represented by other number systems. For example, the ASCII values of characters 'A' and 'k' in hexadecimal are 41 and 6b respectively,

   A = ASCII (0x41)   and   k = ASCII (0x6b)

To distinguish a hexadecimal integer from a decimal, the prefix '0x' is usually appended to the value, as demonstrated in the examples above.

Table 1.1 ASCII character codes

	0	1	2	3	4	5	6	7	8	9
3			space	!	"	#	$	%	&	'
4	(	)	*	+	,	-	.	/	0	1
5	2	3	4	5	6	7	8	9	:	;
6	<	=	>	?	@	A	B	C	D	E
7	F	G	H	I	J	K	L	M	N	O
8	P	Q	R	S	T	U	V	W	X	Y
9	Z	[	\	]	^	_	`	a	b	c
10	d	e	f	g	h	i	j	k	l	m
11	n	o	p	q	r	s	t	u	v	w
12	x	y	z	{			}	~			

With ASCII code, characters and messages can be processed and manipulated easily. For example, in terms of ECMAScript, the following program fragment can be used to print out the characters 'A' and 'k' from their corresponding ASCII code.

```
<script>
 document.write( String.fromCharCode(65) )
 document.write( String.fromCharCode(107) )
</script>
```

The first line instructs the browser that the code is ECMAScript. The function `document.write()` will send the string inside the bracket to the browser. Consider the function

```
String.fromCharCode( 65 )
```

This function returns the character which has ASCII value 65 (i.e. A). Together with the `document.write()` function, character 'A' is displayed.

By using a simple for-loop, the character codes in Table 1.1 can be displayed easily. Consider the following program fragment:

```
<script>
 for (ii=33;ii<127;ii++)
 {
    document.write(String.fromCharCode(ii) + " ")
 }
</script>
```

This is a simple for-loop in ECMAScript. When the variable `ii` takes the value 33, the `String.fromCharCode(33)` returns the character '!'. In order to separate the characters, a space is added at the end (+ " "). The plus sign in ECMAScript is used to concatenate strings. As the variable `ii` runs through the values from 33 to 126, we generate the list of characters as in Table 1.1. Consider `ex01-05.htm`. This is an XHTML page to print out the printable ASCII character set ranging from 33 to 126. As you can see, a simple for-loop is used in lines 14–17 to loop through the ASCII code set. In order to pack the characters together, all characters and the ECMAScript are inside a division element `<div>` with `width=380` pixels (line 12). Note that the attribute `align="center"` in line 8 is for backward compatibility with some older browsers. A screenshot of this example is shown in Figure 1.10.

Example: ex01-05.htm: ASCII character codes

```
1: <?xml version="1.0" encoding="iso-8859-1"?>
2: <!DOCTYPE html PUBLIC "-//W3C//DTD XHTML 1.0 Transitional//EN"
3:     "http://www.w3.org/TR/xhtml1/DTD/xhtml1-transitional.dtd">
4: <html xmlns="http://www.w3.org/1999/xhtml" xml:lang="en"
   lang="en">
5: <head><title>Example: ex01-05.htm</title></head>
6: <body style="font-family:'Courier New';font-weight:bold;
7:       font-size:23pt;text-align:center">
8: <div align="center">

9:  Printable ASCII Character Set <br />
10: (From 33 To 126 Decimal Format)<br /><br />
11:
12: <div style="text-align:left;width:380px">
13:  <script>
14:   for (ii=33;ii<127;ii++)
15:   {
16:     document.write(String.fromCharCode(ii) + " ");
17:   }
18:  </script>
19: </div></div>
20: </body>
21: </html>
```

Fig. 1.10 ASCII codes

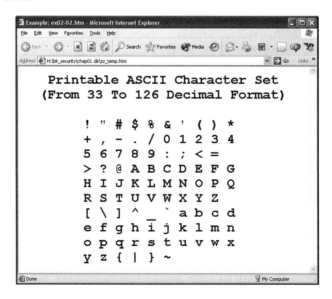

To put ASCII into action, let's consider a page to display a message with a sequence of ASCII codes. Consider `ex-01-06.htm`.

```
Example: ex01-06.htm: Display a message with ASCII codes

 1: <?xml version="1.0" encoding="iso-8859-1"?>
 2: <!DOCTYPE html PUBLIC "-//W3C//DTD XHTML 1.0 Transitional//EN"
 3:     "http://www.w3.org/TR/xhtml1/DTD/xhtml1-transitional.dtd">
 4: <html xmlns="http://www.w3.org/1999/xhtml" xml:lang="en"
       lang="en">
 5: <head><title>Message With ASCII Codes -
      ex01-06.htm</title></head>
 6: <body style="font-family:arial;font-size:24pt;text-align:center;
 7:        background:#000088;color:#ffff00"><br />
 8:  Display Message With ASCII Codes <br />
 9: <img alt="pic" src="line1.gif" height="7"
      width="550" /><br /><br />
10:  <div style="font-size:20pt">
11:   <script>
12:     var charArray = new Array(72,101,108,108,111,32,
13:                              87,111,114,108,100,33);
14:     for (ii=0;ii< charArray.length; ii++) {
15:       document.write( charArray[ii]+" " );
16:     }
17:       document.write("<br /><br />");
18:     for (ii=0;ii< charArray.length; ii++) {
19:       document.write( String.fromCharCode(charArray[ii]));
20:     }
21:   </script>
22:   <br /><br />(The Two Messages Above Are Equivalent)<br />
23:  </div>
24: </body> </html>
```

The main part of the page is the script block defined in lines 11–21. First, an array called charArray is declared in lines 12–13 with a sequence of numbers. That is

```
charArray[0]=72, charArray[1]=101,... ..., charArray[11]=33
```

The for-loop in lines 14–16 is used to display these numbers in the browser window. Note that the variable charArray.length has the value 12 representing the total number of elements in the array. After the two line breaks defined in line 17, another for-loop is used to display the message represented by the sequence of numbers stored inside the array. For example, when ii=0, consider the statement in line 19:

```
document.write( String.fromCharCode(charArray[0]))
```

Fig. 1.11   A message using ASCII codes

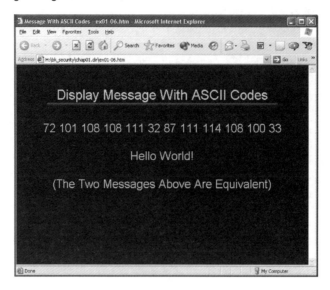

The `charArray[0]` returns the value 72 and the function `String.fromCharCode(72)` will return the character 'H'. This character will then be output by the `document.write()` function. When the for-loop runs through the entire array, the message 'Hello World!' is displayed. A screenshot of this example is shown in Figure 1.11.

One of the main objectives of a Web page is to reach every corner of the world. To do that, ASCII code is clearly not sufficient to satisfy the hundreds of millions of people speaking and writing hundreds (if not thousands) of different languages. For this purpose, ASCII was expanded and Unicode was created.

1.3.3   Using Unicode on the Web

Before Unicode was developed and accepted in the early 1990s, no single encoding system could contain enough characters to accommodate all the different languages in the world. The 8-bit ASCII code can only have $2^8 = 256$ possibilities for encoding and is already stretched to the limit with all English characters, punctuation, technical and drawing symbols. For example, in Europe a number of different encoding schemes were developed to cope with the different European languages. As a result, most of them conflict with each other with 'one to many' and/or 'many to one' inconsistencies. Information exchange, such as emails, documents and data, between non-English countries and computer platforms was a nightmare for programmers.

Unicode provides a solution to the problem by a huge expansion of ASCII code so that a unique number can be assigned to every character, no matter what the language. The Unicode standard has been adopted by almost all computer organizations and is used worldwide. In particular, Unicode features are supported by all the browsers (IE6+, NS7+ and Opera 6+) mentioned in an earlier section of this chapter.

Basically, Unicode works by adding another 8 bits on top of the ASCII code. That is:

Table 1.2 ASCII and Unicode characters

ASCII text	Unicode text
A – 0100 0001 (0x41)	A – 0000 0000 0100 0001 (0x41)
B – 0100 0010 (0x42)	B – 0000 0000 0100 0010 (0x42)
... ...	... ...
Y – 0101 1001 (0x59)	Y – 0000 0000 0101 1001 (0x59)
Z – 0101 1010 (0x5a)	Z – 0000 0000 0101 1010 (0x5a)

As you can see from Table 1.2, ASCII and Unicode are identical for English alphabets. By adding another 8 bits on top of the ASCII code, Unicode has more than 65 000 codes to cope with the characters, scripts, technical and drawing symbols of all the languages in the world. In fact, the Unicode v.3 standard contains 49 194 characters and can be used to define the full sets of alphabetic symbols of many non-English speaking countries in Europe, the Middle East and Asia. In particular, Unicode contains a subset of 27 484 ideographic characters which are defined and used in China, Japan, Korea, Taiwan, Vietnam and Singapore. In addition to language features, Unicode also provides standard encoding for mathematical symbols, punctuation, technical symbols and many geometric shapes. To see Unicode in action, consider ex01-07.htm.

```
Example: ex01-07.htm - Unicode characters

1:  <?xml version="1.0" encoding="iso-8859-1"?>
2:  <!DOCTYPE html PUBLIC "-//W3C//DTD XHTML 1.0 Transitional//EN"
3:     "http://www.w3.org/TR/xhtml1/DTD/xhtml1-transitional.dtd">
4:  <html xmlns="http://www.w3.org/1999/xhtml" xml:lang="en"
       lang="en">
5:  <head>
6:      <title> ASCII Code: ex01-04.htm</title>
7:  </head>
8:  <body style="font-family:arial;font-size:28pt;text-align:center;
9:      background:#000088;color:#ffff00">
```

```
10:
11:   Unicode Characters
12:   <img alt="pic" src="line1.gif" height="7" width="650" />
13:   <div style="font-size:20pt;width=660px">
14:   <script>
15:     document.write("<br /><br />\(0x0041-0x0050\) -- ");
16:     for (ii=0x0041;ii<=0x0050;ii++) {
17:       document.write(String.fromCharCode(ii)+" ");
18:     }
19:     document.write("<br /><br />\(0x3041-0x3050\) -- ");
20:     for (ii=0x3041;ii<=0x3050;ii++) {
21:       document.write(String.fromCharCode(ii)+" ");
22:     }
23:     document.write("<br /><br />\(0x0621-0x0630\) -- ");
24:     for (ii=0x0621;ii<=0x0630;ii++) {
25:       document.write(String.fromCharCode(ii)+" ");
26:     }
27:     document.write("<br /><br />\(0x03b1-0x03c0\) -- ");
28:     for (ii=0x03b1;ii<=0x03c0;ii++) {
29:       document.write(String.fromCharCode(ii)+" ");
30:     }
31:     document.write("<br /><br />\(0x6141-0x6150\) -- ");
32:     for (ii=0x6141;ii<=0x6150;ii++) {
33:       document.write(String.fromCharCode(ii)+" ");
34:     }
35:   </script>
36:   </div>
37: </body> </html>
```

This page contains five sequences of Unicode in hexadecimal representation. The first set of Unicode is defined and displayed by the for-loop in lines 16–18. By looping through the hexadecimal values 0x0041–0x0050, the following Unicode characters are generated:

(0x0041–0x0050) – A B C D E F G H I J K L M N O P

The Unicode of this sequence is identical to ASCII. The second sequence of Unicode is specified in lines 20–22 covering the range 0x3041–0x3050. This Unicode sequence generates the following characters:

(0x3041–0x3050) – ぁ あ ぃ い ぅ う ぇ え ぉ お か が き ぎ く ぐ

This Unicode set can be used to define Japanese characters. The remaining three Unicode sequences are defined in lines 24–26, 28–30, and 32–34. As a result, the following character sets are generated:

(0x0621–0x0630) – ﻥ ﺭ ﺥ ﺡ ﺝ ﺕ ﺕ ﺓ ﺏ ا ئ إ أ آ ء

(0x03b1–0x03c0) – α β γ δ ε ζ η θ ι κ λ μ ν ξ ο π

(0x6141–0x6150) – 恩 憑 愮 慄 愯 愰 慇 慈 慉 慊 態 慌 慍 慎 慏 憙

A screenshot of this example in action is shown in Figure 1.12.

If you are using Microsoft Windows XP, you can use the Character Map utility to select and copy Unicode characters. For example, you can activate the Character Map program from

```
Start | All Programs | Accessories | System Tools | Character Map
```

Inside the map, you can locate and select any character, for example 'α' (see Figure 1.13). At the bottom of the map, you will see the hexadecimal value of this Unicode as 03B1 (i.e. 0x03b1).

For a more interesting example using Unicode, let's develop a page which can take an arbitrary character and return the corresponding Unicode value. Consider the first part of ex01-08.htm.

Fig. 1.12 Unicode characters

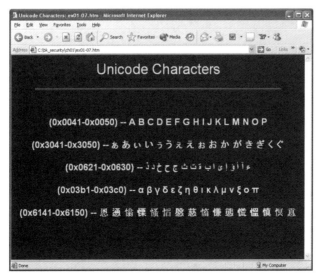

Fig. 1.13 The character map of Windows XP

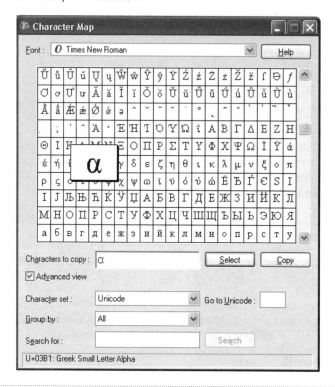

```
Example: ex01-08.htm - Getting unicode values

1:  <?xml version="1.0" encoding="iso-8859-1"?>
2:  <!DOCTYPE html PUBLIC "-//W3C//DTD XHTML 1.0 Transitional//EN"
3:    "http://www.w3.org/TR/xhtml1/DTD/xhtml1-transitional.dtd">
4:  <html xmlns="http://www.w3.org/1999/xhtml" xml:lang="en"
    lang="en">
5:  <head><title>Getting Unicode - ex01-07.htm</title></head>
6:
7:  <body style="font-family:arial;font-size:26pt;text-align:center;
8:       background:#000088;color:#ffff00">
9:  Getting Unicode Values <br /><br />
10: <img alt="pic" src="line1.gif" height="7"
    width="650" /><br /><br />
11:
12: <table style="text-align:left;font-size:18pt" align="center">
13:  <tr><td>Please Enter A Character: </td>
```

```
14:     <td><input size="1" id="unicode_c" maxlength="1"
15:         onkeyup="getUnicode()"style="font-size:18pt;width=40px;
16:         font-weight:bold;height:30px;background:#dddddd;
            color:#ff0000" /> </td></tr>
17:   <tr><td>The Decimal Value Of Unicode: </td>
18:     <td><input size="8" id="unicode_dec" readonly
19:         style="font-size:18pt;width:140px;height:30px;
            background:#aaffaa"/></td></tr>
20:   <tr><td>The Hexadecimal Value Of Unicode: </td>
21:     <td><input size="8" id="unicode_hex" readonly
22:         style="font-size:18pt;width:140px;height:30px;
            background:#aaffaa" /></td></tr>
23:   <tr><td>The Binary Value Of Unicode: </td>
24:     <td><input size="16" id="unicode_bin" readonly
25:         style="font-size:18pt;width:200px;height:30px;
            background:#aaffaa" /></td></tr>
26: </table>
27:
```

The main part of this page is the XHTML table declared in lines 12–26. You can define an XHTML table using the element `<table>`. Table rows and table cells (or table data) are defined by the elements `<tr>` and `<td>` respectively. Consider the table element in line 12:

```
<table style="text-align:left;font-size:18pt" align="center">
```

This statement will instruct the browser to create a table using a font size of 18 points. The text alignment in the table is left. This table will be placed at the centre of the browser window as declared by the attribute `align="center"`. In fact, the attribute 'align' is used only for backward compatibility with some older browsers. If you want to write a page that will run on many browser families and versions, backward compatibility is an important issue.

From this page, you can see that four `<tr>` elements are used to define four table rows. Inside each row, two table data items are specified using `<td>`. Consider the first table row defined in lines 13–16. The first data item in the first row will display the message 'Please Enter A Character'. The second table data item is an input element:

```
<input size="1" id="unicode_c" maxlength="1" onkeyup="getUnicode()"
    style="font-size:18pt;width=40px;font-weight:bold;
    height:30px;background:#dddddd;color:#ff0000" /> </td></tr>
```

By default, if there is no type attribute, `type="text"` is assumed and a text box is created. This element will create an input field for you to enter some text. In this case, only one character can be input since the attributes of `size` and `maxlength` are set to be 1 (`size="1"` and `maxlength="1"`). This input element has an identity defined by the attribute `id="unicode_c"`. This `id` can be used to capture the character inside the field. After you have entered a character and released the key, the statement in line 15

```
onkeyup = getUnicode()
```

and the user defined function `getUnicode()` will be activated immediately. This function captures the character inside the input field and displays the corresponding Unicode value. The second table row in this page is specified in lines 17–19. The first data item of this row displays the message 'The Decimal Value Of Unicode:'. The second data item is also an input element:

```
<input size="8" id="unicode_dec" readonly style="font-size:18pt;
    width=140px;height:30px;background:#aaffaa" />
```

This input element creates a field with identity `unicode_dec`. This identity is used to display the decimal value of the Unicode. The `readonly` attribute means that the element can only be read and no input is allowed.

The remaining two table rows defined in lines 20–22 and 23–25 specify two areas for displaying the hexadecimal and binary values of the Unicode and should be easy to understand.

To capture the character in the input field and display the corresponding Unicode values, the function `getUnicode()` is used. The details of this function are listed in the continuation of `ex01-08.htm`.

```
Example: Continuation of ex01-08.htm

28: <script>
29:   function getUnicode()
30:   {
31:     var str=document.getElementById("unicode_c").value;
32:     if (str!="") {
33:       unicode = str.charCodeAt(0);
34:     }
35:     document.getElementById("unicode_dec").value=unicode;
36:     document.getElementById("unicode_hex").value
                                          =unicode.toString(16);
37:     document.getElementById("unicode_bin").value
                                          =unicode.toString(2);
38:   }
39: </script>
40: </body>
41: </html>
```

Fig. 1.14 Getting Unicode values

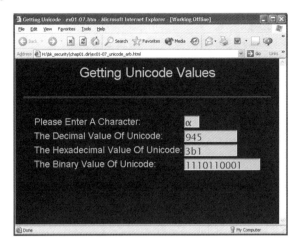

Inside the script block (lines 28–39), the user defined function `getUnicode()` is declared. The first job of this function is to capture the character in the input field with `id="unicode_c"`. Consider the statement in line 31:

```
str=document.getElementById("unicode_c").value
```

The function will locate the XHTML element with `id="unicode_c"` and get the value stored in this element. The value is then assigned to the variable `str`. That is, the character in the input field is captured and assigned to `str`. If `str` is not empty, the statement in line 33 is activated:

```
unicode = str.charCodeAt(0)
```

This statement gets the Unicode of the first character in `str` and assigns it to another variable, `unicode` in decimal format. Therefore, by executing the statement in line 35, the text field or element with `id="unicode_dec"` will have the decimal Unicode value. Similarly, the elements with `id="unicode_hex"` and `"unicode_bin"` will have the hexadecimal and binary values of the Unicode. A screenshot of this example is shown in Figure 1.14.

With Unicode, data and messages in any language can be represented numerically in the Web environment and manipulated by mathematical operations.

1.3.4 Numerical representations of messages

Messages can be considered to be a sequence of characters. If we can break the message down to character level, all the skills in the previous sections can be applied. Breaking a message down into individual characters is a simple task with for-loops. Consider the first part of example `ex01-09.htm`.

Example: ex01-09.htm - Numerical representations of a message

```
 1: <?xml version="1.0" encoding="iso-8859-1"?>
 2: <!DOCTYPE html PUBLIC "-//W3C//DTD XHTML 1.0 Transitional//EN"
 3:    "http://www.w3.org/TR/xhtml1/DTD/xhtml1-transitional.dtd">
 4: <html xmlns="http://www.w3.org/1999/xhtml" xml:lang="en"
    lang="en">
 5: <head><title>Num. Rep. of Message - ex01-09.htm</title></head>
 6: <body style="font-family:arial;font-size:26pt;text-align:center;
 7:    background:#000088;color:#ffff00">
 8: Numerical Representations Of A Message <br />
 9: <img alt="pic" src="line1.gif" height="7"
    width="650" /><br /><br />
10:
11: <table style="font-size:18pt;text-align:left" align="center">
12:    <tr><td>Please Enter A Message Below And Press the
    Button: </td></tr>
13:    <tr><td><input size="30" id="in_mesg" maxlength="30"
14:       style="font-size:16pt;width=340px;font-weight:bold;
15:       height:40px;background:#dddddd;color:#ff0000" />
16:       <input type="button" value="OK" onclick="toUnicode()"
17:       style="font-size:16pt;font-weight:bold;width:80px;
18:       height:40px;background:#dddddd;
          color:#ff0000" /></td></tr>
19:
20:    <tr><td>The Decimal Representation Of The Message: </td><tr>
21:    <tr><td><textarea rows="3" cols="40" id="unicode_dec" readonly
22:          style="font-size:16pt;font-weight:bold;width:540px;
23:          height:60px;background:#aaffaa"></textarea></td></tr>
24:
25:    <tr><td>The Hexadecimal Representation Of The Message: </td></tr>
26:    <tr><td><textarea rows="3" cols="40" id="unicode_hex" readonly
27:          style="font-size:16pt;font-weight:bold;width:540px;
28:          height:60px;background:#aaffaa"></textarea></td></tr>
29:
30:    <tr><td>The Binary Representation Of The Message: </td></tr>
31:    <tr><td><textarea rows="3" cols="40" id="unicode_bin" readonly
32:          style="font-size:16pt;font-weight:bold;width:540px;
33:          height:80px;background:#aaffaa"></textarea></td></tr>
34: </table>
35:
```

This page contains an XHTML table of eight rows. The first row, defined in line 12, is used to display the message 'Please Enter A Message Below And Press the Button:'. The second row, in lines 13–18, contains two input elements. The first defines an input field for the user to type a message. The second input element is a button called OK. Once the user finishes a message and the OK button is clicked, the following statement is activated (line 16)

```
onclick="toUnicode()"
```

This function will capture the message and convert it into Unicode representation. The decimal, hexadecimal and binary Unicode representations of the message are then displayed in the 4th, 6th, and 8th rows of the table respectively. In order to display the entire numerical representation, we have used an XHTML text area element <textarea> in this case. For example, consider the text area defined in the 4th row (i.e. lines 21–23):

```
<textarea rows="3" cols="50" id="unicode_dec" readonly
    style="font-size:16pt;font-weight:bold;width=540px;
    height:60px;background:#aaffaa"></textarea>
```

This <textarea> element creates a small text area in the browser window with 3 rows and 50 columns. The readonly attribute specifies that the text area can be used only to display information and that no user input is allowed. You can send information to this text area by using the identity id="Unicode_dec" and the document.getElementById() function. Similarly, hexadecimal and binary representations are displayed in the text areas defined in lines 26–28 and 31–33.

Without a doubt, the power engine of this example is the ECMAScript function toUnicode(). The details of this function are defined in the continuation of ex01-09.htm.

```
Example: Continuation of ex01-09.htm

36: <script>
37:  function toUnicode()
38:  {
39:     var sstring2="";
40:     var sstring16="";
41:     var sstring10="";
42:
43:     var sstr=document.getElementById("in_mesg").value;
44:     var ii =0, str, unicode;
45:     for (ii=0;ii<sstr.length;ii++) {
46:        unicode = sstr.charCodeAt(ii);
47:        sstring2 = sstring2 + unicode.toString(2) +" ";
48:        sstring16 = sstring16 + unicode.toString(16) +" ";
49:        sstring10 = sstring10 + unicode +" ";
```

```
50:    }
51:    document.getElementById("unicode_bin").value=sstring2;
52:    document.getElementById("unicode_hex").value=sstring16;
53:    document.getElementById("unicode_dec").value=sstring10;
54: }
55: </script>
56: </body> </html>
```

The function `toUnicode()` is defined inside the script block in lines 36–55. First, three strings are declared and they are `sstring2`, `sstring16` and `sstring10`. These variables are used to store the binary, hexadecimal and decimal representations of the message. After execution of the statement in line 43, the user input message will be stored in variable `sstr`. A simple for-loop on this variable will capture each character and convert it into numerical representation.

Consider the for-loop in lines 45–50. The Unicode of the ii[th] character of the `sstr` string is obtained by the `sstr.charCodeAt(ii)` function and stored in the variable `unicode` (line 46). This `unicode` value is added into the strings `sstring2`, `sstring16` and `sstring10`. After the for-loop, all three numerical representations of the message `sstr` are obtained. A screenshot of this example at work is shown in Figure 1.15.

Now, we have everything ready to implement one of our very first message encryption schemes – the Caesar code.

Fig. 1.15   Numerical representations of a message

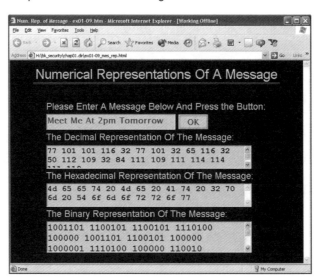

1.3.5 Implementation of the Caesar code

As we have mentioned earlier, messages from the emperor of ancient Rome were sometimes shifted by 3 from the character table to maintain security and secrecy. This coding method is known as the Caesar code. With the knowledge of numerical representation of messages, Caesar code can be implemented easily by the following steps:

- get the Unicode of each character from the original message;

- increment the Unicode using the Caesar shifting number;

- obtain the new character from the modified Unicode and display it.

Consider ex01-10.htm. This page is the first part of the implementation and the main object is the content of the XHTML table in lines 11–30. Using tables to organize page objects such as messages, input boxes and other shapes is simple, efficient and popular among professionals. This table has six rows and is divided into three groups according to their functionalities. The first group defined in lines 12–15 contains an input element (or text box) and is responsible for getting the user input of the original message. The second group in lines 17–24 has two input elements. The first input element (lines 19–21) is a text box to get the Caesar shifting value. This number will determine the extent of character shifting. Along with the shifting value, we also have an OK button defined in lines 22–24. Once the original message and the shifting value fields are filled, the OK button is used to execute the function caesar_code() to perform the Caesar code encryption. The result will be displayed in the text area (lines 27–29) in the third group.

```
Example: ex01-10.htm - Implementation of Caesar code

 1: <?xml version="1.0" encoding="iso-8859-1"?>
 2: <!DOCTYPE html PUBLIC "-//W3C//DTD XHTML 1.0 Transitional//EN"
 3:    "http://www.w3.org/TR/xhtml1/DTD/xhtml1-transitional.dtd">
 4: <html xmlns="http://www.w3.org/1999/xhtml" xml:lang="en"
    lang="en">
 5: <head><title>Caesar Code - ex01-10.htm</title></head>
 6: <body style="font-family:arial;font-size:26pt;text-align:center;
 7:       background:#000088;color:#ffff00">
 8:   Implementation Of Caesar Code<br />
 9:   <img alt="pic" src="line1.gif" height="7"
     width="650" /><br /><br />
10:
11: <table style="font-size:18pt;text-align:left" align="center">
12:   <tr><td>Please Enter A Message Below:</td></tr>
13:   <tr><td><input id="in_mesg" size="50" maxlength="50"
14:           style="font-size:16pt;width:540px;font-weight:bold;
```

```
15:                    height:40px;background:#dddddd;color:#ff0000" />
16:
17: <tr><td>Please Enter The Caesar Shifting Value Here:</td></tr>
18: <tr><td style="text-align:center">
19:        <input id="caesar_v" size="3" maxlength="3"
20:          style="font-size:16pt;width:50px;height:40px;
21:          font-weight:bold;background:#dddddd;color:#ff0000" />
22:        <input type="button" value="OK" onclick="caesar_code()"
23:          style="font-size:16pt;font-weight:bold;width:80px;
24:          height:40px;background:#dddddd;color:#ff0000" /></td></tr>
25:
26: <tr><td>The Caesar Encryption Of The Message: </td><tr>
27: <tr><td><textarea rows="3" cols="38" id="unicode_dec" readonly
28:              style="font-size:16pt;font-weight:bold;width:540px;
29:              height:60px;background:#aaffaa"></textarea></td></tr>
30: </table>
31:
```

The driving force for this page is the ECMAScript function `caesar_code()` and is specified in the continuation of `ex01-10.htm`.

Example: Continuation of ex01-10.htm

```
32: <script>
33:  function caesar_code()
34:  {
35:    var sstring10="", sstr, caesarV, ii, unicode, str;
36:    sstr=document.getElementById("in_mesg").value;
37:    caesarV=parseInt(document.getElementById("caesar_v").value);
38:
39:    for (ii=0;ii<sstr.length;ii++)
40:    {
41:      unicode = sstr.charCodeAt(ii);
42:      sstring10 = sstring10 + String.fromCharCode(unicode
                                                        +caesarV);
43:    }
44:    document.getElementById("unicode_dec").value=sstring10;
45:  }
46: </script>
47: </body> </html>
```

This page contains one script block and one function, `caesar_code()`. Inside the function, the statement in line 36 is used to obtain the original message and store it in the string variable `sstr`. Consider the statement in line 37:

```
caesarV=parseInt(document.getElementById("caesar_v").value)
```

The function `document.getElementById("caesar_v").value` captures the Caesar shifting number stored from the text box where `id="caesar_v"`. Since the returned value is a string, the `parseInt()` function is employed to convert it to an integer and assign it to variable `caesarV`.

Once the original message and the Caesar shifting number are well defined, a simple for-loop is activated to perform the encryption. For each character of the original message, the following statements are executed (lines 41–42):

```
unicode = sstr.charCodeAt(ii)
sstring10 = sstring10 + String.fromCharCode(unicode + caesarV)
```

First, the Unicode of the ii[th] character is obtained and stored in the variable `unicode`. To perform the encryption, all we have to do is to add the `unicode` to the shifting number (i.e. `caesarV`) and convert the resulting number back to a character. Finally, the encrypted character is concatenated into the string `sstring10`. The statement in line 44 is simply to output the encrypted string `sstring10` back to the text box defined in lines 27–29. A screenshot of this example in action is shown in Figure 1.16.

Fig. 1.16   Caesar encryption I

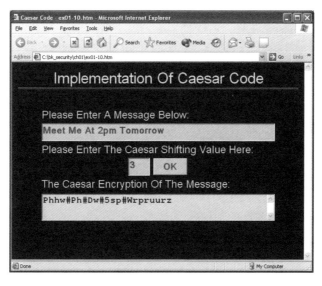

From Figure 1.16, you can see that if you enter the text 'Meet Me At 2pm Tomorrow' and the Caesar shifting number is 3, you will have the encrypted message Phhw#Ph#Dw#5sp#Wrpruurz.

Now, try to make a copy of the encrypted message 'Phhw#Ph#Dw#5sp#Wrpruurz' and paste it into the input message box. If you enter −3 as the shifting value and click the OK button, you will have the original message 'Meet Me At 2pm Tomorrow' back, as in Figure 1.17.

This example demonstrates an important point – if the Caesar shifting number 3 is the encryption key (or password), then −3 will be the decryption key.

Although still in a pre-mature stage, you can use this example to practise encryption/decryption on the Web with your friends. For example, you and your friends could publish encrypted messages inside a Web page and use this page as a utility to perform decryption.

One interesting feature of Caesar code is that if you have shifted the characters forward by 6, you can have the original message back by two separate backward shifts of 3. However, if you have shifted the original message too much, say 1 000 000, you will have moved the characters beyond the bounding range of Unicode. In this case, your computer will clip the number and destroy the encryption/decryption scheme. This is one of the reasons why we have restricted the input field for the shifting value to 3 digits (line 19 of ex01-10.htm). Also, for most browsers and operating systems, some characters such as '^Z' (end of file) may have special meaning. When you print these characters on the screen, they

Fig. 1.17 Caesar encryption II

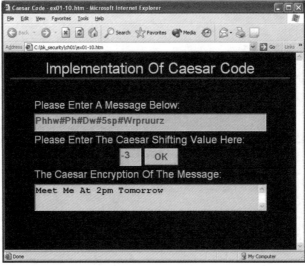

will not print but perform some special function other instead. These characters may, sometimes, damage your encryption algorithms.

To print characters safely onto screen the use of an escape code and, even better, hexadecimal representation are recommended. They will be discussed in Section 1.5.1.

Now, we have some hands-on experience of encryption/decryption on the Web. To prepare you for more advanced topics, message manipulation down to the bit level (or bitwise operators) is necessary.

1.4 Bitwise operators and Base64 encoding/decoding

1.4.1 An introduction to bitwise operators

Mathematical operations such as addition and subtraction on Unicode will result in some kind of encryption. If the mathematical operations are reversible, the decryption scheme is feasible. More advanced operations, or algorithms, will produce more sophisticated encryption schemes. To understand more about modern encryption, some fundamental knowledge of bitwise operations is needed.

Bitwise operators are designed to work with the binary digit (bit). The bit is the most basic unit used by computers. A single bit can hold only one of two values, 0 or 1. More bits are concatenated together to form a larger value called a binary number. ECMAScript provides extensive bit manipulation capabilities, so that programmers can get down into the so-called 'bits' (or bits-and-bytes) level. Some frequently used bit operators in ECMAScript are listed in Table 1.3.

Table 1.3 Basic bitwise operators in ECMAScript

Operator	Name	Description
~	Bitwise NOT	Sets all 0 bits to 1 and all 1 bits to 0. e.g. if α = 0100 0101 → ~ α = 1011 1010
<<	Bitwise left shift	Shifts the bits of the first operand left by the number of bits specifies by the second operand. e.g. if α = 0100 0101 → α << 2 = 0001 0100
>>	Sign propagating right shift	Shifts the bits of the first operand right by the number of bits specifies by the second operand. The copies of the leftmost bit are added on from the left e.g. if α = 0100 0101 → α >> 2 = 0001 0001
>>>	Zero right shift	Similar to >> but bits shifted off to the right are discarded and zeros are added on to the left.
&	Bitwise AND	The resultant bits are set to 1 only when both corresponding bits in the two operands are 1. Otherwise bits are set to 0. e.g. α =0100 0101, β = 0101 0110 → α & β = 0100 0100
|	Bitwise OR	The resultant bits are set to 1 when either one of corresponding bits in the two operands is 1. Otherwise bits are set to 0. e.g. α =0100 0101, β = 0101 0110 → α | β = 0101 0111
^	Bitwise XOR	The resultant bits are set to 1 if exactly one of the corresponding bets in the two operands is 1. e.g. α =0100 0101, β = 0101 0110 → α ^ β = 0001 0011

The bitwise operator NOT (~) is a unary operator and only one operand is needed. It sets all 0 bits in its operand to 1 and all 1 bits to 0 in the result. Consider 8-bit ASCII: every ASCII character is represented by an 8-bit binary value. If we have an 8-bit ASCII value 0100 0101 (i.e. character 'E'), the result of the NOT operation is:

~ 0100 0101 = 1011 1010

If the same character 'E' is represented by 16-bit Unicode as 0000 0000 0100 0101, the NOT operation turns out to be:

~ 0000 0000 0100 0101 = 1111 1111 1011 1010

Note that these two results are different. In many cases, the length of a bit plays an important role in bitwise operations. However, no matter what kind of bit-length you are using, two NOT operations together will always get the original value back. That is, for any binary value α, we have

$$\sim (\sim\alpha) = \alpha$$

Note that the zero right shift operator '>>>' is equivalent to '>>' for positive integers.

As you can see from the examples in Table 1.3, bitwise operators manipulate the most fundamental unit of computers and digital message – bits. Most cryptographic algorithms use them, big or small, advanced or not so advanced. Let's see how these three bitwise operators can be implemented on the Web. If you are an 'ordinary' Web or ECMAScript programmer, chances are that you will never use bit operations. However, if you are programming security or encryption, bitwise operations will be a powerful tool.

1.4.2 Bitwise operations and encryptions on the Web

To implement the three bitwise operators &, |, and ^ on the Web, consider the first part of ex01-11.htm.

One of the great strengths of HTML/XHTML is that it can be used as a user interface. In other words, it is one of the ideal languages for designing user input and communication with users.

After the usual page title, a table is defined in lines 17–24. Inside the table, input elements are used to design two input fields. These two fields are identified by the identities a_v and b_v. They are used to get two binary values from users. In order to include the bitwise operators, three radio buttons (sometimes called radio boxes) are used to represent each of the bitwise operators &, |, and ^. The bitwise operation will be shown in the field specified in lines 43–44. Consider the first two radio buttons defined in lines 29–32.

Example: ex01-11.htm - Bitwise operators

```
 1: <?xml version="1.0" encoding="iso-8859-1"?>
 2: <!DOCTYPE html PUBLIC "-//W3C//DTD XHTML 1.0 Transitional//EN"
 3:    "http://www.w3.org/TR/xhtml1/DTD/xhtml1-transitional.dtd">
 4: <html xmlns="http://www.w3.org/1999/xhtml" xml:lang="en"
     lang="en">
 5: <head><title>Bitwise Operations - ex01-11.htm</title></head>
 6: <style>
 7:   .butSt{font-size:16pt;width:250px;height:40px;
 8:          font-weight:bold;background:#dddddd;color:#ff0000}
 9:   .radSt{font-size:16pt;width:35px;height:30px;
10:          font-weight:bold;background:#88ff88;color:#ff0000}
11: </style>
12: <body style="font-family:arial;font-size:26pt;text-align:center;
13:        background:#000088;color:#ffff00">
14:  Bitwise Operations On The Web<br />
15:  <img alt="pic" src="line1.gif" height="7"
     width="650" /><br /><br />
16:
17: <table style="font-size:18pt" align="center">
18: <tr><td>Enter The Binary Value For A :</td>
19:    <td style="text-align:center">
20:    <input type="text" class="butSt" id="a_v" /></td></tr>
21: <tr><td>Enter The Binary Value For B :</td>
22:    <td style="text-align:center">
23:    <input type="text" class="butSt" id="b_v"
        name="b_v" /></td></tr>
24: </table><br />
25:
26: <div style="font-size:18pt">Pick One Of The Bitwise
     Operators<br /><br />
27: <form action="">
28: <table style="font-size:18pt" cellspacing="10" align="center">
29: <tr><td style="width:280px;text-align:left"><input type="radio"
30:        id="b_rad" name="b_rad" class="radSt" /> Bitwise
           AND ( & )</td>
31:    <td style="width:280px;text-align:left"><input type="radio"
32:        id="b_rad" name="b_rad" class="radSt" />
           Bitwise XOR ( ^ )</td>
33: </tr>
34: <tr><td style="width:280px;text-align:left"><input type="radio"
35:        id="b_rad" name="b_rad" class="radSt" />
           Bitwise OR ( | )</td>
```

```
36:    <td style="width:280px;text-align:left"><input size="20"
37:      type="button"class="butSt" style="width:180px" value="OK"
       onclick="bit_op()" />
38:  </tr>
39:  </table>
40:  </form>
41:
42:  <br />The Bitwise Operation Result is:<br /> <br />
43:  <input size="20" id="result" style="text-align:center;
44:      width:450px" class="butSt" />
45:
```

```
  <input type="radio" id="b_rad"
     name="b_rad" class="radSt" /> Bitwise AND (&)
  <input type="radio" id="b_rad"
     name="b_rad" class="radSt" /> Bitwise XOR (^)
```

The first input element will generate a radio box since the attribute type is set to 'radio'. Both the identity and name of this radio box are set to b_rad. Soon after the radio box, the text 'Bitwise AND (&)' is displayed. If the user checks this radio box, the bitwise AND operation will be performed. The second input element defines a similar radio box. The same id and name attributes are used here to indicate that only one radio button can be checked. If this box is checked, the operation is bitwise XOR. The third operation, bitwise OR, is defined by another radio box in lines 34–35. Note that this radio box also has the same id and name attributes so that only one radio box can be checked by the user. Adjacent to this radio box is an OK button (lines 36–37). This button will trigger the ECMAScript function bit_op() to perform the operation.

Note that we have put all radio buttons inside the form element defined in lines 27 and 40. Some browsers, such as NS, will not generate a radio box properly if they are not declared inside a form.

The definition of this bit_op() function is specified in the continuation of ex01-11.htm.

Example: Continuation of ex01-11.htm

```
46: <script>
47:  function bit_op()
48:  {
49:    var aV, bV, llV, dispSt="", cV;
50:    aV=parseInt(document.getElementById("a_v").value,2);
51:    bV=parseInt(document.getElementById("b_v").value,2);
52:    llV = document.getElementsByName("b_rad");
53:
```

```
54:    if (11V.item(0).checked) {
55:        dispSt = "A \& B = ";
56:        cV = aV & bV;
57:    }
58:    if (11V.item(1).checked) {
59:        dispSt = "A \^ B = ";
60:        cV = aV ^ bV;
61:    }
62:    if (11V.item(2).checked) {
63:        dispSt = "A \| B = ";
64:        cV = aV | bV;
65:    }
66:    dispSt = dispSt + cV.toString(2);
67:    document.getElementById("result").value = dispSt;
68: }
69: </script>70: </body> </html>
```

Consider the first statement (line 50) inside the function `bit_op()`:

```
aV=parseInt(document.getElementById("a_v").value,2)
```

The function `document.getElementById("a_v").value` returns the string stored in the input field where `id="a_v"`. Since the stored string represents a binary value, the function

```
parseInt(xxx,2)
```

is employed to convert the string into a number. The value '2' in the second argument indicates that the input string is in binary format and we want a binary number. The binary number is stored in the variable `aV`. Similarly, the statement in line 51 will get the binary number and store it in variable `bV`. Consider the statement in line 51:

```
11V = document.getElementsByName("b_rad")
```

This `document.getElementsByName()` is a collection function recommended by W3C to deal with radio buttons. It is specified in W3C's Document Object Model (DOM) specification. Basically, this function will return all HTML/XHTML elements of the same name `b_rad` and store them in `11V`. Variable `11V` is considered as a collection which, roughly speaking, is similar to an array. For example, `11V.item(0)` is the first element (or radio box) with identity `b_rad` and therefore the property

```
11V.item(0).checked
```

will return the check status of that radio box. Consider the `if` statement in lines 54–57.

```
if (llV.item(0).checked) {
    dispST = "A \& B = "
    cV = aV & bV
}
```

This conditional statement means that if the first radio box is checked, we

- set the display string `dispSt` as `"A & B = "`;

- perform the bitwise operation `aV & bV` and store the result in variable `cV`.

The other two conditional statements in lines 58–61 and 62–65 are dealt with in a similar manner. The operation result `cv` is added into the string `dispSt` by the statement in line 66

```
dispSt = dispSt + cV.toString(2)
```

Finally, the string `dispSt` is output to the field where `id="result"`. Screenshots of this example in action are shown in Figures 1.18 and 1.19.

In addition to the bitwise operations, this example also shows how to use radio buttons on Web pages. In fact, for security on the Web, page design, programming and security algorithms are equally important. Now, let's see how to use bitwise operations to develop a well-known encoding.

Fig. 1.18 Bitwise operator I

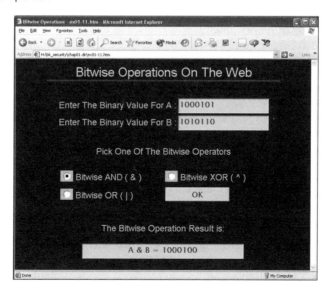

Fig. 1.19 Bitwise operator II

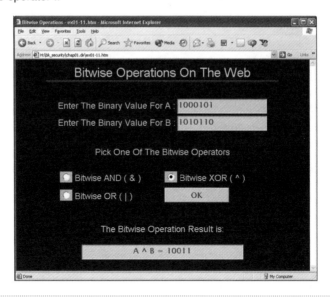

1.4.3 Base64 encoding and decoding

Computers are designed to handle binary data efficiently. Binary data is typically stored in bytes of 8 bits. Under the standard ASCII code, one character occupies one byte (8 bits) although only 7 bits are used. This is why ASCII can define only $2^7 = 128$ characters. Of these 128 characters, not all are printable on your screen or printer. Many other documents or files such as executable programs, pictures, music, video clips and movies, are stored in a truly binary data fashion. In general, they are not printable and you will have a problem editing them using your favoured editor, such as Notepad. More importantly, it is not easy to transmit them from one computer to another.

Base64 encoding is a way of overcoming this problem. It takes a sequence of binary data and converts them into a sequence of printable characters. Each character is one of the following 64 (Base64 string) ranging from 0–63, and therefore the process is called 'Base64'.

ABCDEFGHIJKLMNOPQRSTUVWXYZabcdefghijklmnopqrstuvwxyz0123456789+/

Surprisingly, this simple algorithm is widely used. Your email system uses it for attachments. HTTP uses it to display a login window on your browser communicating your username and password. This process can protect your Web site in a standard way, called 'HTTP Authentication'. Also, many strong encryption/decryption algorithms in this book use it to display encrypted results.

Base64 (sometimes called Radix-64) is so popular that there is a standard for it called 'Internet Engineering Task Force (IEFT) RFC 2440'. The algorithm is simple and can be summarized in one sentence:

A sequence of 8-bit bytes are converted to 6-bit chunks and then into characters.

Consider an example to encode the word 'secrets'.

Step 1   convert the characters into decimal and binary representations.

```
s        e        c        r        e        t        s        (char)
115      101      99       114      101      116      115      (deci)
01110011 01100101 01100011 01110010 01100101 01110100 01110011 (bin)
```

Step 2   regroup the binary format into 6-bit chunks, padding with zeros (0s) at the end if necessary

```
011100 110110 010101 100011 011100 100110 010101 110100 011100 110000
```
(In this case, we have put two pairs of zeros (**00 00**) at the end to form a perfect 6-bit chunk).

Step 3   change the 6-bit chunks into decimal and then look up the character from the Base64 string

```
28   54   21   35   28   38   21   52   28   48    (deci)
c    2    V    j    c    m    V    0    c    w
```
(The first two numbers (28, 54) give the characters 'c' and '2' in the Base64 string. There are ten characters in total.)

Since we have padded two pairs of zeros (**00 00**) in step 2, two equal signs '==' are added at the end of the encoded result to reflect the padding. If one pair of zeros (00) is padded, one equal sign '=' is needed at the end. In this example, we have the following transformation

$$\text{secrets} \xrightarrow{\text{Base64 Encoding}} \text{c2VjcmV0cw} ==$$

The decoding process is just the reverse of the three steps above. To develop a Web page for Base64 encoding/decoding, consider part I of ex01-12.htm.

Example: ex01-12.htm Base64 encoding and decoding   **(Part I)**

```
1: <?xml version="1.0" encoding="iso-8859-1"?>
2: <!DOCTYPE html PUBLIC "-//W3C//DTD XHTML 1.0 Transitional//EN"
3:    "http://www.w3.org/TR/xhtml1/DTD/xhtml1-transitional.dtd">
4: <html xmlns="http://www.w3.org/1999/xhtml" xml:lang="en"
      lang="en">
5: <head><title> Base64 Encoding and Decoding -
      ex01-12.htm</title></head>
```

```
 6: <style>
 7:  .butSt{font-size:16pt;width:250px;height:40px;
 8:          font-weight:bold;background:#dddddd;color:#ff0000}
 9:  .radSt{font-size:16pt;width:35px;height:30px;
10:          font-weight:bold;background:#88ff88;color:#ff0000}
11: </style>
12: <body style="font-family:arial;font-size:26pt;text-align:center;
13:      background:#000088;color:#ffff00">
14:  Base64 Encoding and Decoding<br />
15:  <img alt="pic" src="line1.gif" height="7" width="650" /><br />
16:
17: <table style="font-size:18pt" cellspacing="10" align="center">
18:  <tr><td colspan="3"><br />Enter The Input Message: </td></tr>
19:  <tr><td colspan="3"><textarea rows="5" cols="40" id="in_mesg"
20:     style="width:570px;height:100px;font-size:16pt;
21:     font-weight:bold;background:#dddddd"></textarea></td></tr>
22:  <tr><td style="width:180px;text-align:left">
23:      <input type="radio" checked id="b_rad" name="b_rad"
           class="radSt" />
24:      Encoding</td>
25:      <td style="width:180px;text-align:left">
26:       <input type="radio" id="b_rad" name="b_rad" class="radSt" />
27:       Decoding</td>
28:      <td style="width:180px;text-align:left">
29:       <input size="20" type="button" class="butSt"
           style="width:180px"
30:       value="OK" onclick="base64_fun()" /></td></tr>
31:  <tr><td colspan="3">The Output Message is: </td></tr>
32:  <tr><td colspan="3">
33:   <textarea rows="5" cols="40" id="out_mesg" readonly
34:    style="width:570px;height:100px;font-size:16pt;
          font-weight:bold;background:#aaffaa">
35:   </textarea></td></tr>
36: </table>
```

This XHTML fragment is a modification of ex01-11.htm to act as an interface for the page. The table element in lines 17–36 defines two text areas, two radio buttons and one OK button. The first text area in lines 19–21 would allow you to enter a message to be processed. The statements in lines 23–27 define two radio buttons – one for 'Encoding' and the other for 'Decoding'. When you enter a message in the text area, check one of the radio boxes (e.g. 'Encoding') and click the OK button the encoding result will be displayed in the second text area specified in lines 33–35.

When you click the OK button defined in lines 29–30, the function base64_fun() is executed. The detail of this function is in part II of ex01-12.htm.

```
Example: Continuation of ex01-12.htm                        (Part II)

37: <script src="ex01-12.js"></script>
38: <script>
39:  function base64_fun()
40:  {
41:    var llV, message="",llst="";
42:    llV = document.getElementsByName("b_rad");
43:    if (llV.item(0).checked) {
44:      message = document.getElementById("in_mesg").value;
45:      llst = base64_en(message);
46:      document.getElementById("out_mesg").value = llst;
47:    }
48:    if (llV.item(1).checked) {
49:      message = document.getElementById("in_mesg").value;
50:      llst = base64_de(message);
51:      document.getElementById("out_mesg").value = llst;
52:    }
53:  }
54: </script>
55: </body> </html>
```

The function base64_fun() is defined in lines 39–53. As mentioned in ex01-11.htm, by executing the statement in line 42 all the results of radio buttons are stored in the local variable llv. By checking the status of llV.item(0).checked (line 43), we will know whether the first radio box has been checked. If this statement returns a true value, Base64 encoding will be performed. In this case, the user input text is captured and stored in the variable message (line 44). The function in line 45

```
llst = base64_en(message);
```

will carry out Base64 encoding on message and store the result in the variable llst. The result llst will be displayed in the text area by the statement in line 46. Similarly, if the second radio box is checked (line 48), Base64 decoding is performed by the function base64_de(message) as illustrated in line 50. The decoding result will be displayed by the statement in line 51. Screenshots of this example are shown in Figures 1.20 and 1.21.

The encoding engine, or function base64_en(), is defined in part I of the external file ex01-12.js and included by the statement in line 37.

Fig. 1.20 Base64 encoding

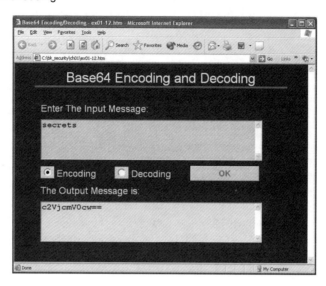

Fig. 1.21 Base64 decoding

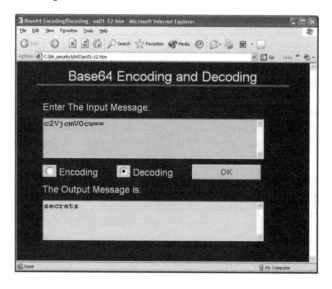

```
 1: var b64Char =
 2:  "ABCDEFGHIJKLMNOPQRSTUVWXYZabcdefghijklmnopqrstuvwxyz0123456789+/";
 3:
 4: function base64_en(inStr)
 5: {
 6:   var bitV, twoChar, strLength, outStr = "";
 7:   var ii=0
 8:   inStr=escape(inStr);
 9:   strLength = inStr.length;
10:   while(strLength >= ii + 3)
11:   {
12:     bitV = (inStr.charCodeAt(ii++) & 0xff) <<16 |
13:             (inStr.charCodeAt(ii++) & 0xff) <<8  |
14:              inStr.charCodeAt(ii++) & 0xff;
15:
16:     outStr += b64Char.charAt((bitV & 0x00fc0000) >>18) +
17:               b64Char.charAt((bitV & 0x0003f000) >>12) +
18:               b64Char.charAt((bitV & 0x00000fc0) >> 6) +
19:               b64Char.charAt((bitV & 0x0000003f));
20:   }
21:   if(strLength -ii > 0 && strLength -ii < 3)
22:   {
23:     twoChar = Boolean(strLength -ii-1);
24:     bitV = ((inStr.charCodeAt(ii++) & 0xff) <<16) |
25:             (twoChar ? (inStr.charCodeAt(ii) & 0xff) <<8 : 0);
26:
27:     outStr +=   b64Char.charAt((bitV & 0x00fc0000) >>18) +
28:                 b64Char.charAt((bitV & 0x0003f000) >>12) +
29:       (twoChar ? b64Char.charAt((bitV & 0x00000fc0) >>6) : "=")
                                                         + "=";
30:   }
31:   return outStr;
32: }
33:
```

To perform Base64 encoding, the first thing is to define the Base64 string. This string is declared as variable `b64Char` in lines 1–2. The program code of the function `base64_en()` is followed in lines 4–31. In order to handle Unicode other than ASCII, the input string `inStr` is converted to an escape sequence first (line 8). The while-loop in lines 10–20 is used to take every three characters (8-bit) from the input string and transform them into four characters with 6-bits each. The three statements in lines 12–14 combine three characters into one 24-bit value stored in the variable `bitV`. The four statements in lines 16–19 break this `bitV` value into four 6-bit characters. For example, consider the statement in line 16:

```
b64Char.charAt((bitV & 0x00fc0000) >>18)
```

The hexadecimal 0xfc has binary value as 11111100. The bitwise & operation between `bitV` and 0x00fc0000 will only keep the first 6 bits of `bitV` since `bitV` is only 24 bits. After shifting 18 bits, using the `>> 18` operation, only the first 6 bits of `bitV` is left. This 6-bit value is then used to map the corresponding character in the Base64 string using the `b64Char.charAt()` function.

After the while-loop, only the last one or two characters needed to be processed (line 20). The statement in line 23 determines whether we have a 2-character case. If the value of variable `twochar` is `true`, the second 8-bit character is also added into `bitV` as illustrated in line 25. If we have a 2-character case, the statement in line 29 guarantees that only one equal sign '=' is added into the output string. Otherwise two equal signs '==' are added.

Compared to the encoding, the decoding process is slightly simpler and is listed in part II of `ex01-12.js`.

```
Example: Continuation of ex01-12.js                          (Part II)

34:  function base64_de(inStr)
35:  {
36:    var bitV, outStr="", tmpStr="";
37:    var strLength = inStr.length;
38:    for(ii=0; ii< strLength; ii += 4)
39:    {
40:      bitV = (b64Char.indexOf(inStr.charAt(ii)) & 0xff) <<18 |
41:             (b64Char.indexOf(inStr.charAt(ii+1)) & 0xff) <<12 |
42:             (b64Char.indexOf(inStr.charAt(ii+2)) & 0xff) << 6 |
43:              b64Char.indexOf(inStr.charAt(ii+3)) & 0xff;
44:
45:      tmpStr += String.fromCharCode((bitV & 0xff0000) >>16,
46:                                    (bitV & 0xff00) >>8,
47:                                     bitV & 0xff);
48:    }
49:    if(inStr.charCodeAt(ii-2) == 0x3d)
50:      outStr=tmpStr.substring(0, tmpStr.length -2);
51:    else if(inStr.charCodeAt(ii-1) == 0x3d)
52:      outStr=tmpStr.substring(0, tmpStr.length -1);
53:    else outStr=tmpStr;
54:
55:    return unescape(outStr);
56:  }
```

The decoding is just the reverse of the encoding process. For every 4-character chunk of the encoded string, the four statements in lines 40–43 are used to change them back into a 24-bit value `bitV`.

Since `bitV` is 24-bit, the operation `(bitV & 0xff0000) >>16` in line 45 will extract the value of the first 8 bits. Similarly, the operations `(bitV & 0xff00) >>8` and `bitV & 0xff` extract the second and third 8-bit values. These three 8-bit values are converted into three characters by `String.fromCharCode()` in one function call. After the for-loop in lines 38–48, all encoded characters are decoded and stored in a temporary string `tmpStr`.

Finally, the if-statement in lines 49–53 will make sure that the equal sign(s) generated by the encoding process are properly cut off from `tmpStr`. For example, if the second last character of the input is '=' (hexadecimal 0x3d), the statement in line 50 will cut off two characters from `tmpStr` and store the new result in `outStr`. From the encoding process, the string `outStr` is, in fact, coding with an `escape()` function. The `unescape()` function is called in line 55 before returning the decoded string.

Many people do not consider Base64 encoding is an encryption process due to the fact that no encryption key is involved. You don't need a key for Base64 decoding. However, we consider encryption to be a process of transforming readable text into unreadable gibberish. Under this general definition, Base64 encoding is considered as one kind of encryption, called 'keyless encryption'. Now, let's consider some encryptions with keys.

1.5 The XOR and PkZip/WinZip encryption schemes

1.5.1 XOR encryption/decryption

The bitwise XOR (^) operator has a special property and can be used directly on encryption. Given two arbitrary numbers α and β, the following expression for bitwise XOR holds:

$$(\alpha \wedge \beta) \wedge \beta = \alpha$$

That is, a number XOR another number twice will be itself. For example, if $\alpha = 0110$ and $\beta = 1101$, then

$$\alpha \wedge \beta = 0110 \wedge 1101 = 1011$$

$$(\alpha \wedge \beta) \wedge \beta = 1011 \wedge \beta = 1011 \wedge 1101 = 0110 = \alpha$$

If α is the original character and β a chosen character, then α can be encrypted by the XOR operation, i.e. $\alpha \wedge \beta$. More importantly, you can use the same character β to decrypt the message. This characteristic leads to an important encryption/decryption method called symmetric-key encryption.

In modern cryptography terms, if one key (i.e. digital password) is used for both encryption and decryption, the scheme (or encryption method) is called symmetric-key encryption. The most powerful (or strongest) encryption schemes belong to the symmetric type. A more formal discussion of symmetric-key encryptions and algorithms is presented in Chapters 4 and 6. For now, let's see how bitwise XOR is used to derive one of the simplest symmetric-key encryption schemes.

Suppose you have a message 'M' with p characters and a chosen key 'K' with q characters, i.e.

$$M = (m_0, m_1, m_2, \ldots, m_{p-1})$$

$$K = (k_0, k_1, k_2, \ldots, k_{q-1})$$

Message M can be encrypted by the key K using the following bitwise XOR operations on each character of M:

$$E = (m_0 \wedge k_0, m_1 \wedge k_1, \ldots, m_q \wedge k_0, m_{q+1} \wedge k_1, \ldots, m_p \wedge k_{p\%q})$$

where the symbol $p\%q$ at the end is the remainder of p divided by q. The result is an encrypted string E. This encryption scheme is described by the algorithm shown in `1x01-04.txt`.

```
Example: 1x01-04.txt - The XOR encryption algorithm

 1:      get the original string M (length of M is p)
 2:      get the encryption key K  (length of K is q)
 3:
 4:      for i =0 to p-1 (i.e. length of M-1)
 5:         calculate i%q (the remainder of i divided by q)
 6:         get the ith character of M: M(i)
 7:         get the i%q th character of K: K(i%q)
 8:         perform the bitwise XOR on M(i) ^ K(i%q) and
 9:         output the encrypted character
10:      next i
```

In fact, the for-loop in this algorithm is to calculate the ith character of the encrypted string E above, (i.e. $m_i \wedge k_{i\%q}$). Given the encrypted string E and the same key K below:

$$E = (e_0, e_1, e_2, \ldots, e_{p-1})$$

$$K = (k_0, k_1, k_2, \ldots, k_{q-1})$$

String E can be decrypted by the key K using the following bitwise XOR operations on each character of E:

$$(e_0 \wedge k_0, e_1 \wedge k_1, \ldots, e_q \wedge k_0, e_{q+1} \wedge k_1, \ldots, e_p \wedge k_{p\%q})$$

$$= (m_0 \wedge k_0 \wedge k_0, m_1 \wedge k_1 \wedge k_1, \ldots, m_p \wedge k_{p\%q} \wedge k_{p\%q})$$

$$= (m_0, m_1, m_2, \ldots, m_{p-1})$$

where the symbol $p\%q$ is the remainder of p divided by q. The result is the same string of M. The decryption algorithm is described in 1x01-05.txt.

```
Example: 1x01-05.txt - The XOR decryption algorithm

 1:      get the encrypted string E (length of E is p)
 2:      get the encryption key K   (length of K is q)
 3:
 4:      for i =0 to p-1 (i.e. length of E -1)
 5:         calculate i%q (the remainder of i divided by q)
 6:         get the ith character of E: E(i)
 7:         get the i%q th character of K: ·K(i%q)
 8:         perform the bitwise XOR on E(i) ^ K(i%q) and
 9:         output the decrypted character
10:      next i
```

This algorithm is very similar to its encryption counterpart and should be easy to read. Since the encryption key (or password) is defined by the user, a certain degree of security is maintained. This is probably one of the simplest XOR (or symmetric-key) encryption schemes. An implementation of the scheme on Web pages is provided in the next section.

1.5.2 Implementation of the XOR scheme on the Web

The first thing to do when implementing the XOR encryption on a Web page is to generate some boxes for the user to enter the original message and encryption password (or key). A text field for the encrypted message, or outcome, is also needed. For this kind of application, HTML/XHTML code is an ideal choice. Consider ex01-13.htm.

```
Example: ex01-13.htm - The XOR encryption scheme

 1: <?xml version="1.0" encoding="iso-8859-1"?>
 2: <!DOCTYPE html PUBLIC "-//W3C//DTD XHTML 1.0 Transitional//EN"
 3:    "http://www.w3.org/TR/xhtml1/DTD/xhtml1-transitional.dtd">
 4: <html xmlns="http://www.w3.org/1999/xhtml" xml:lang="en"
       lang="en">
 5: <head><title>The XOR Encryption Scheme -
       ex01-13.htm</title></head>
 6: <body style="font-family:arial;font-size:26pt;text-align:center;
 7:        background:#000088;color:#ffff00">
 8:   My XOR Encryption Page<br />
 9:   <img alt="pic" src="line1.gif" height="7"
       width="640" /><br /><br />
10:
11: <table style="font-size:18pt;text-align:left" align="center">
12:   <tr><td>Please Enter A Message Below:</td></tr>
13:   <tr><td><textarea id="in_mesg" rows="5" cols="40"
14:        style="font-size:16pt;width:540px;font-weight:bold;
15:        height:100px;background:#dddddd;
            color:#ff0000"></textarea>
16:
17:   <tr><td><br />Enter The Encryption password (or Key)
       Here:</td></tr>
18:   <tr><td style="text-align:center">
19:        <input id="key_v" size="10" maxlength="10"
20:         style="font-size:16pt;width:250px;height:40px;
21:         font-weight:bold;background:#dddddd;color:#ff0000" />
22:         <input type="button" value="OK" onclick="xor_encode()"
```

```
23:              style="font-size:16pt;font-weight:bold;width:80px;
24:              height:40px;background:#dddddd;
                 color:#ff0000" /></td></tr>
25:
26:  <tr><td><br />The Encrypted Message is: </td><tr>
27:  <tr><td><textarea rows="5" cols="40" id="en_str" readonly
28:              style="font-size:16pt;font-weight:bold;width:540px;
29:              height:100px;background:#aaffaa"></textarea></td></tr>
30: </table>
31: <script src="ex01-13.js"></script>
32: </body></html>
```

Inside this code fragment, a text area <textarea> is defined in lines 13–15 to generate an area so that a user can enter the original message. Soon after this, two input elements are declared. The first input element (lines 19–21) generates a smaller input field for the user to enter the encryption password (or key). The purpose of this key is to encrypt the original message. The second input element is an OK button to trigger the encryption action. When this button is clicked, the function xor_encode() is called. The result of the encrypted message is then displayed in the text area defined in lines 27–29. The details of the function xor_encode() are defined in part I of ex01-13.js.

```
Example: ex01-13.js - External ECMAScript for ex01-13.htm     (Part I)

 1: function xor_encode()
 2: {
 3:   var enSt="";
 4:   var mSt=document.getElementById("in_mesg").value;
 5:   var keySt=document.getElementById("key_v").value;
 6:   var ii, mCh,mCode, kCh, kCode,ind;
 7:   for (ii=0;ii< mSt.length;ii++) {
 8:      mCode = mSt.charCodeAt(ii);
 9:      ind = ii % keySt.length;
10:      kCh = keySt.charAt(ind);
11:      kCode = kCh.charCodeAt(0);
12:      enSt = enSt + String.fromCharCode(mCode ^ kCode);
13:   }
14:   document.getElementById("en_str").value=unicodeCharToHex(enSt);
15: }
16:
```

Using the encryption algorithm mentioned in 1x01-04.txt, this function is easy to read. Lines 4–5 get the original message and the encryption key. The for-loop in lines 7–13 performs the bitwise XOR operations and ultimately does the encryption. For each character in the original string mSt, Unicode mCode is obtained. The next step is to calculate the index (ind). This value is the remainder of ii divided by the length of the encryption key. This index is used to obtain the corresponding character kCh and Unicode kCode of the encryption key. The XOR operation

```
mCode ^ kCode
```

produces the encrypted character and appends it to the string enSt. The statement in line 14 displays the string enSt to where id="en_str".

It is important to note that the bitwise operation can produce any character code. Some of them may be well beyond the ASCII range or have special meaning for the browser and operating system. When a browser interprets these characters, it may stop processing the encryption and perform some special functions instead. This will destroy the integrity of the encryption scheme and security. In order to make sure that the encrypted message is safe to print on the screen, the function unicodeCharToHex() is used in line 14 to convert the Unicode character to hexadecimal representation. The function call

```
unicodeCharToHex(enSt)
```

will convert each Unicode character into two bytes (four digits) hexadecimal form, i.e. XXXX. A screenshot of this page in action is shown in Figure 1.22.

Fig. 1.22 Bitwise XOR encryption

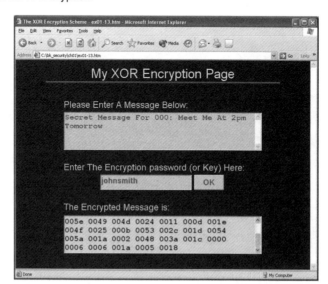

Alternatively, you can use a standard ECMAScript function such as `escape(enSt)` to produce a safety output of characters. However, some browsers such as NS7+ have difficulties handling large character code. The definition of the function `unicodeCharToHex()` is provided in part II of `ex01-13.js`.

```
Example: Continuation of ex01-13.js                          (Part II)

17: function unicodeCharToHex (s)
18: {
19:  var r = "";
20:  var hexes = new Array ("0","1","2","3","4","5","6","7",
21:                          "8","9","a","b","c","d","e","f");
22:  for (var i=0; i<s.length; i++) {
23:   r += hexes [s.charCodeAt(i) >> 16 & 0xf] +
24:         hexes [s.charCodeAt(i) >> 8 & 0xf] +
25:         hexes [s.charCodeAt(i) >> 4 & 0xf] +
26:         hexes [s.charCodeAt(i) & 0xf] + " ";
27:  }
28:  return r;
29: }
```

This function is easy to read. First, an array `hexes` is declared for the 16 hexadecimal digits in lines 20–21. For each Unicode character, the for-loop in lines 22–27 constructs the hexadecimal string. The two statements in lines 23–24 extract the most significant byte (MSB) of the Unicode code represented by two hexadecimal digits, i.e. XX. The next two lines (lines 25–26) extract the least significant byte (LSB) of the Unicode into hexadecimal form. The result, i.e. XXXX with a space, is added into a string `s` and then returned to the function caller. One of the reasons for using this function is that we can clearly see all the encoded characters one by one.

Being a symmetric process to encryption, decryption is similar. First, we make a copy of example `ex01-13.htm` and call it `ex01-14.htm`. The next step is to modify the following five lines to reflect that the page is a decryption page.

```
 8:    My XOR Decryption Page<br />
22:        <input type="button" value="OK" onclick="xor_decode()"
26:  <tr><td><br />The Decrypted Message is: </td><tr>
27:  <tr><td><textarea rows="5" cols="40" id="de_str" readonly
31:  <script src="ex01-14.js"></script>
```

Note that when the OK button in line 22 is clicked, the function `xor_decode()` will be triggered to perform the decryption. The decrypted result will be displayed in the text area defined in line 27.

This decryption function `xor_decode()` is specified in the external file `ex01-14.js`.

```
 1: function xor_decode()
 2: {
 3:   var deSt="";
 4:   var eSt=hexToUnicodeChar(document.getElementById
        ("in_mesg").value);
 5:   var keySt=document.getElementById("key_v").value;
 6:   var ii, eCh, eCode, kCh, kCode,ind;
 7:   for (ii=0;ii<eSt.length;ii++) {
 8:       eCode = eSt.charCodeAt(ii);
 9:       ind = ii % keySt.length;
10:       kCh = keySt.charAt(ind);
11:       kCode = kCh.charCodeAt(0);
12:       deSt = deSt + String.fromCharCode(eCode ^ kCode);
13:   }
14:   document.getElementById("de_str").value=deSt;
15: }
```

Since the encrypted message is a two byte hexadecimal string, as mentioned in the encryption process, the `hexToUnicodeChar()` function (line 4) is used to convert it back to a Unicode string and characters. If you use the standard function `escape()` in the encryption process, you should use the `unescape()` function here. After the encryption password is obtained, the for-loop in lines 7–13 starts the decryption process. For each encrypted character in the string `eSt`, Unicode `eCode` is obtained. Based on the position of this `eCode`, the corresponding Unicode `kCode` in the password string is found (lines 8–12). The bitwise XOR operation `eCode^kCode` (line 12) returns the original (or plaintext) character.

This character is then added to the decrypted string `deSt` in line 12. When the entire string is decoded, the string is output by the statement in line 14 to the text area where `id="de_str"`. A screenshot is shown in Figure 1.23. In this you can see that the same encoded message from `ex01-12.htm` is copied into this example. After you have entered the password 'johnsmith' and the OK button is clicked, the original message 'Secret Message For 000: Meet Me At 2pm Tomorrow' appears in the bottom field. The details of the function `hexToUnicodeChar()` are defined in part II of `ex01-14.js`.

Fig. 1.23 Bitwise XOR decryption

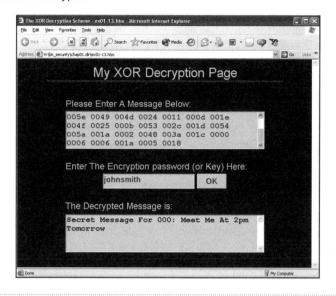

```
Example: Continuation of ex01-14.js                    (Part II)

16: function hexToUnicodeChar(s)
17: {
18:  var r="", jj=0;
19:  while (jj < s.length)
20:  {
21:    r += String.fromCharCode(parseInt(s.substring(jj,jj+4),16));
22:    jj = jj+5;
23:  }
24:  return r;
25: }
```

Since each Unicode in the string s is represented by four hexadecimal digits plus a
space, the while-loop in lines 19–23 extracts the hexadecimal value for every five
characters in the input string s. Consider the statement

```
String.fromCharCode(parseInt(s.substring(jj,jj+4),16))
```

This statement first extracts four characters from string s using the substring
function. The function parseInt(xx,16) parses the substring into an integer with
base 16. The function String.fromCharCode() converts the integer into Unicode.
The Unicode is then added to the string r and returns to the function caller as
illustrated in lines 21 and 24.

From now on, we will put these `hexToUnicodeChar()` and `unicodeCharToHex()` functions in an ECMAScript file called `hexlib.js` so that they can be used in later sections. Note that these hexadecimal conversion functions are elementary. Some more practical conversion functions are provided. Consider the function in `hexlib.js` below.

```
Example: hexlib.js - some hexadecimal functions                    (Part I)

26: function myParseHex(inSt)
27: {
28:    var ii,idx=0,startL=0,endL=0, flag;
29:    var hexV = new Array();
30:
31:    stLen = inSt.length;
32:    for (ii=0;ii< stLen;ii++) {
33:       while ( (inSt.charCodeAt(startL)==32) && (startL < stLen))
                    startL++;
34:       endL=0;
35:       while ( (inSt.charCodeAt(startL+endL) !=32) && (startL+endL
                    < stLen))
36:       {
37:          flag = 1;
38:          endL++;
39:       }
40:       if (flag ==1) {
41:          hexV[idx]= parseInt(inSt.substring(startL,startL+endL),16);
42:          flag = 0;
43:          startL =startL + endL;
44:          idx++;
45:       }
46:    }
47:    return(hexV);
48: }
49:
```

The line numbers in `hexlib.js` continue from the function `hexToUnicodeChar()` in `ex01-04.js`. A hexadecimal conversion function called `myParseHex()` is listed. Given a hexadecimal string (`inSt`) with each value separated by one or more spaces, this function can read the string, parse each hexadecimal value into the array `hexV[]` and then return to the function caller.

The length of the input string is captured by the variable `stLen` in line 31. The for-loop in lines 32–46 process each character of the string. The while-loop in line 33 finds the starting position of the character which is not a space and stores it in variable `startL`. The second while-loop in lines 35–39 finds the ending position of character (`endL`), which is again a space. In other words, the hexadecimal value is from the position `startL` to `endL`. This value is extracted by the statement in line 41 and stored in array `hexV[]`. By adding the positons `startL` and `endL`, as in line 43, the searching and converting process can continue until the end of the input string. The array `hexV[]` is returned by the statement in line 47.

In some cases, the ECMAScript standard function `parseInt()` is not a reliable function for parsing a hexadecimal value. To convert the integer ourselves, the functions shown in part II of `hexlib.js` are needed.

```
Example: Continuation of hexlib.js                          (Part II)

50: function byteToHex (s)
51: {
52:   var r = "";
53:   var hexes = new Array ("0","1","2","3","4","5","6","7",
54:                          "8","9","a","b","c","d","e","f");
55:   r += hexes [s >> 4 & 0xf] + hexes [s & 0xf];
56:   return r;
57: }
58:
59: function byteStToHex(ss)
60: {
61:   var ii, retSt="";
62:   for (ii=0;ii<ss.length;ii++)
63:       retSt += byteToHex(ss.charCodeAt(ii)) + " ";
64:   return retSt;
65: }
66:
67: function hexStToByteSt(ss)
68: {
69:   var ii, retSt="";
70:   var hexArr = new Array();
71:   hexArr = myParseHex(ss);
72:   for (ii=0;ii<hexArr.length;ii++)
73:     retSt += String.fromCharCode(hexArr[ii]);
74:   return retSt;
75: }
```

The first function `byteToHex()` in lines 50–57 converts a single byte into a hexadecimal value. It is simply a bit manipulation, as illustrated in line 55. The second function `byteStToHex()` uses the `byteToHex()` function to convert a byte string into a hexadecimal string. Each hexadecimal value is separated by a space.

The third function `hexStToByteSt()` converts a hexadecimal string `ss` to a byte (or character) string. First the hexadecimal string is parsed by the `myParseHex()` function in part I of hexlib.js. For each array element in `hexArr[]`, the for-loop in lines 72–73 is used to convert them into a string called `retSt` and then return to the function caller. These functions will be used in this book.

The XOR encryption/decryption scheme gives you the freedom of inputting your own password and creating certain flexibilities for applications.

This bitwise XOR encryption is one of the most fundamental schemes in cryptography. Many encryption/decryption algorithms are based on this operation. In fact, if the encryption key is random, only used once, and if the length of the key is the same as the plaintext, the encryption is known as 'one-time-pad'. One-time-pad is the only encryption that has been proved to be unbreakable. The well-known hotline between Washington and Moscow was protected by one-time-pad. Many advanced encryption algorithms are based on the same principle – try to make the encryption key random and as long as possible. In next section, we consider how this scheme is used on commercial products such as PkZip and WinZip.

1.5.3   Encryption/decryption in PkZip and WinZip

If you have sent email with attachments or downloaded files from the Internet and Web, chances are that you are already familiar with a special file format called 'zip'.

In fact, most of the files available for download on the Internet and Web are stored as zip files. Storing files in the zip format provides two advantages:

- several files can be packed into one file;
- files stored in the zip format are compressed and the file size is usually much smaller.

General speaking a zip file is one or more files compressed into a single, smaller file. There are several tools and commercial products (such as WinZip and PkZip) available to zip and unzip files. PkZip, from PKWARE Inc, is the original program that creates zip files stretching back to a decade ago. The founder of PKWARE is Phil Katz. PkZip was so widely used that 'zipping' became the standard and all zip files have the file extension `.zip`. The success of PkZip led to the launch of other competing zip products, such as WinZip. These two products are compatible technically.

In order to provide security for zip files, an encryption scheme was introduced in the early versions of the PkZip program. Encryption is activated by entering a password. For example, you can select the password option in the 'Add Files' menu of PkZip to add encryption. A password window will be activated as shown in Figure 1.24. For WinZip users, you can select Options | Password to see the password window as shown in Figure 1.25.

Fig. 1.24 PkZip password window

Fig. 1.25 WinZip password window

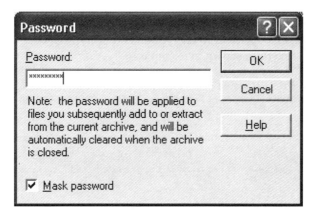

To enable compatibility of the two types of software, the encryption used in PkZip and WinZip is the same. The encryption scheme described here is based on the application note file (appnote.txt) provided by the PkZip package. The scheme will be implemented on a Web page using ECMAScript in the next section. The scheme has a simple presentation and is shown below.

```
The encryption algorithm          The decryption algorithm

1: Initialization()               1: Initialization()
2: loop until end of input        2: loop until end of input
3:    read a character into C     3:    read an encrypted character E
4:       temp = C ^ decrypt_byte() 4:       temp = E ^ decrypt_byte()
5:       update_keys(C)           5:       update_keys(temp)
6:    output temp                 6:    output temp
7: end loop                       7: end loop
```

As you can see from the algorithms, both the encryption and decryption processes are based on the bitwise XOR operation of two characters and therefore can be considered as the XOR type.

The interesting part of the algorithms is the use of functions decrypt_byte() and undate_keys(). Based on three values (or keys), namely keys_0, keys_1, and keys_2, the decrypt_byte() function returns a character (or a byte) which is used to perform the XOR operations. The update_keys() function takes the original character and updates all three keys. In order to guarantee the decryption process, the same original character must be input into the function update_keys() as illustrated in line 5 of the decryption algorithm. The details of the functions decrypt_byte() and update_keys() are discussed in the following section.

1.5.4 Implementation of the PkZip/WinZip encryption scheme

To implement Pkzip/WinZip encryption and decryption on a Web page, we use the XHTML interface shown in example ex01-15.htm.

```
Example: ex01-15.htm - The PkZip/WinZip encryption scheme

 1: <?xml version="1.0" encoding="iso-8859-1"?>
 2: <!DOCTYPE html PUBLIC "-//W3C//DTD XHTML 1.0 Transitional//EN"
 3:    "http://www.w3.org/TR/xhtml1/DTD/xhtml1-transitional.dtd">
 4: <html xmlns="http://www.w3.org/1999/xhtml" xml:lang="en"
    lang="en">
 5: <head><title> ZIP/PKZIP/WINZIP Encryption -
    ex01-15.htm</title></head>
 6: <body style="font-family:arial;font-size:26pt;text-align:center;
 7:       background:#000088;color:#ffff00">
 8:    The PkZip / WinZip Encryption Scheme<br />
 9:    <img alt="pic" src="line1.gif" height="7"
    width="640" /><br /><br />
10:
```

```
11:  <table style="font-size:16pt;text-align:left" align="center">
12:   <tr><td colspan=2>Please Enter A Message Below:</td></tr>
13:   <tr><td colspan=2><textarea id="in_mesg" rows="5" cols="40"
14:          style="font-size:16pt;width:600px;font-weight:bold;
15:          height:70px;background:#dddddd;
              color:#ff0000" ></textarea>
16:
17:   <tr><td><br />Enter Encryption Key</td><td>Enter Decryption
       Key</td></tr>
18:   <tr><td>
19:          <input id="en_key" size="40" maxlength="40"
20:            style="font-size:16pt;width:250px;height:40px;
21:            font-weight:bold;background:#dddddd;
              color:#ff0000" /></td><td>
22:          <input id="de_key" size="40" maxlength="40"
23:            style="font-size:16pt;width:250px;height:40px;
24:            font-weight:bold;background:#dddddd;color:#ff0000" />
25:          <input type="button" value="OK" onclick="zip_code()"
26:            style="font-size:16pt;font-weight:bold;width:80px;
27:            height:40px;background:#dddddd;
              color:#ff0000" /></td></tr>
28:
29:   <tr><td>Encrypted Message:</td><td>Decrypted Message: </td></tr>
30:   <tr><td><textarea rows="5" cols="40" id="en_str" readonly
31:            style="font-size:16pt;font-weight:bold;width:300px;
32:            height:170px;background:#aaffaa"></textarea></td><td>
33:          <textarea rows="5" cols="40" id="de_str" readonly
34:            style="font-size:16pt;font-weight:bold;width:300px;
35:            height:170px;background:#aaffaa"></textarea></td></tr>
36:  </table>
37:  <script src="ex01-15.js"></script>
38:  <script src="hexlib.js"></script>
38:  </body></html>
```

This page generates three text areas, one text box and an OK button. The first text area `<textarea>` in lines 13–15 allows you to enter an original message. The two text boxes defined in lines 19–21, 22–24 are used to get the encryption and decryption key (or password) respectively. The two read-only text areas in lines 30–32 and 33–35 are used to display the encrypted and decrypted messages. Screenshots are shown in Figures 1.26 and 1.27.

One of the strengths of this scheme is that if you have made a minor mistake on the password then the output will be quite different and the decrypted message will be nothing like the original message. This is because the scheme uses a powerful

Fig. 1.26 WinZip encryption scheme I

Fig. 1.27 WinZip encryption scheme II

security enhancement called 'pseudo-random sequence'. We will cover this pseudo-random topic later in Chapter 5.

From line 25, you can see that when the OK button is clicked, the function zip_code() is activated and both the encryption and decryption are performed. The details of this ECMAScript zip_code() function are specified in the external file ex01-15.js as indicated in line 37.

The first part of this ECMAScript file is listed in ex01-15.js.

```
Example: ex01-15.js - ECMAScript for ex01-15.htm          (Part I)

 1: function zip_code()
 2: {
 3:    var enStr="", deStr="", mesg="", pass="";
 4:    mesg=document.getElementById("in_mesg").value;
 5:    en_pass=document.getElementById("en_key").value;
 6:    de_pass=document.getElementById("de_key").value;
 7:
 8:    if ((en_pass !="") && (de_pass !="") && ( mesg !="")) {
 9:       enStr = zip_encode(mesg,en_pass);
10:       deStr = zip_decode(enStr,de_pass);
11:       document.getElementById("en_str").value=unicodeCharToHex
                                                            (enStr);
12:       document.getElementById("de_str").value=deStr;
13:    }
14: }
15:
16: function zip_encode(inSt,pass)
17: {
18:   var enSt="", ch, ch1;
19:   init_keys(pass);
20:   for (ii=0;ii< inSt.length;ii++) {
21:      ch1 = inSt.charCodeAt(ii);
22:      ch = inSt.charCodeAt(ii) ^ decrypt_byte();
23:      update_keys(ch1);
24:      enSt= enSt + String.fromCharCode(ch);
25:   }
26:   return (enSt);
27: }
28:
29: function zip_decode(inSt,pass)
30: {
31:   var deSt="", ch, ch1;
32:   init_keys(pass);
```

```
33:    for (ii=0;ii< inSt.length ;ii++) {
34:       ch1 = inSt.charCodeAt(ii);
35:       ch = inSt.charCodeAt(ii) ^ decrypt_byte();
36:       update_keys(ch);
37:       deSt= deSt + String.fromCharCode(ch);
38:    }
39:    return (deSt);
40: }
41:
```

This code fragment contains three functions. The first function `zip_code()` controls the entire process. First, the statements in lines 4–6 capture the original message, encryption and decryption key and store them in strings `mesg`, `en_pass` and `de_pass` respectively. If all three strings are not empty (line 8), encryption/decryption are executed. Consider the statement in line 9:

```
enStr = zip_encode(mesg,en_pass)
```

This statement passes the original message `mesg` and password `en_pass` into the function `zip_encode()` for encryption. The result is stored in variable `enStr`. Similarly, the statement in line 10:

```
deStr = zip_decode(enStr,de_pass)
```

passes the encrypted string `enStr` and password `de_pass` into the function `zip_decode()` to do the decryption. The result is stored in the string `deStr`. Both the encrypted and decrypted strings are output by the statements in lines 11–12. Since the encrypted string `enStr` may contain non-printable characters, the `unicodeCharToHex()` function covered in previous section is used for a safety output (line 11).

Consider the encryption function `zip_encode()` in lines 16–27. This function takes an input string `inSt` and a password `pass`. The password string is used in the `init_keys()` function to initialize the three keys, namely `keys[0]`, `keys[1]` and `keys[3]`. With these keys, the function `decypt_byte()` can return a byte to perform the bitwise XOR operation on a character of the input string. The encrypted character `ch` is then appended at the end of the encrypted string. The `update_keys()` function in line 23 uses the original character `ch1` and generates a new set of keys. Using the same process, another encrypted character is generated and appended in `enSt`.

The decryption process, or function, `zip_decode()` in lines 29–40 is similar. The same `decrypte_byte()` and `update_keys()` functions are employed. As long as the `decrypte_byte()` function generates the same value (or byte) as in the encryption process, the decryption is guaranteed. In order to do that, the original or decrypted character `ch` is used in the function `update_keys()` as in line 36.

The purpose of the `decrypt_byte()` and `update_keys()` functions is to generate the so-called pseudo-random value (or sequence) so that the security of the XOR scheme is greatly enhanced. Based on the PkZip documentation `appnote.txt`, the functions `decrypt_byte()` and `update_keys()` are given in part II of `ex01-15.js`.

```
Example: Continuation of the ECMAScript ex01-15.js          (Part II)

42: var keys=new Array(0,0,0);
43:
44: function decrypt_byte()
45: {
46:    var temp;
47:    temp = (keys[2] & 0xffff) [*140] 2;
48:    return (((temp * (temp ^ 1)) >> 8) & 0xff);
49: }
50:
51: function update_keys(c)
52: {
53:        keys[0] = CRC32(keys[0], c);
54:        keys[1] = (keys[0] & 0xff) + keys[1];
55:        keys[1] = bit32_mult(keys[1],134775813)+1;
56:        keys[2] = CRC32(keys[2], keys[1] >> 24);
57: }
58:
59: function bit32_mult(a,b)
60: {
61:    var tmp = ((a * (b>>16)) << 16);
62:    tmp += a * (b & 0xffff);
63:    return (tmp & 0xffffffff);
64: }
65:
```

As you can see, the `decrypt_byte()` is governed by a number called `Key_2` (or `Keys[2]`). In order to obtain a different `Key_2` for each step, the function `update_keys()` in lines 51–57 is used. This `update_keys()` function takes an input character variable `c` (usually from the original message) and updates the values of three 4-byte integers `keys[0]`, `keys[1]` and `keys[2]`. The updated value of `keys[2]` will be used by the `decrypt_byte()` function in lines 44–49.

From the XOR operation, we know that as long as the same character is input to `update_keys()`, the encryption and decryption processes are guaranteed by the XOR operation. This function involves a multiplication of two large (32-bit) integers and a `CRC()` function. The purpose is to generate the so-called pseudo-random sequence. The pseudo-random sequence (discussed in Chapter 5) is an important subject in cryptography and can be used to enhance the security of a scheme. In order to prevent the ECMAScript changing the result of the multiplication to a floating point number (or real number), a multiplication function called `bit32_mult()` is used as shown in part III of `ex01-15.js`.

```
Example: Continuation of the ECMAScript ex01-15.js          (Part III)

66: function CRC32(c,b)
67: {
68:    var tmp = crc_32_tab[(c ^ b) & 0xff];
69:    return( ((c >> 8 ) & 0xffffff) ^ tmp);
70: }
71:
72: function init_keys(passwd)
73: {
74:       keys[0] = 0x12345678;
75:       keys[1] = 0x23456789;
76:       keys[2] = 0x34567890;
77:       for (ii=0;ii< passwd.length; ii++) {
78:          tmp1 = parseInt(passwd.charCodeAt(ii));
79:          update_keys(tmp1);
80:       }
81: }
82:
```

The `CRC32()` function takes a 4-byte integer `c` and a single byte character `b` as arguments. By using a predefined cyclic redundancy check (CRC) table `crc_32tab[]`, a value is returned. CRC is not really needed for encryption. It is used to ensure transmission accuracy by checking the CRC sums.

In order to prepare the keys for both the encryption and decryption processes, the input password is used in the `init_keys()` function (lines 72–81) to generate the first set of `keys[0]`, `keys[1]` and `keys[2]`. First, initial values of the keys are set. The for-loop in lines 77–80 illustrate that for each character of the password, the function `update_keys()` is called to further update `keys[0]`, `keys[1]` and `keys[2]`. Based on these algorithms, the two functions `CRC32()` and `init_keys()` can be implemented easily. This is listed in part III of the ECMAScript `ex01-15.js`.

For completeness of the program, the 32-bit CRC table is listed in part IV of the ECMAScript `ex01-15.js`.

CRC values are often used as transmission signatures or to detect errors during electronic transmission of data.

By today's cryptography standard, this encryption scheme is not very sophisticated. It can be attacked and cracked by a number of methods such as

```
 83: var crc_32_tab = new Array(
 84:    0x00000000, 0x77073096, 0xee0e612c, 0x990951ba, 0x076dc419,
 85:    0x706af48f, 0xe963a535, 0x9e6495a3, 0x0edb8832, 0x79dcb8a4,
 86:    0xe0d5e91e, 0x97d2d988, 0x09b64c2b, 0x7eb17cbd, 0xe7b82d07,
 87:    0x90bf1d91, 0x1db71064, 0x6ab020f2, 0xf3b97148, 0x84be41de,
 88:    0x1adad47d, 0x6ddde4eb, 0xf4d4b551, 0x83d385c7, 0x136c9856,
 89:    0x646ba8c0, 0xfd62f97a, 0x8a65c9ec, 0x14015c4f, 0x63066cd9,
 90:    0xfa0f3d63, 0x8d080df5, 0x3b6e20c8, 0x4c69105e, 0xd56041e4,
 91:    0xa2677172, 0x3c03e4d1, 0x4b04d447, 0xd20d85fd, 0xa50ab56b,
 92:    0x35b5a8fa, 0x42b2986c, 0xdbbbc9d6, 0xacbcf940, 0x32d86ce3,
 93:    0x45df5c75, 0xdcd60dcf, 0xabd13d59, 0x26d930ac, 0x51de003a,
 94:    0xc8d75180, 0xbfd06116, 0x21b4f4b5, 0x56b3c423, 0xcfba9599,
 95:    0xb8bda50f, 0x2802b89e, 0x5f058808, 0xc60cd9b2, 0xb10be924,
 96:    0x2f6f7c87, 0x58684c11, 0xc1611dab, 0xb6662d3d, 0x76dc4190,
 97:    0x01db7106, 0x98d220bc, 0xefd5102a, 0x71b18589, 0x06b6b51f,
 98:    0x9fbfe4a5, 0xe8b8d433, 0x7807c9a2, 0x0f00f934, 0x9609a88e,
 99:    0xe10e9818, 0x7f6a0dbb, 0x086d3d2d, 0x91646c97, 0xe6635c01,
100:    0x6b6b51f4, 0x1c6c6162, 0x856530d8, 0xf262004e, 0x6c0695ed,
101:    0x1b01a57b, 0x8208f4c1, 0xf50fc457, 0x65b0d9c6, 0x12b7e950,
102:    0x8bbeb8ea, 0xfcb9887c, 0x62dd1ddf, 0x15da2d49, 0x8cd37cf3,
103:    0xfbd44c65, 0x4db26158, 0x3ab551ce, 0xa3bc0074, 0xd4bb30e2,
104:    0x4adfa541, 0x3dd895d7, 0xa4d1c46d, 0xd3d6f4fb, 0x4369e96a,
105:    0x346ed9fc, 0xad678846, 0xda60b8d0, 0x44042d73, 0x33031de5,
106:    0xaa0a4c5f, 0xdd0d7cc9, 0x5005713c, 0x270241aa, 0xbe0b1010,
107:    0xc90c2086, 0x5768b525, 0x206f85b3, 0xb966d409, 0xce61e49f,
108:    0x5edef90e, 0x29d9c998, 0xb0d09822, 0xc7d7a8b4, 0x59b33d17,
109:    0x2eb40d81, 0xb7bd5c3b, 0xc0ba6cad, 0xedb88320, 0x9abfb3b6,
110:    0x03b6e20c, 0x74b1d29a, 0xead54739, 0x9dd277af, 0x04db2615,
111:    0x73dc1683, 0xe3630b12, 0x94643b84, 0x0d6d6a3e, 0x7a6a5aa8,
112:    0xe40ecf0b, 0x9309ff9d, 0x0a00ae27, 0x7d079eb1, 0xf00f9344,
113:    0x8708a3d2, 0x1e01f268, 0x6906c2fe, 0xf762575d, 0x806567cb,
114:    0x196c3671, 0x6e6b06e7, 0xfed41b76, 0x89d32be0, 0x10da7a5a,
115:    0x67dd4acc, 0xf9b9df6f, 0x8ebeeff9, 0x17b7be43, 0x60b08ed5,
116:    0xd6d6a3e8, 0xa1d1937e, 0x38d8c2c4, 0x4fdff252, 0xd1bb67f1,
117:    0xa6bc5767, 0x3fb506dd, 0x48b2364b, 0xd80d2bda, 0xaf0a1b4c,
118:    0x36034af6, 0x41047a60, 0xdf60efc3, 0xa867df55, 0x316e8eef,
119:    0x4669be79, 0xcb61b38c, 0xbc66831a, 0x256fd2a0, 0x5268e236,
120:    0xcc0c7795, 0xbb0b4703, 0x220216b9, 0x5505262f, 0xc5ba3bbe,
121:    0xb2bd0b28, 0x2bb45a92, 0x5cb36a04, 0xc2d7ffa7, 0xb5d0cf31,
122:    0x2cd99e8b, 0x5bdeae1d, 0x9b64c2b0, 0xec63f226, 0x756aa39c,
123:    0x026d930a, 0x9c0906a9, 0xeb0e363f, 0x72076785, 0x05005713,
124:    0x95bf4a82, 0xe2b87a14, 0x7bb12bae, 0x0cb61b38, 0x92d28e9b,
```

```
125:    0xe5d5be0d, 0x7cdcefb7, 0x0bdbdf21, 0x86d3d2d4, 0xf1d4e242,
126:    0x68ddb3f8, 0x1fda836e, 0x81be16cd, 0xf6b9265b, 0x6fb077e1,
127:    0x18b74777, 0x88085ae6, 0xff0f6a70, 0x66063bca, 0x11010b5c,
128:    0x8f659eff, 0xf862ae69, 0x616bffd3, 0x166ccf45, 0xa00ae278,
129:    0xd70dd2ee, 0x4e048354, 0x3903b3c2, 0xa7672661, 0xd06016f7,
130:    0x4969474d, 0x3e6e77db, 0xaed16a4a, 0xd9d65adc, 0x40df0b66,
131:    0x37d83bf0, 0xa9bcae53, 0xdebb9ec5, 0x47b2cf7f, 0x30b5ffe9,
132:    0xbdbdf21c, 0xcabac28a, 0x53b39330, 0x24b4a3a6, 0xbad03605,
133:    0xcdd70693, 0x54de5729, 0x23d967bf, 0xb3667a2e, 0xc4614ab8,
134:    0x5d681b02, 0x2a6f2b94, 0xb40bbe37, 0xc30c8ea1, 0x5a05df1b,
135:    0x2d02ef8d
136: );
```

'brute-force' and 'known plaintext'. We will discuss some attacks in the next chapter. However, this PkZip/WinZip scheme is a good starting point for learning about modern encryption/decryption since it demonstrates a number of the cryptographic features used in cryptology.

At the start of 2004, in addition to this encryption, WinZip adopted a more secure encryption scheme called 'Advanced Encryption Standard' (AES), which was promoted by the US government. The AES encryption/decryption will be discussed in Chapter 6.

2

Cryptology, Web site protection and attacks

2.1 An overview of cryptology

2.1.1 What is cryptology?

In Chapter 1 you learned some basic ideas and skills on encryption/decryption and how to use them on the Web to maintain the confidentiality of messages. Encryption and decryption are part of a technology called cryptography. In fact, in terms of security, cryptography is only half the story. A scientific study of security also involves attacks forming a wider subject called 'cryptology' (Figure 2.1).

Fig. 2.1 An overview of cryptology

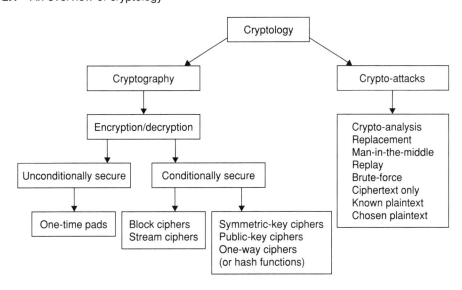

In terms of cryptography, any technique that can transform a readable document (or plaintext) to unreadable gibberish is called encryption. The data after the encryption is called ciphertext. In the same terminology, encryption schemes are sometimes also called ciphers. Encryption is, in fact, a data processing technique to disguise the plaintext. If an encryption is reversible, the reverse process to convert ciphertext back to plaintext is called decryption. Not all encryptions are reversible. One-way encryption does exist and plays an equally important role as encryption and decryption in modern cryptography and security applications.

In the digital world of cryptography, both encryption and decryption are usually controlled by digital keys. A key is referred to a value that works with an algorithm to encrypt or decrypt data. Normally, keys are strings or big numbers measured in bits. Bigger keys (in bits) will result in stronger security. In practice, keys sometimes are regarded as passwords. An encryption scheme is said to be breakable if a third party (adversary) can determine the key or plaintext from ciphertext. An attack is defined as the process or technique for recovering the key or plaintext from an encryption scheme. In an attack, you can assume that your adversary knows everything about your scheme (including the process and some plaintext) except for the key. This is called Kerckhoff's principle and dates back to more than 100 years ago. The openness of this principle is the fundamental form of modern cryptology and well suited to our World Wide Web environment. Some examples are presented in the next section. More attacks and implementations are presented in Sections 2.4 and 2.5.

Unconditionally secure ciphers

In general, security can be measured by risks which, in many cases, are calculable. In fact, unconditional risk-free (or unconditionally secure) encryption does exist. A cipher is said to be unconditionally secure if the plaintext is statistically independent of the ciphertext. In other words, examination of the ciphertext provides no information whatsoever to an adversary. From a scientific point of view, these schemes are risk free even with unlimited computational power and resources. Some necessary conditions for such a cipher are that the key must be truly random, used once only and at least as long as the plaintext. One (and only one) famous example is the One-time pad, which will be discussed in Chapter 5.

Conditionally secure ciphers

Another risk measurement is computational or practical security. An encryption scheme is said to be computationally secure if the amount of computational effort to defeat the system, even in the best attack, is well beyond the computing capability of the adversary or exceeds the usefulness of the plaintext. Computationally secure ciphers are the most important ciphers in modern cryptology. There are two reasons for this. First, they are not safe (not absolutely safe). By giving up the unconditionally safe criterion, key administrations are lowered to a manageable level. We are only human and we all want memorable, reusable and short keys. These user-friendly requirements lead to a whole range of different ciphers in cryptology.

Symmetric-key ciphers

In general, symmetric-key schemes use one key for both encryption and decryption. In order to maintain security, the key must be kept secret all the time. Therefore these schemes are also called secret-key ciphers. The encryptions discussed in Chapter 1 are symmetric-key ciphers and there are many stronger symmetric-key ciphers available today. Although symmetric-key ciphers are strong, they all have the so-called key distribution problem. You are running a risk when you expose the secret key to other people, including the message receiver. The more people you share information with, the more difficult the key distribution problem is to handle.

Public-key ciphers

Another class of computationally secure encryptions is the public-key cipher. These schemes use two keys – one key is for encryption and the other for decryption. In other words, if you use one key to encrypt the plaintext, you must use the other key to decrypt the ciphertext. Using two different keys enables you to make one key public and keep one key secret. This family of ciphers not only solves the key distribution problem but also generates a new series of applications. For example, public-key schemes can be used for digital signatures, authentication, certificate, certificate authority, live Web connection with security, digital contracts, opening a new chapter for cryptology and applications.

One-way ciphers

In dealing with computers (big or small), most people have come across passwords. Usually, a password is a unique encrypted string (a short ciphertext) used to restrict access to certain computer areas or resources. The main purpose is to identify authorized users and to protect against intruders. When you enter a password, the system generates the same encrypted string to identify you. This process is called 'user authentication'. Since there is no decryption needed, passwords are usually generated by one-way encryptions (or one-way ciphers).

As a starting point for Web security, the application of one-way ciphers or passwords for Web site protection, user authentications and their attacks is studied comprehensively in this chapter. Again, step-by-step application examples are provided throughout.

Crypto-attacks

The scientific study of ciphers for the purpose of launching attacks is also an important part of cryptology. Cryptography and crypto-attacks (or simply attacks) are the two central topics of cryptology. One of the classic crypto-attacks in history is crypto-analysis. It is a subject which analyzes ciphertext for patterns or phrase matching. The result can be used to find the key and launch an attack on the cipher. Some elementary examples are given in the next section. A number of operating systems, including Windows, are vulnerable to replacement attacks. For example, by replacing the password records in the password file, an attacker can access the system without knowing your password. To steal your password, the Man-in-the-middle (MITM) is often used. Sometimes, an attacker can intentionally mirror an entire organization's (e.g. bank) site to get your password. Since the Web client–server dialog is public, Web applications, in general, are particularly vulnerable to replay attacks. By replaying your Web dialog to a server, an attacker can get access to your account in a protected Web site. By studying crypto-attacks, crypto-systems can be improved.

When keys with a fixed length are used, the ciphers are vulnerable to the so-called 'brute-force' (try-them-all) attack. In principle, your adversary can simply try all possible combinations of keys to get your encryption/decryption password. Depending on computing power and time resources, brute-force schemes are generally considered to be infallible. Another interesting feature is that a scheme that was computationally secure 20 years ago may not be safe now. According to Moore's law 'computing power doubles every 18 months': this multiplication by 2 is equivalent to increasing 1 bit of your key length. Also, attacks like brute-force or 'known plaintext' were well beyond the reach of ordinary people 10 or 15 years ago but can now comfortably be performed on desktop or portable machines. Another essential condition by which to judge a good cipher is whether it can be broken only by brute-force attacks. From the cryptology point of view, ciphers and attacks are natural competitors. The struggle and competition between them form the beauty of the subject.

Now, let's start with some examples on classic ciphers and attacks. The ideas of these ciphers can be used to design many strong ciphers, as discussed later in Chapters 4 and 5.

2.1.2 Examples of classic ciphers and attacks

One of the most popular encryption methods across history has been the symbolic substitution. Encryption methods using symbolic substitution are also called substitution ciphers. For this cipher to work, symbolic pictures, drawings or symbols are used to replace the plaintext characters forming an unreadable ciphertext. An example is shown in Table 2.1.

Table 2.1 A substitution cipher

A	B	C	D	E	F	G	H	I	J	K	L	M	N	O	P	Q	R	S	T	U	V	W	X	Y	Z
ç	Γ	Η	Π	Σ	Ν	Β	Τ	ϑ	Λ	Ζ	Α	Δ	Χ	Π	Φ	Κ	Ι	Ξ	Ε	Μ	Ο	Υ	Ω	Ψ	Θ

If the same set of characters is used on both plaintext and ciphertext, the encryption is called permutation encryption. For example, Table 2.2 specifies a permutation cipher.

Table 2.2 A permutation cipher

A	B	C	D	E	F	G	H	I	J	K	L	M	N	O	P	A	R	S	T	U	V	W	X	Y	Z
V	G	H	R	S	N	B	T	J	L	Z	A	D	C	P	F	K	I	X	E	M	O	U	W	Y	Q

It defines a permutation key and specifies a permutation cipher. The encryption is basically a rearrangement (permutation) of the plaintext symbols. One of the characteristics of the permutation cipher is that the decryption always exists provided that no character in the table is repeated. In this case, the decryption is achieved by simply reversing the permutation cipher table.

If the character set of plaintext contains 26 symbols, the total number of permutations is 26!

$$26! = 403\ 291\ 461\ 126\ 605\ 635\ 584\ 000\ 000$$

$$\approx 4.03 \times 10^{26}$$

This number is called the key-space containing all the possible keys for decryption. In order words, in order to break in the cipher system with the brute-force (or Try-them-all) attack, the intruder has to try 26! times in order to obtain the specific decryption key as in Table 2.2.

Among all those permutations, one that is particularly popular and simple to program is the transposition cipher. The characteristic of this cipher is that the permutation is actually a position shift (transposition). For example, Table 2.3 demonstrates a transposition cipher with a forward character shift of three, (i.e. a type of Caesar code).

Table 2.3 A transposition cipher

A	B	C	D	E	F	G	H	I	J	K	L	M	N	O	P	A	R	S	T	U	V	W	X	Y	Z
D	E	F	G	H	I	J	K	L	M	N	O	P	A	R	S	T	U	V	W	X	Y	Z	A	B	C

By today's standards, encryptions using permutations and transpositions are very simple to attack since they all have a pattern to follow. As an example, consider the following encrypted message:

'ΩΚΛς Λς ΩΚΗ ςΗΦΥΗΩ ΠΗςςΔϑΗ Λ ςΗΘΩ'

To attack this cipher (encrypted message), you can try to get the key of the encryption method, such as the substitution and transposition. On the other hand, you could use a good dictionary and the following instructions to perform the crypto-analysis:

- substitute the single character symbol to 'I' or 'A';

- try to determine the words with just two characters;

- substitute the most occurring symbol to 'E';

- try to determine the words with three characters;

- try to determine the whole sentence.

After a little trial and error, it is easy to work out that the plaintext is

'THIS IS THE SECRET MESSAGE I SENT'

This is just a simple example working on the assumption that the message is in English. The decryption rules have long-used characteristics of the English language, such as that the most frequently used character is 'E'. In fact, long before this book was written, people had already compiled a statistical table on every character used in the English language. Statistical tables also exist for every language. In modern terms, this attack is called crypto-analysis.

This attack has been used on several occasions in history to attack encryptions and demonstrates an important point. That is, the attack is independent of probability in the so-called key-space. In other words, no matter what kinds of substitution and transposition are used and how difficult it is to get the decryption key, this attack works. The longer the sentence the more accurate will be the patterns for the attack.

To increase the security or the encryption or confidentiality of the message, the patterns of the plaintext and ciphertext have to be minimized or destroyed.

One improvement to eliminate patterns of character occurrence is to use two or more transposition ciphers. Suppose we have two transposition ciphers – the first is specified in Table 2.4a.

Table 2.4a Forward transposition by 3

A	B	C	D	E	F	G	H	I	J	K	L	M	N	O	P	A	R	S	T	U	V	W	X	Y	Z	[]
D	E	F	G	H	I	J	K	L	M	N	O	P	A	R	S	T	U	V	W	X	Y	Z	[]	A	B	C

This table is a forward transposition with a value of 3. Note that the empty space character [] is added at the end of the plaintext. Table 2.4b defines a forward transposition cipher of 5.

Table 2.4b Forward transposition by 5

A	B	C	D	E	F	G	H	I	J	K	L	M	N	O	P	A	R	S	T	U	V	W	X	Y	Z	[]
F	G	H	I	J	K	L	M	N	O	P	Q	R	S	T	U	V	W	X	Y	Z	[]	A	B	C	D	F

If you apply the transposition in Table 2.4a to every odd-numbered character in the plaintext, and the transposition in Table 2.4b to the even-numbered characters, you will have the following encryption result:

```
THIS IS THE SECRET MESSAGE I SENT
WMLXCNVFWMHFVJFWHYCQHXVFJJCNCXHSW
```

As you can see, the occurrence (or frequency) of the character E in the plaintext is reduced in the ciphertext, and this therefore increases the difficulty for the crypto-analysis. From the transposition cipher point of view, this encryption is equivalent to a transposition scheme with two transpositions:

Transposition encryption = (P_1, P_2)
where P_1 = transpose (3) and P_2 = transpose (5)

The first transposition, P_1, is a forward transposition of 3 and the second transposition, P_2, is 5. To attack this scheme, an able intruder can, for example, divide the encrypted message into two parts and perform crypto-analysis instead of trying all the combinations of decryption keys.

Even the most general transposition cipher below offers little protection against attack:

Transposition encryption = $(P_1, P_2, \ldots, P_t)$
where $P_1, P_2, \ldots, P_t$ are transposition functions

Once the value of t is determined, crypto-analysis can be performed. This attack is known as 'cut and join'. This example demonstrates one important point – that is, that the size of the key-space is only a necessary condition for a secure cipher.

One of the problems with these ciphers is that they preserve the language features or character frequency distribution of the plaintext, which is vulnerable under crypto-analysis. Also, with the computing power of today, an entire English dictionary with 100000 entries can be searched within a fraction of a second. Encryptions with language features are no longer considered to be safe.

Although the classic ciphers are not safe, the techniques of permutation, substitution and combinations of them provide a fundamental framework for advanced encryption. In fact, some skills covered in this section will be used to develop a number of advanced ciphers, such as the Data Encryption Standard (DES), in Chapters 4 and 5. Now, let's see how modern ciphers can be used to protect Web sites against unauthorized access.

2.2 Basic user authentication and Web site protection

2.2.1 The beginning of cipher-based authentication

In 1972, the National Institute of Standards and Technology (NIST) (called the National Bureau of Standards at that time) decided that they need a cryptographic system to protect electronic data, documents and transmission. They turned to the commercial and public sectors asking for an encryption algorithm that was practical, computationally cheap, widely available and very secure. In answer to their request, IBM submitted the Lucifer algorithm in 1974. Two years later, the modified Lucifer algorithm was adopted by NIST as a federal standard (on November 23, 1976) but they changed the name to 'Data Encryption Standard' (DES). The algorithmic specification was published in January 1977 and became the official encryption mechanism for the US government and was quickly used world wide. The second version is the Federal Information Processing Standards Publication 46-2 (FIPS 46-2), published in December 1993. The latest version is FIPS 46-3, which was published in October 1999. This remarkable scheme marked an important milestone in modern ciphering and is still actively used today.

Inspire by the classic ciphers, the DES algorithm uses permutations and substitutions heavily. In fact, it uses seven permutation tables, eight substitution tables and one selection table to perform encryption:

- permutation tables: `PC1-C`, `PC1-D`, `PC2-C`, `PC2-D`, `IP`, `IP⁻¹`, and `P`;
- substitution tables: `S1`, `S2`, `S3`, `S4`, `S5`, `S6`, `S7`, and `S8`;
- bit selection table: `E`.

The scheme takes an 8-character (or 64-bit) key and some plaintext as input. In fact, only 56 bits of the key are used. The algorithm uses your key and the tables above to perform encryption on 8-character plaintext strings (64-bit chunks) a time. When all the chunks of plaintext have been processed, you have a complete ciphertext. DES is, therefore, a block cipher with block length 64 bits. The use of permutation and substitution tables guarantees that the ciphertext cannot be decrypted easily without knowing the original encryption key. The DES algorithm and its implementation will be discussed in detail in Chapter 3.

As soon as DES became available, the UNIX operating system adapted the algorithm to develop a user authentication scheme known as `Crypt()` to identify authorized users. `Crypt()` is the very first authentication algorithm used in the computing industry and is still active and available on almost every UNIX/LINUX machine.

The algorithm that `Crypt()` uses is based on the operations of DES. Unlike DES, which is a reversible encryption scheme, the `Crypt()` function takes the user's password as the encryption key to DES-encrypt a block of 64 zeros in bit format.

The resulting 64-bit block of ciphertext is then DES encrypted a total of 25 times. In order to make the decryption process even more difficult, the `Crypt()` function also uses two characters known as 'salt' to perturb the encryption. As a result, the `Crypt()` algorithm is virtually irreversible. In cryptology terms, it is called a one-way encryption (or one-way cipher). The final 64 bits are unpacked into a string of 11 printable characters (6-bits each). With the 2-character 'salt' at the beginning followed by the 11-character ciphertext, the entire 13-character string is stored in the password file (usually in `/etc/passwd`).

As an example, some entries of the password file on a Red Hat LINUX system are shown in `lx02-01.txt`.

Example: lx02-01.txt: UNIX/LINUX password file /etc/passwd

```
1: root:t1Gyyq0guHImk:0:0:Super User:/root:/bin/csh
2: cs006:8kiluiZYvEy6I:502:10:arthur:/users/arthur:/usr/bin/csh
3: cs005:cdan1WJA6xjtE:505:10:rody:/users/rody:/usr/bin/csh
4: cs001:abOs8/PTEL6Ag:508:10:john:/users/john:/usr/bin/csh
```

This password file contains four users. Each has an entry with a number of fields separated by colons. The first two fields are the 'user name' and 'encrypted password' of the user. For example, the user name of the fourth person is 'cs001' and the `Crypt()` encrypted password is 'abOs8/PTEL6Ag'. This ciphertext has 13 characters and the salt is the first 2 characters, i.e. 'ab'.

When you try to login, the UNIX/LINUX system does not actually decrypt your password. Instead, it performs the following tasks:

■ take the password that you typed;

■ get the first two characters from the `/etc/passwd` file entry as salt;

■ encrypt the password with the salt using the `Crypt()` function to product a ciphertext;

■ compare the new ciphertext with the ciphertext stored in the `/etc/passwd` file.

If the two encrypted results match, the system lets you in. This process is called 'user authentication'. This process has been used to identify UNIX/LINUX users for more than 25 years and is still employed on almost every UNIX/LINUX system. Not surprisingly, the same authentication is widely accepted on the Web to identify authorized users in compliance with the 'basic HTTP authentication' standard. Before discussing that, let's see how to generate `Crypt()` encrypted passwords using Web pages.

Suppose we have developed the `Crypt()` function in ECMAScript inside the file `zz_crypt3.js`. The details of this file will be discussed in Chapter 3 (`ex03-04.js`).

The Web page `ex02-01.htm` can be used to generate encrypted passwords, as in the password file `1x02-01.txt`.

Example ex02-01.htm: Generating UNIX/LINUX encrypted passwords

```
 1: <?xml version="1.0" encoding="iso-8859-1"?>
 2: <!DOCTYPE html PUBLIC "-//W3C//DTD XHTML 1.0 Transitional//EN"
 3:    "http://www.w3.org/TR/xhtml1/DTD/xhtml1-transitional.dtd">
 4: <html xmlns="http://www.w3.org/1999/xhtml" xml:lang="en"
    lang="en">
 5: <head><title> Gen. Crypt() Password - ex02-01.htm</title></head>
 6: <style>
 7: .butSt{font-size:18pt;width:150px;height:35px;
 8:        font-weight:bold;background:#dddddd;color:#ff0000}
 9: .txtSt{font-size:16pt;font-weight:bold}
10: </style>
11: <body style="font-family:arial;font-size:22pt;text-align:center;
12:        background:#000088;color:#ffff00"><br />
13: Generating Crypt() Password<br />
14: <img alt="pic" src="line1.gif" height="7" width="500" /><br />
15:
16: <table class="txtSt" cellspacing="25">
17:  <tr><td>Enter The Password <br />(max 8-char):</td>
18:     <td><input id="keySt" type="text" class="butSt"
19:             maxlength="8" /></td></tr>
20:  <tr><td>Enter The Salt <br />(max 2-char):</td>
21:     <td><input id="saltSt" type="text" class="butSt"
22:             style="width:40px" maxlength="2" /></td></tr>
23:  <tr><td>Generate Encrypted <br />Password</td>
24:     <td><input type="button" class="butSt" value="OK"
25:             onclick="genCrypt()" /></td></tr>
26:  <tr><td>The Encrypted <br />Password Is</td>
27:     <td><input id="outMsg" type="text" class="txtSt"
            readonly /></td></tr>
28: </table>
29:
30: <script src="zz_crypt3.js"></script>
31: <script>
32: function genCrypt()
33: {
34:   var key_st, salt_st, out_st="";
35:   var result= new Array();
36:
37:   key_st = document.getElementById("keySt").value;
```

```
38:    salt_st = document.getElementById("saltSt").value;
39:
40:    result = crypt(key_st,salt_st);
41:    for (i=0; i<result.length; i++) {
42:      out_st += String.fromCharCode(result[i]);
43:    }
44:    document.getElementById("outMsg").value = out_st;
45:  }
46: </script>
47: </body>
48: </html>
```

This page contains a simple table with three input text boxes and one OK button (lines 16–28). The first two boxes, defined in lines 17–22, are used to get the input for the password and the salt. The maximum length for the password is restricted to eight characters specified by the attribute `maxlength="8"` in line 19. The maximum length for the salt is set to 2. Once you have entered the password, the salt, and the button defined in lines 24–25 is clicked, the function `genCrypt()` is activated. The encrypted password is displayed in the `readonly` text box defined in lines 26–27.

The `genCrypt()` function is defined by the ECMAScript in lines 32–45. First, the input password and salt are captured by the string variables `key_st` and `salt_st` (lines 37–38). These two variables are used to call the function `crypt()` in line 40. This function is defined in the ECMAScript file `zz_crypt3.js` and the general calling syntax is

```
result = crypt(password,salt);
```

This is the main function of the page and takes two arguments – one is the password and the other is the 2-character salt. The encrypted password is returned as an array of Unicode and, in this case, stored in the array variable `result`. The for-loop in lines 41–43 will convert the Unicode series into a string called `out_st`. This `out_st` is then output to the text box by the statement in line 44. Screenshots of this example in action are shown in Figures 2.2 and 2.3.

From these two figures, you can see that the encrypted passwords for users cs005 and cs001 are 'rody' and 'john'. If you create a new encrypted password using this page and change the encrypted password fields in lx02-01.txt, you have changed the password of that user instantly. If the record or the entire file is replaced by an unauthorized intruder, the system is under replacement attack.

If you are using Microsoft Windows the password situations are slightly different. Each Windows product, such as NT/2000/XP, employs different password algorithms for encryption. However, they all use the same password file called 'SAM' located inside the `windows\system32\config` folder. This file is also

Fig. 2.2 Generating `Crypt()` password I

Fig. 2.3 Generating `Crypt()` password II

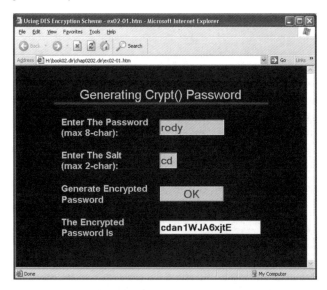

replaceable. The username/password entries of 'cs005' and 'cs001' of an XP system are shown in `lx02-02.txt`.

```
Example: lx02-02.txt: Windows XP Password File windows\system32\
config\SAM

1: cs005:1004:0f438dafac6c86fdaad3b435b51404ee:
   29e513c7c2b83d18f87efc584779f0ce:::
2: cs001:1005:2a1ce55e2c0663cee034c60fa8ac8477:
   ff86e487b6139798fab0eda23aac6c96:::
```

The passwords, in this case, are protected by the so-called 'message digest' (MD) algorithm. Message digest is an important subject and the Web uses it to perform the so-called 'digest' user authentication. We will discuss it in Section 2.3.

If the UNIX/LINUX passwords are protected by a shadowed password file, the password information is in the file /etc/shadow. For example, the entries of the root information may look like

```
/etc/passwd:
root:x:0:0:Super User:/root:/bin/csh
/etc/shadow    for shadowed /etc/passwd:
root:t1Gyyq0guHImk:9955::::::-1
```

The root password, in this case, is in file /etc/shadow. Now, let's see how Crypt() can be used to perform standard user authentication on the Web.

2.2.2   Basic HTTP authentication with Apache

As we have mentioned in Chapter 1, Web communication is governed by the browser–server dialog and ultimately by the HTTP protocol. The HTTP specifications known as IETF RFC 1945, RFC 2068 and RFC 2069 define two authentication methods, namely 'basic authentication' and 'digest authentication'.

Basic authentication is supported by almost all HTTP servers and browsers. It is by far the most widely supported authentication method.

To use basic authentication, you must configure your HTTP server to know that certain documents are protected and access to them will require authentication. How this is done varies with different HTTP servers. We will show you how it is done for both UNIX/LINUX and Microsoft Windows using Apache. Unless stated otherwise, we will use Apache as the default server software in this book, simply because it is free and the most popular Web server on the Internet. Whether you are using Windows 9.x/Me/2000/XP or UNIX/LINUX, you can download a working copy of Apache from the official Web site www.apache.org.

In addition, the source code of Apache is freely available so that modifications of the software are possible.

First, all documents or Web pages that need to be protected are placed in a common directory under your server's document root. In this case, the document root of Apache is assumed to be /apache/htdocs. This directory (and all beneath it) can be protected either by a password file or by an access file. The default password and access files on a UNIX/LINUX system are called .htpasswd and .htaccess. Since these files have a period in front of them, some Windows systems may have difficulties in creating or handling them. In order to ensure that the authentication works for both systems, we call the password and access file 'htpass.wd' and 'htacc.ess' respectively. You can, in fact, use any file name you like.

One of the simplest ways of generating passwords in htpass.wd is to use the password utility htpasswd of Apache. For example, you can open a shell window (or a DOS prompt if you are using Windows) and run the following commands.

```
htpasswd -cb htpass.wd root  peter
htpasswd -b  htpass.wd cs006 arthur
htpasswd -b  htpass.wd cs005 rody
htpasswd -b  htpass.wd cs001 john
```

The option -c of the first line will create the password file called htpass.wd. The second option b will generate a user called 'root' and the encrypted password 'peter'. The result will be stored in htpass.wd. The second line will effectively generate the username and password for 'cs006' in htpass.wd. After you have processed all users, you will see the entries in the password file shown in 1x02-03.txt.

Example: 1x02-03.txt: The basic password file htpass.wd (or .htpasswd)

```
1:   root:qwUz5jttxGJNk
2:   cs006:afMas1RMTeywU
3:   cs005:2kIi0DkibHn/o
4:   cs001:5t0ckoMheqAT6
```

Since the salt is generated randomly by the system at run time, you will see a different encrypted password, even if you have the same original. For Windows users, the entries in htpass.wd will be

```
root:$apr1$VY2.....$FDbVgTbR2jd0QpO.YTtXR.
cs006:$apr1$VY2.....$UbAC7eP/worBScsaWHhic/
cs005:$apr1$VY2.....$ejyqMp39hLhRN18B9Nixv/
cs001:$apr1$VY2.....$WCJvn0hwVZECppFKp4M0p1
```

Apache for Windows uses a different password encryption called `md5crypt` and therefore the results are different. In other words, password files for Windows and UNIX/LINUX may not be interchangeable for the basic method. The encryption details are not important here and MD5 encryption will be covered in more detail Section 2.3.

In order to use `htpass.wd` in the access file (e.g. `htacc.ess`), the instructions shown in `lx02-04.txt` are needed.

```
Example: lx02-04.txt: The basic access file htacc.ess (or .htaccess)

1: AuthType Basic
2: AuthName "private"
3: AuthUserFile /apache/htdocs/basic/htpass.wd
4: require valid-user
```

The first line states that the authentication type is `Basic`. The realm name of this basic authentication is called 'private', as illustrated in line 2. When you request a page from the protected directory, the realm name will appear in the login `username/password` window. The third line instructs Apache to use the password file `htpass.wd` inside the directory `/apache/htdocs/basic` for authentication. The last line allows only authorized users – in order words, only users with a valid password account in the password file can access the documents or Web pages.

Since we have used an access file name other than `.htaccess`, we need to instruct Apache to look for the new access file `htacc.ess`. To do that, we need to edit the global Apache configuration file `httpd.conf` located in `/apache/config` directory. You can edit the file and search for the string '`AccessFileName`'. The next step is to add the new file `htacc.ess` before the default `.htaccess` as illustrated in line 2 in `lx02-05.txt`.

```
Example: lx02-05.txt: Modified contents in Apache file - httpd.conf

1: ### AccessFileName .htaccess
2: AccessFileName htacc.ess .htaccess
3:
4: <Directory "\apache\htdocs\basic">
5:     AllowOverride All
6:     Options None
7:     Order deny,allow
8: </Directory>
```

You also need to add a directory section to tell Apache that the directory `/apache/htdocs/basic` is protected (lines 4–8). If you put the files `htpass.wd` and

htacc.ess and some Web pages inside the directory /apache/htdocs/basic, all
Web pages are protected by the basic authentication. To test the authentication,
a simple Web page is constructed and the body part of the page is shown in
ex02-02.htm.

```
Example: ex02-02.htm - Testing a Web page for basic authentication
1: <body style="font-family:arial;font-size:22pt;text-align:center;
2:    color:#ffff00;background:#000088"><br /><br />
3:    Basic HTTP Authentication<br />This Page Is Protected<br />
4: </body>
```

If you request the page by the instruction

http://www.pws-ex.com/basic/ex02-02.htm

you will see a login window asking for a username and a password. Screenshots of
this authentication in IE are shown in Figures 2.4 and 2.5.

Since basic HTTP authentication is supported by all browsers across all platforms,
the login windows for NS (7.1) and Opera (7.2) are shown in Figures 2.6 and 2.7.
Be careful with the use of the 'Remember my password' tickbox as it will store
your password inside the operating system and this can be retrieved by a capable
intruder.

Fig. 2.4   The username/password authentication window of Internet Explorer

Fig. 2.5 Access the protected document?

Fig. 2.6 The username/password authentication window of Netscape

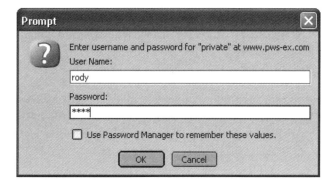

Now we can control who can access pages and documents. Apache can also perform access control concerning where the visitors are coming from and to what group they belong.

2.2.3 Using access directives and group files

Authentication by username and password is only part of the authentication process. In many cases, you want to control access depending on where people are

Fig. 2.7 The username/password authentication window of Opera

coming from and to what group (or category) they belong. Apache has a powerful set of commands, or directives, allowing you better control of Web site access. Some of them are listed in Table 2.5. Those we have used already are emboldened.

The use of `allow` and `deny`

The `allow` and `deny` directives will let you allow or deny access based on the host name, domain name or IP address that the request is coming from. For example, the following directive would allow two sites to access the documents.

```
allow from www.pws-ex.com 172.165.88.103
```

If you want to keep someone out, you could do the following:

```
deny from 172.252.46.165 abc.xxx.com
```

Visitors coming from these addresses would not be able to access anything behind this directive. If you want to block access from an entire domain, you can issue just part of an address or domain name. You can also block all access except from some specified address. Some examples are shown below.

```
deny from 162.101.205              order deny,allow
deny from bargain.com      or      deny from all
deny from .gov xxx.com             allow from db.llxt.com
```

     Deny some domains   Deny all but one

Table 2.5 Apache access file configuration directives

Directive	Argument type	Default value	Purpose
`allow from`	List of hosts	–	Allows access to this directory from the designated IP hosts
`deny from`	List of hosts	–	Denies access to this directory from the designated IP hosts
`require user`	List of user IDs	–	List of IDs of users who can access a directory
`require group`	List of groups	–	Groups that can access a directory
`require valid-user`	NA	–	Only authorized user ID and password can access
`AuthGroupFile`	File name	–	Name of file containing list of user groups **(basic authentication)**
`AuthName`	Authorization name	–	Name of authorization or domain for a directory, e.g. `AuthName="private"`
`AuthType`	Basic digest	**Basic**	Type of user authorization (digest authentication is experimental)
`AuthUserFile`	File name	–	Absolute path of file with users and passwords **(basic authentication)**
`AuthDBMUserFile`	File name		Name of DBM database file containing users and passwords
`AuthDBMGroupFile`	File name		Name of DBM database file containing groups
`Options`	List of options	–	Defines which server features are allowed in a given directory

The order directives, together with `deny` and `allow`, would let you exclude all access except by some specified sites. You can also use the files feature (or `<files>`) of Apache to control access to certain files. The following directives will deny all links to `jpg` files.

```
<files "*.jpg">
deny from All
</files>
```
Deny all links to JPG files

```
deny from all
<files "index.htm">
allow from All
</files>
```
Controlling file access

If you try to request an image file with a `.jpg` extension, such as

```
http://www.pws-ex.com/basic/02.jpg
```

you will receive the 'Forbidden' message, as shown in Figure 2.8, which has a respond code 403.

Similarly, you can use `<files>` to deny access for all files but one. Now, let's see how to perform access controls depending on which group the visitors belong to.

Fig. 2.8 Forbidden access

Controlling access with group files

Consider the directives used in the access file (see `1x02-04.txt`):

```
AuthType Basic
AuthName "private"
AuthUserFile /apache/htdocs/basic/htpass.wd
require valid-user
```

These directives allow only a valid user to get in. All valid users are defined in the password file `htpass.wd`. If you just want to let 'root' and 'cs001' in, you can change the last line to

```
require user root cs001
```

If you want to classify authorized people into groups, you may need to use group files. A group file is simply a text file containing group names and a list of users associated with that group. For example, the contents of a group file called `mygroup` are shown in `1x02-06.txt`.

```
Example: 1x02-06.txt: Group file: mygroup

1: group6: root cs006
2: group5: root cs005
3: group1: root cs001
```

This file contains three groups. The first group is called 'group6' and contains two users, namely 'root' and 'cs006'. If you modified the access file as shown in `lx02-07.txt` access would be limited to the users in group6.

```
Example: lx02-07.txt - Basic access using groups

1: AuthType Basic
2: AuthName "private"
3: AuthUserFile "/apache/htdocs/basic/htpass.wd"
4: AuthGroupFile "/apache/htdocs/basic/mygroup"
5: require group group6
```

To test this set up, a simple Web page called `ex02-03.htm` is used. This page is the same as `ex02-02.htm` with a modification to line 3:

```
Example: Modification to ex02-02.htm to produce ex02-03.htm

3:   Basic HTTP Authentication<br />Using Group File<br />
```

Now, although users cs005 and cs001 have valid password accounts in the password file, they cannot access the directory because they are not in the authorized group. Screenshots of this example in action are shown in Figures 2.9 and 2.10.

Up to now, all password and group files have been text based. Searching a big text file, in many cases, is not efficient. If you have a large number of users divided into many groups, you may want to use the database features of Apache.

2.2.4 Using DBM database files

The Apache implementation of database features is through a module called `auth_dbm_module`. You may need to check the availability of this module in your Apache software. Open the configuration file `httpd.conf` and locate the following string

```
#LoadModule auth_dbm_module modules/mod_auth_dbm.so
```

If you find a hash symbol '#' in front of this string, you may need to delete it so that the dbm module is ready for action. You may also need to reactivate Apache.

By default, Apache uses the UNIX/LINUX database feature called DataBase Manager (DBM) to handle data. If you are using Apache for UNIX/LINUX, you already have everything installed including the utility program dbmmanage. This program is similar to the utility htpasswd and can generate password files but in

Fig. 2.9 Using a group file

Fig. 2.10 Unauthorized access

DBM format. For example, the following command will add the user 'root' to the database file mydbmfile

```
dbmmanage mydbmfile adduser root
```

You will be prompted for the password and the user 'root' will be added to the existing database file mydbmfile or a new file will be created if one does not exist. If you want to change the password in the file mydbmfile, you can use the update option

```
dbmmanage mydbmfile update root
```

Password accounts can also be deleted by using the dbmmanage utility

```
dbmmanage mydbmfile delete cs006
```

To create a database file with four accounts root, cs006, cs005 and cs001 as in htpass.wd, you can use

```
dbmmanage mydbmfile adduser root
dbmmanage mydbmfile adduser cs006
dbmmanage mydbmfile adduser cs005
dbmmanage mydbmfile adduser cs001
```

If you put this new database file mydbmfile in the directory /apache/basic and change the access file htacc.ess as shown in lx02-08.txt, the directory is protected by the basic method using the database records.

```
Example: lx02-08.txt: Basic authentication - using DBM file

1: AuthType Basic
2: AuthName "private"
3: AuthDBMUserFile "/apache/htdocs/basic/mydbmfile"
4: require valid-user
```

A test page for this DBM database file is provided in ex02-04.htm. This page is the same as ex02-03.htm with a modification to line 3:

```
Example: Modification to ex02-03.htm to produce ex02-04.htm

3: Basic HTTP Authentication<br />With Database DBM User File<br />
```

Screenshots of this example are shown in Figures 2.11 and 2.12.

When adding a user, you may optionally specify the groups belonged to. Multiple groups can be defined and separated by commas. That is, you can put the group

Fig. 2.11 Using a DBM database file

Fig. 2.12 Authentication with a DBM database file

names into the database file. For example, the following command adds the user root and a number of groups to the database file `mydbmgroup`:

```
dbmmanage mydbmgroup adduser root - group6,group5,group1
```

This command generates an account called 'root'. The hyphen '-' will instruct the utility to prompt you for the password. The root account now belongs to group6, group5 and group1. To create the same group structure for other users, but with DBM features, you can use

```
dbmmanage mydbmgroup adduser cs006 - group6
dbmmanage mydbmgroup adduser cs005 - group5
dbmmanage mydbmgroup adduser cs001 - group1
```

Now, the file `mydbmgroup` contains the username/password as well as the group information. If you put this file in the directory `/apache/htdocs/basic` and modify the access file as shown in `lx02-09.txt`, you are ready to use basic authentication with DBM database features.

Example: lx02-09.txt: Access file using DBM groups

```
1: AuthType Basic
2: AuthName "private"
3: AuthDBMUserFile "/apache/htdocs/basic/mydbmgroup"
4: AuthDBMGroupFile "/apache/htdocs/basic/mydbmgroup"
5: require group group6
```

The test page is `ex02-05.htm` and is the same as `ex02-04.htm` with a new line 3:

Example: Modification to ex02-04.htm to produce ex02-05.htm

```
3: Basic HTTP Authentication<br />With Database DBM Group File<br />
```

Any request to this page will be challenged by a login window. User login will be checked against the username, password and group in the DBM file `mydbmgroup`.

The utility `dbmmanage` from the Apache package is a script written in the Practical Extraction and Report Language (Perl). If you are using Apache for Windows, you need Perl to run it. A popular Perl package for Windows is called 'ActiveState Perl' and can be downloaded free from the official site www.activestate.com. After the Perl installation, you also need to install the `Crypt-PasswdMD5` package to run `dbmmanage`. Suppose you have installed Perl in the `c:\Perl` directory: you can run the following two commands to install it.

```
C;\Perl\bin> ppm
PPM> install Crypt-PasswdMD5
```

Now, you can run dbmmanage, for example:

```
perl dbmmanage.pl mydbmfile adduser root
```

where perl is the Perl language processor and dbmmanage.pl is the Perl script. Perl is a practicable technology for the Web and can be used to generate the so-called 'Common Gateway Interface' (CGI) script. CGI and Web databases will be covered in Chapter 7.

If you are using Apache 2 or later, you don't need Perl or dbmmanage to handle DBM passwords. Apache 2+ comes with a utility called htdbm to generate DBM password files. The calling syntax for htdbm is similar to htpasswd.

On the whole, the entire basic authentication is an amazingly simple process which doesn't rely on any encryption or cookies. More importantly, you don't need to change your Web pages at all. However, basic HTTP authentication has a fundamental security flaw and this security risk may discourage most users.

2.2.5   Inside the basic method and security attacks

In order to understand the security of basic authentication, a good starting point is the client–server dialog. When your browser, such as IE, NS or Opera, requests a secure document, the server looks to see if the request contains a username and password to identify you as an authorized user. If not, it responds with an HTTP 401 response code. Your browser then displays a dialog box asking for a username and password. For an illustrated example, consider the HTTP command

```
http://www.pws-ex.com/mybasic/ex02-02.htm
```

You are asking your browser to fetch a Web page /mybasic/ex02-02.htm from the host www.pws-ex.com. In doing so, your browser connects to www.pws-ex.com on TCP port 80 and issues a request as shown in 1x02-10.txt.

Example: lx02-10.txt: HTTP client-server dialog – request a document

```
1: GET /mybasic/ex02-02.htm HTTP/1.1
2: Host: www.pws-ex.com
```

Since your browser doesn't know, initially, that the Web page is in a password-protected directory, it doesn't send any authentication information with the request above. Therefore the server, www.pws-ex.com, simply sends back an error and asking for authentication with a header like that shown in 1x02-11.txt.

```
Example: lx02-11.txt: Client-server dialog: server response

1: HTTP/1.1 401 Authorization Required
2: Date: Tue, 07 Dec 2004 12:08:10 GMT
3: Server: Apache/2.0
4: WWW-Authenticate: Basic realm="private"
5: Connection: close
6: Content-Type: text/html
```

First, the server returns a 401 status ('unauthorized'). This 401 response code tells your browser you are not allowed to fetch the document requested. The WWW-Authenticate header in line 4 requests the document using basic authentication with realm name "private". This realm name is a string that you have entered in your access file. In these circumstances, your browser should display a dialog box with the name 'private' asking for username and password input. For IE, NS and Opera you will see Figures 2.4, 2.6 and 2.7, in Section 2.2.2, respectively.

After you enter a username, a password and press the OK button your browser will try to submit the request again. This time it will send the request together with the 'authentication' header shown in lx02-12.txt.

```
Example: lx02-12.txt: Client-server dialog: Transmitting
username:password

1: GET /mybasic/ex02-02.htm HTTP/1.1
2: Host: www.pws-ex.com
3: Authorization: Basic cm9vdCUzQXBldGVy
```

The authentication header in line 3 contains the keyword Basic and an encoded string. The encoded string is the username and password separated by a colon. The HTTP server then looks up the login name and checks the password against the one stored in the password file. If the account doesn't exist or the passwords don't match, the server sends a rejection back to the browser and asks the user for a new username/password pair. If the passwords match and the target is an HTML page, the server transmits the page.

Unfortunately, the entire authentication is done on the server. This means that the browser is transmitting raw username:password data for processing. Now, consider the Authentication header in line 3:

```
Authorization: Basic cm9vdCUzQXBldGVy
```

The string that comes after the word Basic is simply a Base64 encoding of username:password. This is the same encoding method we discussed

Fig. 2.13 Decoding the username and password

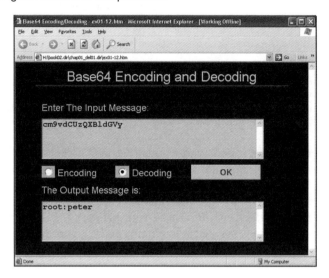

in Section 1.4.3. If you copy the encoded string into the page ex01-12.htm (in Section 1.4.3) and perform Base64 decoding, the original username and password will be displayed. A screenshot is shown in Figure 2.13.

As you can see from the figure, the decoded string cm9vdCUzQXBldGVy is simply root:peter. In other words, the plaintext password for the root is transmitted and is peter.

No matter what kind of security measures you are using regarding password and access files, the transmission itself is vulnerable. Using basic authentication is, therefore, not considered to be safe. In order to improve security during transmission, the HTTP standard provides another authentication method, known as 'digest authentication'.

2.3   Digest user authentication

2.3.1   What is digest authentication?

Digest authentication was added to HTTP in 1999 and became the IETF RFC 2617 standard. The purpose is to provide a method of authenticating users without transmitting a password as unprotected text. This standard fixes the major security weakness in basic authentication.

Basically, digest authentication works through an enhancement of the basic method. It uses a message digest function called `md5()`. Like `Crypt()`, `md5()` is a one-way encryption which can be used to generate encrypted passwords. Unlike `Crypt()`, the function `md5()` takes a string (a long string) and produces an encrypted string with a fixed length of 32 hexadecimal characters. For example:

```
md5("johnsmith")   = cd4388c0c62e65ac8b99e3ec49fd9409
md5("john")        = 527bd5b5d689e2c32ae974c6229ff785
```

For basic authentication the reject code is 401 – for digest authentication the rejection message is different. The respond message of digest authentication includes a new string called 'nonce'. Basically, nonce is a random number that doesn't repeat within a defined interval. Nonce, in this case, is an encrypted (MD5 encryption) string containing the time of day and the IP address of the requester. Nonce is different for each request made.

After the reject message, the browser may prompt the user for a username and password. Instead of just sending the information as described in the basic method, the browser uses the information `username`, `realm`, `password`, `URI`, `request method`, and the `nonce` to produce an MD5 encrypted string called `response`.

The main idea is to send this `response` string to the server. To perform the authentication, the server tries to get information from the password file and compute the same `response` string. If the two response strings match, the server transmits the document. Otherwise, the server rejects the request with the same respond code. Full details of the process including the security, client–server dialog, and attacks will be discussed in Section 2.3.4.

Compared to the basic method, this digest process is much safer. Firstly, no plaintext password is transmitted to the server. Authentication will be carried out based on the `response` string. It is difficult for an intruder to sniff the password even if the entire client–server dialog can be captured. Secondly, since the nonce, and hence the response string, is different for every request, replaying the client–server dialog to the server (i.e. replay attack) does not help. The idea of the nonce is an effective tool to fight against replay attack in the Web environment.

2.3.2 Setting up digest HTTP authentication

In spite of its many improvements over the basic method, the application of digest authentication has only recently become popular. One of the reasons is that not all browsers implemented it in the past. For example, Netscape didn't implement it until version 7+ (NS7+) in early 2003. If you are using IE6+, NS7+ or Opera 7+, you have the ability to perform digest authentication on the Web.

Although Apache has supported digest authentication for a long time (since version 1.3.9), not all the features in specification RFC 2617 are implemented. At the time of this writing, the official Apache implementations (versions 1.3.29 and 2.0.48) of the digest authentication are still considered to be experimental. Before we get into details of how the digest method improves the security of the basic method, let's see how to use and set up the digest process for user authentication.

Like the basic method, digest authentication also uses password files (e.g. htpass.wd or .htpasswd) and access files (e.g. htacc.ess or .htaccess) to restrict access. But the format of the password file is different – it uses 'Message Digest' (or MD5) encryption to generate encrypted passwords and is therefore called 'digest authentication'.

The Apache implementation of digest authentication is achieved through a module called auth_digest_module. You may need to check the availability of this module in your Apache software. Open the configuration file httpd.conf and locate the following string

```
#LoadModule auth_digest_module modules/mod_auth_digest.so
```

If there is a hash symbol '#' in front of this string, you should delete the hash so that the module can be loaded and be made ready for action.

One of the best ways to generate password accounts for digest authentication is to use the Apache utility htdigest. The calling syntax is

```
htdigest [-c] passwordfile realm username
```

where
-c	option whether to create a new file
passwordfile	file name to store the password
realm	name to identify the authentication
username	user's name for the password account

Apart from the option -c, you have to provide names for all three arguments. If you have entered the passwordfile, realm and a username, the utility will ask you to type in the password and confirm it. If everything is OK, a password account for the user will be created in the password file. For example, the following will create the password file htpass.wd and a password account for root.

```
htdigest -c htpass.wd private root
Adding password for root in realm private.
New password: *****
Re-type new password: *****
```

After you have generated password accounts for cs006, cs005 and cs001, the records of the password file `htpass.wd` will look as shown in `1x02-13.txt`.

```
Example: 1x02-13.txt: The digest password file htpass.wd
(or .htpasswd)

1: root:private:eb08565779611216c0c9d374f7546e62
2: cs006:private:d1643a59a07d421eb4fdf5a5f5723bb5
3: cs005:private:d7fd6df99a9d591859f698a87d310da2
4: cs001:private:a86845ee12898f7635ebe6eb02280568
```

This password file contains four password accounts (or records), and each record has three fields separated by a colon. The first two fields are the username and realm name. The final field is an encrypted string containing information to identify the user. Unlike the basic method, the realm name is incorporated in the password file. This file structure and format are the same across all operating systems and platforms using Apache. In other words, the password files of digest authentication for Windows and UNIX/LINUX are interchangeable.

Now, you can put this password file into the directory (or folder) that you want to protect. If you put the file into the directory `/apache/htdocs/mydigest`, all documents or Web pages will be protected by digest authentication. The next step is to include the directory in the Apache configuration file `httpd.conf`. For example, you can make another directory block `<Directory>` similar to the basic method as in `1x02-05.txt`. Continuing the line numbers of `1x2-05.txt`, the new directory block is listed in `1x02-14.txt`.

```
Example: 1x02-14.txt: Continuation of 1x02-05.txt (httpd.conf)

 9: <Directory "/apache/htdocs/mydigest">
10:     AllowOverride All
11:     Options None
12:     Order deny,allow
13: </Directory>
```

The directory `/apache/htdocs/mydigest` and all its subdirectories will be protected. Note that the path name should be an absolute path. If you are using Apache for Windows you should include the drive name as well, e.g. `c:/apache/htdocs/mydigest`. Constructing the access file is simple and is shown in `1x02-15.txt`.

```
Example: 1x02-15.txt: The digest access file htacc.ess (or .htaccess)

1: AuthType Digest
2: AuthName "private"
3: AuthDigestFile "/apache/htdocs/mydigest/htpass.wd"
4: AuthDigestDomain http://www.pws-ex.com/mydigest
5: require valid-user
```

Line 1 defines the authentication type as `digest`. The realm name is specified as `"private"` in line 2 – as in the basic method, the realm name will appear in the login window. In line 3, the absolute path of the digest password file is declared. If you are using Apache for Windows you should include the drive name, such as `c:\`, in the path. Line 4 declares an authentication domain, and you should declare at least one domain. The access restriction is defined in line 5. In this case, only the authorized users in the digest password file can access the documents or Web pages.

Now, you can put this access file in the folder `/apache/htdocs/mydigest` and start using digest authentication. A test page for digest authentication is provided in `ex02-06.htm`. This page is the same as `ex02-05.htm` with a new line 3:

```
Example: Modification to ex02-05.htm to produce ex02-06.htm

3: Digest HTTP Authentication<br />This Page Is Protected<br />
```

If you request this page using the HTTP command:

```
http://www.pws-ex.com/mydigest/ex02-06.htm
```

you will see a login window to ask you for a username and password. Screenshots are shown in Figures 2.14 and 2.15.

Note that the IE login window is different from the basic method (see Figure 2.4). The login windows for NS and Opera are the same as for basic authentication (see Figures 2.6 and 2.7).

Now we have some ideas on digest authentication, it's time to learn more commands, or directives, for the access file to ensure better protection on Web sites against unauthorized access.

2.3.3   Using access directives and group files

Like the basic method, Apache has a number of directives allowing you to perform access control depending on groups and the time available for the nonce. These are summarized in Table 2.6.

Fig. 2.14 The digest login window

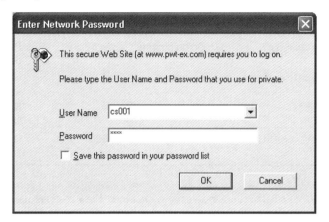

Fig. 2.15 Digest authentication

The group file used in digest authentication is exactly the same as that used in the basic method. It is simply a text file containing group names and a list of users associated with each group. For example, you can use the same group file `mygroup` as used in the basic method for digest authentication. If you modify the access file as shown in `1x02-16.txt`, only the users in group6 can gain access the to directory. A test page for using group files is `ex02-07.htm`, which is the same as `ex02-06.htm` with a simple modification at line 3.

Table 2.6   Apache access file configuration directives

Directive	Argument type	Default value	Purpose
AuthDigestDomain	Domain name	–	Domain name for the digest authentication
AuthDigestFile	File name	–	Name of file with users and passwords
AuthDigestGroupFile	File name	–	Name of file containing list of user groups
AuthDigestNonceLifetime	Seconds	300	Controls how long the server nonce is valid

```
Example: lx02-16.txt: The digest access file for groups of people

1: AuthType Digest
2: AuthName "private"
3: AuthDigestFile        "/apache/htdocs/mydigest/htpass.wd"
4: AuthDigestGroupFile "/apache/htdocs/mydigest/mygroup"
5: AuthDigestDomain    http://www.pws-ex.com/mydigest
6: require group group6
```

```
Example: Modification to ex02-06.htm to produce ex02-07.htm

3: Digest HTTP Authentication<br />Using Group File<br />
```

Figures 2.16 and 2.17 show that user cs005 is trying to access page ex02-07.htm. After several attempts, the unauthorized message is displayed.

Fig. 2.16   Using a group file

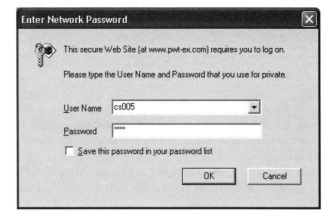

Fig. 2.17 Unauthorized access

Although users cs005 and cs001 have valid password accounts in the digest password file, they cannot access documents in the directory because they are not in the authorized group.

2.3.4   Inside the digest method and security attacks

One of the best ways of studying the security of the digest method is to read the actual client–server dialog during the authentication process. When your browser requests a digest-protected document, the server returns a 401 respond code together with a different WWW-Authenticate message. An example of the server response is given in 1x02-17.txt.

```
Example: lx02-17.txt: Digest authentication - server response

1: HTTP/1.1 401 Authorization Required
2: Date Tue, 07 Dec 2004 12:08:10 GMT
3: Server: Apache/2.0
4: WWW-Authenticate: Digest
5:    realm="private",
6:    nonce="bc02c65dfcabdb278111c84cbe9c9923"
7: ... ... ...
8: Connection: close
9: Content-Type: text/html
```

The WWW-Authenticate header indicates that a digest authentication is required and also provides a special string called 'nonce'. Nonce is an encrypted (MD5 encryption) string containing the time of day and the IP address of the requester. Since time is involved, nonce is different for each request made.

To respond to the request, the browser may prompt the user for a username and password. Instead of just sending that information as described in the basic method, the browser does the following:

1 compute the MD5 encrypted string on username, the realm name and the password;

2 compute the MD5 encrypted string on the request method and URI of the request;

3 compute the final MD5 encrypted string called response on the two previous encrypted strings together with the nonce supplied by the server

MD5 encryption (or simply MD5) can take a string (a long string) and produce a one-way ciphertext with a fixed length (32 characters). MD5 is irreversible and is one of the most important encryptions in cryptography. We will discuss it in detail in Chapter 3. The three steps above and the computation of response can be summarized in one formula:

```
md5(md5(<username>+":"+<realm>+":"+<password>)+
    ":"+<nonce> +":"+
    md5(<method>+":"+<uri>))
```

This response string (final MD5) is then sent to the server together with the nonce and some other request headers to form a new request. Note that the MD5 string generated in step 1 is the same as the encrypted information stored in the password file. The new request may look like that shown in 1x02-18.txt.

```
Example: 1x02-18.txt: Digest method - transmitting the
response string

1: GET /digest/ex02-06.htm HTTP/1.1
2: Host: www.pws-ex.com
3: Authorization: Digest username="root",
4:     realm="private",
5:     nonce="bc02c65dfcabdb278111c84cbe9c9923",
6:     uri="/mydigest/ex02-03.htm",
7:     response="6629fae49393a05397450978507c4ef1",
8: ... ... ...
```

To perform the authentication, the server will get the MD5 encrypted information from the password file and compute the response string as described in steps 2 and 3. The server compares the `response` strings for a match. If they match, the server transmits the document. Otherwise, the server rejects the request with a 401 (or 'authorization required') respond code.

The main security idea involved in digest authentication is transmitting the message digest (or MD5) string over the Web. MD5 is a sophisticated one-way encryption for generating passwords, and there is no known decryption method. Unless you have a good brute-force attack scheme and a huge amount of time and computing resources, getting a well-chosen plaintext password is not going to be easy.

In addition, the `nonce` is different for every new request, and capturing the entire client–server conversation is not going to help much. Even if you can perform a replay attack while the `nonce` is still alive, you can only access the one-off static Web page. Therefore, the digest authentication is, in general, considered to be much safer than the basic method.

There is one situation in which digest authentication is *less* secure than basic authentication. To crack the basic method, an intruder has to wait for someone to login and capture the plaintext password. Even if they can get into the password file or database inside the server, the intruder still needs to crack the encryption for the plaintext password to login. Compare this to the digest method – if someone gets into the password file stored in server, they can use the information directly to compute the `response` string asking for digest authentication. Since there is no plaintext password involved, there is no need to crack or decrypt the plaintext password.

Suppose you have developed an ECMAScript function `md5()` to compute the MD5 string. The program code of this function is stored in an external file called `zz_md5.js`. You can use this function to develop a simple page to generate the MD5 encrypted password of the digest method. Consider example `ex02-08.htm`.

```
Example: ex02-08.htm - generating digest passwords

1:  <?xml version="1.0" encoding="iso-8859-1"?>
2:  <!DOCTYPE html PUBLIC "-//W3C//DTD XHTML 1.0 Transitional//EN"
3:     "http://www.w3.org/TR/xhtml1/DTD/xhtml1-transitional.dtd">
4:  <html xmlns="http://www.w3.org/1999/xhtml" xml:lang="en"
       lang="en">
5:  <head><title>Generating Digest Passwords --
       ex02-08.htm</title></head>
6:  <style>
7:    .butSt { font-size:16pt;width:250px;height:35px;font-weight:bold;
8:             background:#dddddd;color:#ff0000}
9:  </style>
```

```
10:  <body style="font-family:arial;font-size:22pt;background:#000088;
11:            text-align:center;color:#00ff00">
12:     Generating Passwords For <br />Digest Authentication <br />
13:  <img alt="pic" src="line1.gif" height="7"
     width="530" /><br /><br />
14:  <table style="font-size:16pt" cellspacing="20px" align="center">
15:  <tr><td style="width:120px;color:#ffff00">User Name</td>
16:      <td><input id="usrname" size="30" maxlength="30"
            class="butSt" />
17:  <tr><td style="width:120px;color:#ffff00">Realm Name</td>
18:      <td><input id="realm" size="30" maxlength="30"
            class="butSt" />
19:  <tr><td style="width:120px;color:#ffff00">Password</td>
20:      <td><input id="passwd" size="30" maxlength="30"
            class="butSt" />
21:      <input type="button" value="OK"
22:       style="font-size:16pt;font-weight:bold;width:80px;
23:       height:35px;background:#dddddd;color:#ff0000"
            onclick="digest_md5()" /></td></tr>
24:  <tr><td colspan="2" style="width:360px;color:#ffff00">
25:       Digest Password</td></tr>
26:   <tr><td colspan="2"><input id="dis_mesg" size="55"
27:       maxlength="55" style="font-size:16pt;width:480px;
            height:35px;font-weight:bold;
28:       background:#dddddd;color:#ff0000" /> </td> </tr>
29:  </table>
30:  </body>
31:  <script src="zz_md5.js"></script><br />
32:  <script>
33:  function digest_md5()
34:  {
35:   var usrSt = document.getElementById("usrname").value;
36:   var realmSt = document.getElementById("realm").value;
37:   var passSt = document.getElementById("passwd").value;
38:   document.getElementById("dis_mesg").value=md5(usrSt+":"+
39:                                    realmSt+":"+passSt);
40:  }
41:  </script>
42:  </html>
```

This is a simple interface page containing four text boxes and one push button.
The first three text boxes in lines 15–20 are to get the username, realm name and
password. Once you have entered these fields and clicked the OK button defined in

lines 21–23, the function `digest_md5()` is activated and the digest password will be displayed in the final text box (lines 26–28).

The ECMAScript function `digest_md5()` is defined in lines 33–40. Inside the function, lines 35–37 are used to obtained the user input username, realm name and password from the text boxes. They are stored in the string variables `usrSt`, `realmSt` and `passSt` respectively. Consider the function call in line 38

```
md5(usrSt+":"+realmSt+":"+passSt)
```

This statement first will concatenate the username, realm name and password together with colons separating them. The `md5()` function encrypts (one-way) it and returns a string of 32 hexadecimal characters. This encrypted password is output by the statement in line 38. The program code of the function `md5()` is defined in the script `zz_md5.js` and is included in this page by the statement in line 31. Details of this file and `md5()` will be discussed in Chapter 3. Screenshots of this example are shown in Figures 2.18 and 2.19.

From these figures, you can see that the output is the same as the encrypted string (or hash) stored in the digest password file (see `lx02-13.txt`). With a page like this, password records for digest authentication can be generated independently, and hence the authentication is vulnerable from replacement attack. One of the efficient ways of protecting against replacement attack is to restrict the physical access to the server. This is particularly true when you are using Windows systems. In

Fig. 2.18 Digest password for the user 'root'

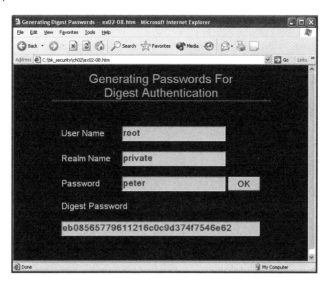

Fig. 2.19   Digest password for the user 'cs001'

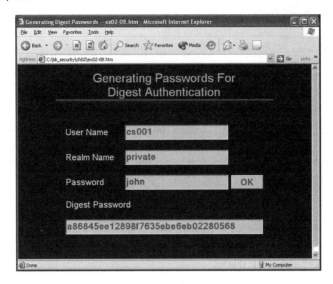

general, servers should be used and maintained by administrators or related personnel, and not ordinary users.

Most of the crypto-attacks discussed above have their specific working areas and limitations, and do not always work. For most ciphers, the first infallible attack is the so-called 'brute-force' attack.

2.4   Brute-force attacks

2.4.1   What is brute-force attack?

Brute-force attack (also known as brute-force cracking) is a trial and error method used by application programs to decrypt a cipher by an exhaustive search for the password (or key). If you consider a cipher to be a message in a safe protected by a number lock, then it is a process for breaking into the safe by trying all the possible number keys. Brute-force, in general, is considered to be infallible, although it is a time- and resource-consuming approach. An old saying in cryptology is

> a well-designed encryption is a scheme that can only be defeated by brute-force attack.

Before 1995, brute-force schemes were tools used by governments and big organizations to solve intelligence or scientific problems. Ordinary desktop machines of that time couldn't search and test more than 500 keys a second. With this kind of computing power, performing brute-force attack is not an option for most attackers. Now, even an ordinary portable PC can search more than 100 000 keys a second comfortably. With this processing power, brute-force schemes became one of the most popular types of attack in cryptology. The reason is simple – computers have made it easier to attack ciphertext by using brute-force rather than by attacking the mathematics behind the encryption. With a brute-force attack, the attacker merely generates every possible key and applies it to the ciphertext. Any resulting plaintext that makes sense reveals a candidate for a legitimate key so that further analysis can be carried out.

Another driving force for the development of brute-force schemes in the early 1990s was the challenge to crack the Data Encryption Standard (DES). The DES cipher was the world-wide encryption standard used by the US government and the international community. Instead of employing intellectual strategies to solve the mathematical problem behind the DES, brute force was used intensively. In fact, a number of brute-force challenges to the DES scheme were launched in the late 1990s. In January 1999, a brute-force scheme known as 'Deep Crack' was able to crack the DES scheme within one day and effectively raise a big question mark over the security of 56-bit DES encryption. However, DES is still one of the most popular encryptions used today.

In cryptography, size does matter. The larger the key, the harder it is to crack. For example, if your password consists of 26 English (lower case) letters, the key-symbol (or key-code) string is defined by

[a–z] = abcdefghijklmnopqrstuvwxyz

In this case, the number of the key-code is 26 and each password, or key, is composed of elements of this key-code string. If your password length (or key length) is between one and three characters, the brute-force attacker has to try all these combinations of strings:

a, b, c, . . . , z, (keys with one character)
aa, ab, . . . , zz, (keys with two characters)
aaa, aab, . . . , zzz (keys with three characters)

By trying all the combinations, a collision, in theory, is guaranteed.

Given a key length, the collection of all keys of this length is called the key-space with respect to key length. If the key length is denoted by the variable `key-length`, the total number of keys in the key-space is

(number of key-code)$^{\text{key-length}}$

For example, if the key-length = 3 and the key-code = [a–z], we have $(26)^3 = 17\,576$ keys. This number also represents the total number of tests (or exhaustive tests) for the attack. In practice, the 10 numeric symbols 0, 1, 2, . . . , 9 are also frequently used. If 36 key symbols are considered, the key-code turns out to be

[a–z, 0–9] = abcdefghIjklmnopqrstuvwxyz0123456789

When the key length is 3, the total number of keys in this key-space is $(36)^3 = 46\,656$. If the key length is from 1 to 3 (or [1, 3]), the number of keys in the key-space is

$$36 + (36)^2 + (36)^3 = 47\,988$$

In general, we will use [a–z, 0–9] for most brute-force examples in this chapter. For brute-force attacks, the key length, and hence the number of keys, is often used as a numerical guide to the security of a cipher under attack. For example, if your PC can process 100 000 keys a second, Table 2.7 shows the key length, the number of keys in the key-space and the time needed to perform the attack. From this you can see that the time taken to test all combinations of keys of 5 characters is 10 minutes. If you increase the key length to 10 characters, the time is 1159 years.

Obviously, expansion of the key-code also increases the number of keys in a key-space dramatically. For example, the key-space can be expanded by adding the upper case alphabet set – [a–z, A–Z, 0–9]. Sometimes, you can add punctuation marks as well. If you take the entire ASCII character set into account, ASCII values

Table 2.7 Key length and number of keys in the key-space

Key length	Number of keys	Time	Key length	Number of keys	Time
1	36	<1 sec	6	2176782336	6 hours
2	1296	<1 sec	7	78364164096	9 days
3	46656	<1 sec	8	2821109907456	10 Months
4	1679616	16 sec	10	3656158440062976	1159 years
5	60466176	10 Minutes	16	7958661109946400884391936	2523 billion years

32–126 represent the 95 frequently used characters in English. To perform brute-force attack on this key-space will be even more time consuming, even if you have a dedicated chip-set that can test 200 million keys a second. Now, it's time to consider how to generate the key-space for the attacks.

2.4.2 The key-space of brute-force attacks

There are a number of ways of generating the key-space. As a starting point, a simple brute-force method based on a for-loop is presented in this section. More flexible and practical implementations will be presented in Section 2.5. For simplicity, but not limiting the key length much, we will consider the 36 key-code [a–z, 0–9] case. The key-space for one character contains 36 keys. The key-space for three characters has $(36)^3 = 46\,656$ keys and they are

aaa, aab, . . . , aaz, aa0, . . . , aa9, aba . . . , . . . , . . . , 999

One of the simplest ways to generate the key-space for three characters is to use for-loops in ECMAScript. Consider example ex02-09.htm.

```
Example: ex02-09.htm - A simple key-space scheme using for-loops

 1: <?xml version="1.0" encoding="iso-8859-1"?>
 2: <!DOCTYPE html PUBLIC "-//W3C//DTD XHTML 1.0 Transitional//EN"
 3:    "http://www.w3.org/TR/xhtml1/DTD/xhtml1-transitional.dtd">
 4: <html xmlns="http://www.w3.org/1999/xhtml" xml:lang="en"
      lang="en">
 5: <head><title> Gen. Key-Space Using For Loops --
      ex02-01.htm </title></head>
 6: <style>
 7:   .bx {color:#ff0000;font-size:16pt;font-weight:bold;width:50px;
 8:        height:30px;background-color:#eeeeee" }
 9: </style>
10: <body style="font-family:arial;font-size:22pt;text-align:center;
11:        color:#ffff00;background:#000088">
12: A Brute-force Key-Space Scheme <br />Using Simple For Loops<br />
13: <img alt="pic" src="line1.gif" height="7"
      width="640" /><br /><br />
14:
15: <table style="font-size:18pt;text-align:left" align="center">
16:   <tr><td style="width:200px">Key Symbols: </td>
17:        <td colspan="3">[ a-z,0-9 ] (36 English)</td></tr>
18:   <tr><td>Min. Key Length</td>
19:     <td><input type="text" id="minK" class="bx" value=" 3"
            readonly /></td>
```

```
20:    <td>Max. Key Length</td>
21:    <td><input type="text" id="maxK" class="bx" value=" 3"
          readonly /></td>
22:  </tr>
23:  <tr><td colspan="2">Generating The Key-Space: </td>
24:      <td colspan="2"><input type="button" class="box" value="OK"
25:           style="width:120px" onclick="key_space()" /></td></tr>
26:  <tr><td colspan="4"><textarea rows="5" cols="50" id="out_mesg"
27:       readonly style="font-size:16pt;font-weight:bold; width:620px;
28:       height:250px;background:#aaffaa"></textarea></td></tr>
29:  </table>
30:  <script src="ex02-01.js"></script>
31:  </body> </html>
```

This is a simple Web page containing two text boxes, one text area and one OK button. The two text boxes are used to get the minimum and maximum key length from the user. In this example, we use the 36 characters [a–z, 0–9] as key-code (line 17). Both the text boxes (lines 19 and 21) have the same default value of 3 to indicate that the key-space is fixed at 3. Once the OK button is pressed, the entire key space of $(36)^3 = 46\,656$ keys will be generated and displayed in the text area defined in lines 26–28. This is a general interface and we will use it as a framework for brute-force attacks in the coming sections.

When the OK button defined in lines 25–26 is pressed, the function key_space() is activated. This function is declared in the ECMAScript file ex02-09.js.

```
Example: ex02-09.js - ECMAScript file for ex02-09.htm

 1: var keyC = Array("a","b","c","d","e","f","g","h","i","j","k","l",
 2:                   "m","n","o","p","q","r","s","t","u","v","w","x",
 3:                   "y","z","0","1","2","3","4","5","6","7","8","9");
 4: var shSt="";
 5:
 6: function key_space()
 7: {
 8:   var myTime01 = new Date();
 9:   var startTime = myTime01.getTime();
10:   shSt="";
11:
12:   key_space_gen();
13:
14:   var myTime02 = new Date();
```

```
15:    var endTime= myTime02.getTime();
16:    shSt +="\n *** Time = " + (endTime - startTime);
17:    document.getElementById("out_mesg").value = shSt;
18: }
19:
20: function key_space_gen()
21: {
22:    for (ss=0; ss < keyC.length; ss++) {
23:      for (kk=0; kk < keyC.length; kk++) {
24:        for (jj=0; jj < keyC.length; jj++) {
25:          keySt="";
26:          keySt = keyC[ss] + keyC[kk] + keyC[jj];
27:          shSt +=keySt + " "
28:    }}}
29: }
```

Since brute force is such a time-consuming process, efficiency plays an important role in the implementation. A device to measure the execution time in milliseconds is used inside the function key_space(). Line 8 declares a date object variable called myTime01. With this variable, the function myTime01.getTime() will get the time in milliseconds and store it in startTime (line 9). After the entire key-space is generated by the function key_space_gen(), the statements in lines 14–15 return the final time (also in milliseconds) to variable endTime. The difference of the variables endTime and startTime represents the time to execute the program. The execution time is displayed by the statement in line 17.

The central block of this program is the function key_space_gen() in lines 20–29. In this function, a triple for-loop is used. Since the 36 symbols [a–z, 0–9] are defined by the array keyC in lines 1–3, the property variable keyC.length contains the value 36. The three for-loops on variables ss, kk, and jj compose all the combinations of $(36)^3$ element and the statement in line 26

```
keySt = keyC[ss] + keyC[kk] + keyC[jj]
```

combines all three characters into a key string called keySt. This key string is added to the display string shSt in line 27. In fact all key strings are added into shSt after the execution of the function. This string is output to the Web page by the statement in line 17. Screenshots of this example are shown in Figures 2.20 and 2.21.

As you can see from these two screenshots, the execution time in NS7 is shorter than in IE(6+).

With this page, you can perform brute-force tests on any password of three characters against a cipher. However, this program code is not very flexible. The hard-wired for-loops in this program can only compute three rounds. It may not be easy to modify it to accept an arbitrary key length. Also, this program didn't use the information about minimum and maximum key length from the Web page.

Fig. 2.20 `ex02-09.htm` in Internet Explorer

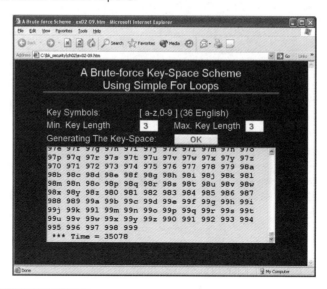

Fig. 2.21 `ex02-09.htm` in Netscape

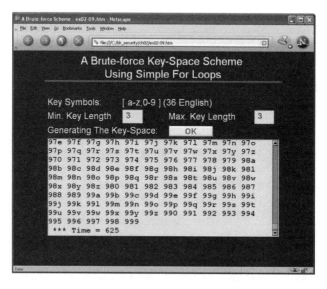

2.5   Implementation and application of brute-force schemes

Brute force, in many cases, is harder to implement than you might think. Most schemes are not easy to follow due to the fact that efficiency of the implementation is essential. In many cases, machine structure and hardware coding (or machine codes) are heavily involved.

We will introduce two brute-force implementations in this section, namely 'quotient and remainder' and 'position updating'. These two schemes are neither very efficient nor up to industrial strength. However, they are easy to understand and can help master brute-force skills step by step. These two schemes are implemented with Web technologies based on the same rationale. Porting to other languages such as C/C++ is not a difficult task.

2.5.1   The quotient and remainder method

One of the simple ways of modifying the for-loop program in the previous section to accept an arbitrary key length is to use the quotient and remainder method. Suppose we have an array of 36 key codes:

```
keyC = new Array("a","b","c","d","e","f","g","h","i","j","k","l","m",
                 "n","o","p","q","r","s","t","u","v","w","x","y","z",
                 "0","1","2","3","4","5","6","7","8","9")
```

Given an arbitrary key length, say three, the total number of keys, $36^3 = 46\ 656$, can be generated by a single for-loop with variable ii (ii for-loop) running through from 0 to $36^3 - 1$. The three characters ch1, ch2 and ch3 of the arbitrary ii^{th} key can be calculated by the following four steps.

1 ch1 = keyC [the quotient of $(ii/36^2)$]

2 tmp = the remainder of $(ii/36^2)$

3 ch2 = keyC [the quotient of $(tmp/36)$]

4 ch3 = keyC [the remainder of $(tmp/36)$]

When ii=0, ch1=keyC[0], ch2=keyC[0] and ch3=keyC[0] and therefore the key is 'aaa'. When ii=36^3 - 1, we have

1 ch1 = keyC [quotient of $(36^3 - 1)/36^2$] = keyC [35]= "9"

2 tmp = the remainder of $(36^3 - 1)/36^2 = 1295$

3 ch2 = keyC [quotient of 1295/36] = keyC[35]= "9"

4 ch3 = keyC [remainder of 1295/36] = keyC[35]= "9"

Therefore the key string is '999'. Based on this, we can construct a more general key space scheme, and this is shown in lx02-19.txt.

```
Example: lx02-19.txt - the quotient and remainder algorithm

 1: Step 1:
 2:   Defines the key codes e.g. keyC=[a-z,0-9]
 3:
 4: Step 2:
 5:   Get the minimum and maximum key length e.g. minKeyL, maxKeyL
 6:
 7: Step 3: Generating All Key Strings From minKeyL to maxKeyL
 8:
 9:  for (noD = minKeyL; noD <=maxKeyL; noD++)
10:    total_key = (keyC.length)^{noD}
11:    for (jj=0; jj < total_key; jj++)
12:       tmp1 = jj;
13:       keySt=""
14:       for (kk=0; kk <= noD; kk++)
15:          tmp1 = Quotient of ( tmp1 / keyC.length ^{(noD - kk)} )
16:          keySt = keySt + keyC[tmp1]
17:          tmp1 = Remainder of ( jj / keyC.length ^{(noD - kk)} )
18:       end-for
19:          //** keySt = key string and attacks can be here **/
20:    end-for
21: end-for
```

This algorithm consists of three steps. Step 1 is to define the key codes for the key-space. In this case, the key-code is [a–z, 0–9]. Step 2 of the algorithm is to get the minimum and maximum key lengths, used to control the beginning and end of the process.

Step 3 of the algorithm generates all keys with key lengths from minKeyL to maxKeyL (lines 7–21). For a particular key length noD, the total number of keys is calculated by line 10. The jj for-loop in lines 11–20 will generate all key strings using the quotient and remainder method. The kk for-loop (lines 14–18) produces each individual key and stores them in variable keySt. Applications related to the key including the brute-force attacks can be added in line 19. To put this algorithm into action, you can construct a brute-force page as follows.

First, make a copy of ex02-09.htm and call it ex02-10.htm. Modify the following four lines:

```
12: A Brute-force Key-Space Scheme <br />Using Quotient and
    Remainder<br />
19:   <td><input type="text" id="minK" class="bx" value=" 1" /></td>
21:   <td><input type="text" id="maxK" class="bx" value=" 3" /></td>
30: <script src="ex02-10.js"></script>
```

Line 12 is to change the display of the page. Lines 19 and 21 are basically the same as `ex02-09.htm` except that we have removed the `readonly` attribute so that users are allowed to change the values of minimum and maximum key lengths. Once the OK button is pressed, the `key_space()` function will be activated. This function is declared in the ECMAScript file `ex02-10.js`.

```
Example: ex02-10.js - ECMAScript file for ex02-10.htm
 1: var keyC = Array("a","b","c","d","e","f","g","h","i","j","k","l",
 2:                   "m","n","o","p","q","r","s","t","u","v","w","x",
 3:                   "y","z","0","1","2","3","4","5","6","7","8","9");
 4: var shSt="";
 5:
 6: function key_space()
 7: {
 8:  var myTime01 = new Date();
 9:  var startTime = myTime01.getTime();
10:  var vMinKeyL=1, vMaxKeyL=3;
11:
12:  vMinKeyL = parseInt(document.getElementById("minK").value);
13:  vMaxKeyL = parseInt(document.getElementById("maxK").value);
14:
15:  if ((vMinKeyL > 0) && (vMaxKeyL < 7) && (vMinKeyL <= vMaxKeyL))
16:    shSt = "Minimum Key Length = "+ vMinKeyL + "\n";
17:    shSt += "Maximum Key Length = "+ vMaxKeyL + "\n";
18:
19:    key_space_gen(vMinKeyL,vMaxKeyL);
20:
21:    var myTime02 = new Date();
22:    var endTime= myTime02.getTime();
23:    shSt +="\nTotal Time In Milliseconds = " + (endTime -
                                              startTime) +"\n";
24:    document.getElementById("out_mesg").value= shSt;
25:  } else {
26:    alert("Invalid Key Range! \n Please Check");
27:  }
28: }
29:
30: function key_space_gen(minKeyL,maxKeyL)
31: {
32:    var total_key,jj,kk,keySt;
33:    for(noD=minKeyL; noD <=maxKeyL; noD++) {
34:      total_key = Math.pow(keyC.length,noD);
35:      for (jj=0; jj < total_key; jj++) {
```

```
36:          keySt="";
37:          tmp1 = jj;
38:          for(kk=1;kk<=noD;kk++) {
39:             divd = Math.pow(keyC.length,noD-kk);
40:             tmp1 = Math.floor(tmp1/divd);
41:             keySt = keySt+ keyC[tmp1];
42:             tmp1 = jj % divd;
43:          }
44:          //-- Now keySt stores the key string e.g.
             shSt+=keySt + " " --//
45:     }
46:   }
47: }
```

This program contains two functions. The first function `key_space()` in lines 6–28 controls the program execution and measures the running time. The `key_space_gen()` function generates all the key strings. The two statements in lines 12–13 get the minimum and maximum key lengths. In order to keep the execution time reasonable, we have clipped the key length to less than 7 in this example (line 15). By calling the function `key_space_gen(vMinKeyL,vMaxKeyL)` in line 19, all the keys between the key lengths `vMinkeyL` and `vMaxKeyL` are generated. The program execution time is measured in lines 21–23 and displayed by the statement in line 24.

The function `key_space_gen()` uses variables `minKeyL` and `maxKeyL` as parameters. The variable `noD` (number of digit) and the for-loop in lines 33–46 run through the key length from `minKeyL` to `maxKeyL`. For example, when the variable `noD=3`, all keys of three characters are generated. The array `keyC` in lines 1–3 defines the key-code characters and therefore the property `keyC.length` has the value 36. The total number of keys in the key-space is calculated by the statement in line 34,

```
total_key = Math.pow(keyC.length,noD)
```
$$= (keyC.length)^{noD} = (36)^3 = 46656$$

The `jj` for-loop in lines 35–45 computes all the keys. For each value of `jj`, the corresponding key string is computed by the inner `kk` for-loop in lines 38–43. For example when `jj=257`, the first character (when `kk=1`) of the key is computed by the statements in line 39–40, which is equivalent to

```
Math.floor(jj/Math.pow(keyC.length,noD-kk))=Math.floor( 257/(26)²)
```

This number is the integer part (i.e. quotient) of $257/(26)^2$ and equals 0. Therefore the first digit of the key string is `keyC[0]=a`. When the variable `tmp1` assigns the remainder of $257/(26)^2$, the value is 257 (line 42). The second digit of the key is calculated by line 39. In this case, the second digit is determined by the integer part of $257/26$, which is 9, and therefore the second character is `keyC[9]=j`. The third digit is calculated by the remainder of $257/26$, which equals 23, and therefore keyC[23]=x. The key string for value 257 is 'ajx'. Continuing the jj for-loop provides all the 46 656 keys, which is the key-space for three characters. As in the previous example, the execution time is generated and output to the screen by the statements in lines 23–24. Screenshots of this example in action are shown in Figures 2.22 and 2.23.

Fig. 2.22 ex02-10.htm in Internet Explorer

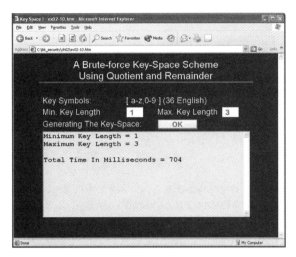

Fig. 2.23 ex02-10.htm in Netscape

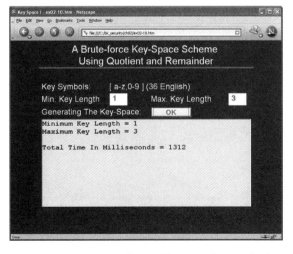

This quotient and remainder method of generating key space is simple and easy to understand. However, it is not very efficient since too many mathematical functions are involved. Another disadvantage of this method is that putting the value of total number of keys as one integer, sometimes, may be too big for your system to handle. Don't forget that no integer in a 32-bit system can be more than $2^{32} = 4\,294\,967\,296$. This number is sufficiently big enough for general computing, but a bit low for cryptology and security applications. To overcome this problem, let's consider a more practical scheme, the 'position updating method'.

2.5.2 The position updating method

The basic idea of the position updating method (or digit update method) is simple. We consider the space (or collection) of key-code used in the brute-force scheme to be a number system. A decimal number system has only 10 symbols, namely $0, 1, \ldots, 9$. Any three-digit number, such as pqr, in the decimal system can be represented by the polynomial

$$pqr = p(10)^2 + q(10)^1 + r$$

When the value of r is greater than 9, it reverts to 0 and the value of q increases by 1. For the hexadecimal system the symbols are $0, 1, 2, \ldots, 9, a, b, c, d, e, f$. An arbitrary three-digit number xyz can be represented by

$$xyz = x(16)^2 + y(16)^1 + z$$

This polynomial represents all three-digit numbers in the hexadecimal system (i.e. the space of 3-digit numbers). Like the decimal case, one characteristic of these representations is that when the least significant digit, say z, runs through all the 16 symbols, the next digit (or the value of y) will be increased by 1. In other words, the first element in this space is 000, the next one is 001 and the last element is fff. Based on this digit, or position, updating feature, we can construct a more general algorithm to generate the key-space. The idea is straightforward – we can treat the key-code as a number system. Consider the algorithm and pseudo-code in 1x02-20.txt with the key length equal to 3 so that it is easy to understand.

```
Example: 1x02-20.txt - The position updating algorithm when key
length = 3

1: Step 1:
2:    Defines the key codes e.g. keyC=[a-z,0-9]
3: Step 2:
4:    Defines an array of 3 elements e.g. s[0]=0, s[1]=0, and s[2]=0
5:
6: Step 3: Generating All Key Strings Using Position Update
7:    c=1
```

```
 8:   while (c > 0 )
 9:     (A) Fixed the first 2 digits i.e. s[0], s[1]
10:         and generate keys by changing the 3rd digit
            i.e. obtaining keys
11:             keyC[s[0]] keyC[s[1]] a, ..., keyC[s[0]] keyC[s[1]] 9
12:         When finished, update the second digit by 1
13:         s[1] = s[1] +1
14:
15:     (B) Check all previous digits for an update i.e. for p = 1 to 0
16:         if (s[p] > keyC.length  // if one the digit > code length
17:             s[p]=0              // set the current digit to zero
18:             s[p-1]++            // increase the previous digit by 1
19:         end-if
20:
21:     (C) When first digit s[0] > code length stop the while loop
22:         if (s[0] > keyC.length)
23:             c =0                // stop the while loop
24:         end-if
25:   end-while
```

This algorithm also contains three steps. Step 1 is to set up the key-code as usual. Step 2 is to define an array to represent the digit position. In this case, we have three array elements s[0], s[1] and s[2], representing each character of the key string. If you have key length = k, you should declare an array of k elements.

Step 3 of the algorithm is basically a while-loop (lines 8–25) and will generate all the keys using the position updating method. Inside the while-loop, there are three processes. Process (A) in lines 9–13 is to generate the first set of keys. By fixing the first two array elements s[0] and s[1], the key strings can be constructed by changing the third element s[2]. As a result, the first set of key strings are 'aaa, aab, aac, . . . , aa8, aa9'. When these keys are generated, the second array s[1] is increased by 1. Now the new set of keys will be generated: 'aba, abb, abc, . . . , ab8, ab9'. This feature is the same as updating the previous digit of the key.

Process (B) is to check all previous digits (or positions) to see whether an update is needed. For example, when the value of s[1] (or second last position) is bigger than the key length, you have generated the last round of keys related to the second character s[1], i.e. 'a9a, a9b, a9c, . . . , a98, a99'. In this case, element s[0] needed to be updated and the key string set is 'baa, aab, aac, . . . , aa8, ba9'.

Process (C) checks whether we have generated all the keys. When the first array s[0] is bigger than the key length, as illustrated in lines 21–24, the last set of keys '99a, 99b, 99c, . . . , 998, 999' has been generated. In other words, all keys in the key-space with length = 3 have been constructed and the while-loop is terminated. We have considered the algorithm when the key length equals 3 so that the process is easy to understand and remember. Once you understand the algorithm, modification to any arbitrary key length can be achieved without difficulty.

For a practical example, let's consider the following Web page. First, copy the page ex02-10.htm to ex02-11.htm and modify the following two lines:

```
12: A Brute-force Key-Space Scheme <br />Using Position Updating
                                                      Method<br />
30: <script src="ex02-11.js"></script>
```

Line 12 is to change the display at the top of the page. Once the OK button is pressed, the key_space() function will be activated. This function is declared in the ECMAScript file ex02-03.js. This file contains two functions, key_space() and key_space_gen(). The key_space() function is the same as ex02-10.js and therefore the first 29 lines of the codes are unchanged. Only the remaining code of the function key_space_gen() is listed in ex02-11.js.

Example: ex02-11.js – The ECMAScript program fragment for ex02-11.htm

```
30: function key_space_gen(minKeyL,maxKeyL)
31: {
32:  var keySt="", c=1;
33:  var noD,noD01,noD02,symL,symL01,ii,jj,p,tmp;
34:  var s= new Array(32);
35:
36:  for (noD = minKeyL; noD <= maxKeyL ; noD++) {
37:    c=1;
38:    for (ii=0;ii< noD;ii++) { s[ii]=0; }
39:    noD01 = noD -1;
40:    noD02 = noD -2;
41:    symL = keyC.length;
42:    symL01 = keyC.length -1;
43:
44:    while (c > 0) {
45:      for (ii=0;ii< symL;ii++) {
46:        keySt ="";
47:        for(jj=0; jj < noD01 ; jj++) {
48:          tmp = s[jj];
49:          keySt += keyC[tmp];
50:        }
51:        keySt += keyC[ii];
52:        //-- Now keySt Stores The Key String        --//
53:        //-- Brute-Force Attack Can Be Here          --//
54:      }
```

```
55:        s[noD02] += 1;
56:
57:        if ( noD > 1) {
58:           if ( s[noD02] > symL01) {
59:              for (p=noD02; p > 0; p--) {
60:                 if (s[p] > symL01 ) {
61:                    s[p] =0;
62:                    s[p-1] +=1;
63:                 }
64:              }
65:              if ( s[0] > symL01 ) { c=0; }
66:           }
67:        } else { c=0; }
68:     }    // end while-loop
69:  }        // end noD-for-loop
70: }
```

This program fragment provides the definition of the function `key_space_gen()`. In this function, the `noD` for-loop in lines 36–69 runs through key lengths `minKeyL` to `maxKeyL` to generate all the keys.

For a specified key length, `noD` (or number of digit), the `ii` for-loop in line 38 is used to initialize the digit array `s[]`. This array is used to control individual digits. As mentioned in algorithm `1x02-20.txt`, an infinite while-loop is set in lines 44–68 to generate all the keys until it is done. With the digit array `s[]`, the inner `jj` for-loop in lines 47–50 generates the key string with first `noD-1` digits. The last digit is generated by the statement in line 51 and added to the key string (lines 45–54). Next, the element or digit `s[noD-2]` is increased by 1 so the corresponding digit of the key string is updated. If this digit `s[noD-1]` or any of the values in the array `s[]`, say `s[p]`, is bigger than the key-code, the value `s[p]` is set to 0 and `s[p-1]` is increased by 1 (lines 58–67). When the first digit `s[0]` is bigger than `noD-1`, all the keys with `length = noD` will have been generated. In this case, the value of `c` is set to zero to stop the while-loop at line 65. Screenshots of this example are shown in Figures 2.24 and 2.25.

From these two figures, we can see that IE is faster than NS in this situation. For a simple comparison of the two methods, Table 2.8 measures the execution time in milliseconds for some popular browsers and key lengths.

From Table 2.8, you can see that the digit updating method is faster than the quotient and remainder method. Also, with key lengths 1–4 to 1–5, the execution times increase dramatically. In order to generate all the keys from one to four characters, the IE6.x browser needs only 8 seconds. Increasing the key length to 1–5 characters increases the time to more than 3 minutes (203 seconds). The digit updating method is also more efficient than the quotient and remainder method.

Fig. 2.24 `ex02-11.htm` in Internet Explorer

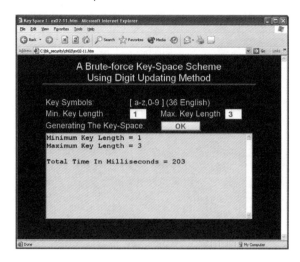

Fig. 2.25 `ex02-11.htm` in Netscape

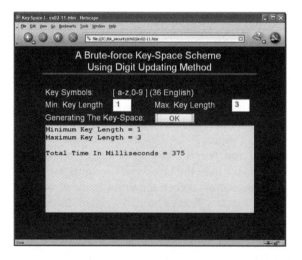

Source: Netscape Communicator browser window © 2005 Netscape Communications Corporation. Used with permission. Netscape Communications has not authorized, sponsored, endorsed, or approved this publication and is not responsible for its content.

Compared to browsers, the C/C++ program implementation runs much faster. A simple C/C++ implementation will be discussed in Section 2.5.4. Table 2.8 is just a rough guideline. For a more appropriate comparison, more tests on different platforms are needed.

Table 2.8 Comparison of the two key-space schemes

	Quotient and remainder method			Digit updating method		
	1–3	1–4	1–5	1–3	1–4	1–5
IE 6.x	421	15 432	447 178	220	8 041	203 062
NS 7.x	871	29 973	957 073	441	15 482	564 642
Opera	5388	183 184	12 875 466	2173	75 158	833 074
C/C++	30	197	3 335	0	30	1 232

Now, let's consider how to use the brute-force scheme to perform some attacks on ciphers and passwords.

2.5.3 Attacking passwords using brute-force schemes

For attacking password schemes, such as MD5, the brute-force method described in Section 2.5.2 can be employed. The basic idea behind the attack is that once the MD5 string is known, exhaustive tests against the entire key-space can be applied. If the original password is within the key length range, a collision or hit is guaranteed. Consider example ex02-12.htm.

```
Example: ex02-12.htm - MD5 password attacks using brute-force

 1: <?xml version="1.0" encoding="iso-8859-1"?>
 2: <!DOCTYPE html PUBLIC "-//W3C//DTD XHTML 1.0 Transitional//EN"
 3:    "http://www.w3.org/TR/xhtml1/DTD/xhtml1-transitional.dtd">
 4: <html xmlns="http://www.w3.org/1999/xhtml" xml:lang="en"
       lang="en">
 5: <head><title></title></head>
 6: <style>
 7:   .bx {color:#ff0000;font-size:16pt;font-weight:bold;width:50px;
 8:       height:30px;background-color:#eeeeee}
 9:   .bx2 {width:30px;height:30px;background-color:#ff88ff}
10: </style>
11: <body style="font-family:arial;font-size:22pt;text-align:center;
12:       color:#ffff00;background:#000088">
13: A Brute-Force Scheme <br />For MD5 Strings<br />
14: <img alt="pic" src="line1.gif" height="7"
       width="640" /><br /><br />
15:
16: <table style="font-size:18pt;text-align:left" align="center">
```

```
17:  <tr><td colspan="5" style="width:360px;color:#ffff00">
18:       Enter md5 Encrypted String</td></tr>
19:   <tr><td colspan="5"><input id="key_v" size="55" maxlength="55"
20:       style="font-size:16pt;width:450px;height:35px;
21:       font-weight:bold;background:#dddddd;color:#ff0000"
22:       value= "187ef4436122d1cc2f40dc2b92f0eba0" /><br /><br />
         </td></tr>
23:  <tr><td>Key Code : </td><td>[0-9]</td><td>
24:      <input type="radio" id="keyS" name="keyS" class="bx2"
         checked /></td>
25:      <td> [a-z,0-9]</td><td>
26:      <input type="radio" id="keyS" name="keyS"
         class="bx2" /></td></tr>
27:  <tr><td>Key Length: </td><td>Min.</td>
28:      <td><input type="text" id="minK" class="bx"
             value=" 1" /></td>
29:      <td>Max.</td>
30:      <td><input type="text" id="maxK" class="bx"
             value=" 3" /></td></tr>
31:  <tr><td>Finding A Match: </td>
32:      <td colspan=4><input type="button" class="bx" value="OK"
33:        style="width:120px" onclick="brute_force()" /></td></tr>
34:  <tr><td colspan="5"><textarea rows="5" cols="50" id="out_mesg"
35:      readonly style="font-size:16pt;font-weight:bold;width:620px;
36:      height:250px;background:#aaffaa"></textarea></td></tr>
37: </table>
38: <script src="zz_md5.js"></script>
39: <script src="ex02-12.js"></script>
40: </body>
41: </html>
```

This XHTML page contains three text boxes, two radio buttons and one OK button.
The first text box defined in lines 19–22 allows you to type in an MD5 string.
The two radio buttons (lines 23–26) are used to specify the key-code. You can pick
one of them, [0–9] or [a–z, 0–9]. Another two text boxes, in lines 27–30, let you
type in the range of key lengths. The default key lengths are minimum 1 and
maximum 3. Once the ok button, declared in lines 32–33, is pressed, the function
brute_force() is executed. The original text matched to the MD5 string will be
displayed in the text area specified in lines 34–36.

The driving force for this page is the ECMAScript function brute_force(). This
function is defined in the ECMAScript file ex02-12.js.

Example: ex02-12.js – The ECMAScript program for ex02-06.htm (Part I)

```
 1: var keyC= new Array()
 2: var shSt="", searchSt = "";
 3:
 4: function brute_force()
 5: {
 6:  var myTime01 = new Date();
 7:  var startTime = myTime01.getTime();
 8:  var vMinKeyL=1, vMaxKeyL=3, keyStV="";
 9:
10:  vMinKeyL = parseInt(document.getElementById("minK").value);
11:  vMaxKeyL = parseInt(document.getElementById("maxK").value);
12:  searchSt = "Password NOT Found \n";
13:  keyStV = document.getElementById("key_v").value;
14:  if ((vMinKeyL > 0) && (vMaxKeyL < 7) &&
         (vMinKeyL <= vMaxKeyL)) {
15:   shSt  = "Minimum Key Length = "+ vMinKeyL + "\n";
16:   shSt += "Maximum Key Length = "+ vMaxKeyL + "\n";
17:
18:   key_symbol()
19:   brute_force_test(vMinKeyL,vMaxKeyL,keyStV);
20:
21:   var myTime02 = new Date();
22:   var endTime= myTime02.getTime();
23:   shSt +="\n"+searchSt;
24:   shSt +="\nTotal Time In Milliseconds = " +
            (endTime - startTime) +"\n";
25:   document.getElementById("out_mesg").value= shSt;
26:  } else {
27:   alert("Invalid Key Range! \n Please Check");
28:  }
29: }
30:
```

First we define an array `keyC[]` and two strings (`shSt` and `searchSt`) in lines 1–2. The brute-force attack function `brute_force()` then follows. If you compare this `brute_force()` function with the `key_space()` function in previous examples, you will find that they are very similar. Lines 6–7 are used to get the program starting time in milliseconds. Lines 8–11 get the range of the key lengths. The variables `vMimKeyL` and `vMaxKeyL` store the minimum and maximum key length respectively. Naturally, the initial value for the search string `searchSt` is set to `"Password NOT Found"` in line 12. If the key length is legal, the statements inside the conditional-if block (i.e. lines 14–25) would perform the brute-force attack. The input key for comparison is captured by line 13. The main attack procedures are the following two functions:

```
key_symbol()
brute_force_test(vMinKeyL,vMaxKeyL,keyStV);
```

The `key_symbol()` function selects the key symbols used for the attack. If you have selected the symbols [0–9] or [a–z, 0–9] in the XHTML page `ex02-12.htm`, the set of symbols will be used to form the key space for the attack. The `brute_force_test()` function is similar to the `key_space_gen()` function in previous examples. The main purpose is to generate the key-space and perform the exhaustive test for a match with input key `keyStV`. The solution will be stored in the variable `searchSt` and then added to the string `shSt` in line 23. Together with the execution time, the result is displayed to the text area specified in line 25. The function `key_symbol()` is listed in part II of the ECMAScript file `ex02-12.js`.

```
Example: Continuation of ex02-12.js                        (Part II)
31: function key_symbol()
32: {
33:    symV = document.getElementsByName("keyS")
34:    for (ii=0;ii< symV.length;ii++) {
35:       if (symV.item(ii).checked) vOption=ii;
36:    }
37:    if (vOption ==0) {
38:       keyC = Array("0","1","2","3","4","5","6","7","8","9");
39:       shSt += "Key Code = [0-9]\n";
40:    }
41:    else {
42:       keyC = Array("a","b","c","d","e","f","g","h","i","j","k","l",
43:                    "m","n","o","p","q","r","s","t","u","v","w","x",
44:                    "y","z","0","1","2","3","4","5","6","7","8","9");
45:       shSt += "Key Code = [a-z,0-9]\n";
46:    }
47: }
48:
```

First, a function call to `document.getElementsByName("keyS")`, in line 33, will get all radio buttons into a collection `symV`. The for-loop in lines 34–36 checks through all radio buttons to see which one has the status as checked. The checked radio button will be assigned to the variable `vOption` in line 35. Since we have only two radio buttons defined in `ex02-06.htm`, a simple conditional-if is employed in lines 37–46 to perform the task. If the first radio button is checked (i.e. `vOption` =0) we assign the key symbol array `keyC[]` to symbols [0-9] as illustrated in lines 37–40.

If not, the set of symbols [a–z, 0–9] is assigned to the key code array `keyC[]` in lines 42–46.

After this function, the main brute-force attack function `brute_force_test()` is defined as shown in part III of `ex02-12.js`.

```
Example: Continuation of ex02-12.js                          (Part III)
49: function brute_force_test(minKeyL,maxKeyL,inKeySt)
50: {
51:   var keySt="",  c=1;
52:   var noD,noD01,noD02,symL,symL01,ii,jj,p,tmp;
53:   var s= new Array(32);
54:
55:   for (noD = minKeyL; noD <= maxKeyL ; noD++) {
56:     c=1;
57:     for (ii=0;ii< noD;ii++) { s[ii]=0; }
58:     noD01 = noD -1;
59:     noD02 = noD -2;
60:     symL = keyC.length;
61:     symL01 = keyC.length -1;
62:
63:     while (c > 0) {
64:       for (ii=0;ii< symL;ii++) {
65:         keySt ="";
66:         for(jj=0; jj < noD01 ; jj++) {
67:           tmp = s[jj];
68:           keySt += keyC[tmp];
69:         }
70:         keySt += keyC[ii];
71:         //-- Now keySt Stores The Key String --//
72:         if (check_key(keySt,inKeySt)== true) { ii=symL;
                                                  c=0; noD=maxKeyL+1;}
73:       }
74:       s[noD02] += 1;
75:
76:       if ( noD > 1) {
77:           if ( s[noD02] > symL01) {
78:               for (p=noD02; p > 0; p--) {
79:                   if (s[p] > symL01 ) {
80:                       s[p] =0;
81:                       s[p-1] +=1;
82:                   }
83:               }
```

```
84:                if ( s[0] > symL01 ) { c=0; }
85:           }
86:        } else { c=0; }
87:      } // end while-loop
88:   }    // end noD-for-loop
89: }
90:
```

If you compare this `brute_force_test()` function with the `key_space_gen()` function in previous examples, you will that they are exactly the same except for line 72. In other words, we have added one statement only, at line 72. From knowledge of key-space, we know that the variable `keySt` in line 71 contains the individual key-string generated by the key-space. To perform brute-force attack, all we need to do is to perform the attack, or exhaustive test, on the key `keySt` at line 72. We generate a function call `check_key(keySt,inKeySt)`. This function will perform the actual search for every key `keySt` against `inkeySt`. If the attack is successful, the return status is `true`. In this case, the remaining statements in line 72 reset the variables below and stop execution of the program.

`ii=symL;` — stops the `ii` for-loop

`c=0;` — stops the while-loop

`noD = maxKeyL+1;` — stops the `noD` for-loop

The idea here is to show a clear structure of the brute-force attack. For this purpose, the `check_key()` function is listed in part IV of `ex02-12.js`.

```
Example: Continuation of ex02-12.js                      (Part IV)

 91: function check_key(pa_Id,inKeySt)
 92: {
 93:   var tmpSt1 = inKeySt;
 94:   var tmpSt2 = md5(pa_Id);
 95:   if (tmpSt1 == tmpSt2) {
 96:      tmp3 = true;
 97:      searchSt="Password Found: "+pa_Id+"\n "+pa_Id+" --> "+
                   tmpSt2+"\n";
 98:   } else {
 99:      tmp3 = false;
100:   }
101:   return (tmp3);
102: }
```

This check_key() function has a simple structure. First, the input MD5 string from the XHTML page inKeySt is stored in variable tmpSt1. Next, the key from the key-space is used to generate an MD5 string in tmpSt2. If the input MD5 string equals the original MD5 string (i.e. inKeySt), the brute-force attack is successful and we have a collision. In this case, the text 'Password Found', together with the password, is stored in the search string searchSt (line 97) for display purposes. The variable tmp3 is set to true and returns to the main program. If the MD5 strings are not matched, the variable tmp3 is set to false and the exhaustive test continues until all keys are tested. Screenshots of this brute-force attack in action are shown in Figures 2.26 and 2.27.

To summarize the strategy of attacking passwords with a brute-force scheme, we have

XHTML → brute_force() → brute_force_test() → check_key()

The XHTML page obtains information from users, such as the MD5 string, key symbols and search key lengths. The function brute_force() gets the information from XHTML and calls the brute_force_test() function to generate the key-space. For each key string, a call to the check_key() function is made to check the key. In this case, check_key() employs the MD5 routine to produce a MD5 string on the generated key looking for a match. Therefore, for different attacks, you only need to change the check_key() function.

The brute-force scheme above is for demonstration only. For time-critical applications such as brute-force, Web page implementation in many cases is not

Fig. 2.26 Brute-force attack on MD5 strings I

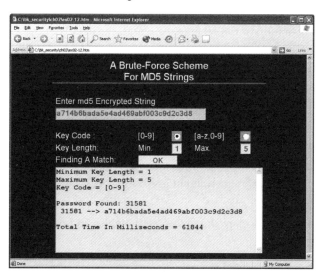

Fig. 2.27 Brute-force attack on MD5 strings II

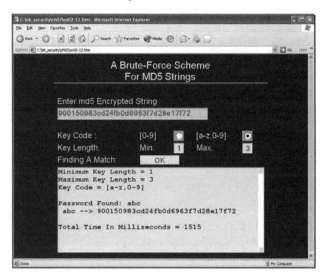

very efficient. From Table 2.8, a C/C++ implementation of the scheme can run up to 100 times faster. Now, let's consider a brute-force utility using the C language.

2.5.4 A brute-force utility to search MD5 passwords

Since MD5, or md5(), is so widely used, it is also known as the IETF standard RFC 1321. In addition to the algorithm, the RFC 1321 specification also contains a C implementation of the scheme. Although the details of the algorithm and implementation will be discussed in Chapter 3, we need to use it now.

Suppose we have extracted the C program from RFC 1321 and call it md5.c. To use the utility inside RFC 1321, you first need to put the following two statements in your C program:

```
#include "global.h"
#include "md5.h"
```

These two programs (or header files) are provided along with the MD5 package in RFC 1321. The first statement includes some global data types for the MD5 scheme. The second statement declares an MD5 structure and some function settings.

The next step is to declare the following variables and make the function calls:

```
1: Variables:
2:    MD5_CTX context;
```

```
3:    String inSt, outSt;
4:    Int len;
5: Functions:
6:    MD5Init (&context);
7:    MD5Update (&context, inSt, len);
8:    MD5Final (outSt, &context);
```

Line 2 defines a structure (data) type called MD5_CTX. The detail of this data type is in the file md5.h. With this type, a variable context is defined. Next, two user-defined strings inSt and outSt are required. Variable inSt stores the message you want to digest (or encrypt) by the MD5 and the output is sent to outSt. The integer variable len is the length of the message you want to digest (i.e. inSt).

The function in line 6 is to initialize the MD5 utility. The update function MD5Update() in line 7 is to put the message inSt and length into the structure variable context. The final function MD5Final() will digest the message stored in context and store the result (an MD5 string) into variable outSt.

Although we are going to develop the utility in the C language, you may find that the codes are similar to the script (ECMAScript or JavaScript) statements used in Web pages. In fact, apart from the variable types and a few differences, many operational and structure statements of script are identical to the C language. In this book, we will use some elementary C language when utilities of encryption/decryption schemes are developed. The C codes are carefully selected so that they are similar to script and readable, even if you are not familiar with the C language. C++ users should have no difficulty in understanding some C code since C is a subset of C++.

Now, let's use the instructions above to develop a brute-force utility. Consider the C program shown in example brute-force.c.

Example: brute-force.c – A brute-force utility for MD5   (Part I)

```
 1: #include "stdio.h"
 2: #include "global.h"
 3: #include "md5.h"
 4:
 5: void md5String (unsigned char *sstr, unsigned char *md5St)
 6: {
 7:    MD5_CTX context;
 8:    unsigned int len = strlen (sstr);
 9:    MD5Init (&context);
10:    MD5Update (&context, sstr, len);
11:    MD5Final (md5St, &context);
12: }
13:
```

```
14: void md5Hex(unsigned char *iinSt,unsigned char *outSt)
15: {
16:    unsigned char * hexV="0123456789abcdef";
17:    unsigned int i,m=0;
18:    unsigned char tmp[32];
19:    md5String(iinSt,tmp);
20:    for (i = 0; i < 16; i++) {
21:       outSt[m++] = hexV[(tmp[i] >> 4) & 0xf];
22:       outSt[m++] = hexV[tmp[i] & 0xf];
23:    }
24:    outSt[m]='\0';
25: }
```

Line 1 includes some standard (input and output) functions from the C language. Lines 2–3 include the MD5 header files so that the functions related to the MD5 scheme can be called. The remaining code defines two functions md5String() and md5Hex(). The function md5String() in lines 5–12 takes two strings as parameters. The first parameter is a string sstr storing the message to be MD5 digested. The second string variable md5St is to store the result or the MD5 string. The MD5_CTX type variable context is declared in line 7 and the length of the message is captured by the statement in line 8. The next three function calls in lines 9–11 are used to digest the string sstr and the result is stored in md5St as described earlier.

Since the result, md5St, is a string containing ASCII code, the function md5Hex() in lines 14–25 is used to call md5String() and produce the result as a hexadecimal string for our brute-force utility. First, a hexadecimal symbol string is declared in line 16. After the function is called in line 19, the variable tmp contains the MD5 string. The for-loop in lines 20–23 converts this ASCII string tmp into a hexadecimal string stored in outSt. The statement in line 24 puts an end to outSt. The main brute-force function is shown in part II of brute-force.c.

Example: brute-force.c   **(Part II)**

```
26:
27: int brute_force(int minKeyL, int maxKeyL,
28:                 char * keyc, int keyL, unsigned char *keyTest)
29: {
30:    unsigned char ch, md5St[32], tmpKey[32];
31:    int ii, jj, kk,tmp1,p,k,noD, a[30],c;
32:
```

```
33:    for (noD=minKeyL; noD <=maxKeyL; noD++) {
34:    for(kk=0;kk<20;kk++) a[kk]=0;
35:    c=1;
36:    while (c>0) {
37:      for (ii=0;ii<keyL;ii++) {
38:        for (jj=0;jj<noD-1;jj++) {
39:          tmp1 = a[jj];
40:          tmpKey[jj]=keyc[tmp1];
41:        }
42:        tmpKey[noD -1]=keyc[ii];
43:        tmpKey[noD]='\0';
44:        if (check_key(tmpKey,keyTest)==0) {ii=keyL+1; c=0;
                                              noD=maxKeyL+1;}
45:      }
46:    if ( noD > 1) {
47:        a[noD-2] +=1;
48:        if ( a[noD-2] > keyL -1) {
49:          for (p=noD-2; p > 0; p--) {
50:            if (a[p] > keyL-1 ) {
51:              a[p] =0;
52:              a[p-1] +=1;
53:            }
54:          }
55:          if ( a[0] > keyL-1 ) c=0;
56:        }
57:    } else { c=0; }
58:    } // end while
59:    }  // end noD-for-loop
60: }
61:
```

This C program fragment contains one function `brute-force()`. This function is similar to part III of script `ex02-12.js` to perform the brute-force search. In fact, the statements from line 33 to the end are almost identical to the script counterpart. The only difference is that an MD5 string called `keyTest` is included (line 28) for the brute-force tests. When the key `tmpKey` is generated in line 43, this `tmpKey` is checked with the input MD5 `keyTest` for a match. If they are identical, the function `check_key()` will printout the result, and the codes at the end of line 44 terminate any further brute-force search. The details of the function `check_key()` are given in part III of `brute-force.c`.

```
62: int check_key(unsigned char *pa_id, unsigned char *inKeySt)
63: {
64:   unsigned char *tmpSt1 = inKeySt;
65:   unsigned char *tmpSt2;
66:   unsigned int status;
67:   md5Hex(pa_id,tmpSt2);
68:   status = strcmp(tmpSt1,tmpSt2);
69:   if (!status) output_result(pa_id,tmpSt2);
70:   return (status);
71: }
72:
73: int output_result(unsigned char *genKey, unsigned char *md5Str)
74: {
75:   printf("A Match Has Been Found\n");
76:   printf("   Potential Key = %s\n",genKey);
77:   printf("   Matched Key = %s\n",md5Str);
78: }
79:
```

The check_key() function in lines 62–71 is used to compare the generated key pa_id and MD5 string inKeySt for a match. First, the MD5 input string inKeySt is copied to local variable tmpSt1 (line 64) and the MD5 digest of pa_id is obtained by the statement in line 67. The hexadecimal result is stored in variable tmpSt2. The statement in line 68 compares the two strings tmpSt1 and tmpSt2. If the two strings match, the function output_result() in line 69 is executed. This function, defined in lines 73–78, contains three output statements. The first output statement is to print the message 'A Match Has Been Found' on the screen. The symbol '\n' in the C language produces a new line. The second output statement in line 76 prints out the generated key genKey and the MD5 string stored in md5Str.

In order to use the functions above effectively, some interface functions are required. One such interface is shown in part IV of brute-force.c.

```
80: int main(int argc, char *argv[])
81: {
82:   int minKeyL=1, maxKeyL=6;
83:   unsigned char *keyC0="abcdefgihijlmnopqrstuvwxyz";
84:   unsigned char *keyTest, *keyC;
85:   unsigned long clock01=0, clock02=0;
```

```
 86:   int cOL=26, keySymL=26, keyType=1;
 87:   FILE *inf;
 88:
 89:   if (argc != 2) {
 90:     printf("\r\nUsage: brute_force <infile> \n");
 91:     return 2;
 92:   }
 93:   if((inf=fopen(argv[1],"r"))==NULL){
 94:       printf("\r\nCould not open input file: %s",argv[1]);
 95:       return 2;
 96:   }
 97:   fscanf(inf,"%d %d %d %s",&minKeyL,&maxKeyL,&keyType,keyTest);
 98:   printf("Starting Brute Force Search: \n %d %d %d %s \n",
 99:       minKeyL,maxKeyL,keyType,keyTest);
100:   if ( keyType !=1) {
101:       printf("\r\nError.. Only Type 1 is allowed\n");
102:       fclose(inf);
103:       return 2;
104:   } else {
105:       keySymL = cOL;
106:       keyC = keyC0;
107:   }
108:   clock01 = clock();
109:   brute_force(minKeyL,maxKeyL,keyC,keySymL,keyTest);
110:   clock02 = clock();
111:   printf("Execution Time = %ld",clock02-clock01);
112:   fclose(inf);
113: }
```

Compared to the original interface functions provided in RFC 1321, this program fragment is a simple one. Basically, this function `main()` reads a file and uses the information in the file to perform a brute-force search. For example, the data of a typical testing file (e.g. `brute_force.txt`) is

    1   5   1   0679a6d86d1a1f0a4df2e1280655f9d6

The first two parameters are the starting and ending key length for the brute-force attack. In this case, the brute-force search will test all keys from 1 to 5 characters. The third parameter is the `keyType`. When `keyType` is 1 the following key symbol is used for the search:

    abcdefgihijlmnopqrstuvwxyz

For our simple interface function, the only key symbols used are [a–z]. The last parameter is the input MD5 string for a brute-force match.

The input file, such as `brute_force.txt`, will be opened by lines 93–96. If the file does not exist or cannot be opened, the statements in lines 94–95 print out the error message and terminate the program. If the file is opened successfully, the statement in line 97

```
97: fscanf(inf,"%d %d %d %s",&minKeyL,&maxKeyL,&keyType,keyTest);
```

will read the data from file into variables `minKeyL`, `maxKeyL`, `keyType` and `keyTest` respectively. If the `keyType` is not 1, an error message is printed and the program is terminated by lines 101–103. Otherwise, the key symbol `keySymL` is set to `coL` (i.e. [a–z]) and the number of key symbols is set to `keyC0` (i.e. 26). The statement in line 108 starts the clock and gets the current time so that the execution time is monitored. The `brute-force()` function in line 109 performs a brute-force search trying to find a match to string `keyTest`. The `clock()` function gets the updated time. The execution time is printed out by line 111.

The statements in lines 89–92 make sure that the program needs an input file. If no file is input as parameter or argument, a usage message is printed and the program is terminated by lines 90–91.

If you have a C/C++ compiler such as Borland C/C++, Microsoft C/C++ or UNIX/Linux C/C++, you can compile this `brute-force.c` program and build an brute-force utility for MD5.

For example, if you are using the Microsoft C/C++ compiler, you can build the utility using the command

```
cl brute-force.c md5.c
```

This command would perform the following:

- compile the C programs `brute-force.c` and `md5.c` into object files `brute-force.obj` and `md5.obj`. The md5.c file is extracted from the RFC 1321;

- use the object files to build the executable program `brute-force.exe`.

If you are using UNIX/LINUX with a `gcc` or `cc` compiler, you can compile the utility with the command

```
gcc -o brute-force brute-force.c md5.c
```

This command will compile the C programs `brute-force.c` and `md5.c`. Instead of the traditional executable file name 'a.out', this command will name the executable file as brute-force.

Since `gcc` is freely available and widely used in both UNIX/LINUX and Windows, we will use `gcc` as the default C/C++ compiler in this book.

After the compilation, you should have an executable file called `brute-force.exe`, or `brute-force` if you are using UNIX/LINUX in your local directory. The compiling and running session using the `gcc` compiler in Windows XP are captured and shown in Figure 2.28.

Fig. 2.28 Brute-force utility

```
H:\ch02>gcc -o brute-force brute-force.c md5.c
H:\ch02>brute-force

Usage: brute_force <infile>

H:\ch02>brute-force brute_force.txt

Starting Brute Force Search:
 1 5 1 0679a6d86d1a1f0a4df2e1280655f9d6
A Match Has Been Found
    Potential Key = rody
    Matched Key = 0679a6d86d1a1f0a4df2e1280655f9d6
Execution Time = 1592

H:\ch02>
```

As you can see from Figure 2.28, if no file is input, the usage message is displayed. When the data file brute_force.txt is read, the data is also shown on the screen. In this case, a match with the MD5 is found and the potential key (or password) of the MD5 string is 'rody'. The execution time is 1.6 seconds.

Note that the execution time will increase dramatically when you increase the search key length or expand the key symbol. For a long search, some coding to show that the program is still alive may be needed.

Now we have some idea about cryptology, and it's time to consider some encryptions.

3

One-way encryptions, hash functions and message digests

3.1   One-way functions and encryptions

3.1.1   Passwords and one-way functions

This chapter gives a comprehensive study of passwords and how to generate them in practice. From detailed algorithm to programming, some of the most popular password schemes on computer systems and the World Wide Web are presented including `Crypt()`, MD5, `md5Crypt()` and SHA-1. Step-by-step examples are provided throughout so that using them in applications can be done smoothly. From the cryptology viewpoint, a password is, in many cases, generated by a one-way function $f(x)$ which has the following mathematical characteristics:

■ for all x, the function y or $f(x)$ is easy to compute;

■ for virtually all y, it is extremely difficult to find an x such that $f(x) = y$.

Roughly speaking, if the result of a one-way function is a ciphertext, the function is regarded as a one-way encryption. As we have seen in Chapter 2, using one-way encryption to generate passwords is common practice in security. However, a truly one-way function is difficult to find. With all kinds of one-way functions around today, it is not easy to prove they are satisfying the second condition given in the definition above simply because the condition itself is not well defined. It is not easy to define what is meant by 'extremely difficult' mathematically or scientifically. In general, we will accept that a function or a process is difficult if it is linked or related to a known difficult mathematical problem, such as factorization of a large number. For a simple example, consider the following function:

$$f(x) = x^2 \bmod n$$

where $n = pq$, p and q are two random prime numbers

Given the value (integer value) of x, it is easy to compute $x^2 \bmod n$. It is the remainder of x^2 divided by n. Without the knowledge of the primes p and q, it is not easy to compute the integer value of x from a value of $x^2 \bmod n$. This problem is also related to the following one-way function:

$h(p, q) = pq$

where p and q are two (carefully chosen) big prime numbers

Given the two big primes p and q, the product $n = pq$ is easy to compute. However, given n it is difficult to compute the primes p and q. This integer factorization problem is well known in number theory and not easy to tackle without assumptions. Many RSA (the creators of MD5) encryptions and other cryptographic systems rely on this property.

Another interesting point is that many ciphers can also be considered as one-way functions depending or how you look at them. For example, consider the Data Encryption Standard (DES) mentioned in Chapter 2. The DES function can be written as

$y = \mathrm{des}(x, k)$

where x is the input plaintext and k is the key. This function will return a ciphertext y. The function $\mathrm{des}(x, k)$ is not a one-way function of x if k is known. Given y and k, decryption using k can be easily done to obtain x. However, if you can hide the key k (or k is an externally unknown quantity), then $\mathrm{des}(x, k)$ is a one-way function. That is, given y and x, it is not easy to find the key k. In other words, $\mathrm{des}(x, k)$ is a one-way function of k. For this reason, many early one-way encryptions to generate encrypted passwords, including `Crypt()`, are DES based.

3.1.2   A step-by-step single DES scheme

By the time you read this, you'll probably have realized that DES is an important cipher. It is reasonably strong and practically viable for many crypto-applications. The construction of DES and the use of bit-manipulation tables mark a cornerstone of modern cryptography and cryptology. The first step in really understanding modern ciphers or cryptographic systems is to understand DES. For this reason, a step-by-step look at how DES works is provided in this section.

DES is a block cipher which works on bits. It operates on a chunk (64-bit) of plaintext M and a 64-bit key K. The returned ciphertext is also 64-bit. All the possible arrangements of 64 bits produce a permutation of $2^{64} = 18\,446\,744\,073\,709\,551\,616$ values. The entire message can be encrypted by DES as a sequence of 64-bit chunks. Suppose we have the 64-bit M and K as follows:

```
M = 00000001 00100011 01000101 01100111 10001001 10101011 11001101 11101111

K = 00010011 00110100 01010111 01111001 10011011 10111100 11011111 11110001
```

M and K are represented by 8 bytes and each byte is 8 bits long. In terms of hexadecimal values, we have M = '01 23 45 67 89 AB CD EF' and K = '13 34 57 79 9B BC DF F1'. The first step in the DES algorithm is to generate 16 subkeys (each 48 bits long) from the key K.

Generating the DES 16 subkeys

Given the key K, DES uses the two 'permuted choice' (PC1) tables below to permute the key.

<table>
<tr><td colspan="7" align="center">Table PC1-C</td></tr>
<tr><td>57</td><td>49</td><td>41</td><td>33</td><td>25</td><td>17</td><td>9</td></tr>
<tr><td>1</td><td>58</td><td>50</td><td>42</td><td>34</td><td>26</td><td>18</td></tr>
<tr><td>10</td><td>2</td><td>59</td><td>51</td><td>43</td><td>35</td><td>27</td></tr>
<tr><td>19</td><td>11</td><td>3</td><td>60</td><td>52</td><td>44</td><td>36</td></tr>
</table>

<table>
<tr><td colspan="7" align="center">Table PC1-D</td></tr>
<tr><td>63</td><td>55</td><td>47</td><td>39</td><td>31</td><td>23</td><td>15</td></tr>
<tr><td>7</td><td>62</td><td>54</td><td>46</td><td>38</td><td>30</td><td>22</td></tr>
<tr><td>14</td><td>6</td><td>61</td><td>53</td><td>45</td><td>37</td><td>29</td></tr>
<tr><td>21</td><td>13</td><td>5</td><td>28</td><td>20</td><td>12</td><td>4</td></tr>
</table>

When you apply tables PC1-C and PC1-D to K, you have two bit-strings C_0 and D_0. The first bit of C_0 is the 57th bit of K, which is 1, and the second bit of C_0 is the 49th bit of K (i.e. 1) and so on. The manipulation and the first seven bits of C_0 are highlighted in key K above. The C_0 and D_0 bit strings turn out to be

```
PC1-C(K) = C₀ = 1111000 0110011 0010101 0101111
PC1-D(K) = D₀ = 0101010 1011001 1001111 0001111
```

Note that the numbers {8, 16, 24, 32, 40, 48, 56, 64} are missing in tables PC1-C and PC1-D. The corresponding 8th, 16th, 24th, 32th, 40th, 48th, 56th and 64th bits of the key K are not used. DES is indeed a 56-bit encryption. Based on the bit string pair (C_0, D_0), another shift table is used:

```
1 1 2 2 2 2 2 2 1 2 2 2 2 2 2 1 – The shifts table
```

This table contains 16 left-shifting numbers. The first number means that if you left-shift (C_0, D_0) by 1, the pair (C_1, D_1) is obtained. Similarly, left-shifting (C_1, D_1) by 1 gives (C_2, D_2). Again, left-shifting (C_2, D_2) by 2 gives the pair (C_3, D_3). The shift table produces the 17 pairs below.

```
C₀  = 1111000 0110011 0010101 0101111   D₀  = 0101010 1011001 1001111 0001111
C₁  = 1110000 1100110 0101010 1011111   D₁  = 1010101 0110011 0011110 0011110
C₂  = 1100001 1001100 1010101 0111111   D₂  = 0101010 1100110 0111100 0111101
C₃  = 0000110 0110010 1010101 1111111   D₃  = 0101011 0011001 1110001 1110101
C₄  = 0011001 1001010 1010111 1111100   D₄  = 0101100 1100111 1000111 1010101
C₅  = 1100110 0101010 1011111 1110000   D₅  = 0110011 0011110 0011110 1010101
C₆  = 0011001 0101010 1111111 1000011   D₆  = 1001100 1111000 1111010 1010101
C₇  = 1100101 0101011 1111110 0001100   D₇  = 0110011 1100011 1101010 1010110
C₈  = 0010101 0101111 1111000 0110011   D₈  = 1001111 0001111 0101010 1011001
C₉  = 0101010 1011111 1110000 1100110   D₉  = 0011110 0011110 1010101 0110011
C₁₀ = 0101010 1111111 1000011 0011001   D₁₀ = 11110001 1110101 0101011 001100
```

```
C₁₁ = 0101011 1111110 0001100 1100101   D₁₁ = 11000111 1010101 0101100 110011
C₁₂ = 0101111 1111000 0110011 0010101   D₁₂ = 00011110 1010101 0110011 001111
C₁₃ = 0111111 1100001 1001100 1010101   D₁₃ = 01111010 1010101 1001100 111100
C₁₄ = 1111111 0000110 0110010 1010101   D₁₄ = 11101010 1010110 0110011 110001
C₁₅ = 1111100 0011001 1001010 1010111   D₁₅ = 10101010 1011001 1001111 000111
C₁₆ = 1111000 0110011 0010101 0101111   D₁₆ = 01010101 0110011 0011110 001111
```

For each pair (C_n, D_n), the 'permuted choice 2' tables PC2-C and PC2-D below are used to produce the corresponding subkey.

<table>
<tr><td colspan="6" align="center">Table PC2-C</td></tr>
<tr><td>14</td><td>17</td><td>11</td><td>24</td><td>1</td><td>5</td></tr>
<tr><td>3</td><td>28</td><td>15</td><td>6</td><td>21</td><td>10</td></tr>
<tr><td>23</td><td>19</td><td>12</td><td>4</td><td>26</td><td>8</td></tr>
<tr><td>16</td><td>7</td><td>27</td><td>20</td><td>13</td><td>2</td></tr>
</table>

<table>
<tr><td colspan="6" align="center">Table PC2-D</td></tr>
<tr><td>41</td><td>52</td><td>31</td><td>37</td><td>47</td><td>55</td></tr>
<tr><td>30</td><td>40</td><td>51</td><td>45</td><td>33</td><td>48</td></tr>
<tr><td>44</td><td>49</td><td>39</td><td>56</td><td>34</td><td>53</td></tr>
<tr><td>46</td><td>42</td><td>50</td><td>36</td><td>29</td><td>32</td></tr>
</table>

To produce the first subkey, say K_1, you need to concatenate the string C_1D_1 and apply tables PC2-C and PC2-D to it. The combining result is the subkey K_1, i.e.

```
C₁D₁ = 1110000 1100110 0101010 1011111 1010101 0110011 0011110 0011110
K₁   = PC2-C(C₁D₁) + PC2-D(C₁D₁)
     = 000110 110000 001011 101111 111111 000111 000001 110010
```

For example, the first bit of K_1 is the 14th bit of C_1D_1 which is 0, and so on. The operation and the first six bits of K_1 are highlighted above. Following the same procedure, the remaining subkeys are

```
K₂  = 011110 011010 111011 011001 110110 111100 100111 100101
K₃  = 010101 011111 110010 001010 010000 101100 111110 011001
K₄  = 011100 101010 110111 010110 110110 110011 010100 011101
K₅  = 011111 001110 110000 000111 111010 110101 001110 101000
K₆  = 011000 111010 010100 111110 010100 000111 101100 101111
K₇  = 111011 001000 010010 110111 111101 100001 100010 111100
K₈  = 111101 111000 101000 111010 110000 010011 101111 111011
K₉  = 111000 001101 101111 101011 111011 011110 011110 000001
K₁₀ = 101100 011111 001101 000111 101110 100100 011001 001111
K₁₁ = 001000 010101 111111 010011 110111 101101 001110 000110
K₁₂ = 011101 010111 000111 110101 100101 000110 011111 101001
K₁₃ = 100101 111100 010111 010001 111110 101011 101001 000001
K₁₄ = 010111 110100 001110 110111 111100 101110 011100 111010
K₁₅ = 101111 111001 000110 001101 001111 010011 111100 001010
K₁₆ = 110010 110011 110110 001011 000011 100001 011111 110101
```

Note that there are only 24 elements in each of tables PC2-C and PC2-D so that each subkey is 48 bits long. Some implementations combine tables PC1-C and PC1-D (or PC2-C and PC2-D) into one table. Now, let us consider how to use the subkeys to perform encryption on plaintext.

Encrypting each 64-bit chunk of plaintext

DES first applies table IP below to the plaintext M.

		Table IP					
58	50	42	34	26	18	10	2
60	52	44	36	28	20	12	4
62	54	46	38	30	22	14	6
64	56	48	40	32	24	16	8
57	49	41	33	25	17	9	1
59	51	43	35	27	19	11	3
61	53	45	37	29	21	13	5
63	55	47	39	31	23	15	7

		Table IP^{-1}					
40	8	48	16	56	24	64	32
39	7	47	15	55	23	63	31
38	6	46	14	54	22	62	30
37	5	45	13	53	21	61	29
36	4	44	12	52	20	60	28
35	3	43	11	51	19	59	27
34	2	42	10	50	18	58	26
33	1	41	9	49	17	57	25

Consider the same 64-bit plaintext M above: the IP(M) transformation is

```
M     = 00000001 00100011 01000101 01100111 10001001 10101011 11001101 11101111
IP(M) = 11001100 00000000 11001100 11111111 11110000 10101010 11110000 10101010
```

The result of IP(M) is then split into two halves called (L_0, R_0)

```
L0 = 11001100 00000000 11001100 11111111
R0 = 11110000 10101010 11110000 10101010
```

Based on the pair (L_0, R_0), 16 rounds of iterations are employed to produce the pair (L_{16}, R_{16}). The iteration formula is

```
Ln = Rn-1    and    Rn = Ln-1    XOR    f(Rn-1,Kn)    where n = 1 to 16
```

For n = 1, we have

```
L1 = R0 = 1111 0000 1010 1010 1111 0000 1010 1010
K1 = 000110 110000 001011 101111 111111 000111 000001 110010
R1 = L0 XOR f(R0,K1)
```

We will define the function f() later. The first pair (L_1, R_1) is used to calculate (L_2, R_2). The iteration is repeated 16 times until the pair (L_{16}, R_{16}) is obtained.

The next step is to concatenate the pair (L_{16}, R_{16}) in reverse order to form the single bit string $R_{16}L_{16}$. The ciphertext is obtained by applying table IP^{-1} to $R_{16}L_{16}$

```
C = IP-1(R16L16)
```

The bit string C is the ciphertext corresponding to the plaintext M under DES encryption. Note that table IP^{-1} is the inverse of table IP so that IP^{-1}[IP(a)] = a. Now, consider the DES iteration formula.

The DES iteration formula

Consider the iteration formula

```
Ln = Rn-1    and    Rn = Ln-1    XOR    f(Rn-1,Kn)    where n = 1,16
```

The calculation of $f(R_{n-1}, K_n)$ is divided into three steps:

Step 1 For a given n, expand the bit string R_{n-1} by applying the expansion table E. Perform the XOR operation on the key K_n and divide the result into eight equal parts, namely $B_1 B_2 B_3 B_4 B_5 B_6 B_7 B_8$, i.e.

$$K_n \text{ XOR } E(R_{n-1}) = B_1 B_2 B_3 B_4 B_5 B_6 B_7 B_8$$

Step 2 For each B_i in step 1, apply the corresponding tables $S1$ $S2$ $S3$ $S4$ $S5$ $S6$ $S7$ $S8$ to obtain strings

$$S1(B_1) \quad S2(B_2) \quad S3(B_3) \quad S4(B_4) \quad S5(B_5) \quad S6(B_6) \quad S7(B_7) \quad S8(B_8)$$

Step 3 Concatenate all the $S_i(B_i)$ strings in step 2 to form a single string and apply another table P to it

$$f = P[\ S1(B_1)S2(B_2)\ldots S8(B_8)\ ]$$

This string f is used in the iteration formula to continue the process. After 16 rounds (or iterations), the resultant pair (L_{16}, R_{16}) is obtained. This pair can be used to calculate the ciphertext c mentioned above. To compute f, the expansion table (or bit selection table) E in step 1 is defined by:

Table E

32	1	2	3	4	5
4	5	6	7	8	9
8	9	10	11	12	13
12	13	14	15	16	17
16	17	18	19	20	21
20	21	22	23	24	25
24	25	26	27	28	29
28	29	30	31	32	1

As you can see, the first two columns in Table E are repeated in the final columns. This table will take a 32-bit string and expand it into a 48-bit string.

Consider the first iteration

```
L₁ = R₀ = 1111 0000 1010 1010 1111 0000 1010 1010
K₁ = 000110 110000 001011 101111 111111 000111 000001 110010
R₁ = L₀ XOR f(R₀,K₁)
```

The operation $f(R_0, K_1)$ in step 1 yields

```
K₁           = 000110 110000 001011 101111 111111 000111 000001 110010
E(R₀)        = 011110 100001 010101 010101 011110 100001 010101 010101
K₁ XOR E(R₀) = 011000 010001 011110 111010 100001 100110 010100 100111
```

The XOR result is then divided into eight equal parts, namely B_1, B_2, B_3, B_4, B_5, B_6, B_7, B_8. In this case, we have $B_1 = 011000$, $B_2 = 010001$ ... etc. To compute the strings

$S1(B_1)$, $S2(B_2)$, $S3(B_3)$, $S4(B_4)$, $S5(B_5)$, $S6(B_6)$, $S7(B_7)$, $S8(B_8)$,

eight tables, called 'S-boxes', are employed. The first S-table `s1` is specified as follows:

Table S1

Row	0	1	2	3	4	5	6	7	8	9	10	11	12	13	14	15
no.																
0	14	4	13	1	2	15	11	8	3	10	6	12	**5**	9	0	7
1	0	15	7	4	14	2	13	1	10	6	12	11	9	5	3	8
2	4	1	14	8	13	6	2	11	15	12	9	7	3	10	5	0
3	15	12	8	2	4	9	1	7	5	11	3	14	10	0	6	13

(Column number)

Table P

16	7	20	21
29	12	28	17
1	15	23	26
5	18	31	10
2	8	24	14
32	27	3	9
19	13	30	6
22	11	4	25

To use this table, the row and column numbers are needed. Since B_i is 6 bits long, the row number (row) and column number (col) are calculated as

row = 1st and 6th bit   col = middle 4 bits

Given B_1=011000, we have `row=00` (1st and 6th bits together) and `col=1100` (middle 4 bits). The decimal values are `row=0` and `col=12`. Using row and col, the corresponding value of the 0th row and 12th column in table S1 is 5. This value 5 is output as a 4-bit binary 0101, i.e.

`S1(011000)=`**`0101`**

The remaining seven S-boxes, `s2`, `s3`, `s4`, `s5`, `s6`, `s7`, `s8`, are given below.

Table S2

15	1	8	14	6	11	3	4	9	7	2	13	12	0	5	10
3	13	4	7	15	2	8	14	12	0	1	10	6	9	11	5
0	14	7	11	10	4	13	1	5	8	12	6	9	3	2	15
13	8	10	1	3	15	4	2	11	6	7	12	0	5	14	9

Table S3

10	0	9	14	6	3	15	5	1	13	12	7	11	4	2	8
13	7	0	9	3	4	6	10	2	8	5	14	12	11	15	1
13	6	4	9	8	15	3	0	11	1	2	12	5	10	14	7
1	10	13	0	6	9	8	7	4	15	14	3	11	5	2	12

Table S4

7	13	14	3	0	6	9	10	1	2	8	5	11	12	4	15
13	8	11	5	6	15	0	3	4	7	2	12	1	10	14	9
10	6	9	0	12	11	7	13	15	1	3	14	5	2	8	4
3	15	0	6	10	1	13	8	9	4	5	11	12	7	2	14

Table S5

2	12	4	1	7	10	11	6	8	5	3	15	13	0	14	9
14	11	2	12	4	7	13	1	5	0	15	10	3	9	8	6
4	2	1	11	10	13	7	8	15	9	12	5	6	3	0	14
11	8	12	7	1	14	2	13	6	15	0	9	10	4	5	3

Table S6

12	1	10	15	9	2	6	8	0	13	3	4	14	7	5	11
10	15	4	2	7	12	9	5	6	1	13	14	0	11	3	8
9	14	15	5	2	8	12	3	7	0	4	10	1	13	11	6
4	3	2	12	9	5	15	10	11	14	1	7	6	0	8	13

Table S7

4	11	2	14	15	0	8	13	3	12	9	7	5	10	6	1
13	0	11	7	4	9	1	10	14	3	5	12	2	15	8	6
1	4	11	13	12	3	7	14	10	15	6	8	0	5	9	2
6	11	13	8	1	4	10	7	9	5	0	15	14	2	3	12

Table S8

13	2	8	4	6	15	11	1	10	9	3	14	5	0	12	7
1	15	13	8	10	3	7	4	12	5	6	11	0	14	9	2
7	11	4	1	9	12	14	2	0	6	10	13	15	3	5	8
2	1	14	7	4	10	8	13	15	12	9	0	3	5	6	11

If you apply all eight tables to strings B_1, B_2, B_3, B_4, B_5, B_6, B_7, B_8, the combined string in step 2 is

$$S_1(B_1)\,S_2(B_2)\,S_3(B_3)\,S_4(B_4)\,S_5(B_5)\,S_6(B_6)\,S_7(B_7)\,S_8(B_8) = 0101\ 1100\ 1000\ 0010$$
$$1011\ 0101\ 1001\ 0111$$

The final stage (step 3) to calculate f is to apply table P to the string above, i.e.

```
f = P[ S1(B₁)S2(B₂) ... S8(B₈) ]
```

Table P produces a 32-bit output and is the final value for f (first four bits are highlighted)

```
f = 0010 0011 0100 1010 1010 1001 1011 1011
```

This value f is, in fact, the value of the function $f(R_0, K_1)$ and is used to calculate R_1 from the iteration formula,

```
R₁ = L₀ XOR f(R₀,K₁)
   =     1100 1100 0000 0000 1100 1100 1111 1111
   XOR 0010 0011 0100 1010 1010 1001 1011 1011
   =     1110 1111 0100 1010 0110 0101 0100 0100
```

Continuing the iteration formula for 16 rounds, we have

$$L_{16} = 0100\ 0011\ 0100\ 0010\ 0011\ 0010\ 0011\ 0100$$
$$R_{16} = 0000\ 1010\ 0100\ 1100\ 1101\ 1001\ 1001\ 0101$$

From these two strings, $R_{16}L_{16}$ can be easily obtained:

$$R_{16}L_{16} = 00001010\ 01001100\ 11011001\ 10010101\ 01000011\ 01000010\ 00110010\ 00110100$$

Applying table IP^{-1} to $R_{16}L_{16}$ gives the desired ciphertext C:

$$
\begin{aligned}
C = IP^{-1}(R_{16}L_{16}) &= \mathbf{10000101}\ 11101000\ 00010011\ 01010100 \\
&\quad 00001111\ 00001010\ 10110100\ 00000101 \quad \text{(binary)} \\
&= 85\ E8\ 13\ 54\ 0F\ 0A\ B4\ 05 \quad \text{(hexadecimal)}
\end{aligned}
$$

Using this process for all 64-bit chunks of plaintext, you have the entire DES ciphertext C. Figure 3.1 summarizes all the procedures above in this DES encryption scheme.

For DES decryption, all you have to do is consider the ciphertext as input and apply the subkeys in reverse order.

Consider the ciphertext C above as input. If we apply the subkeys in reverse order (i.e. $K_{16}, K_{15}, \ldots, K_1$) in the iteration formula for 16 rounds, the new $R_{16}L_{16}$ turns out to be

$$R_{16}L_{16} = 11001100\ 00000000\ 11001100\ 11111111\ 11110000\ 10101010\ 11110000\ 10101010$$

Applying table IP^{-1} on top of this $R_{16}L_{16}$ will give you back the original plaintext M:

$$
\begin{aligned}
IP^{-1}(R_{16}L_{16}) &= 00000001\ 00100011\ 01000101\ 01100111 \\
&\quad 10001001\ 10101011\ 11001101\ 11101111 \quad \text{(plaintext M)} \\
&= 01\ 23\ 45\ 67\ 89\ AB\ CD\ EF \quad \text{(hexadecimal of M)}
\end{aligned}
$$

Fig. 3.1 The DES encryption scheme

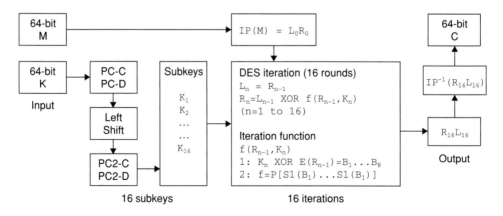

Note that this 56-bit DES scheme (or single DES) is not superstrong for encryption/decryption. If you put three DES procedures together to form the so-called 'Tri-DES' (Triple DES), the cryptostrength will be enhanced. Tri-DES will be discussed in Chapter 4.

Now, we have some idea about DES encryption/decryption and how it works. Most DES-based schemes, including the one-way encryption `crypt()` widely used in UNIX/LINUX systems, can be handled. But first, we need to know how the single DES scheme is implemented.

3.2 The single DES scheme and my first one-way encryption: `Crypt()`

3.2.1 Table lookup techniques and the DES sub-keys

In this section, we consider a special implementation of the single DES scheme which operates on one chunk (64-bit) of data. Many people may refer to this development as the 'core' of DES encryption since it can be used to perform many other DES schemes and applications.

The first thing in performing a DES operation is to generate all 16 DES subkeys. With the benefit of the previous section, we know that DES uses bit-manipulation tables heavily. One of the simplest ways to implement table lookup is to use arrays. Consider the script ex03-01.js.

Example: ex03-01.js – ECMAScript file to generate DES subkeys   (Part I)

```
 1: var PC1_C = new Array(
 2:    57, 49, 41, 33, 25, 17,  9,
 3:     1, 58, 50, 42, 34, 26, 18,
 4:    10,  2, 59, 51, 43, 35, 27,
 5:    19, 11,  3, 60, 52, 44, 36 );
 6:
 7: var PC1_D = new Array(
 8:    63, 55, 47, 39, 31, 23, 15,
 9:     7, 62, 54, 46, 38, 30, 22,
10:    14,  6, 61, 53, 45, 37, 29,
11:    21, 13,  5, 28, 20, 12,  4 );
12:
13: var shifts = new Array( 1,1,2,2,2,2,2,2,1,2,2,2,2,2,2,1);
14:
15: var PC2_C = new Array(
16:    14, 17, 11, 24,  1,  5,
17:     3, 28, 15,  6, 21, 10,
18:    23, 19, 12,  4, 26,  8,
19:    16,  7, 27, 20, 13,  2 );
20:
21: var PC2_D = new Array(
22:    41, 52, 31, 37, 47, 55,
23:    30, 40, 51, 45, 33, 48,
24:    44, 49, 39, 56, 34, 53,
25:    46, 42, 50, 36, 29, 32 );
26:
```

This is a simple ECMAScript file containing the necessary tables to generate DES subkeys. All of tables `PC1-C`, `PC1-D`, `shifts`, `PC2-C`, and `PC2-D` are implemented with arrays so that permutations or bit-manipulations can be performed using table lookup. Once we have the table data, the subkeys can be generated using part II of `ex03-01.js`.

Example: Continuation of ex03-01.js   (Part II)

```
27: var C = new Array(28);
28: var D = new Array(28);
29: var KS = new Array();
30:
31: function des_subKey(key)
32: {
33:     var i, j, k, t, index;
34:     if (KS == null) KS = new Array(16*48);
35:     for (i = 0; i < 28; i++) {
36:         C[i] = key[PC1_C[i]-1];
37:         D[i] = key[PC1_D[i]-1];
38:     }
39:     for (i = 0; i < 16; i++) {
40:         for (k = 0; k < shifts[i]; k++) {
41:             t = C[0];
42:             for (j = 0; j < 28-1; j++) C[j] = C[j+1];
43:             C[27] = t;
44:             t     = D[0];
45:             for (j = 0; j < 28-1; j++) D[j] = D[j+1];
46:             D[27] = t;
47:         }
48:         for (j = 0; j < 24; j++) {
49:             index = i * 48;
50:             KS[index+j]    = C[PC2_C[j]-1];
51:             KS[index+j+24] = D[PC2_D[j]-28-1];
52:         }
53:     }
54: }
55:
```

The arrays `C[]` and `D[]` in lines 27–28 are used to store the string pairs (C_i, D_i). The elements of `KS[]` will store the DES subkeys. The `des_subKey()` in lines 31–54 is the main function for computing all the subkeys. It will take a 64-bit argument `key` and generate all the subkeys in `KS[]`.

The first for-loop in lines 35–38 uses table lookup skills to compute the first pair (C_0, D_0). Note that the DES table data starts with index 1, and all arrays in ECMAScript start with 0. We need to subtract 1 when applying DES table data to arrays. Consider the statements in lines 36–37

```
C[i] = key[PC1_C[i]-1];   and   D[i] = key[PC1_D[i]-1];
```

The value in the first statement `PC1_C[i]-1` represents the ith data in table `PC1-C`. Substituting this value into array `key[]` will get the corresponding bit value stored in `C[i]`. A simple for-loop with these two simple statements will compute all values of the first pair (C_0, D_0).

The `i` for-loop in lines 39–53 uses the first pair (C_0, D_0) to compute all the subkeys. Consider the case when `i=0`. The value `shifts[0]` in line 40 picks up the shift value. The two for-loops in lines 41–46 perform the left-shifting on C_0 and D_0. After left-shifting, the for-loop in lines 48–52 apply tables `PC2-C` and `PC2-D` on `c[]` and `D[]` respectively to get the first subkey. Since we want to store all 16 subkeys (each 48-bit) into one array, the value `index` in line 49 ensures that all elements are stored correctly. Continuing the `i` for-loop, all the subkeys are calculated and stored in array `KS[]`.

To test this ECMAScript, consider the body part of Web page `ex03-01.htm`.

```
Example: ex03-01.htm - Generating DES subkeys

 1: <body style="font-family:arial;font-size:26pt;text-align:center;
 2:       background:#000088;color:#ffff00">
 3: Generating The 16 DES Sub-Keys<br />
 4: <img alt="pic" src="line1.gif" height="7" width="640" /><br />
 5: <table style="font-size:18pt;text-align:left" align="center">
 6:   <tr><td><br />Enter The DES Key (8-Characters) Here:</td></tr>
 7:   <tr><td style="text-align:center">
 8:     <input id="key_v" size="8" maxlength="8"
 9:         style="font-size:16pt;width:250px;
           height:40px;font-weight:bold;
10:         background:#dddddd;color:#ff0000" value="agent001" />
11:     <input type="button" value="OK" onclick="gen_subkeys()"
12:         style="font-size:16pt;font-weight:bold;width:80px;
13:         height:40px;background:#dddddd;color:#ff0000" /></td></tr>
14:   <tr><td><br />The 16 DES Sub-Keys are: </td></tr>
15:   <tr><td><textarea rows="16" cols="40" id="outMsg" readonly
16:           style="font-size:14pt;font-weight:bold;width:630px;
17:           height:380px;background:#aaffaa"></textarea></td></tr>
18: </table>
19: <script src="hexlib.js"></script>
```

```
20: <script src="ex03-01.js"></script>
21: <script>
22:  function gen_subkeys()
23:  {
24:     var r,ii,jj,kk;
25:     var outSt="", kkeySt="";
26:     var hexV = new Array(), block = new Array(66);
27:     kkeySt = document.getElementById("key_v").value
28:     hexV = myParseHex(kkeySt);
29:
30:     for (ii=0;ii<66;ii++) block[ii]=0;
31:     jj=0;
32:     for (ii=0;jj<hexV.length && ii < 64;jj++) {
33:       r = hexV[jj];
34:       for(kk=0; kk < 8; kk++, ii++) {
35:         block[ii] = ((r>>(7-kk)) & 01);
36:       }
37:     }
38:     des_subKey(block);
39:
40:     outSt += "DES Sub-Keys";
41:     for (ii=0;ii<16;ii++) {
42:         outSt +="\nK"+ (ii+1) +" = ";
43:         for (jj = 0; jj < 48; jj++) {
44:             index = ii * 48;
45:             outSt += KS[index+jj];
46:         }
47:     }
48:     document.getElementById("outMsg").value=outSt;
49:  }
50: </script>
51: </body>
```

From now on, only the body part of the XHTML page will be listed and the first
line number will be the first line of the body part of the page. The XHTML/HTML
header will be assumed. For many browsers, such as IE, you can add <html> and
</html> to both ends to make it work. The XHTML code defined in lines 5–18
contains a table with one text box, one OK button and one text area. The first text
box (lines 8–10) gets the eight hexadecimal values as the key. Once the OK button, in
lines 12–13, is clicked, the function gen_subKeys() is activated and all the subkeys
are displayed in the text area defined in lines 15–17. The details of this function are
specified inside the script block in lines 22–49.

Fig. 3.2 DES subkeys

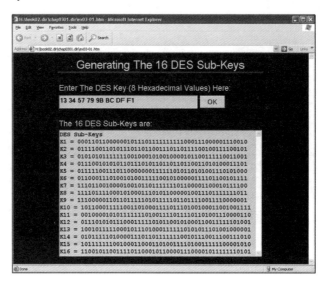

In the function gen_subKeys(), the user input string is captured by the statement in line 27 and stored in variable kkeySt. The statement in line 28 calls the function myParseHex() to parse kkeySt into an array of hexadecimal values stored in hexV[]. The next step is to convert each element in hexV[] into binary, forming a total 64-bit binary value. This process is done by the double for-loops in lines 31–37, and the result is stored in the array block[]. This block[] can be input into the function des_subKey() to generate all the subkeys (line 38) stored in array KS[]. To output the subkeys, an string called outSt and a double for-loop are used in lines 40–47. The inner jj for-loop in lines 43–46 output all the bit values of a subkey into outSt. The outer ii for-loop outputs all 16 subkeys into outSt. The statement in line 48 displays outSt, containing all the subkeys, to the text area. A screenshot of this example is shown in Figure 3.2.

As you can see from this figure, the subkeys are the same as those in Section 3.1.2. This indicates that the ECMAScript ex03-01.js is working properly. Now, we can continue the implementation of Crypt() by performing DES encryption on one chunk (64-bit) of data.

3.2.2 DES encryption on one chunk (64-bit) of data

This encryption is the 'core' of the DES algorithm. First, make a copy of ex03-01.js and call it ex03-02.js. At the end of this new file, add the script ex03-02.js.

```
56: var IP = new Array(
57:       58, 50, 42, 34, 26, 18, 10, 2,
58:       60, 52, 44, 36, 28, 20, 12, 4,
59:       62, 54, 46, 38, 30, 22, 14, 6,
60:       64, 56, 48, 40, 32, 24, 16, 8,
61:       57, 49, 41, 33, 25, 17,  9, 1,
62:       59, 51, 43, 35, 27, 19, 11, 3,
63:       61, 53, 45, 37, 29, 21, 13, 5,
64:       63, 55, 47, 39, 31, 23, 15, 7 );
65:
66: var FP = new Array(
67:     40, 8, 48, 16, 56, 24, 64, 32,
68:     39, 7, 47, 15, 55, 23, 63, 31,
69:     38, 6, 46, 14, 54, 22, 62, 30,
70:     37, 5, 45, 13, 53, 21, 61, 29,
71:     36, 4, 44, 12, 52, 20, 60, 28,
72:     35, 3, 43, 11, 51, 19, 59, 27,
73:     34, 2, 42, 10, 50, 18, 58, 26,
74:     33, 1, 41,  9, 49, 17, 57, 25 );
75:
76: var E = new Array(48);
77: var e2 = new Array(
78:     32,  1,  2,  3,  4,  5,
79:      4,  5,  6,  7,  8,  9,
80:      8,  9, 10, 11, 12, 13,
81:     12, 13, 14, 15, 16, 17,
82:     16, 17, 18, 19, 20, 21,
83:     20, 21, 22, 23, 24, 25,
84:     24, 25, 26, 27, 28, 29,
85:     28, 29, 30, 31, 32,  1 );
86:
87: var S = new Array(0,0,0,0,0,0,0,0);
88: S[0] = new Array(
89:    14, 4,13, 1, 2,15,11, 8, 3,10, 6,12, 5, 9, 0, 7,
90:     0,15, 7, 4,14, 2,13, 1,10, 6,12,11, 9, 5, 3, 8,
91:     4, 1,14, 8,13, 6, 2,11,15,12, 9, 7, 3,10, 5, 0,
92:    15,12, 8, 2, 4, 9, 1, 7, 5,11, 3,14,10, 0, 6,13);
93: S[1] = new Array(
94:    15, 1, 8,14, 6,11, 3, 4, 9, 7, 2,13,12, 0, 5,10,
95:     3,13, 4, 7,15, 2, 8,14,12, 0, 1,10, 6, 9,11, 5,
96:     0,14, 7,11,10, 4,13, 1, 5, 8,12, 6, 9, 3, 2,15,
97:       13, 8,10, 1, 3,15, 4, 2,11, 6, 7,12, 0, 5,14, 9);
```

```
 98: S[2] = new Array(
 99:     10, 0, 9,14, 6, 3,15, 5, 1,13,12, 7,11, 4, 2, 8,
100:     13, 7, 0, 9, 3, 4, 6,10, 2, 8, 5,14,12,11,15, 1,
101:     13, 6, 4, 9, 8,15, 3, 0,11, 1, 2,12, 5,10,14, 7,
102:      1,10,13, 0, 6, 9, 8, 7, 4,15,14, 3,11, 5, 2,12);
103: S[3] = new Array(
104:      7,13,14, 3, 0, 6, 9,10, 1, 2, 8, 5,11,12, 4,15,
105:     13, 8,11, 5, 6,15, 0, 3, 4, 7, 2,12, 1,10,14, 9,
106:     10, 6, 9, 0,12,11, 7,13,15, 1, 3,14, 5, 2, 8, 4,
107:      3,15, 0, 6,10, 1,13, 8, 9, 4, 5,11,12, 7, 2,14);
108: S[4] = new Array(
109:      2,12, 4, 1, 7,10,11, 6, 8, 5, 3,15,13, 0,14, 9,
110:     14,11, 2,12, 4, 7,13, 1, 5, 0,15,10, 3, 9, 8, 6,
111:      4, 2, 1,11,10,13, 7, 8,15, 9,12, 5, 6, 3, 0,14,
112:     11, 8,12, 7, 1,14, 2,13, 6,15, 0, 9,10, 4, 5, 3);
113: S[5] = new Array(
114:     12, 1,10,15, 9, 2, 6, 8, 0,13, 3, 4,14, 7, 5,11,
115:     10,15, 4, 2, 7,12, 9, 5, 6, 1,13,14, 0,11, 3, 8,
116:      9,14,15, 5, 2, 8,12, 3, 7, 0, 4,10, 1,13,11, 6,
117:      4, 3, 2,12, 9, 5,15,10,11,14, 1, 7, 6, 0, 8,13);
118: S[6] = new Array(
119:      4,11, 2,14,15, 0, 8,13, 3,12, 9, 7, 5,10, 6, 1,
120:     13, 0,11, 7, 4, 9, 1,10,14, 3, 5,12, 2,15, 8, 6,
121:      1, 4,11,13,12, 3, 7,14,10,15, 6, 8, 0, 5, 9, 2,
122:      6,11,13, 8, 1, 4,10, 7, 9, 5, 0,15,14, 2, 3,12);
123: S[7] = new Array(
124:     13, 2, 8, 4, 6,15,11, 1,10, 9, 3,14, 5, 0,12, 7,
125:      1,15,13, 8,10, 3, 7, 4,12, 5, 6,11, 0,14, 9, 2,
126:      7,11, 4, 1, 9,12,14, 2, 0, 6,10,13,15, 3, 5, 8,
127:      2, 1,14, 7, 4,10, 8,13,15,12, 9, 0, 3, 5, 6,11);
128:
129: var P = new Array(
130:            16,  7, 20, 21,
131:            29, 12, 28, 17,
132:             1, 15, 23, 26,
133:             5, 18, 31, 10,
134:             2,  8, 24, 14,
135:            32, 27,  3,  9,
136:            19, 13, 30,  6,
137:            22, 11,  4, 25);
138:
```

This is a simple program fragment containing all the remaining table data for performing DES encryption. Lines 56–74 define tables IP and FP. Table FP is the same as table IP⁻¹ (the inverse of IP).

Table E is declared in line 76 and the data inside will be copied from array e2[] in lines 77–85. Lines 87–127 define tables s1 to s8. First, the array s is declared as a one-dimensional array (line 87) containing eight elements, namely S[0], S[2], ..., S[7]. For each of these elements, another one-dimensional array with 64 elements is defined. As a result, tables s1 to s8 are defined as two-dimensional arrays. Elements of the s tables can be assessed by standard two-dimensional methods. For example, the first two elements of table S1 are

$$S[0][0] = 14 \quad \text{and} \quad S[0][1] = 4$$

At the end of this script is Table P. With all these DES tables, we can perform the DES encryption. Consider part II of ex03-02.js.

```
Example: Continuation of ex03-02.js - DES encryption          (Part II)

139: var L     = new Array(64);
140: var tempL = new Array(32);
141: var f     = new Array(32);
142: var preS  = new Array(48);
143: var block = new Array(66);
144:
145: function init()
146: {
147:    var ii;
148:    for (ii=0;ii<32;ii++)
149:    {
150:      L[ii]=0; f[ii]=0;
151:    }
152:    for (ii=0;ii<46;ii++) preS[ii]=0;
153:    for (ii=0;ii<64;ii++) L[ii]=0;
154:    for (ii=0;ii<66;ii++) block[ii]=0;
155:    for (ii=0;ii<48;ii++) E[ii] = e2[ii];
156: }
157:
158: function des_encrypt()
159: {
160:   var i;
161:   var t, j, k;
162:   var R = 32;
163:   if (KS == null)      KS   = new Array(16*48);
164:   for(j=0;j< 64;j++)   L[j] = block[IP[j]-1];
```

```
165:   for(i=0;i< 16;i++) {
166:     index = i * 48;
167:     for(j=0;j<32;j++) tempL[j] = L[R+j];
168:     for(j=0;j<48;j++) preS[j] = (L[R+E[j]-1] ^ KS[index+j]);
169:     for(j=0;j< 8;j++) {
170:       t = 6*j;
171:       k = S[j][(preS[t+0]<<5)+
172:                (preS[t+1]<<3)+
173:                (preS[t+2]<<2)+
174:                (preS[t+3]<<1)+
175:                (preS[t+4]<<0)+
176:                (preS[t+5]<<4)];
177:       t = 4*j;
178:       f[t+0] = ((k>>3)&01);
179:       f[t+1] = ((k>>2)&01);
180:       f[t+2] = ((k>>1)&01);
181:       f[t+3] = ((k>>0)&01);
182:     }
183:     for(j=0;j<32;j++) L[R+j] = (L[j] ^ f[P[j]-1]);
184:     for(j=0;j<32;j++) L[j] = tempL[j];
185:   }
186:   for(j=0;j<32;j++) {
187:     t       = L[j];
188:     L[j]    = L[R+j];
189:     L[R+j]  = t;
190:   }
191:   for(j=0;j<64;j++) block[j] = L[FP[j]-1];
192: }
193:
```

In lines 139–143, the following operational arrays are declared.

- L   – an array to store the pairs (L_i, R_i).

- preS – to compute and store the result of the S boxes

- f   – to compute and store the result of the DES function $f(R_{n-1}, K_n)$

- block – to store the one chunk of data for processing.

The function init() in lines 145–156 is to initialize all the arrays above. In particular, the for-loop in line 155 will copy all elements from table e2 into table E so that E is operational in the DES algorithm. The main function in this script is des_encrypt(). This function performs DES iteration and ultimately encrypts the data in the array block[].

The for-loop in line 164 computes the data $IP(M)$ (i.e. $L_0 R_0$ in Figure 3.1) and stores it in array $L[]$. $L[]$ is a single array containing both L_i and R_i, and therefore an index variable R in line 162 is needed to separate the data. Suppose we have all 16 DES subkeys defined as in the last section. The statements in lines 165–185 perform the DES iteration

```
L_n = R_{n-1}
R_n = L_{n-1} XOR f(R_{n-1}, K_n)   n = 1 to 16
```

The two for-loops in lines 167 and 184 carry out the first assignment. Another two for-loops in lines 168 and 169–182 calculate the function $f(R_{n-1}, K_n)$. The for-loop in line 183 computes the second iteration formula. To compute the function $f(R_{n-1}, K_n)$, the for-loop in line 169 calculate the values

$$E(R_{n-1}) \quad \text{and} \quad [K_n \text{ XOR } E(R_{n-1})] = B_1 B_2 B_3 B_4 B_5 B_6 B_7 B_8$$

The values of B_i above are stored in array $preS[]$ and the values of S boxes on B_i are computed by the for-loop in lines 169–182. For example, suppose $B_1 = 011000$ and $j=0$, the expressions in lines 171–176 (see also the DES iteration formula in Section 3.1.2)

```
k = S[j][ (preS[t+0]<<5)+ (preS[t+1]<<3)+
          (preS[t+2]<<2)+ (preS[t+3]<<1)+
          (preS[t+4]<<0)+ (preS[t+5]<<4)];
```

compute $S1(B_1)$ (or $S[0][12]$), which has the value of 5 (i.e. $k=5$). The statements in lines 178–181 convert this k into binary (or 0101) and it is stored in array $f[]$. When all values of $f[]$ are available, the for-loop in line 183 finishes the job of one round of the iteration. The for-loop in line 184 prepares for another round up to a total of 16 iterations. The for-loop in lines 186–190 arranges the results in reverse order, i.e. $R_{16} L_{16}$. Finally, another for-loop in line 191 applies table IP^{-1} (or FP) to $R_{16} L_{16}$, producing the result ciphertext C. The ciphertext C is then stored in array $block[]$.

To test this script, consider ex03-02.htm.

Example: ex03-02.htm – DES encryption on one chunk of data   (Part I)

```
1: <body style="font-family:arial;font-size:26pt;text-align:center;
2:        background:#000088;color:#ffff00">
3: DES Encryption On 64 Bits Data<br />
4: <img alt="pic" src="line1.gif" height="7" width="600" /><br />
5: <table style="font-size:18pt;text-align:left" align="center">
6: <tr><td><br />Enter One Chunk (8 Hex Values) of Data:</td></tr>
7: <tr><td><input type="text" id="in_msg"
                              value="01 23 45 67 89 AB CD EF"
8:          style="font-size:14pt;font-weight:bold;width:430px;
9:          height:40px;background:#aaffaa" /></td></tr>
```

```
10:     <tr><td><br />Enter The DES Key (8 Hex Values) Here:</td></tr>
11:     <tr><td><input type="text" id="key_v"
                                          value="13 34 57 79 9B BC DF F1"
12:           style="font-size:14pt;font-weight:bold;width:430px;
13:           height:40px;background:#aaffaa" />
14:        <input type="button" value="OK" onclick="des_encode()"
15:         style="font-size:16pt;font-weight:bold;width:80px;
16:         height:40px;background:#dddddd;color:#ff0000" /></td></tr>
17:     <tr><td><br />The DES CipherText Is (Hexadecimal): </td></tr>
18:     <tr><td><input type="text" id="outMsg"
19:           style="font-size:14pt;font-weight:bold;width:430px;
20:           height:40px;background:#aaffaa" /></td></tr>
21: </table>
```

This is the body part of a simple page containing three text boxes and one OK button. The first two text boxes in lines 7–9 and 11–13 capture the input data and the key respectively. Both the input data and the key are eight bytes long (64-bit) and are represented by hexadecimal values. Once these fields are filled and the OK button is clicked, the function des_encode() in line 14 is activated. The DES encryption result (also 64-bit) will be displayed in the text box in lines 18–20. This des_encode() function is defined in part II of ex03-02.htm.

Example: Continuation of ex03-02.htm (Part II)

```
22: <script src="hexlib.js"></script>
23: <script src="ex03-02.js"></script>
24: <script>
25:  function des_encode()
26:  {
27:    var r,ii,jj,kk;
28:    var outSt="", kkeySt="";
29:    var hexV = new Array();
30:    inMsg = document.getElementById("in_msg").value
31:    kkeySt = document.getElementById("key_v").value
32:    hexV = myParseHex(kkeySt);
33:
34:    init();
35:    jj=0;
36:    for (ii=0;jj<hexV.length && ii < 64;jj++) {
37:      r = hexV[jj];
38:      for(kk=0; kk < 8; kk++, ii++) {
39:        block[ii] = ((r>>(7-kk)) & 01);
```

```
40:        }
41:      }
42:      des_subKey(block);
43:
44:      hexV = myParseHex(inMsg);
45:      for (ii=0;ii<66;ii++) block[ii]=0;
46:      jj=0;
47:      for (ii=0;jj<hexV.length && ii < 64;jj++) {
48:        r = hexV[jj];
49:        for(kk=0; kk < 8; kk++, ii++) {
50:          block[ii] = ((r>>(7-kk)) & 01);
51:        }
52:      }
53:      des_encrypt();
54:
55:      outSt += "";
56:      for (ii=0;ii<8;ii++) {
57:        tmpV = 0;
58:        for (jj = 0; jj <8; jj++) {
59:          tmpV += (block[ii*8+jj] & 01) << (7-jj);
60:        }
61:        outSt += byteToHex(tmpV) + " ";
62:      }
63:      document.getElementById("outMsg").value=outSt;
64:    }
65: </script>
66: </body>
```

Line 22 includes the hexadecimal library hexlib.js into the page so that functions related to hex values can be called. The DES encryption script ex03-02.js discussed earlier in this section is included by the statement in line 23. The main function des_encode() is defined in lines 25–64.

The statements in lines 30 and 31 capture the input data and the DES key in variables inMsg and kkeySt respectively. Since both inMsg and kkeySt are in string form, we need to convert them into binary bits before the encryption.

The function myParseHex() in line 32 parses the key string kkeySt into individual hexadecimal values in hexV[]. After the initialization function init(), the double for-loop in lines 36–41 converts the hexadecimal values in hexV[] into binary bits and stores them in array block[]. The block[] is then used to call the function des_subkey() to generate the 16 subkeys. Once we have the subkeys, the statements in lines 44–53 perform the encryption. Before encryption, the statements in lines 44–52 are used to parse and convert the plaintext string inMsg into binary bits which are stored in `block[]`. With this global variable `block[]`, the function `des_encrypt()` in line 53 is called to encrypt the data and store the result in the array `block[]`.

In order to display the encrypted results in `block[]`, a string called `outSt` is used in line 55. For each eight bits in `block[]`, the for-loop in lines 58–60 converts it into one byte called `tmpV`. The hexadecimal representation of this one-byte value is obtained by the function `byteToHex()` in line 61 and appended to `outSt`. The details of this hexadecimal function is given in the `hexlib.js` library.

This final string `outSt` is displayed on the Web page by the statement in line 63. Screenshots of this example in action are shown in Figures 3.3 and 3.4.

As you can see from Figure 3.3, the encryption result is the same as the step-by-step example in Section 3.1.2. Since DES is an algorithm operating on a full 8 bytes (64-bit) of data, hexadecimal values are selected for input and output rather than 8-bit ASCII for display purposes. If you enter the following information into the page

```
M = 6d 79 73 65 63 72 65 74    i.e. M = "mysecret"
K = 61 67 65 6e 74 30 30 31    i.e. K = "agent001"
```

you will see the encrypted result as shown in Figure 3.4.

You can use `ex01-09.htm` to obtain the hexadecimal values if you wish. Again, the DES implementation here is for one chunk (64-bit) of data and is the core component of the algorithm. Now, let's see how to perform DES decryption on one chunk of data.

Fig. 3.3 DES encryption I

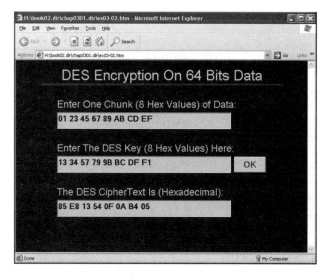

Fig. 3.4 DES encryption II

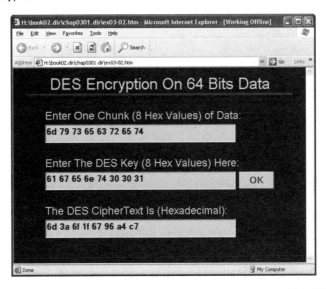

3.2.3 Performing DES decryption

Performing DES decryption on one chunk of data is simple – all you have to do is apply the subkeys in reverse order. As a quick example, let's make a copy of the ECMAScript `ex03-02.js` and call it `ex03-03.js`. Now, make the simple modifications below:

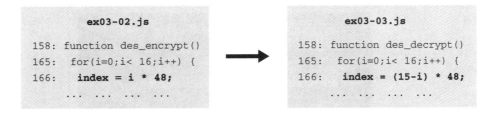

The first modification of `ex03-02.js` is to change the function name to `des_decrypt()` (line 158). If you look at the lines 165–166 in `ex03-02.js`, you will find that the 16 subkeys (each 48 bits long) are applied in ascending order from `i=0` to `15`. When you modify the code as shown in line 166 of `ex03-03.js`, the variable `index` is equivalent to applying the 16 subkeys in reverse order and ultimately performing the DES decryption.

To test this new script `ex03-03.js`, you can make a copy of `ex03-02.htm` and call it `ex03-03.htm`. Now change the following lines:

```
 3: DES Decryption On 64 Bits Data<br />
 6: <tr><td><br />Enter One Chunk (8 Hex Values) of
    ciphertext:</td></tr>
14:    <input type="button" value="OK" onclick="des_decode()"
17: <tr><td><br />The Plaintext Is (Hexadecimal): </td></tr>
25: function des_decode()
53: des_decrypt();
```

The first four lines are actually the simple XHTML code. Lines 3–6 tell the user that DES decryption will be performed in this page. When the OK button is clicked, the function `des_decode()` in line 14 is activated and the decrypted result is displayed on the page, as indicated by the statement in line 17. To carry out the decryption, all you need do is change the function names to `des_decode()` and `des_decrypt()`, in lines 25 and 53 respectively. Screenshots are shown in Figures 3.5 and 3.6.

The decryption results shown in Figures 3.5 and 3.6 correspond to the encryptions in Figures 3.3 and 3.4. Note that this decryption example is simple and for demonstration purposes only. For a more practical example, the encryption and decryption should be combined as a single function. With this DES script, many DES-related encryptions, including the one-way encryption `Crypt()`, are easy to follow.

Fig. 3.5 DES decryption I

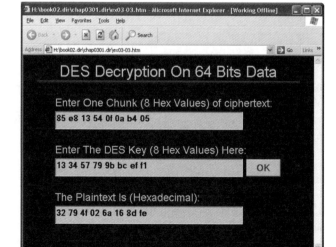

Fig. 3.6 DES decryption II

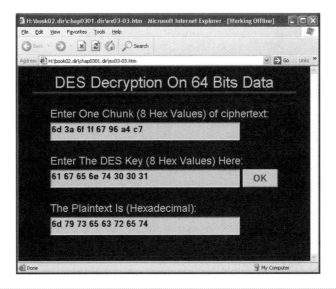

3.2.4   My first one-way encryption: Crypt()

During a system administration error at MIT in the early 1960s, the plaintext passwords (password file) of every user were disclosed on each terminal where people used to login. This accident raises a security alarm not just for software or operating systems, but also for how people handle passwords. In fact, no matter how well you hide the password file or all the backup copies, human error, machine malfunctioning and sabotage can all compromise the entire security situation. Once a password is stolen, by whatever means, all passwords must be changed. Hiding the password file is a nightmare for many system administrators and no longer an option for modern operating systems in a network environment. A solution known as Crypt() was developed and used by UNIX systems. The development was documented by two UNIX pioneers, Robert Morris and Ken Thompson, in an article 'Password Security: A Case History' in 1979. Today, all UNIX/LINUX machines are equipped with this function to handle encrypted passwords.

Note that Crypt() is a function for generating encrypted passwords, and is not the same as the UNIX program Crypt, which is for encryption of file data.

Once you understand the operations of DES, Crypt() is easy to follow. Unlike DES encryption/decryption, Crypt() is a one-way encryption which takes your plaintext password and a 2-character (each 6-bit) string called 'salt' to produce an encrypted password. Basically, the Crypt() function involves 25 DES encryptions, and the salt is used to permute table E so that the encryption is not reversible. The algorithm is divided into three steps.

Step 1 The salt is used to permute the expansion table E inside the DES scheme. Consider the DES iteration formula below:

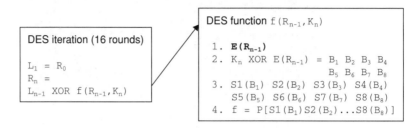

The expansion table (E) in the DES scheme is used to expand the bit string R_n from 32-bit to 48-bit. The result is for the computation of the function $f(R_{n-1}, K_n)$ in the DES iteration formula. Suppose table E is stored as an array E[]. Considering the 2-character salt as a 12-bit string, if one of the bits, say the kth, of the salt is not zero, swap the elements E[k] and E[k+24]. This can be done easily by the following double for-loop:

```
for(i=0; i < 2; i++) {
    c = salt.charCodeAt(i);
    for(j=0; j < 6; j++) {
        if( ((c>>j) & 01) != 0) {
            temp = E[6*i+j];
            E[6*i+j] = E[6*i+j+24];
            E[6*i+j+24] = temp;
} } }
```

The 12-bit salt can have a total of $2^{12} = 4096$ ways of changing table E so the decryption is no longer easy (one-way encryption).

Step 2 Use your plaintext password as the key and perform DES encryption on a zero string to obtain a ciphertext. Again perform DES encryption on the ciphertext a total of 25 times.

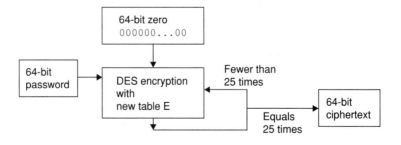

Step 3   The final 64-bit ciphertext is arranged into 11 (6-bit) printable characters to form a printable string. The 2-character salt is added to the front of the string so that the final output is a string with 13 printable characters.

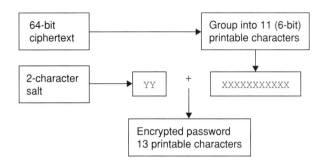

Now, we have a clear idea of the Crypt() algorithm. Let's see how to implement it on the Web.

3.2.5   Implementation of Crypt() on the Web

Crypt() is a one-way encryption and, therefore, only the DES encryption is needed. Make a copy of the DES script ex03-02.js and call it ex03-04.js. At the end of this ECMAScript file, the three-step implementation in the last section is added (ex03-04.js).

```
Example: ex03-04.js - The Crypt() algorithm                    (Part I)

194: function crypt(pw, salt)
195: {
196:   var c, i, j, pwi;
197:   var temp;
198:   var iobuf = new Array(13);
199:
200:   init();
201:   pwi = 0;
202:   for(i=0; pwi < pw.length && i < 64; pwi++) {
203:     c = pw.charCodeAt(pwi);
204:     for(j=0; j < 7; j++, i++) {
205:     block[i] = ((c>>(6-j)) & 01);
206:     }
207:     i++;
208:   }
209:   des_subKey(block);
210:
```

This script contains the first part of the function called `Crypt()` with two arguments `pw` (password) and `salt` (2-character). The variable `pw` is used to generate the DES subkeys and the `salt` is used to permute table `E` in DES encryption. The encrypted result or the `Crypt()` password will be returned by the array `iobuf` defined in line 198.

Unlike ordinary DES encryption, which operates on full 8-bit code, `Crypt()` operates on printable characters and will consider the first seven bits of each character of `pw` as the most significant bits to generate the subkeys. The for-loop in lines 203–206 captures one character of `pw` and stores the seven bits into the first seven elements of the array `block[]`. This `block[]` is used to generate the DES subkeys in line 209.

Now, consider how to use the salt and perform the 25 DES encryptions, as described in Section 3.2.4. Consider part II of script `ex03-04.js`.

```
Example: Continuation of ex03-04.js - the Crypt() algorithm   (Part II)
211:   for(i=0;i<66;i++) block[i] = 0;
212:   for(i=0;i<2;i++) {
213:     c = salt.charCodeAt(i);
214:     iobuf[i] = c;
215:     if(c > 90)    c -= 6;        // char code of 'Z'
216:     if(c > 57)    c -= 7;        // char code of '9'
217:     c -= 46;                     // char code of '.'
218:     for(j=0;j<6; j++) {
219:       if( ((c>>j) & 01) != 0) {
220:         temp = E[6*i+j];
221:         E[6*i+j] = E[6*i+j+24];
222:         E[6*i+j+24] = temp;
223:       }
224:     }
225:   }
226:   for(i=0;i<25;i++) des_encrypt(); // 25 Encryptions
227:
228:   for(i=0;i<11;i++) {
229:     c = 0;
230:     for(j=0;j< 6; j++) {
231:       c <<= 1;
232:       c |= block[6*i+j];
233:     }
234:     c += 46;                      // char code of '.'
235:     if(c > 57)    c += 7;         // char code of '9'
236:     if(c > 90)    c += 6;         // char code of 'Z'
```

```
237:     iobuf[i+2] = c;
238:   }
239:   if(iobuf[1] == 0) iobuf[1] = iobuf[0];
240:   return(iobuf);
241: }
```

Line 211 generates a zero array in `block[]` to be encrypted. Each character of the salt is captured by the statement in line 213 and added into the array `iobuf[]` so that the first two characters of the encrypted password are the salt. The statements in lines 215–217 adjust the gaps of the salt character. For example, the ASCII values of 'Z' and 'a' are 90 and 97 respectively. If the character in variable c is bigger than 90 (i.e. 'Z'), a minus 6, as illustrated in line 215, will fill the gap and append the 'a' at the end of 'Z'. The for-loop in lines 218–224 will check each bit of c. If one of the bits is not zero, the statements in lines 220–222 swap the elements in table E as described in step 1 of Section 3.2.4. After table E is permuted by the salt, the for-loop in line 226 performs the 25 DES encryptions.

At the end of the operation, the encrypted result is stored in array `block[]`. Since `block[]` is declared as an array of 66 elements, it can be converted into 11 characters; each of them is 6 bits long. The double for-loop in lines 228–238 converts the bit array `block[]` into 11 encrypted characters in `iobuf[]`. This `iobuf` containing the `Crypt()` encrypted password will be returned to the function caller by the statement in line 240.

One of the quickest ways to test this script is to make a copy of `ex02-01.htm`, modifying the following two lines and then calling it `ex03-04.htm`:

```
 5: <head><title>Gen. Crypt() Password - ex03-04.htm</title></head>
30: <script src="ex03-04.js"></script>
```

The title message in line 5 will display in the title bar of the browser window. Line 30 includes the script file `ex03-04.js` into the page so that the functions inside are available. Screenshots are shown in Figures 3.7 and 3.8.

Now, we have the `Crypt()` scheme in the browser. As mentioned in Chapter 2, if you have a password scheme in the browser, the password can be encrypted locally. Only the ciphertext password is transmitted over the Internet or Web without exposing the plaintext password during communication, and hence security risks are highly reduced. With this capability, many of the authentications discussed in Chapter 2 can be implemented on the server by using CGI technologies. Security with CGI and related skills will be discussed in Chapter 7.

Some people may consider `Crypt()` to be a special application of DES. In fact, you can easily modify the algorithm by applying more DES encryptions to form your own proprietary one-way (or password) encryption and use it for your security application. Note that using your imagination on top of a standard encryption scheme can, in many cases, cause a major headache for experts.

Fig. 3.7 `Crypt()` password I

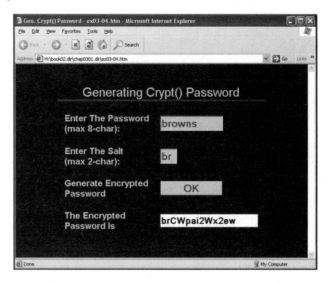

Fig. 3.8 `Crypt()` password II

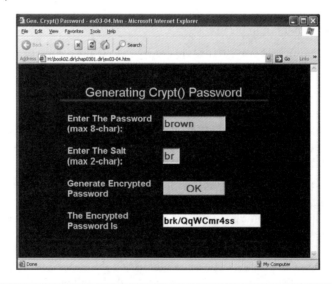

Another feature of `Crypt()` is that even a minor change in the password will produce a completely different result. This property is called 'random' behaviour. The random and one-way nature of `Crypt()` yield a wider and more secure class of one-way encryption called 'hash functions'.

3.3 Hash functions and the message digest: MD5

3.3.1 What are hash functions?

One of the fundamental primitives in modern cryptography is the cryptographic hash function. Sometimes, it is also called the 'one-way hash function' due to the fact that they are often irreversible.

Basically, a hash function is a computationally efficient function which takes a binary string of arbitrary length and outputs a binary string of some fixed length. The result is called a hash value or simply hash.

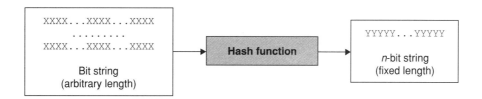

In practice, the term 'arbitrary length' is well defined only within the computational power of machine. Since the output is a bit string with a fixed length, hash functions cannot be one-to-one. In other words, given a hash function h(), there is a chance that for two different binary strings, x and y, they may have the same hash, i.e. h(x) = h(y). Therefore, not all hash functions are useful. A good cryptographic hash function should have the following properties.

- Random: given two similar binary strings x and y, the hash results h(x) and h(y) are NOT similar.

- One-way: for a given hash value z, it is computationally infeasible to find a binary string x such that h(x) = z.

- No-collision: it is computationally infeasible to find two distinct binary strings x and y such that h(x) = h(y).

These three properties and the requirements of one-way encryption match perfectly well and, therefore, hash functions can be used to generate encrypted passwords. More importantly, a carefully designed hash function can be used to produce the so-called 'digital signature of a document'. If you want to put a signature on an electronic document or file just like you sign a piece of paper so that no one can alter it, the following steps can be used.

- Obtain the hash value of the file or electronic document. This binary string (hash) with a fixed length represents the signature of the document.

- Send your document and the signature separately to the one intended.

- The receiver obtains the hash value from the document and looks for a match with the signature. If the new hash matches the signature, the document is genuine.

Any modifications to the document will produce a different hash as a result. This feature is widely used to maintain data integrity of files, documents and downloads on the Web. One of the most popular hash functions on the World Wide Web is message digest (MD).

3.3.2   The 128-bit MD5 algorithm

We have discussed some of the properties and applications of message digest in Chapter 2. In fact, the MD5 function md5() used previously is a hash function which produces a 128-bit hash value. Some examples are

```
md5("")          = d41d8cd98f00b204e9800998ecf8427e
md5("a")         = 0cc175b9c0f1b6a831c399e269772661
md5("johnsmith") = cd4388c0c62e65ac8b99e3ec49fd9409
md5("john")      = 527bd5b5d689e2c32ae974c6229ff785
```

The 128-bit hashes (or digests) above are represented by 32 hexadecimal values. The digest values can also be considered as one-way encryptions of plaintext passwords and can be transmitted over the Web environment safely. Since MD5 is so widely used, it is also known as the IETF standard RFC 1321.

The message digest algorithm was first developed by Ronald L. Rivest in the MIT Laboratory for Computer Science and RSA Data Security Inc. in the early 1990s. It is a family of algorithms known as 'MD'. The algorithm has gone through a number of versions and the most popular ones are MD4 and MD5. In this section we will cover the details of MD5.

In general the MD5 algorithm takes a message of arbitrary length as input and produces an output of a 128-bit hash or message digest. Suppose we have a b-bit message as input. The number b is an arbitrary non-negative integer, and every bit can be represented by the sequence

$$m\{0\}, m\{1\}, \ldots, m\{b-1\}$$

Note that each ASCII character is represented by an 8-bit sequence. The algorithm can be described by the three steps below.

Step 1 Appending padding bits and add length

The input message sequence is always padded and extended by a bit '1' and an optional sequence of bit '0' so that congruent to 448 modulo 512 is achieved. If the message sequence is already congruent to 448 modulo 512, a new chunk of 512 bits is added.

The reason for making it congruent to 448 modulo 512 is that a 64-bit representation of b (the length of the input message before the padding) is then added into the padded sequence to make it a multiple of 512 bits. The 64-bit representation of b is appended as two 32-bit words with the low-order word first. This means that the message digest algorithm can digest a message of 2^{64} = 184 467 440 737 095 516 16 length in terms of bits. This is a big number and it is unlikely that your message would have more bits than this. If b is greater than 2^{64} bits then only the low-order 64 bits of b are used. The result of the extended message is an exact multiple of 512 bits and is represented as an exact multiple of 16 (32-bit) words. In this case we can store the message in terms of words of 32-bit quantity. Now, let the sequence

$M[0], M[1], \ldots, M[N-1]$

denote the padded and extended plaintext in 32-bit words, where N is a multiple of 16.

Step 2 Defining data and functions for MD5

To process the message, some variables and functions are required. First, four primary variables a, b, c and d are defined with initial values:

a = 0x67452301 b = 0xefcdab89

c = 0x98badcfe d = 0x10325476

These variables are 32-bit (4 bytes or 1 word) quantities in hexadecimal format. They will eventually store the 128-bit message digest string that we want. Along with the primary variables, a 4×4 table of constants is defined as

```
S11 = 7      S21 = 5      S31 = 4      S41 = 6
S12 = 12     S22 = 9      S32 = 11     S42 = 10
S13 = 17     S23 = 14     S33 = 16     S43 = 15
S14 = 22     S24 = 20     S34 = 23     S44 = 21
```

This table is used for the left-rotation operation in the algorithm. Next, four functions are defined as follows:

$$F(x, y, z) = (((x) \& (y)) \mid ((\sim x) \& (z)))$$

$$G(x, y, z) = (((x) \& (z)) \mid ((y) \& (\sim z)))$$

$$H(x, y, z) = ((x) \wedge (y) \wedge (z))$$

$$I(x, y, z) = ((y) \wedge ((x) \mid (\sim z)))$$

Each function takes three words (each 32-bit) and produces one 32-bit value. These four functions are used to specified another set of functions:

$$FF(a, b, c, d, k, s, i) = b + ((a + F(b, c, d) + k + i) <<\!\!\text{-} s)$$

$$GG(a, b, c, d, k, s, i) = b + ((a + G(b, c, d) + k + i) <<\!\!\text{-} s)$$

$$HH(a, b, c, d, k, s, i) = b + ((a + H(b, c, d) + k + i) <<<- s)$$

$$II(a, b, c, d, k, s, i) \quad = b + ((a + I(b, c, d) + k + i) <<<- s)$$

The operation '$x <<<- s$' is specified by the following bitwise shift in ECMAScript:

$$X <<<- s = (((x) << (s)) \mid ((x) >>> (32-(s))))$$

which is equivalent to left-rotating x by s. Also, an array of 64 elements is populated by the formula

$$T[i] = int(4\,294\,967\,296 \times abs(sin(i))) \qquad where\ i = 1\ to\ 64$$

$T[i]$, in fact, is the integer part of an enlarged sine function (absolute valued). In practice, the 64 values are stored in hexadecimal and will be used as constants for functions FF(), GG(), HH() and II().

Step 3 Processing a message to produce a digest

Given a padded and extended sequence $M[0], M[1], \ldots, M[N-1]$ as described in Step 1, the 128-bit digested string can be calculated by the pseudo-code outlined in the following example, which shows how to process a message to produce a digest.

```
Example: The pseudo-code of MD5 - processing a message to produce
a digest

 1: for (i=0, i<=N/16 - 1;i++)
 2:   for (j=0; j<=15; j++)
 3:      x[j] = M[i*16+j];
 4:   end-for
 5:
 6:  aa = a;    bb = b;   cc = c;   dd = d;
 7:
 8:  a=FF(a,b,c,d,x[ 0],S11,T[ 1]);    d=FF(d,a,b,c,x[ 1],S12,T[ 2]);
 9:  c=FF(c,d,a,b,x[ 2],S13,T[ 3]);    b=FF(b,c,d,a,x[ 3],S14,T[ 4]);
10:  a=FF(a,b,c,d,x[ 4],S11,T[ 5]);    d=FF(d,a,b,c,x[ 5],S12,T[ 6]);
11:  c=FF(c,d,a,b,x[ 6],S13,T[ 7]);    b=FF(b,c,d,a,x[ 7],S14,T[ 8]);
12:  a=FF(a,b,c,d,x[ 8],S11,T[ 9]);    d=FF(d,a,b,c,x[ 9],S12,T[10]);
13:  c=FF(c,d,a,b,x[10],S13,T[11]);    b=FF(b,c,d,a,x[11],S14,T[12]);
14:  a=FF(a,b,c,d,x[12],S11,T[13]);    d=FF(d,a,b,c,x[13],S12,T[14]);
15:  c=FF(c,d,a,b,x[14],S13,T[15]);    b=FF(b,c,d,a,x[15],S14,T[16]);
16:
17:  a=GG(a,b,c,d,x[ 1],S21,T[17]);    d=GG(d,a,b,c,x[ 6],S22,T[18]);
18:  c=GG(c,d,a,b,x[11],S23,T[19]);    b=GG(b,c,d,a,x[ 0],S24,T[20]);
19:  a=GG(a,b,c,d,x[ 5],S21,T[21]);    d=GG(d,a,b,c,x[10],S22,T[22]);
20:  c=GG(c,d,a,b,x[15],S23,T[23]);    b=GG(b,c,d,a,x[ 4],S24,T[24]);
31:  a=GG(a,b,c,d,x[ 9],S21,T[25]);    d=GG(d,a,b,c,x[14],S22,T[26]);
32:  c=GG(c,d,a,b,x[ 3],S23,T[27]);    b=GG(b,c,d,a,x[ 8],S24,T[28]);
```

```
33:    a=GG(a,b,c,d,x[13],S21,T[29]);    d=GG(d,a,b,c,x[ 2],S22,T[30]);
34:    c=GG(c,d,a,b,x[ 7],S23,T[31]);    b=GG(b,c,d,a,x[12],S24,T[32]);
35:
36:    a=HH(a,b,c,d,x[ 5],S31,T[33]);    d=HH(d,a,b,c,x[ 8],S32,T[34]);
37:    c=HH(c,d,a,b,x[11],S33,T[35]);    b=HH(b,c,d,a,x[14],S34,T[36]);
38:    a=HH(a,b,c,d,x[ 1],S31,T[37]);    d=HH(d,a,b,c,x[ 4],S32,T[38]);
39:    c=HH(c,d,a,b,x[ 7],S33,T[39]);    b=HH(b,c,d,a,x[10],S34,T[40]);
40:    a=HH(a,b,c,d,x[13],S31,T[41]);    d=HH(d,a,b,c,x[ 0],S32,T[42]);
41:    c=HH(c,d,a,b,x[ 3],S33,T[43]);    b=HH(b,c,d,a,x[ 6],S34,T[44]);
42:    a=HH(a,b,c,d,x[ 9],S31,T[45]);    d=HH(d,a,b,c,x[12],S32,T[46]);
43:    c=HH(c,d,a,b,x[15],S33,T[47]);    b=HH(b,c,d,a,x[ 2],S34,T[48]);
44:
45:    a=II(a,b,c,d,x[ 0],S41,T[49]);    d=II(d,a,b,c,x[ 7],S42,T[50]);
46:    c=II(c,d,a,b,x[14],S43,T[51]);    b=II(b,c,d,a,x[ 5],S44,T[52]);
47:    a=II(a,b,c,d,x[12],S41,T[53]);    d=II(d,a,b,c,x[ 3],S42,T[54]);
48:    c=II(c,d,a,b,x[10],S43,T[55]);    b=II(b,c,d,a,x[ 1],S44,T[56]);
49:    a=II(a,b,c,d,x[ 8],S41,T[57]);    d=II(d,a,b,c,x[15],S42,T[58]);
50:    c=II(c,d,a,b,x[ 6],S43,T[59]);    b=II(b,c,d,a,x[13],S44,T[60]);
51:    a=II(a,b,c,d,x[ 4],S41,T[61]);    d=II(d,a,b,c,x[11],S42,T[62]);
52:    c=II(c,d,a,b,x[ 2],S43,T[43]);    b=II(b,c,d,a,x[ 9],S44,T[64]);
53:
54:    a = a + aa
55:    b = b + bb
56:    c = c + cc
57:    d = d + dd
58: end-for
```

The message sequence M[0], M[1], ..., M[N-1] is processed in chunks of 16 elements. The pseudo-code for-loop in lines 2–4 copies 16 elements into an array called x[]. This x[] is then digested by the functions FF(), GG(), HH() and II() in lines 8–52. The result is then added to the primary variables a, b, c and d as illustrated in lines 54–57. When the i for-loop has finished, variables a, b, c and d contain the characteristics (or digest) of the entire message sequence and return to the caller function as a 128-bit digest or hash string. In practice, the digest is usually returned in hexadecimal format.

This MD5 algorithm is implemented widely and used in security applications. Many Web server technologies, such as such as Perl and PHP, include it as a standard function. Also, the RFC 1321 specification has provided a C implementation of the algorithm. We will discuss this C implementation in Section 3.3.4 on building a utility. As discussed in Chapter 2, security on the Web client is just as important as on the server and in many cases can enhance security for Web traffic. For this reason, the MD5 implementation on the browser is discussed in the next section.

3.3.3 The implementation of MD5 on the Web

Compared to DES, the MD5 algorithm described in Section 3.3.2 (or RFC 1321) has a simpler structure and therefore is straightforward to program. In this section, a slightly modified implementation is provided.

Consider the following main functions in MD5:

$$FF(a, b, c, d, k, s, i) = b + ((a + F(b, c, d) + k + i) <<\text{-} s)$$

$$GG(a, b, c, d, k, s, i) = b + ((a + G(b, c, d) + k + i) <<\text{-} s)$$

$$HH(a, b, c, d, k, s, i) = b + ((a + H(b, c, d) + k + i) <<\text{-} s)$$

$$II(a, b, c, d, k, s, i) = b + ((a + I(b, c, d) + k + i) <<\text{-} s)$$

If we define the core function KK() as

$$KK(q, a, b, x, s, t) = [(a + q) + (x + t) <<\text{-} s] + b$$

the four functions above turn out to be

$$FF(a, b, c, d, k, s, i) = KK(F(b, c, d), a, b, k, s, i)$$

$$GG(a, b, c, d, k, s, i) = KK(G(b, c, d), a, b, k, s, i)$$

$$HH(a, b, c, d, k, s, i) = KK(H(b, c, d), a, b, k, s, i)$$

$$II(a, b, c, d, k, s, i) = KK(I(b, c, d), a, b, k, s, i)$$

Using the definition of F(), G(), H() and I(), the functions above can be written as:

$$FF(a, b, c, d, k, s, i) = KK([(b \,\&\, c) \mid ((\sim b) \,\&\, d)] , a, b, k, s, i)$$

$$GG(a, b, c, d, k, s, i) = KK([(b \,\&\, d) \mid (c \,\&\, (\sim d))] , a, b, k, s, i)$$

$$HH(a, b, c, d, k, s, i) = KK([b \wedge c \wedge d] , a, b, k, s, i)$$

$$II(a, b, c, d, k, s, i) = KK([c \wedge (b \mid (\sim d))] , a, b, k, s, i)$$

Consider part I of ex03-05.js.

Example: ex03-05.js - Implementation of message digest md5() (Part I)

```
1: function kk(q, a, b, x, s, t)
2: {
3:   var tmp1 = bit32_add(bit32_add(a, q), bit32_add(x, t));
4:   tmp1 = rot_l(tmp1, s);
5:   tmp1 = bit32_add(tmp1, b);
6:   return tmp1;
7: }
8:
```

```
 9: function ff(a, b, c, d, x, s, t)
10: {
11:   var tmp = (b & c) | ((~b) & d);
12:   return kk(tmp, a, b, x, s, t);
13: }
14:
15: function gg(a, b, c, d, x, s, t)
16: {
17:   var tmp = (b & d) | (c & (~d));
18:   return kk(tmp, a, b, x, s, t);
19: }
20:
21: function hh(a, b, c, d, x, s, t)
22: {
23:   var tmp = b ^ c ^ d;
24:   return kk(tmp, a, b, x, s, t);
25: }
26:
27: function ii(a, b, c, d, x, s, t)
28: {
29:   var tmp = c ^ (b | (~d));
30:   return kk(tmp, a, b, x, s, t);
31: }
32:
33: function bit32_add(x, y)
34: {
35:   var low = (x & 0xffff) + (y & 0xffff);
36:   var hig = (x >> 16) + (y >> 16) + (low >> 16);
37:   return (hig << 16) | (low & 0xffff);
38: }
39:
40: function rot_l(val, s)
41: {
42:   return (val << s) | (val >>> (32 - s));
43: }
44:
```

Note that, for our script implementation, all function names are in lower case. Lines 1–7 define the function kk(). Since this function uses 32-bit addition and rotation operations, the binary addition function bit32_add() and left-rotation function rot_l() are defined in lines 33–43. Once the function kk() is specified, the corresponding functions ff(), gg(), hh() and ii() are defined in lines 9–31.

To generate the message digest, consider part II of script ex03-05.js.

```
45: function md5_raw(x, len)
46: {
47:   /* Append Padding Bits & Length */
48:   x[len >> 5] |= 0x80 << ((len) % 32);
49:   x[(((len + 64) >>> 9) << 4) + 14] = len;
50:
51:     var a = 0x67452301, b = 0xefcdab89;
52:     var c = 0x98badcfe, d = 0x10325476;
53:
54:     var S11=7, S12=12, S13=17, S14=22;
55:     var S21=5, S22=9, S23=14, S24=20;
56:     var S31=4, S32=11, S33=16, S34=23;
57:     var S41=6, S42=10, S43=15, S44=21;
58:
59:   for(var i = 0; i < x.length; i += 16)
60:     {
61:     var aa = a, bb = b, cc = c; dd = d;
62:
63: a=ff(a,b,c,d,x[i+ 0],S11,0xd76aa478);
    d=ff(d,a,b,c,x[i+ 1],S12,0xe8c7b756);
64: c=ff(c,d,a,b,x[i+ 2],S13,0x242070db);
    b=ff(b,c,d,a,x[i+ 3],S14,0xc1bdceee);
65: a=ff(a,b,c,d,x[i+ 4],S11,0xf57c0faf);
    d=ff(d,a,b,c,x[i+ 5],S12,0x4787c62a);
66: c=ff(c,d,a,b,x[i+ 6],S13,0xa8304613);
    b=ff(b,c,d,a,x[i+ 7],S14,0xfd469501);
67: a=ff(a,b,c,d,x[i+ 8],S11,0x698098d8);
    d=ff(d,a,b,c,x[i+ 9],S12,0x8b44f7af);
68: c=ff(c,d,a,b,x[i+10],S13,0xffff5bb1);
    b=ff(b,c,d,a,x[i+11],S14,0x895cd7be);
69: a=ff(a,b,c,d,x[i+12],S11,0x6b901122);
    d=ff(d,a,b,c,x[i+13],S12,0xfd987193);
70: c=ff(c,d,a,b,x[i+14],S13,0xa679438e);
    b=ff(b,c,d,a,x[i+15],S14,0x49b40821);
71:
72: a=gg(a,b,c,d,x[i+ 1],S21,0xf61e2562);
    d=gg(d,a,b,c,x[i+ 6],S22,0xc040b340);
73: c=gg(c,d,a,b,x[i+11],S23,0x265e5a51);
    b=gg(b,c,d,a,x[i+ 0],S24,0xe9b6c7aa);
74: a=gg(a,b,c,d,x[i+ 5],S21,0xd62f105d);
    d=gg(d,a,b,c,x[i+10],S22, 0x2441453);
75: c=gg(c,d,a,b,x[i+15],S23,0xd8a1e681);
    b=gg(b,c,d,a,x[i+ 4],S24,0xe7d3fbc8);
```

```
76: a=gg(a,b,c,d,x[i+ 9],S21,0x21e1cde6);
    d=gg(d,a,b,c,x[i+14],S22,0xc33707d6);
77: c=gg(c,d,a,b,x[i+ 3],S23,0xf4d50d87);
    b=gg(b,c,d,a,x[i+ 8],S24,0x455a14ed);
78: a=gg(a,b,c,d,x[i+13],S21,0xa9e3e905);
    d=gg(d,a,b,c,x[i+ 2],S22,0xfcefa3f8);
79: c=gg(c,d,a,b,x[i+ 7],S23,0x676f02d9);
    b=gg(b,c,d,a,x[i+12],S24,0x8d2a4c8a);
80:
81: a=hh(a,b,c,d,x[i+ 5],S31,0xfffa3942);
    d=hh(d,a,b,c,x[i+ 8],S32,0x8771f681);
82: c=hh(c,d,a,b,x[i+11],S33,0x6d9d6122);
    b=hh(b,c,d,a,x[i+14],S34,0xfde5380c);
83: a=hh(a,b,c,d,x[i+ 1],S31,0xa4beea44);
    d=hh(d,a,b,c,x[i+ 4],S32,0x4bdecfa9);
84: c=hh(c,d,a,b,x[i+ 7],S33,0xf6bb4b60);
    b=hh(b,c,d,a,x[i+10],S34,0xbebfbc70);
85: a=hh(a,b,c,d,x[i+13],S31,0x289b7ec6);
    d=hh(d,a,b,c,x[i+ 0],S32,0xeaa127fa);
86: c=hh(c,d,a,b,x[i+ 3],S33,0xd4ef3085);
    b=hh(b,c,d,a,x[i+ 6],S34, 0x4881d05);
87: a=hh(a,b,c,d,x[i+ 9],S31,0xd9d4d039);
    d=hh(d,a,b,c,x[i+12],S32,0xe6db99e5);
88: c=hh(c,d,a,b,x[i+15],S33,0x1fa27cf8);
    b=hh(b,c,d,a,x[i+ 2],S34,0xc4ac5665);
89:
90: a=ii(a,b,c,d,x[i+ 0],S41,0xf4292244);
    d=ii(d,a,b,c,x[i+ 7],S42,0x432aff97);
91: c=ii(c,d,a,b,x[i+14],S43,0xab9423a7);
    b=ii(b,c,d,a,x[i+ 5],S44,0xfc93a039);
92: a=ii(a,b,c,d,x[i+12],S41,0x655b59c3);
    d=ii(d,a,b,c,x[i+ 3],S42,0x8f0ccc92);
93: c=ii(c,d,a,b,x[i+10],S43,0xffeff47d);
    b=ii(b,c,d,a,x[i+ 1],S44,0x85845dd1);
94: a=ii(a,b,c,d,x[i+ 8],S41,0x6fa87e4f);
    d=ii(d,a,b,c,x[i+15],S42,0xfe2ce6e0);
95: c=ii(c,d,a,b,x[i+ 6],S43,0xa3014314);
    b=ii(b,c,d,a,x[i+13],S44,0x4e0811a1);
96: a=ii(a,b,c,d,x[i+ 4],S41,0xf7537e82);
    d=ii(d,a,b,c,x[i+11],S42,0xbd3af235);
97: c=ii(c,d,a,b,x[i+ 2],S43,0x2ad7d2bb);
    b=ii(b,c,d,a,x[i+ 9],S44,0xeb86d391);
98:
```

```
 99:        a = bit32_add(a, aa);
100:        b = bit32_add(b, bb);
101:        c = bit32_add(c, cc);
102:        d = bit32_add(d, dd);
103:      }
104:      return Array(a, b, c, d);
105: }
106:
```

This script fragment contains a function `md5_raw()` with two arguments, namely `x` and `len`. Variable `x` is the input message represented as an array. Each element `x[i]` contains one word (32-bit) of the message. The variable `len` is the length of the input message in bits. Lines 48–49 pad and extend the input message by 1 and 0 bits as described in Step 1 of the algorithm. The expression `(((len+64)>>> 9) <<4)+14` in line 49 performs the 448 modulo 512 operation on 32-bit words. In fact, 14 words (32-bit) is 448 bits and the statement in line 49 appends the value `len` to the end of the extended sequence `x[]`. Lines 51–57 define the constants as in Step 2 of the algorithm. Apart from some minor modifications, the rest of the program codes are basically the same as Step 3 of the algorithm.

In Step 3 of the algorithm, double for-loops are used and chunks of 512 bits of the message are copied out for processing. The implementation here uses a single for-loop with a step of 16 (line 59) and therefore all the indices of `x[]` between lines 63 and 97 require incrementing by variable `i`. Also, the hexadecimal constants inside functions `ff()`, `gg()`, `hh()` and `ii()` are the corresponding values of `T[i]` described in Step 3. They are hard coded here for efficiency. After the message is digested, the result is stored in variables `a`, `b`, `c` and `d`. These four variables are returned to the function caller as an array (line 104).

In order to use this function effectively, a user-friendly interface is required. This is shown in part III of `ex03-05.js`.

Example: Continuation of ex03-05.js   **(Part III)**

```
107: function strToBin(str)
108: {
109:   var binArr = Array();
110:   var mask = (1 << 8) - 1;
111:   for(var i = 0; i < str.length * 8; i += 8)
112:   {
113:     binArr[i>>5] |= (str.charCodeAt(i / 8) & mask) << (i%32);
114:   }
```

```
115:    return binArr;
116: }
117:
118: function binToHex(binArr)
119: {
120:    var hexes = "0123456789abcdef";
121:    var hexSt = "";
122:    for(var i = 0; i < binArr.length * 4; i++)
123:    {
124:      hexSt += hexes.charAt((binArr[i>>2] >> ((i%4)*8+4)) & 0xf) +
125:               hexes.charAt((binArr[i>>2] >> ((i%4)*8 )) & 0xf);
126:    }
127:    return hexSt;
128: }
129:
130: function md5(s)
131: {
132:    return (binToHex(md5_raw(strToBin(s), s.length * 8)));
133: }
```

This script fragment contains three functions. The first, strToBin(), in lines 107–116 takes a string and returns an array of 32-bit words to the caller. The second function binToHex() in lines 118–128 takes an array of 32-bit words and returns it in hexadecimal format. The main function is md5() defined in lines 130–133. It takes a string s as argument and returns the MD5 digest to the caller. If you call this function with a string, e.g. 'john', the function strToBin("john") in line 132 will convert the string into a 32-bit binary array. Together with the bit length, the statement in line 132 calls the function md5_raw() to obtain the message digest, and finally the function binToHex() is called to transform it into hexadecimal values. Note that the function md5_raw() returns an array of four 32-bit elements and the function binToHex(binSt) would generate 32 hexadecimal characters. This can be seen from the for-loop in lines 122–126. For the input string 'john', the caller should receive the following string:

```
md5("john") = 527bd5b5d689e2c32ae974c6229ff785
```

Using this script, you can develop a general Web page to obtain MD5 digests. The body part of this page is shown in example ex03-05.htm.

```
Example: ex03-05.htm - generating an MD5 digest

 1: <body style="font-family:arial;font-size:22pt;background:#000088">
 2: <div style="text-align:center;color:#00ff00"><br />
 3:     Generating MD5 Message Digest</div><br />
 4: <table style="font-size:16pt" cellspacing="10px" align="center">
 5: <tr><td style="width:100px;color:#ffff00">Input Message</td>
 6:     <td><input type="button" value="OK" style="font-size:16pt;
 7:         font-weight:bold;width:80px;height:35px;
            background:#dddddd;
 8:         color:#ff0000" onclick="get_md5()" /></td></tr>
 9: <tr><td colspan="2"style="width:60px;color:#ffff00">
10:     <textarea id="key_v" style="font-size:16pt;width:450px;
11:       height:60px;font-weight:bold;
12:       background:#ddffdd;color:#ff0000"></textarea></td></tr>
13: <tr><td colspan="2" style="width:360px;color:#ffff00">
14:     md5 Message Digest</td></tr>
15: <tr><td colspan="2"><input id="dis_mesg" size="55" maxlength="55"
16:     style="font-size:16pt;width:450px;height:35px;
        font-weight:bold;
17:     background:#dddddd;color:#ff0000" /> </td> </tr>
18: </table>
19: <script src="ex03-05.js"></script>
20: <script>
21: function get_md5()
22: {
23:   var tmp = document.getElementById("key_v").value;
24:   document.getElementById("dis_mesg").value=md5(tmp);
25: }
26: </script>
27: </body>
```

This page contains one OK button (lines 6–8), a text area (lines 10–12) and one text box (lines 15–17). Once you have entered a string in the text area and clicked the OK button, the function get_md5() (line 8) is activated. The details of the get_md5() function are specified in lines 21–25. The statement in line 23 captures the string in the text area and stores it in variable tmp. The function md5(tmp) in line 24 will obtain the MD string and display it in the text box with the statement in line 24. The main function md5() is defined in the script file ex03-05.js, as illustrated in line 19. Screenshots are shown in Figures 3.9 and 3.10.

In Chapter 2, MD5 was used to generate encrypted passwords to identify users for authentication purposes. In fact, MD5 can also be used to identify a document (or file) so that no alteration or modification can be made. To do that we need to build an MD5 utility.

Fig. 3.9 MD5 string I

Fig. 3.10 MD5 string II

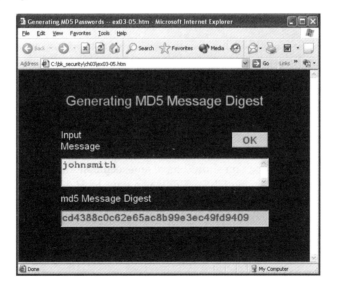

3.3.4   Building a utility from the MD standard programs

The MD5 specification RFC 1321 includes a C implementation of the algorithm. It provides the following program files:

`global.h`   – contains all constants and generic types

`md5.h`   – header file for `md5.c`

`md5.c`   – the primary program to implement the MD5 algorithm

`mddriver.c` – a driver program to use `md5.c` (Utility)

If you have a C/C++ compiler such as Borland C/C++, Microsoft C/C++ or UNIX/Linux C/C++, you can compile this `md5.c` program and build an MD5 utility. Since the `md5.c` program is not designed to be an executable program, the standard also provides a driver program called `mddriver.c` so that an executable program can be built. For example, if you are using the Microsoft C/C++ compiler, you can build the utility using the command

```
cl -D MD=5 mddriver.c md5.c
```

This command would perform the following tasks.

- Compile the C programs `mddriver.c` and `md5.c` and build the executable program `mddriver.exe`.

- The standard programs can also be used to build some older versions of the message digest schemes such as MD4 and MD2. The directive `-D MD=5` above defines a macro in `mddriver.c` to make sure that MD5 (version 5) is built.

If you are using UNIX/LINUX with a `gcc` or `cc` compiler, you can compile the utility with the command

```
gcc -o mddriver -D MD=5 mddriver.c md5.c
```

This command will define the macros `MD=5` and compile the C programs. Instead of the traditional executable file name `a.out`, the option '-o' will name the executable file as `mddriver`.

After the compilation, you should have an executable file called `mddriver.exe` or `mddriver` if you are using UNIX/LINUX in your local directory. For our default C/C++ compiler `gcc` on Windows, a compiling session is captured and is shown in Figure 3.11.

Suppose the executable program mddriver.exe is built in your local directory. To test this program, you can activate the test suite by issuing the command

```
mddriver -x
```

If you can see the following messages, as in Figure 3.12, on your screen, you have a working MD5 utility.

Fig. 3.11 Compiling MD5 programs

```
F:\chap03>gcc -o mddriver -D MD=5 mddriver.c md5.c

F:\chap03>mddriver -sabc
MD5 ("abc") = 900150983cd24fb0d6963f7d28e17f72

F:\chap03>mddriver -s"message digest"
MD5 ("message digest") =
f96b697d7cb7938d525a2f31aaf161d0

F:\chap03>mddriver -sjohnsmith
MD5 ("johnsmith") =
cd4388c0c62e65ac8b99e3ec49fd9409

F:\chap03>
```

Fig. 3.12 Testing the MD5 utility

```
F:\chap03>mddriver -x
MD5 test suite:
MD5 ("") = d41d8cd98f00b204e9800998ecf8427e
MD5 ("a") = 0cc175b9c0f1b6a831c399e269772661
MD5 ("abc") = 900150983cd24fb0d6963f7d28e17f72
MD5 ("message digest") =
f96b697d7cb7938d525a2f31aaf161d0
MD5 ("abcdefghijklmnopqrstuvwxyz") =
c3fcd3d76192e4007dfb496cca67e13b
MD5 ("ABCDEFGHIJKLMNOPQRSTUVWXYZabcdefghijklmnopq
rstuvwxyz0123456789") = d174ab98d277d9f5a5611c2c9f419d9f
MD5 ("12345678901234567890123456789012345678901234
567890123456789012345678901234567890") =
57edf4a22be3c955ac49da2e2107b67a

F:\chap03>
```

In fact, the following are the standard testing results to verify an MDS
implementation known as the 'MDS test suite':

```
MD5 test suite:
MD5 ("") = d41d8cd98f00b204e9800998ecf8427e
MD5 ("a") = 0cc175b9c0f1b6a831c399e269772661
MD5 ("abc") = 900150983cd24fb0d6963f7d28e17f72
MD5 ("message digest") = f96b697d7cb7938d525a2f31aaf161d0
MD5 ("abcdefghijklmnopqrstuvwxyz") = c3fcd3d76192e4007dfb496cca67e13b
MD5 ("ABCDEFGHIJKLMNOPQRSTUVWXYZabcdefghijklmnopqrstuvwxyz0123456789")
= d174ab98d277d9f5a5611c2c9f419d9f
```

```
MD5 ("1234567890123456789012345678901234567890123456
789012345678901234567890") = 57edf4a22be3c955ac49da2e2107b67a
```

Now you have a utility that can produce MD5 strings. The utility `mddriver` also includes a directive '-s' to generate an MD5 string from a command line. For example, you can use the following command to generate an MD5 string 'johnsmith':

```
mddriver -sjohnsmith
```

You will have the following output on your screen (see Figure 3.11):

```
MD5 ("johnsmith") = cd4388c0c62e65ac8b99e3ec49fd9409
```

This result can be verified easily using the Web page `ex03-05.htm`. Don't put any empty spaces between your text and the directive -s above. If you do, the utility will generate an MD5 string based on your text with an empty space. The result will be a completely different MD5 string.

Application of MD5 for Web site protection and authentication has been discussed in Chapter 2. In fact, these are just one kind of application of `Crypt()` and MD5. Some other popular applications are introduced in the next section.

3.4 Applications of message digests and the `md5Crypt` password scheme

3.4.1 The MD5 checksum and document signatures

A popular application of the MD5 string is to obtain the digital signature of a document or file. If you run the MD utility `mddriver` above without any directive then it will assume the input is a file and try to produce an MD string of the file contents.

For example, if you have written a letter with your favourite editor to your personal banker as shown in example banker.txt, when you use the MD utility and issue the command

```
mddriver banker.txt
```

you will obtain the MD5 string (or checksum) below:

```
MD5 (banker.txt) = 884b41c1978ad78941a0d7beceae2432
```

This MD5 string can be used as a signature (or checksum) for your letter. When you send the letter and checksum to the banker, your banker will be able to use `mddriver`, or any other MD5 program, to ascertain whether the letter has been altered in any way.

```
Example: banker.txt - a letter to a banker

Dear Mr. John Brown (personal banker)

I would like to transfer US$2500 from my account:

    Bank Name:      XXX Bank
    Account Name:   John Smith
    Account Number: 8765-4321

to the following charity account:

    Bank Name:      XXX Bank
    Account Name:   AAA Children Charity
    Account Number: 1234-5678

Regards
John Smith
```

If someone had altered the receiving account name and number to

```
Account Name:   ABC Children Charity
Account Number: 8551-4231
```

the MD5 string of the altered letter would turn out to be

```
MD5 (banker.txt) = 76ad89d3f76274383685cbf3df34ee6f
```

From this example, you can see that even a minor change in the contents would produce a completely different MD5 string. The MD5 string is, in fact, a 'digest' of a document or file and can be used as signature in almost all file formats. MD5 strings are popular on the Web and are known as the MD5 checksum.

If you have used email, chances are that you are already familiar with email attachments. Another popular use of MD5 checksums is to protect attachments against alterations.

Suppose you have an important letter (tender.txt) containing the tendering value of a project. You may want to send this letter to your boss with some kind of protection.

```
Example: tender.txt - an important business letter

Dear Mr. John Brown

The following is the tendering value recommended by our team

  Project Name:        MMV-Airport Security Project
  Recommended Value:   US$:xxxxxxx

Good Luck!

Evaluation Team Manager
John Smith
```

One popular method can be described as follows.

Step 1 Compress the letter, tender.txt, using PkZip/WinZip with a password. The result is a zip file, tender.zip.

Step 2 Obtain the MD5 checksum on the zip file. For example

```
MD5 (tender.zip) = 6a8b17809561c33b0d92b0322f1a2633
```

Step 3 Write an email to the receiver with the checksum and send the zip file, tender.zip, as attachment or, preferably, through a separate channel.

Although the PkZip/WinZip encryption in step 1 is not very sophisticated, it provides at least a minimal protection. Message security and encryption are important subjects and will be discussed in Chapter 4. The MD5 checksum makes sure that no one has altered the zip file and reduces the chances for attack by intruders, to a certain degree. A screenshot is shown in Figure 3.13.

Since MD5 strings can be considered as document (or file) signatures against modification, they are used almost universally on the Web to protect the downloading of documents, files and programs against virus infection and alteration.

Fig. 3.13 Protecting an attachment

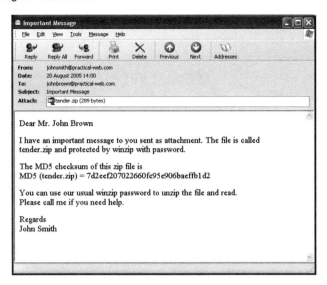

3.4.2   Protecting downloads against viruses and alterations

Another use of the MD5 checksum on the Web is to protect download files from virus infection and alteration. The idea is simple – suppose you have the following files on your site, or page, ready for someone to download

- an executable file   – `mddriver.exe`

- digest authentication – `rfc2617.txt`

- MD5 source package – `mddriver.c, md5.c, md5.h, global.h`

- a GIF image file   – `logo.gif`

You can run PkZip/WinZip to zip all these files with or without passwords depending on your requirement. The next step is to obtain the MD5 signature of each zip file using the MD utility mddriver developed in the last section. The result is listed in Table 3.1.

Table 3.1 MD5 checksum of some downloadable files

Original file	Zip file	MD5 checksum of the zip file
`mddriver.exe`	`mddriver.zip`	`3c4fddb6ab5927ef9f90d063303f6174`
`rfc2617.txt`	`rfc2617.zip`	`9f63664ade60b574d8084f437ff74207`
MD5 package	`md5.zip`	`da17a409a64a5732dc08e00a382b2a48`
`logo.gif`	`logo.zip`	`32d4f587946231a685c949a604b074f3`

Now, you can develop a simple page to display the checksums and allow the download operation by clicking on the files. Consider the main body part of the page ex03-06.htm.

Example: ex03-06.htm – Protect download files against virus infection and alteration

```
 1: <style>
 2:    .txtSt{font-family:arial;font-weight:bold; text-align:left;
 3:       font-size:18pt;color:#ffff00}</style>
 4: <body style="background:#000088;text-align:center" class="txtSt">
 5: <div style="text-align:center">
 6:    A Page To Protect Downloadable Files<br />
 7:    From Viruses And Alterations
 8:    <img src="line1.gif" style="width:630px;
          height:7px" /><br /></div>
 9:    <table class="txtSt" cellspacing="10">
10:    <tr><td colspan="2" style="text-align:left">
11:       You are welcome to download the following files. <br />
12:       Please check the MD5 signature (or MD5 CheckSum) <br />
13:       against viruses and alterations: <br /><br /> </td></tr>
14:    <tr><td>File Name</td><td>MD5 Signature of Zip File</td></tr>
15:    <tr><td><a href="mddriver.zip"
             style="color: #00ff00">mddriver.exe</a>
16:       </td><td>3c4fddb6ab5927ef9f90d063303f6174</td></tr>
17:    <tr><td><a href="rfc2617.zip"
             style="color:#00ff00">Digest Auth.</a>
18:       </td><td>9f63664ade60b574d8084f437ff74207</td></tr>
19:    <tr><td><a href="md5.zip" style="color:#00ff00">MD5 Package</a>
20:       </td><td>da17a409a64a5732dc08e00a382b2a48</td></tr>
21:    <tr><td><a href="logo.zip" style="color:#00ff00">Logo
             Picture</a>
22:       </td><td>32d4f587946231a685c949a604b074f3</td></tr>
23:    </table>
24: </body>
```

This is a simple page to list all the zip files for downloading. The MD5 strings of the zip files are displayed alongside each file. A screenshot of this example is shown in Figure 3.14.

The user can double click any file to download it. Once the file is on the user's hard disk, the user can obtain an MD5 string of the file with any MD5 utility. If the string generated by the user matches the MD5 string listed in the page, the file is intact. Any modification of the zip file will result in a different MD5 checksum.

Fig. 3.14 Protection against virus and alteration

Another important application of MD5 is the development of the so-called 'md5Crypt' password scheme. UNIX BSD uses this password scheme to identify users, and Apache uses it worldwide in the Web environment.

3.4.3 The md5Crypt password algorithm

Recall from Section 2.2.2 that when you use the Apache utility htpasswd to generate encrypted passwords, you will get different results depending on what kind of Apache you are using. For example, the following commands

```
htpasswd -cb htpass.wd root peter
htpasswd -b htpass.wd cs006 arthur
htpasswd -b htpass.wd cs005 rody
htpasswd -b htpass.wd cs001 john
```

will produce one set of results on Apache for UNIX/LINUX and another set on Apache for Windows, as shown below

Apache For UNIX/LINUX	Apache For Windows
root:qwUz5jttxGJNk	root:$apr1$VY2.....$FDbVgTbR2jd0QpO.YTtXR.
cs006:afMas1RMTeywU	cs006:$apr1$VY2.....$UbAC7eP/worBScsaWHhic/
cs005:2kli0DkibHn/o	cs005:$apr1$VY2.....$ejyqMp39hLhRN18B9Nixv/
cs001:5t0ckoMheqAT6	cs001:$apr1$VY2.....$WCJvn0hwVZECppFKp4M0p1

If you are using Apache for UNIX/LINUX, the default password encryption is `Crypt()`, which has been covered in earlier sections in this chapter.

Apache for Windows uses a different password encryption, called `md5crypt`, and this is why the results are different. If you examine the `md5crypt` password closely, you will find that the Apache for Windows version contains the following fields and explanations:

```
root:$apr1$VY2.....$FDbVgTbR2jd0QpO.YTtXR.
```

Account name:	`root`	
Magic string:	`$apr1$`	(6 characters)
Salt:	`VY2.....`	(8 characters)
Encrypted password:	`FDbVgTbR2jd0QpO.YTtXR.`	(22 characters)

In this case, the magic string (a fixed string), salt (8-character) and the plaintext password 'peter' will produce the `md5crypt` encrypted password 'FDbVgTbR2jd0QpO.YTtXR.' The salt and plaintext password are user defined.

As soon as the MD5 algorithm became available and spread among the computing community, the UNIX development quickly adopted the scheme and used it to derive a more secure password encryption, known as `md5crypt`.

The original UNIX `md5crypt` algorithm used the magic string as '1' and still widely uses that today. Apache adopted the same algorithm, but with a different magic string, '$apr1$'. The UNIX `md5crypt` algorithm can be described in a series of steps.

Step 1 Input and output specifications

Three specific variables are used and specified as follows:

■ `magic:`   the magic string is 1

■ `password:` the input plaintext password as a byte string

■ `salt:`   user-input character string (maximum 8 characters).
            If the input is less than 8 characters, pad with symbol '.'.
            e.g. if input ="VY2" → salt ="VY2....."

The output is encoded using the following character set:

```
charSet = "./0123456789ABCDEFGHIJKLMNOPQRSTUVWXYZabcdefghijklmnopqrstuvwxyz"
```

This set is the same as that used by the UNIX `Crypt()` algorithm.

Step 2 Computing the md5Crypt string

First, the MD5 of the following combined string is computed:

```
foo = MD5(password + salt + password);
```

The MD5 result, `foo`, is represented as a 16-byte string and each byte is 8 bits. Next, some characters of `foo` are added to the end of 'password+1+salt',

```
bar = password + "$1$" + salt + extend(foo, length(password));
```

The function `extend(str, len)` is defined by

```
extend(str, len) is str repeated to fill len bytes.
```

If the value of `len` is bigger than `length(str)`, multiple `str` characters are added. The next process is to add either `charCode(0)`, or the first character of the password, to the end of the variable `bar`. More precisely, we have the pseudo-code below:

```
i = length(password);
while (i > 0) {
   if (i mod 2 != 0)    bar = bar + charCode(0);
      else              bar = bar + password[0];
   i = i >>> 1;
}
```

There is no obvious reason why this process is necessary. In the original md5Crypt documentation, they quote 'yes, this makes absolutely no sense'. The final md5Crypt string is obtained by iterating 1000 repetitions of MD5 as follows.

```
baz = MD5(bar);
i = 0;
while (i < 1000) {
   baz = MD5(baz + ifnz(i mod 3,salt) + ifnz(i mod 7,password) +
           password);
   i++;
   baz = MD5(password + ifnz(i mod 3,salt) + ifnz(i mod 7,password) + baz);
   i++;
}
```

where the function `ifnz(i,s)` is defined by

```
ifnz(i, s)  = "",    if i == 0
            = s,     otherwise
```

The main purpose of these 1000 iterations is to slow down the execution and hence make the brute-force or dictionary attack a bit more time-consuming. Now, the variable `baz` contains the md5Crypt encrypted password and can be formatted.

Step 3 Formatting the `md5Crypt` string output

The output string is formatted by the following pseudo-code.

```
output = "$1$" + salt + "$" +
        encode(                      baz[12]        & 0x3F ) +
        encode((baz[12] >>> 6) | ((baz[ 6] << 2) & 0x3F)) +
        encode((baz[ 6] >>> 4) | ((baz[ 0] << 4) & 0x3F)) +
        encode( baz[ 0] >>> 2                      ) +
        encode(                      baz[13]        & 0x3F ) +
        encode((baz[13] >>> 6) | ((baz[ 7] << 2) & 0x3F)) +
        encode((baz[ 7] >>> 4) | ((baz[ 1] << 4) & 0x3F)) +
        encode( baz[ 1] >>> 2                      ) +
        encode(                      baz[14]        & 0x3F ) +
        encode((baz[14] >>> 6) | ((baz[ 8] << 2) & 0x3F)) +
        encode((baz[ 8] >>> 4) | ((baz[ 2] << 4) & 0x3F)) +
        encode( baz[ 2] >>> 2                      ) +
        encode(                      baz[15]        & 0x3F ) +
        encode((baz[15] >>> 6) | ((baz[ 9] << 2) & 0x3F)) +
        encode((baz[ 9] >>> 4) | ((baz[ 3] << 4) & 0x3F)) +
        encode( baz[ 3] >>> 2                      ) +
        encode(                      baz[ 5]        & 0x3F ) +
        encode((baz[ 5] >>> 6) | ((baz[10] << 2) & 0x3F)) +
        encode((baz[10] >>> 4) | ((baz[ 4] << 4) & 0x3F)) +
        encode( baz[ 4] >>> 2                      ) +
        encode(                      baz[11]        & 0x3F ) +
        encode( baz[11] >>> 6                      );
```

where the function `encode(x)` converts the character x to the character set in Step 1,

```
encode(x) = charSet[x]
```

The value `0x3F` guarantees that the output is 6 bits. Since a total of 22 `encode()` functions are called, the encrypted password contains 22 characters. If you input `salt="VY2"` and `password="peter"`, the output string from this `md5Crypt` algorithm would be

```
output = "$1$VY2.....$UshwCSPgNFKSZYTETpoaM/"
```

Although this algorithm is 'plain weird', as commented by the original developers, it is supported worldwide by the Web and crypto-community. More and more security applications have used this password scheme in recent years. One advantage is that you can create your own scheme by just changing the magic string. If you change the magic string to `magic="$apr1$"`, the output string above turns out to be

```
output = "$apr1$VY2.....$FDbVgTbR2jd0Qp0.YTtXR."
```

This string is known as the Apache `md5Crypt` password. Let's see how to implement this generic algorithm on the Web.

3.4.4 Generating UNIX and Apache `md5Crypt` passwords

As described in the previous section, the `md5Crypt` algorithm uses MD5 heavily. To implement it on the Web you first make a copy of MD5 (or `ex03-05.js`) and call it `ex03-07.js`. The original implementation of MD5, or the `md5_raw()` function, returns four 32-bit words. In order to convert them to a 16-byte string, as required by `md5Crypt`, a function is added to the end of `ex03-07.js`.

```
Example: ex03-07.js - Implementation of md5Crypt on the Web    (Part I)

136: function md5_byteStr(xx, llen)
137: {
138:   var tmp1 = new Array();
139:   var tmp2 = "",ii,jj;
140:   tmp1 = md5_raw(xx,llen);
141:   for (ii=0; ii < 4; ii++) {
142:    for (jj=0; jj < 4; jj++) {
143:      tmp2 +=String.fromCharCode((tmp1[ii] >> (jj*8)) & 0xff);
144:    }
145:   }
146:   return tmp2;
147: }
148:
```

This script contains one function, namely `md5_byteStr()`. When the function `md5_raw()` is called in line 140, the returned variable, `tmp1`, is an array of four elements, each being a 32-bit word. The double for-loops in lines 141–145 convert `tmp1` into a string `tmp2`. This string has 16 characters and each is represented by 1 byte (or 8 bits). With this MD5 byte string, the string manipulation as described in `md5Crypt` algorithm can be performed. The second part of the implementation is listed in part II of `ex03-07.js`.

This script contains the partial coding of the function `md5Crypt_core()`. This function takes three variables, namely `pw`, `salt` and `magic`, and will return the `md5Crypt` password to the function caller. Lines 153–163 perform the computation of the following two statements mentioned in the `md5Crypt` algorithm:

```
final= MD5(password + salt + password);
ctx  = password + "$1$" + salt + extend(final, length(password));
```

Since the variable `final` is a string of 16 characters (or bytes), the `extend()` function can be implemented as a for-loop in lines 158–163. The while-loop in lines 165–172 appends either `charCode(0)` or the first character of the password at the end of `ctx`. The resulting `ctx` is used to compute another MD5 string, `final`, as illustrated in line 173. The statements in lines 175–188 convert the following pseudo-code of the algorithm into a single for-loop:

Example: Continuation of ex03-07.js – md5Crypt algorithm   (Part II)

```
149: function md5Crypt_core(pw, salt, magic)
150: {
151:   var final="", pwl, pl, tmp1, i, ctx, ctx1, passwd;
152:
153:   tmp1 = pw + salt + pw;
154:   final = md5_byteStr(strToBin(tmp1), tmp1.length * 8);
155:
156:   ctx = pw + magic + salt;
157:   pwl = pw.length;
158:   for (pl = pwl; pl >0 ; pl = pl -16) {
159:       if (pl > 16)
160:           ctx = ctx + final.substring(0,16);
161:       else
162:         ctx = ctx + final.substring(0,pl);
163:   }
164:
165:   i= pwl;
166:   while ( i > 0) {
167:     if (i & 1)
168:           ctx = ctx + String.fromCharCode(0);
169:     else
170:           ctx = ctx + pw.charAt(0);
171:     i = i >>> 1;
172:   }
173:   final = md5_byteStr(strToBin(ctx), ctx.length * 8);
174:
175:   for( i=0; i< 1000;i++) {
176:     ctx1 = ""
177:     if (i & 1)
178:       ctx1 = ctx1 + pw;
179:     else
180:       ctx1 = ctx1 + final.substring(0,16);
181:     if (i % 3) ctx1 = ctx1 + salt;
182:     if (i % 7) ctx1 = ctx1 + pw;
183:     if (i & 1)
184:       ctx1 = ctx1 + final.substring(0,16);
185:     else
186:       ctx1 = ctx1 + pw;
187:       final = md5_byteStr(strToBin(ctx1), ctx1.length * 8);
188:   }
189:
```

```
   i = 0;
   while (i < 1000) {
      final = MD5(final + ifnz(i mod 3,salt) + ifnz(i mod 7,password) +
            password);
      i++;
      final = MD5(password + ifnz(i mod 3,salt) + ifnz(i mod 7,password)
            + final);
      i++;
   }
```

To combine the two calculations above, two if-else statements are used in lines 177–180 and 183–186. The function `ifnz()` in the algorithm is also implemented by a conditional-if statement. For example, the function `ifnz(i mod 3,salt)` can be implemented by (line 181)

```
   if (i % 3) ctx1 = ctx1 + salt;
```

At the end of the for-loop, variable `final` contains the md5Crypt string. This string can be formatted into 22 characters and output by part III of ex03-07.js.

```
Example: Continuation of ex03-07.js - md5Crypt algorithm   (Part III)

190:   passwd = "";
191:   passwd += to64((final.charCodeAt(0) << 16)|
                     (final.charCodeAt(6) << 8) |
192:                  (final.charCodeAt(12)), 4);
193:   passwd += to64((final.charCodeAt(1) << 16)|
                     (final.charCodeAt(7) << 8) |
194:                  (final.charCodeAt(13)), 4);
195:   passwd += to64((final.charCodeAt(2) << 16)|
                     (final.charCodeAt(8) << 8) |
196:                  (final.charCodeAt(14)), 4);
197:   passwd += to64((final.charCodeAt(3) << 16)|
                     (final.charCodeAt(9) << 8) |
198:                  (final.charCodeAt(15)), 4);
199:   passwd += to64((final.charCodeAt(4) << 16)|
                     (final.charCodeAt(10) << 8)|
200:                  (final.charCodeAt(5)), 4);
201:   passwd += to64((final.charCodeAt(11)), 2)
202:
203:   return magic + salt + "$" + passwd;
204: }
205:
206: var ITOA64 = "./0123456789ABCDEFGHIJKLMNOPQRSTUVWXYZ"+
207:              "abcdefghijklmnopqrstuvwxyz";
```

```
208: function to64 (v, n)
209: {
210:    var ret = "";
211:    while (n - 1 >= 0) {
212:       n = n - 1;
213:       ret = ret + ITOA64.charAt(v & 0x3f);
214:       v = v >> 6;
215:    }
216:    return ret;
217: }
218:
```

Lines 190–204 format the output according to Step 3 of the algorithm. Consider the following four statements.

```
encode(                       final[12]     & 0x3F ) +
encode((final[12] >>> 6) | ((final[ 6] << 2) & 0x3F)) +
encode((final[ 6] >>> 4) | ((final[ 0] << 4) & 0x3F)) +
encode( final[ 0] >>> 2                       ) +
```

The operation of these four statements is equivalent to

■ concatenating the 8-bit characters final[0], final[6] and final[12] to form a 24-bit value, i.e. final[0]+final[6]+final[12];

■ outputting this 24-bit value as four 6-bit characters.

This operation is the same as the statement in lines 191–192. The actual conversion function is defined by to64() in lines 206–217. The statements in lines 190–201 convert the MD5 string final into 22 6-bit characters stored in variable passwd. Finally, the md5Crypt result is returned by the statement (line 203)

```
return magic + salt + "$" + passwd;
```

With the core function md5_Cryptcore(), an md5Crypt password for UNIX and Apache can be generated by the two interface functions given in part IV of ex03-07.js.

Example: Continuation of ex03-07.js – md5Crypt algorithm   (Part IV)

```
219: function md5Crypt_UNIX(pw,salt)
220: {
221:    var saltV="";
222:    saltV = salt + ".........";
223:    saltV = saltV.substring(0,8);
224:    return md5Crypt_core(pw,saltV,"$1$");
225: }
```

```
226:
227: function md5Crypt_Apache(pw,salt)
228: {
229:   var saltV="";
230:   saltV = salt + "........";
231:   saltV = saltV.substring(0,8);
232:   return md5Crypt_core(pw,saltV,"$apr1$");
233: }
```

The function `md5Crypt_UNIX()` takes the variables `pw` and `salt` as input. The statement in line 222 appends an 8-character string `"........"` to the variable `salt`. After cutting the first eight characters of `salt`, this variable is in the format required by the algorithm. Calling the function `md5Crypt_core()` with magic string `"$1$"` (line 224) would generate and return the UNIX `md5Crypt` password. Similarly, the function `md5Crypt_Apache()` would generate and return the Apache `md5Crypt` password.

For a testing example, consider the body section of `ex03-07.htm`.

```
Example: ex03-07.htm

 1: <style>
 2:   .butSt{font-size:16pt;width:250px;height:40px;
 3:           font-weight:bold;background:#dddddd;color:#ff0000}
 4:   .radSt{font-size:16pt;width:35px;height:30px;
 5:           font-weight:bold;background:#88ff88;color:#ff0000}
 6: </style>
 7: <body style="font-family:arial;font-size:26pt;text-align:center;
 8:         background:#000088;color:#ffff00">
 9:   Generating md5Crypt Password<br />
10:   <img alt="pic" src="line1.gif" height="7" width="650" /><br />
11:
12: <table style="font-size:18pt" cellspacing="10" align="center">
13:   <tr><td colspan="3"><br />Enter The Password: </td></tr>
14:   <tr><td colspan="3"><textarea rows="3" cols="40" id="in_mesg"
15:         style="width:570px;height:50px;font-size:16pt;
16:         font-weight:bold;background:#dddddd"></textarea></td></tr>
17:   <tr><td>Enter The Salt</td>
18:       <td colspan=2><input type="text" id="in_salt"
19:         style="width:150px;height:40px;font-size:16pt;
20:         font-weight:bold;background:#dddddd" /></td></tr>
```

```
21:  <tr><td style="width:180px;text-align:left">
22:      <input type="radio" checked id="b_rad" name="b_rad"
        class="radSt" />
23:      Apache</td>
24:      <td style="width:180px;text-align:left">
25:      <input type="radio" id="b_rad" name="b_rad" class="radSt" />
26:      UNIX</td>
27:      <td style="width:180px;text-align:left">
28:       <input size="20" type="button" class="butSt"
          style="width:100px"
29:       value="OK" onclick="get_md5Crypt()" /></td></tr>
30:  <tr><td colspan="3">The md5Crypt Password Is: </td></tr>
31:  <tr><td colspan="3">
32:    <textarea rows="5" cols="40" id="out_mesg" readonly
33:    style="width:570px;height:50px;font-size:16pt;
34:    font-weight:bold;background:#ccffcc"></textarea></td></tr>
35:  </table>
36:  <script src="ex03-07.js"></script>
37:  <script>
38:  function get_md5Crypt()
39:  {
40:    var llV, message="", llst="";
41:    llV = document.getElementsByName("b_rad");
42:    if (llV.item(0).checked) {
43:        password = document.getElementById("in_mesg").value;
44:        salt    = document.getElementById("in_salt").value;
45:        llst    = md5Crypt_apache(password,salt);
46:        document.getElementById("out_mesg").value = llst;
47:    }
48:    if (llV.item(1).checked) {
49:        password = document.getElementById("in_mesg").value;
50:        salt    = document.getElementById("in_salt").value;
51:        llst    = md5Crypt_UNIX(password,salt);
52:        document.getElementById("out_mesg").value = llst;
53:    }
54:  }
55:  </script>
56:  </body>
```

This is a simple test page. The XHTML codes in lines 1–35 contain two text areas, one text box, two radio buttons and one OK button. The text area in lines 14–16 allows a user to enter the password. The salt can be entered in the text box in lines 18–20. The two radio buttons defined in lines 22–26 represent the two options

'Apache' and 'UNIX'. Only one radio button can be selected. When the OK button is clicked, the function get_md5Crypt() is activated and the corresponding md5Crypt password will be displayed in the read-only text area specified in lines 32–34.

The details of the function get_md5Crypt() are given in lines 38–55. First, the options of the radio buttons are captured by the statement in line 41. If the 'Apache' radio button is checked, password and salt are captured in lines 43–44. The function call in line 45 gets the Apache md5Crypt password in llst. This password is displayed by the statement in line 46. Similarly, if the 'UNIX' radio button is checked, the function md5Crypt_UNIX() function gets the UNIX md5Crypt password. This password will be output by the statement in line 52. Screenshots of this example in action are shown in Figures 3.15 and 3.16.

Fig. 3.15   Apache md5Crypt password

Fig. 3.16 UNIX md5Crypt password

3.5 The secure hash algorithm

3.5.1 What is SHA?

The secure hash algorithm, SHA, is basically a family of algorithms to produce hash values for security purposes. It was designed by the National Security Agency (NSA) and promoted by the National Institute of Standards and Technology (NIST). The first specification of the algorithm was published in 1993 and known as the Federal Information Processing Standards (FIPS-180). Due to a security flaw, the first version of SHA (SHA-0) was withdrawn soon after its publication. A much improved version was published in 1995, as FIPS 180-1, and is commonly known as SHA-1 today.

The idea of SHA was based on the message digest (MD4) developed by Ronald L. Rivest in MIT, and therefore they share the same structure and application as message digest. SHA-1 produces a 160-bit digest from a message with a maximum size of 2^{64} bits and is considered more secure than MD5. For a simple example, the results of performing MD5 and SHA-1 on the string 'abc' are

```
md5("abc")  = "900150983cd24fb0d6963f7d28e17f72"
sha1("abc") = "a9993e364706816aba3e25717850c26c9cd0d89d"
```

These digests are represented in hexadecimal format. As you can see, the digest of SHA-1 is 8 hexadecimal characters (or 32 bits) longer. Recall that the MD5 algorithm returns four 32-bit words to form a 128-bit digest. For SHA-1, the algorithm returns five 32-bit words, so is a 160-bit hash.

Based on SHA-1, NIST has published three more versions, each with longer digests. They are named according to their digest lengths (in bits): SHA-256, SHA-384 and SHA-512. Together with SHA-1, the SHA family was released as an official standard in 2002. Of all those SHA algorithms, only SHA-1 has been examined very closely by the cryptographic community and has proved to be secure. For this reason, SHA-1 has had the worldwide support of security sectors. In practice, the secure hash algorithm is, in general, referred to as SHA-1.

3.5.2 The SHA-1 algorithm

The SHA-1 algorithm originally came from MD4 and therefore has a similar structure to MD5. As you will see in this section, the algorithm itself is similar to MD5 as described in Section 3.3.2. The 160-bit hash provides more security and the execution is at the same time more expansive.

The SHA-1 algorithm takes a message of arbitrary length as input and produces an output of a 160-bit hash or message digest. Suppose we have a b-bit message as input. The number b is an arbitrary non-negative integer and every bit can be represented by the sequence

$$m\{0\}, m\{1\}, \ldots, m\{b-1\}$$

In normal circumstances, a character can be represented by an 8-bit ASCII sequence. Like MD5, the SHA-1 algorithm can be described by three steps.

Step 1 Appending, padding bits and add length

This step is the same as that for MD5 (Section 3.3.2). The message sequence is padded and extended by a bit '1' and an optional sequence of bit '0' so that congruence to 448 modulo 512 is achieved. At the end of the padding, a 64-bit representation of b is appended as two 32-bit words with the low-order word first. This means that the message digest algorithm can digest a message of 2^{64} length in terms of bits. The result of the message is an exact multiple of 512 bits so that it can be represented as an exact multiple of 16 (32-bit) words. We can store the message in terms of words, and each word is a 32-bit quantity. Now, let the sequence (or array)

$$M[0], M[1], \ldots, M[N-1]$$

denote the padded and extended plaintext in 32-bit words, where N is a multiple of 16.

Step 2 Defining data and functions for SHA-1

To process the message, a number of predefined constants and functions are specified. First, five constants, namely $h0, h1, h2, h3$ and $h4$, are defined:

$h0 = 0x67452301$ $h1 = 0xefcdab89$ $h2 = 0x98badcfe$

$h3 = 0x10325476$ $h4 = 0xc3d2e1f0$

The algorithm also uses 80 constants in four equal intervals,

$$k_i = \begin{cases} 0x5a827999 & 0 \leq i \leq 19 \\ 0x6ed9eba1 & 20 \leq i \leq 39 \\ 0x8f1bbcdc & 40 \leq i \leq 59 \\ 0xca62c1d6 & 60 \leq i \leq 79 \end{cases}$$

Each value is a 32-bit integer. For each interval i above, the corresponding function $f_i(b, c, d)$ is defined:

$$f_i(b, c, d) = \begin{cases} (b \text{ and } c) \text{ or } ((\sim b) \text{ and } d) & 0 \leq i \leq 19 \\ b \text{ xor } c \text{ xor } d & 20 \leq i \leq 39 \\ (b \text{ and } c) \text{ or } (b \text{ and } d) \text{ or } (c \text{ or } d) & 40 \leq i \leq 59 \\ b \text{ xor } c \text{ xor } d & 60 \leq i \leq 79 \end{cases}$$

where the input b, c and d are 32-bit values. All the bitwise operations inside the function are performed as 32 bits. Technically, 80 functions are specified. In practice, constants k_i and functions $f_i(b, c, d)$ are implemented as functions $k(i)$ and $f(i, b, c, d)$, putting the variable i as the argument.

Step 3 Processing a message to produce a digest

Given a padded and extended sequence $M[0]$, $M[1]$, . . . , $M[N-1]$ as described in Step 1, the 160-bit digested string can be calculated by the following pseudo-code.

```
Example: The Pseudo-code of SHA-1 - Processing a message to produce
a digest

 1: a = h0 = 0x67452301
 2: b = h1 = 0xEFCDAB89
 3: c = h2 = 0x98BADCFE
 4: d = h3 = 0x10325476
 5: e = h4 = 0xC3D2E1F0
 6:
 7: for (i=0;i<length(M) i+=16)
 8:      aa = a
 9:      bb = b
10:      cc = c
11:      dd = d
12:      ee = e
13:
14:      for (j=0;j<80;i++)
15:           if (j < 16)
16:                w[j] = M[i+j]
17:           else
18:                w[j] = ( w[j-3] xor w[j-8] xor w[j-14] xor
                          w[j-16] ) <<<- 1
19:           end-if
20:
21:           temp = (a <<<- 5) + f(j,b,c,d) + e + k(j) + w[j]
22:           e = d
23:           d = c
24:           c = b <<<- 30
25:           b = a
26:           a = temp
27:      end-for
28:
29:      a = aa + a
30:      b = bb + b
```

```
31:    c = cc + c
32:    d = dd + d
33:    e = ee + e
34: end-for
```

Lines 1–5 specify the five predefined constants k_i into variables a, b, c, d and e. The pseudo-code for-loop in lines 7–34 processes the entire message M and produces the 160-bit hash. The input message M is digested into a chunk of 16 elements (512-bit) a time. The idea is to extend the 16 elements of M[] into 80 elements.

The first 16 elements of M[] are copied into array w[0]...w[15] at line 16 and are processed by the statements in lines 21–26 with function f(j,b,c,d) and constant k(j). The processed results are stored in variables a, b, c, d and e. The second set of elements w[16]...w[79] are obtained by the statement in line 18 and processed by the same operations in lines 21–26. The processed results are stored in a, b, c, d and e in lines 29–33. When the for-loop in lines 7–34 is exhausted, the 32-bit variables a, b, c, d and e contain the digest of the entire message M[] and return together as a 160-bit hash.

The operation x <<<- s used in the algorithm is specified by the following bitwise shift:

```
x <<<- s = (((x) << (s)) | ((x) >>> (32-(s)))))
```

which is equivalent to left-rotating x by s. Now, let's see how to implement this SHA-1 algorithm on the Web.

3.5.3   Implementation of SHA-1 on the Web

From the previous section, you can see that the algorithmic structure of SHA-1 is similar to MD5. Apart from the details of constants and functions, both algorithms have the same implementation steps. Therefore the implementation presented here is also parallel to ex03-05.js. First, we need to define all the constants and functions used in the SHA-1 algorithm. Consider the script fragment in part I of ex03-08.js.

Example: ex03-08.js – Implementation of the SHA-1 digest   (Part I)

```
1: function fun_ft(t, b, c, d)
2: {
3:    if(t < 20) return (b & c) | ((~b) & d);
4:    if(t < 40) return b ^ c ^ d;
5:    if(t < 60) return (b & c) | (b & d) | (c & d);
6:    return b ^ c ^ d;
7: }
```

```
 8:
 9: function const_kt(t)
10: {
11:   if(t < 20) return 0x5A827999;
12:   if(t < 40) return 0x6ED9EBA1;
13:   if(t < 60) return 0x8F1BBCDC;
14:   return 0xCA62C1D6;
15: }
16:
17: function bit32_add(x, y)
18: {
19:   var low = (x & 0xffff) + (y & 0xffff);
20:   var hig = (x >> 16) + (y >> 16) + (low >> 16);
21:   return (hig << 16) | (low & 0xffff);
22: }
23:
24: function rot_l(val, s)
25: {
26:   return (val << s) | (val >>> (32 - s));
27: }
28:
```

This script fragment defines all the 80 constants and functions used by the SHA-1 algorithm. Function `fun_ft(t,b,c,d)` in lines 1–7 is the same as the function `fi(b,c,d)` described in Step 2 of Section 3.5.2. For example, if the parameter `t` has a value $0 \le t \le 19$, the statement in line 3 will be executed and return the value '(b&c) | ((~b)&d)' to the caller. Similarly, the constants used in the algorithm are specified in lines 9–15. Since SHA-1 uses 32-bit addition and left-rotation functions, these are defined in lines 17–27.

To generate the SHA-1 digest, consider part II of script `ex03-08.js`.

```
Example: Continuation of ex03-08.js - SHA-1 digest          (Part II)

29: function sha1_raw(x, len)
30: {
31:   /* append padding */
32:   x[len >> 5] |= 0x80 << (24 - len % 32);
33:   x[((len + 64 >> 9) << 4) + 15] = len;
34:
35:   var w = Array(80);
36:   var a=0x67452301, b=0xefcdab89, c=0x98badcfe, d=0x10325476,
         e=0xc3d2e1f0;
37:
```

```
38:  for(var i = 0; i < x.length; i += 16) {
39:      var aa = a, bb = b, cc = c, dd = d, ee = e;
40:      for(var j = 0; j < 80; j++) {
41:        if(j < 16) w[j] = x[i + j];
42:        else      w[j] = rot_l( w[j-3] ^ w[j-8] ^ w[j-14] ^
                      w[j-16], 1);
43:
44:        t = bit32_add( bit32_add(rot_l(a, 5), fun_ft(j, b, c, d)),
45:                       bit32_add(bit32_add(e, w[j]), const_kt(j)));
46:        e = d;
47:        d = c;
48:        c = rot_l(b, 30);
49:        b = a;
50:        a = t;
51:      }
52:      a = bit32_add(a, aa);
53:      b = bit32_add(b, bb);
54:      c = bit32_add(c, cc);
55:      d = bit32_add(d, dd);
56:      e = bit32_add(e, ee);
57:  }
58:  return Array(a, b, c, d, e);
59: }
60:
```

This script fragment contains a function called sha1_raw() with two input arguments
x and len. Variable x is the input message represented as an array of words (32-bit).
The variable len is the length of the input message in bits. Lines 32–33 are to pad
and extend the input message by bit '1' followed by a sequence of bit '0' as
described in Step 1 of the algorithm. Note that this message padding is the same as
MD5 and the purpose is to extend the length of the message so that it is congruent
to 448 bits modulo 512. At the end of the message, a 64-bit representation of the
message length is added so that the entire message is a multiple of 512 represented
as 32-bit words.

The original design of SHA-1 was for big-endian machines, the least significant
word being stored first. For little-endian machines, such as Intel and PC, the
number 24 and 15 in lines 32 and 33 respectively are used to reverse the word
order. By default, implementations in this book are little-endian based. Each
16 words of the message are copied to the 80-element array w[] and are processed
by the double for-loops in lines 38–57. The statements inside the for-loops are
parallel to the pseudo-code in Section 3.5.2 with the following replacements:

- bit addition x+y is replaced by function bin32_add(x,y);

- the left rotation operation x<<<-s is replaced by function rot_l(x,s);

- function $f_j(b,c,d)$ is replaced by function `fun_ft(t,b,c,d)`;

- constants k_i are replaced by function `constant_kt(i)`.

The five 32-bit variables `a`, `b`, `c`, `d` and `e` are finally returned as an array by the statement in line 58. Using this `sha1_raw()` function, an interface function to generate SHA-1 hash values can be developed. Consider part III of `ex03-08.js`.

```
Example: Continuation of ex03-08.js - SHA-1 digest          (Part III)
61: function strToBinBig(str)
62: {
63:    var binArr = Array();
64:    var mask = (1 << 8) - 1;
65:    for(var i = 0; i < str.length * 8; i += 8)
66:    {
67:      binArr[i>>5] |= (str.charCodeAt(i / 8) & mask) << (24 - i%32);
68:    }
69:    return binArr;
70: }
71:
72: function binToHexBig(binArr)
73: {
74:    var hexes = "0123456789abcdef";
75:    var str = "";
76:    for(var i = 0; i < binArr.length * 4; i++) {
77:      str += hexes.charAt((binArr[i>>2] >> ((3 - i%4)*8+4)) & 0xf) +
78:             hexes.charAt((binArr[i>>2] >> ((3 - i%4)*8 )) & 0xf);
79: }
80:    return str;
81: }
82:
83: function sha1(s)
84: {
85:    return binToHexBig( sha1_raw(strToBinBig(s), s.length * 8));
86: }
```

This script fragment contains three functions. Again the SHA-1 algorithm is designed for big-endian machines; the first function `strToBinBig()` in lines 61–70 takes a string and converts it to an array of big-endian words. That is, each 32-bit word will have the least significant byte first. The second function `binToHexBig()`, in lines 72–81, converts an array of big-endian words to a hex string. The main function is `sha1()` defined in lines 83–86. It takes a string `s` as argument and returns the 160-bit SHA-1 digest in hexadecimal format to the caller.

If you call this function with a string, e.g. 'abc', the function `strToBinBig("abc")` in line 61 will convert the string into a big-endian array. Together with the bit length, the statement in line 85 calls the function `sha1_raw()` to obtain the SHA-1 digest, and finally the function `binToHexBig()` is called to transform it into hexadecimal values to return to the caller. The 160-bit hash is returned as 40 hexadecimal values. For the input string 'abc', the caller should receive the string

```
sha1("abc") = "a9993e364706816aba3e25717850c26c9cd0d89d"
```

Note that this implementation, including the structure, function names and calling syntax, is consistent with the MD5 described in `ex03-05.js`. With this script, we can develop a general Web page to obtain SHA-1 digests. The body part of this page is listed in `ex03-08.htm`.

```
Example: ex03-08.htm - Generating an SHA-1 digest
 1: <body style="font-family:arial;font-size:22pt;background:#000088">
 2: <div style="text-align:center;color:#00ff00"><br />
 3:    Generating SHA-1 Hash Values</div><br />
 4: <table style="font-size:16pt" cellspacing="10px" align="center">
 5:   <tr><td style="width:100px;color:#ffff00">Input Message</td>
 6:      <td><input type="button" value="OK" style="font-size:16pt;
 7:          font-weight:bold;width:80px;height:35px;
             background:#dddddd;
 8:          color:#ff0000" onclick="get_sha1()" /></td></tr>
 9:   <tr><td colspan="2" style="width:60px;color:#ffff00">
10:        <textarea id="key_v" style="font-size:16pt;width:450px;
11:         height:60px;font-weight:bold;
12:         background:#ddffdd;color:#ff0000"></textarea></td></tr>
13:   <tr><td colspan="2" style="width:360px;color:#ffff00">
14:        The SHA-1 Hash Value (160-Bit) Is</td></tr>
15:   <tr><td colspan="2"><textarea id="dis_mesg" size="55"
16:        maxlength="55" style="font-size:16pt;width:450px;
            height:80px;font-weight:bold;
17:        background:#dddddd;color:#ff0000"></textarea> </td> </tr>
18: </table>
19: <script src="ex03-08.js"></script>
20: <script>
21: function get_sha1()
22: {
23:  var tmp = document.getElementById("key_v").value;
24:  document.getElementById("dis_mesg").value=sha1(tmp);
25: }
26: </script>
27: </body>
```

Fig. 3.17 SHA-1 digest I

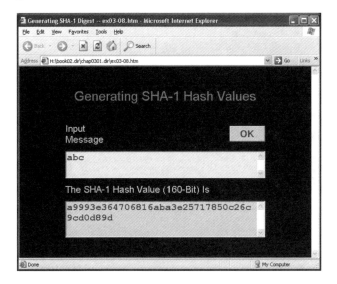

This page contains one OK button (lines 6–8) and two text areas (lines 10–12 and 15–17). Once you have entered a string in the first text area and clicked the OK button, the function get_sha1() (line 8) is activated. The details of the get_sha1() function are specified in lines 21–25. The statement in line 23 captures the string in the text area and stores it in variable tmp. The function sha1(tmp) in line 24 returns the SHA-1 digest and displays it in the second text area by the statement in line 24. The details of the function sha1() are defined in the script file ex03-08.js, which is included in line 19. Screenshots are shown in Figures 3.17 and 3.18.

Sections 3.3.4, 3.4.1 and 3.4.2 have shown how an MD5 utility can be built and used to get the digest string of a file. Such a utility, to read and digest files, is handy for security applications. The next section covers this.

3.5.4 Building an SHA-1 utility

In Section 3.3.4, a utility called mddriver for MD5 was built, based on the C programs provided by the RFC 1321 specification. This program can read a string or an entire file and produce the corresponding MD5 digest. To build a utility for SHA-1, we consider an article known as RFC 3174. This report provides a C implementation of the SHA-1 algorithm with the following program files:

sha1.h – header file for sha1.c;

sha1.c – the C program to implement the SHA-1 algorithm.

Fig. 3.18 SHA-1 digest II

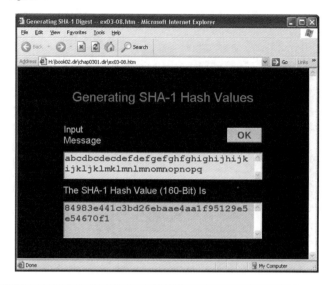

If you have a C/C++ compiler, such as Borland C/C++, Microsoft C/C++ or UNIX/Linux C/C++, you can compile this sha1.c program and build an SHA-1 utility. Since the sha1.c program is not designed to be an executable program, RFC 3174 also provides a test program called sha1test.c so that an executable program can be built. For example, if you are using Microsoft C/C++ compiler you can build the utility using the command

```
cl sha1test.c sha1.c
```

The executable program sha1test.exe will be built in your local directory.

If you are using UNIX/LINUX with a gcc or cc compiler, you can compile the utility with the command

```
gcc -o sha1test sha1test.c sha1.c
```

This command will compile the C programs and produce the executable file as sha1test.

After the compilation, you should have an executable file called sha1test.exe or sha1test in your local directory. The compiling process using a gcc compiler with Windows is shown in the first line of Figure 3.19.

Once you have the executable program sha1test.exe (or sha1test) you can run it – the execution results are shown in Figure 3.19.

Report RFC 3174, however, does not provide a utility similar to the mddriver that can read a file and generate a digest. In this case, you need to write one yourself.

Fig. 3.19 Testing SHA-1 output

```
H:\ch03>gcc -o sha1test sha1test.c sha1.c
H:\ch03>sha1test
Test 1: 1, 'abc'
    A9 99 3E 36 47 06 81 6A BA 3E 25 71 78 50 C2 6C 9C D0 D8 9D
Should match:
    A9 99 3E 36 47 06 81 6A BA 3E 25 71 78 50 C2 6C 9C D0 D8 9D

Test 2: 1, 'abcdbcdecdefdefgefghfghighijhijkijkljklmklmnlmnomnopnopq'
    84 98 3E 44 1C 3B D2 6E BA AE 4A A1 F9 51 29 E5 E5 46 70 F1
Should match:
    84 98 3E 44 1C 3B D2 6E BA AE 4A A1 F9 51 29 E5 E5 46 70 F1

Test 3: 1000000, 'a'
    34 AA 97 3C D4 C4 DA A4 F6 1E EB 2B DB AD 27 31 65 34 01 6F
Should match:
    34 AA 97 3C D4 C4 DA A4 F6 1E EB 2B DB AD 27 31 65 34 01 6F

Test 4: 10,
'0123456701234567012345670123456701234567012345670123456701234567'
    DE A3 56 A2 CD DD 90 C7 A7 EC ED C5 EB B5 63 93 4F 46 04 52
Should match:
    DE A3 56 A2 CD DD 90 C7 A7 EC ED C5 EB B5 63 93 4F 46 04 52
```

If you read the file sha1.c, you will find that the following five statements are needed in order to generate a SHA-1 digest:

```
1: SHA1Context sha1;
2: unsigned char sha1_hash[20];
3: SHA1Reset(&sha1);
4: SHA1Input(&sha1, (const unsigned char *) inStr, strlen(inStr));
5: SHA1Result(&sha1, sha1_hash);
```

The first line declares an SHA-1 structure called sha1. The second line defines an array called sha1_hash[] to hold the SHA-1 digest. The function SHA1Reset(&sha1) resets all constants so that a new SHA-1 digest can be generated. If you have a string stored in variable inStr, the function SHA1Input() in line 4 will put the string into the structure and get ready to generate the corresponding SHA-1 digest. The function SHA1Result() in line 5 is to actually generate the digest and store it in the array sha1_hash.

With this calling information, we can develop a utility for SHA-1. To have the same consistency as for MD5, we are going to use the same program structure and function-calling syntax as described in mddriver.c. Consider the C program sha1driver.c.

Example: sha1driver.c - The C program for SHA-1 utility   (Part I)

```
 1: #include <stdio.h>
 2: #include <string.h>
 3: #include "sha1.h"
 4:
 5: static void sha1Print (unsigned char *hash)
 6: {
 7:   unsigned int i;
 8:   for (i = 0; i < 20; i++)
 9:     printf ("%02x", hash[i]);
10: }
11:
12: int sha1String(char *inStr)
13: {
14:   SHA1Context sha1;
15:   int i;
16:   unsigned char sha1_hash[20];
17:
18:   SHA1Reset(&sha1);
19:   SHA1Input(&sha1, (const unsigned char *) inStr, strlen(inStr));
20:   SHA1Result(&sha1, sha1_hash);
21:
22:   printf ("sha1(\"%s\") = ",inStr);
23:   sha1Print(sha1_hash);
24:   printf("\n");
25:   return (0);
26: }
27:
28: void sha1File (char *filename)
29: {
30:   FILE *file;
31:   SHA1Context context;
32:   int len;
33:   unsigned char buffer[1024], sha1_hash[20];
34:
35:   if ((file = fopen (filename, "rb")) == NULL)
36:       printf ("%s can't be opened\n", filename);
37:   else {
38:       SHA1Reset (&context);
39:       while (len = fread (buffer, 1, 1024, file)) {
40:           SHA1Input(&context, buffer, len);
41:       }
42:       SHA1Result(&context,sha1_hash);
```

```
43:        fclose (file);
44:        printf ("sha1(%s) = ", filename);
45:        sha1Print (sha1_hash);
46:        printf ("\n");
47:    }
48: }
```

This C program contains three simple functions and should be quite easy to read, even if you are not familiar with the C language. The first function `sha1Print()` defined in lines 5–10 takes the SHA-1 hash array as input and prints out the hash string in hex format. The print function in line 9,

```
printf ("%02x", hash[i]);
```

prints out each element `hash[i]` as two characters in hexadecimal format. The second function `sha1String()` is defined in lines 12–26. This function takes a character string (e.g. `inStr`) and generates the corresponding SHA-1 hash. By executing the statements in lines 18–20

```
SHA1Reset(&sha1);
SHA1Input(&sha1, (const unsigned char *) inStr, strlen(inStr));
SHA1Result(&sha1, sha1_hash);
```

the SHA-1 hash is stored in the array `sha1_hash[]`. These three statements are declared in the header file `sha1.h` provided by RFC 3174 and are included in the program by the statement in line 3. If you call this function with a string 'abc', say, you will see the result on the screen as

```
sha1("abc") = "a9993e364706816aba3e25717850c26c9cd0d89d"
```

The third function `sha1File()` defined in lines 28–48 takes a file name as input. It will read the entire file and produce the SHA-1 digest string. The digest string (or hash) will be printed on the screen.

The statement in line 35 opens a file. If the operation is successful, the statements in lines 38–46 will be executed. If the operation fails, an error message will be printed by the statement in line 36. Line 38 calls the function `SHA1Reset()` to reset the constants and parameters. The while-loop in lines 39–41 will effectively read the entire file and put the data into the SHA structure using the function `SHA1Input()`. By calling the function `SHA1Result()` in line 42, the SHA-1 hash corresponding to the input file is stored in array `sha1_hash[]`. This array is then printed to the screen by the function `sha1Print()` in line 45. Note that these three functions are designed to have similar name, structure and calling syntax as functions `MDPrint()`, `MDString` and `MDFile()` in the MD5 (or `mddriver.c`) case. This arrangement can make porting the application from `mddriver` to `sha1driver` easier. The main function of the utility is given in part II of `sha1driver.c`.

```
50: int main (int argc, char *argv[])
51: {
52:    int i;
53:    char *opt1=" -sstring --digest string, e.g. -sabc";
54:    char *opt2=" filename --digest file";
55:
56:    if (argc > 1) {
57:        for (i = 1; i < argc; i++) {
58:            if (argv[i][0] == '-' && argv[i][1] == 's')
59:                sha1String (argv[i] + 2);
60:            else
61:                sha1File(argv[i]);
62:        }
63:    } else {
64:        printf("Usage: sha1driver options \n%s\n%s",opt1,opt2);
65:    }
66:    return (0);
67: }
```

Again, the calling syntax of the `main()` function is similar to that of `mddriver`. For simplicity, only two command line options are implemented. The command line options are stored in array `argv[]` (line 50). If you call this utility with a directive '-s'

```
sha1driver -sjohnsmith
```

the variable `argc` will have the value '2' and the command options are

```
argv[0] = "sha1driver"    and    argv[1] = "-sjohnsmith"
```

In this case, the statements in lines 58–59 will be executed. The function

```
sha1String (argv[i] + 2)
```

will cut the two characters '-s' out and ultimately compute the SHA-1 hash of the string 'johnsmith'. Similarly, if you call this utility with a file name without directive, such as

```
sha1diver sha_f.txt
```

the statement in line 61 will compute the SHA-1 hash of the file `sha_f.txt` accordingly. To compile this utility, you can use the following command if you are using `gcc`:

```
gcc -o sha1driver sha1driver.c sha1.c
```

Fig. 3.20 Compiling and testing `sha1driver`

```
H:\chap03>gcc -o sha1driver sha1driver.c sha1.c

H:\chap03>sha1driver
Usage: sha1driver options
  -sstring --digest string, e.g. -sabc
  filename --digest file

H:\chap03>sha1driver -sabc
sha1("abc") = a9993e364706816aba3e25717850c26c9cd0d89d

H:\chap03>sha1driver sha_f.txt
sha1(sha_f.txt) = a9993e364706816aba3e25717850c26c9cd0d89d

H:\chap03>sha1driver -sabc sha_f.txt
sha1("abc") = a9993e364706816aba3e25717850c26c9cd0d89d
sha1(sha_f.txt) = a9993e364706816aba3e25717850c26c9cd0d89d

H:\chap03>
```

The compilation and some running results with the `gcc` compiler for Windows are shown in Figure 3.20.

Note that the text file `sh1_f.txt` illustrated in Figure 3.20 contains only one string 'abc'. Also from this figure you can see that you can put as many command line options in any order you like.

Now we have a utility for the SHA-1 scheme, many applications with MD5 can be converted directly to SHA-1 for more security strength.

4

Some strong symmetric-key ciphers

4.1 An introduction to strong symmetric-key ciphers

4.1.1 Strong block and stream ciphers

When a single key is used for both encryption and decryption, the cipher is called a symmetric-key scheme. The sender uses the key to encrypt the plaintext and sends the ciphertext to the receiver. The receiver applies the same key to decrypt the message and recover the plaintext. Because a single key is used for both processes, the key must be kept secret in order to maintain security – therefore the symmetric-key scheme is also called secret-key encryption.

All the elementary encryptions in Chapter 1, such as Caesar code, XOR encryption and PkZip/WinZip, are the symmetric type. The single DES scheme introduced in Chapter 3 is an important symmetric-key cipher known as 'Feistel'. It is immediate and obvious that the key must be known to both the sender and the receiver to make the scheme work. The biggest difficulty of these schemes is the distribution of the key. Revealing the secret key to the receiver exposes you to a large number of attacks during the key transmission or exchange process. The more people you share the key with, the higher the resulting security risks. Despite this problem, symmetric-key ciphers are still used widely simply because they produce stronger protection under attack. It is believed that the strongest computationally secure scheme(s) belong to these types.

One of the basic guides to cipher strength is the key length in bits. For example, in the late 1990s, the single DES scheme with maximum 50-bit key length could be attacked by a number of brute-force methods, producing the data in Table 4.1.

You can see that a symmetric-key cipher with a maximum 56-bit key length, with no other support, is no longer considered to be secure. With today's computing

Table 4.1 DES and brute-force attack

Type of attacker	Time per attack (40-bit key)	Time per attack (50-bit key)
Hacker	1 week	Impracticable
Small business	12 minutes	556 days
Corporate department	0.18 seconds	3 hours
Big company	0.005 seconds	6 minutes
Intelligence agency	0.002 seconds	12 seconds

power, a cipher with a key length less than 128 bits will not be considered as strong. By expanding the key length to 128 bits, the execution time (even with the best computing power) will be increased to billions of years. In an ideal case, and with no other assumptions, this will discourage most of the attackers.

Reflecting the operational style, symmetric-key ciphers are generally categorized as being either stream ciphers or block ciphers. Stream ciphers operate on a single character of the plaintext at a time using a stream of encryption characters called a key-stream. In order to create a key-stream, some form of feedback mechanism is employed so that the key is constantly changing. The PkZip/WinZip cipher in Chapter 1 is an example of a stream cipher.

A block cipher operates on one block of plaintext characters at a time using the same key on each block. Block ciphers usually have the so-called block effect. In other words, the same plaintext block will always produce the same ciphertext with the same key. In order to eliminate or reduce the block effect, a number of feedback mechanisms called 'operation modes' can be used. Sometimes, a stream cipher can be considered as a block cipher with block length = 1.

There are a number of strong symmetric-key ciphers (block and stream) in use today. Each has its own advantages and application areas. They are summarized below.

■ **Triple Data Encryption Standard (Tri-DES)**
Tri-DES is the successor of the 56-bit DES scheme from NIST and is known as FIPS46-3. By putting three DES schemes together, the key length is extended to 168-bit, providing extra strength against attacks.

■ **CAST-128 (IETF RFC 2144)**
CAST-128 (also called CAST5) is a DES-like cipher developed by Carlisle Adams and Stafford Tavares (CAST). It is a 128-bit key scheme operating on a 64-bit block. There are no known attacks and it is quite secure. It is now the default cipher in a well-known security package called 'Pretty Good Privacy' (PGP).

■ **International Data Encryption Algorithm (IDEA)**
IDEA is an algorithm developed by X. Lai and J. Massey in the early 1990s. It is based on addition and multiplication modulo and operates on a 64-bit block with key length 128. IDEA was best known as a component of PGP. IDEA was patented by a Swiss firm and is now owned by Entrust.

- **RC4, RC5, and RC6**

  RC4 is a stream cipher from Ron Rivest using variable-sized keys. RC5 and RC6 are block ciphers supporting a variety of block and key sizes. In particular, RC6 is designed as an alternative to the Advanced Encryption Standard, which is the official successor to DES promoted by the US government.

- **Software-optimized Encryption Algorithm (SEAL)**

  SEAL was designed by Rogaway and Coppersmith as a fast stream cipher for 32-bit machines. SEAL has a rather involved initialization phase during which a large set of tables is initialized using the secure hash algorithm (SHA).

- **Blowfish/Twofish**

  Blowfish is a fast symmetric-key scheme from Bruce Schneier. It is a 64-bit block cipher with 32- to 448-bit key length. It is used by a number of commercial products. Twofish is a 128-bit block expansion of Blowfish with variable key lengths. Blowfish is a flexible scheme for small devices.

- **Advanced Encryption Standard (AES)**

  AES is the official successor to DES from Rijndael. In fact, AES was the result of a massive competition organized by the US government, which is one of the fascinating stories in recent crypto-history. AES operates on variable block lengths with variable key lengths. A typical AES scheme uses key length 128-, 192- or 256-bit to encrypt data blocks that are 128, 192 or 256 bits long.

We will cover most of these ciphers in this and the next two chapters. One characteristic of symmetric-key ciphers (block or stream) is that they can be classified by block and key lengths. For example, the triple DES cipher is a 64-bit block cipher with 168-bit key length and is usually called Tri-DES[64:168]. Similarly, we have

$$\text{CAST-128[64:128]} \quad \text{RC4[1:var]} \quad \text{Blowfish[64:var]} \quad \text{and} \quad \text{AES[var:var]}$$

In the early sections of this chapter, an introduction to block ciphers with 128-bit key length, operation modes and their applications is presented. In order to study Tri-DES with 168-bit key length, single DES with coding optimization is discussed in detail. A highly optimized DES program is developed step by step. The development will help you to understand some of the professional DES implementations in industry. Since coding optimization is not an easy subject, some readers may find Section 4.2 challenging.

Along with DES, Tri-DES is implemented as a special application of DES in Section 4.3.4. CAST-128, a DES-like cipher, is also discussed in Section 4.4. By increasing the key length to 128-bit or more, strong security for message confidentiality during exchange or transmission on the World Wide Web is achieved. Application examples and encryption/decryption tools are developed throughout.

4.1.2   Operation modes of symmetric-key ciphers

Whether it is 64 or 128 bits, a block cipher operates on one block of plaintext characters at a time. When the same key is used on identical blocks, the same ciphertext block will be produced. This undesirable feature is known as the block effect. In order to eliminate the block effect and improve the security strength of block ciphers, DES designers have developed a number of operation modes which are included in the official DES publication FIPS 46-3. They are:

- electronic codebook (ECB) mode;

- cipher block chaining (CBC) mode;

- cipher feedback (CFB) mode;

- output feedback (OFB) mode.

Although the operation modes were originally developed for the DES algorithm, they can also be used and implemented by general block ciphers.

Electronic codebook (ECB) mode

The ECB mode of a block cipher is illustrated in Figure 4.1. In ECB encryption, the plaintext message is divided into blocks $(P_1, P_2, \ldots, P_n)$ according to the block length of the cipher. Each block, P_i, is encrypted by the encryption function $E()$ of the cipher producing the ciphertext block C_i, i.e. $C_i = E(P_i)$. The ECB decryption process is the same as encryption except that the ciphertext block C_i is input into the decrypt function $D()$ of the block cipher producing the plaintext block P_i, i.e. $P_i = D(C_i)$. ECB is the default mode for many block ciphers and has no feedback mechanism at all.

Fig. 4.1   The ECB mode

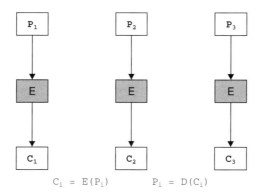

$$C_i = E(P_i) \qquad P_i = D(C_i)$$

Cipher block chaining (CBC) mode

The CBC mode of a block cipher is described in Figure 4.2. In CBC encryption, the plaintext message is divided into blocks $(P_1, P_2, \ldots, P_n)$ according to the block length of the cipher. The first input block for encryption is formed by XORing the first block of the message (P_1) and an initialization vector C_0. The result is encrypted by the encryption function $E()$, producing the first block of ciphertext C_1. This C_1 is XORed with the next plaintext block P_2 and then goes through the same encryption, yielding the following iteration formula:

$$C_1 = E(C_0 \wedge P_1) \quad \text{and} \quad C_i = E(C_{i-1} \wedge P_i) \quad \text{where } i = 1 \text{ to } n$$

In CBC decryption, the first ciphertext block (C_1) is used as the input block to the decryption function $D()$. The result is then XORed with the initialization vector (IV) C_0 to give the first plaintext block P_1. The second ciphertext block C_2 is decrypted by $D()$ and then XORed with C_1, producing plaintext block P_2. The iteration formula is

$$P_1 = C_0 \wedge D(C_1) \quad \text{and} \quad P_i = C_{i-1} \wedge D(C_i) \quad \text{where } i = 1 \text{ to } n$$

From the encryption process, we can see that the corresponding ciphertext blocks of two identical plaintext blocks will not be the same. The first block of feedback C_0 (or IV in FIPS) is a randomly generated block known as an initialization vector. When this is done, each ciphertext block is dependent not only on the plaintext block that generated it but also on each of the preceding blocks as well, including the initialization vector. Identical plaintext blocks will now produce the same ciphertext block only if each of the preceding blocks are identical and the initialization vectors are the same. This feature is popular and widely implemented in many block ciphers.

Some operation modes can also be used to develop a system to deal with variable block lengths.

Fig. 4.2 The CBC mode

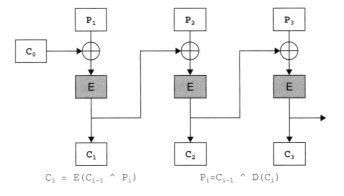

$$C_i = E(C_{i-1} \wedge P_i) \qquad P_i = C_{i-1} \wedge D(C_i)$$

Cipher feedback (CFB) mode

The structure of the CFB mode of a block cipher is described in Figure 4.3. In CFB encryption, the plaintext message is divided into blocks $(P_1, P_2, \ldots, P_n)$ with block length k where k can be from 1 up to the block size of the cipher. When k is equal to the block size of the cipher, an initial vector c_0 is processed by the encryption function $E()$ to produce an output block. This output block is XORed with the first plaintext block P_1 to produce the ciphertext block c_1. Ciphertext c_1 is then encrypted by $E()$ and XORed again with the plaintext P_2. The iteration formula is

$$C_1 = E(C_0) \;\text{^}\; P_1 \quad \text{and} \quad C_i = E(C_{i-1}) \;\text{^}\; P_i \quad \text{where } i = 1 \text{ to } n$$

For the decryption process, the initial vector c_0 is first encrypted by the function $E()$ to produce an output block. This output block is then XORed with the first ciphertext block c_1 to generate the plaintext block P_1. c_1 is encrypted by function $E()$ and XORed with c_2 again to produce the plaintext block P_2. Continuing the process we have

$$P_1 = E(C_0) \;\text{^}\; C_1 \quad \text{and} \quad P_i = E(C_{i-1}) \;\text{^}\; C_i \quad \text{where } n = 1 \text{ to } n$$

From Figure 4.3, one characteristic of the CFB mode is that the function $E()$ is outside the plaintext blocks. The encryption mechanism is used to encrypt the ciphertext block only. This arrangement would allow a block cipher to handle variable block lengths. Now, consider the situation when k is less than the block size of the cipher. Suppose we have the following:

- $E()$ – the encryption function of a block cipher with a block size equal to 64 bits;

- IV – the initialization vector with bit length L, i.e.
    $IV = (IV[1], IV[2], \ldots, IV[L])$, where $L <$ block size;

Fig. 4.3 The CFB mode

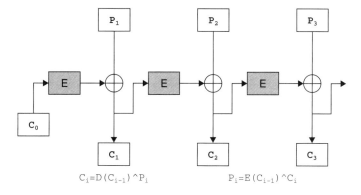

$$C_i = D(C_{i-1})\text{^}P_i \qquad P_i = E(C_{i-1})\text{^}C_i$$

- P_i – the plaintext message represented as k-bit blocks, i.e.

    M (plaintext) = P_1, P_2, P_3, ..., P_n

    P_i = ($P_i[1]$, $P_i[2]$, ..., $P_i[k]$) where k < block size.

The following algorithmic process shows how the CFB mode can be used to perform encryption on P_i.

Step 1   Append the L-bit initialization vector IV to the least significant bits of a zero vector (64-bit) and call it the input vector I:

$$I = (I[1], I[2], ..., I[64]) = (C_0[1], C_0[2], ..., C_0[64])$$
$$= (0, 0, ..., 0, IV[1], IV[2], IV[L])$$

Step 2   Perform encryption on I, i.e. $E(I)$, and take the k most significant bits as the result. Now XOR the result with the first plaintext block P_1 to produce the ciphertext block C_1:

$$C_1 = H_k(E(I)) \; \char94 \; P_1 \qquad \text{where } H_k() \text{ return the } k \text{ most significant bits}$$
$$C_1 = (C_1[1], C_1[2], ..., C_1[k])$$

Step 3   Discard the first k most significant bits of the input block I and append C_1 at the end to form a new I:

$$I = (I[k+1], I[k+2], ..., I[64], C_1[1], C_1[2], ..., C_1[k])$$

This new I contains 64 elements and can go through the same process as Step 2 to obtain another ciphertext block C_2.

Continue the Step 2 – Step 3 process until all message blocks P_i are encrypted. The ciphertext is $C = C_1, C_2, ..., C_n$ and each ciphertext block C_i is k bits long. By using the ciphertext block as input, the three steps above can be used to perform decryption.

Sometimes, particularly for small or real-time devices, encryption must be performed before the full block of data is obtained. With the CFB mode, block ciphers can be adapted to handle these situations.

Output feedback (OFB) mode

The structure of the OFB mode of a block cipher is described in Figure 4.4. In OFB encryption, the plaintext message is divided into blocks (P_1, P_2, ..., P_n) with block length k where k can be from 1 up to the block size of the cipher. First, an initial vector C_0 is processed by the encryption function $E()$ to produce an output block. This output block is XORed with the first plaintext block P_1 to produce the ciphertext block C_1. Then the output of $E(C_0)$ is input to the encryption $E()$ and XORed again with the plaintext P_2. The iteration formula is

$$C_1 = E^1(C_0) \; \char94 \; P_1 \qquad \text{and} \qquad C_i = E^i(C_0) \char94 P_i \qquad \text{where } i = 1 \text{ to } n$$

For the decryption process, the initial vector C_0 is first encrypted by the function $E()$ to produce an output block. This output block is then XORed with the first

Fig. 4.4 The OFB mode

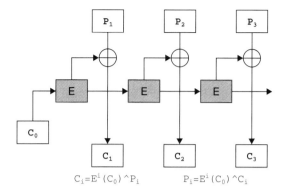

$C_i=E^i(C_0)\char94 P_i$ $P_i=E^i(C_0)\char94 C_i$

ciphertext block C_1 to generate the plaintext block P_1. The output $E^1(C_0)$ is then encrypted by $E()$ again and XORed with C_2 to produce plaintext block P_2. The iteration is

$P_1=E^1(C_0)\char94 C_1$ and $P_i=E^i(C_0)\char94 C_i$ where $i = 1$ to n

Again the encryption function $E()$ of OFB is outside the plaintext blocks. This arrangement would allow us to handle variable block lengths. Consider the situation when k is less than the block size case, and suppose we have the following:

- $E()$ – the encryption function of a block cipher with a block size equal to 64 bits;
- IV – the initialization vector with bit-length L, i.e.
    $IV=(IV[1],IV[2],...,IV[L])$, where $L < 64$;
- P_i – the plaintext message represented as k-bit blocks, i.e.
    M (plaintext) $= P_1,P_2,P_3,...,P_n$
    $P_i=(P_i[1],P_i[2],...,P_i[k])$ where $k < 64$.

The following algorithmic process shows how OFB mode can be used to perform encryption on P_i.

Step 1 Append the L-bit initialization vector IV to the least significant bits of a zero vector (64-bit) and call it the input vector I:

$I = (I[1], I[2],..., I[64]) = (C_0[1],C_0[2],...,C_0[64])$
$= (0,0,...,0,IV[1],IV[2],IV[L])$

Step 2 Perform encryption on I, i.e. $E(I)$, and take the k most significant bits as the result. Suppose the k bits are $O = (O[1], O[2],...,O[k])$. Now perform the XOR operation on O and the first block P_1 to produce the ciphertext block C_1:

$O = H_k(E(I))$ where $H_k()$ return the k most significant bits
$C_1 = (C_1[1],C_1[2],...,C_1[k]) = O \char94 P_1$

Step 3   Discard the first `k` most significant bits of the input block `I` and append `o` at the end to form a new `I`:

$$I = (I[k+1], I[k+2], \ldots, I[64], O[1], O[2], \ldots, O[k])$$

This new `I` contains 64 elements and can go through the same process in Step 2 to obtain another ciphertext block c_2.

Continue the Step 2–Step 3 process until all message blocks P_i are encrypted. The ciphertext is $c = c_1, c_2, \ldots, c_n$ and each ciphertext block c_i is `k` bits long. By using the ciphertext block as input, the three steps above can be used to perform decryption.

This OFB mode uses the output of a function, e.g. `E()`, as a feedback mechanism to perform encryption. The algorithmic structure is similar to the CFB mode and, therefore, it also can be used on small or real-time devices requiring different block lengths.

Another operation mode for block ciphers comes from 'triple DES'. Suppose we have one DES encryption/decryption and three 56-bit keys. The triple DES scheme can be described as follows:

- use the plaintext and key 1 for encryption;

- use the output and key 2 to perform decryption;

- use the output and key 3 to perform encryption.

The final output is the ciphertext of Tri-DES (see Figure 4.5). Since Tri-DES, basically, carries out single DES three times and can be applied to many symmetric-key ciphers, we generally consider Tri-DES as another operation mode.

Provided all three keys are independent, the total key length is 168-bit and, therefore, the strength of the scheme is enhanced. However, the operation is three times slower.

Fig. 4.5   Triple DES scheme

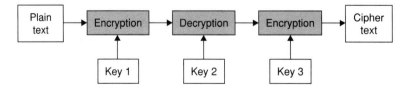

4.2   Coding optimization of the DES scheme

4.2.1   The optimization process for DES

Coding optimization is not an easy subject. Often, it will require a deep understanding of the encryption/decryption scheme and some advanced skills in computing. By studying the coding optimization of DES, you will have a better knowledge of the structure of the algorithm and be one step closer to professional programming. Some readers may find this section challenging.

DES has existed for a long time and has been under public scrutiny for more than 25 years. Although DES is ageing, it is believed that the extent of human resources spent on DES is still greater than the total of all the others. Optimization of DES codes was once a 'hot' research topic. From proprietary to public, from chipset to software implementation, the refinement work on DES has produced many code breakers, interesting results and stories contributing to the beauty of the entire encryption/decryption subject.

For obvious reasons, code breaking is neither the scope nor intention of this chapter. We don't want codes that no one else can read or to be beating our brains for a few instructions faster. The purpose of this section is to provide a step-by-step guide on an optimized DES scheme and to help you to understand and read some of the professional implementations you may find in the public domain, such as IE, NS, Opera, Java and many other security packages.

In Chapter 3, we introduced an implementation of DES according to the standard FIPS-46. If you compare the program code in Sections 3.2.2 and 3.2.3 and the implementation in this section, you will find nothing similar. Here is the explanation. Basically, the DES scheme involves two major processes:

- set up the 16 subkeys;

- perform DES encryption/decryption with known subkeys (or simply the DES encryption in this chapter).

Since key set-up is used only once, we will pay less attention to the first of the processes. There are a number of 'key schedule' optimizations to set up the keys. The key schedule developed in this chapter is not heavily optimized. It may be a factor of five per cent or so slower than it could be but it is a really small one. The most obvious optimization is the DES encryption. It will be performed for every 64-bit chunk of data equivalent to eight characters of input plaintext. Any optimization in this area will improve the performance significantly.

Also, the original FIPS-46 and the implementation in Section 3.2.3 are designed for array manipulations. One array element is used to store one bit. A chunk (64-bit) will need 64 elements. For 32-bit computers, an integer (or an array element) is normally a 32-bit value. To save some internal memory and increase efficiency,

Fig. 4.6 The DES encryption algorithm

```
IP(M) = L₀R₀
Lₙ = Rₙ₋₁
Rₙ = Lₙ₋₁ XOR f(Rₙ₋₁,Kₙ), n = 1 to 16          (16 rounds)

    DES Function f(Rₙ₋₁,Kₙ)
    1. E(Rₙ₋₁)
    2. Kₙ XOR E(Rₙ₋₁) = B₁ B₂ B₃ B₄ B₅ B₆ B₇ B₈ (6 bits each)
    3. S1(B₁) S2(B₂) S3(B₃) S4(B₄) S5(B₅)    (4 bits each)
       S6(B₆) S7(B₇) S8(B₈)
    4. f = P[S1(B₁)S2(B₂)...S8(B₈)]

C = IP⁻¹(R₁₆L₁₆)
```

optimized DES implementations often use 32-bit integers. One chunk (64-bit) of data is stored as two integers of 32 bits each.

One of the most successful optimizations is due to Eric Young. His implementation has been adopted practically by many security applications. We will follow the basic principle developed by him and build an optimized DES implementation using Web pages step by step. From the standard algorithm, the DES scheme is summarized in Figure 4.6.

In the following sections, we will examine and perform the optimization process below.

■ Combine table P with S-boxes S1,S2,...,S8 to form the SP-boxes SP1,SP2,..., SP8. We will generate these data in the next section, and you will find them in a number of professional implementations.

■ Perform optimized table lookup by 'permutation sequences'. Table lookup with permutation sequences was developed by Richard Outerbridge. We will use the optimization results on IP(M) and IP⁻¹(R₁₆L₁₆).

■ Embed table E and perform the bitwise XOR operation with the keys Kᵢ. Together with the SP-boxes, compute the 16 rounds of DES iteration.

■ Generate all subkeys and set up the key schedule to finish the entire DES algorithm.

Now, let's consider how to combine table P with the S-boxes.

4.2.2   Combining Table P with S-boxes to generate SP-boxes

The first and most obvious optimization on the DES scheme is the S-boxes and the P box. Each S-box takes in a 6-bit binary call B_i producing a 4-bit output as S1(B_1),S2(B_2),...,S8(B_8). The combination of these eight 4-bit outputs is submitted to table P producing the 32-bit f value as the result of the iteration function f() defined in the algorithm.

Table P is a permutation performing bit changes. It is invariant (not changing) under the bitwise OR operation. More precisely, for any two 32-bit strings X and Y, we have

```
P ( X | Y ) = P(X) | P (Y)
```

Combining Table P and the S-boxes is done simply by applying P to every S-box: S1,S2,...,S8. The result is a new set of data known as SP-boxes: SP1,SP2,...,SP8 (or spfunctions) in many DES programs.

Before we continue and discuss the coding, let's consider another way of performing permutation with table P. Consider the table stored as an array P[] and a bit array B[] = {$b_0, b_2, ..., b_{31}$}. Table P is a permutation which can be written as

```
16, 7,20,21,29,12,28,17, 1,15,23,26, 5,18,31,10,    <- (bit no.)
01,02,03,04,05,06,07,08,09,10,11,12,13,14,15,16,    <- (position)

 2, 8,24,14,32,27, 3, 9,19,13,30, 6,22,11, 4,25    <- (bit no.)
17,18,19,20,21,22,23,24,25,26,27,28,29,30,31,32    <- (position)
```

This permutation can be read as 'putting the 16th bit into the 1st position, the 7th bit into the 2nd position and so on'. The bit manipulation of P[] on B[] can be done by one simple for-loop:

```
1: newB = new Array(32);
2: for (i=0; i < 32; i++)
3:    newB[i] = B[ P[i] -1 ];
```

Note that we have changed the starting index from 1 to 0 so that the 'minus 1' operation in line 3 is needed. Another, more efficient, way to do the same permutation is that if you rearrange the ordering of bit number of P, you have the following:

```
 1, 2, 3, 4, 5, 6, 7, 8, 9,10,11,12,13,14,15,16,    <- (bit no.)
09,17,23,31,13,28,02,18,24,16,30,06,26,20,10,01,    <- (position)

17,18,19,20,21,22,23,24,25,26,27,28,29,30,31,32    <- (bit no.)
08,14,25,03,04,29,11,19,32,12,22,07,05,27,15,21    <- (position)
```

This is also a permutation and can be interpreted as 'putting the 1st bit into the 9th position, the 2nd bit into the 17th position and so on'. If you store the 'position' as an array called ivP[] = {9,17,23,...,21}, the same permutation of P on a 32-bit integer C with the bit sequence {$b_0, b_2, ..., b_{31}$} can be performed by the following script:

```
1: var newC=0x00000000;  // One 32-bit integer
2: for (j=0;j<32;j++)
3:    if (C & (0x80000000 >>> j)) newC |= 0x00000001 << (31-(ivP[j]-1));
```

The conditional-if in line 3 'c & (0x80000000 >>> j)' will check through every bit of c. If the jth bit is bigger than 0 (i.e. 1), the code '(31- (ivP[j]-1))' computes the position from ivP[j] -1 and left-shifts the bit 0x00000001 into the correct position. The bitwise OR operation will concatenate all the results to form a new integer newC containing the bit sequence after permutation P. Note that the code above is efficient, but still not heavily optimized. It can be considered as a starting point for understanding table lookup optimization that we are going to use it in this section.

To generate the SP-boxes, consider part I of ex04-01.js.

```
Example: ex04-01.js - Generating the data for SP-boxes        (Part I)

 1: var S = new Array(0,0,0,0,0,0,0,0);
 2: S[0]  = new Array(
 3:     14, 4,13, 1, 2,15,11, 8, 3,10, 6,12, 5, 9, 0, 7,
 4:      0,15, 7, 4,14, 2,13, 1,10, 6,12,11, 9, 5, 3, 8,
 5:      4, 1,14, 8,13, 6, 2,11,15,12, 9, 7, 3,10, 5, 0,
 6:     15,12, 8, 2, 4, 9, 1, 7, 5,11, 3,14,10, 0, 6,13);
 7: S[1]  = new Array(
 8:     15, 1, 8,14, 6,11, 3, 4, 9, 7, 2,13,12, 0, 5,10,
 9:      3,13, 4, 7,15, 2, 8,14,12, 0, 1,10, 6, 9,11, 5,
10:      0,14, 7,11,10, 4,13, 1, 5, 8,12, 6, 9, 3, 2,15,
11:     13, 8,10, 1, 3,15, 4, 2,11, 6, 7,12, 0, 5,14, 9);
12: S[2]  = new Array(
13:     10, 0, 9,14, 6, 3,15, 5, 1,13,12, 7,11, 4, 2, 8,
14:     13, 7, 0, 9, 3, 4, 6,10, 2, 8, 5,14,12,11,15, 1,
15:     13, 6, 4, 9, 8,15, 3, 0,11, 1, 2,12, 5,10,14, 7,
16:      1,10,13, 0, 6, 9, 8, 7, 4,15,14, 3,11, 5, 2,12);
17: S[3]  = new Array(
18:      7,13,14, 3, 0, 6, 9,10, 1, 2, 8, 5,11,12, 4,15,
19:     13, 8,11, 5, 6,15, 0, 3, 4, 7, 2,12, 1,10,14, 9,
20:     10, 6, 9, 0,12,11, 7,13,15, 1, 3,14, 5, 2, 8, 4,
21:      3,15, 0, 6,10, 1,13, 8, 9, 4, 5,11,12, 7, 2,14);
22: S[4]  = new Array(
23:      2,12, 4, 1, 7,10,11, 6, 8, 5, 3,15,13, 0,14, 9,
24:     14,11, 2,12, 4, 7,13, 1, 5, 0,15,10, 3, 9, 8, 6,
25:      4, 2, 1,11,10,13, 7, 8,15, 9,12, 5, 6, 3, 0,14,
26:     11, 8,12, 7, 1,14, 2,13, 6,15, 0, 9,10, 4, 5, 3);
27: S[5]  = new Array(
28:     12, 1,10,15, 9, 2, 6, 8, 0,13, 3, 4,14, 7, 5,11,
29:     10,15, 4, 2, 7,12, 9, 5, 6, 1,13,14, 0,11, 3, 8,
30:      9,14,15, 5, 2, 8,12, 3, 7, 0, 4,10, 1,13,11, 6,
31:      4, 3, 2,12, 9, 5,15,10,11,14, 1, 7, 6, 0, 8,13);
```

```
32: S[6] = new Array(
33:     4,11, 2,14,15, 0, 8,13, 3,12, 9, 7, 5,10, 6, 1,
34:    13, 0,11, 7, 4, 9, 1,10,14, 3, 5,12, 2,15, 8, 6,
35:     1, 4,11,13,12, 3, 7,14,10,15, 6, 8, 0, 5, 9, 2,
36:     6,11,13, 8, 1, 4,10, 7, 9, 5, 0,15,14, 2, 3,12);
37: S[7] = new Array(
38:    13, 2, 8, 4, 6,15,11, 1,10, 9, 3,14, 5, 0,12, 7,
39:     1,15,13, 8,10, 3, 7, 4,12, 5, 6,11, 0,14, 9, 2,
40:     7,11, 4, 1, 9,12,14, 2, 0, 6,10,13,15, 3, 5, 8,
41:     2, 1,14, 7, 4,10, 8,13,15,12, 9, 0, 3, 5, 6,11);
42:
43: var P = new Array(
44:    16,  7, 20, 21, 29, 12, 28, 17,
45:     1, 15, 23, 26,  5, 18, 31, 10,
46:     2,  8, 24, 14, 32, 27,  3,  9,
47:    19, 13, 30,  6, 22, 11,  4, 25 );
48:
49: var sp = new Array(0,0,0,0,0,0,0,0);
50:    sp[0] = new Array(64);    sp[1] = new Array(64);
51:    sp[2] = new Array(64);    sp[3] = new Array(64);
52:    sp[4] = new Array(64);    sp[5] = new Array(64);
53:    sp[6] = new Array(64);    sp[7] = new Array(64);
54:
```

This is a simple script for data preparation. Lines 1–41 define a two-dimensional array called `s[][]` for the S-boxes. Table `P` is declared as an array `p[]` in lines 43–47. They are the same as in `ex03-02.js`. To store the SP-boxes, a two-dimensional array called `sp[][]` is declared in lines 50–53. A function to generate the SP-boxes is given in part II of `ex04-01.js`.

Example: Continuation of ex04-01.js   (Part II)

```
55: function spGen()
56: {
57:   var ivP = new Array(32);
58:   var i,j,k,rowcol;
59:   var outV=0;
60:   var spV = 0, tmp1=0;
61:
62:   for (i=0;i<8;i++) {
63:     for (j=0;j< 64;j++) sp[i][j] = 0;
64:   }
65:   for(j=0; j<32; j++) {
66:     for(i=0;i<32;i++) {
```

```
67:            if( P[i]-1 == j ) {
68:                ivP[j] = i & 0xff; break;
69:            }
70:        }
71:    }
72:    for(k = 0; k < 8; k++){
73:        for(i=0; i < 64; i++){
74:            spV = 0;
75:            rowcol = (i & 32) | ((i & 1) ? 16 : 0) | ((i >>> 1) & 0xf);
76:            for(j=0; j < 4; j++){
77:                if(S[k][rowcol] & (8 >>> j)) {
78:                    spV |= 0x00000001 << (31 - ivP[4*k + j]);
79:                }
80:            }
81:            tmp1 = 0;
82:            if (spV >>> 31) tmp1 = 1;
83:            spV = (spV << 1) | tmp1;
84:            sp[k][i] = spV;
85:        }
86:    }
```

This script fragment contains partial codes of the function spGen(). This function is used to generate all the values for SP-boxes. The for-loop in lines 62–64 initializes all elements of the array sp[][] to zero. The double for-loop in lines 65–71 performs the bit re-ordering of table P and stores the value in array ivP[].

The main operation is the k for-loop in lines 72–86, which is used to generate all eight combined tables. The i for-loop in lines 73–85 populates each combined table. Note that each S-box takes a 6-bit input and produces a 4-bit output. One simple way to combine them is to run through all 6-bit (i.e. 0 to 64) values. For each 6-bit, consider the statement in line 75:

```
rowcol = (i & 32) | ((i & 1) ? 16 : 0) | ((i >>> 1) & 0xf);
```

If the 6-bit i is $\{b_1, b_2, b_3, b_4, b_5, b_6\}$, this statement produces an integer rowcol with a bit sequence of $\{b_1, b_6, b_2, b_3, b_4, b_5\}$. In other words, it combines the 1st and 6th bit as row number and the middle 4-bit as column number so that the S-box value can be accessed as S[k][rowcol].

When k=0, there are 64 i and hence 64 rowcol values. Each S[0][rowcol] is a 4-bit binary and only this value is needed for permutation with table P. The inner j for-loop in lines 76–80 runs through 0 to 3 and is permuted with '(31-ivP[j])', which is the first four elements in ivP[]. The result is stored in variable spV. Lines 81–84 rotate this spV left by 1 and store the result in array sp[0][i]. This implementation is equivalent to applying table P on S1 to produce a table SP1.

Similarly, when `k = 1`, each `S[1][rowcol]` value permutes with `'(31-ivP[4*(1)+j])'`, which is the second set of four elements in `ivP[]`. This process is equivalent to applying `P` on `S2` to obtain a table `SP2`. When the `k` for-loop is exhausted, the array `sp[k][i]`, where `k = 0 to 7` and `j = 0 to 63`, represents tables `SP1, SP2, ..., SP8` with 64 values each.

To display the result, consider part III of `ex04-01.js`.

Example: Continuation of ex04-01.js   **(Part III)**

```
87:    spSt = "<br />     "
88:    for (i=0;i<8;i++ ) {
89:      document.write("<br />var SP"+(i+1)+" = new Array ("+spSt);
90:      for (j=0;j<16;j++) {
91:        for (k =0; k< 4; k++) {
92:          outV = sp[i][j*4+k];
93:          vSt = "000000000" + byte4ToHex(outV);
94:          oSt = vSt.substring(vSt.length-8,vSt.length);
95:          if ((j*4+k) < 63) document.write("0x"+ oSt +",  ");
96:          else document.write("0x"+ oSt +" );");
97:        }
98:        document.write(spSt);
99:      }
100:   }
101: }
102:
103: function byte4ToHex (s)
104: {
105:   var r = "";
106:   var hexes = new Array ("0","1","2","3","4","5","6","7",
107:                          "8","9","a","b","c","d","e","f");
108:   r += hexes [s >> 28 & 0xf] + hexes [s >> 24 & 0xf]+
109:        hexes [s >> 20 & 0xf] + hexes [s >> 16 & 0xf]+
110:        hexes [s >> 12 & 0xf] + hexes [s >> 8  & 0xf]+
111:        hexes [s >> 4  & 0xf] + hexes [s      & 0xf];
112:   return r;
113: }
```

We want the SP-box data generated by `ex04-01.js` to be cut and pasted directly into the DES program that we are going to develop. The script block in lines 87–100 contains XHTML and ECMAScript (or Javascript) codes.

Line 87 defines a space variable `spSt` containing XHTML code with a line break and some spaces. The `i` for-loop in lines 88–100 outputs the eight SP-boxes. When `i = 0`, the statement in line 89 produces the string `'var SP1 = new Array ('`, which is the script to define an array called sp1. The double for-loop in lines 90–99 prints out all 64 pieces of data of sp1 in 16 rows and 4 columns format. One of the simplest ways to print out the data as 8 hexadecimal values using script is to use the statements in lines 93–94. The function byte4ToHex() converts the SP-box data into a hexadecimal string. By inserting a sequence of '000000000' at the front and then cutting it to 8 characters from the end will make sure that the string oSt is 8 characters long. This oSt string is output by the document.write() function in line 95. The last data will be printed by line 96 with ending string ');' attached.

To test this script, the body part of a Web page, ex04-01.htm, is used.

```
Example: ex04-01.htm - Generating data for SP-boxes

1:  <body style="font-family:arial;font-size:20pt;text-align:left;
2:    background:#eeffee;color:#0000ff">
3:  Generating DES SP Boxes Data
4:  <img alt="pic" src="line1.gif" height="7" width="600" />
5:  <div style="font-size:16pt">
6:    <script src="ex04-01.js"></script>
7:    <script> spGen() </script>
8:  </div>
9:  </body>
```

This page includes the script ex04-01.js in line 6. Inside the script block, the function spGen() is called and the generated data are displayed. A screenshot is shown in Figure 4.7.

As you can see from Figure 4.7, the data is displayed as an array in script and can be cut and pasted directly into many other Web applications. You will find that these data appear in a number of DES implementations. Also, if you comment the following 3 lines in ex04-01.js as shown below,

```
81:  // tmp1 = 0;
82:  // if (spV >>> 31)     tmp1 = 1;
83:  // spV = (spV << 1) | tmp1;
```

the SP-boxes, now, are not left-rotated (see Figure 4.8). In this case, you will find the data to be identical to that of Eric Young and other DES implementations.

4.2.3   Using permutation sequences for table lookup

The standard DES scheme involves several tables and uses table lookup heavily throughout. The next obvious target is to optimize these operations. There are a number of ways of doing this. The method introduced in Section 4.2.2 is a good starting point. Another table lookup skill will be presented in Section 4.2.5. Both

Fig. 4.7 SP-box data I

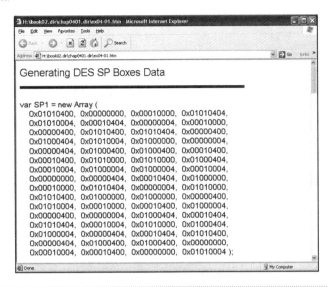

Fig. 4.8 SP-box data II

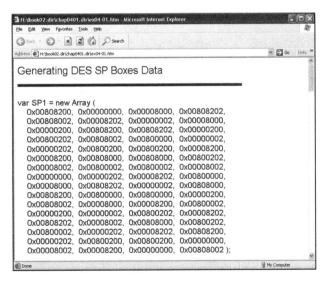

of them are efficient but still not heavily optimized for speed. One of the fastest table lookup techniques is the so-called 'permutation sequence'. It is widely used in industry and professional programming on algorithms like DES.

Basically, given two 32-bit integers `left` and `right`, the bit values in `left` and `right` can be exchanged or swapped by the permutation sequence

```
tmp = ((left >>> size) ^ right) & (mask);
right ^= tmp;
left ^=(tmp << size);
```

The parameter `size` is an integer to control the shifting, and the `mask` is an integer to mask the bits. With `size` and `mask`, bits between `left` and `right` are exchangeable. By combining a number of permutation sequences together, table lookup operation can be achieved.

As an example, table `PC1` lookup in DES can be performed by the permutation sequences, or pseudo-code algorithm, given in `ex04-01.txt`.

Example: ex04-01.txt Permutation sequences for table PC1 (pseudo-code)

```
 1:  Function PC1(left, right) begin
 2:     temp    = ((left >>> 4) ^ right) & 0x0f0f0f0f;
 3:       right ^= temp;
 4:       left  ^= (temp << 4);
 5:     temp    = ((right >>> -16) ^ left) & 0x0000ffff;
 6:       left  ^= temp;
 7:       right ^= (temp << -16);
 8:     temp    = ((left >>> 2) ^ right) & 0x33333333;
 9:       right ^= temp;
10:       left  ^= (temp << 2);
11:     temp    = ((right >>> -16) ^ left) & 0x0000ffff;
12:       left  ^= temp;
13:       right ^= (temp << -16);
14:     temp    = ((left >>> 1) ^ right) & 0x55555555;
15:       right ^= temp;
16:       left  ^= (temp << 1);
17:     temp    = ((right >>> 8) ^ left) & 0x00ff00ff;
18:       left  ^= temp;
19:       right ^= (temp << 8);
20:     temp    = ((left >>> 1) ^ right) & 0x55555555;
21:       right ^= temp;
22:       left  ^= (temp << 1);
23:     temp    = (left << 8) | ((right >>> 20) & 0x000000f0);
24:       left  = (right << 24) | ((right << 8) & 0xff0000) |
25:               ((right >>> 8) & 0xff00) | ((right >>> 24) & 0xf0);
26:       right = temp;
27: return (left, right);
```

Given two 32-bit integers `left` and `right`, this algorithm states that table `PC1` operation of the DES scheme is equivalent to performing a number of permutation sequences, as in `ex04-01.txt`. This algorithm was used in Eric Young's DES C code. He gave credit to John Fletcher for one of the most efficient ways of doing `PC1`.

Note that, in general, not all permutation tables can be converted into permutation sequences nicely like this one. Depending on the randomness of the table data, sometimes, even if you can find the equivalent permutation sequences, it may be complicated and not very practical to use.

To verify the algorithm in `ex04-01.txt`, a simple page is developed in `ex04-02.js` to trace every step of the bit movements.

```
Example: ex04-02.js - The permutation sequence of table PC1

 1: function doPC1(left,right)
 2: {
 3:   var t, l, r;
 4:   l = left; r=right;
 5:   t= ((l >>> 4)   ^ r) & 0x0f0f0f0f; r ^= t; l ^= (t << 4);
 6:   t= ((r >>> -16) ^ l) & 0x0000ffff; l ^= t; r ^= (t << -16);
 7:   t= ((l >>> 2)   ^ r) & 0x33333333; r ^= t; l ^= (t << 2);
 8:   t= ((r >>> -16) ^ l) & 0x0000ffff; l ^= t; r ^= (t << -16);
 9:   t= ((l >>> 1)   ^ r) & 0x55555555; r ^= t; l ^= (t << 1);
10:   t= ((r >>> 8)   ^ l) & 0x00ff00ff; l ^= t; r ^= (t << 8);
11:   t= ((l >>> 1)   ^ r) & 0x55555555; r ^= t; l ^= (t << 1);
12:   t = (l << 8)| ((r >>> 20) & 0x000000f0);
13:   l = (r << 24)            | ((r << 8)   & 0xff0000) |
14:       ((r >>> 8) & 0xff00) | ((r >>> 24) & 0xf0);
15:   r = t;
16:   return Array(l,r);
17: }
```

Basically, this script contains one function and is a direct translation from the sequences algorithm. The variables `l` and `r` are 32-bit values. After the permutation, they are returned as an array in line 16. To test this script, consider the body part of Web page `ex04-02.htm`.

This page includes the script `ex04-02.js` in line 3 so that the function `doPC1()` is available. To test the algorithm, we need to perform the following tasks:

- set up a mechanism to remember every position of the bits from 1 to 64;

- call the function `doPC1()`;

- mark all the movements of the bits.

Example: ex04-02.htm – Testing the PC1 permutation sequences

```
 1: <body style="font-family:'Courier New';font-weight:bold;
    font-size:18pt">
 2:  Verifying Table PC1 With <br /> Permutation Sequences<br />
 3: <script src=ex04-02.js></script>
 4: <script>
 5:   var inL, inR;
 6:   var outV = new Array();
 7:   var outL = new Array();
 8:   var outR = new Array();
 9:   for (jj=0;jj<32;jj++) {
10:      outL[jj]=0; outR[jj]=0;
11:   }
12:   for (i=0;i<32;i++) {
13:    inL = 0x00000001 << (31-i); inR = 0x00000000;
14:    outV = doPC1(inL,inR);
15:    for (jj=0;jj<32;jj++) {
16:       if (outV[0] >>> (31-jj) & 0x1) outL[jj]=i+1;
17:       if (outV[1] >>> (31-jj) & 0x1) outR[jj]=i+1;
18:    }
19:   }
20:   for (i=0;i<32;i++) {
21:    inR = 0x00000001 << (31-i); inL = 0x00000000;
22:    outV = doPC1(inL,inR);
23:    for (jj=0;jj<32;jj++) {
24:       if (outV[0] >>> (31-jj) & 0x1) outL[jj]=i+32+1;
25:       if (outV[1] >>> (31-jj) & 0x1) outR[jj]=i+32+1;
26:    }
27:   }
28:   document.write("Left = <br />   ");
29:   for (jj=0;jj<32;jj+=8) {
30:     for (kk=0;kk<8;kk++) {
31:       document.write(outL[jj+kk]+",");
32:     }
33:     document.write("<br />   ");
34:   }
35:   document.write("<br />Right = <br />   ");
36:   for (jj=0;jj<32;jj+=8) {
37:     for (kk=0;kk<8;kk++) {
38:       document.write(outR[jj+kk]+",");
39:     }
40:     document.write("<br />   ");
41:   }
42: </script>
43: </body>
```

The for-loop in lines 9–10 initializes two arrays outL[] and outR[]. They are used to store the movement of individual bits. The main operation is the for-loop in lines 12–19.

Consider when i = 0: the statement in line 13 generates one bit located at the 1st position of variable inL (i.e. the left). All bits in variable inR (i.e. Right) are zero. After the function doPC1() is called, the one bit is moved somewhere in the array outV[]. The for-loop in lines 15–18 checks through outV[] to find the bit. When the bit is found, the position is stored as (i+1) so that the movement of the 1st bit is recorded as 1. When i = 1, the movement of the 2nd bit is recorded as number 2. Therefore the for-loop will record all the movements of the first 32 bits, i.e. from 0 to 31.

Similarly, the for-loop in lines 20–27 creates another set of bits from 32 to 63 one-by-one in variable inR. Every time after the function doPC1() is called, the specific 1 bit will be moved, searched and recorded by the for-loop in lines 23–26. Note that the expression here is (i+32+1) to indicate that the recorded bits run from 33 to 64.

Lines 28–34 are used to print out the bit movement for the first 32 bits. This should contain the upper part of the table PC1. Similarly, lines 35–41 print out the lower part of table PC1. A screenshot of this example is shown in Figure 4.9.

From Figure 4.9, you can see that when the input table (or bit stream) is {1,2,3,...,64}, the output table representing the bit movements of the

Fig. 4.9 Verifying table PC1

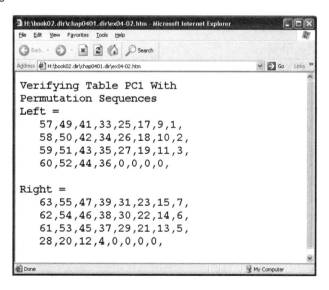

permutation sequences is the same as table PC1. Note that the table PC1 uses only 56 bits of the input 64 bits. The four zeros at the end of `left` and `right` both show this feature.

Compared to other table lookup techniques, these permutation sequences do the same job with bit shifting and swapping. It is fast – as quoted by Eric Young 'It is really quite evil but fast'.

Table PC1 is used to generate DES subkeys. For DES encryption/decryption, we need to optimize tables IP and IP^{-1}. The plaintext message M is first processed by table IP and the final ciphertext is obtained after being processed by IP^{-1}. If you split this 64-bit plaintext M into two 32-bit integers called `left` and `right`, the IP permutation can be written as

$$IP(M) = IP(left, right) = L_0R_0$$

The permutation sequences for IP and IP^{-1} in this chapter were originated by Richard Outerbridge. The permutation sequence for table IP is listed in ex04-02.txt.

```
Example: ex04-02.txt Permutation sequences for table IP  (pseudo-code)
 1:    Function IP(left, right) begin
 2:        tmp       = ((left >>> 4) ^ right) & 0x0f0f0f0f;
 3:          right  ^= tmp;
 4:          left   ^= tmp << 4;
 5:        tmp       = ((left >>> 16) ^ right) & 0x0000ffff;
 6:          right  ^= tmp;
 7:          left   ^= tmp << 16;
 8:        tmp       = ((right >>> 2) ^ left) & 0x33333333;
 9:          left   ^= tmp;
10:          right  ^= (tmp << 2);
11:        tmp       = ((right >>> 8) ^ left) & 0x00ff00ff;
12:          left   ^= tmp;
13:          right  ^= (tmp << 8);
14:        right     = rotate_left(right, 1);
15:        tmp       = (left ^ right) & 0xaaaaaaaa;
16:          left   ^= tmp;
17:          right  ^= tmp;
18:        left      = ((left << 1) | ((left >>> 31) & 1)) & 0xffffffff;
19: return (left, right)
```

This algorithm is widely implemented as a routine called 'IPERM(left,right)'. Table IP^{-1} is the inverse operation of IP. The permutation sequences for IP^{-1} are, basically, the same as `ex04-02.txt` with the reverse order of statements – they are listed in `ex04-03.txt`.

```
Example: ex04-03.txt Permutation sequences for IP⁻¹ or FP (pseudo-code)

 1: Function FP(left, right) begin
 2:     right    = (right << 31) | (right >>> 1);
 3:     work     = (leftt ^ right) & 0xaaaaaaaa;
 4:      left   ^= work;
 5:      right  ^= work;
 6:     left     = (left << 31) | (left >>> 1);
 7:     work     = ((leftt >> 8) ^ right) & 0x00ff00ff;
 8:      right  ^= work;
 9:      left   ^= (work << 8);
10:     work     = ((left >>> 2) ^ right) & 0x33333333;
11:      right  ^= work;
12:      left   ^= (work << 2);
13:     work     = ((right >>> 16) ^ left) & 0x0000ffff;
14:      left   ^= work;
15:      right  ^= (work << 16);
16:     work     = ((right >>> 4) ^ left) & 0x0f0f0f0f;
17:      left   ^= work;
18:      right  ^= (work << 4);
19:  return (left, right);
```

These two algorithms will be implemented in the next section. Now, we have everything to implement the optimized DES encryption/decryption.

4.2.4   Optimized DES encryption/decryption

Now, both the SP-boxes and the permutation sequences for `IP(left,right)` are available. The next optimization target is to handle table `E`. Table `E` is used to perform the operations below before the subkeys and SP-boxes are created.

$$\text{IP}(M) \;=\; L_0 R_0$$
$$L_1 \;=\; R_0$$
$$K_n \;\wedge\; \mathbf{E}(\mathbf{R}_0) \;=\; B_1 B_2 \ldots B_8$$

In fact, soon after table `E`, the result is split into eight chunks and XORed with the subkeys to form the eight 6-bit B_i. We want to build table `E` and all subkeys into

Fig. 4.10 Bit distribution on SP-boxes

```
bit     123456789012345678901234567890012

SP1  XXXXX                                        X
SP2       XXXXXX
SP3           XXXXXX
SP4               XXXXXX
SP5                   XXXXXX
SP6                       XXXXXX
SP7                           XXXXXX
SP8  X                            XXXXX
```

the optimization as well. If you take a closer look at table E, it is a function cycling around values from 1 to 32 (i.e. one 32-bit integer). In other words, it uses only 32 bits of R_0, creating a 48-bit $E(R_0)$. Therefore, only the first 32 bits of R_0 still exist in $E(R_0)$. If you split the result of $E(R_0)$ into 6-bit chunks, the bit distribution against the SP-boxes is as shown in Figure 4.10.

The bit string marked by 'X' in the first row contains the bit sequence 32, 1, 2, 3, 4, 5 of R_0, and they are same as the first six numbers in table E. As you can see, the bit strings are overlapping. With overlapping data, it is not convenient to perform key XORing and extracting bit strings B_i cleanly. One solution for the overlapped data is to split it into odd {SP1,SP3,SP5,SP7} and even {SP2,SP4,SP6,SP8} portions so that calculation can be fitted into 32-bit words with no overlap. Because of the splitting, a simple operation such as '(r << 28)|(r >>> 4)' on the odd portion will fit the data suitable for the SP-boxes input.

Provided the scheduled subkeys are in the same format, we have an optimized DES scheme. Note that we have left-rotated the algorithm by one bit, which included:

- rotating all SP-boxes and entries one bit to the left;

- rotating each word of the key to the left by one element;

- rotating L and R one bit left just after IP; and

- rotating one bit right just before IP^{-1} or (FP).

This operation will save a few more instructions, and that's why the SP-boxes in Section 4.2.2 are rotated one bit left.

To implement this scheme, the first thing is to run page ex04-01.htm to generate the data for the SP-boxes. Next, you can cut and paste all the data from the page into a script file called ex04-03.js. This will define all the SP-boxes SP1, SP2,...,SP8 as arrays. To this add part I of ex04-03.js. The data for SP-boxes contains 144 lines so that the starting line number here is 145.

```
145: function doIP(left,right) {
146:   var t, l, r;
147:   l = left; r = right;
148:
149:   t = ((l >>> 4)  ^ r) & 0x0f0f0f0f; r ^= t; l ^= (t << 4);
150:   t = ((l >>> 16) ^ r) & 0x0000ffff; r ^= t; l ^= (t << 16);
151:   t = ((r >>> 2)  ^ l) & 0x33333333; l ^= t; r ^= (t << 2);
152:   t = ((r >>> 8)  ^ l) & 0x00ff00ff; l ^= t; r ^= (t << 8);
153:
154:   r = ((r << 1) | ((r >>> 31) & 1)) & 0xffffffff;
155:   t = (l ^ r) & 0xaaaaaaaa; l ^= t; r ^= t;
156:   l = ((l << 1) | ((l >>> 31) & 1)) & 0xffffffff;
157:   return Array(l,r);
158: }
159:
160: function doFP(left,right) {
161:   var t, l, r;
162:   l = left; r = right;
163:
164:   r = ((r << 31) | (r >>> 1)) & 0xffffffff;
165:   t = (l ^ r) & 0xaaaaaaaa; l ^= t; r ^= t;
166:   l = ((l << 31) | (l >>> 1)) & 0xffffffff;
167:
168:   t = ((l >>> 8)  ^ r) & 0x00ff00ff; r ^= t; l ^= (t << 8);
169:   t = ((l >>> 2)  ^ r) & 0x33333333; r ^= t; l ^= (t << 2);
170:   t = ((r >>> 16) ^ l) & 0x0000ffff; l ^= t; r ^= (t << 16);
171:   t = ((r >>> 4)  ^ l) & 0x0f0f0f0f; l ^= t; r ^= (t << 4);
172:   return Array(r,l);
173: }
174:
```

This script fragment is not difficult to read. It contains two functions. The first is the direct implementation of ex04-03.txt. It is used to perform table IP lookup on variables left and right. The result is returned as an array of two elements. The second function doFP() in lines 160–173 is the permutation sequences to perform table IP^{-1} lookup as in ex04-03.txt. Table IP^{-1} is also called the 'final permutation' (FP) in the standard specification. This function is the inverse of IP so that the statements inside doFP() are, in general, in the reverse order of doIP().

To perform the DES encryption, consider part II of ex04-03.js.

```
175: function doDesIteration(wKey,left,right)
176: {
177:  var t, l, r;
178:  var f,round;
179:  l = left; r = right;
180:
181:  for ( round = 0; round < 8; round++) {
182:    t  = ((r << 28) | (r >>> 4)) ^ wKey[round * 4 + 0];
183:    f  = SP1[(t >>> 24) & 0x3f]
184:       | SP3[(t >>> 16) & 0x3f]
185:       | SP5[(t >>> 8)  & 0x3f]
186:       | SP7[ t         & 0x3f];
187:
188:    t  = r ^ wKey[round * 4 + 1];
189:    f |= SP2[(t >>> 24) & 0x3f]
190:       | SP4[(t >>> 16) & 0x3f]
191:       | SP6[(t >>> 8)  & 0x3f]
192:       | SP8[ t         & 0x3f];
193:    l ^= f;
194:
195:    t  = ((l << 28) | (l >>> 4)) ^ wKey[round * 4 + 2];
196:    f  = SP1[(t >>> 24) & 0x3f]
197:       | SP3[(t >>> 16) & 0x3f]
198:       | SP5[(t >>> 8)  & 0x3f]
199:       | SP7[ t         & 0x3f];
200:
201:    t  = l ^ wKey[round * 4 + 3];
202:    f |= SP2[(t >>> 24) & 0x3f]
203:       | SP4[(t >>> 16) & 0x3f]
204:       | SP6[(t >>> 8)  & 0x3f]
205:       | SP8[ t         & 0x3f];
206:    r ^= f;
207:  }
208:  return Array(l,r);
209: }
210:
211: function des_64bits(wKey,left,right)
212: {
213:  var lrArr = new Array(2);
214:    lrArr = doIP(left,right);
215:    lrArr = doDesIteration(wKey,lrArr[0],lrArr[1]);
216:    lrArr = doFP(lrArr[0],lrArr[1]);
217:  return lrArr;
218: }
```

This script fragment also contains two functions. The main function is `doDesIteration(wKey, left, right)` in lines 175–209. This function takes all the subkeys and two 32-bit data `left` and `right` as input. The subkeys are represented as an array of 32 elements. Details of the keys will be discussed in the next section. After all the DES iterations, the result is returned as an array of two elements. The iteration process is straightforward following the discussion at the beginning of this section. At the beginning, the right data is shifted by the statement in line 182 and XORed with the first key. Then the result is passed to boxes `SP1`, `SP3`, `SP5` and `SP7` (lines 183–187). Note that SP-boxes are operated on 6-bit data. Lines 188–193 process the even portion, i.e. boxes `SP2`, `SP4`, `SP6`, and `SP8`. Lines 195–206 swap the `left` and `right` as required by the algorithm and go through the same iteration. After eight rounds, all 16 iterations are accomplished. The `l` and `r` results are returned by line 208.

The function `des_64bits(wKey,left,right)` in lines 211–218 is equivalent to performing DES encryption/decryption on one chunk of data. It takes the key sequences and two 32-bit data (`left` and `right`) as input. Line 214 calls the function `doIP()` to do permutation with table `IP`. The result is stored in the array `lrArr[]`. Element `lrArr[0]` contains the integer representing the 'left' data. Similarly, `lrArr[1]` represents the 'right'. These two elements are substituted into the function `doDesIteration()` in line 215 for DES iteration. The iteration results are then substituted into the function `doFP()` to perform permutation with table IP^{-1}. The result is the ciphertext stored in array `lrArr[]` and returned to the caller by the statement in line 217. If the subkey sequence is in reverse order, this function is, in fact, doing decryption and the 64-bit plaintext is returned.

Now, the final part of the task is to set up all the subkeys and schedule them into the correct format used in the algorithm.

4.2.5 Setting up and scheduling all subkeys

As mentioned at the beginning of Section 4.1.1, the key set-up is used only once and is a relatively small part of the DES scheme. The codes present in this section may not be heavily optimized. The implementation in this section originated from James Gillogly and Phil Karn, and involves other interesting skills in table lookup operations.

To generate all the subkeys, tables `PC1` (i.e. permuted table 1) and `PC2` (i.e. permuted Table 2) together with a shift table are used. We will use the original data of `PC1` and `PC2`. The shift table is converted to total rotations. Consider part I of `ex04-04.js`.

This script fragment defines a number of arrays. Lines 1–11 define the arrays for tables `PC1` and `PC2`. They are the original data in the DES standard. Lines 13–15 is an array called `TOTAL_ROTATION`. If you compare this array with the shift table

```
 1: var  PC1 = new Array (
 2:        56,48,40,32,24,16, 8,  0,57,49,41,33,25,17,
 3:         9, 1,58,50,42,34,26, 18,10, 2,59,51,43,35,
 4:        62,54,46,38,30,22,14,  6,61,53,45,37,29,21,
 5:        13, 5,60,52,44,36,28, 20,12, 4,27,19,11, 3 );
 6:
 7: var PC2 = new Array (
 8:        13, 16, 10, 23,  0,  4,  2, 27, 14,  5, 20,  9,
 9:        22, 18, 11,  3, 25,  7, 15,  6, 26, 19, 12,  1,
10:        40, 51, 30, 36, 46, 54, 29, 39, 50, 44, 32, 47,
11:        43, 48, 38, 55, 33, 52, 45, 41, 49, 35, 28, 31 );
12:
13: var TOTAL_ROTATION = new Array (
14:         1,  2,  4,  6,  8, 10, 12, 14,
15:        15, 17, 19, 21, 23, 25, 27, 28 );
16:
17: var BIT_MASK_FOR_BYTE = new Array (
18:        0x80, 0x40, 0x20, 0x10,
19:        0x8,  0x4,  0x2,  0x1 );
20:
21: var BIT_MASK_FOR_24BIT = new Array (
22:        0x800000, 0x400000, 0x200000, 0x100000,
23:        0x80000,  0x40000,  0x20000,  0x10000,
24:        0x8000,   0x4000,   0x2000,   0x1000,
25:        0x800,    0x400,    0x200,    0x100,
26:        0x80,     0x40,     0x20,     0x10,
27:        0x8,      0x4,      0x2,      0x1        );
28:
```

```
Shift = new Array(1,1,2,2,2,2,2,2,1,2,2,2,2,2,2,1)
```

in the standard DES algorithm, you will find that the data in the total rotation is the sum of the shift table. For example, the third element of the total rotation is the sum of the previous three shifting numbers

```
TOTAL_ROTATION[2] = Shift[0]+Shift[1]+Shift[2] = 4
```

The array BIT_MASK_FOR_BYTE[] in lines 17–19 makes it easy to extract a bit within a byte (8-bit). The array BIT_MASK_FOR_24BIT[] in lines 21–27 defines 24 elements so that extracting a bit within a 24-bit quantity is easier. The actual subkey-generating program is shown in part II of ex04-04.js.

```
29: function createKeys(encrypting, key)
30: {
31:   var rKey   = new Array(32);
32:   var pc1m   = new Array(56);
33:   var pcr    = new Array(56);
34:   var i, j, k, m, n, i1, i2;
35:
36:   for (j = 0; j < 56; j++ ) {
37:     k = PC1[j];
38:     pc1m[j]=((key[(k >>> 3)] & BIT_MASK_FOR_BYTE[k & 0x07]) != 0);
39:   }
40:   for (i = 0; i < 16; i++) {
41:     if (encrypting)     m = i << 1;
42:     else                m = (15 - i) << 1;
43:
44:     n = m + 1;   rKey[m] = 0;   rKey[n] = 0;
45:
46:     for (j = 0; j < 28; j++) {
47:       k = j + TOTAL_ROTATION[i];
48:       if ( k < 28 )  pcr[j] = pc1m[k];
49:       else           pcr[j] = pc1m[k - 28];
50:     }
51:     for (j = 28; j < 56; j++) {
52:       k = j + TOTAL_ROTATION[i];
53:       if (k < 56 )   pcr[j] = pc1m[k];
54:       else           pcr[j] = pc1m[k - 28];
55:     }
56:
57:     for (j = 0; j < 24; j++) {
58:       if (pcr[PC2[j]])         rKey[m] |= BIT_MASK_FOR_24BIT[j];
59:       if (pcr[PC2[j + 24]])    rKey[n] |= BIT_MASK_FOR_24BIT[j];
60:     }
61:   }
62:
```

This script fragment contains partial coding of a function called
createKeys(encrypting, key). The first parameter for this function is a boolean
type variable called encrypting. If this variable contains a true value, the function
will generate a set of subkeys suitable for encryption. On the other hand, a false
value will generate a set of decryption subkeys.

The second parameter is called `key`. It is an array `key[]` of eight elements containing the user input 64-bit password or raw key. Each element is one byte or an 8-bit integer. Given an array of eight elements `key[]`, the for-loop in lines 36–39 is used to perform PC1 table lookup. Line 37 gets the value in table PC1 and stores it as variable `k`. This `k` (or the kth bit) represents the bit position within the password. Consider the statement in line 38,

```
pc1m[j]=((key[(k >>> 3)] & BIT_MASK_FOR_BYTE[k & 0x07]) != 0);
```

The expression `(k>>>3)` will find out which element (byte) in array `key[]` contains the kth bit. The `key[(k>>>3)]` will single out that element. The expression `BIT_MASK_FOR_BYTE[k & 0x07]` will find out which bit inside element `key[(k>>>3)]` is the kth bit. If this bit is not zero, the variable `pc1m[j]` stores the bit. This process is equivalent to performing table PC1 permutation on array `key[]`.

The `i` for-loop in lines 40–61 generates all 16 subkeys. If the variable `encrypting` is `true`, the statement in line 41 makes sure that the subkeys are in ascending order for encryption. Otherwise the statement in line 42 will be executed and the subkeys are in reverse order for decryption. Consider when `i = 0`: the first subkey is generated and will be stored in variables `rKey[0]` and `rKey[1]`. Each variable is a 32-bit integer storing half (i.e. 24 bits) of the subkey. Putting it together, the 48-bit subkey is stored. The two for-loops in lines 46–55 are used to perform the shift table. By calculating the total rotation, i.e. `TOTAL_ROTATION[i]`, in line 47, the first 28 elements in `pc1m[]` can be shifted by the for-loop in lines 46–50. Another 28 elements in `pc1m[]` are shifted by the for-loop in lines 51–55. The result is stored in array `pcr[]`. With `pcr[]`, table PC2 permutation can be done by the for-loop in lines 57–60. Consider the statement in line 58:

```
if (pcr[PC2[j]])    rKey[m] |= BIT_MASK_FOR_24BIT[j];
```

This statement is equivalent to checking through all the bits of `pcr[]` via the variable `j` under table PC2 permutation. If the bit is not zero, it is cast into the return key `rKey[]`. This is the trick we have used from time to time to perform table lookup and should be easy to read by now. When `i = 0`, the first subkey is stored in variables `rKey[0]` and `rKey[1]`. When `i = 1`, with the total rotation, the second subkey is generated and stored in `rKey[2]` and `rKey[3]`. At the end, all 16 subkeys are stored in `rKey[0],...,rKey[31]`.

Now, let's see how to schedule these subkeys into the correct format suitable for DES implementation. Consider part III of script `ex04-04.js`.

Consider the first subkey situation (`i = 0`). Each variable `rKey[0]` and `rKey[1]` is 32-bit storing 24 bits of the subkey. If we consider each 6-bit of the subkey as a chunk, the bit streams of `rKey[0]` and `rKey[1]` are

```
i1 = rKey[0] = 0000 0000 p1 p2 p3 p4
i2 = rKey[1] = 0000 0000 p5 p6 p7 p8
```

The symbol `p1` is the first 6-bit of the subkey, `p2` is the second 6-bit and so on. To schedule this subkey for our optimized algorithm, the four statements in

```
63:
64:    for (i = 0; i < 32; i += 2)
65:    {
66:      i1 = rKey[i]; i2 = rKey[i + 1];
67:      rKey[i]    = ((i1 & 0x00fc0000) <<   6)
68:                 | ((i1 & 0x00000fc0) <<  10)
69:                 | ((i2 & 0x00fc0000) >>> 10)
70:                 | ((i2 & 0x00000fc0) >>>  6);
71:
72:      rKey[i + 1] = ((i1 & 0x0003f000) <<  12)
73:                  | ((i1 & 0x0000003f) <<  16)
74:                  | ((i2 & 0x0003f000) >>>  4)
75:                  | (i2 & 0x0000003f);
76:    }
77:    return rKey;
78: }
```

lines 67–70 will extract `p1`, `p3`, `p5` and `p7` and combine them in variable `rKey[0]` with the format

```
rKey[0] = 00p1 00p3 00p5 00p7
```

Each 6-bit p_i is an 8-bit boundary and can be easily extracted to perform an SP-box operation. This is exactly what we want in the algorithm. Similarly, the statements in lines 72–75 compose the subkey `rKey[1]=00p2 00p4 00p6 00p8`. All 32 array elements `rKey[]` containing all 16 subkeys are returned to the caller by the statement in line 77.

You may have already worked out that this script, `ex04-04.js`, together with `ex04-03.js` will form the core program and codes for a completely optimized DES implementation. In fact, we will use it to develop the Tri DES and other DES encryption tools.

4.3 Optimized DES, triple DES and some encryption tools

4.3.1 A functional optimized DES page

To construct a fully functional DES encryption/decryption tool with the optimized codes is straightforward. One simple way is to make a copy of ex04-03.js and ex04-04.js and merge them into a single script called ex04-05.js. At the end of this new script, add the following codes.

```
Example: ex04-05.js - DES encryption/decryption
297: function keyStToSubkeys(encrypt,inKeySt)
298: {
299:   var i, rKeyArr = new Array(8);
300:   for (i=0; i<8; i++) rKeyArr[i] = inKeySt.charCodeAt(i);
301:   return (createKeys(encrypt,rKeyArr));
302: }
303:
304: function des(keySt, msgSt, encrypt)
305: {
306:   var m=0, chunk=0, len = msgSt.length;
307:   var i, tResult="", result="";
308:   var iKeyArr=new Array(8), oKeyArr=new Array(), lrArr=new Array(2);
309:
310:   keySt += "\0\0\0\0\0\0\0\0"; keySt = keySt.substring(0,8);
311:   if (encrypt) oKeyArr = keyStToSubkeys(true,keySt);
312:   else oKeyArr = keyStToSubkeys(false,keySt);
313:
314:   msgSt += "\0\0\0\0\0\0\0\0";
315:   while (m < len) {
316:     lrArr[0]= (msgSt.charCodeAt(m++) << 24)
                  |(msgSt.charCodeAt(m++) << 16)|
317:              (msgSt.charCodeAt(m++) << 8)
                  | msgSt.charCodeAt(m++);
318:     lrArr[1]= (msgSt.charCodeAt(m++) << 24)
                  |(msgSt.charCodeAt(m++) << 16)|
319:              (msgSt.charCodeAt(m++) << 8)
                  | msgSt.charCodeAt(m++);
320:
321:     lrArr= des_64bits(oKeyArr,lrArr[0],lrArr[1]);
322:
323:     tempSt= String.fromCharCode(
324:        ((lrArr[0] >>> 24) & 0xff), ((lrArr[0] >>> 16) & 0xff),
```

```
325:        ((lrArr[0] >>>  8) & 0xff), ( lrArr[0]          & 0xff),
326:        ((lrArr[1] >>> 24) & 0xff), ((lrArr[1] >>> 16) & 0xff),
327:        ((lrArr[1] >>>  8) & 0xff), ( lrArr[1]          & 0xff));
328:
329:    tResult += tempSt; chunk += 8;
330:    if (chunk    512) {
331:       result += tResult; tResult = ""; chunk = 0;
332:     }
333:   }
334:   return result + tResult;
335: }
336:
```

The total number of lines from files ex04-03.js and ex04-04.js is 296. As a continuation, the starting line of this script is 297. This script contains two functions. The first function keyStToSubkeys(encrypt, inKeySt) in lines 297–302 takes two parameters. If the first parameter encrypt is true, the function will process the key string inKeySt and return all 16 subkeys for encryption. If the encrypt value is false, it will return subkeys for decryption.

The second function des(keySt, msgSt, encrypt) has three parameters: the user raw key (keySt), message string (msgSt), and a boolean type variable encrypt to switch between encryption and decryption. First, the key string keyST is expanded and then cut to eight characters so that the key is always 64-bit. If encryption is true, the function keyStToSubkeys() in line 311 will generate a set of subkeys in array oKeyArr[] for encryption. Otherwise, the statement in line 312 will create a set of subkeys for decryption.

When the subkeys are generated, the input message string msgSt is expanded in line 314 so that message padding is available if necessary. The while-loop in lines 315–335 runs through the entire message for processing. The statements in lines 316–319 capture eight characters (64 bits) of msgSt and convert it into two 32-bit integers called lrArr[0] (i.e. 'left') and lrArr[1] (i.e. 'right'). Together with the subkeys oKeyArr[], variables lrArr[0] and lrArr[1] represent one chunk of data (64-bit) to be processed by the function des_64bits() in line 321. The result is returned and stored in array lrArr[].

The statements in lines 323–327 convert lrArr[] into a string of eight characters in tempSt. This tempSt is one chunk of data and is stored in variable tResult in line 329 temporarily. In order to do some administrative work and reduce some string manipulations, the string in tResult is copied to another variable result whenever 512 characters are reached. Therefore, the statement in line 329 always works with small strings with little overhead. When the entire message is processed, the combined result (result + tResult) is returned to the function caller. To test this script, consider part I of ex04-05.htm.

```
 1: <style>
 2:   .butSt{font-size:16pt;width:250px;height:40px;
 3:         font-weight:bold;background:#dddddd;color:#ff0000}
 4:   .radSt{font-size:16pt;width:35px;height:30px;
 5:         font-weight:bold;background:#88ff88;color:#ff0000}
 6: </style>
 7: <body style="font-family:arial;font-size:26pt;text-align:center;
 8:       background:#000088;color:#ffff00">
 9:   DES Encryption/Decryption On The Web<br />
10:   <img alt="pic" src="line1.gif" height="7" width="650" /><br />
11:
12: <table style="font-size:18pt" align="center">
13:   <tr><td><br />Enter The Input Message: </td></tr>
14:   <tr><td><textarea style="font-size:16pt;width:570px;height:100px;
15:           font-weight:bold;background:#dddddd" rows="5" cols="40"
16:           id="in_mesg">Meet Me At 2pm Tomorrow</textarea></td></tr>
17: </table>
18: <form action="">
19: <table style="font-size:18pt" cellspacing="10" align="center">
20:   <tr><td>Enter The Key: </td>
21:       <td style="text-align:center" colspan=2>
22:         <input type="text" id="key_v" size="8" maxlength="8"
23:         style="font-size:16pt;width:370px;height:40px;
24:         font-weight:bold;background:#dddddd;color:#ff0000
            value="agent001" /></td></tr>
25:
26:   <tr><td style="width:180px;text-align:left"><input type="radio"
            checked
27:           id="b_rad" name="b_rad" class="radSt" /> Encryption</td>
28:     <td style="width:180px;text-align:left"><input type="radio"
29:         id="b_rad" name="b_rad" class="radSt" /> Decryption</td>
30:     <td style="width:180px;text-align:left"><input size="20"
31:         type="button" class="butSt" style="width:180px"
            value="OK" onclick="des_fun()" />
32:     </td></tr>
33: </table>
34: </form>
35: <table style="font-size:18pt" align="center">
36:   <tr><td>The Output Message is: </td></tr>
37:   <tr><td><textarea rows="5" cols="40" id="out_mesg" readonly
38:              style="font-size:16pt;font-weight:bold;width:570px;
39:              height:100px;background:#aaffaa"></textarea></td></tr>
40: </table>
```

This XHTML code is a simple interface page to get user input. Basically it contains two text areas, one text box, two radio buttons and one OK button. The first text area defined in lines 14–16 allows a user to enter a message for processing. The default message is 'Meet Me At 2pm Tomorrow' as illustrated in line 16. The text box in lines 22–24 is to get the user raw key (or password). The default password is 'agent001'. The two radio buttons allow a user to switch between encryption and decryption. When one of the radio buttons is checked and the OK button is clicked, the function des_fun() is activated. The message is processed by DES encryption or decryption and the result is displayed in the second text area defined in lines 37–39. The function des_fun() is defined in part II of ex04-05.htm.

```
Example: Continuation of ex04-05.htm                        (Part II)

41: <script src="ex04-05.js"></script>
42: <script src="hexlib.js"></script>
43: <script>
44:  function des_fun()
45:  {
46:    var key="",message="",llst=""
47:    llV = document.getElementsByName("b_rad")
48:    if (llV.item(0).checked) {
49:       key = document.getElementById("key_v").value
50:       message = document.getElementById("in_mesg").value
51:
52:       llst = byteStToHex(des(key, message, 1))
53:       document.getElementById("out_mesg").value = llst
54:    }
55:    if (llV.item(1).checked) {
56:       key = document.getElementById("key_v").value
57:       message = hexStToByteSt(document.getElementById("in_mesg").value)
58:
59:       llst = des(key, message, 0)
60:       document.getElementById("out_mesg").value = llst
61:    }
62:  }
63: </script>
64: </body
```

The function des_fun() is defined in the script block in lines 44–62. The statement in line 47 gets the status of all the radio buttons. If the first radio button (i.e. encryption) is checked, lines 49–53 are executed. In this case, the user input raw key and message are captured by lines 49–50 and stored in variables key and message. Consider the function call in line 52

```
llst = byteStToHex(des(key, message, 1))
```

Fig. 4.11   DES encryption

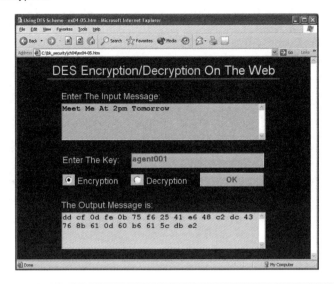

The variables `key` and `message` are used to trigger the function `des()`. The value '1' makes sure that encryption is performed. Since the returned result is a byte string and may contain non-printable characters, the function `byteStToHex()` is called to convert them into a hexadecimal string, which is stored in variable `11st`. This `11st` value will be displayed in the second text area by the statement in line 53.

Similarly, when the second radio button (i.e. decryption) is checked, the statements in lines 56–60 are executed. For decryption, the input message may contain non-printable characters. To handle this problem we use hexadecimal values as input. The statement in line 57 captures the hexadecimal string and the function `hexStToByteSt()` converts it into a byte string, which is stored in variable `message`. Line 59 performs decryption, and the decrypted message is displayed in the second text area by line 60. Screenshots of this example in action are shown in Figures 4.11 and 4.12.

Now, we have a functional DES encryption/decryption Web page. This can be used to protect privacy when using 'real time message exchange' on the Web or Internet, such as chat or instant messaging. In practice, you can open two windows, one for encryption containing your password and the other for decryption containing the password of your partner. Only the encrypted hexadecimal strings are transmitted over the Web environment.

4.3.2   Adding operation modes to eliminate the block effect

In Section 4.1.1, you learned that block ciphers, in general, are characterized by block length and key length. For example, DES can be written as DES[64:56]. Also,

Fig. 4.12 DES decryption

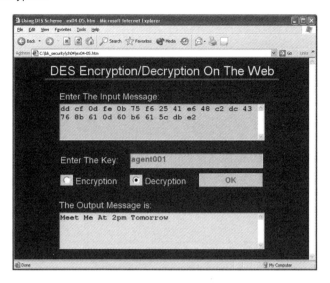

block ciphers with a fixed block length usually have the block effect. In other words, the same block will produce the same ciphertext with the same key. For a simple example, if you run the page ex04-05.htm with the following plaintext:

mysecretmysecretmysecret

you will see three sets (or blocks) of identical ciphertext '6d 3a 6f 1f 67 96 a4 c7' as illustrated in Figure 4.13. In this case, attackers can isolate the ciphertext block and perform brute-force attack more easily.

To eliminate (or reduce) the block effect of DES, the operation modes described in Section 4.1.2 can be applied. Since the most popular operation mode is cipher block chaining (CBC), we are going to implement this mode in this section. The CBC encryption and decryption processes are described in Figures 4.14 and 4.15.

Given an n-block plaintext $\{P_1, P_2, \ldots, P_n\}$, each P_i is 64 bits long. The CBC encryption process is governed by the iteration formula

$$C_1 = E(C_0 \char`^ P_1) \quad \text{and} \quad C_i = E(C_{i-1} \char`^ P_i) \quad \text{where } i = 1 \text{ to } n$$

The first block of ciphertext C_1 is obtained by encrypting P_1 and XORing with an initial predefined vector C_0. In the standard DES specification, the initial vector C_0 is also called IV. The C_1 is then XORed with P_2. The result is an iterative event to generate blocks of ciphertext. The CBC decryption is governed by the formula

$$P_1 = C_0 \char`^ D(C_1) \quad \text{and} \quad P_i = C_{i-1} \char`^ D(C_i) \quad \text{where } i = 1 \text{ to } n$$

The first ciphertext block (C_1) is used as the input block to the decryption function D() and then XORed with the initial vector C_0 to give the first plaintext block P_1. The

Fig. 4.13 DES block effect

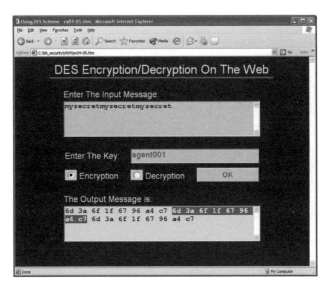

Fig. 4.14 DES CBC encryption process

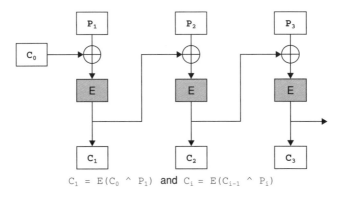

$$C_1 = E(C_0 \wedge P_1) \text{ and } C_i = E(C_{i-1} \wedge P_i)$$

second ciphertext block C_2 is decrypted by $D()$ and then XORed with C_1 producing plaintext block P_2. The process is continued until the entire plaintext is obtained. Provided the raw key and the initial vector are the same for both encryption/decryption, the same plaintext is obtained.

To implement the CBC mode, make a copy of ex04-05.js and call it ex04-06.js. At the end of this script add the program code in ex04-06.js.

Fig. 4.15 DES CBC decryption process

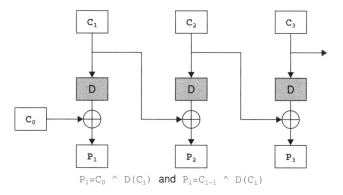

$$P_1=C_0 \text{ ^ } D(C_1) \text{ and } P_i=C_{i-1} \text{ ^ } D(C_i)$$

Example: ex04-06.js – The CBC mode of DES encryption/decryption

```
337: function cbc_des(keySt, msgSt, encrypt,ivSt)
338: {
339:   var m=0, chunk=0, len = msgSt.length;
340:   var tResult="",result="";
341:   var i,left,right, cbc_left, cbc_right, cbc_left2, cbc_right2;
342:   var iKeyArr = new Array(8), oKeyArr = new Array();
343:   var lrArr = new Array(2);
344:
345:   keySt += "\0\0\0\0\0\0\0\0"; keySt = keySt.substring(0,8);
346:   if (encrypt) oKeyArr = keyStToSubkeys(true,keySt);
347:   else         oKeyArr = keyStToSubkeys(false,keySt);
348:   msgSt += "\0\0\0\0\0\0\0\0";
349:
350:   cbc_left =(ivSt.charCodeAt(m++) << 24)
               |(ivSt.charCodeAt(m++) << 16) |
351:            (ivSt.charCodeAt(m++) << 8) |ivSt.charCodeAt(m++);
352:   cbc_right=(ivSt.charCodeAt(m++) << 24)
               |(ivSt.charCodeAt(m++) << 16) |
353:            (ivSt.charCodeAt(m++) << 8) |ivSt.charCodeAt(m++);
354:   m=0;
355:
356:   while (m < len) {
357:    lrArr[0]= (msgSt.charCodeAt(m++) << 24)
               |(msgSt.charCodeAt(m++) << 16)|
358:            (msgSt.charCodeAt(m++) << 8)
               | msgSt.charCodeAt(m++);
```

```
359:      lrArr[1]= (msgSt.charCodeAt(m++) << 24)
                  |(msgSt.charCodeAt(m++) << 16)|
360:               (msgSt.charCodeAt(m++) << 8)
                  | msgSt.charCodeAt(m++);
361:
362:     if (encrypt) {
363:            lrArr[0] ^= cbc_left;
364:            lrArr[1] ^= cbc_right;
365:     } else {
366:            cbc_left2 = cbc_left;
367:            cbc_right2 = cbc_right;
368:            cbc_left = lrArr[0];
369:            cbc_right = lrArr[1];
370:     }
371:
372:     lrArr= des_64bits(oKeyArr,lrArr[0],lrArr[1]);
373:
374:     if (encrypt) {
375:         cbc_left = lrArr[0];
376:         cbc_right = lrArr[1];
377:      } else {
378:         lrArr[0] ^= cbc_left2;
379:         lrArr[1] ^= cbc_right2;
380:      }
381:     tempSt= String.fromCharCode(
382:       ((lrArr[0] >>> 24) & 0xff), ((lrArr[0] >>> 16) & 0xff),
383:       ((lrArr[0] >>>  8) & 0xff), ( lrArr[0]        & 0xff),
384:       ((lrArr[1] >>> 24) & 0xff), ((lrArr[1] >>> 16) & 0xff),
385:       ((lrArr[1] >>>  8) & 0xff), ( lrArr[1]        & 0xff));
386:
387:     tResult += tempSt; chunk += 8;
388:     if (chunk == 512) {
389:        result += tResult; tResult = ""; chunk = 0;
390:      }
391:   }
392:   return result + tResult;
393: }
```

This script fragment contains one function cbc_des(keySt,msgSt,encrypt,ivSt), which is similar to the function des() in the previous section. This new function has one more parameter ivSt at the end so that users can input the initial vector ivSt (or c_0) to perform the encryption/decryption under the CBC mode. If you compare the program codes of this function with function des() in ex04-05.js, you will find that only three small batches of new lines have been added, and these are highlighted above.

The first batch of codes is in lines 350–354. They are used to process the 64-bit initial vector ivSt into two 32-bit integers called cbc_left and cbc_right. These two integers are used in the second batch of code in lines 362–370. When encryption is true, the statements in lines 363–364 will XOR the plaintext block lrArr[0] (i.e. 'left'), lrArr[1] (i.e. 'right') with cbc_left and cbc_right respectively to produce the first block of ciphertext with the function des_64bits().

Before outputting the result, the statements in lines 375–376 store the ciphertext block (or lrArr[0], lrArr[1]) into cbc_left and cbc_right for the next encryption. Therefore, the same process will chain the ciphertext into the encryption, achieving the objective of CBC. The decryption process follows similar lines.

From this example, you can see that adding operation mode is not a difficult task. To test this script, consider ex04-06.htm.

```
Example: ex04-06.htm - Page for DES cipher under CBC mode      (Part I)

 1: <style>
 2:  .butSt{font-size:16pt;width:250px;height:40px;
 3:         font-weight:bold;background:#dddddd;color:#ff0000}
 4:  .radSt{font-size:16pt;width:35px;height:30px;
 5:         font-weight:bold;background:#88ff88;color:#ff0000}
 6: </style>
 7: <body style="font-family:arial;font-size:26pt;text-align:center;
 8:       background:#000088;color:#ffff00">
 9:  DES Encryption/Decryption CBC Mode<br />
10:  <img alt="pic" src="line1.gif" height="7" width="650" /><br />
11:
12: <table style="font-size:18pt" align="center">
13:  <tr><td><br />Enter The Input Message: </td></tr>
14:  <tr><td><textarea style="font-size:16pt;width:570px;height:100px;
15:          font-weight:bold;background:#dddddd" rows="5" cols="40"
16:          id="in_mesg">Meet Me At 2pm Tomorrow</textarea></td></tr>
17: </table>
18: <form action="">
19: <table style="font-size:18pt" cellspacing="10" align="center">
20:  <tr><td>Enter The Key: </td>
21:      <td style="text-align:center" colspan=2>
22:       <input type="text" id="key_v" size="8" maxlength="8"
23:        style="font-size:16pt;width:370px;height:40px;
24:        font-weight:bold;background:#dddddd;
             color:#ff0000" value="agent001" /></td></tr>
```

```
25:  <tr><td>Enter The Initial Vector (IV): </td>
26:       <td style="text-align:center" colspan=2>
27:         <input type="text" id="iv_st" size="8" maxlength="8"
28:          style="font-size:16pt;width:370px;height:40px;
29:          font-weight:bold;background:#dddddd;
             color:#ff0000" value="agent001" /></td></tr>
30:
31:  <tr><td style="width:180px;text-align:left"><input
             type="radio" checked
32:          id="b_rad" name="b_rad" class="radSt" /> Encryption</td>
33:    <td style="width:180px;text-align:left"><input type="radio"
34:          id="b_rad" name="b_rad" class="radSt" /> Decryption</td>
35:    <td style="width:180px;text-align:left"><input size="20"
36:          type="button" class="butSt"
             style="width:180px" value="OK" onclick="cbc_des_fun()" />
37:    </td></tr>
38:  </table>
39:  </form>
40:  <table style="font-size:18pt" align="center">
41:   <tr><td>The Output Message is: </td></tr>
42:   <tr><td><textarea rows="5" cols="40" id="out_mesg" readonly
43:              style="font-size:16pt;font-weight:bold;width:570px;
44:              height:100px;background:#aaffaa"></textarea></td></tr>
45:  </table>
```

If you compare this page with ex04-05.htm, you will find that lines 25–29 are added. These XHTML codes generate another text box (line 27) on the screen. This box is used to get the initialization vector (IV) required by the CBC operation mode. Once the OK button defined in lines 35–36 is clicked, the function cbc_des_fun() is activated and the encryption is displayed in the text area in lines 42–44.

The function cbc_des_fun() is defined in part II of ex04-06.htm.

```
Example: Continuation of ex04-06.htm                        (Part II)

46: <script src="ex04-06.js"></script>
47: <script src="hexlib.js"></script>
48: <script>
49:  function cbc_des_fun()
50:  {
51:    var ivSt = ""
```

```
52:     var key="",message="",llst="";
53:     llV = document.getElementsByName("b_rad");
54:     if (llV.item(0).checked) {
55:        key = document.getElementById("key_v").value;
56:        ivSt = document.getElementById("iv_st").value;
57:        message = document.getElementById("in_mesg").value;
58:
59:        llst = byteStToHex(cbc_des(key, message, 1,ivSt));
60:        document.getElementById("out_mesg").value = llst;
61:     }
62:     if (llV.item(1).checked) {
63:        key = document.getElementById("key_v").value;
64:        ivSt = document.getElementById("iv_st").value;
65:        message = hexStToByteSt(document.getElementById("in_mesg").value);
66:
67:        llst = cbc_des(key, message, 0, ivSt);
68:        document.getElementById("out_mesg").value = llst;
69:     }
70:  }
71: </script>
72: </body>
```

This page fragment is similar to the second part of `ex04-05.htm`. The differences are the modified four lines highlighted. Line 56 is used to get the initialization vector and store it in variable `ivSt`. Line 59 calls the function `cbc_des(key,message,1,ivSt)` with an additional parameter `ivSt` to operate the encryption with CBC mode. Similarly, if the second radio box (i.e. decryption) is checked, line 64 gets the initial vector `ivSt`, and the function call in line 67 decrypts the message under CBC mode. Screenshots are shown in Figures 4.16 and 4.17.

From these two figures, we can see that there is no block effect under the CBC operation mode even if you have used the same initialization vector as the raw key. Some encryption/decryption results on a general message are shown in Figures 4.18 and 4.19.

In `ex04-06.js`, functions `des()` and `cbc_des()` are put together into one script. This arrangement makes it easy to develop a page with radio boxes which can be used to select DES or DES with CBC.

4.3.3   Double DES and the meet-in-the-middle attack

Soon after the DES algorithm was officially broken at the end of 1990s, a scheme known as 'double DES' was introduced to strengthen the DES algorithm. A direct,

Fig. 4.16 Block effect I

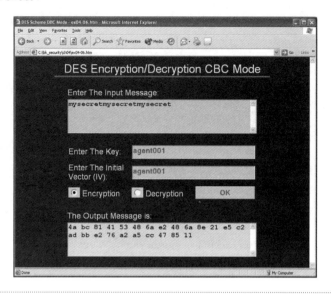

Fig. 4.17 Block effect II

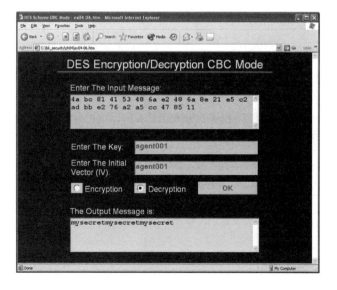

Fig. 4.18 DES CBC encryption

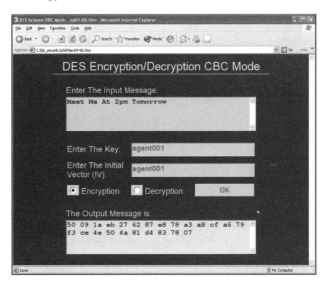

Fig. 4.19 DES CBC decryption

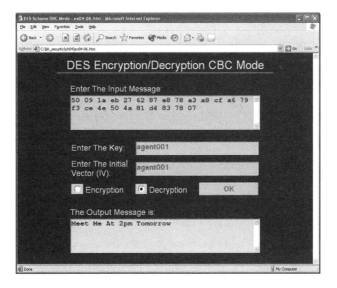

Fig. 4.20 The double DES scheme

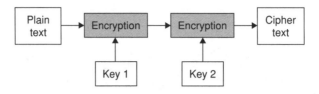

and reasonable, approach is to use two keys instead of one. Putting two 56-bit keys together, hopefully, would achieve the effect of 112-bit encryption strength. The construction is described in Figure 4.20.

Basically, the encryption result from the first key is encrypted again using the second key to produce the ciphertext. If one key, such as the first, is broken by a brute-force search, the attackers still need to crack the system with the second key. The double DES encryption scheme is governed by the formula below

$$C_i = E(k_2, E(k_1, P_i)) \qquad \text{where } i = 1 \text{ to } n$$

$E(k_1, P_i)$ is the DES encryption function on plaintext P_i using key k_1. However, the second key provides virtually no security improvement under the so-called 'meet–in–the–middle' (MITM) attack. The MITM attack is based on the following mathematical observation. The double DES scheme on a plaintext block P can be written as

$$C = E(k_2, E(k_1, P))$$

Let the encrypted result of $E(k_1, P) = X$; we have

$$C = E(k_2, X) \Rightarrow X = D(k_2, C)$$

The function $D()$ is the DES decryption. In other words, it says that you can perform encryption on P with key k_1 and decryption on C with key k_2. If the two sets of blocks match, you have found the keys (or potential keys) for k_1 and k_2. In fact, the matched block X will meet in the middle as

$$X = E(k_1, P) \qquad \text{and} \qquad X = D(k_2, C)$$

If the effort to defeat DES is 56-bit (or 2^{56}) trials, the total number of trials to crack double DES under MITM attack is $2^{56} + 2^{56} = 2^{57}$. The MITM attack is described below.

Given a plaintext P and a ciphertext C:

- encrypt P for all 2^{56} possible values of the first key k_1;
- store the results in a table and sort the table by the values of X;
- decrypt C using all 2^{56} possible values of the second key k_2;
- as each decryption is produced, check the result against the table. If two matching keys produce the correct block X, they are to be accepted as a candidate for the correct keys.

From a cryptology point of view, the second key provides little security for the system, and the improvement of double DES is not a lot compared with single DES. To overcome this MITM attack, three DES schemes are employed: hence the scheme is known as triple DES.

4.3.4   Implementation of triple DES

Triple DES (or Tri-DES) is a standard officially released as FIPS 46-3. The structure of Tri-DES is simple and is illustrated in Figure 4.21.

It takes three 64-bit keys, forming an overall key length of 192 bits. The upper part of Figure 4.20 describes the encryption process and the lower part is for decryption. Consider the Tri-DES encryption. The data P_i is encrypted with the first key k_1, decrypted with the second key k_2, and finally encrypted again with the third key k_3 to obtain the ciphertext C_i. The individual encryption/decryption functions $E()$ and $D()$ are exactly the same as single DES. The process is similar to performing three DES and, therefore, is called triple DES.

By default, you simply type in the entire 192-bit (24 character) raw key rather than each of the three keys individually. The algorithm will break the key into three individual keys, padding them if necessary so they are each 64 bits long and suitable for the DES action. Since single DES uses 56 bits of each key, the total key length of Tri-DES is, in fact, 168 bits.

Although Tri-DES runs three times slower than standard DES, it is much more secure if used properly. The procedure for decryption is the reverse order of encryption, as illustrated in Figure 4.21. There is no particular attack that can crack Tri-DES easily. It is, indeed, a strong block cipher and can be classified as Tri-DES[64:168].

Because three keys are used independently, the so-called 'weak key' cases may occur. For example, when the first and second, or the second and third, keys are

Fig. 4.21   Tri-DES encryption and decryption

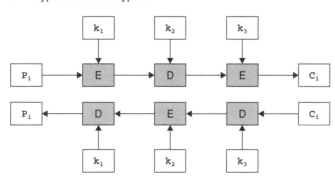

the same, the encryption procedure is essentially the same as standard DES. In this situation, the entire Tri-DES is equivalent to a really slow version of DES. Note that the weak key described here is not the same as the weak key for single DES in the literature. The weak key for single DES is, generally, referred to as a raw key that will generate some trivial 16 subkeys in the key schedule procedure. Weak keys for single DES are rather rare.

To implement Tri-DES on the Web, make a copy of ex04-05.js and call it ex04-07.js. At the end of this script, add the program codes listed in ex04-07.js.

```
Example: ex04-07.js - Triple DES encryption/decryption
337: function tri_des(keySt, msgSt, encrypt)
338: {
339:   var m=0, chunk=0 , len = msgSt.length;
340:   var i , result="", tResult="";
341:   var oKeyArr1= new Array(), oKeyArr2= new Array(),
       oKeyArr3=new Array();
342:   var tmpSt = new Array(3),lrArr = new Array(2);
343:
344:   keySt += "\0\0\0\0\0\0\0\0\0\0\0\0\0\0\0\0\0\0\0\0\0\0\0\0";
345:   for (j=0;j<3;j++) tmpSt[j] = keySt.substring(j*8,j*8+8);
346:
347:   if (encrypt) {
348:       oKeyArr1 = keyStToSubkeys(true, tmpSt[0]);
349:       oKeyArr2 = keyStToSubkeys(false,tmpSt[1]);
350:       oKeyArr3 = keyStToSubkeys(true, tmpSt[2]);
351:   } else {
352:       oKeyArr1 = keyStToSubkeys(false,tmpSt[0]);
353:       oKeyArr2 = keyStToSubkeys(true, tmpSt[1]);
354:       oKeyArr3 = keyStToSubkeys(false,tmpSt[2]);
355:   }
356:
357:   msgSt += "\0\0\0\0\0\0\0\0";
358:   while (m < len) {
359:    lrArr[0]= (msgSt.charCodeAt(m++) << 24)|
                  (msgSt.charCodeAt(m++) << 16)|
360:              (msgSt.charCodeAt(m++) << 8) |
                   msgSt.charCodeAt(m++);
361:    lrArr[1]= (msgSt.charCodeAt(m++) << 24)|
                  (msgSt.charCodeAt(m++) << 16)|
362:              (msgSt.charCodeAt(m++) << 8) |
                   msgSt.charCodeAt(m++);
363:
```

```
364:    if (encrypt) {
365:        lrArr= des_64bits(oKeyArr1,lrArr[0],lrArr[1]);
366:        lrArr= des_64bits(oKeyArr2,lrArr[0],lrArr[1]);
367:        lrArr= des_64bits(oKeyArr3,lrArr[0],lrArr[1]);
368:    } else {
369:        lrArr= des_64bits(oKeyArr3,lrArr[0],lrArr[1]);
370:        lrArr= des_64bits(oKeyArr2,lrArr[0],lrArr[1]);
371:        lrArr= des_64bits(oKeyArr1,lrArr[0],lrArr[1]);
372:    }
373:
374:    tempSt= String.fromCharCode(
375:        ((lrArr[0] >>> 24) & 0xff), ((lrArr[0] >>> 16) & 0xff),
376:        ((lrArr[0] >>>  8) & 0xff), ( lrArr[0]         & 0xff),
377:        ((lrArr[1] >>> 24) & 0xff), ((lrArr[1] >>> 16) & 0xff),
378:        ((lrArr[1] >>>  8) & 0xff), ( lrArr[1]         & 0xff));
379:
380:    tResult += tempSt; chunk += 8;
381:    if (chunk == 512) {
382:        result += tResult; tResult = ""; chunk = 0;
383:    }
384:    }
385:    return result + tResult;
386: }
```

This script fragment contains one function `tri_des(keySt,msgSt,encrypt)`, which is similar to the regular DES function `des()`. The differences are highlighted above.

First, three arrays are declared in line 341 to accommodate the three keys used in triple DES operation. Line 344 expands the key string `keySt` with zeros so that `keySt` can always be cut into three keys by the for-loop in line 345. Each key is eight characters long and is stored in array `tmpSt[]`. If encryption is `true`, the three sets of subkeys are created. The first set is for encryption. The second set is for decryption and the third is again for encryption, as illustrated by the statements in lines 348–350. Once all three sets of subkeys for encryption are ready, the statements in lines 365–367 are executed. These three statements just do DES three times according to the three sets of subkeys. As a result, the ciphertext from triple DES is produced in array `lrArr[]` in line 367. This array is printed out by the remaining lines.

For decryption, three sets of subkeys are generated by lines 352–254 following the order of decryption, encryption and decryption. Following the algorithm in Figure 4.20, the statements in lines 369–371 use these three sets of subkeys in reverse order to produce the plaintext.

Now, we have a workable script for triple DES encryption/decryption. To test this script, make a copy of ex04-05.htm, in Section 4.3.1, call it ex04-07.htm and modify the following six lines:

```
 9: Triple DES Encryption/Decryption<br />
22:           <input type="text" id="key_v" size="24" maxlength="24"
32:           class="butSt" style="width:180px" value="OK"
              onclick="tri_des_fun()" />
45: function tri_des_fun()
53:     llst = byteStToHex(tri_des(key, message, 1))
60:     llst = tri_des(key, message, 0)
```

Line 9 is to change the display text to indicate that we are working with the triple DES scheme. Line 22 is to extend the length of the input key to a maximum of 24 characters. Therefore users can input 24 or fewer characters in the text box provided. When the OK button is clicked, line 32 activates the function tri_des_fun(). This function is declared in line 45. Inside the function block, lines 53–60 change the function call to tri_des() so that triple DES is performed. Screenshots are shown in Figures 4.22 and 4.23.

From these two figures, you can see that triple DES is used and the input key is 24 characters (192-bit) long. One interesting feature of triple DES is that when the input key is eight characters long, it will reduce to single DES encryption/decryption automatically. The reason is that when the input key is eight characters long, the second and third keys are the same. In this case, the

Fig. 4.22 Triple DES encryption

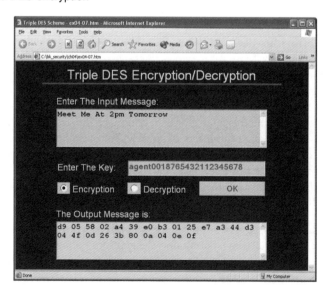

Fig. 4.23 Triple DES decryption

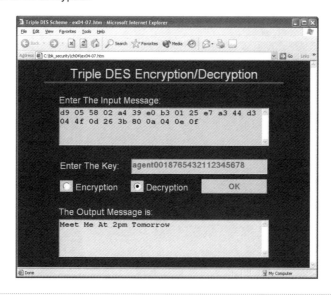

DES operations with the second and third keys are cancelled out by the algorithm design. Screenshots showing this feature are in Figures 4.24 and 4.25. If you change the `type` in line 22 from

    type="text"   to   type="password"

Fig. 4.24 Triple DES with one key

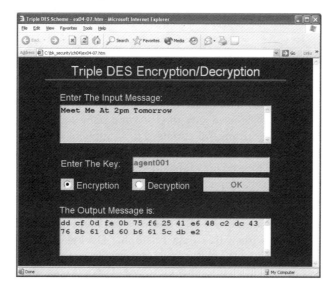

Fig. 4.25   Triple DES decryption

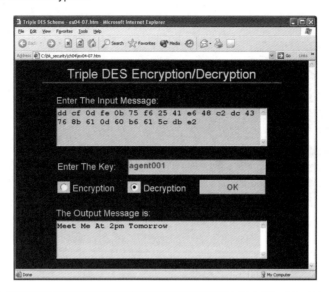

the text in the box will be replaced by big dots to increase security. In this book we will use clear text in the password field for demonstration purposes. In practice, all password fields should be protected by `type="password"`.

Now, we have a page to perform triple DES encryption/decryption on the Web. This is particularly practical for exchanging encrypted messages in real time over the Web, using software such as chat or instant messaging. If you want to encrypt or decrypt a file and exchange it over the Web, a utility may be more convenient.

4.3.5   Building a Tri-DES utility

The script implementations of DES and Tri-DES in the last few sections are only good for protecting small messages on the web and not practical for file applications. They can be used as a good starting point for demonstrating and understanding the algorithm. All you need is a couple of Web pages and you can use them almost anywhere, regardless of machine platforms and operating systems. If you want to use DES and Tri-DES on file type applications such as email attachments, exchanging files on the Web or protecting an entire directory for downloading, then a utility working on files may be what you are looking for.

There are many DES and/or Tri-DES software packages on the Internet. The one we are going to use is freeware from Christopher Devine under the GNU General Public License. A copy of the software is available from the book-supporting site and a number of search engines, including www.google.com. Basically you are free to use, modify and distribute the software as you like. Some readers may find that reference to search engines is provided instead of the holding site (URI or IP address) of the software. One reason is that some of the software- or package-holding sites change frequently. Searching through engines for the software and the author's information, in many cases, may be more reliable.

The Devine package implements the DES and Tri-DES schemes compliant to the FIPS 46-3 standard and comes with the two C program files below:

- `des.h` – header file for `des.c`;

- `des.c` – the C program to implement DES and Tri-DES algorithms.

If you have a C/C++ compiler such as Borland C/C++, Microsoft C/C++ or UNIX/Linux C/C++, you can compile this `des.c` program and build a DES/Tri-DES utility. By default the `des.c` program is not designed to generate an executable program to work with files. It contains the core functions for DES/Tri-DES operations instead. Also, there is a self-testing mechanism defined as a macro 'TEST' inside `des.c` so that you can determine whether you have a working package or not.

For our default `gcc` compiler for Windows, the following command is use to test the program:

```
gcc -D TEST -o des des.c
```

The macro TEST will force the compiler to generate an executable program called `des.exe` with testing codes. The compiling and testing processes are shown in Figure 4.26.

If you issued the command 'des', the test result is as shown in Figure 4.26.

Fig. 4.26 Testing `des.c`

```
H:\ch04>gcc -D TEST -o des des.c
H:\ch04>des

Triple-DES Monte Carlo Test (ECB mode) – encryption

    Test 1, key size =  64 bits: passed.
    Test 2, key size = 128 bits: passed.
    Test 3, key size = 192 bits: passed.

Triple-DES Monte Carlo Test (ECB mode) – decryption

    Test 1, key size =  64 bits: passed.
    Test 2, key size = 128 bits: passed.
    Test 3, key size = 192 bits: passed.

H:\chap04.dir>
```

The program des.c does not provide a utility allowing you to read files and generate encrypted results. In this case, you may need to write one yourself. If you read the file des.c, you will find that the following six statements are basically needed in order to do a Tri-DES encryption/decryption:

```
1: des3_context ctx3;
2: unsigned char buf[8];
3: unsigned char kkey1[8], kkey2[8], kkey3[8];
4: des3_set_3keys( &ctx3, kkey1,kkey2,kkey3 );
5: des3_encrypt( &ctx3, buf, buf );
6: des3_decrypt( &ctx3, buf, buf );
```

The first line defines a structure called des3_context. This structure is to store the subkeys. The second line defines a character array (or string) buf[] with eight characters. This array is used to store one chunk of plaintext for the Tri-DES scheme. The three keys are specified in line 3, and the function in line 4 uses these keys to set up all the subkeys. If you want encryption, you call the function in line 5; for decryption, the function in line 6 should be used instead.

To develop a driver to encrypt files, consider part I of the C program called des3driver.c.

Example: des3driver.c - A Tri-DES utility to work with files (Part I)

```
 1: #include <stdio.h>
 2: #include "des.h"
 3: #include "des.c"
 4:
 5: int main(int argc, char *argv[])
 6: {
 7:   int i, n;
 8:   des3_context ctx3;
 9:   unsigned char buf[8];
10:   unsigned char *kkey, kkey1[8], kkey2[8], kkey3[8];
11:   FILE *inK, *inP, *outF;
12:
13:   if (argc!=5) {
14:   printf("\nUsage:\n des3driver (e)|(d) <infile>
      <outfile> <keyfile>\n");
15:   return 2;
16: }
17: for (i=0;i<8;i++) {
18:   kkey1[i]=0; kkey2[i]=0; kkey3[i]=0; buf[i]=0;
19: }
20:
21: if((inK=fopen(argv[4],"rb"))==NULL){
22:     printf("\r\nCould not open input file: %s",argv[4]);
23:     return 2;
```

```
24: } else {
25:      fread(kkey1,1,8,inK);
26:      fread(kkey2,1,8,inK);
27:      fread(kkey3,1,8,inK);
28:      fclose(inK);
29: }
30: des3_set_3keys( &ctx3, kkey1,kkey2,kkey3 );
31:
```

This is a simple C program and should be easy to read even if you are not familiar with the language. First, the software package is included in this program in lines 2–3. After the variable declarations in lines 7–11, the usage of the program is set in lines 13–16. To use this program, four command line parameters are needed. The general calling syntax is

```
des3driver (e)|(d) <infile> <outfile> <keyfile>
```

For example, if you want to encrypt the infile called 'plain.txt' and send the output to outfile 'en.txt' using the keyfile 'kkey.txt', you can use the command

```
des3driver e plain.txt en.txt kkey.txt
```

Note that the key file 'kkey.txt' should contain three keys forming a maximum of 24 characters. The for-loop in lines 17–19 is to initialize the key arrays and the working chunk of data buf[]. The open file statement in line 21 opens the key file and the three keys are read by the statements in lines 25–27. The keys are used to call the function des3_set_3keys() in line 30 to set up all the subkeys. Now, the encryption and decryption are ready to be called. Consider part II of des3driver.c.

```
Example: Continuation of des3driver.c                          (Part II)

32:  if((inP=fopen(argv[2],"rb"))==NULL){
33:      printf("\r\nCould not open input file: %s",argv[2]);
34:      return 2;
35:  }
36:  if((outF=fopen(argv[3],"wb"))==NULL){
37:      printf("\r\nCould not open output file: %s",argv[3]);
38:      return 2;
39:  }
40:
41:  if(argv[1][0]=='e') {
42:    while ((n=fread(buf,1,8,inP)) >0) {
43:      if (n < 8) {
44:          for(i=n;i<8;i++) buf[i]=0;
45:      }
```

```
46:        des3_encrypt( &ctx3, buf, buf );
47:        if(fwrite(buf,1,8,outF) < 8) {
48:            printf("\r\nError writing to output file\r\n");
49:            return(3);
50:        }
51:    }
52: }
53: if(argv[1][0]=='d') {
54:    while ((n=fread(buf,1,8,inP)) >0) {
55:        des3_decrypt( &ctx3, buf, buf );
56:        if(fwrite(buf,1,8,outF) < 8){
57:            printf("\r\nError writing to output file\r\n");
58:            return(3);
59:        }
60:    }
61: }
62: fclose(inP); fclose(outF);
63: return 0;
64: }
```

Lines 32–39 open the `infile` and `outfile` files. If the first command line parameter
is 'e', the while-loop in lines 42–52 is executed to process the entire `infile`. The
read statement in line 42 reads in every eight characters to variable `buf`. If the
length of `buf` is not eight characters, the if-statement in lines 43–45 pads the string
with zeros. The function call in line 46 is to perform encryption on `buf`, and the
result is printed to `outfile` in line 47. The while-loop continues this process until
all the characters in the `infile` are exhausted. Likewise, if the first command line
parameter is 'd', the while-loop in lines 54–61 performs the decryption and the
result is saved in the `outfile`.

To compile the program, you can use the simple command 'gcc -o des3driver
des3driver.c' using the gcc compiler. If the two files `infile="plain.txt"` and
`keyfile ="kkey.txt"` contain the strings

```
plain.txt = "Meet Me At 2pm Tomorrow"
kkey.txt = "agent0018765432112345678"
```

the commands below will perform encryption and decryption accordingly:

```
des3driver e plain.txt en.txt kkey.txt
des3driver d en.txt   de.txt kkey.txt
```

The execution process is captured and shown in Figure 4.27.

The encrypted file from `des3driver` can be sent as an email attachment or as a file
downloaded from a Web page. If you have a large number of documents to protect,
you can encrypt all the files using the program `des3driver`. Then zip them, and put
them into a directory (e.g. `des3protected.dir`). The next step is to use the browsing

Fig. 4.27 Running the `des3driver` program

```
H:\ch04>gcc -o des3driver des3driver.c
H:\ch04>des3driver

Usage:

  des3driver (e)|(d) <infile> <outfile> <keyfile>

H:\ch04> des3driver e plain.txt en.txt kkey.txt
H:\ch04> des3driver d en.txt de.txt kkey.txt
H:\ch04>type de.txt

Meet Me At 2pm Tomorrow
H:\ch04>
```

capability of the browser (IE, NS or Opera) on the directory to download and unzip the individual file. Only the person with the password can decrypt the files easily (see Figure 4.28).

Compared to script on the Web environment, C implementation is much faster. For example, using this `des3driver` tool it takes less than one second to both encrypt and decrypt a 2MB Acrobat `pdf` file on a low-end portable PC (2.0 GHz).

There are two DES-like ciphers popular in the security sector and they are CAST-128 and IDEA. The IDEA algorithm is patented and only CAST-128 is described in the next section.

Fig. 4.28 Protecting all files

4.4 A DES-like cipher: CAST-128

4.4.1 What is CAST-128?

CAST-128 (also called CAST5) is a block cipher developed by Carlisle Adams and Stafford Tavares (CAST). It is a DES-like cipher simply because both of them belong to the 'Feistel' type ciphers using (L_0, R_0) representing the block, a set of subkeys and iterative functions to compute the ciphertext. In fact, they work on the so-called 'substitution–permutation network' (SPN). The structure of a general Feistel cipher and the SPN are illustrated in Figure 4.29.

The basic operation is that a plaintext P with block length = $2n$ bits is split into a two-half pair (L1,R1). The right half R1 and a subkey K1 are input to a so-called 'round function', f1; the output is then used to XOR with the left half L1. Swapping the left and right halves generates another pair (L2,R2). This process is called round 1 of the cipher. The operations can continue to as many rounds as are defined by the cipher. After the final round, the pair (Ln+1,Rn+1) are concatenated to form the ciphertext block c. Ciphers with Feistel structure have been studied for many years. A good example is the DES.

In general, the security strength of this type of cipher is proportional to the number of 'rounds' involved. However, using more rounds slows down the operations. Also, good S-box design alone for function does not necessarily produce good crypto-strength. The key schedule is another important aspect in designing a good Feistel cipher. Using part of the S-boxes to generate subkeys is another good example, which is a characteristic of a cipher called CAST-128.

CAST-128 operates on 64-bit blocks with key length 128 bits. Unlike Tri-DES, the 128-bit key length of CAST-128 is continuous as a single string. There are no known attacks and it is quite secure. It is known as the RFC 2144 standard and is the default cipher in a well-known security package called 'Pretty Good Privacy' (PGP).

Fig. 4.29 Feistel cipher and the substitution–permutation network

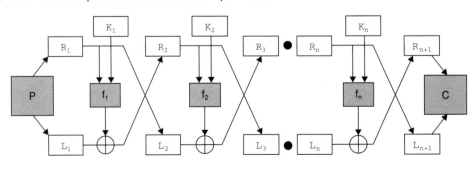

4.4.2 The CAST-128 encryption/decryption algorithm

Like the DES algorithm, the CAST-128 scheme involves two processes. The first is the 'key schedule' and the other is '16 rounds of iteration' (see Figure 4.30).

Given the 64-bit plaintext $M=(m1\ldots m64)$ and the 128-bit key $K=(k1,\ldots,k128)$, the algorithm produces a 64-bit ciphertext $C = (c1,\ldots,c64)$ in the following steps.

Step 1 Compute 16 pairs of subkeys {Kmi, Kri} from K (key schedule) (details will be discussed later).

Step 2 Split the plaintext into left and right 32-bit halves (L_0, R_0) where $L_0 = m1\ldots m32$ and $R_0 = m33\ldots m64$.

Step 3 For $i = 1$ to 16, compute L_i and R_i as follows:
$L_i = R_{i-1}$;
$R_i = f(L_{i-1},R_{i-1},Kmi,Kri)$, where the function f() is one of f1(), f2(), or f3(), depending on i.

Step 4 Exchange final blocks L_{16}, R_{16} and concatenate to form the ciphertext, i.e. $(R_{16},L_{16}) = c1,\ldots,c64$

The decryption process is identical to the encryption algorithm given above, except that the rounds of subkey pairs are applied in reverse order.

The iterative function $f(L_{i-1},R_{i-1},Kmi,Kri)$ used by CAST-128

The iteration function f() is defined by three functions f1(), f2() and f3(). The pseudo-codes are:

```
f1(L,R,Kmi,Kri) {
  I = ((Kmi + R) <<<- Kri)            // Symbol <<<- is left rotation
  I = Ia,Ib,Ic,Id                     // represent I as 4 bytes Ia,Ib,Ic,Id
  Return L ^ (((S1[Ia] ^ S2[Ib]) - S3[Ic]) + S4[Id])
}
```

Fig. 4.30 The CAST-128 encryption scheme

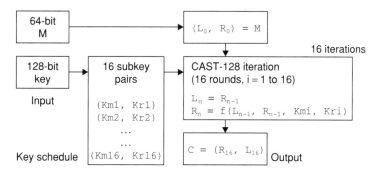

```
f2(L,R,Kmi,Kri) {
  I = ((Kmi ^ R) <<<- Kri)
  I = Ia,Ib,Ic,Id
  Return L ^ (((S1[Ia] - S2[Ib]) + S3[Ic]) ^ S4[Id])
}
f3(L,R,Kmi,Kri) {
  I = ((Kmi - R) <<<- Kri)
  I = Ia,Ib,Ic,Id
  Return L ^ (((S1[Ia] + S2[Ib]) ^ S3[Ic]) - S4[Id])
}
```

The usage of the function f() is governed by the iteration formula below:

$$f(L, R, Kmi, Kri) = \begin{cases} f1\ (L, R, Kmi, Kri) & \text{Rounds } (1, 4, 7, 10, 13) \\ f2\ (L, R, Kmi, Kri) & \text{Rounds } (2, 5, 8, 11, 14) \\ f3\ (L, R, Kmi, Kri) & \text{Rounds } (3, 6, 9, 12, 15) \end{cases}$$

The S-boxes S1[], S2[], S3[] and S4[] are predefined and provided in RFC 2144. Compared to RFC 2144, we have built the XOR operation of L into the functions f1(), f2() and f3() so that all functions are working on left (L) and right (R) fashion.

Key schedule for CAST-128

To generate all the key pairs (Kmi, Kri), the 128-bit key K is first represented as 16 bytes, i.e.

```
K= x0x1x2x3x4x5x6x7x8x9xAxBxCxDxExF
```

where x0 is the most significant byte, x1 is the second significant byte and so on. Together with a temporary variable T (also 16 bytes)

```
T= z0z1z2z3z4z5z6z7z8z9zAzBzCzDzEzF
```

the subkeys are generated by the following algorithm (from RFC 2144).

```
for (n=0;n<2;n++) {
    z0z1z2z3 = x0x1x2x3 ^ S5[xD] ^ S6[xF] ^ S7[xC] ^ S8[xE] ^ S7[x8]
    z4z5z6z7 = x8x9xAxB ^ S5[z0] ^ S6[z2] ^ S7[z1] ^ S8[z3] ^ S8[xA]
    z8z9zAzB = xCxDxExF ^ S5[z7] ^ S6[z6] ^ S7[z5] ^ S8[z4] ^ S5[x9]
    zCzDzEzF = x4x5x6x7 ^ S5[zA] ^ S6[z9] ^ S7[zB] ^ S8[z8] ^ S6[xB]
            K[1+n*16] = S5[z8] ^ S6[z9] ^ S7[z7] ^ S8[z6] ^ S5[z2]
            K[2+n*16] = S5[zA] ^ S6[zB] ^ S7[z5] ^ S8[z4] ^ S6[z6]
            K[3+n*16] = S5[zC] ^ S6[zD] ^ S7[z3] ^ S8[z2] ^ S7[z9]
            K[4+n*16] = S5[zE] ^ S6[zF] ^ S7[z1] ^ S8[z0] ^ S8[zC]
    x0x1x2x3 = z8z9zAzB ^ S5[z5] ^ S6[z7] ^ S7[z4] ^ S8[z6] ^ S7[z0]
    x4x5x6x7 = z0z1z2z3 ^ S5[x0] ^ S6[x2] ^ S7[x1] ^ S8[x3] ^ S8[z2]
    x8x9xAxB = z4z5z6z7 ^ S5[x7] ^ S6[x6] ^ S7[x5] ^ S8[x4] ^ S5[z1]
    xCxDxExF = zCzDzEzF ^ S5[xA] ^ S6[x9] ^ S7[xB] ^ S8[x8] ^ S6[z3]
```

```
        K[5+n*16]  = S5[x3] ^ S6[x2] ^ S7[xC] ^ S8[xD] ^ S5[x8]
        K[6+n*16]  = S5[x1] ^ S6[x0] ^ S7[xE] ^ S8[xF] ^ S6[xD]
        K[7+n*16]  = S5[x7] ^ S6[x6] ^ S7[x8] ^ S8[x9] ^ S7[x3]
        K[8+n*16]  = S5[x5] ^ S6[x4] ^ S7[xA] ^ S8[xB] ^ S8[x7]
 z0z1z2z3 = x0x1x2x3 ^ S5[xD] ^ S6[xF] ^ S7[xC] ^ S8[xE] ^ S7[x8]
 z4z5z6z7 = x8x9xAxB ^ S5[z0] ^ S6[z2] ^ S7[z1] ^ S8[z3] ^ S8[xA]
 z8z9zAzB = xCxDxExF ^ S5[z7] ^ S6[z6] ^ S7[z5] ^ S8[z4] ^ S5[x9]
 zCzDzEzF = x4x5x6x7 ^ S5[zA] ^ S6[z9] ^ S7[zB] ^ S8[z8] ^ S6[xB]
        K[9+n*16]  = S5[z3] ^ S6[z2] ^ S7[zC] ^ S8[zD] ^ S5[z9]
        K[10+n*16] = S5[z1] ^ S6[z0] ^ S7[zE] ^ S8[zF] ^ S6[zC]
        K[11+n*16] = S5[z7] ^ S6[z6] ^ S7[z8] ^ S8[z9] ^ S7[z2]
        K[12+n*16] = S5[z5] ^ S6[z4] ^ S7[zA] ^ S8[zB] ^ S8[z6]
 x0x1x2x3 = z8z9zAzB ^ S5[z5] ^ S6[z7] ^ S7[z4] ^ S8[z6] ^ S7[z0]
 x4x5x6x7 = z0z1z2z3 ^ S5[x0] ^ S6[x2] ^ S7[x1] ^ S8[x3] ^ S8[z2]
 x8x9xAxB = z4z5z6z7 ^ S5[x7] ^ S6[x6] ^ S7[x5] ^ S8[x4] ^ S5[z1]
 xCxDxExF = zCzDzEzF ^ S5[xA] ^ S6[x9] ^ S7[xB] ^ S8[x8] ^ S6[z3]
        K[13+n*16] = S5[x8] ^ S6[x9] ^ S7[x7] ^ S8[x6] ^ S5[x3]
        K[14+n*16] = S5[xA] ^ S6[xB] ^ S7[x5] ^ S8[x4] ^ S6[x7]
        K[15+n*16] = S5[xC] ^ S6[xD] ^ S7[x3] ^ S8[x2] ^ S7[x8]
        K[16+n*16] = S5[xE] ^ S6[xF] ^ S7[x1] ^ S8[x0] ^ S8[xD]
    }
```

The S-boxes `S5[]`, `S6[]`, `S7[]` and `S8[]` are predefined and provided by the standard RFC 2144. The `n` for-loop generates 32 keys, namely `K[1]`–`K[32]`. The key pairs (`Kmi,Kri`) are extracted from the 16 key arrays by the pseudo-code

```
for (i=1; i<=16; i++) { Kmi = K[i]; Kri = K[16+i]; }
```

In other words, the first 16 keys `K1`–`K16` are stored in `Kmi` and another 16 keys are stored in `Kri`. For those `Kri` keys, only the least 5 bits are used. A typical implementation of CAST-128 uses 32-bit words so that the 4 bytes, such as z0z1z2z3, can be represented by one 32-bit word (or one integer).

Variable key size issues

The design of the CAST-128 algorithm allows us to have some control on the key length. The rules are

- for key length from 40 bits to 80 bits with increment of eight bits (i.e., 40, 48, 56, 64, 72 and 80 bits), the algorithm runs 12 rounds instead of the full 16 rounds;

- for key length from 80 bits to the full 128 bits, the algorithm uses the full 16 rounds;

- if the key length is less than 128 bits, the key is padded with zeros.

If the key is implemented as a byte (8-bit) character stream, this key length issue simply detects how many characters are in the key. If the number of characters is fewer than or equal to 10, then 12 rounds of iteration are run. Otherwise, the full 16 rounds of iterations are run. Now, let's see how to implement the scheme on the Web.

4.4.3   Implementation of CAST-128 on the Web

Following the algorithm in the last section, the implementation of CAST-128 is not difficult.

The first thing is to copy the data of S-boxes `S1[]` to `S8[]` from RFC 2144 into a new script called `ex04-08.js`. Define them as arrays such as

```
  1: var S1 = new Array (
  2: 0x30FB40D4, 0x9FA0FF0B, 0x6BECCD2F, 0x3F258C7A,
  3: 0x1E213F2F, 0x9C004DD3, 0x6003E540, 0xCF9FC949,
     ... ...        ... ...        ... ...     ... ...
463: var S8 = new Array (
     ... ...        ... ...        ... ...     ... ...
526: 0x04F19130, 0xBA6E4EC0, 0x99265164, 0x1EE7230D,
527: 0x50B2AD80, 0xEAEE6801, 0x8DB2A283, 0xEA8BF59E );
528:
```

Yes, the S-box data occupy a total of 527 lines. To the end of this data, attach part I of `ex04-08.js`.

Example: ex04-08.js – CAST-128 encryption/decryption   (Part I)

```
529: function Ia(x) { return (x>>>24); }
530: function Ib(x) { return ((x>>>16) & 0xff); }
531: function Ic(x) { return ((x>>>8) & 0xff); }
532: function Id(x) { return ((x) & 0xff); }
533: function ROL(x, n) { return ((x)<<(n)) | ((x)>>>(32-(n))) }
534:
535: var xkey= new Array(32);
536: var rounds;
537:
538: function F1(l, r, i)
539: {
540:   t = ROL(xkey[i] + r, xkey[i+16]);
541:   l ^= ((S1[Ia(t)] ^ S2[Ib(t)]) - S3[Ic(t)]) + S4[Id(t)];
542:   return l;
543: }
544:
```

```
545: function F2(l, r, i)
546: {
547:     t = ROL(xkey[i] ^ r, xkey[i+16]);
548:     l ^= ((S1[Ia(t)] - S2[Ib(t)]) + S3[Ic(t)]) ^ S4[Id(t)];
549:   return l;
550: }
551:
552: function F3(l, r, i)
553: {
554:     t = ROL(xkey[i] - r, xkey[i+16]);
555:     l ^= ((S1[Ia(t)] + S2[Ib(t)]) ^ S3[Ic(t)]) - S4[Id(t)];
556:   return l;
557: }
558:
```

Given a 32-bit word containing four bytes `Ia`, `Ib`, `Ic` and `Id`, the functions `Ia()`, `Ib()`, `Ic()` and `Id()` in lines 529–532 are used to extract the individual bytes. Line 533 defines a left-rotation function for any 32-bit word. The global variable `xkey[]` in line 535 stores the key pairs `(Kmr, Kri)`. The variable `rounds` records the number of rounds needed. The functions `F1()`, `F2()` and `F3()` in lines 538–557 are direct coding from the algorithm. The encryption and decryption are implemented in part II of `ex04-08.js`.

Example: Continuation of ex04-08.js   (Part II)

```
559: function cast128_encrypt(inblock)
560: {
561:   var t, l, r;
562:   var outblock = new Array();
563:
564:   l=(inblock[0]<<24)|(inblock[1]<<16)|(inblock[2]<<8)|inblock[3];
565:   r=(inblock[4]<<24)|(inblock[5]<<16)|(inblock[6]<<8)|inblock[7];
566:
567:   l=F1(l,r,0); r=F2(r,l,1); l=F3(l,r, 2); r=F1(r,l,3);
568:   l=F2(l,r,4); r=F3(r,l,5); l=F1(l,r, 6); r=F2(r,l,7);
569:   l=F3(l,r,8); r=F1(r,l,9); l=F2(l,r,10); r=F3(r,l,11);
570:   if (rounds > 12) {
571:       l=F1(l, r, 12); r=F2(r, l, 13);
572:       l=F3(l, r, 14); r=F1(r, l, 15);
573:   }
574:
```

```
575:    outblock[0] = Ia(r); outblock[1] = Ib(r);
576:    outblock[2] = Ic(r); outblock[3] = Id(r);
577:    outblock[4] = Ia(l); outblock[5] = Ib(l);
578:    outblock[6] = Ic(l); outblock[7] = Id(l);
579:    t = l = r = 0;
580:    return outblock;
581: }
582:
583: function cast128_decrypt(inblock)
584: {
585:    var t, l, r;
586:    var outblock = new Array();
587:
588:    r=(inblock[0]<<24)|(inblock[1]<<16)|(inblock[2]<<8)|inblock[3];
589:    l=(inblock[4]<<24)|(inblock[5]<<16)|(inblock[6]<<8)|inblock[7];
590:
591:    if (rounds > 12) {
592:         r= F1(r,l,15); l= F3(l,r,14);
593:         r= F2(r,l,13); l= F1(l,r,12);
594:    }
595:    r= F3(r,l,11); l= F2(l,r,10); r= F1(r,l,9); l= F3(l,r,8);
596:    r= F2(r,l, 7); l= F1(l,r, 6); r= F3(r,l,5); l= F2(l,r,4);
597:    r= F1(r,l, 3); l= F3(l,r, 2); r= F2(r,l,1); l= F1(l,r,0);
598:
599:    outblock[0] = Ia(l); outblock[1] = Ib(l);
600:    outblock[2] = Ic(l); outblock[3] = Id(l);
601:    outblock[4] = Ia(r); outblock[5] = Ib(r);
602:    outblock[6] = Ic(r); outblock[7] = Id(r);
603:    t = l = r = 0;
604:    return outblock;
605: }
606:
```

This script fragment contains two functions. The function cast128_encrypt() is for encryption. It takes a 64-bit block called inblock as a parameter. The encrypted result is returned by variable outblock. Lines 564–565 split the inblock into left (i.e. l) and right (i.e. r). Lines 567–569 perform 12 rounds of iteration. If the variable rounds is bigger than 12, the conditional-if statement is executed and four more rounds are run in lines 571–572. When finished, the result is stored in variable outblock (lines 575–578). This variable is returned to the function caller by the statement in line 580. The decryption function cast128_decrypt() is similar to the encryption and should be easy to read. The program codes for the key schedule process are defined in part III of ex04-08.js.

Example: Continuation of ex04-08.js   **(Part III)**

```
607: function cast128_setkey(rawkey,keybytes)
608: {
609:   var t = new Array(4), z = new Array(4), x = new Array(4), i;
610:
611:   rounds = (keybytes <= 10 ? 12 : 16);
612:   for (i=0; i< 32; i++) { xkey[i]=0;}
613:   for (i = 0; i < 4; i++) {
614:     x[i] = 0;
615:     if ((i*4+0) < keybytes) x[i]  = rawkey[i*4+0] << 24;
616:     if ((i*4+1) < keybytes) x[i] |= rawkey[i*4+1] << 16;
617:     if ((i*4+2) < keybytes) x[i] |= rawkey[i*4+2] << 8;
618:     if ((i*4+3) < keybytes) x[i] |= rawkey[i*4+3];
619:   }
620:   for (i = 0; i < 32; i+=4) {
621:    switch (i & 4) {
622:     case 0:
623:       t[0]=z[0]=x[0] ^ S5[Ib(x[3])] ^ S6[Id(x[3])] ^
                          S7[Ia(x[3])] ^
624:                      S8[Ic(x[3])] ^ S7[Ia(x[2])];
625:       t[1]=z[1]=x[2] ^ S5[Ia(z[0])] ^ S6[Ic(z[0])] ^
                          S7[Ib(z[0])] ^
626:                      S8[Id(z[0])] ^ S8[Ic(x[2])];
627:       t[2]=z[2]=x[3] ^ S5[Id(z[1])] ^ S6[Ic(z[1])] ^
                          S7[Ib(z[1])] ^
628:                      S8[Ia(z[1])] ^ S5[Ib(x[2])];
629:       t[3]=z[3]=x[1] ^ S5[Ic(z[2])] ^ S6[Ib(z[2])] ^
                          S7[Id(z[2])] ^
630:                      S8[Ia(z[2])] ^ S6[Id(x[2])];
631:     break;
632:     case 4:
633:       t[0]=x[0]=z[2] ^ S5[Ib(z[1])] ^ S6[Id(z[1])] ^
                          S7[Ia(z[1])] ^
634:                      S8[Ic(z[1])] ^ S7[Ia(z[0])];
635:       t[1]=x[1]=z[0] ^ S5[Ia(x[0])] ^ S6[Ic(x[0])] ^
                          S7[Ib(x[0])] ^
636:                      S8[Id(x[0])] ^ S8[Ic(z[0])];
637:       t[2]=x[2]=z[1] ^ S5[Id(x[1])] ^ S6[Ic(x[1])] ^
                          S7[Ib(x[1])] ^
638:                      S8[Ia(x[1])] ^ S5[Ib(z[0])];
639:       t[3]=x[3]=z[3] ^ S5[Ic(x[2])] ^ S6[Ib(x[2])] ^
                          S7[Id(x[2])] ^
640:                      S8[Ia(x[2])] ^ S6[Id(z[0])];
641:     break;
642:    }
```

```
643:        switch (i & 12) {
644:     case 0:
645:     case 12:
646:        xkey[i+0]=S5[Ia(t[2])]^S6[Ib(t[2])]^S7[Id(t[1])]^S8[Ic(t[1])];
647:        xkey[i+1]=S5[Ic(t[2])]^S6[Id(t[2])]^S7[Ib(t[1])]^S8[Ia(t[1])];
648:        xkey[i+2]=S5[Ia(t[3])]^S6[Ib(t[3])]^S7[Id(t[0])]^S8[Ic(t[0])];
649:        xkey[i+3]=S5[Ic(t[3])]^S6[Id(t[3])]^S7[Ib(t[0])]^S8[Ia(t[0])];
650:        break;
651:     case 4:
652:     case 8:
653:        xkey[i+0]=S5[Id(t[0])]^S6[Ic(t[0])]^S7[Ia(t[3])]^S8[Ib(t[3])];
654:        xkey[i+1]=S5[Ib(t[0])]^S6[Ia(t[0])]^S7[Ic(t[3])]^S8[Id(t[3])];
655:        xkey[i+2]=S5[Id(t[1])]^S6[Ic(t[1])]^S7[Ia(t[2])]^S8[Ib(t[2])];
656:        xkey[i+3]=S5[Ib(t[1])]^S6[Ia(t[1])]^S7[Ic(t[2])]^S8[Id(t[2])];
657:        break;
658:     }
659:     switch (i & 12) {
660:      case 0:
661:        xkey[i+0] ^= S5[Ic(z[0])]; xkey[i+1] ^= S6[Ic(z[1])];
662:        xkey[i+2] ^= S7[Ib(z[2])]; xkey[i+3] ^= S8[Ia(z[3])];
663:        break;
664:      case 4:
665:        xkey[i+0] ^= S5[Ia(x[2])]; xkey[i+1] ^= S6[Ib(x[3])];
666:        xkey[i+2] ^= S7[Id(x[0])]; xkey[i+3] ^= S8[Id(x[1])];
667:        break;
668:      case 8:
669:        xkey[i+0] ^= S5[Ib(z[2])]; xkey[i+1] ^= S6[Ia(z[3])];
670:        xkey[i+2] ^= S7[Ic(z[0])]; xkey[i+3] ^= S8[Ic(z[1])];
671:        break;
672:      case 12:
673:        xkey[i+0] ^= S5[Id(x[0])]; xkey[i+1] ^= S6[Id(x[1])];
674:        xkey[i+2] ^= S7[Ia(x[2])]; xkey[i+3] ^= S8[Ib(x[3])];
675:        break;
676:     }
677:     if (i >= 16) {
678:      xkey[i+0] &= 31; xkey[i+1] &= 31;
679:      xkey[i+2] &= 31; xkey[i+3] &= 31;
680:     }
681:   }
682:   for (i = 0; i < 4; i++) { t[i] = x[i] = z[i] = 0; }
683: }
684:
```

This script contains one function called `cast128_setkey(rawkey,keybytes)`. This function uses the user key and key length in bytes as parameters. The purpose is to generate all key pairs (Kmi, Kri) in the algorithm. This script is a direct implementation of the 'key schedule' in Section 4.4.2 and is not difficult to read. Line 611 determines the number of iteration rounds depending on the key length in bytes (i.e. keyBytes). Lines 614–618 store the raw key into array elements x[0], x[1], x[2] and x[3]. Since these elements are 32-bit, they represent a total of 128 bits (16 bytes) keys, i.e.

```
X[0]=x0x1x2x3     X[1]=x4x5x6x7     X[2]=x8x9xAxB     X[3]=xCxDxExF
```

A similar setting is applied to arrays z[0],z[1],z[2] and z[3] so that the operations in lines 621–642 are parallel to the algorithm. The for-loop in lines 620–681 runs the loop eight times (i = 0 to 31 with step 4). Each loop generates four elements so that a total of 32 elements in xkey[] are generated. The first 16 elements in xkey[] are for Kmi. The remaining elements are for Kri. The statements in lines 677–680 make sure that the keys Kri are only 5 bits compliant to the algorithm mentioned in Section 4.1.1. Now, we have the core functions for a CAST-128 scheme. To use the script in practice, let's develop some tools and Web pages.

4.5 Encryption/decryption tools with CAST-128

4.5.1 A functional page for CAST-128 encryption/decryption

In order to develop a general purpose Web page to use CAST-128, some interface functions which make use of script ex04-08.js are needed. Following the programming structure for the DES and Tri-DES cases, these functions are added to the end of ex04-08.js, as shown in part IV.

```
Example: Continuation of ex04-08.js                        (Part IV)
685: function keyStToSubkeys(inSt)
686: {
687:   var i, rKeyArr = new Array();
688:   for (i=0; i< inSt.length ; i++) rKeyArr[i] = inSt.charCodeAt(i);
689:   cast128_setkey(rKeyArr,inSt.length);
690: }
691:
692: function cast128(keySt, msgSt, encrypt)
693: {
694:   var m=0, chunk=0, len = msgSt.length;
695:   var i, tResult="", result="", tempSt="";
696:   var msgArr = new Array(8), outArr = new Array(8);
697:
698:   keyStToSubkeys(keySt);
699:
700:   while (m < len) {
701:     for (i=0;i<8;i++) msgArr[i] = msgSt.charCodeAt(m++);
702:     if (encrypt) {
703:        outArr= cast128_encrypt(msgArr);
704:     } else {
705:        outArr= cast128_decrypt(msgArr);
706:     }
707:     tempSt = "";
708:     for (i=0;i<8;i++) {
709:       tempSt += String.fromCharCode(outArr[i]);
710:     }
711:     tResult += tempSt; chunk += 8;
712:     if (chunk == 512) {
713:        result += tResult; tResult = ""; chunk = 0;
714:     }
715:   }
716:   return result + tResult;
717: }
718:
```

The first function in this script fragment is keyStToSubkeys(inSt). This function takes the user input key as variable inSt and generates all the key pairs (Kmi, Kri) which are stored in array xkey[] (see Part I of ex04-08.js). Since the key schedule process is designed to work with byte streams, the for-loop in line 688 converts inSt into a series of bytes in rKeyArr[]. This array is then submitted to function cast128_setkey() to generate all the keys.

The second function cast128() is the main interface. Users call this function with the raw key (keySt), the message to be processed (msgSt) and a boolean type variable encrypt. If the value in encrypt is true, this function will encrypt the message msgSt. A false value will decrypt the message. In fact, the structure of this function is similar to the interface functions for the DES and Tri-DES cases. Line 698 calls the function keyStToSubkeys() to set up all the subkeys. The while-loop in lines 700–715 processes the message msgSt block by block. The for-loop in line 701 copies one block of data into array msgArr[]. If encryption is true, the statement in line 703 encrypts the block msgArr[]. Otherwise, decryption is performed in line 705. The for-loop in lines 708–710 combines the block msgArr[] into one single string in tempSt. The remaining program codes are for display purposes and are the same as ex04-06.js and ex04-07.js.

To test this script, make a copy of ex04-07.htm and call it ex04-08.htm. In this page, modify the following lines:

```
 9: The CAST-128 Encryption/Decryption<br />
22:          <input type="text" id="key_v" size="16" maxlength="16"
32:          class="butSt" style="width:180px" value="OK"
             onclick="cast128_fun()" />
45:  function cast128_fun()
53:       llst = byteStToHex(cast128(key, message, 1))
60:       llst = cast128(key, message, 0)
```

Line 9 changes the display so that we are working with the CAST-128 cipher. Line 22 changes the size and maxlength of the key box to 16 characters. In this case, the maximum number of characters the user can input is 16 (128 bits). When the OK button is clicked, the function activated by line 32 is cast128_fun(). This function is defined in line 45. Inside this function, all you need to do is change the function call in lines 53 and 60. Since we are using the same structure, these lines are exactly the same as the modified lines for the Tri-DES case, i.e. ex04-07.js. Screenshots are shown in Figures 4.31 and 4.32.

In order to do encryption and decryption on files, a CAST-128 scheme is built in the next section.

4.5.2   Building a CAST-128 utility

In this section, a CAST-128 utility to work with files is built using the same program design as DES/Tri-DES so that the same calling syntax and applications

Fig. 4.31 CAST-128 encryption

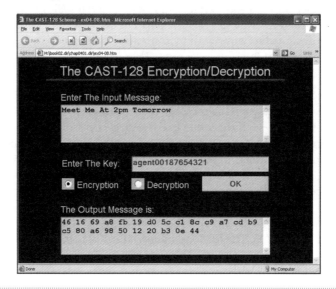

Fig. 4.32 CAST-128 decryption

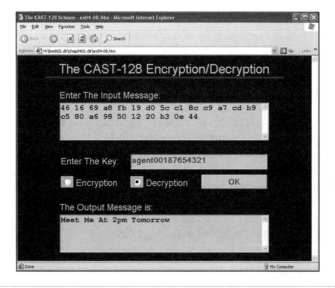

are achieved. The software package that we are going to use is a public domain program from Steve Reid. The software implements the CAST-128 scheme according to the RFC 2144 standard. The following files are included in the package:

- cast128.h – header file for cast128.c;

- cast128sb.h – header file containing the S-box data (included in cast128.c);

- cast128.c – the C program to implement the CAST-128 algorithm.

The program cast128.c contains the core functions for the scheme, and there is no entry point for the function main(). Therefore, you may need to write a utility or driver to work with files yourself. If you read the file cast128.c, you will find that the following five statements are needed in order to do CAST-128 encryption/decryption:

```
1: cast128_key castkey;
2: unsigned char kkey[8], buf[8], obuf[8];
3: cast128_setkey(&castkey, kkey, m);        // m length of kkey
4: cast128_encrypt(&castkey, buf, obuf);
5: cast128_decrypt(&castkey, buf, obuf);
```

The first line is to define a structure called castkey: this stores the subkeys. The second line defines the arrays for the raw key (kkey[]), the plaintext (buf[]) and output block (obuf[]). If you want encryption, you call the function in line 4; for decryption, the function in line 5 should be used instead.

To develop a driver to encrypt files, consider part I of a C program called cast128driver.c.

```
Example: cast128driver.c - A utility for CAST-128              (Part I)

 1: #include <stdio.h>
 2: #include "cast128.h"
 3: #include "cast128.c"
 4:
 5: int main(int argc, char *argv[])
 6: {
 7:   int i, n, m=-1;
 8:   cast128_key castkey;
 9:   unsigned char buf[8];
10:   unsigned char kkey[8];
11:   unsigned char obuf[8];
12:   FILE *inK, *inP, *outF;
13:
14:   if (argc!=5) {
15:   printf("\nUsage:\n cast128driver (e)|
             (d) <infile> <outfile> <keyfile>\n");
16:   return 2;
17:   }
```

```
18:    for (i=0;i<8;i++) {
19:        kkey[i]=0; buf[i]=0; obuf[i]=0;
20:    }
21:    if((inK=fopen(argv[4],"r"))==NULL) {
22:        printf("\r\nCould not open input file: %s",argv[4]);
23:        return 2;
24:    } else {
25:
26:    while (!feof(inK) && m < 16) { kkey[++m] =(unsigned char)
                                              fgetc(inK); }
27:    fclose(inK);
28:
29:    }
30:    cast128_setkey(&castkey, kkey, m);
31:
```

This is a simple C program similar to des3driver.c and should be easy to read even if you are not familiar with the language. First, the software package is included in this program in lines 2–3. After the variable declarations in lines 7–12, the use of the program is defined in lines 14–17. To use this program, four command line parameters are needed. The general calling syntax is

```
cast128driver (e)|(d) <infile> <outfile> <keyfile>
```

For example, the following command will encrypt the file plain.txt, and output the ciphertext to file en.txt using the key file kkey.txt:

```
cast128driver e plain.txt en.txt kkey.txt
```

Note that the key file kkey.txt should contain a key string of no more than 16 characters. The for-loop in lines 18–20 is to initialize the arrays kkey[], buf[] and obuf[]. The open file statement in line 21 opens the key file. The statement in line 26 reads the key file, to a maximum 16 characters (128-bit), to array kkey[]. The length is stored in variable m. Line 27 closes the key file. The array kkey[] and m are input to the function call cast128_setkey(&castkey, kkey,m) in line 30 to generate all the subkeys. Now, the encryption and decryption are ready to be called. Consider part II of cast128driver.c.

Example: Continuation of cast128driver.c (Part II)

```
32:    if((inP=fopen(argv[2],"rb"))==NULL){
33:        printf("\r\nCould not open input file: %s",argv[2]);
34:        return 2;
35:    }
```

```
36:       if((outF=fopen(argv[3],"wb"))==NULL){
37:          printf("\r\nCould not open output file: %s",argv[3]);
38:          return 2;
39:   }
40:
41:   if(argv[1][0]=='e') {
42:      while ((n=fread(buf,1,8,inP)) >0) {
43:         if (n < 8) {
44:            for(i=n;i<8;i++) buf[i]=0;
45:         }
46:         cast128_encrypt(&castkey, buf, obuf);
47:         if(fwrite(obuf,1,8,outF) < 8) {
48:            printf("\r\nError writing to output file\r\n");
49:            return(3);
50:         }
51:      }
52:   }
53:   if(argv[1][0]=='d') {
54:      while ((n=fread(buf,1,8,inP)) >0) {
55:         cast128_decrypt(&castkey, buf, obuf);
56:         if(fwrite(obuf,1,8,outF) < 8){
57:            printf("\r\nError writing to output file\r\n");
58:            return(3);
59:         }
60:      }
61:   }
62:   fclose(inP); fclose(outF);
63:   return 0;
64: }
```

Lines 32–39 open the files infile and outfile. If the first command line parameter
is 'e', the while-loop in lines 42–52 is executed to process the entire infile. The
read statement in line 42 reads in every eight characters to variable buf. If the
length of buf is not eight characters, the if-statement in lines 43–45 pads the string
with zeros. The function call in line 46 is to perform encryption on buf, and the
result is printed to the outfile in line 47. The while-loop continues this process
until all the characters in the infile are exhausted. Likewise, if the first command
line parameter is 'd', the while-loop in lines 54–61 performs decryption and the
result is saved in the outfile.

To compile the program, you can use the following simple command with a gcc
compiler

```
gcc -o cast128driver cast128driver.c
```

Fig. 4.33 CAST-128 working on files

```
H:\>gcc -o cast128driver cast128driver.c
H:\>cast128driver
Usage:
  cast128driver (e)|(d) <infile> <outfile> <keyfile>

H:\>cast128driver e plain.txt en.txt kkey.txt
H:\>cast128driver d en.txt    de.txt kkey.txt
H:\>type de.txt

Meet Me At 2pm Tomorrow
H:\>
```

to compile the driver. If `infile` and `keyfile` contain the following message and key

```
plain.txt = "Meet Me At 2pm Tomorrow"
kkey.txt = "agent00187654321"
```

the command below will use the driver to perform encryption and decryption:

```
cast128driver e plain.txt en.txt kkey.txt
cast128driver d en.txt    de.txt kkey.txt
```

In this case, the encrypted file is `en.txt` and the decrypted file is `de.txt`. The execution process is captured and shown in Figure 4.33.

Now, let's see how to add operation modes to the CAST-128 encryption/decryption scheme.

4.5.3 CAST-128 encryption/decryption with operation modes

CAST-128 is a block cipher with block length 64 bits equivalent to eight characters. Like most block ciphers, it has block effects. For example, if you have two identical plaintext blocks of eight characters, the ciphertext blocks will be the same. If you run page `ex04-08.htm` with the following:

```
plain.txt: "mysecretmysecretmysecret"
Key      : "agent00187654321"
```

you will see three sets of identical ciphertext block:

```
Ciphertext: a9 23 b3 45 09 4d 85 35 a9 23 b3 45 09 4d 85 35
            a9 23 b3 45 09 4d 85 35
```

One efficient way of eliminating block effects is to use operation modes. As we have seen in Section 4.3.2, adding modes to a block cipher is not difficult. In this section, we will show you how to add the CBC mode to CAST-128. First, make a copy of ex04-08.js and call it ex04-09.js. At the end of this script, add the following program code.

```
Example: ex04-09.js - CAST-128 With operation modes

719: function cbc_cast128(keySt, msgSt, encrypt,ivSt)
720: {
721:    var m=0, chunk=0, len = msgSt.length;
722:    var i, tResult="", result="", tempSt="";
723:    var msgArr = new Array(8), outArr = new Array(8);
724:    var cbcArr = new Array(8), tmpArr = new Array(8);
725:
726:    for (i=0;i<8;i++) {
727:         msgArr[i]=0; cbcArr[i]=0;
728:         outArr[i]=0; tmpArr[i]=0;
729:    }
730:    for (i=0;i<8;i++) cbcArr[i] = ivSt.charCodeAt(i);
731:
732:    keyStToSubkeys(keySt);
733:
734:    while (m < len) {
735:      for (i=0;i<8;i++) msgArr[i] = msgSt.charCodeAt(m++);
736:      if (encrypt) {
737:          for (i=0;i<8;i++) msgArr[i] = msgArr[i] ^ cbcArr[i];
738:          outArr= cast128_encrypt(msgArr);
739:          for (i=0;i<8;i++) cbcArr[i] = outArr[i];
740:      } else {
741:          for (i=0;i<8;i++) tmpArr[i] = cbcArr[i];
742:          for (i=0;i<8;i++) cbcArr[i] = msgArr[i];
743:          outArr= cast128_decrypt(msgArr);
744:          for (i=0;i<8;i++) outArr[i] = outArr[i] ^ tmpArr[i];
745:      }
746:      tempSt = "";
747:      for (i=0;i<8;i++) {
748:       tempSt += String.fromCharCode(outArr[i]);
749:      }
750:      tResult += tempSt; chunk += 8;
751:      if (chunk == 512) {
752:          result += tResult; tResult = ""; chunk = 0;
753:      }
754:    }
755:    return result + tResult;
756: }
```

This script has one function `cbc_cast128()`. It is used to perform the CBC mode on a CAST-128 cipher. If you compare this function with `cast128()` in `ex04-08.js`, they are similar. The differences are highlighted in the program code for `ex04-09.js`.

The function declaration in line 719 contains an additional parameter `ivSt`, which is the initialization vector used in CBC operations. Two more arrays are added in line 724. The array `cbcArr[]` stores the ciphertext result and is used to perform the XOR operation with the plaintext block as required by CBC operations. Initially, the for-loop in line 730 converts the initialization vector (IV) to eight character codes in array `cbcArr[]`. If encryption is `true`, the statements in lines 737–739 are executed. The for-loop in line 737 will XOR the plaintext block `msgArr[]` and the CBC block `cbcArr[]` together and encrypt them in line 738. The for-loop in line 739 stores the ciphertext block `outArr[]` back to the CBC block `cbcArr[]` for the next round of encryption. For decryption, the statements in lines 741–744 are executed and the operations are similar to encryption in reverse order. To test this script, consider the Web page `ex04-09.htm`.

Example: ex04-09.htm - CAST128 encryption/decryption with modes (Part I)

```
 1: <style>
 2:   .butSt{font-size:16pt;width:250px;height:40px;
 3:          font-weight:bold;background:#dddddd;color:#ff0000}
 4:   .radSt{font-size:16pt;width:35px;height:30px;
 5:          font-weight:bold;background:#88ff88;color:#ff0000}
 6: </style>
 7: <body style="font-family:arial;font-size:26pt;text-align:center;
 8:       background:#000088;color:#ffff00">
 9:   CAST-128 With Operation Modes<br />
10:   <img alt="pic" src="line1.gif" height="7" width="620" /><br />
11:
12: <table style="font-size:18pt" align="center" >
13: <tr><td>Enter The Input Message: </td></tr>
14:   <tr><td><textarea style="font-size:16pt;width:620px;height:80px;
15:          font-weight:bold;background:#dddddd" rows="5" cols="40"
16:          id="in_mesg">Meet Me At 2pm Tomorrow</textarea></td></tr>
17: </table>
18: <form action="">
19: <table style="font-size:18pt" cellspacing="10" align="center">
20: <tr><td>Enter The Key: </td>
21:     <td style="text-align:center" colspan=2>
22:         <input type="text" id="key_v" size="8" maxlength="16"
23:         style="font-size:16pt;width:370px;height:40px;
24:         font-weight:bold;background:#dddddd;
            color:#ff0000" value="agent00187654321" /></td></tr>
```

```
25:    <tr><td>Initial Vector: </td>
26:        <td style="text-align:center" colspan=2>
27:            <input type="text" id="iv_st" size="8" maxlength="8"
28:             style="font-size:16pt;width:370px;height:40px;
29:             font-weight:bold;background:#dddddd;
               color:#ff0000" value="agent001" /></td></tr>
30:
31:    <tr><td style="width:180px;text-align:left"><input
           type="radio" checked
32:           id="m_rad" name="m_rad" class="radSt" /> ECB Mode</td>
33:       <td colspan="2" style="width:180px;text-align:left"><input
           type="radio"
34:           id="m_rad" name="m_rad" class="radSt" /> CBC Mode</td>
35:
36:    </td></tr>
37:    <tr><td style="width:180px;text-align:left"><input
           type="radio" checked
38:           id="b_rad" name="b_rad" class="radSt" /> Encryption</td>
39:       <td style="width:180px;text-align:left"><input type="radio"
40:           id="b_rad" name="b_rad" class="radSt" /> Decryption</td>
41:       <td style="width:180px;text-align:left"><input size="20"
           type="button"
42:           class="butSt" style="width:180px" value="OK"
           onclick="mcast128_fun()" />
43:    </td></tr>
44: </table>
45: </form>
46: <table style="font-size:18pt" align="center">
47:  <tr><td>The Output Message is: </td></tr>
48:  <tr><td><textarea rows="5" cols="40" id="out_mesg" readonly
49:            style="font-size:16pt;font-weight:bold;width:620px;
50:            height:80px;background:#aaffaa"></textarea></td></tr>
51: </table>
```

This page is similar to ex04-06.htm, and the differences are highlighted. The additional XHTML codes in lines 31–34 add two more radio buttons to the page so that users can select from operation modes ECB or CBC. When the OK button is clicked, the function mcast128_fun() in line 42 is activated and the result is displayed in the second text area defined in lines 48–50. The function mcast128_fun() is defined in part II of ex04-09.htm.

```
52: <script src="ex04-09.js"></script>
53: <script src="hexlib.js"></script>
54: <script>
55:  function mcast128_fun()
56:  {
57:    var ivSt = "", mlV, llV;
58:    var key="",message="",llst="";
59:    mlV = document.getElementsByName("m_rad");
60:    llV = document.getElementsByName("b_rad");
61:    if (llV.item(0).checked) {
62:      key = document.getElementById("key_v").value
63:      ivSt = document.getElementById("iv_st").value
64:      message = document.getElementById("in_mesg").value
65:      if ( mlV.item(1).checked)
66:         llst = byteStToHex(cbc_cast128(key, message, 1,ivSt));
67:      if ( mlV.item(0).checked)
68:         llst = byteStToHex(cast128(key, message, 1));
69:      document.getElementById("out_mesg").value = llst
70:    }
71:    if (llV.item(1).checked) {
72:      key = document.getElementById("key_v").value
73:      ivSt = document.getElementById("iv_st").value
74:      message = hexStToByteSt(document.getElementById("in_mesg").value)
75:      if ( mlV.item(1).checked)
76:         llst = cbc_cast128(key, message, 0,ivSt);
77:      if ( mlV.item(0).checked)
78:         llst = cast128(key, message, 0);
79:      document.getElementById("out_mesg").value = llst
80:    }
81:  }
82: </script>
83: </body>
```

The script function `mcast128_fun()` is similar to `cast128()` in `ex04-08.htm` and not difficult to read. The only new statements are to handle the newly created radio buttons. Line 59 checks the status of all radio buttons with `id="m_rad"` and stores them in variable `mlV`. Note that the first radio button with `id="m_rad"` runs ECB mode and is stored in `mlV[0]`. Now, if encryption is `true`, the statements in lines 65–68 are executed. If the CBC radio button is checked (line 65), the function `cbc_cast128()` in line 66 will run to perform encryption with the CBC mode. If the ECB button is checked, the function `cast128()` in line 68 will run to do encryption with the ECB mode. A similar decryption process is defined in lines 75–78. Screenshots of this example in action are shown in Figures 4.34–4.35.

In Figures 4.34 and 4.35, you can see that block effects appear in the ciphertext when you enter identical plaintext blocks. If you use the CBC mode, the block effects disappear, as illustrated in Figures 4.36 and 4.37.

Fig. 4.34 Encryption with ECB

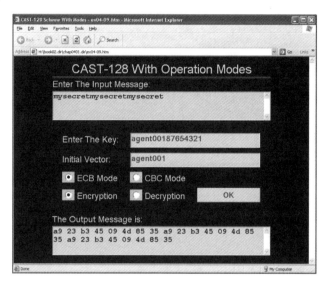

Fig. 4.35 Decryption with ECB

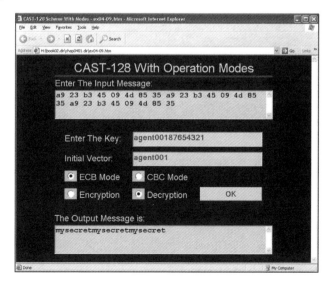

Fig. 4.36 Encryption with CBC

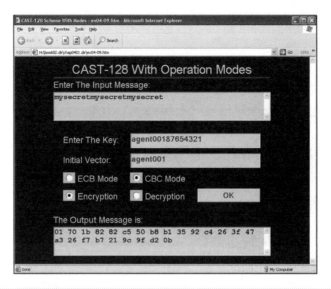

Fig. 4.37 Decryption with CBC

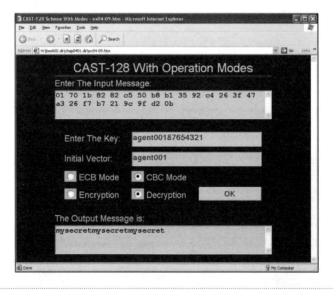

For practice, you may want to change the type of the 'key' and 'initial vector' boxes (lines 22 and 27 of ex04-09.htm) from

```
type="text" to type="password"
```

The characters of these two fields will be hidden and replaced by big dots so that people cannot see the original password texts.

An encryption tool like this is handy when exchanging sensitive information in real time via the chat capability of the Internet or Web environment. For example, a company's staff overseas can use this tool to discuss sensitive business information such as prices, contracts and tendering with the bosses in headquarters using an ordinary chat room. Encrypted messages from this page can be copied and pasted into the chat and then decrypted using the tool on your computer. Only the encrypted message is transmitted over the Internet or Web, achieving privacy and secrecy.

5

Practical software-based stream ciphers

5.1 An introduction to stream ciphers

5.1.1 The main characteristics of stream ciphers

In Chapter 4, you learned about some block ciphers. One characteristic of these is that they try to encrypt a block or a number of characters simultaneously. The number of characters that they can encrypt at one time is called the block length. When the block length is reduced to one, the cipher is equivalent to one which encrypts a stream of individual characters and is called a 'stream cipher'. The stream cipher is an important class of cipher in the crypto-community due to the fact that they are, in general, faster than ordinary block ciphers. Also, most stream ciphers are more suitable for hardware implementations since they have simpler hardware circuitry. For this reason they are appropriate for small devices when processing power, memory and buffering are limited.

The XOR and PkZip/WinZip encryptions introduced in Chapter 1 are good examples of stream ciphers. The PkZip/WinZip encryption process uses the input key to generate an arbitrary long string called a 'key-stream'. The key-stream is then used to perform bitwise XOR operation with the plaintext character by character, producing the ciphertext. In general, the structure of a stream cipher is like that illustrated in Figure 5.1.

From Figure 5.1, you can see that the plaintext is considered to be an input stream. When the input data p_i is XORed with the key-stream k_i, the result is the ciphertext character c_i. When the ciphertext character c_i is XORed with the key-stream k_i again, the plaintext character p_i is obtained, i.e.

$$p_i \; \hat{} \; k_i \; = \; c_i \quad \text{and} \quad c_i \; \hat{} \; k_i \; = \; p_i$$

The symbol '$\hat{}$' is the XOR operation and we will use this convention in this chapter. By definition, the encryption/decryption of the stream cipher need not

Fig. 5.1 The encryption/decryption process of a stream cipher

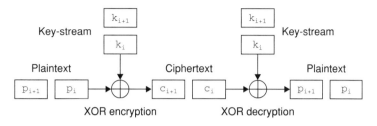

be an XOR operation. However, most of the stream ciphers just use the bitwise XOR (or the XOR gate). One characteristic of the XOR design is that the encryption and decryption operations are exactly the same. As you will see, all the stream ciphers discussed in this chapter employ a similar structure to that in Figure 5.1.

Encrypting character by character, stream ciphers are fast, compact and more unlikely to have errors. However, despite the vast theoretical knowledge about stream ciphers, very few software-based algorithms or implementations are available in the public domain. Most of the stream ciphers used today are trade secrets and under heavy protection by the companies involved. In this chapter, we will discuss some of them. Examples and step-by-step implementation are provided throughout.

From Figure 5.1, the security of a stream cipher is completely determined by the key-stream it uses. When the key-stream is truly random, as long as the plaintext stream is used only once, the stream cipher is known as 'one-time-pad' (OTP). Although OTP was designed almost a century ago, it is still the only proven unbreakable (or unconditionally secure) cipher available today.

The crypto-strength of OTP, or generally stream ciphers, comes from the randomness of the key-stream. Most stream ciphers, in fact, employ a random number generator (RNG) to produce a random key-stream based on the input key. Attackers, on the other hand, are looking for weakness in the corresponding RNG. Since truly random numbers are extremely difficult (if possible at all) to obtain using computers or algorithms, a perfect stream cipher is difficult to construct.

In fact, block ciphers operating with operation modes other than ECB can be consider as stream ciphers. This feature is discussed in Section 5.1.2; OTP will be discussed in Section 5.2. Random numbers, or pseudo-random numbers, are a big subject with many applications well beyond the scope of this book. Only a basic discussion of the skills and techniques needed to generate them is presented in Section 5.3; its contents can be used as a background to understanding the stream ciphers in this chapter. In Section 5.4, a fast and compact stream cipher, known as RC4 from Ron Rivest, is introduced and implemented. This cipher is surprisingly secure and claims to be more than 10 times faster than the standard implementation of DES. A competitor of RC4, known as ISAAC, is also discussed in detail. Based on the secure hash algorithm (SHA-1) in discussed Chapter 3, a heavyweight stream cipher called SEAL is implemented in Section 5.5.

5.1.2   Using a block cipher to implement a stream cipher

Stream ciphers are usually divided into two categories, namely 'synchronising' and 'self-synchronising'. When the generated key-stream of a stream cipher is independent of the plaintext and ciphertext, it is called a 'synchronizing' stream cipher. The key-stream of a synchronized stream cipher usually depends on the key only. One characteristic of these ciphers is that the sending and receiving ends must be synchronized. In other words, as long as the same key and the same position of the key-stream are used, the decryption is well defined and proceeds accordingly.

In particular, when the key-stream and the plaintext are XORed at the binary level to produce the binary ciphertext, the synchronized stream cipher is called a 'binary additive stream cipher'. Binary additive stream ciphers are popular in industry. The structure of the cipher is simple: all you need is a good pseudo-random number generator which can take an input key and produce a sequence of random bits. In fact, most of the practical and commercial stream ciphers belong to this type.

Note that most of the random number generators or pseudo-random number generators (PRNG) found in computer languages such as C/C++ are for general programming purposes. They are not suitable for serious cryptography or cryptology applications since they are predictable in some ways and not random enough to produce a crypto-strength which discourages attackers. A better way to generate random numbers is to use one-way ciphers (Chapter 3) or block ciphers as a secure PRNG. For example, ANSI and FIPS have used SHA-1 and Tri-DES as standard ways of generating random numbers with crypto-strength – they are known as X9.17 and FIPS 186. RNG and PRNG will be discussed in Section 5.3.

When the generated key-stream is a function of (or related to) the key and some parts of the previous ciphertext, the stream cipher is called 'self-synchronizing'. Using part of the ciphertext data for encryption is the idea behind operation modes to eliminate block effects for a block cipher. If you take a look at the operation modes of block ciphers (Section 4.1), you will find that the cipher feedback mode (CFB) can be modified easily to operate as a stream cipher. All you need do is employ the encryption only in the cipher to produce the same key-stream.

Using CFB mode as a self-synchronous stream cipher

The modifications of using CFB to perform encryption and decryption as a stream cipher are illustrated in Figures 5.2 and 5.3.

Fig. 5.2 CFB mode encryption

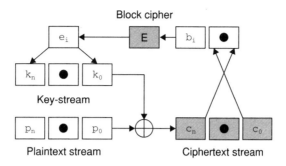

Fig. 5.3 CFB mode decryption

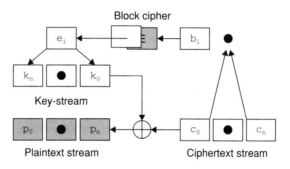

The main idea is to use the block cipher to produce the same key-stream. From Figure 5.2, a block b_i is sent to the block cipher to produce a cipher block called e_i. The e_i is then split and represented as a key-stream $\{k_o, \ldots, k_n\}$. Together with a section of plaintext stream $\{p_o, \ldots, p_n\}$, the XOR operation is carried out to produce a section of the ciphertext stream $\{c_o, \ldots, c_n\}$. This ciphertext is grouped into a block and fed back to the block cipher for the next round as illustrated in Figure 5.2.

For decryption, a section of the ciphertext stream is converted into a block for the block cipher encryption. Since the same block is input to the block cipher, the same output e_i is obtained. The e_i is then represented as a section of the key-stream $\{k_o, \ldots, k_n\}$. This key-stream is XORed with the ciphertext stream $\{c_o, \ldots, c_n\}$ to produce the plaintext block. Again, the same plaintext section $\{p_o, \ldots, p_n\}$ is obtained because the same key-stream is used.

The output feedback mode (OFB) of a block cipher is independent of the ciphertext or plaintext and can be used to implement a synchronous stream cipher.

Using OFB mode as a synchronous stream cipher

As in the CFB case, implementing OFB mode as a stream cipher is simple. All you need do is employ the encryption of the cipher to produce the same key-stream. This process is illustrated in Figures 5.4 and 5.5.

In Figure 5.4, the user key is considered as a block b_i and input to the block cipher. The result is a block e_i. The next step is to represent e_i in a key-stream $\{k_o, \ldots, k_n\}$. The key-stream is XORed with the plaintext stream $\{p_o, \ldots, p_n\}$ to produce the ciphertext stream $\{c_o, \ldots, c_n\}$. To obtain the next section of the key-stream, block e_i is fed back to the block cipher again, as illustrated in Figure 5.4.

For the decryption process, the same block (the user key) is input to the block cipher to produce e_i. The same key-stream $\{k_o, \ldots, k_n\}$ is produced. When you perform an XOR operation on $\{k_o, \ldots, k_n\}$ and $\{c_o, \ldots, c_n\}$, the same plaintext stream $\{p_o, \ldots, p_n\}$ is obtained. To demonstrate this process, let's implement an example.

Fig. 5.4 OFB mode encryption

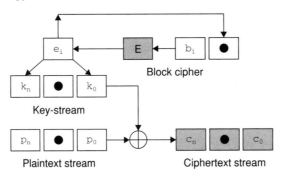

Fig. 5.5 OFB mode decryption

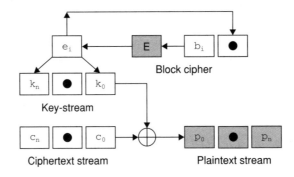

5.1.3 Implementation of output feedback mode as a stream cipher

One of the quickest ways of implementing OFB as a stream cipher is to use the optimized DES program developed in Chapter 4. DES is a secure and reliable cipher with a good reputation and it is not easy to find one to replace it. Now, make copies of `ex04-05.htm` and `ex04-05.js`, and call them `ex05-01.htm` and `ex05-01.js` respectively. At the end of `ex05-01.js`, insert the following program code.

```
Example: ex05-01.js - Implementing OFB mode as a stream cipher
337: function ofb_des_stream(keySt, msgSt, encrypt)
338: {
339:   var m=0, chunk=0, len = msgSt.length;
340:   var i, tResult="", result="";
341:   var iKeyArr=new Array(8), msgArr=new Array(8), lrArr=new Array(2);
342:   var omsgArr= new Array(8);
343:   var tempSt = "", tResult=""; result="";
344:
345:   keySt += "\0\0\0\0\0\0\0\0"; keySt = keySt.substring(0,8);
346:   oKeyArr = keyStToSubkeys(true,keySt);
347:
348:   lrArr[0]= (keySt.charCodeAt(m++) << 24) |
                  (keySt.charCodeAt(m++) << 16)|
349:              (keySt.charCodeAt(m++) << 8) |
                  keySt.charCodeAt(m++);
350:   lrArr[1]= (keySt.charCodeAt(m++) << 24) |
                  (keySt.charCodeAt(m++) << 16)|
351:              (keySt.charCodeAt(m++) << 8) |
                  keySt.charCodeAt(m++);
352:   m=0;
353:   msgSt += "\0\0\0\0\0\0\0\0";
354:
355:   while (m < len) {
356:     lrArr= des_64bits(oKeyArr,lrArr[0],lrArr[1]);
357:
358:     for (i=0;i<8;i++) msgArr[i] =msgSt.charCodeAt(m++) & 0xff;
359:     for (i=0;i<8;i++) iKeyArr[i]=(lrArr[i/4] >>> (8* ((7-i) % 4))
                                                      & 0xff);
360:     for (i=0;i<8;i++) omsgArr[i] = msgArr[i] ^ iKeyArr[i];
361:     if ( m < len )
362:       for (i=0;i<8;i++) tempSt += String.fromCharCode(omsgArr[i]);
363:     else
364:       for (i=0;i<len-(m-8);i++) tempSt +=
                                        String.fromCharCode(omsgArr[i]);
365:
366:     tResult += tempSt; chunk += 8; tempSt = "";
```

```
367:    if (chunk == 512) {
368:        result += tResult; tResult = ""; chunk = 0;
369:     }
370:   }
371:  return result + tResult;
372: }
```

This script fragment contains one function ofb_des_stream() which is used to implement the output feedback mode of DES as a stream cipher. If you compare this function with the function des() in lines 304–335, the programming styles are similar and the differences are highlighted. We have included both functions in this script file for educational and demonstration purposes.

In line 346, the user input key keySt is used to set up the DES subkeys. This is just a convenient setting and you should use the initial vector (i.e. IV) of your choice. Since our DES program uses 32-bit words for both encryption and decryption, keySt is converted into words stored in array lrArr[] by lines 348–351.

The while-loop in lines 355–370 performs the encryption and decryption of the stream cipher. First, the key array lrArr[] is put into the DES cipher in line 356 to obtain an encrypted block. It is an array of two 32-bit words. The for-loop in line 359 converts this array into a stream of eight bytes. This stream is our key-stream and is stored in iKeyArr[]. The for-loop in line 358 gets the incoming plaintext and converts it into an array of eight elements (plaintext stream) called msgArr[]. The for-loop in line 360 performs the XOR operations on the two streams to produce a section of the ciphertext stream. The statement in line 362 is used to convert the ciphertext stream into string and return it for display purposes. Note that DES is a block cipher working on a block of eight elements. If the length of the incoming plaintext is not a multiple of 8, the remaining ciperhext characters are output by the statement in line 364.

Note that, using OFB mode as a stream cipher, only the encryption process is needed, and therefore only the encryption subkeys are set in line 346.

To test this script, edit the Web page ex05-01.htm and modify the following lines:

```
 9: DES OFB Mode AS A Stream Cipher<br />
31: class="butSt" style="width:180px" value="OK"
       onclick="cfb_des_fun()" />
41: <script src="ex05-01.js"></script>
44: function cfb_des_fun()
52:      llst = byteStToHex(ofb_des_stream(key, message, 1))
59:      llst = ofb_des_stream(key, message, 0)
```

Line 9 changes the display to show that we are working with OFB mode as a stream cipher. When the OK button is clicked, line 31 will activate the function cfb_des_fun(). This function is defined in line 44. Line 52 calls function `ofb_des_stream()` to do the encryption and line 59 calls the same function for the decryption. Screenshots are shown in Figures 5.6 and 5.7.

In order to understand more about stream ciphers, we need to investigate the nature and crypto-strength of stream ciphers. A good starting point is the one-time-pad developed almost a century ago.

Fig. 5.6 OFB mode encryption

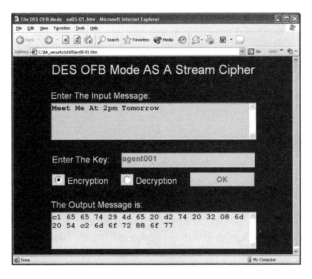

Fig. 5.7 OFB mode decryption

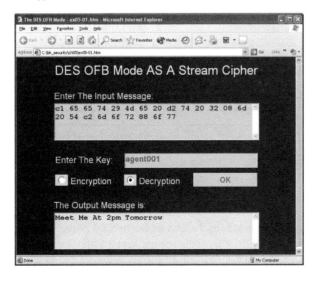

5.2 An unbreakable cipher: the one-time-pad

5.2.1 One-time-pad vs brute-force attack

One-time-pad (OTP) was invented by Mauborgne and Vernam in AT&T near the end of World War I (1917) to provide a secure cipher system for use in the military context. What was devised at that time was the only proven unbreakable encryption scheme known. The original design of OTP consists of a large set of truly random letters written on sheets of paper glued together into a pad or pads. To use OTP, you need two copies of the 'pad' and you use a truly random data set at least as long as the message you wish to encode using XOR encryption. To decode the data, the same key is needed. The key, or letters on the pad, is used once and is then destroyed. Since the key is used only once, the process is called One-time-pad. To summarize the characteristics of OTP, we have:

- truly random letters (or keys);

- the length of the key at least as long as the plaintext;

- the key is used only once.

'Truly random' means that all keys (or pads) are equally probable. In other words, there is no information to assist in crypto-analysis. This arrangement effectively provides perfect security against analysis of the cipher (or the so-called ciphertext-only attack).

Suppose the key bit is truly random: the probability of a key bit being 1 or 0 is exactly equal to $1/2$. Assume that the plaintext bits are not balanced. In this case, let the probability of the plaintext bit being 0 be p. The probability of the plaintext bit being 1 turns out to be $1 - p$. By combining all plaintext bits, key bits and cipher bits, we have the following probability table:

Table 5.1 The probabilities in OTP

Plaintext bit	Probability	Key bit	Probability	XOR	Cipher bit	Probability
0	p	0	$1/2$	^	0	p/2
0	p	1	$1/2$	^	1	p/2
1	1 - p	0	$1/2$	^	1	(1 - p)/2
1	1 - p	1	$1/2$	^	0	(1 - p)/2

From Table 5.1, the probability of a ciphertext bit being 1 or 0 is equal to $(1/2)p + (1/2)(1 - p) = 1/2$. This means that an attacker can't compute the plaintext from the ciphertext without knowledge of the key.

Since the length of the key is at least as long as the plaintext, trying all possible keys, or searching the whole key-space, using a brute-force scheme doesn't help at all. This is because all possible plaintexts are equally likely decryptions of the ciphertext. This result is particularly true regardless of:

- the length of the key, so long as the key length is greater than or equal to the plaintext;

- how much you know about the structure of the plaintext.

As a result, no useful information about the plaintext is available for a brute-force search. In other words, brute-force attack will not work on OTP.

For example, suppose you intercept an important OTP message from the enemy. The ciphertext is a one-character message encoded by one character key. Assume that you also know that the corresponding plaintext character can only be 'E' or 'N', determining the attacking direction as 'east' or 'north' respectively. If you try to decrypt the OTP ciphertext using a brute-force test through the 256 ASCII character key space you will find that there is a character key giving you the 'E' result and another character key giving the 'N' result. You still need to determine the attacking direction of the enemy.

If the key is not reused, there is virtually no possibility of getting information on the key(s) or the plaintext, and therefore OTP is unconditionally secure (or unbreakable). As mentioned in Chapter 1, the hotline between Washington and Moscow during the Cold War was protected by the OTP mechanism.

Another practical use of OTP is found in the community of Swiss banks. They accept electronic payment, transactions and orders using a mechanism similar to OTP to verify the identity of an issuer. When a client authorizes the bank to accept electronic transactions, the bank provides a list of passwords, or keys (usually numbers of 4 to 6 digits), to the client. The customer agrees to keep the list of passwords physically safe, and not to hold the bank liable for any unauthorized usage. Each time an order is given, the next key from the list must be entered and then crossed off by the user. The bank verifies the key against a copy of the list stored in their computer. Action will be taken by the bank only if the keys match. Multiple incorrect entries automatically block all activities in the account until reactivated by the bank.

Compared to other encryption schemes, the structure and implementation of OTP is simple provided that a good (or truly) random number generator is available. OTP encryption/decryption can be described by the following steps:

- generate a series of random keys with length longer than or equal to the plaintext;

- perform XOR encryption/decryption using one key;

- cross out or destroy the key after it is used.

5.2.2   Generating one-time-pad

To generate a perfect OTP, you need a truly random number generator. However, a truly random key or RNG is extremely difficult (if possible at all) to obtain. In fact, many people doubt the existence of such a perfect random scheme. Usually, random numbers generated by computers are called 'pseudo-random numbers' and the mechanism is called a pseudo-random number generator (PRNG).

Also, random numbers generated by ordinary computing languages, such as C/C++, are predictable in many ways and, therefore, not suitable for serious OTP and cryptology applications. This feature is well documented in an Internet Engineering Task Force (IETF) report known as RFC 1750. A popular way of producing more truly random numbers is to add natural noise and entropy such as radioactive decay or hard-drive air turbulence to the algorithm. We are not going into the details here. RNG and PRNG will be discussed in Section 5.3.

We are going to use a simple PRNG based on time to generate OTP. The function is called `random()` inside the `Math` object of ECMAScript (or Javascript). The calling syntax is

```
var01 = Math.random()
```

This statement returns a random value between 0 and 1. Since time is involved, the value is different every time you call the function. A random number between 0 and 100 can be generated by

```
var01 = Math.round( Math.random() * 100 )
```

The function `Math.round()` rounds a supplied value to the nearest integer. This random technique has been widely used in the Web environment for displaying random pictures, generating random motions, and even random links that can completely disrupt your screen or work.

To generate random keys with a length longer or equal to the plaintext, consider `ex05-02.htm`.

Example: ex05-02.htm - Generating random keys for OTP

```
 1: <style>
 2:    .bx {color:#ff0000;font-size:16pt;font-weight:bold;width:50px;
 3:         height:30px;background-color:#eeeeee}
 4:    .bx2 {width:30px;height:30px;background-color:#ff88ff}
 5: </style>
 6: <body style="font-family:arial;font-size:20pt;text-align:center;
 7:         font-weight:bold;color:#ffff00;background:#8888fe">
 8:  A Simple One-Time-Pad<br />Random Key Generation Scheme<br />
 9:  <img alt="pic" src="line1.gif" height="7" width="680" /><br /><br />
10:
```

```
11:    <table style="font-size:18pt;font-weight:bold" align="center">
12:    <tr><td>Key Code : </td><td>[a-z,0-9]</td><td>
13:       <input type="radio" id="keyS" name="keyS" class="bx2" /></td>
14:       <td> [a-z,A-Z,0-9]</td><td> <input type="radio" id="keyS"
15:          name="keyS" class="bx2" checked /></td></tr>
16:    <tr><td colspan="2">Number of Keys: </td>
17:       <td><input type="text" id="noKey" class="bx" value="5" /></td>
18:       <td>Key Length</td>
19:       <td><input type="text" id="keyL" class="bx"
             value="90" /></td></tr>
20:    <tr><td colspan="2">Generating OTP Random Keys: </td>
21:       <td colspan="3"><input type="button" class="bx" value="OK"
22:          style="width:120px" onclick="randomKeyGen()" /></td></tr>
23:    <tr><td colspan="5"><textarea rows="15" cols="60" id="out_mesg"
24:          readonly style="font-size:15pt;font-weight:bold;width:640px;
25:          height:300px;background:#aaffaa"></textarea></td></tr>
26: </table>
27: <script src="ex05-02.js"></script>
28: </body>
```

This simple page contains two radio boxes, two text boxes and one text area.
The two radio boxes defined in lines 13–15 allow the user to select the key codes
[a–z, 0–9] or [a–z, A–Z, 0–9]. The key codes define the key symbols used in the
key-space. The first text box specified in lines 16–17 is designed to get the user
input for the number of keys. The default value is 5 and in this case five random
keys are generated. The second text box in lines 18–23 specifies the key length.
The default value is 90. Once the OK button in lines 21–22 is clicked, the function
randomKeyGen() is activated. The random keys are generated and displayed in the
text area defined in line 23.

The details of the random key function randomKeyGen() are provided in the
ECMAScript file ex05-02.js.

```
Example: ex05-02.js - Generating one-time-pad keys

1: function ran_fun()
2: {
3:    return Math.random();
4: }
5:
6: function randomKeyGen()
7: {
8:    var dispKeySt="", ranKeyC="", keySt="";
9:    var keySize, noKeys, rnd, ii,jj;
```

```
10:
11:    if ( document.getElementsByName("keys").item(0).checked) {
12:      ranKeyC = "abcdefghiklmnopqrstuvwxyz1234567890";
13:    }
14:    if ( document.getElementsByName("keys").item(1).checked) {
15:      ranKeyC = "abcdefghiklmnopqrstuvwxyzABCDEFGHIJKLMNOPQRSTUVWXTZ"+
16:                "1234567890";
17:    }
18:    keySize = parseInt(document.getElementById("keyL").value);
19:    noKeys = parseInt(document.getElementById("noKey").value);
20:
21:    for (jj=0; jj < noKeys; jj++) {
22:      keySt = "";
23:      for (ii=0; ii< keySize; ii++) {
24:        rnd = Math.floor(ran_fun() * ranKeyC.length);
25:        keySt += ranKeyC.substring(rnd,rnd+1);
26:      }
27:      dispKeySt += keySt +" -- ("+ (jj+1) + ") \n";
28:    }
29:    document.getElementById("out_mesg").value= dispKeySt;
30: }
31:
```

Inside the function `randomKeyGen()`, three string variables are declared in line 8. The variable `dispKeySt` stores all the keys to be displayed on the screen. Variable `ranKeyC` stores the key codes and `keySt` is used to store one key. The conditional-if statement in lines 11–13 checks the status of the first radio box. If the box is checked, the key code [a–z, 0–9] is used. The key code string `ranKeyC` is then defined in line 12. If the second radio box is checked, the key code is [a–z, A–Z, 0–9] and the key symbols are assigned to `ranKeyC` by the statement in lines 15–16.

The two statements in lines 18–19 store the key length and number of keys in variables `keySize` and `noKey` respectively. The `jj` for-loop in lines 21–28 runs through the value of `noKey` to generate all the keys. The inner `ii` for-loop in lines 23–26 generates each key with size `keySize`. Consider the statements inside the `ii` for-loop:

```
rnd = Math.floor(ran_fun() * ranKeyC.length);
keySt += ranKeyC.substring(rnd,rnd+1);
```

The first statement calls the function `ran_fun()` defined in lines 1–4. This function, in fact, calls `Math.random()` and returns a random number between 0 and 1. By multiplying the random number by `ranKeyC.length`, the length of the key code is stored in variable `rnd`. The second statement extracts the corresponding character stored in variable `ranKeyC` and appends the character to `keySt`. When the `ii` for-loop is exhausted, the variable `keySt` will contain one random key. This random key is then appended to the displaying string `dispKeySt` in line 27. When all the random keys have been generated, `dispKeySt` is output to the screen by the statement in line 29. Screenshots of this example are shown in Figures 5.8 and 5.9.

Fig. 5.8 Generating OTP I

Fig. 5.9 Generating OTP II

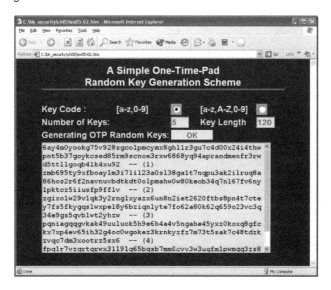

In the script `ex05-02.js`, we have used the function `ran_fun()` to represent a random function. If you have another PRNG, all you have to do is to put your random function inside. Although the random function used is simple, the results can also be used to encrypt/decrypt message for OTP.

5.2.3   A page for OTP encryption/decryption

With the OTP generator in last section, you can develop a page to use OTP encryption/decryption on the Web. Now, let's use `ex05-02.htm` to generate a random pad containing, say, 300 characters. We will use this pad to encrypt and decrypt messages. You can, for example, generate a number of pads and give each of them a name. When communicating with your friends, a different pad can be used. As long as the same pad is used for encryption and decryption, the results will be the same. In order to simulate the crossing out of the used characters, a pad index is implemented so that the current position of the pad is kept in the ciphertext. When the random characters in the pad are used up, a message is displayed so that a new pad can be generated.

The first thing to do is design the interface using XHTML codes. A typical implementation page would include text areas for the OTP random numbers and the input message. A text box for the pad index and two radio buttons for the encryption or decryption options are also required. An OK button and a text area to display the result are useful. Consider `ex05-03.htm`.

```
Example: ex05-03.htm - A page for OTP encryption/decryption   (Part I)

 1: <style>
 2:   .butSt{font-size:16pt;width:250px;height:40px;
 3:           font-weight:bold;background:#dddddd;color:#ff0000}
 4:   .radSt{font-size:16pt;width:35px;height:30px;
 5:           font-weight:bold;background:#88ff88;color:#ff0000}
 6: </style>
 7: <body style="font-family:arial;font-size:26pt;text-align:center;
 8:       background:#000088;color:#ffff00">
 9:  The OTP Encryption/Decryption<br />
10:  <img alt="pic" src="line1.gif" height="7"
     width="700" /><br /><br />
11:
12: <table style="font-size:18pt" align="center">
13:  <tr><td>Enter The Input Message: </td>
         <td>Enter The One-Time-Pad</td></tr>
14:  <tr><td><textarea style="font-size:16pt;width:350px;height:220px;
15:           font-weight:bold;background:#dddddd" rows="50" cols="40"
```

```
16:                 id="in_mesg"></textarea></td>
17:         <td><textarea style="font-size:16pt;width:350px;height:220px;
18:             font-weight:bold;background:#dddddd" rows="50" cols="40"
19:             id="key_v"></textarea></td></tr>
20: </table>
21: <form action="">
22: <table style="font-size:18pt" align="center" style="width:700px">
23:   <tr><td style="width:180px;text-align:left"><input
            type="radio" checked
24:         id="b_rad" name="b_rad" class="radSt" /> Encryption</td>
25:     <td style="width:180px;text-align:left"><input type="radio"
26:         id="b_rad" name="b_rad" class="radSt" /> Decryption</td> </tr>
27:   <tr>
28:     <td style="width:180px;text-align:left">Pad Index</td>
29:     <td style="width:180px;text-align:left"><input size="20"
            type="text"
30:         id="idx" class="butSt" style="width:180px" value="0" /> </td>
31:
32:     <td style="width:180px;text-align:left"><input size="20"
33:         type="button" class="butSt" style="width:180px" value="OK"
            onclick="otp_fun()" />
34:     </td></tr>
35: </table>
36: </form>
37: <table style="font-size:18pt" align="center">
38:   <tr><td>The Output Message is: </td></tr>
39:   <tr><td><textarea rows="5" cols="40" id="out_mesg" readonly
40:             style="font-size:16pt;font-weight:bold;width:700px;
41:             height:100px;background:#aaffaa"></textarea></td></tr>
42: </table>
```

This page fragment is the body part of ex05-03.htm. It contains two text areas (lines 14–19), two radio buttons (lines 23–26) and a text box for the pad index (lines 28–30). The two text areas are for the OTP random numbers and the input message. The radio buttons are for the encryption and decryption options. When the OK button in lines 32–33 is clicked, the function otp_fun() is activated and the result is displayed in the text area in lines 39–41.

Remembering the position in the pad is important for OTP encryption/decryption. For our simple implementation, we are going to build the pad position, or pad index, into the ciphertext. When the ciphertext is transmitted to your friends, the pad index is available and decryption can be done effortlessly. Our implementation is simple: the pad index is stored as a number at the beginning of the ciphertext as a string of eight characters. Consider part II of ex05-03.htm.

```
Example: Continuation of ex05-03.htm                    (Part II)

43: <script src="ex05-03.js"></script>
44: <script src="hexlib.js"></script>
45: <script>
46:  function otp_fun()
47:  {
48:    var key="",message="",llst="";
49:    var idxSt,idV,idxSt="";
50:    llV = document.getElementsByName("b_rad")
51:    if (llV.item(0).checked) {
52:      key = document.getElementById("key_v").value
53:      message = document.getElementById("in_mesg").value
54:      idV = parseInt(document.getElementById("idx").value,10);
55:      idV = idV + message.length;
56:      idxSt = "0000000000"+ idV;
57:      idxSt = idxSt.substring(idxSt.length - 8, idxSt);
58:      llst = byteStToHex(otp_encrypt(message,key,idV))
59:      if (llst !="") llst = idxSt + " " + llst;
60:      else llst = "Error.. The Pad May Have Been Used Up..Check.."
61:      document.getElementById("out_mesg").value = llst
62:    }
63:    if (llV.item(1).checked) {
64:      key = document.getElementById("key_v").value
65:      mesg_st = document.getElementById("in_mesg").value;
66:      idV = parseInt(mesg_st.substring(0,8),10);
67:      message = mesg_st.substring(9,mesg_st.length);
68:      message = hexStToByteSt(message);
69:
70:      llst = otp_decrypt(message,key,idV);
71:      if (llst =="") llst = "Error.. The Pad May Have Been Used
          Up..Check.."
72:      document.getElementById("out_mesg").value = llst;
73:    }
74:  }
75:  mesgSt = "Corba Has Been Cancelled. Contact Greentrack "+
76:          "In The Mountain Immediately.";
77:  otpSt = "WhdxegiRSo9xiGU6muqZ9oTso044BDKVTvvRy0PEHrs0vn3awe" +
78:          "mB1BPfvFwCwIUEo1TbdrxSWB3K4feNyFL2hQropKzKVcoovRIi" +
79:          "V69o8bHOtoFAu3lqUuqtMlOt7OHUNHqXZ8Lx1cHHGcAvodxCA1" +
80:          "DKOGQq5n4vv7wFW1dHZ3wAxkoxCF2wo620iJwHygbnrcRIcsGX" +
81:          "P1OXcz5LeFCTpZREVDDO8bgh9AXwato6v0Ga3pSDOOcendcRKy" +
82:          "HXJZgxaiFaryPKlv9mJt7ulJ9VAsyR2DbskZrTKhbfhf3WyPTv";
83:  document.getElementById("in_mesg").value=mesgSt;
84:  document.getElementById("key_v").value=otpSt;
85: </script>
86: </body>
```

This page fragment defines the function `otp_fun()`. When activated, the input message and the OTP pad are captured by the lines 52–53. The pad index, `idv`, is captured by the statement in line 54. Note that, in ECMAScript, if the first character of a string is '0', the `parseInt()` function will consider it to be an octal number. To obtain a decimal value, the radical 10 is needed at the end of line 54. The pad index is added to the length of the input message so that the program will know whether the pad is long enough to encrypt the message. Lines 56–57 are used to add some zeros in front of the pad index and then cut the string to eight characters so that the pad index is represented by an 8-character numeric string. In this case, the pad index is recording the ending position of the OTP. The input message, the OTP (or key) and the pad index are submitted to the function `otp_encrypt()` for encryption. If the OTP random numbers (or keys) have been used up, the function returns an empty string. In this case, the error message in line 60 will be displayed.

For decryption, the statements in lines 64–72 will be executed. Since the pad index is built into the ciphertext, we don't need the information in the index text box. The input message (ciphertext) and the OTP random numbers are captured by lines 64–65. The pad index is extracted from the input ciphertext by line 66. The real ciphertext is also extracted by line 67. Lines 68–70 call the function `otp_decrypt()` to decrypt the ciphertext. If the length of ciphertext is longer than the remaining OTP random numbers, the function returns an empty string and the error message in line 71 will be displayed.

To test the page, a default message and the 300-character pad are added in lines 75–82. The statements in lines 83–84 will send these test strings to the corresponding text area so that we can test them.

The actual encrypting and decrypting functions are defined in script `ex05-03.js` and included in the page as illustrated in line 43.

Example: ex05-03.js – Implementation of OTP encryption/decryption

```
 1: function otp_encrypt(mSt,keySt,idxx)
 2: {
 3:   var enSt=""
 4:   var ii, mCh,mCode, kCh, kCode,ind, diff;
 5:
 6:   if ( idxx < keySt.length) {
 7:     diff = idxx - mSt.length;
 8:     for (ii=0;ii< mSt.length;ii++) {
 9:       mCode = mSt.charCodeAt(ii);
10:       ind = ii + diff;
11:       kCh = keySt.charAt(ind);
12:       kCode = kCh.charCodeAt(0) & 0xff;
13:       enSt = enSt + String.fromCharCode(mCode ^ kCode);
```

```
14:     }
15:     } else enSt = ""
16:     return (enSt);
17: }
18:
19: function otp_decrypt(eSt,keySt,idxx)
20: {
21:     var deSt="";
22:     var ii, eCh, eCode, kCh, kCode,ind, diff;
23:
24:     if ( idxx < keySt.length) {
25:         diff = idxx - eSt.length;
26:         var ii, eCh, eCode, kCh, kCode,ind;
27:         for (ii=0;ii<eSt.length;ii++) {
28:             eCode = eSt.charCodeAt(ii)
29:             ind = ii + diff;
30:             kCh = keySt.charAt(ind);
31:             kCode = kCh.charCodeAt(0);
32:             deSt = deSt + String.fromCharCode(eCode ^ kCode);
33:         }
34:     } else deSt = ""
35:     return (deSt);
36: }
```

This script contains two functions and is basically same as the XOR encryption and decryption in Chapter 1 (see ex01-13.js and ex01-14.js). The main difference is that there is an index parameter, idxx, in both functions. Consider the encryption function otp_encrypt(). There are two reasons for using idxx. First, it can be used to measure whether the remaining OTP key (keySt) is long enough to encrypt the message mSt. If not, the encrypted string enSt returns an empty string as illustrated in line 15. If the length is OK, the index idxx is used as a difference (or a offset) for the OTP (line 7). For each character of the plaintext message, the offset character in the OTP is used for the XOR encryption (line 13). The result is returned by line 16. The decryption function otp_decrypt() is similar and should be easy to read. Screenshots of this example in action are shown in Figures 5.10 and 5.11.

In Figure 5.10, you can see that the test message and OTP are inserted into the two text areas. The pad index is 10. When the OK button is clicked, the encrypted message, in hexadecimal, is displayed at the bottom text area. The first 8-character block of the ciphertext is '00000083', indicating that the ending index of the OTP is at the 83 character position. If you or your friend copy this ciphertext into the message box, check the decryption radio button and click the OK button, the decrypted message is displayed. For OTP decryption only the ciphertext is needed.

Fig. 5.10 OTP encryption

Fig. 5.11 OTP decryption

Note that the pad index is storing the ending position of the ciphertext. Suppose you want to continue the encryption after you have generated an encrypted message. You can copy the first eight characters of your last ciphertext to the pad index box to start a new encryption (see Figure 5.12).

Fig. 5.12 Continue OTP encryption

You can see that the index from the ciphertext is now '00000156', representing the correct index in the OTP. When the OTP is used up, an error message is shown (see Figure 5.13).

For a more automatic pad index, you can implement them as 'cookies' or use CGI techniques. However, storing the index permanently without protection may be a risk.

Using OTP to communicate an encrypted message confers maximum security (unbreakable). Recall the characteristics of OTP:

- the key from the OTP must be as long as the message;

- the data inside the pad is truly random;

- the key of the OTP is used only once.

The first two conditions make sure that no statistical information can be obtained from the cipher, including the infallible brute-force attack (see Section 5.2.1). However, a truly random number sequence is difficult to obtain. For example, if you use a date-and-time-based random function, such as `Math.random()` in Section 5.2.1, an attacker can estimate and simulate the date and time to produce the same random sequence. Random numbers are important in cryptology and will be discussed in Section 5.3.

Why can't the pad be used more than once? The answer is interesting. When the key (or key-stream) of the OTP is used more than once, it can be subject to a

Fig. 5.13 Run out of OTP data

number of crypto-analyses and attacks for pattern matching. As a simple example, suppose you have intercepted two encrypted messages c_1, c_2 from OTP with the same key k, i.e.

$$c_1 = m_1 \,\hat{}\, k \quad \text{and} \quad c_2 = m_2 \,\hat{}\, k \quad (\hat{}\; \text{is the XOR operation})$$

This simple XOR operation produces $c_1 \,\hat{}\, c_2 = m_1 \,\hat{}\, m_2$ containing plaintext information. Many crypto-analyses on patterns can be performed on $m_1 \,\hat{}\, m_2$.

An interesting story involving OTP is the code name 'VENONA' during the Cold War. Soviet intelligence once reused OTP keys years after they had already used them. The British intelligence service noticed some patterns and began searching against a complete archive of all coded intercepts. Together with the FBI and CIA, a huge and top secret project called VENONA (meaning 'Decoding Soviet Espionage in America') was set up. Over a period of years, various secret communications were compromised. The NSA has declassified parts of the story and published them on the Web.

If you are intending to send highly secure or confidential information over non-secure channels such as telephone, radio, post, Internet or Web, you require absolute security. You want the ciphertxt sent by you to have no chance (no chance at all) of being decrypted, even if intercepted by a third party. In this case, you may have no choice but to use OTP. Now, let's see some OTP applications on the Web.

5.2.4   Two OTP applications on the Web

In this section, two OTP programs in the public domain are introduced. The first is an OTP generator similar to ex05-03.htm with more control over the output formats. The second is a more sophisticated and completed OTP application which can be used to generate the pad and perform OTP encryption and/or decryption simultaneously.

A large number of OTP generators are available today that allow you to generate random passwords. A popular one for the public domain was developed by John Walker called 'One-Time Pad Generator.htm'. A copy of this page can be obtained from the accompanying site of this book along with a number of public domain sites. The random number generator used by this page will be discussed in Section 5.3. Screenshots of this page are shown in Figures 5.14 and 5.15.

Apart from some numeric, alphabetic and gibberish characters on this page it also includes an algorithm to generate English-like OTP keys. The page can be used to generate random passwords and one-time-pads for OTP encryption/decryption.

Another OTP package in the public domain is otp094.zip. A copy of the package can be obtained from the book, supporting site or search engine. This package is a more complete implementation of OTP in C language. It can use an external source such as a 'zip' file to generate a more secure and random pad. This pad is stored as a data file and needs to be copied to your friend for OTP decryption. When the pad is used for encryption, it will be updated so that the next encryption is

Fig. 5.14   Generating OTP data I

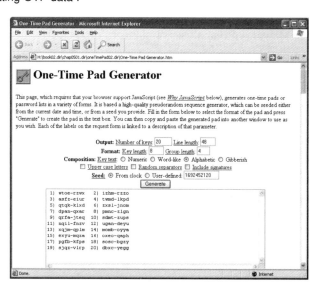

Fig. 5.15 Generating OTP Data II

well defined. When the data in the pad is used up, a new pad must be generated. To compile the program, you can use the command

```
gcc -o otp otp.c
```

The executable file `otp.exe` will be in your local directory. To see the command line options for the program, you can just type 'otp' without parameter. An operation session is captured and shown in `ex05-01.txt`.

```
Example: ex05-01.txt - One-time-pad package

1: H:\ch05>gcc -o otp otp.c
2: H:\ch05>otp
3: OTP: One Time Pad Encryption (Version 0.9.4):
        Usage Notes: General
4:
5: \-------------------------------------------------------/
6: |OTP is safe ONLY IF: 1. BOTH COPIES of the pad, your HARD DISK
   and MONITOR|
7: |are hidden from spies; 2. Pads are NEVER RE-USED; 3. Pads are
   TRULY RANDOM|
8: |- or simply unpredictable, without pattern, unrecreatable...
   (see RFC1750)|
9: /-------------------------------------------------------\
```

```
10:
11: Options summary: (use /M or /E or /D or /B on their own for more help)
12:
13: To make the one time pad: OTP /M[n] TEMP1.ZIP [TEMP2.ZIP ...]
14: To encrypt a message use: OTP /E PLAIN.TXT CIPHER.TXT
                                                          [D:\OTP.DAT]
15: To decrypt a message use: OTP /D CIPHER.TXT PLAIN.TXT
16: To get status of the pad: OTP /S     (Is the pad random/used up?)
17: To test if pad is random: OTP /T [INFILE.DAT]
                                         (more thorough than OTP /S)
18: To zap disk's free space: OTP /Z
19: To base-64 encode a file: OTP /BE INFILE.TXT OUTFILE.TXT
                                                     (NOT encryption!)
20: To base-64 decode a file: OTP /BD INFILE.TXT OUTFILE.TXT
21: H:\ch05>
```

The program otp also contains a detailed explanation of every operational command. One of the best ways to show how to use this program is by an example.

Suppose we want to encrypt a file with size 700kB to be downloaded from the Web. The first thing to do is to generate an OTP longer than this size. In order to generate a more random pad, an external file is used. In this case, we use the zip file of Chapter 4 (chap04.zip) for the external source since zip files produce good random data. To make the pad, you can use the command 'otp /m chap04.zip'. If the operation is OK, the OTP data 'otp.dat' and 'otp.cnt' will be created (see ex05-02.txt).

```
Example: ex05-02.txt - Generating OTP random numbers

1: H:\ch05>otp /m chap04.zip
2:
3:   For 1048576 bytes, mean value = 127.4749 (random = 127.5) - PASS
4:   Serial correlation = -0.0019 (random = 0.0) - PASS
5:   Maurer's universal = -0.0004 (random = 0.0) - PASS
6:   Chi-square = 250.5, exceeded by ~75% of random sequences - PASS
7:   OTP: Make: OTP.DAT and OTP.CNT successfully created.
8: H:\ch05>
```

As you can see from ex05-02.txt, the program will check the randomness of the input data. If you want a detailed report, you can use 'otp /s' and you will see the listing in ex05-03.txt.

```
Example: ex05-03.txt - OTP help manu

 1: H:\ch05>otp /s
 2:
 3:    PASS: (9725 < ok < 10275) Of 20000 bits sampled, 1's  = 9901
 4:    PASS: (2.16 < ok < 46.17) Chi-sq of 4-bit nibbles      = 17.08
 5:    PASS: (2342 < ok <  2658) 1 bit runs of 0's            = 2483
 6:    PASS: (2342 < ok <  2658) 1 bit runs of 1's            = 2548
 7:    PASS: (1134 < ok <  1366) 2 bit runs of 0's            = 1260
 8:    PASS: (1134 < ok <  1366) 2 bit runs of 1's            = 1222
 9:    PASS: ( 541 < ok <   709) 3 bit runs of 0's            = 638
10:    PASS: ( 541 < ok <   709) 3 bit runs of 1's            = 660
11:    PASS: ( 250 < ok <   374) 4 bit runs of 0's            = 336
12:    PASS: ( 250 < ok <   374) 4 bit runs of 1's            = 308
13:    PASS: ( 110 < ok <   202) 5 bit runs of 0's            = 161
14:    PASS: ( 110 < ok <   202) 5 bit runs of 1's            = 155
15:    PASS: ( 110 < ok <   202) 6+ bit runs of 0's           = 149
16:    PASS: ( 110 < ok <   202) 6+ bit runs of 1's           = 134
17:    PASS: (   0 < ok <    26) Longest run of 0's or 1's    = 16
18: OTP: Status: Pad passes FIPS 140-2 tests for randomness.
19: OTP: Status: You can encrypt 1048576 more bytes.
20: H:\ch05>
```

The program uses the testing method in the standard specification FIPS 140-2 for randomness. The program will tell you if the test fails. In our case, we can encrypt about 1MB of data. To encrypt the plaintext file chap04.zip, the following command can be used:

```
otp /e chap04.zip chap04.cit
```

This command will encrypt the data file chap04.zip producing the ciphertext file called chap04.cit using the OTP data file otp.dat in the local directory. If the OTP data file is in another directory, you may need to include the file and path as well. If the encryption is successful, you will see listing ex05-04.txt.

```
Example: ex05-04.txt - OTP encryption

1: H:\chap05>otp /e chap04.zip chap04.cit
2:
3: OTP: Encrypt: Warning! chap04.cit fails FIPS 140-2 tests for
                 randomness.
4: OTP: Encrypt: chap04.cit successfully created.
5: H:\chap05>
```

After the OTP encryption, the randomness of the ciptertext is also checked against the FIPS 140-2 test. In this case, the program creates the file chap04.cit even if the test fails. After the file chap04.zip is encrypted, the random number of otp.dat is decreased. To see how many random data remain in data file otp.dat, you can use the command 'otp /s' and the listing is shown in ex05-05.txt.

```
Example: ex05-05.txt - OTP status report

 1: H:\ch05>otp /s
 2:
 3:  PASS: (9725 < ok < 10275) Of 20000 bits sampled, 1's   = 9948
 4:  PASS: (2.16 < ok < 46.17) Chi-sq of 4-bit nibbles      = 12.97
 5:  PASS: (2342 < ok <  2658) 1 bit runs of 0's            = 2455
 6:  PASS: (2342 < ok <  2658) 1 bit runs of 1's            = 2520
 7:  PASS: (1134 < ok <  1366) 2 bit runs of 0's            = 1278
 8:  PASS: (1134 < ok <  1366) 2 bit runs of 1's            = 1271
 9:  PASS: ( 541 < ok <   709) 3 bit runs of 0's            = 658
10:  PASS: ( 541 < ok <   709) 3 bit runs of 1's            = 613
11:  PASS: ( 250 < ok <   374) 4 bit runs of 0's            = 311
12:  PASS: ( 250 < ok <   374) 4 bit runs of 1's            = 297
13:  PASS: ( 110 < ok <   202) 5 bit runs of 0's            = 163
14:  PASS: ( 110 < ok <   202) 5 bit runs of 1's            = 157
15:  PASS: ( 110 < ok <   202) 6+ bit runs of 0's           = 145
16:  PASS: ( 110 < ok <   202) 6+ bit runs of 1's           = 153
17:  PASS: (   0 < ok <    26) Longest run of 0's or 1's    = 17
18:
19: OTP: Status: Pad passes FIPS 140-2 tests for randomness.
20: OTP: Status: You can encrypt 350889 more bytes.
21: H:\chap05>
```

Now, only 350 899 more random bytes left! To decrypt the ciphertext chap04.cit, the same otp.dat is needed. Let's copy the files otp.exe, otp.dat, and chap04.cit onto another computer and issue the command

```
otp /d chap04.cit chap04.zip
```

If the operation is successful, the plaintext file chap04.zip is obtained. A session of the operation is shown in ex05-06.txt.

```
Example: ex05-06.txt

1: C:\>otp /d chap04.cit chap04.zip
2:
3: OTP: Decrypt: chap04.zip successfully created.
4: C:\>
```

Fig. 5.16 OTP decryption result

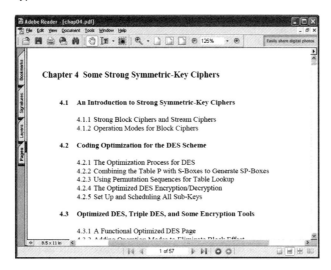

If you unzip the file `chap04.zip`, you will see an Acrobat file called `chap04.pdf` in your local folder. When you open it with Acrobat reader, you will see a figure similar to that shown in Figure 5.16.

Now, we have some experience of OTP and its application to encryption/ decryption, it is time to study the root of stream ciphers: that is, random numbers and how to generate them.

5.3 Techniques for generating random key-streams

5.3.1 Linear feedback shift registers

Generating random numbers is a big subject with so many applications well beyond the scope of this book. In this section, only a few selected topics on random numbers and how to generate them are presented. The purpose is simply to provide a foundation for understanding the ciphers discussed in this chapter.

Since computers are more or less predictable, it is extremely difficult (if possible at all) to produce truly random numbers. Random numbers generated by computers via algorithms are called 'pseudo-random numbers'. The algorithm or program producing pseudo-random numbers is called a 'pseudo-random number generator' (PRNG).

One of the classic PRNGs used by stream ciphers is the 'linear feedback shift register' (LFSR). It is a hardware device to produce random bits using the XOR gate. To understand the LFSR, let's consider an example.

Consider a hardware design containing four registers as shown in Figure 5.17. Together with starting value of $R_1 R_2 R_3 R_4$ as 1111, a simple LFSR can be constructed as follows. Within a particular time interval (one tick):

■ perform the XOR operation on the rightmost two bits;

■ place the result to be the leftmost bit;

■ shift the stream one bit to the right;

■ use the dropped rightmost bit to XOR with the plaintext.

This device contains shift and feedback functions and is called LFSR. This simple LFSR generates the following stream cycle before repeating itself.

1111, 0111, 0011, 0001, 1000, 0100, 0010, 1001, 1100, 0110, 1011, 0101, 1010, 1101, 1110, 1111

Fig. 5.17 A simple LFSR for a stream cipher

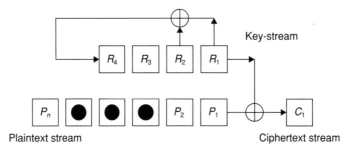

The generated key-stream is {1,1,1,1,0,0,0,1,0,0,1,1,0,1,0,1}. The starting value is usually part of the system and, in many cases, is the input key. In order to generate a non-predictable sequence, some initial values, such as '0000', should be avoided. It is believed that LFSR was one of the earliest mechanisms used to generate a key-stream for an encryption process. Some people consider LFSR to be the origin of stream ciphers. For a good key-stream generator, the following three conditions must be met:

- the generator should have long periods without repetition;

- the sequence should be statistically unpredictable;

- the sequence should be random, or the number of 1s equal to the number of 0s.

A more general LFSR is also made up of two parts – a shift register and a feedback function. The shift register is initialized with n bits (called the key), and each time a key-stream bit is required all the bits in the register are shifted 1 to the right. The dropped, or least significant, bit is the output bit for the encryption. The new leftmost bit is computed as the XOR of certain bits in the register.

Consider an LFSR with length L. The design can be written as a polynomial in modulo 2 below

$$c_L D^L + c_{(L-1)} D^{(L-1)} + \ldots + c_1 D + 1$$

where the coefficients c_i are either '0' or '1' describing the connection of the LFSR, and the polynomial is called the 'connection polynomial'. Given an initial set state $\{s_0, s_1, \ldots, s_{(L-1)}\}$, the subsequent state can be calculated by the formula

$$s_j = c_1 s_{(j-1)} + c_2 s_{(j-1)} + \ldots + c_L s_{(j-L)} \qquad \text{mod } 2 \qquad \text{for } j \geq L$$

Since the calculation is under modulo 2, it can easily be carried out by hardware (and software) to produce the output bit. This formula is usually used to implement LFSR. For an LFSR with length n, it can potentially produce a $2^n - 1$ bit-long pseudo-random sequence (referred to as the period) before repeating. This number is the maximum period for the LFSR. In other words, designing an LFSR to have a maximum period is important.

LFSRs have been studied for many years and, as stated, they are related to polynomials in modulo 2. One classic result is that in order to have an LFRS design with maximum period, the design must be a primitive polynomial in modulo 2. Some mod 2 primitive polynomials are

$$x^8 + x^4 + x^3 + x^2 + 1, \qquad x^{11} + x^2 + 1, \qquad x^{13} + x^4 + x^3 + x^1 + 1$$

Using the first polynomial for the 8-bit case, the design in Figure 5.18 produces an LFSR with maximum period. In other words, it will cycle through $2^8 - 1$ values before repeating.

Most early hardware implementations of stream ciphers belong to the LFSR type. In many cases, multiple LFSRs can work together to form more secure ciphers.

Fig. 5.18 An LFSR for 8 bits

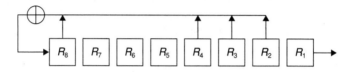

The characteristics of LFSR design and corresponding primitive polynomials are well known. This knowledge, however, is also available to attackers.

Given an initial value x_0, the operation of an LFSR of length n can be modified or generalized as

$$x_{i+1} = ((x_i * 2) + R_1 \text{ XOR } R_j \dots) \pmod{2^n}$$

This formula leads to a more general iterative form:

$$x_{i+1} = (a * x_i + c) \bmod m$$

With some carefully chosen constants a, c and m, this formula can produce sequences of pseudo-random numbers with good random statistics. The formula above is known as the 'linear congruential algorithm' for generating random numbers and is found in many computer languages, such as C/C++.

5.3.2 Linear congruential and related algorithms

As mentioned earlier, computers are more or less predictable, and it is extremely difficult to produce truly random numbers. One of the most popular PRNGs is the linear congruential algorithm.

The linear congruential algorithm

The linear congruential algorithm is the most popular PRNG. It has the following simple form:

$$x_{i+1} = (a * x_i + c) \bmod m$$

Given an initial value x_0, called the 'seed', this formula can generate a sequence of numbers

$$x_1, x_2, \dots, x_n, \dots$$

Because of the modulo operation, the values generated are in the interval $[0, m - 1]$. The parameters a, c and m determine the characteristics of the generator. The choice of the seed, x_0, determines the particular sequence of random numbers it generates. If the generator is run with the same values of a, c, m and seed, the generated sequence will be identical to the previous one. For this reason, the numbers generated are not truly random (i.e. pseudo-random). The implementation of the linear congruential algorithm is simple and can be written as the following two lines:

```
SEED = ( a * SEED + c) mod m
x = SEED /m
```

The second line is used to produce a random number between 0 and 1. Most random functions in computer languages are of this type. For example, the random functions used in ANSI C and Microsoft C are:

```
ANSI C: function rand()

        #define RAND_MAX 32767      /* i.e. (2¹⁵ - 1) */
        SEED = (1103515245 * SEED + 12345) mod 2¹⁵
        X = SEED
        Returns an integer in range from 0 to RAND_MAX

Microsoft C: function rand()

        SEED = (214013 * SEED + 2531011) mod 2³¹
        X = int( SEED/2¹⁶ )
        Returns an integer in range from 0 to 2¹⁵ - 1
```

In both cases, the output range is from 0 to 32767. The random number cycle may be too short for many crypto-applications. For some other C implementations, the following is used instead:

```
SEED = (1103515245 * SEED + 12345) mod 2³¹
X = SEED
Returns an integer in range 0 to 2³¹ - 1
```

The RNG using the linear congruential algorithm is called a 'linear congruential generator' (LCG). Not all LCGs are useful. For example, consider the following LCG:

```
SEED = 5        //initial value
SEED = ( 4 * SEED + 3 ) mod 16
```

This LCG can only produce the sequence '5, 7, 15, 15, 15, 15 . . .' and clearly is not an ideal choice for applications.

One necessary condition for a good linear congruential formula is that it will generate a long sequence of numbers before repeating itself. Also, if the seed is repeated, or is the same as the one previously generated, the sequence locks itself in a cycle. Obviously, the maximum length a sequence can be is m (the modulus operation).

It is also well known that a linear congruential formula will generate a sequence of maximum length m if, and only if, the following three conditions are met:

- c is relatively prime to m;

- $a - 1$ is a multiple of p, for every prime p dividing m;

- $a - 1$ is a multiple of 4, if m is a multiple of 4.

Consider the two generators above. They satisfy all three conditions, and only the Microsoft case (i.e. $a = 214013$, $c = 2531011$, $m = 2^{31}$) is shown below.

- The prime factorization of $2531011 = (7)(17)(21269)$. This number has no common divisor with 2^{31} other than 1. That is, the greatest common divisor of 2531011, 2^{31} is 1, i.e. they are relatively prime.

- The only prime dividing $m = 2^{31}$ is 2 and $a - 1 = 214012$ is a multiple of 2.

- $m = 2^{31}$ is a multiple of 4 and so is $a - 1 = 214012 = 2^2 (53503)$.

All the generators above enjoy a maximum sequence no matter what kind of seed and are sufficient for general applications. However, the random numbers generated by these schemes are predictable (not random enough). The crypto-strength is rather weak and hence they are not very practical to be used by ciphers.

A modified LCG

Based on the linear congruential algorithm, a modified version to generate random numbers was developed by Park and Miller at the beginning of the 1990s. This version can generate uniformly distributed pseudo-random numbers in the range 0 to $2^{31} - 1$. Although the scheme is not very strong, a number of applications have been found on ciphers. The algorithm has the simple formula

$$\hat{x}_n = a * (x_{n-1} \bmod q) - r * (x_{n-1}/q)$$

where the division in this algorithm is integer division and

$$x_n = \begin{cases} \hat{x}_n + m & \hat{x}_n < 0 \\ \hat{x}_n & \hat{x}_n \geq 0 \end{cases}$$

Compared to the linear congruential algorithm, the additonal parameters r and q are defined by

$$r = m \bmod a \qquad q = m/a \qquad \text{(integer)}$$

In a normal situation, the seed value x_0 can be set to the clock time. In order to provide better statistical and random properties, it is recommended that the parameters m and a are

$$m = 2^{31}; \qquad a = 48271 \rightarrow r = 3399 \qquad \text{and} \qquad q = 44488$$

For some early version of browsers and Javascript, the random function `Math.random()` is not available and you may need to implement a random function yourself. This algorithm is considered to be a good alternative.

Next, we want to implement this LCG and use it in the OTP example `ex05-01.htm`. First, make copies of `ex05-02.htm` and `ex05-02.js`, and call them `ex05-04.htm` and `ex05-04.js` respectively. In `ex05-04.htm`, modify line 32 so that the page loads the proper script:

```
32: <script src="ex05-04.js"></script>
```

In `ex05-04.js`, change line 3:

```
3: return myRandom();
```

In this case, the function `ran_fun()` will call a new random function called `myRandom()`. Finally, at the end of `ex05-04.js`, add the following program code:

```
Example: ex05-04.js - Generating random numbers using LCG

32: var lc_a = 48271, lc_m = 2147483647;
33: var lc_r = 3399; lc_q = 44488;
34: var lc_seed = 1234567;
35:
36: function myRandom()
37: {
38:   var tmp1, tmp2, ret
39:   if ( lc_seed == 1234567) mySeed();
40:
41:   tmp1 = lc_seed   / lc_q;
42:   tmp2 = lc_seed   % lc_q;
43:   ret  = lc_a * tmp2 - lc_r * tmp1;
44:
45:   if (ret < 0) lc_seed = ret + lc_m;
46:   else          lc_seed = ret;
47:
48:   tt = 1.0/lc_m;
49:   return (lc_seed *tt);
50: }
51:
52: function mySeed()
53: {
54:   var d = new Date();
55:   lc_seed = 2345678901
56:             + (d.getSeconds() * 0xffffff)
57:             + (d.getMinutes() * 0xffff);
58: }
```

This simple script fragment is a direct implementation of the modified LCG. Lines 32–34 define all the necessary variables a, m, r, q and the seed. The seed has an initial value which is used in line 39 to check whether a function call to `mySeed()` is needed. Lines 41–46 are direct programming of the Park and Miller formula above. Since we want to simulate the script function `Math.random()`, the variable `tt` is used to perform the division and return a floating point number between 0 and 1. The function `mySeed()` in lines 52–58 is a simple function to place the seed according to time. This page can produce random numbers similar to `ex05-01.htm`.

In addition to the constants used in the modified LCG formula above, some other constants can also be considered.

```
a = 1588635695,    m = 4294967291U,    q = 2,         r = 1117695901
a = 1223106847,    m = 4294967291U,    q = 3,         r = 625646750
a = 279470273,     m = 4294967291U,    q = 15,        r = 102913196
a = 1583458089,    m = 2147483647,     q = 1,         r = 564025558
a = 784588716,     m = 2147483647,     q = 2,         r = 578306215
a = 16807,         m = 2147483647,     q = 127773,    r = 2836
a = 950706376,     m = 2147483647,     q = 2,         r = 246070895
```

The PRNG page used in Section 5.3.4 belongs to this type. In general, the randomness of a PRN can be enhanced by the so-called 'shuffle' technique.

The shuffle technique

To understand the shuffle technique, we need to construct a function that can return a random value within a given interval such as `[min,max]`. Such a random function can easily be constructed using the script

```
1: function myRand(min,max)
2: {
3:      var range=max-min;
4:      return Math.round(myRandom()*range+min);
5: }
```

If the function `myRandom()` used in line 4 returns a floating-point random value in [0, 1], the statement in line 4 will return a random integer value in the interval `[min,max]`.

The random function `myRand(a,b)` returns a random integer from `a` to `b`. If you want to generate 100 random selections from values 1, 2, . . . , 99, 100, the shuffle technique is used and described by the following two for-loops:

```
for (i=1; i <= 100; i++) a[i] = i;
for (i=1; i <= 100; i++) swap(a[i], a[myRand(i,100)]);
```

The first for-loop generates an array `a[1]=1,a[2]=2,...,a[100]=100`. The second for-loop generates a random number on array `a[rand(i,100)]` and swaps it with `a[i]`. After the shuffling, the values (e.g. 1 to 100) inside array `a[]` are uniformly distributed. Although this technique is simple, you will find it (or similar techniques) in many ciphers.

All the techniques mentioned above are generally predictable and fail the so-called 'cryptographically secure pseudo-random number tests' as documented in RFC 1750. Depending on the form of the PRNG, the sequence, in many cases, can be determined by observing certain portions of the sequence. In other words, the initial seed x_0 can be determined by certain values of x_i.

If you have an external file containing some physical source of unpredictable numbers, such as radioactive decay, thermal noise or even some big pictures of your choice zipped together as a big file, the situation may be different. In this case, the PRNGs and shuffle techniques above can be used with the help of a physical source generating a random sequence which may cause a major headache for many crypto-experts.

Next we ask: can we have more secure pseudo-random numbers and generators, and how do we know which is more secure and random? To answer this question, some testing methods are needed. In general they test on the bits of a PRNG. If the generator passes all the randomness tests, the generator is considered to be a cryptographically secure pseudo-random bit generator (CSPRBG). Note that a CSPRBG is also a cryptographically secure pseudo-random number generator simply because random bits can produce random numbers.

5.3.3 Randomness tests and cryptographically secure pseudo-random bit generators

The basic randomness tests used by FIPS 140

Randomness tests have been studied for years. The first was proposed by Golomb and was known as the 'Golomb randomness postulates'. For our practical purposes, we are not going to discuss every aspect of the tests. Only a brief description of the test proposed by FIPS 140 is provided here.

One popular randomness test was proposed by the FIPS 140 specification, later revised as FIPS 140-2. Given a sequence of 20000 bits or elements, FIPS 140-2 employs the following four tests.

■ **Frequency test (or mono-bit test)**
This test is to see whether a sequence contains approximately the same numbers of 0s and 1s. The test is passed if the number of 1s is between 9725 and 10275.

■ **Poker test**
Divide the 20 000 bit stream into 5000 consecutive 4-bit segments. Count and store the number of occurrences of the 16 possible 4-bit values. Denote n_i as the number of each 4 bit value i, where $0 \le i \le 15$. Evaluate the following:

$$X = \frac{16}{5000}\left(\sum_{i=0}^{15} n_i^2\right) - 5000$$

The test is passed if $2.16 < X < 46.17$.

- **Runs test**

  A run is defined as a maximal sequence of consecutive bits of either all 1s or all 0s that is part of the 20 000 bit sample stream. The incidences of runs (for both consecutive 0s and consecutive 1s) of all lengths (≥ 1) in the sample stream are counted and stored.

  The test is passed if the runs that occur (of lengths 1 through 6) are each within the corresponding interval specified in the table below.

Run length	Interval	Run length	Interval
1	2343–2657	4	251–373
2	1135–1365	5	111–201
3	542–708	6+	111–201

  The test must hold for both the 0s and 1s (i.e. all 12 counts must lie in the specified interval). Runs of greater than 6 are considered to be of length 6.

- **Long run test**

  A long run is defined to be a run of length 26 or more (of either 0s or 1s). On the sample of 20 000 bits, the test is passed if there are no long runs.

These tests are specific and not difficult to implement. If one of the tests is failed, the FIPS 140-2 test is failed.

There are many other tests for randomness. If a sequence passes all the tests proposed in FIPS 140-2 above, the sequence is recommended as random and generally regarded to be secure. The OTP application in Section 5.2.4 uses FIPS 140-2 to test randomness. Note that most of the tests are specific for one sequence. Proving a general random algorithm is another matter.

Cryptographically secure pseudo-random bit generators

Although some methods have not been proven to be cryptographically secure, they appear to be quite secure and are recommended by standard organizations such as FIPS and ANSI. Also, most block ciphers are considered to be secure. Using block ciphers such as Tri-DES and CAST-128 to generate random numbers is considered to be secure. In particular, consider using a block cipher as a PRNG in Figure 5.19.

If the least significant bit (one bit) is output for every iteration, it is similar to the LFSR design. The difference is that the registers are replaced by a cipher (a complex non-linear function) of all bits rather than a simple linear or polynomial combination of output device. It is believed that this design is secure and is recommended by the US government. The generator outputs one bit a time and is called a cryptographically secure pseudo-random bit generator (CSPRBG). In fact, not just block ciphers but most of the hash functions can be used as well.

Fig. 5.19 Using a block cipher for PRNG

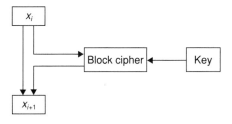

To predict the values of a sequence generated by these techniques is equivalent to breaking the cryptosystem. The well-known stream cipher SEAL2 uses secure hash algorithm SHA-1 as a generator and belongs to this type.

Quadratic residue and Blum-Blum-Shub CSPRBG

In addition to the linear congruential random number generator above, a quadratic generator of the following form can also be considered:

$$x_{n+1} = a * (x_n)^2 + b * x_n + c \qquad \text{mod } m$$

The expression is a quadratic form with a modulus and is called a 'quadratic residue'. Since this is not linear, it is harder to crack. A publicly known CSPRBG called Blum-Blum-Shub (BBS) belongs to this type. The algorithm has a simple description.

■ Find two large prime numbers, p and q, both of which are congruent 3 mod 4.

■ Find a seed x_0 which is relatively prime to $n = pq$.

■ Output the least significant bit of the iterative formula

$$x_{n+1} = x_n^2 \qquad \text{mod } n$$

(Sometime, several low-order bits can be used as output).

This algorithm is not very fast and, therefore, not suitable for simulation applications. However, this generator has generally proven to be strong and suitable for cryptographically applications. It is considered to be a CSPRBG. As long as the two primes are big and remain secret, it is hard to crack the system. However, implementation with big numbers can be complicated.

5.3.4 Implementation discussions on big numbers

This section uses BBS as an example for providing a simple discussion on implementation involving big numbers. When an algorithm such as BBS involves the square of a big number or integer, the choice of primes p, q to form the product $n = pq$ and x must be made carefully. If you have a big n or x, the square of x (i.e. x^2), in many cases, can be so big that your computer cannot handle it. In this case, the number will usually be truncated by the machine or compiler to fit to the maximum boundary. Don't forget, for a 32-bit machine, the biggest integer is normally $2^{32} - 1 = 4294967295$. Care must be taken when picking the primes and starting number x_0. Consider the following example. Given two primes $p = 5323$, $q = 7411$, $n = p * q = 39448753$ and the seed $x_0 = 8285383$, you may find the C codes of BBS (in ex05-05.c) in some implementations.

Example: ex05-05.c − Blum-Blum-Shub pseudo-random number

```
 1: #include "stdio.h"
 2: int main()
 3: {
 4: unsigned long x = 8285383, n=39448753;
 5: int i,j,s, noBytes;
 6: noBytes = 10;
 7:
 8:   for(j=0; j<noBytes; j++) {
 9:      s=0;
10:      for (i=0;i<8;i++) {
11:         x = (x * x ) % n;
12:         s |= (x & 1) << (7-i);
13:      }
14:      printf("%02lx ",s);
15:      if ((j&7)==7) printf("\n");
16:   }
17: }
```

This simple C program uses the product $n = p * q$ and the seed above to produce some random numbers in byte format. Variables n and x are defined in line 4. The variable noBytes in line 6 is set to 10 so that 10 bytes (8 bits each) will be generated by the double for-loops in lines 8–16. The inner for-loop in lines 10–13 executes the BBS algorithm producing one bit a time. When eight bits have been collected by line 12, a byte s is formed and output by the statement in lines 14–15. The random bytes are

'cf 78 54 f1 b2 65 e1 d8 f6 14'

and may be used in a stream cipher. However, there is a problem in this implementation. The program uses two large numbers x and n. In C, the data type unsigned long (or unsigned int) is a 32-bit integer. If x is a big number, the square of x can be well beyond 32 bits and will be truncated by the program. Although only 1 bit (the least significant bit) is output and used, it may affect the cycle.

Implementing this C program on the Web with ECMAScript will be even more complicated. On top of the difficulties above, ECMAScript doesn't have any data type such as unsigned long or integers. Sometimes, for two big numbers a and b, ECMAScript can give you a confusing result on whether a > b or not. The reason is that when a big number goes into the ECMAScript engine, it may change its sign without your consent. This is a general problem for a computing language without data types. The situation may drive you mad when your boss asks you to write a Web page using script that is compatible with the C program above. In other words, he is asking you to simulate the truncated result as in the C program. The reason is, simply, without the same random number sequence as in the C program, the plaintext on the Web page will be different. Compatibility is, in many cases, a vital issue for practicality and business. To write a compatible page, you can use ex05-06.htm.

```
Example: ex05-06.htm - BBS with Web page                    (Part I)

 1:  <body style="font-family:arial;font-size:20pt">
 2:  <script src="hexlib.js"></script>
 3:  <script>
 4:  function bbs_test()
 5:  {
 6:   var x = 8285383, n=39448753;
 7:   var i, j, s;
 8:   var rSt = "", noBytes=10;
 9:
10:   for(j=0;j< noBytes;j++)
11:   {
12:     s=0;
13:     for (i=0;i<8;i++)
14:     {
15:       x = bbs(n,x);
16:       s |= (x & 1) << (7-i);
17:     }
18:     rSt += byteToHex(s) + " ";
19:   }
20:   document.write(rSt);
21:  }
22:
23:  function bbs(n,x)
24:  {
25:   var x1;
26:   x1 = bit32_mult(x,x);
27:   x = bit32_mod(x1,n);
28:   return x;
29:  }
30:
```

This page contains a number of functions to produce the same random sequence as in ex05-05.c. The function bbs_test() in lines 4–21 uses the same x and n and produces the 10 bytes specified by the variable noBytes in line 8. The bbs() function is called in line 15 with n and x, and 1 bit of the result is extracted. When 8 bits have been collected, the byte is stored in a string variable rst and directly displayed by the document.write() function in line 20.

The bbs() function is defined in lines 23–29 with the two parameters n and x. The function bit32_mult() is called to compute x^2 in line 26. This function is similar to the C language so that a similar result as produced in ex05-05.c. When the numbers are big, the type of the data may be changed by ECMAScript and, therefore, the modulus operation may not operate as you expect. In this case, we need to program the modulus ourselves. This function and others are listed in part II of ex05-06.htm.

```
Example: Continuation of ex05-06.htm                    (Part II)

31: function bit32_mult(a,b)
32: {
33:  var tmp1,tmp2;
34:    tmp1 = b >>> 16;
35:    tmp2 = (a * tmp1 << 16) & 0xffffffff;
36:    tmp2 += a * (b & 0xffff);
37:    tmp2 = tmp2 & 0xffffffff;
38:    return (tmp2);
39: }
40:
41: function bit32_mod(x,n)
42: {
43:    while (bit32_bigger(x,n))
44:    {
45:      x = x - n;
46:    }
47:  return x;
48: }
49:
50: function bit32_bigger(x,y)
51: {
52:  var hw1, lw1, hw2, lw2;
53:  var status = false;
54:
55:  hw1 = x >>> 16 & 0xffff;    lw1 = x & 0xffff;
56:  hw2 = y >>> 16 & 0xffff;    lw2 = y & 0xffff;
57:
```

```
58:    if (hw1 > hw2) status = true;
59:    else {
60:      if ( hw1 == hw2) {
61:        if ( lw1 > lw2) status = true;
62:      }
63:    }
64:    return status;
65:  }
66:
67:  bbs_test()
68:  </script>
69:  </body>
```

The first function in this page is `bit32_mult()`, which can be used for multiplication of 32-bit integers. The behaviour is similar to the C language. The `bit32_mod()` function in lines 41–48 performs the modulus operation with big numbers. Basically, it is a while-loop to compare x and n and do the subtraction. The returned result x is the remainder. The function `bit32_bigger(x,y)` in lines 50–65 is used to determine whether integer x is bigger than y. Lines 55–56 split the values x and y into 16-bit components. The conditional-if statement in lines 58–63 compares the components and returns the status (`true` or `false`) of the comparison to the caller. A screenshot of this example is shown in Figure 5.20.

To avoid truncation problems, one solution is to use a small n to restrict the maximum value of $x * x$. However, this will reduce the period of the random

Fig. 5.20 `ex05-06.htm`

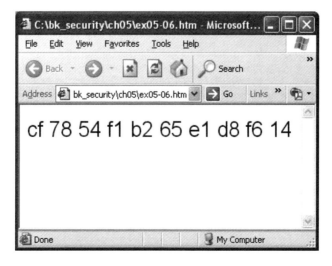

number sequence. Even if you have a smaller n, the starting value x_0 cannot be too big. You can replace the code '$x * x \bmod n$' by

$$y = (x \bmod n); \qquad y = y * y \bmod n$$

If you have a starting value x_0 bigger than n, it can be written as $x_0 = kn + r$. Taking the square of x_0, you have $(kn)^2 + 2(kn)r + r^2$. The same result is obtained by $r^2 \bmod n$.

Another solution is to use precision mathematics and symbolic programming. Symbolic programming is beyond the scope of this chapter and only a simple example is provide here. Consider the seed $x = 8285383$, which has a hexadecimal representation '7e6cc7'. The square of x should be

$$x^2 = 68\ 647\ 571\ 456\ 689 \text{ or } 3E6F421C82B1 \text{ (in hexadecimal)}$$

The truncated version of the C program and Web page above produces '1109164721' or '421c82b1' in hexadecimal. To compute the true value, you need a high precision or symbolic package. For a 64-bit case, you can program it yourselves with the 64-bit multiplication example shown in ex05-07.htm.

```
Example: ex05-07.htm - 64-bit multiplication

 1: <body style="font-family:arial;font-size:18pt">
 2: <script src="hexlib.js"></script>
 3: <script>
 4: function mult_test()
 5: {
 6:   var x = 8285383;
 7:   var outArr = new Array(2);
 8:   var rSt = "The Square of " + x + " In Hex is <br /><br />";
 9:   outArr = bit64_mult(x,x);
10:   rSt += " The High 32-Bit = " + byte4ToHex(outArr[0]) + "<br />"+
11:          " The Low 32-Bit = " + byte4ToHex(outArr[1]);
12:   document.write(rSt);
13: }
14:
15: function bit64_mult(inA,inB)
16: {
17:   var hw1,lw1, hw2,lw2;
18:   var ho1,ho2,ho3;
19:
20:   var tmp1, tmp2;
21:
22:   hw1 = (inA >>> 16 ) & 0xffff;
23:   lw1 = inA & 0xffff;
```

```
24:
25:    hw2 = (inB >>> 16 ) & 0xffff;
26:    lw2 = inB & 0xffff;
27:
28:    ho1 = hw1 * hw2;
26:    lw2 = inB & 0xffff;
27:
28:    ho1 = hw1 * hw2;
29:    ho2 = (hw1 * lw2) + (hw2 * lw1)
30:    ho3 = lw1 * lw2;
31:
32:    add01 = (ho3 >>> 16 ) & 0xffff;
33:    ho3 = ho3 & 0xffff;
34:
35:    ho2 = (ho2 + add01);
36:    add01 = (ho2 >>> 16) & 0xffff;
37:    ho2 = ho2 & 0xffff;
38:    ho1 = ho1 + add01;
39:    ho2 = (ho2 << 16) + ho3;
40:
41:  return Array(ho1,ho2);
42: }
43:
44: mult_test()
45: </script>
46: </body>
```

The function in this page is `mult_test()`, which is used to test the square of $x = 8285383$. The function `bit64_mult()` in line 9 computes the square of x and returns it as an array of two elements `outArr[0]` and `outArr[1]`. This function is defined in lines 15–42. When you calculate the multiplication of two large numbers x and y, say, you can split the numbers into two parts (or components) such as '$x = (a + b)$' and '$y = (c + d)$'. Then apply the simple algebraic formula on the components below:

```
(a + b) (c + d) = ac + ad + bc + bd
```

After the multiplication on components, all you have to do is to add them back according to the order of bits. Lines 22–26 split the variables `inA` and `inB` into two parts each. The multiplications on the parts are computed by the statements in lines 28–30. Lines 32–39 are used to merge the components back together to form two 32-bit words. The result is similar to a 64-bit integer and is returned to the caller as an array of two elements. A screenshot of this example is shown in Figure 5.21.

Fig. 5.21 ex05-07.htm

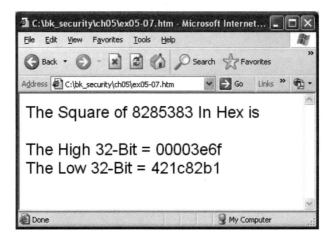

The implementation of algorithms such as BBS would involve precision problems and care should be taken. Since we are not going to use BBS in this chapter, we will not go through further details in this section. Mathematics with arbitrary precision will be discussed further in Chapter 8. Now, let's see some fast and compact stream cipher designs for serious crypto-applications. They are easy to implement and, more importantly, produce high security strength ciphertext (no efficient known attack).

5.4   Two fast and compact stream ciphers: RC4 and ISAAC

5.4.1   The RC4 algorithm and discussions on strength

RC4 is a symmetric-key stream cipher invented by Ron Rivest, co-founder of RSA Data Security. According to RSA, the official name of RC4 is 'Rivest Cipher 4'. In the cryptology community, the RC acronym is generally taken to mean 'Ron's code' forming a family of ciphers. Other publicly known ciphers in the family are RC5 and RC6. Unlike RC4, these two ciphers are block based. In particular, RC6 was one of the best candidates for the Advanced Encryption Standard (AES) challenge promoted by the US government and will be introduced in Section 6.5.

RC4 is a fast and compact stream cipher which operates on one byte of data at a time. In general, the speed of RC4 is up to 10 times faster than the standard DES. It was designed in 1987 and was initially used as a trade secret. In September 1994, the algorithm was anonymously posted on the Internet on the Cyperpunks' 'anonymous remailers' list. The algorithm was then posted on the sci.crypt newsgroup for scrutiny and verification. It was soon available from many sites. Once an algorithm is known, it is no longer a trade secret. It is believed that 'unofficial' implementations of the algorithm are legal but cannot use the name RC4 since it is a trademark. To avoid such problems, RC4 implementations are usually called 'alleged RC4' (ARC4).

Just like many other stream ciphers, RC4 is essentially a pseudo-random number generator initialized by a short key (compared to OTP) of up to 256 bytes. The algorithm generates a key-stream of arbitrary length. The key-stream is simply XORed with the plaintext to produce the ciphertext stream. This process is similar to OTP. Since XOR operations are used for encryption, decryption is exactly the same as encryption with the same key.

Another reason for its popularity is that the algorithm is simple. Not many serious encryption algorithms in cryptology can be memorized by heart and implemented as quickly as RC4. Apart from the first few hundred bytes of the key-stream (see later in this section), it is surprisingly secure.

RC4 is a cipher with variable key length. The key length can be 1 to 256 bytes forming a maximum of 2048 bits. The main operation is to initialize a 256-byte state table. The state table is used for subsequent generation of pseudo-random bytes XORing with the plaintext to give the ciphertext. The state table `S[0]` to `S[255]` occupies 256 bytes of memory. The algorithm is described in `ex05-07.txt`.

```
Example: ex05-07.txt - The RC4 algorithm

 1: Step1: Initialize the pseudo-random number generator
 2:    for i = 0 ... 255 do S[i] = i End for
 3:    j=0
 4:    for i = 0 ... 255 do
 5:        j = (j + S[i] + key[i mod key_length]) mod 256
 6:      swap (S[i],S[j])
 7:    End for
 8:
 9: Step2: Generating byte k for encryption and decryption
10:    i = 0
11:    j = 0
12:    loop until the entire message is encrypted/decrypted
13:      i = (i + 1) mod 256
14:      j = (j + S[i]) mod 256
15:      swap(S[i],S[j])
16:      k = S[(S[i] + S[j]) mod 256]
17:      output the XOR of k with the next byte of input
18:    End loop
```

Yes, the algorithm is less than 20 lines. The two for-loops in Step1 are used to initialize the random number generator with the user input key[]. The key is represented as an array of bytes (or characters) and therefore is easy to implement. From the second for-loop, in lines 4–7, you can see that the key length can be 1 to 256. If the key is less than 256 characters, the key will be repeated by the modulus operation (i.e. i mod key-length) in line 5. If the key is longer than 256, only the first 256 characters are used. The main purpose is to use 256 key characters to get some disturbed values of j. The variable j is to swap the elements between S[i] and S[j] in line 6. At the end, we have a permuted state table S[]. Since there are 256 elements in S[], a total of 256 * 8 = 2048 bits is achieved.

In Step2, a fixed mechanism is designed to change around the data in S[] to produce a byte called k. The value of k is, in fact, one of the elements inside table S[] obtained by the four simple statements (PRNG) in lines 13–16. The byte k is then used to perform an XOR operation with the incoming plaintext character. The values of k form a stream (or a key-stream) for the XOR encryption. Given the same key in key[], it is easy to see that the key-stream will be the same and, therefore, the XOR decryption remains the same as the encryption. Sometimes, you don't even need to distinguish the encryption or decryption.

This simple scheme has been under public scrutiny since its appearance in the middle of 1990s and it has been found to be surprisingly secure. Many serious works use RC4 for protection.

The security strength comes from the simple PRNG in lines 13–16. Yes! Just four lines with simple swaps. The difficulties of cracking the system are that firstly it is difficult to know where any value is in s[]. It is also difficult to know which locations in s[] are used in selecting each value in the sequence. Finally, the swap of a known position with an unknown position paralyzes many attacks based on elimination methods. There is, basically, no efficient known attack for RC4.

In 2001, a discovery was made by Fluhrer, Martin and Shamir (known as the Fluhrer, Martin and Shamir attack). By studying all possible RC4 input keys and the corresponding key-streams, the statistics tables for the first few bytes of output key-stream are seriously non-random. As a result, an attack is possible to recover the RC4 key if a large number of messages are encrypted with this key. In other words, you are taking a risk if you use the same key to encrypt many messages or over a long time. This effect had an impact on the security of the IEEE 802.11 Wireless Networks standard and led to the specification IEEE 802.11i. Apart from this minor flaw, no other attacks have been found for the last couple years.

In fact, this drawback can be avoided easily. Most of the implementations just ignore the first few hundreds of bytes so that the numbers generated by the random number generator are random enough to have high crypto-strength. Now, let's see how to implement the scheme.

5.4.2   Implementations of the RC4 scheme

Based on the algorithm in the previous section, the implementation of the scheme is straightforward. In order to maintain the same calling syntax, we will use the same program structure developed in Chapter 4. Consider the script ex05-08.js.

```
Example: ex05-08.js - The implementation of ARC4            (Part I)

 1: var rc4_p = 0, rc4_q=0;
 2: var rc4_S = new Array(256);
 3:
 4: function rc4_setup(key,length)
 5: {
 6:     var i, j, k, a;
 7:     rc4_p = 0; rc4_q = 0;
 8:     for( i = 0; i < 256; i++ ) rc4_S[i] = i;
 9:
10:     j = k = 0;
11:     for( i = 0; i < 256; i++ ) {
12:        a = rc4_S[i];
13:        j = ( j + a + key[k] ) & 0xff;
```

```
14:
15:        rc4_S[i] = rc4_S[j];
16:        rc4_S[j] = a;
17:
18:        if( ++k >= length ) k = 0;
19:      }
20: }
21:
22: function rc4_crypt(data,length)
23: {
24:   var i, p1, q1, a, b, k;
25:   var odata = new Array()
26:
27:     p1 = rc4_p;
28:     q1 = rc4_q;
29:
30:     for( i = 0; i < length; i++ ) {
31:         p1 = ( p1 + 1) & 0xff;
32:         a = rc4_S[p1];
33:         q1 = ( q1 + a) & 0xff;
34:         rc4_S[p1] = b = rc4_S[q1];
35:         rc4_S[q1] = a;
36:         k = rc4_S[( a + b ) & 0xff];
37:         data[i] = data[i] ^ k;
38:     }
39:     rc4_p = p1;
40:     rc4_q = q1;
41:   return data;
42: }
43:
```

This script fragment contains two functions and is a direct implementation of the scheme described in `ex05-07.txt`. At the top of the script, the state table `rc4_S[]` is declared in line 2 as an array of 256 elements. Together with variables `rc4_p` and `rc4_q`, the state table `rc4_S[]` can be indexed easily. The `rc4_setup()` function takes in two parameters. The first is the byte (or character) array of the key and the second is the length of the key. Inside the function is a line-by-line programming of the RC4 scheme. The for-loop in line 8 fills up the state table `rc4_S[]`. The for-loop in lines 11–19 initializes table `rc4_S[]` using the array `key[]`. The two statements in lines 12–13 compute `j` and lines 15–17 are used to swap the elements `rc4_S[i]` and `rc4_S[j]`. Note that the mod 256 operation is replaced by the bitwise AND, i.e. '`&0xff`'. If the input key is less than 256 bytes, the key will be reused by the statement in line 18.

The second function `rc4_crypt()` has two parameters. The first is the byte array `data[]` and the second is the `length`. Inside this function is a line-by-line translation from the RC4 algorithm. The for-loop in lines 30–38 performs the encryption/decryption byte by byte using the state table `rc4_S[]`. Lines 31–36 are the mechanism to compute the value `k`. This value `k` is then XORed with the incoming byte `data[i]` in line 37.

Note that the implementation here is based on the original RC4 scheme. To prevent the Fluhrer, Martin and Shamir attack mentioned in Section 5.4.1, a number of values of `k` should be ignored. One of the simplest ways to do it is to copy lines 30–38 and modify the program as follows:

```
30: for( i = 0; i < 256; i++ ) {
31:     p1 = ( p1 + 1 ) & 0xff;
32:     a = rc4_S[p1];
33:     q1 = ( q1 + a ) & 0xff;
34:     rc4_S[p1] = b = rc4_S[q1];
35:     rc4_S[q1] = a;
36:     k = rc4_S[( a + b ) & 0xff];
37:     //data[i] = data[i] ^ k;
38: }
```

If you want to ignore the first 256 bytes, you simply change the `i` index in line 30 to a different value such as 256. Also, don't forget to comment out the statement in line 37 so that no XOR operation is done. Now, you can insert this program block at line 29 in `ex05-08.js`. To be compliant with the standard RC4 scheme, we left the implementation as it is. To use this script, an interface given in part II of `ex05-08.js` is developed.

```
Example: Continuation of ex05-08.js                          (Part II)

44: function rc4_keys(inSt,length)
45: {
46:   var i, rKeyArr = new Array();
47:   for (i=0; i< length ; i++) { rKeyArr[i] = inSt.charCodeAt(i)
                                        & 0xff; }
48:   rc4_setup(rKeyArr,length);
49: }
50:
51: function rc4(keySt, msgSt)
52: {
53:   var len = msgSt.length;
54:   var i, tempSt="";
55:   var msgArr = new Array(), outArr = new Array();
56:   for (i=0;i<256;i++) rc4_S[i]=0;
```

```
57:    rc4_p1=0; rc_q1=0;
58:
59:    rc4_keys(keySt,keySt.length);
60:
61:    for (i=0;i< len;i++) msgArr[i] = msgSt.charCodeAt(i) & 0xff;
62:    outArr = rc4_crypt(msgArr,len);
63:
64:    tempSt = "";
65:    for (i=0;i< len;i++) {
66:       tempSt += String.fromCharCode(outArr[i] & 0xff);
67:    }
68:    return tempSt;
69: }
```

This script contains two functions rc4_keys() and rc4(). These two functions have the same name, calling syntax and structure as in a number of our previous programs. The function rc4_keys() performs all the subkey (or key-stream) settings. In this case, the for-loop in line 47 converts the key string into an array of bytes and then calls the rc4_setup() in part I of the script.

The second function rc4() takes two strings, keySt and msgSt, from the Web page. Lines 56–57 initialize the state table rc4_s[], and the function call in line 59 ultimately initializes the table with the user key. The for-loop in line 61 converts the message string into a byte array. The function call in line 62 performs the encryption/decryption and the result is stored in array outArr[]. The for-loop in lines 65–68 converts the byte array into a string and returns to the function caller.

To test this script, a Web page is required. Make a copy of ex05-01.htm and call it ex05-08.htm. Modify the following lines of the new file.

```
 9: ARC4 Encryption/Decryption<br />
41: <script src="ex05-08.js"></script>
52:      l1st = byteStToHex(rc4(key, message))
59:      l1st = rc4(key, message)
```

Line 9 changes the display to reflect that we are working with the ARC4 scheme. Line 41 is to include the proper script file. Lines 52 and 59 are used to make the correct function calls. Note that there is no difference between encryption and decryption in an RC4 scheme. Screenshots are shown in Figures 5.22 and 5.23.

Web page application is ideal for communicating encrypted messages in real time on the Web, where messages are usually short and speed is not critical. For a fast program which can work with big files, an implementation using a compiled language such as C is handy.

To implement RC4 in the C language is not difficult. Consider the program given in ex05-09.c.

Fig. 5.22 ARC4 encryption

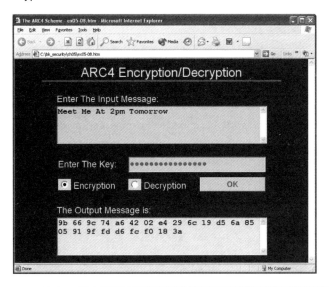

Fig. 5.23 ARC4 decryption

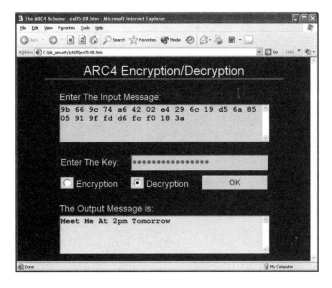

Example: ex05-09.c - C implementation of the ARC4 scheme

```c
 1: struct rc4_context
 2: {
 3:     int p, q;
 4:     int S[256];
 5: };
 6:
 7: void rc4_keys(struct rc4_context *c, unsigned char *key,int keyLen )
 8: {
 9:     int i, j, k, a;
10:     c->p = 0;
11:     c->q = 0;
12:     for( i = 0; i < 256; i++ ) c->S[i] = i;
13:     j = k = 0;
14:     for( i = 0; i < 256; i++ ) {
15:         a = c->S[i];
16:         j = ( j + a + key[k] ) & 0xff;
17:         c->S[i] = c->S[j]; c->S[j] = a;
18:         if( ++k >= keyLen ) k = 0;
19:     }
20: }
21:
22: void rc4_cipher(struct rc4_context *c,unsigned char
                    *data,int dataLen )
23: {
24:     int i, p1, q1, a, b;
25:     p1 = c->p;
26:     q1 = c->q;
27:     for( i = 0; i < dataLen; i++ ) {
28:         p1 = ( p1 + 1 ) & 0xff;
29:         a = c->S[p1];
30:         q1 = ( q1 + a ) & 0xff;
31:         c->S[p1] = b = c->S[q1];
32:         c->S[q1] = a;
33:         data[i] ^= c->S[( a + b ) & 0xff];
34:     }
35:     c->p = p1;
36:     c->q = q1;
37: }
```

As you can see, the entire C implementation is less than 40 lines. In order to maintain a similar calling syntax to other programs in this book, the state table is implemented by a structure called `rc4_context` in C (lines 1–5). For example, the statement in line 10 'c->p' is referred to the value p in the structure. Similarly, c->S[i] is referred to the value in state table S[i] in structure c. The functions in the program are line-by-line translations from the script ex05-05.js and can be read quite easily.

To use this program, a driver program called rc4driver.c is developed.

```
Example: rc4driver.c - A driver program for ARC4 encryption/decryption

 1: #include <stdio.h>
 2: #include "ex05-09.c"
 3:
 4: int main(int argc, char *argv[])
 5: {
 6:   int i, n, m=-1;
 7:   struct rc4_context s;
 8:   unsigned char buf[4096];
 9:   unsigned char kkey[256];
10:   FILE *inK, *inP, *outF;
11:
12:   if (argc!=5) {
13:     printf("\nUsage:\n rc4driver (e)|(d) <infile> <outfile>
              <keyfile>\n");
14:     return 2;
15:   }
16:   for (i=0;i< 4096;i++)    buf[i]=0;
17:   for (i=0;i<256;i++)      kkey[i]=0;
18:
19:   if((inK=fopen(argv[4],"rb"))==NULL){
20:       printf("\r\nCould not open input file: %s",argv[4]);
21:       return 2;
22:   } else {
23:
24:     while (!feof(inK) && m < 256) { kkey[++m] = fgetc(inK) & 0xff; }
25:     fclose(inK);
26:
27:   }
28:
29:   rc4_keys( &s, kkey, m);
30:
31:   if((inP=fopen(argv[2],"rb"))==NULL){
32:       printf("\r\nCould not open input file : %s",argv[2]);
33:       return 2;
34:   }
```

```
35:   if((outF=fopen(argv[3],"wb"))==NULL){
36:       printf("\r\nCould not open output file : %s",argv[3]);
37:       return 2;
38:   }
39:   if(argv[1][0]=='e') {
40:     while ((n=fread(buf,1,4096,inP)) >0) {
41:         rc4_cipher( &s, buf, n );
42:         if(fwrite(buf,1,n,outF) < n) {
43:             printf("\r\nError writing to output file \r\n");
44:             return(3);
45:         }
46:     }
47:   }
48:   if(argv[1][0]=='d') {
49:     while ((n=fread(buf,1,4096,inP)) >0) {
50:         rc4_cipher( &s, buf, n );
51:         if(fwrite(buf,1,n,outF) < n){
52:             printf("\r\nError writing to output file\r\n");
53:             return(3);
54:         }
55:     }
56:   }
57:   fclose(inP); fclose(outF);
58:   return 0;
59: }
```

This program is similar to the driver program in the DES case and the modifications are highlighted in bold. First, in line 2, the program ex05-09.c is included so that its functions for RC4 can be called. We have changed the buffer buf[] to 4096 in line 8 so that the program will read data faster. The key array kkey[] is also increased to 256 in line 9. The for-loops in lines 16–17 initialize the arrays buf[] and kkey[] to 0. The while-loop in line 24 reads all the key data from the key file into array kkey[]. The function call in line 29 passes the key array, the key length and m into the function rc4_keys() to set up the key-stream.

If encryption is true, the while-loop in line 40 reads 4096 pieces of data into array buf[]. The function call in the next line encrypts the data and returns it to array buf[]. The data in buf[] is then written into the outfile by line 42. Similarly, if decryption is true, the lines 48–56 are executed to decrypt the data from infile. Note that the encryption function in line 41 is the same as the decryption function in line 50. Some results of this program in action are shown in Figure 5.24.

Fig. 5.24 ARC4 encryption/decryption

```
 1: H:\ch05>gcc -o rc4driver rc4driver.c
 2: H:\ch05>rc4driver
 3: Usage:
 4: rc4driver (e)|(d) <infile> <outfile> <keyfile>
 5:
 6: H:\ch05>rc4driver e zplain.txt zen.txt zkey.txt
 7: H:\ch05>rc4driver d zen.txt zde.txt zkey.txt
 8: H:\ch05>type zde.txt
 9:
10: Meet Me At 2pm Tomorrow
11:
12: H:\ch05>tohex zen.txt
13:
14: 9b 66 9c 74 a6 42 02 e4 29 6c 19 d5
15: 6a 85 05 91 9f fd d6 fc f0 18 3a
26: H:\ch05>
```

As you can see, a gcc compiler is used to compile the driver rc4driver.c in line 1. The program is used to encrypt the file zplain.txt in line 6 using the key file zkey.txt. The ciphertext file zen.txt is then decrypted by the command in line 7. The decryption result is shown in line 10. We use a hexadecimal utility tohex to read the ciphertext zen.txt as illustrated in line 12. The hexadecimal values are the same as those shown in Figure 5.22 for the Web case.

RC4 scheme is fast: a 5 MB file in pdf format can be encrypted and decrypted by the rc4driver in less than 0.1 second on a low-end portable PC (2.0 GHz).

Surprisingly, there is another stream cipher that can seriously challenge the speed and compactness of RC4. It is ISAAC from Robert Jenkins. First, let's look at the random number generator it uses.

5.4.3 The PRNG used by ISAAC

Apart from the initialization code, the PRNG used in RC4 is described by lines 13–16 in ex05-07.txt:

```
13: i = (i + 1) mod 256
14: j = (j + S[i]) mod 256
15: swap(S[i],S[j])
16: k = S[(S[i] + S[j]) mod 256]
```

The variables `i` and `j` are the pointer and accumulator of the generator. Given an initial state table `s[]` of 256 values, this PRNG produce a key-stream `k`. Each `k` is 8-bit to perform encryption/decryption. The operations in the algorithm are mainly swap, or indirection (I) and accumulate (A), so that it is a IA generator.

The ISAAC pseudo-random number algorithm from Robert Jenkins is a high-quality generator with the following properties:

■ crypto-secure (no efficient known attack);

■ no bias;

■ minimal guaranteed period of 2^{40};

■ average period is 2^{8295};

■ 8192 bits key length for encryption;

■ generates 32-bit random numbers.

It uses the operations indirection, shift, accumulate, add and count (ISAAC) on 32-bit words to generate the 32-bit pseudo-random numbers. Given two internal state arrays, `randrsl[256]` and `mm[256]`, and four parameters `aa`, `bb`, `cc` and `randcnt`, the PRNG can be described by the pseudo-code below:

```
Example: ex05-08.txt - The ISACC pseudo-random number algorithm

 1: cc = cc + 1;
 2: bb = bb + cc;
 3: for (ii=0; ii<256; ++ii) do
 4:    x = mm[ii];
 5:    switch (ii mod 4) do
 6:       case 0: aa = aa ^ (aa << 13); break;
 7:       case 1: aa = aa ^ (aa >>> 6); break;
 8:       case 2: aa = aa ^ (aa << 2); break;
 9:       case 3: aa = aa ^ (aa >>> 16); break;
10:    end-switch
11:
12:    aa             = mm[(ii + 128) mod 256] + aa;
13:    mm[ii]   = y = mm[(x >>> 2)   mod 256] + aa + bb;
14:    randrsl[ii] = bb = mm[(y >>> 10) mod 256] + x;
15: end-for
```

The for-loop in lines 3–15 can generate 256 32-bit random numbers stored in array `randrsl[]` in one round. Although it uses more operations than RC4, one 32-bit random number is equivalent to four 8-bit random numbers in RC4. If all the bits are used, it is a really fast cipher.

Similar to many PRNGs used by stream ciphers, this algorithm has a relatively long initialization code before you can use it. To use the generator, the script ex05-10.js is constructed.

Example ex05-10.js – The ISAAC pseudo-random number generator (Part I)

```
 1: var randrsl = new Array(256);
 2: var mm      = new Array(256);
 3: var aa=0, bb=0, cc=0, randcnt;
 4:
 5: function isaac()
 6: {
 7:   var i,x,y;
 8:   cc = cc + 1;
 9:   bb = bb + cc;
10:   for (i=0; i<256; ++i)
11:   {
12:     x = mm[i];
13:     switch (i%4)
14:     {
15:       case 0: aa = aa ^ (aa << 13); break;
16:       case 1: aa = aa ^ (aa >>> 6); break;
17:       case 2: aa = aa ^ (aa << 2); break;
18:       case 3: aa = aa ^ (aa >>> 16); break;
19:     }
20:     aa              = mm[(i + 128) % 256] + aa;
21:     mm[i]     = y = mm[(x >>> 2) % 256] + aa + bb;
22:     randrsl[i] = bb = mm[(y >>> 10) % 256] + x;
23:   }
24: }
25:
```

At the top of this script fragment, some global variables, namely aa, bb, cc and randcnt, are declared. The arrays randrsl[] and mm[] are the internal states of the generator.

The generator is defined as a function called isaac() in lines 5–25. Inside this function is the line-by-line programming of the generator in ex05-08.txt, which should be easy to read. The array mm[] is populated by the lines 20–21, and the random numbers are stored in randrsl[] in line 22. The initialization codes are defined in part II of ex05-10.js.

```
26: function mix(inArr)
27: {
28:   var a,b,c,d,e,f,g,h;
29:   a = inArr[0]; b = inArr[1]; c = inArr[2]; d = inArr[3];
30:   e = inArr[4]; f = inArr[5]; g = inArr[6]; h = inArr[7];
31:
32:   a ^= b << 11; d += a; b +=c; b ^= c >>> 2;  e += b; c += d;
33:   c ^= d << 8;  f += c; d +=e; d ^= e >>> 16; g += d; e += f;
34:   e ^= f << 10; h += e; f +=g; f ^= g >>> 4;  a += f; g += h;
35:   g ^= h << 8;  b += g; h +=a; h ^= a >>> 9;  c += h; a += b;
36:
37:   return Array(a,b,c,d,e,f,g,h);
38: }
39:
40: function randinit(flag)
41: {
42:  var i;
43:  var lrArr = new Array(8);
44:
45:  aa = bb = cc = 0;
46:  for (i=0;i<8;i++) lrArr[i] = 0x9e3779b9;
47:
48:  for (i=0; i<4; ++i) lrArr = mix(lrArr);
49:  for (i=0; i<256; i+=8)
50:  {
51:    if (flag) {
52:        lrArr[0] +=randrsl[i  ]; lrArr[1] +=randrsl[i+1];
53:        lrArr[2] +=randrsl[i+2]; lrArr[3] +=randrsl[i+3];
54:        lrArr[4] +=randrsl[i+4]; lrArr[5] +=randrsl[i+5];
55:        lrArr[6] +=randrsl[i+6]; lrArr[7] +=randrsl[i+7];
56:    }
57:    lrArr = mix(lrArr);
58:    mm[i ]=lrArr[0]; mm[i+1]=lrArr[1]; mm[i+2]=lrArr[2];
59:    mm[i+3]=lrArr[3]; mm[i+4]=lrArr[4]; mm[i+5]=lrArr[5];
       mm[i+6]=lrArr[6]; mm[i+7]=lrArr[7];
60:  }
61:
62:  if (flag)
63:  {
64:   for (i=0; i<256; i+=8)
65:   {
66:     lrArr[0] +=mm[i  ]; lrArr[1] +=mm[i+1];
```

```
67:        lrArr[2] +=mm[i+2]; lrArr[3] +=mm[i+3];
68:        lrArr[4] +=mm[i+4]; lrArr[5] +=mm[i+5];
69:        lrArr[6] +=mm[i+6]; lrArr[7] +=mm[i+7];
70:
71:        lrArr = mix(lrArr);
72:
73:        mm[i ]=lrArr[0]; mm[i+1]=lrArr[1]; mm[i+2]=lrArr[2];
74:        mm[i+3]=lrArr[3]; mm[i+4]=lrArr[4]; mm[i+5]=lrArr[5];
           mm[i+6]=lrArr[6]; mm[i+7]=lrArr[7];
75:     }
76:   }
77:   isaac();
78:   randcnt=256;
79: }
80:
```

The initialization code consists of two functions. The first is called `mix()`. It will take an array of eight elements as input. After mixing them, the array is returned. The initialization function is `randninit()` in lines 40–79. This function has a boolean type parameter called `flag`. If `flag` is `true`, the random numbers will be stored in array `randrsl[]` ready to be used. Following the standard algorithm, we will assume that `flag` always has a `true` value. An array `lrArr[]` of eight elements is declared in line 43. Together with the global variables `aa`, `bb` and `cc`, they all have an initial value set by the statements in lines 45–46. The for-loop in line 48 mixes the array `lrArr[]` four times. The for-loop in lines 49–60 fills up the 256 elements of the internal state array `mm[]`. The for-loop in lines 64–75 manipulates the array `mm[]` further to finish the initialization process. Now, `mm[]` has been initialized. The statement in line 77 calls the PRNG `isaac()` to produce 256 random numbers in `randrsl[]`. The last statement in line 78 sets the count parameter to 256, indicating that a set of 256 32-bit random numbers are ready to be used.

To test the script, consider the page defined in `ex05-10.htm`.

Example: ex05-10.htm – A page for ISACC pseudo-random numbers

```
1: <body style="font-family:courier;font-size:20pt;font-weight:bold">
2: <script src="hexlib.js"></script>
3: <script src="ex05-10.js"></script>
4: <script>
5: function isaac_test()
6: {
7:   var i,j,rSt = "";
8:   aa = bb = cc = 0;
```

```
 9:    for (i=0; i<256; ++i) mm[i] = randrsl[i]=0;
10:    randinit(true);
11:    for (i=0; i<2; ++i) {
12:       isaac();
13:       for (j=0; j<256; ++j) {
14:          rSt += byte4ToHex(randrsl[j])+" ";
15:          if ((j&3)==3) rSt += "<br />"
16:       }
17:       rSt += "<br />"
18:    }
19:    document.write(rSt);
20: }
21: isaac_test()
22: </script>
23: </body>
```

This page includes ex05-10.js in line 3 so that the functions in that script can be called. The script block in lines 4–23 has only one function, isaac_test(). This function is to test the ISAAC generator and demonstrate how to use it. The global variables and the internal state arrays mm[] and randrsl[] are initially set to zero by the statement in lines 8–9. The function randinit(true) in line 10 uses mm[] and randrsl[] to initialize the random number generator. The for-loop in lines 11–20 calls the function isaac() twice so that two sets of 256 32-bit random numbers are generated. The random numbers are stored in array randrsl[]. To see the random number, the statement

```
byte4ToHex(randrsl[j])
```

converts the 32-bit random number in randrsl[j] into four hexadecimal values. When the two sets of random numbers are generated in the string variable rSt, this string will be output to the screen directly by the document.write() function in line 19. To test this function in this page you may need to execute the function by calling its name as illustrated by the statement in line 21. A screenshot of this example is shown in Figure 5.25.

In fact, the isaac_test() function is the standard way of testing the generator recommended by the original designer. Now, let's see how to use this generator to construct a stream cipher.

5.4.4 The ISAAC stream cipher and implementations

One of the quickest ways to develop a stream cipher using ISAAC algorithm is to make a copy and call it ex05-11.js. At the end of this file add the following codes.

Fig. 5.25 ISAAC PRNG

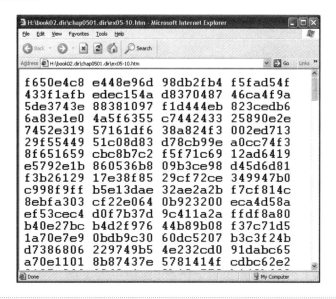

```
Example: ex05-11.js - Script for the ISACC stream cipher

81: function init()
82: {
83:   var i;
84:   for (i=0;i< 256;i++) { mm[i]=0; randrsl[i]=0;}
85:   aa = bb = cc = 0;
86:   randcnt = 0;
87: }
88:
89: function isaac_crypt(data,llen)
90: {
91:   var i,j, m=0, k, aByte;
92:   randinit(true);
93:   while (m < llen)
94:   {
95:     isaac();
96:     for (j=0; j<256; ++j) {
97:       for (i=0;i<4;i++) {
98:         k = m++;
99:         aByte = (randrsl[j] >>> (4-i)) & 0xff;
100:         if ( k < llen) data[k] = (data[k] ^ aByte) & 0xff;
101:         else { i=4; j=256;}
```

```
102:          }
103:      }
104:    }
105:    return data;
106: }
107:
```

Lines 81–87 are to initialize the internal variables, including the state arrays mm[] and randrsl[]. The simple function isaac_crypt() performs encryption and decryption. When the data and length are input to this function, the initialization function randinit(true) is called. Then the while-loop in lines 93–104 processes the data with the XOR operation. First, the function call isaac() in line 95 generates a set of 256 32-bit random numbers. Note that the function randinit() has already generated the first set. The random numbers are 32-bit and are stored in array randrsl[]. To perform the XOR operation with randrsl[] and the plaintext stream data, the double for-loop in lines 96–103 is used. The main idea is to use the inner for-loop in lines 97–102 to extract the bytes from randrsl[j] one-by-one – these are called aByte (action byte). The action byte is XORed with the plaintext byte data[k] in line 100. Therefore, for 256 32-bit random numbers, 1024 8-bit characters can be encrypted in one round.

To use the script with a Web page, some interface functions are needed. Consider part II of ex05-11.js.

Example: Continuation of ex05-11.js   **(Part II)**

```
108: function isaac_keys(inSt,length)
109: {
110:   var i, rKeyArr = new Array(), len;
111:   for (i=0; i< length; i++) rKeyArr[i] = inSt.charCodeAt(i) & 0xff;
112:   if ( length > 256 ) len = 256;
113:   else len = length;
114:   for (i=0;i<len;i++) randrsl[i] = rKeyArr[i];
115: }
116:
117: function isaac_cipher(keySt, msgSt)
118: {
119:   var len = msgSt.length;
120:   var i, tempSt="";
121:   var msgArr = new Array(), outArr = new Array();
122:   init();
123:   isaac_keys(keySt,keySt.length);
124:   for (i=0;i< len;i++) msgArr[i] = msgSt.charCodeAt(i) & 0xff;
```

```
125:    outArr = isaac_crypt(msgArr,len);
126:    tempSt = "";
127:    for (i=0;i< len;i++) {
128:        tempSt += String.fromCharCode(outArr[i]);
129:    }
130:    return tempSt;
131: }
```

The interface function `isaac_keys()` sets up the ISAAC PRNG with the input key. The procedure is simple: we just convert the key string into an array called `rKeyArr[]` and copy this array to `randrsl[]`, as illustrated in line 114. Note that we have set a 256 maximum for the key string characters. In fact, since each element of `randrsl[]` is a 32-bit integer (or word), the algorithm can have 8192 key string characters.

The function `isaac_cipher()` is the main interface function with the Web page. The Web page captures the key and message strings and passes them into this function. After the initial function call in line 122, the function `isaac_keys()` in line 123 uses the key to set up the arrays `mm[]` and `randrsl[]`. The for-loop in line 124 converts the message string into a byte array called `msgArr[]`. With this byte array, the function call in line 125 performs the encryption or decryption. The result is stored in `tempSt` and returned to the caller. Since the encryption and decryption of this cipher are the same, we consider them to be one function.

To test this script a Web page is required. Make a copy of `ex05-08.htm` and call it `ex05-11.htm`. Modify the following lines of this new page.

```
 9: The ISAAC Stream Cipher<br />
41: <script src="ex05-11.js"></script>
52:        llst = byteStToHex(isaac_cipher(key, message))
59:        llst = isaac_cipher(key, message)
```

Line 9 changes the display to reflect that we are working with ISAAC. Line 41 includes the proper script file. Lines 52 and 59 are used to make the correct function calls. Screenshots are shown in Figures 5.26 and 5.27.

The designer of the algorithm also provides a number of C programs to demonstrate how to use the ISAAC PRNG. One of them is called `randport.c`, which is a portable C implementation of ISAAC. This program produces the same random sequence as shown in Figure 5.25. To use the program, all you need is the code below.

```
1: randctx ctx;
2: ctx.randa=ctx.randb=ctx.randc=(ub4)0;
3: for (i=0; i<256; ++i) ctx.randrsl[i]=(ub4)0;
4: randinit(&ctx, TRUE);
5: isaac(&ctx);
```

Fig. 5.26 ISAAC encryption

Fig. 5.27 ISAAC decryption

The first line declares a structure to accommodate the internal variables and arrays. Lines 2–3 initialize the variables in the structure. Lines 4–5 generate a set of 256 random numbers for use. To convert this program to a stream cipher is not difficult. You need some interface functions. Consider the C program `isaac-driver.c`.

Example: isaac_driver.c - The driver for the ISAAC stream cipher (Part I)

```c
 1: #include <stdio.h>
 2: #include "randport.c"
 3:
 4: int isaac_keys(randctx *ctx, unsigned char *key, ub4 kl)
 5: {
 6:    ub4 i, len;
 7:    ctx->randa = ctx->randb = ctx->randc = (ub4) 0;
 8:    if (kl > 256 ) len=256;
 9:    else len = kl;
10:    for (i=0; i<len; i++) ctx->randrsl[i]=key[i];
11: }
12:
13: int isaac_cipher(randctx *ctx, unsigned char *data, ub4 dl)
14: {
15:    ub4 j,i;
16:    ub4 m=0, k, aByte;
17:    randinit(ctx, TRUE);
18:    while (m < dl)
19:    {
20:      isaac(ctx);
21:      for (j=0; j<256; ++j) {
22:        for (i=0; i < 4;i++) {
23:          k = m++;
24:          aByte = (ctx->randrsl[j] >> (4-i)) & 0xff;
25:          if ( k < dl) data[k] = (data[k] ^ aByte) & 0xff;
26:          else { i=4; j=256; }
27:        }
28:      }
29:    }
30: }
31:
```

First, `randport.c` is included in the program in line 2. The function `isaac_keys()` in lines 4–11 uses the user input key to set up all the internal variables and arrays in the structure `ctx`. The procedure is simple: just copy the key elements into the array `randrsl[]` referenced by the structure `ctx` as in line 10.

The function `isaac_cipher()` is the encryption/decryption function. The structure is similar to that in `ex05-11.js` for the Web case. For a set of 256 32-bit random numbers, the for-loop in lines 22–27 extracts the bytes one by one as `aByte` (action byte). This action byte is used to perform the XOR operation with the plaintext byte stream in line 25.

Part II of `isaac-driver.c` is similar to the RC4 case – the differences are highlighted in the listing.

```
Example: Continuation of isaac_driver.c                          (Part II)

32: int main(int argc, char *argv[])
33: {
34:  int i, n, m=-1;
35:  struct randctx s;
36:  unsigned char buf[4096];
37:  unsigned char kkey[256];
38:  FILE *inK, *inP, *outF;
39:
40:  for (i=0;i<256;i++) {s.randmem[i]=s.randrsl[i]=0; }
41:  s.randcnt=s.randa=s.randb=s.randc = (ub4) 0;
42:
43:  if (argc!=5) {
44:   printf("\nUsage:\n Isaac_driver (e)|(d) <infile> <outfile>
            <keyfile>\n");
45:   return 2;
46:  }
47:  for (i=0;i< 4096;i++)   buf[i]=0;
48:  for (i=0;i<256;i++)     kkey[i]=0;
49:
50:  if((inK=fopen(argv[4],"rb"))==NULL){
51:      printf("\r\nCould not open input file: %s",argv[4]);
52:      return 2;
53:  } else {
54:
55:    while (!feof(inK) && m < 256) { kkey[++m] = fgetc(inK) & 0xff; }
56:    fclose(inK);
57:  }
58:
59:  isaac_keys( &s, kkey, m);
60:
61:  if((inP=fopen(argv[2],"rb"))==NULL){
62:      printf("\r\nCould not open input file : %s",argv[2]);
63:      return 2;
64:  }
65:  if((outF=fopen(argv[3],"wb"))==NULL){
66:      printf("\r\nCould not open output file : %s",argv[3]);
67:      return 2;
68:  }
69:  if(argv[1][0]=='e') {
70:    while ((n=fread(buf,1,4096,inP)) >0) {
71:        isaac_cipher( &s, buf, n );
72:        if(fwrite(buf,1,n,outF) < n) {
73:            printf("\r\nError writing to output file \r\n");
```

```
74:            return(3);
75:        }
76:    }
77: }
78: if(argv[1][0]=='d') {
79:    while ((n=fread(buf,1,4096,inP)) >0) {
80:        isaac_cipher( &s, buf, n );
81:        if(fwrite(buf,1,n,outF) < n){
82:            printf("\r\nError writing to output file\r\n");
83:            return(3);
84:        }
85:    }
86: }
87: fclose(inP); fclose(outF);
88: return 0;
89: }
```

Lines 40–41 initialize all the internal variables, including the state arrays, to zero. The function call in line 59 uses the key to set up the generator. Lines 71 and 80 make the correct function call for encryption and decryption purposes. A section of the compiling and running of this program is shown in Figure 5.28.

From this you can see that if you use a utility such as tohex to take a look at the encrypted file zen.txt in hexadecimal format, the result shown in Figure 5.28 is the same as that in Figure 5.26. In other words, the driver and the Web page can communicate with each other.

Fig. 5.28 The ISAAC driver program

```
H:\ch05>gcc -o isaac_driver isaac_driver.c
H:\ch05>isaac_driver

Usage:
 Isaac_driver (e)|(d) <infile> <outfile> <keyfile>

H:\ch05>isaac_driver e zplain.txt zen.txt zkey.txt
H:\ch05>isaac_driver d zen.txt zde.txt zkey.txt

H:\ch05>type zde.txt
Meet Me At 2pm Tomorrow

H:\ch05>tohex zen.txt
f9 0d b4 d7 f6 e1 3d 90 86 fa 3d 08 f1 6e
27 5b ce 2e e8 7c 22 ce 34

H:\ch05>
```

5.5 A heavyweight stream cipher: SEAL2

5.5.1 The software-optimized encryption algorithm

The software-optimized encryption algorithm (SEAL) was proposed by Rogaway and Coppersmith in 1993. It is a stream cipher relying on randomness of key-stream for crypto-strength. Compared to RC4, it has a much longer initialization process. SEAL uses a 160-bit key to generate a larger set of tables. After more than ten years of public scrutiny, and having gone through two versions (SEAL1 and SEAL2), the SEAL2 algorithm is considered safe.

In order to achieve a better (and more secure) random generator, SEAL2 uses the secure hash algorithm SHA-1 in the initialization process. Recall from Section 3.5 that SHA-1 is a hash function similar to message digest (MD). It can read or digest an arbitrarily long message and produce a 160-bit hash value. The hash is usually represented by five 32-bit words.

The key-stream initialization of the SEAL2 algorithm is a long one and can be described by three processes:

- table generation function;
- filling the tables;
- key-stream generation.

The table generation function is, basically, an application of the SHA-1 hash function. Usually, table generation is implemented as a function G(inSt,ii), where the string inSt is a 160-bit (20-character) string and ii is an integer in the interval $[0, 2^{32} - 1]$, i.e. $[0, 2^{32}]$. The pseudo-code of function G(inSt,ii) is listed in ex05-09.txt.

```
Example: ex05-09.txt - SEAL2: table generation function

 1:  Function G(inSt,ii) // inSt - 160-Bit String, ii - int in [0,2**32)
 2:  Begin
 3:    k1 = 0x5a827999, k2 = 0x6ed9eba1, k3 = 0x8f1bbcdc, k4 = 0xca62c1d6.
 4:    w[0]=ii;
 5:    for (i=1;i<16;i++) w[i] = 0x00000000; end-for
 6:    for (i=16;i<80;i++) do w[i] = w[i] = w[i-3]^w[i-8]^w[i-14]^w[i-16];
 7:
 8:    inSt = (h0,h1,h2,h3,h4)
 9:    a = h0; b = h1; c = h2; d = h3; e = h4;
10:
11:    for(i=0;i<20;i++) do:          //Round 1
12:      temp = ROT27(a) + F1(b, c, d) + e + w[i] + k1;
13:      e = d; d = c; c = ROT2(b); b = a; a = temp; end-for
```

```
14:
15:    for (i=20;i<40;i++) do:      //Round 2
16:       temp = ROT27(a) + F2(b, c, d) + e + w[i] + k2;
17:       e = d; d = c; c = ROT2(b); b = a; a = temp; end-for
18:
19:    for (i=40;i<60;i++) do:      //Round 3
20:       temp = ROT27(a) + F3(b, c, d) + e + w[i] + k3;
21:       e = d; d = c; c = ROT2(b); b = a; a = temp; end-for
22:
23:    for (i=60;i<80;i++) do:      //Round 4
24:       temp = ROT27(a) + F4(b, c, d) + e + w[i] + k4;
25:       e = d; d = c; c = ROT2(b); b = a; a = temp; end-for
26:
27:    h0=h0 +a; h1=h1 +b; h2=h2 +c; h3=h3 +d; h4=h4 +a;
28:    return (h0,h1,h2,h3,h4);
28: End
```

If you compare this pseudo-code with step 2 and step 3 of the SHA-1 algorithm in Section 3.5.2, you will find that the following are the same:

- the constants k1, k2, k3 and k4;

- the for-loop in line 6;

- the assignment in line 9;

- the four rounds of computation in lines 11–27 with the same functions F1(), F2(), F3() and F4(), where the right-rotation ROT27(a) is equivalent to symbol a <<<- 5 (i.e. left-rotation) used in the SHA-1 algorithm;

- the assignment in line 27 produces the 160-bit value in five 32-bit words h0, h1, h2, h3 and h4.

The main differences are in lines 4, 5 and 8 of ex05-09.txt. In SHA-1, the first 16 values for w[] are obtained from the input message. Here, the first element w[0] is the input variable ii and the remaining w[1],...,w[15] are initialized as zero in line 5. In SHA-1, variables h0, h1, h2, h3 and h4 in line 8 are predefined constants. For SEAL2, these values are obtained from the user input key, which is a 160-bit string. The statement in line 8,

```
inSt = (h0,h1,h2,h3,h4)
```

is the operation to convert a 160-bit string into five 32-bit words.

The second process is to fill up the SEAL2 tables. SEAL2 uses three tables, namely s_t[512], s_s[265] and s_r[20]. They are all 32-bit word arrays. In our implementation, the function to fill the tables is called seal_init(key). It will use the user input key and the function in ex05-09.txt to populate the tables. The listing is shown in ex05-10.txt.

```
Example: ex05-10.txt - Filling the SEAL2 tables

 1: Function seal_init(key)       // key is the 160-Bit input key
 2: Begin
 3:   for (i=0; i<510; i+=5)  do
 4:       tt= g(key,i/5);
 5:       for (k=0; k<5; k++)  do  s_t[i+k]= tt[k]; end-for
 6:   end-for
 7:   h = g(key,510/5);
 8:   for(i=510; i<512; i++)  do  s_t[i] = h[i-510] end-for
 9:
10:   h = g(key,(-1+0x1000)/5);
11:   for (i=0; i<4; i++)      do  s_s[i] = h[i+1]; end-for
12:   for (i=4; i<254; i+=5)  do
13:       tt= g(key,(i+0x1000)/5);
14:       for (k=0; k<5; k++)  do  s_s[i+k]= tt[k]; end-for
15:   end-for
16:   h = g(key, (254+0x1000)/5);
17:   for (i=254; i<256; i++) do  s_s[i] = h[i-254]; end-for
18:
19:   h = g(key, (-2+0x2000)/5);
20:   for(i=0; i<3; i++)       do  s_r[i] = h[i+2]; end-for
21:   for (i=3; i<13; i+=5)   do
22:       tt= g(key, (i+0x2000)/5);
23:       for (k=0; k<5; k++)  do  s_r[i+k]= tt[k]; end-for
24:   end-for
25:   h = g(key, (13+0x2000)/5);
26:   for (i=13; i<16; i++)    do  s_r[i] = h[i-13]; end-for
27: End
```

Listing ex05-10.txt contains the pseudo-code of the SEAL2 initialization function, called seal_init(). Basically, this uses the generating function g() to fill up tables s_t[], s_s[] and s_r[]. Inside the function, two temporary arrays tt[5] and h[5] are used, together with three blocks of code. Lines 3–8 populate table s_t[] with 512 elements. The second block is in lines 10–17 and fills up table s_s[]. Table s_r[] is populated by lines 19–26 with 16 elements.

The SEAL2 algorithm generates the key-stream by rounds. One round generates 64 32-bit words forming a 256-byte stream. The number of rounds can be used to control how many bytes are in the key-stream, and ultimately determine how many bytes you can read in as one section and process by the algorithm. For example, if you want to generate a key-stream with 1024 bytes in array ks_buf[1024], four rounds are needed (l_rounds = 4). The pseudo-code for this key-stream generation function is listed in ex05-11.txt.

Example: ex05-11.txt — Generating SEAL2 key-stream

```
 1: Function seal(iin)
 2: Begin
 3: for (l=0; l<l_rounds; l++) do
 4:       a = iin ^ s_r[4*l];
 5:       b = ROT8(iin)  ^ s_r[4*l+1];
 6:       c = ROT16(iin) ^ s_r[4*l+2];
 7:       d = ROT24(iin) ^ s_r[4*l+3];
 8:
 9:       for (j=0;j<2;j++) do
10:         p = a & 0x7fc; b += s_t[p/4]; a = ROT9(a);
11:         p = b & 0x7fc; c += s_t[p/4]; b = ROT9(b);
12:         p = c & 0x7fc; d += s_t[p/4]; c = ROT9(c);
13:         p = d & 0x7fc; a += s_t[p/4]; d = ROT9(d);
14:       end-for
15:       n1=d; n2=b; n3=a; n4=c;
16:       p = a & 0x7fc; b += s_t[p/4]; a = ROT9(a);
17:       p = b & 0x7fc; c += s_t[p/4]; b = ROT9(b);
18:       p = c & 0x7fc; d += s_t[p/4]; c = ROT9(c);
19:       p = d & 0x7fc; a += s_t[p/4]; d = ROT9(d);
20:
21:       for (i=0;i<64;i++) do // One Round: 64 32-Bit Words (256 bytes)
22:         p = a & 0x7fc;     b += s_t[p/4]; a = ROT9(a); b ^= a;
23:         q = b & 0x7fc;     c ^= s_t[q/4]; b = ROT9(b); c += b;
24:         p = (p+c) & 0x7fc; d += s_t[p/4]; c = ROT9(c); d ^= c;
25:         q = (q+d) & 0x7fc; a ^= s_t[q/4]; d = ROT9(d); a += d;
26:         p = (p+a) & 0x7fc; b ^= s_t[p/4]; a = ROT9(a);
27:         q = (q+b) & 0x7fc; c += s_t[q/4]; b = ROT9(b);
28:         p = (p+c) & 0x7fc; d ^= s_t[p/4]; c = ROT9(c);
29:         q = (q+d) & 0x7fc; a += s_t[q/4]; d = ROT9(d);
30:
31:         ks_buf [m] = b + s_s[4*i];   m++;
32:         ks_buf [m] = c ^ s_s[4*i+1]; m++;
33:         ks_buf [m] = d + s_s[4*i+2]; m++;
34:         ks_buf [m] = a ^ s_s[4*i+3]; m++;
35:           if(i&1) do
36:               a += n3; c += n4;
37:           else
38:               a += n1; c += n2;
39:           end-if
40:       end-for
41: end-for
42: End
```

This key-stream generating function `seal()` has one parameter, `iin`. It is an integer which controls how many sections of key-stream are generated. For example, if you want to generate key-stream `ks_buf[1024]`, `l_rounds` should be 4. The first 1024 bytes of the key-stream is `seal(0)` and so on. The statements in lines 4–19 are sometimes called the 'initialization' function in other implementations of SEAL2. It produces results in eight variables, namely `a, b, c, d, n1, n2, n3` and `n4`. These variables are used by the for-loop in lines 21–40 to generate 256 bytes (one round) of key-stream. After four rounds, a key-stream of 1024 bytes is produced and stored in array `ks_buf[]`.

Once we have the key-stream, encryption and decryption can be performed with the byte stream from the incoming plaintext. Now, let's see how to implement this SEAL2 algorithm on the Web.

5.5.2   Implementation of SEAL2 on the Web

With the description and pseudo-code in `ex05-09.txt`, `ex05-10.txt`, and `ex05-11.txt`, the implementation of SEAL2 algorithm is now not difficult. Consider script `ex05-12.js`.

```
Example: ex05-12.js - SEAL2 encryption and decryption        (Part I)

 1: var s_t = new Array(520);
 2: var s_s = new Array(265);
 3: var s_r = new Array(20);
 4: var s_counter;
 5: var s_ks_pos;
 6:
 7: var s_h = new Array(5);
 8: var words_per_call = 256
 9: var l_rounds = words_per_call / 256;
10: var s_ks_buf = new Array(words_per_call);
11:
12: function ROT2(x) {
13:   return (((x) >>>2)   | ((x) << 30));
14: }
15: function ROT8(x) {
16:   return (((x) >>>8)   | ((x) << 24));
17: }
18: function ROT9(x) {
19:   return (((x) >>>9)   | ((x) << 23));
20: }
```

```
21: function ROT16(x) {
22:   return (((x) >>> 16) | ((x) << 16));
23: }
24: function ROT24(x) {
25:   return (((x) >>> 24) | ((x) << 8));
26: }
27: function ROT27(x) {
28:   return (((x) >>> 27) | ((x) << 5));
29: }
30:
31: function F1(x, y, z)
32: {
33:   return (((x) & (y)) | ((~(x)) & (z)));
34: }
35: function F2(x, y, z)
36: {
37:   return ((x) ^ (y) ^ (z));
38: }
39: function F3(x, y, z)
40: {
41:   return (((x) & (y)) | ((x) & (z)) | ((y) & (z)));
42: }
43: function F4(x, y, z)
44: {
45:   return ((x) ^ (y) ^ (z));
46: }
47:
```

This script fragment contains some of the variable declarations and basic functions used by SEAL2. Tables s_t[], s_s[] and s_r[] are declared in lines 1–3. Variable s_count is used to count how many key-streams have been generated. In order to perform the XOR operation with the plaintext, the position of the key-stream is stored in variable s_ks_pos. The s_h[] array is used to store the user input key (20-character) as five 32-bit words. The words_per_call and l_rounds are used to control the length of the key-stream. Initially, words_per_call is assigned to 1024 so that l_rounds=4 and the key-stream buffer is an array of 1024 bytes, i.e. s_ks_buf[1024].

Lines 12–29 define six rotation functions. Note that they are right rotations on a 32-bit word. Lines 31–47 specify the functions for the SHA-1 algorithm discussed in Section 3.5.2. Consider part II of ex05-12.js.

```
48: function byteStToWord (cpSt) {
49:   var cp = new Array(4);
50:   var i;
51:   for (i=0; i<4;i++) cp[i] = cpSt.charCodeAt(i) & 0xff;
52:   return ((cp[0]<<24)|(cp[1]<<16)|(cp[2]<<8)|(cp[3]));
53: }
54:
55: function proKeySt(inSt)
56: {
57:   s_h[0] = byteStToWord(inSt.substring(0,4));
58:   s_h[1] = byteStToWord(inSt.substring(4,8));
59:   s_h[2] = byteStToWord(inSt.substring(8,12));
60:   s_h[3] = byteStToWord(inSt.substring(12,16));
61:   s_h[4] = byteStToWord(inSt.substring(16,20));
62: }
63:
64: function g(ii)
65: {
66:   var h0,h1,h2,h3,h4,a,b,c,d,e,temp;
67:   var w = new Array(80);
68:   var hh = new Array(5);
69:
70:   h0=s_h[0]; h1=s_h[1]; h2=s_h[2]; h3=s_h[3]; h4=s_h[4];
71:
72:   w[0] = ii;
73:   for (i=1;i<16;i++) w[i] = 0;
74:   for (i=16;i<80;i++) w[i] = w[i-3]^w[i-8]^w[i-14]^w[i-16];
75:   a = h0; b = h1; c = h2; d = h3; e = h4;
76:
77:   for(i=0;i<20;i++) {
78:     temp = ROT27(a) + F1(b, c, d) + e + w[i] + 0x5a827999;
79:     e = d; d = c; c = ROT2(b); b = a; a = temp;
80:   }
81:   for (i=20;i<40;i++) {
82:     temp = ROT27(a) + F2(b, c, d) + e + w[i] + 0x6ed9eba1;
83:     e = d; d = c; c = ROT2(b); b = a; a = temp;
84:   }
85:   for (i=40;i<60;i++) {
86:     temp = ROT27(a) + F3(b, c, d) + e + w[i] + 0x8f1bbcdc;
87:     e = d; d = c; c = ROT2(b); b = a; a = temp;
88:   }
```

```
89:    for (i=60;i<80;i++) {
90:       temp = ROT27(a) + F4(b, c, d) + e + w[i] + 0xca62c1d6;
91:       e = d; d = c; c = ROT2(b); b = a; a = temp;
92:    }
93:    hh[0]= h0+a; hh[1]= h1+b; hh[2]= h2+c; hh[3]= h3+d; hh[4]= h4+e;
94:    return (hh);
95: }
96:
```

The first function in lines 48–53 converts a string of four characters into one 32-bit word. The function proKeySt(inSt) in lines 55–62 processes the 20-character key into five 32-bit words and stores them in global array s_h[]. Since global array s_h[] is used, there is no need to pass the key to the table generation function g() as described in the algorithm in the previous section. Now, the table generation function g(ii) contains one parameter ii which is used to index the function to produce an SHA-1 hash value in hh[] and is returned to the caller by line 94.

The next step is to fill up the SEAL2 tables s_t[], s_s[] and s_r[]. This function is implemented in part III of ex05-12.js.

Example: Continuation of ex05-12.js   **(Part III)**

```
 97: function seal_init(key )
 98: {
 99:    var i;
100:    var h = new Array(5), tt = new Array(5);
101:
102:    proKeySt(key);
103:
104:    for (i=0;i<5;i++) { h[i]=0; tt[i]=0;}
105:
106:    for (i=0;i<510;i+=5) {
107:       tt= g(i/5);
108:       for (k=0;k<5;k++) s_t[i+k]= tt[k];
109:    }
110:    h = g(510/5);
111:    for(i=510;i<512;i++) s_t[i]  = h[i-510];
112:
113:    h = g((-1+0x1000)/5);
114:    for (i=0;i<4;i++)      s_s[i]  = h[i+1];
115:    for (i=4;i<254;i+=5) {
116:       tt= g((i+0x1000)/5);
117:       for (k=0;k<5;k++) s_s[i+k]= tt[k];
118:    }
```

```
119:    h = g((254+0x1000)/5);
120:    for (i=254;i<256;i++) s_s[i] = h[i-254];
121:
122:    h = g((-2+0x2000)/5);
123:    for(i=0;i<3;i++)        s_r[i] = h[i+2];
124:    for (i=3;i<13;i+=5) {
125:       tt= g((i+0x2000)/5);
126:          for (k=0;k<5;k++) s_r[i+k]= tt[k];
127:    }
128:    h = g((13+0x2000)/5);
129:    for (i=13;i<16;i++) s_r[i] = h[i-13];
130: }
131:
```

To populate the SEAL2 tables, the user key is used as the input parameter.
The key is processed by the function proKeySt() in line 102 and the results are five
32-bit words stored in array s_h[]. This array is used by every function call g()
producing an SHA-1 hash. The hashes are used to populate the tables. Table s_t[]
is filled by lines 106–111, s_s[] by lines 113–121 and s_r[] by lines 122–129.

When the SEAL2 tables are available, the key-stream can be generated by the main
function seal() as shown in part IV of ex05-12.js.

```
Example: Continuation of ex05-12.js                          (Part IV)

132: function seal(iin)
133: {
134:    var i,j,l;
135:    var a,b,c,d,n1,n2,n3,n4;
136:    var p,q;
137:    var m=0;
138:
139:    for (l=0;l<l_rounds;l++) {
140:       a = iin ^ s_r[4*l];
141:       b = ROT8(iin)  ^ s_r[4*l+1];
142:       c = ROT16(iin) ^ s_r[4*l+2];
143:       d = ROT24(iin) ^ s_r[4*l+3];
144:
145:       for (j=0;j<2;j++) {
146:          p = a & 0x7fc; b += s_t[p/4]; a = ROT9(a);
147:          p = b & 0x7fc; c += s_t[p/4]; b = ROT9(b);
148:          p = c & 0x7fc; d += s_t[p/4]; c = ROT9(c);
149:          p = d & 0x7fc; a += s_t[p/4]; d = ROT9(d);
150:       }
```

```
151:        n1 = d; n2=b; n3=a; n4=c;
152:
153:        p = a & 0x7fc; b += s_t[p/4]; a = ROT9(a);
154:        p = b & 0x7fc; c += s_t[p/4]; b = ROT9(b);
155:        p = c & 0x7fc; d += s_t[p/4]; c = ROT9(c);
156:        p = d & 0x7fc; a += s_t[p/4]; d = ROT9(d);
157:
158:        for (i=0;i<64;i++) {
159:            p = a & 0x7fc;      b += s_t[p/4]; a = ROT9(a); b ^= a;
160:            q = b & 0x7fc;      c ^= s_t[q/4]; b = ROT9(b); c += b;
161:            p = (p+c) & 0x7fc; d += s_t[p/4]; c = ROT9(c); d ^= c;
162:            q = (q+d) & 0x7fc; a ^= s_t[q/4]; d = ROT9(d); a += d;
163:            p = (p+a) & 0x7fc; b ^= s_t[p/4]; a = ROT9(a);
164:            q = (q+b) & 0x7fc; c += s_t[q/4]; b = ROT9(b);
165:            p = (p+c) & 0x7fc; d ^= s_t[p/4]; c = ROT9(c);
166:            q = (q+d) & 0x7fc; a += s_t[q/4]; d = ROT9(d);
167:
168:            s_ks_buf[m] = b + s_s[4*i]; m++;
169:            s_ks_buf[m] = c ^ s_s[4*i+1]; m++;
170:            s_ks_buf[m] = d + s_s[4*i+2]; m++;
171:            s_ks_buf[m] = a ^ s_s[4*i+3]; m++;
172:
173:            if(i&1) {
174:                a += n3; c += n4;
175:            } else {
176:                a += n1; c += n2;
177:            }
178:        }
179:    }
180: }
181:
```

This function `seal()` generates the key-stream to perform bitwise XOR operation with the plaintext stream. The statements in lines 140–156 produce eight values: `a,b,c,d,n1,n2,n3` and `n4`. These variables are then used by the for-loop in lines 158–178 (one round) to produce a stream of 64 32-bit words or 256 bytes stored in `s_ks_buf[]`. Together with the `l_rounds` used in the for-loop, the key-stream array is stored in `s_ks_buf[]`.

In order to use all the functions above for SEAL2 encryption and decryption effectively, some interface functions are required. The interface is defined in part V of `ex05-12.js`.

```
182: function seal_key(keySt)
183: {
184:   seal_init(keySt);
185:   s_counter = 0;
186:   s_ks_pos = words_per_call;
187: }
188:
189: function seal_refill_buffer()
190: {
191:   seal(s_counter);
192:   s_counter++;
193:   s_ks_pos = 0;
194: }
195:
196: function seal_encrypt(inMsg,w)
197: {
198:   var i;
199:   var lArr = new Array();
200:   for (i = 0; i < w; i++) {
201:     if(s_ks_pos >= words_per_call  seal_refill_buffer();
202:     lArr[i] = inMsg[i] ^ s_ks_buf[s_ks_pos];
203:     s_ks_pos++;
204:   }
205:   return lArr;
206: }
207:
208: function seal_decrypt(inMsg, w)
209: {
210:   return seal_encrypt(inMsg, w);
211: }
212:
213: function seal2(keySt, msgSt, encrypt)
214: {
215:   var len = msgSt.length;
216:   var i, tempSt="";
217:   var msgArr = new Array(), outArr = new Array();
218:
219:   keySt +="\0\0\0\0\0\0\0\0\0\0\0\0\0\0\0\0\0\0\0\0"
220:   keySt = keySt.substring(0,20);
221:   for (i=0;i<len;i++) msgArr[i] = msgSt.charCodeAt(i);
222:
```

```
223:    if (encrypt) {
224:        seal_key(keySt);
225:        outArr = seal_encrypt(msgArr,len);
226:    } else {
227:        seal_key(keySt);
228:        outArr = seal_decrypt(msgArr,len);
229:    }
230:    for (i=0;i<len;i++) {
231:      tempSt += String.fromCharCode(outArr[i] & 0xff);
232:    }
233:    return tempSt;
234: }
```

The first function defined in lines 182–187 is `seal_key(keySt)`. This function uses the key string from the Web page and calls the function `seal_init()` to fill up all tables. By setting `s_counter` to 0, the first key-stream will be created. Also, setting the key-stream position `s_ks_pos` equal to `words_per_call` (i.e. 1024) will ensure that the key-stream will be created by function `seal_refill_buffer()` defined in lines 189–194. This function refills the key-stream buffer `s_ks_buf[]`. After the buffer is refilled, the counter and key-stream position is reset.

To perform encryption, the function `seal_encrypt()` defined in lines 196–206 should be called with plaintext and length as parameters. This function will perform an XOR operation on the plaintext with the key-stream producing the ciphertext. The key-stream buffer will be refilled if necessary. The ciphertext is stored in array `lArr[]` and returned to the function caller. The decryption function in lines 208–211 is the same as the encryption, calling the function `seal_encrypt()`.

The main user interface function is `seal2()` defined in lines 213–234. This function uses the key and plaintext from the Web page to perform encryption and decryption accordingly. First, the key is appended by a series of 0s and cut to 20-character length so that the keylength is 160-bit. The for-loop in line 221 converts the plaintext into an array of bytes. If encryption is `true`, the statements in lines 224–225 encrypt the data. The ciphertext is stored in `outArr[]`. This byte array is converted to a string by the for-loop in lines 230–232 and returned. Similarly, the statements in lines 227–228 will decrypt the data and return to the caller.

To test this script make a copy of `ex05-11.htm` and call it `ex05-12.htm`, modifying the following lines of the new file:

```
 9: SEAL2 Encryption/Decryption<br />
41: <script src="ex05-12.js"></script>
52:      llst = byteStToHex(seal2(key, message,true))
59:      llst = seal2(key, message,false)
```

Fig. 5.29 SEAL2 encryption

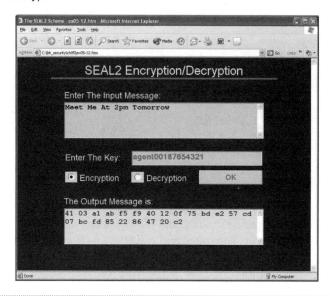

Line 9 changes the display so that the user knows that the SEAL2 scheme is used. Line 41 includes the proper script file. Lines 52 and 59 are used to make the correct function calls. When encryption is `true`, the function `seal2()` is called to encrypt the message. Similarly, when the `false` value is set, the function will perform decryption. Screenshots are shown in Figures 5.29 and 5.30.

SEAL2 is a stream cipher using the hash function SHA-1 to provide randomness and security strength. As you can see from `ex05-12.js`, these kinds of cipher are relatively complicated and generally regarded as heavyweight ciphers.

5.5.3 Building a SEAL2 utility

There are a number of SEAL2 ciphers implemented in the public domain. One such implementation in C language is called `seal2.c`. You can find a copy of this program in a number of public sites, search engines or from the supporting site of this book. To use this program, you can use the following code:

```
1: seal_ctx sc;
2: seal_key(&sc, kkey);
3: seal_encrypt(&sc, buf, n, obuf);
4: seal_decrypt(&sc, buf, n, obuf);
```

Fig. 5.30 SEAL2 decryption

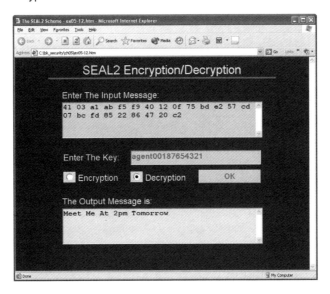

The first line defines a structure to accommodate the variables used in the cipher. The function in line 2 uses the input key to set up the PRNG. With the plaintext stored in `buf` the functions in lines 3 and 4 are used to perform encryption and decryption respectively. The result is stored in the output stream `obuf`. To use this program, the driver file `seal2driver.c` is constructed.

```
Example: seal2driver.c - The driver for the SEAL2 stream cipher

1: #include <stdio.h>
2: #include <string.h>
3: #include "seal2.c"
4: #define COUNT 4096
5: int main(int argc, char *argv[])
6: {
7:   int i, n, m=-1;
8:   seal_ctx sc;
9:   unsigned char buf[COUNT];
10:  unsigned char obuf[COUNT];
11:  unsigned char kkey[20];
12:  FILE *inK, *inP, *outF;
13:
```

```
14:  if (argc!=5) {
15:   printf("\nUsage: seal2driver (e)|(d) <infile> <outfile>
             <keyfile>\n");
16:   return 2;
17:  }
18:  for (i=0;i<20;i++) kkey[i]=0;
19:  for (i=0;i<COUNT;i++) { buf[i]=obuf[i]=0; }
20:  if((inK=fopen(argv[4],"rb"))==NULL){
21:      printf("\r\nCould not open input file: %s",argv[4]);
22:      return 2;
23:  } else {
24:      n=fread(kkey,1,20,inK);
25:      fclose(inK);
26:  }
27:  if((inP=fopen(argv[2],"rb"))==NULL){
28:      printf("\r\nCould not open input file 2: %s",argv[2]);
29:      return 2;
30:  }
31:  if((outF=fopen(argv[3],"wb"))==NULL){
32:      printf("\r\nCould not open output file 3: %s",argv[3]);
33:      return 2;
34:  }
35:  seal_key(&sc, kkey);
36:  if(argv[1][0]=='e') {
37:    while ((n=fread(buf,1,1024,inP)) >0) {
38:        seal_encrypt(&sc, buf, n, obuf);
39:        if(fwrite(obuf,1,n,outF) < n) {
40:            printf("\r\nError writing to output file \r\n");
41:            return(3);
42:        }
43:    }
44:  }
45:  if(argv[1][0]=='d') {
46:    while ((n=fread(buf,1,1024,inP)) >0) {
47:        seal_decrypt(&sc, buf, n, obuf);
48:        if(fwrite(obuf,1,n,outF) < n) {
49:            printf("\r\nError writing to output file \r\n");
50:            return(3);
51:        }
52:    }
53:  }
54:  fclose(inP); fclose(outF);
55:  return 0;
56: }
```

Fig. 5.31 SEAL 2 stream cipher

```
H:\ch05>gcc -o sea12driver sea12driver.c
H:\ch05>sea12driver
Usage:
  sea12driver (e)|(d) <infile> <outfile> <keyfile>

H:\ch05>sea12driver e zplain.txt zen.txt zkey.txt
H:\ch05>sea12driver d zen.txt zde.txt zkey.txt

H:\ch05>type zde.txt

Meet Me At 2pm Tomorrow

H:\ch05>tohex zen.txt

41 03 a1 ab f5 f9 40 12 0f 75 bd e2
57 cd 07 bc fd 85 22 86 47 20 c2

H:\ch05>
```

Line 3 includes seal2.c in the driver. Two buffers, buf[] and obuf[], are declared with 4096 elements in lines 9–10. After reading the input key string in lines 20–26, the input key is to initialize the SEAL2 cipher by the function call in line 35. When encryption is true, the function seal_encrypt() in line 38 is called to encrypt buf[] producing ciphertext in obuf[]. For decryption, the function seal_decrypt in line 47 is called instead. The output buffer obuf[] will be saved into the corresponding outfile. A section of the operations is captured in Figure 5.31.

6

Block ciphers with variable key lengths

6.1 A flexible and adaptive block cipher: Blowfish

6.1.1 A block cipher for small devices

This chapter focuses on some block ciphers with variable lengths and concludes our investigation of practical symmetric-key ciphers. First, a block cipher known as 'Blowfish' is introduced. Blowfish is not just another block cipher – its variable key length (from 32-bit to 448-bit) design provides a flexible and adaptive structure which can be used by many small devices, such as microprocessors with very limited memory. Blowfish uses a very long value for pi (more than 8000 digits in hexadecimal format) for key scheduling or key initialization. In addition to the algorithm, generating decimal digits in hexadecimal format is also introduced. In Section 6.3, another cipher with variable lengths called RC6 is presented. It is generally accepted as a fully parameterized block cipher with good speed, security, flexibility and adaptivity. The designer of RC6 is Ron Rivest, the creator of RC4 in Chapter 5. RC6 is the successor of RC5, forming a family of ciphers. The simplicity of RC6 makes it a popular choice for many application developers.

Any study on symmetric-key ciphers will not be considered to be complete without a detailed discussion of the Advanced Encryption Standard (AES) scheme. AES is the official successor to DES. The AES 'challenge' is one of the most fascinating stories in the crypto-community. In particular, the RC6 scheme was one of the best candidates for winning the competition. The AES winner was a mathematical cipher designed by Rijndael. The algorithmic design and mathematical background of AES are introduced in Section 6.4, including a step-by-step demonstration of the scheme and operation. The implementations and applications of AES are provided in Section 6.5. As we mentioned at the beginning of Chapter 4, every cipher has its own characteristics and application areas. Although AES is an important cipher, it is believed that many other ciphers will also be active in the crypto-community for years to come. Now, let's consider Blowfish.

Like DES and CAST-128, the Blowfish scheme belongs to the Feistel type. The general characteristic of a Feistel cipher is that a block of plaintext, usually $2n$-bit, is represented by a pair of blocks called (L_0, R_0). A set of subkeys and iterative functions are employed to compute the ciphertext. In fact, they work in the 'substitution-permutation network' (SPN) fashion. A general diagram of a Feistel cipher and the SPN is presented in Figure 4.28 in Chapter 4. The design of Blowfish is slightly different from both DES and CAST-128. The main modification is to simplify the operational structure and use more secure key scheduling to enhance the security at the same time. Some of the characteristics of Blowfish design are:

- operates on 64-bit or 128-bit variable blocks;

- variable key lengths from 32-bit to 448-bit;

- only simple operations are used, e.g. XOR, addition, table lookup, modular multiplication (there is no bit-wise permutation or conditional jumps);

- efficient on software and can be implemented on 8-bit small microprocessors;

- variable number of iterations.

It is well known that one of the security strengths of Feistel ciphers comes from the key scheduling and S-boxes. A complex (slower) key generation, in general, produces better security of the cipher. Blowfish has an exceptionally long process on key initialization and scheduling. It uses 18 32-bit element arrays called p[] and four S-boxes. Each S-box has 256 32-bit elements. The p[] array and all the S-boxes comprise a total of 18 + 1024 32-bit elements. All elements are initialized by the fractional part digits (more than 8000) of π. Given a user input key, key scheduling will be performed with p[] and the S-boxes and then be used for the encryption. For decryption, the process is similar but the keys are applied in reverse order.

6.1.2   The Blowfish algorithm

The encryption/decryption algorithm

Blowfish is a Feistel cipher working on a network as shown in Figure 6.1. A typical implementation of Blowfish is that the plaintext is divided into 64-bit blocks called P. P is then divided into two halves (left and right) forming a pair (L_1, R_1) – each of them is a 32-bit value.

A simple encryption function f (or F()) is employed to operate on (L_1, R_1) for 16 rounds producing a pair (L_{17}, R_{17}). The ciphertext is obtained by combining the pair together. For the first 15 rounds, a key scheduling array p[i] is used to XOR with the left part L_i and then input to the encryption function F(). The result is XORed with R_i and stored in L_{i+1} to complete one round of the iteration. After 15 rounds, we have a pair (L_{16}, R_{16}). The last round is slightly different, L_{16} is XORed with p[16] first. The result is used in two processes. The first is to XOR with p[18] to form L_{17}. The second process is to enter the encryption function F() and then XOR with R_{16}

Fig. 6.1 The encryption process of the Blowfish scheme

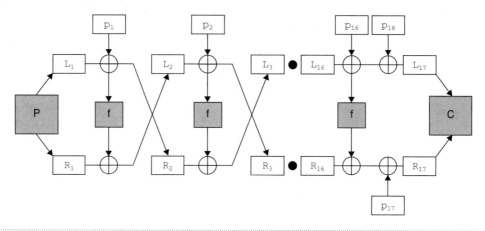

and XOR with p[17] producing R_{17}. The last step is to concatenate (L_{17}, R_{17}) to form a block of ciphertext c.

If you compare this scheme with the Feistel structure of DES, you may find that function F() and the key schedule p[] of Blowfish operate on the left half L_i and DES operates on the right half. One of the reasons for this confusion is that DES was designed with big-endian machines in mind. Big-endian is a computer structure which stores the least significant bit first. Most Intel machines, including PCs, are little-endian based.

With this discussion and using Figure 6.1, the encryption process is easy to understand and can be written as the pseudo-code given in ex06-01.txt.

```
Example: ex06-01.txt - The pseudo-code of Blowfish encryption

 1: Input: A block of 64-bit data P
 2: Divide P into two 32-bit halves (xL,xR)
 3:
 4: for (i=1;i<=16;i++) do
 5:    xL = xL XOR p[i]
 6:    xR = F(xL) XOR xR
 7:    Swap xL and xR
 8: end-for
 9:
10:    Swap xL and xR (Undo the last swap.)
11:    xR = xR XOR P[17]
12:    xL = xL XOR P[18]
13:
14: Recombine xL and xR to a 64-bit block C
```

The algorithm listed in ex06-01.txt is based on the original design of the Blowfish scheme. Given two 32-bit values xL and xR, the for-loop in lines 4–8 executes 16 rounds of iteration using the encryption function F(x). Since there is a swap for each round, the statement in line 10 is needed to undo the swap for the final round. Lines 11–12 are used to XOR xR and xL with the key scheduling elements p[17] and p[18] respectively, as described by the algorithm. The final result is combined as a ciphertext block c and returned.

As in many Feistel ciphers, the decryption process is symmetric to encryption. All you need to do is to apply the scheduled keys p[1] to p[18] in reverse order. The encryption function F() is a simple one described below.

The encryption function

The Blowfish algorithm has four S-boxes: S1[], S2[], S3[] and S4[]. Each of them contains 256 elements of 32-bit value. The encryption function takes a 32-bit value, or integer, and splits it into four bytes a, b, c and d. Each byte is a value from 0 to 255. Using these four bytes, the corresponding values in the S-boxes S1[a], S2[b], S3[c] and S4[d] are computed. The encryption function F is defined by the simple operation

```
F = ( ( S1[a] + S2[b] ) XOR S3[c] ) + S4[d]
```

A graphical representation of the encryption function F() is presented in Figure 6.2.

As you can see from Figure 6.2, the encryption function employed by Blowfish is very simple, involving addition and XOR efficient operations for processors (big or small). For our implementation, the S-boxes are declared as one two-dimensional array S[][]. The pseudo-code of the function F(x) is given in ex06-02.txt.

First, the input 32-bit value x is split into four bytes. The least significant byte d is extracted by line 4. Similarly, bytes c, b and a are extracted by lines 5–10. The statement in line 11 computes the function result value F.

From ex06-02.txt, you can see that the operations used in the encryption function are simple and efficient for both software and hardware implementations.

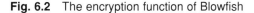

Fig. 6.2 The encryption function of Blowfish

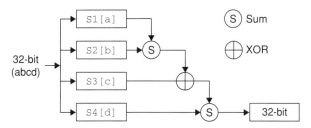

The key generation process

The key generation process used by Blowfish is slightly more complicated. The purpose is to use a user input key to initialize the 18 elements in `p[]` and four S-boxes. The values in `p[]` and the four S-boxes are called subkeys. The process is shown in Figure 6.3.

First, the user input key is taken for key expansion. The aim is to make the key into 18 32-bit values so that the user input key can be of any length up to 72 bytes. If the input key is less than 72 bytes, the key is repeated as often as necessary so that the 18 32-bit elements are filled. The 18 key elements `k[]` are used to XOR with the 18 elements of `p[]` (see Key expansion in Figure 6.3).

Fig. 6.3 The key generation process of Blowfish

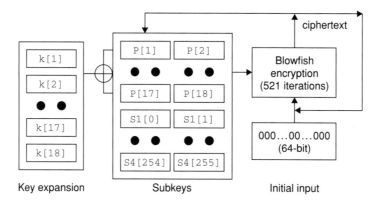

The next step is to use a 64-bit block of zeros as plaintext and perform Blowfish encryption. The output is a 64-bit block ciphertext. This 64-bit ciphertext is used to replace the subkey elements p[1] and p[2] and then input to the Blowfish encryption again for the next iteration. The output ciphertext of the next iteration is used to replace the next pair of subkeys p[3] and p[4] and so on. In other words, after one iteration two subkeys are replaced. This process is continued through all the elements in p[] and S-boxes. After a total of 521 iterations, the final subkeys S4[254] and S4[255] are replaced. The final set of subkeys is used for Blowfish encryption/decryption on the input message. This key generation process is described by the pseudo-code in ex06-03.txt.

```
Example: ex06-03.txt - The key generation Of Blowfish

 1: Function Blowfish_Init(key, keyLen)
 2: Begin
 3:    j = 0;
 4:    for (i = 0; i < N + 2; ++i) do // N is Blowfish iteration = 16
 5:       data = 0;
 6:
 7:       for (k = 0; k < 4; ++k) do
 8:          data = (data << 8) | key[j];
 9:          j = j + 1;
10:          if (j >= keyLen ) j = 0;
11:       end-for
12:
13:       P[i] = P[i] ^ data;
14:    end-for
15:
16:    dataArr[0]=0;    dataArr[1]=0;
17:
18:    for (i = 0; i < N + 2; i += 2) do
19:       dataArr = Blowfish_Encrypt(dataArr[0], dataArr[1]);
20:       P[i]     = dataArr[0];
21:       P[i + 1] = dataArr[1];
22:    end-for
23:
24:    for (i = 0; i < 4; ++i) do
25:       for (j = 0; j < 256; j += 2) do
26:          dataArr = Blowfish_Encrypt(dataArr[0],dataArr[1]);
27:          S[i][j]     = dataArr[0];
28:          S[i][j + 1] = dataArr[1];
29:       end-for
30:    end-for
31: End
```

The pseudo-code in `ex06-03.txt` defines a function called `Blowfish_Init()`. This function uses two parameters, namely `key` and `keyLen`. The `key` is an array of bytes containing the user input key and `keyLen` is its length. The aim of this function is to generate all the subkeys in arrays `p[]` and S-boxes `S[][]`.

The double for-loop in lines 4–14 uses `key[]` to initialize the 18 subkeys in `p[]`. The inner for-loop in lines 7–11 combines four bytes in `key[]` to form a 32-bit word called `data`. By using the XOR operation on `data` and `p[]`, the element `p[]` is initialized (line 13). The conditional-if statement in line 10 makes sure that the array `key[]` is repeated for the initialization process. When the initialization length is longer than the key length, the variable `j` is set to 0 so that array `key[]` is reused.

Line 16 sets up a 64-bit block of zeros. This block is split into two 32-bit words represented by array elements `dataArr[0]` and `dataArr[1]`. These two elements are used as the left and right parts in the Blowfish encryption algorithm. The for-loop in lines 18–22 performs 18 Blowfish encryptions on `dataArr[0]` and `dataArr[1]`. The resultant ciphertext is stored back to `dataArr[]` (line 19). The two values `dataArr[0]` and `dataArr[1]` are used to replace subkeys `p[i]` and `p[i+1]` respectively. When the for-loop is exhausted, all 18 subkeys in `p[]` are initialized. Similarly, the double for-loop in lines 24–30 replaces all the elements in the S-boxes. When the double for-loop is exhausted, all the elements in S-boxes are initialized. All subkeys, including `p[]` and `S[][]`, are ready for Blowfish encryption/decryption on data.

The starting values for subkeys

For the Blowfish scheme, the starting values for the subkeys in `p[]` and `S[][]` are interesting. The starting values of `p[]` and `S[][]` are the fractional part of π in hexadecimal format. Since each element of `p[]` and `S[][]` is a 32-bit value represented as eight hexadecimal digits, the entire set of subkeys consists of $(18 + 1024) \times 8 = 8336$ digits. This means that the Blowfish scheme uses more than 8000 digits (hexadecimal) of π.

If you consider the fractional part of π to be a sequence, it is a good random number sequence. Using the digits of π as starting values for subkeys is a good choice. Together with a slow and non-linear subkey generation the process is considered to be strong.

In many cases, the starting values for subkeys are precomputed. One such set is provided by Mike Schaudies and is listed in `ex06-04.txt`. We will use this set for our implementation.

```
Example: ex06-04.txt - The Fractional values Of π stored in array p[]
    0x243F6A88,    0x85A308D3,    0x13198A2E,    0x03707344,
    0xA4093822,    0x299F31D0,    0x082EFA98,    0xEC4E6C89,
    0x452821E6,    0x38D01377,    0xBE5466CF,    0x34E90C6C,
    0xC0AC29B7,    0xC97C50DD,    0x3F84D5B5,    0xB5470917,
    0x9216D5D9,    0x8979FB1B
```

More discussions on this data and how to generate it will be given in Section 6.2.3. Now, let's implement the Blowfish scheme on the Web.

6.2 Implementation of the Blowfish scheme

6.2.1 A Web page for Blowfish encryption/decryption

With the algorithm and pseudo-code described in the previous section, implementation of the Blowfish scheme is straightforward. Consider script ex06-01.js.

```
Example: ex06-01.js - Implementation of the Blowfish scheme    (Part I)

 1: var b_P = new Array(18); // i.e. 16+2
 2: var b_S = new Array(0,0,0,0);
 3:    b_S[0] = new Array(256);
 4:    b_S[1] = new Array(256);
 5:    b_S[2] = new Array(256);
 6:    b_S[3] = new Array(256);
 7:
 8: var N=16;
 9:
10: var ORIG_P = new Array(
11:          0x243F6A88, 0x85A308D3, 0x13198A2E, 0x03707344,
12:          0xA4093822, 0x299F31D0, 0x082EFA98, 0xEC4E6C89,
13:          0x452821E6, 0x38D01377, 0xBE5466CF, 0x34E90C6C,
14:          0xC0AC29B7, 0xC97C50DD, 0x3F84D5B5, 0xB5470917,
15:          0x9216D5D9, 0x8979FB1B );
16:
17: var ORIG_S = new Array(0,0,0,0);
18:    ORIG_S[0] = new Array (
19:          0xD1310BA6, 0x98DFB5AC, 0x2FFD72DB, 0xD01ADFB7,
20:          0xB8E1AFED, 0x6A267E96, 0xBA7C9045, 0xF12C7F99,
   ... ... ...    ... ... ...    ... ... ...    ... ... ...
   ... ... ...    ... ... ...    ... ... ...    ... ... ...
214:          0xD79A3234, 0x92638212, 0x670EFA8E, 0x406000E0);
215:
216:    ORIG_S[3] = new Array (
217:          0x3A39CE37, 0xD3FAF5CF, 0xABC27737, 0x5AC52D1B,
   ... ... ...    ... ... ...    ... ... ...    ... ... ...
   ... ... ...    ... ... ...    ... ... ...    ... ... ...
279:          0x90D4F869, 0xA65CDEA0, 0x3F09252D, 0xC208E69F,
280:          0xB74E6132, 0xCE77E25B, 0x578FDFE3, 0x3AC372E6);
281:
```

This script fragment is the first part of the implementation containing the data used by the Blowfish scheme. Line 1 declares an array called b_P[18] of 18 elements.

Line 2 defines an array called b_S with four elements. For each element of b_S[], another array of 256 elements is defined by the statements in lines 3–6. This process effectively defines a two-dimensional array b_S[][] for the S-boxes. They are used to store the Blowfish subkeys. The variable N=16 in line 8 specifies that 16 iterations are used for encryption/decryption.

The remaining codes define another set of data called ORIG_P[] and ORIG_S[][]. These two arrays contain the starting data of the subkeys (i.e. the fractional part of π). The starting values will be copied to b_P[] and b_S[][] at the beginning of the algorithm. If a new set of subkeys is needed, the starting data can be copied again. Lines 10–15 populate the 18 elements in ORIG_P[]. Similarly, the elements of the S-boxes ORIG_S[][] are defined and populated by lines 17–280.

The encryption and decryption operations are defined in part II of ex06-01.js.

```
Example: Continuation of ex06-01.js                          (Part II)

282: function F(x)
283: {
284:    var a, b, c, d;
285:
286:            d = x & 0x00FF;
287:    x >>= 8; c = x & 0x00FF;
288:    x >>= 8; b = x & 0x00FF;
289:    x >>= 8; a = x & 0x00FF;
290:
291:    return ((b_S[0][a] + b_S[1][b]) ^ b_S[2][c]) + b_S[3][d];
292: }
293:
294: function Blowfish_Encrypt(xl, xr)
295: {
296:    var Xl, Xr, temp, i;
297:    Xl = xl; Xr = xr;
298:    for (i = 0; i < N; ++i) {
299:        Xl = Xl ^ b_P[i];
300:        Xr = F(Xl) ^ Xr;
301:        temp = Xl; Xl = Xr; Xr = temp;
302:    }
303:    temp = Xl;    Xl = Xr; Xr = temp;
304:    Xr = Xr ^ b_P[N];
305:    Xl = Xl ^ b_P[N + 1];
306:
307:    return Array(Xl,Xr);
308: }
309:
```

```
310: function Blowfish_Decrypt(xl,xr)
311: {
312:   var Xl, Xr, temp, i;
313:     Xl = xl; Xr = xr;
314:     for (i = N + 1; i > 1; --i) {
315:         Xl = Xl ^ b_P[i];
316:         Xr = F(Xl) ^ Xr;
317:         temp = Xl; Xl = Xr; Xr = temp;
318:     }
319:     temp = Xl; Xl = Xr; Xr = temp;
320:     Xr = Xr ^ b_P[1];
321:     Xl = Xl ^ b_P[0];
322:
323:     return Array(Xl,Xr);
324: }
325:
```

The second part of the script contains three functions. The function `F(x)` in lines 282–292 defines the encryption function with one parameter x. Variable x is a 32-bit value and will be converted into four bytes, namely d, c, b and a, by lines 286–289. The function value `F(x)` is computed by

```
((S1[a] + S2[b]) ^ S3[c]) + S4[d]
```

and returned (line 291).

The encryption process is carried out by the function `Blowfish_Encrypt()` in lines 294–308. This function has two parameters, namely xl and xr. Each parameter is a 32-bit word representing the left and right halves of the 64-bit plaintext block. The variables xl and xr are first copied to local variables for processing in line 297. The for-loop in lines 298–302 performs the 16 rounds of iteration. Each round is calculated as follows:

- the left block is XORed with `P[i]` and stored back in the left block;
- the left block passes to the encryption function `F()` and is XORed with the right block;
- the left and right blocks are swapped.

After 16 rounds, the statements in line 303 undo the swap of the last round. The right and left blocks are XORed with `P[17]` and `P[18]` respectively to produce the ciphertext. The ciphertext xl and xr are returned as an array by the statement in line 307. For the decryption process, the function `Blowfish_Decrypt()` is executed and is similar to the encryption case. Note that the for-loop in lines 314–318 uses the variable N to apply the keys in reverse order.

The key generation process is given in part III of script `ex06-01.js`.

```
326: function Blowfish_Init(key, keyLen)
327: {
328:   var i, j, k, data;
329:   var dataArr = new Array(2);
330:
331:   for (i = 0; i < 4; i++) {
332:     for (j = 0; j < 256; j++)
333:       b_S[i][j] = ORIG_S[i][j];
334:   }
335:   j = 0;
336:   for (i = 0; i < N + 2; ++i) {
337:     data = 0x00000000;
338:     for (k = 0; k < 4; ++k) {
339:       data = (data << 8) | key[j];
340:       j = j + 1;
341:       if (j >= keyLen)
342:         j = 0;
343:     }
344:     b_P[i] = ORIG_P[i] ^ data;
345:   }
346:   dataArr[0]=0x00000000; dataArr[1]=0x00000000;
347:
348:   for (i = 0; i < N + 2; i += 2) {
349:     dataArr = Blowfish_Encrypt(dataArr[0], dataArr[1]);
350:     b_P[i]     = dataArr[0];
351:     b_P[i + 1] = dataArr[1];
352:   }
353:   for (i = 0; i < 4; ++i) {
354:     for (j = 0; j < 256; j += 2) {
355:       dataArr = Blowfish_Encrypt(dataArr[0],dataArr[1]);
356:       b_S[i][j]     = dataArr[0];
357:       b_S[i][j + 1] = dataArr[1];
358:     }
359:   }
360: }
361:
```

Given the key generation process discussed in Section 6.1.2 and the pseudo-code in ex06-03.txt, this part of the script is not difficult to follow. The left and right blocks are defined by the array dataArr[] in line 329. The double for-loop in lines 331–334 copies the starting values from the S-boxes ORIG_S[][] into the two-dimensional array b_s[][]. They are used for encryption/decryption. The double for-loop in lines 336–345 carries out line-by-line translation from the pseudo-code in ex06-03.txt for the key expansion and XORing and storing the result in b_P[].

A 64-bit block of zeros is defined in line 346 as the initial plaintext. The for-loop in lines 348–352 encrypts the block nine times. Each encryption result is used to replace the values in b_P[] as the initialization process described in the algorithm. The double for-loop in lines 353–359 performs the encryption 512 times and the result is used to replace the elements of the S-boxes. The subkeys in b_P[] and b_S[][] are then ready to carry out encryption/decryption on user data.

In order to use the above program effectively, some interface functions are required and they are provided in part IV of ex06-01.js.

```
Example: Continuation of ex06-01.js                        (Part IV)

362: function keyStToSubkeys(inKeySt)
363: {
364:   var i, rKeyArr = new Array();
365:   var len = inKeySt.length;
366:   for (i=0; i<len; i++) rKeyArr[i] = inKeySt.charCodeAt(i);
367:   Blowfish_Init (rKeyArr, len);
368: }
369:
370: function blowfish(keySt, msgSt, encrypt)
371: {
372:   var m=0, chunk=0, len = msgSt.length;
373:   var i, tResult="", result="";
374:   var iKeyArr=new Array(8), oKeyArr=new Array(), lrArr=new Array(2);
375:
376:   keyStToSubkeys(keySt)
377:
378:   msgSt += "\0\0\0\0\0\0\0\0";
379:   while (m < len) {
380:     lrArr[0]=(msgSt.charCodeAt(m++) << 24)|
                  (msgSt.charCodeAt(m++) << 16)|
381:              (msgSt.charCodeAt(m++) << 8) |
                   msgSt.charCodeAt(m++);
382:     lrArr[1]=(msgSt.charCodeAt(m++) << 24)|
                  (msgSt.charCodeAt(m++) << 16)|
383:              (msgSt.charCodeAt(m++) << 8) |
                   msgSt.charCodeAt(m++);
384:
385:     if (encrypt) lrArr = Blowfish_Encrypt(lrArr[0],lrArr[1]);
386:     else         lrArr = Blowfish_Decrypt(lrArr[0],lrArr[1]);
387:
388:     tempSt= String.fromCharCode(
```

```
389:        ((lrArr[0] >>> 24) & 0xff), ((lrArr[0] >>> 16) & 0xff),
390:        ((lrArr[0] >>>  8) & 0xff), ( lrArr[0]          & 0xff),
391:        ((lrArr[1] >>> 24) & 0xff), ((lrArr[1] >>> 16) & 0xff),
392:        ((lrArr[1] >>>  8) & 0xff), ( lrArr[1]          & 0xff));
393:
394:    tResult += tempSt; chunk += 8;
395:    if (chunk == 512) {
396:        result += tResult; tResult = ""; chunk = 0;
397:      }
398:  }
399:  return result + tResult;
400: }
401:
```

This script fragment contains two familiar interface functions as used in DES and CAST-128 cases. The first function is keyStToSubkeys() in lines 362–368. This function takes a user input key from the Web page and uses it to generate all the necessary subkeys. The user key is converted into a byte string in array rKeyArr[] (line 366). This array is submitted to function Blowfish_Init() for the key generation process. Once all the subkeys are available, the second function blowfish(), defined in lines 370–400, is called for encryption/decryption.

The function blowfish() takes three parameters, namely keySt, msgSt and a boolean type variable called encrypt. When the variable encrypt has a true value, the plaintext msgSt will be encrypted using the key string keySt.

Like many Feistel schemes, Blowfish implementation operates on a 64-bit block divided into two 32-bit words. After the key generation in line 376, eight bytes from the input plaintext are extracted into two 32-bit words lrArr[0] and lrArr[1] representing the left and right pair of the plaintext block. When encryption is true, this pair is encrypted by calling the function Blowfish_Encrypt() in line 385. Otherwise decryption is performed. The result is stored back in array lrArr[]. The statements in lines 388–392 convert the encrypted (or decrypted) result into a string tempSt. The remaining code is to combine the string together and return it to the function caller.

To test this script, a Web page is needed. One such page can be developed easily by copying ex05-01.htm to ex06-01.htm. Modify the following lines in the new file:

```
 9: Blowfish Encryption/Decryption<br />
31:  class="butSt" style="width:180px" value="OK"
       onclick="blowfish_fun()" />
41: <script src="ex06-01.js"></script>
44:  function blowfish_fun()
52:      llst = byteStToHex(blowfish(key, message,true))
59:      llst = blowfish(key, message,false)
```

Line 9 changes the display of the page to show that we are working with the Blowfish scheme. When the OK button is clicked, the function `blowfish_fun()` is called. This new function is defined in line 44. Inside this function, all you have to do is change the calling functions in lines 52 and 59 to function `blowfish()` with the `key`, `message` and the status of encryption or decryption. Screenshots of this example are shown in Figures 6.4 and 6.5.

Fig. 6.4   Blowfish encryption

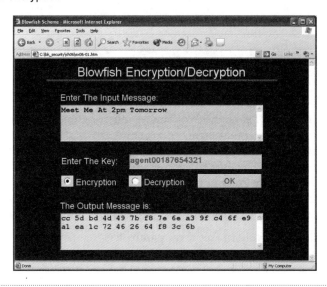

Fig. 6.5   Blowfish decryption

Once you have an implementation of a scheme, it is also important to test it and compare it with the standard test vectors provided by the scheme designer.

6.2.2 Standard results and building a utility

Comparison with some standard results

In order to test the implementation, some test vectors from the Blowfish scheme are used. Since the standard testing vectors are in hexadecimal format, a page that can take hexadecimal input for the key and message is required.

You can, for example, make a copy of ex06-01.htm and call it ex06-02.htm. In the new example ex06-02.htm, modify the following lines:

```
 9:  Blowfish Encryption/Decryption (Hex Input)<br />
16:            id="in_mesg"> </textarea></td></tr>
24:  background:#dddddd;color:#ff0000" value=""/></td></tr>
31:  class="butSt" style="width:180px" value="OK"
      onclick="blowfish_hex()" />
44:  function blowfish_hex()
49:      key = hexStToByteSt(document.getElementById("key_v").value);
50:      message = hexStToByteSt(document.getElementById
                              ("in_mesg").value);
56:      key = hexStToByteSt(document.getElementById("key_v").value);
57:      message = hexStToByteSt(document.getElementById
                              ("in_mesg").value);
59:      llst = byteStToHex(blowfish(key, message,false));
63: var kSt= "FE DC BA 98 76 54 32 10";
64: var pSt="01 23 45 67 89 AB CD EF";
65: document.getElementById("key_v").value=kSt;
66: document.getElementById("in_mesg").value=pSt;
```

Line 9 changes the display to indicate that the page can take only hexadecimal input. In lines 16 and 24 no initial values are specified. The test vectors are defined in new lines 63–64 and put into position by statements in lines 65–66. When the OK button is clicked, the function blowfish_hex() is called. Inside this function the hexadecimal strings of key and message are captured by lines 49–50 and converted into byte strings immediately for the encryption. As in ex06-01.htm, the result of encryption is already in hexadecimal format and there is no need to change.

When decryption is true, the hexadecimal strings key and message are captured by lines 56–57 and converted into byte strings immediately for decryption. Since the decrypted result is returned as a byte string, the last line (line 59) changes the byte string back to hexadecimal values and displays it.

The conversion function hexStToByteSt() defined in the script hexlib.js is included in the page as usual. Screenshots are shown in Figures 6.6 and 6.7.

Fig. 6.6 Standard encryption test

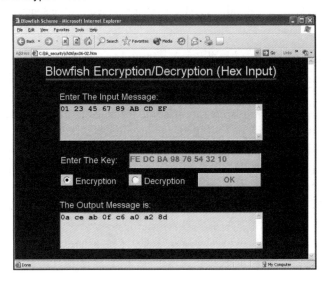

Fig. 6.7 Standard decryption test

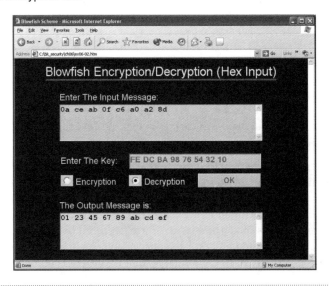

As you can see from Figure 6.6, the encryption result for message '01 23 45 67 89 AB CD EF' and key 'FE DC BA 98 76 54 32 10' is the ciphertext '0a ce ab 0f c6 a0 a2 8d'. There are lots of test vectors available. Given the plaintext block

    p = 'FEDCBA9876543210'

some test ciphertexts c against the variable key strings k are listed below:

```
c=E8 7A 24 4E 2C C8 5E 82   k=F0 E1 D2 C3 B4 A5 96 87
c=15 75 0E 7A 4F 4E C5 77   k=F0 E1 D2 C3 B4 A5 96 87 78
c=12 2B A7 0B 3A B6 4A E0   k=F0 E1 D2 C3 B4 A5 96 87 78 69
c=3A 83 3C 9A FF C5 37 F6   k=F0 E1 D2 C3 B4 A5 96 87 78 69 5A
c=94 09 DA 87 A9 0F 6B F2   k=F0 E1 D2 C3 B4 A5 96 87 78 69 5A 4B
c=88 4F 80 62 50 60 B8 B4   k=F0 E1 D2 C3 B4 A5 96 87 78 69 5A 4B 3C
c=1F 85 03 1C 19 E1 19 68   k=F0 E1 D2 C3 B4 A5 96 87 78 69 5A 4B 3C 2D
c=79 D9 37 3A 71 4C A3 4F   k=F0 E1 D2 C3 B4 A5 96 87 78 69 5A 4B 3C 2D 1E
c=93 14 28 87 EE 3B E1 5C   k=F0 E1 D2 C3 B4 A5 96 87 78 69 5A 4B 3C 2D 1E 0F
```

For the following even longer keys:

```
k1=F0 E1 D2 C3 B4 A5 96 87 78 69 5A 4B 3C 2D 1E 0F 00
k2=F0 E1 D2 C3 B4 A5 96 87 78 69 5A 4B 3C 2D 1E 0F 00 11
k3=F0 E1 D2 C3 B4 A5 96 87 78 69 5A 4B 3C 2D 1E 0F 00 11 22
k4=F0 E1 D2 C3 B4 A5 96 87 78 69 5A 4B 3C 2D 1E 0F 00 11 22 33
k5=F0 E1 D2 C3 B4 A5 96 87 78 69 5A 4B 3C 2D 1E 0F 00 11 22 33 44
k6=F0 E1 D2 C3 B4 A5 96 87 78 69 5A 4B 3C 2D 1E 0F 00 11 22 33 44 55
k7=F0 E1 D2 C3 B4 A5 96 87 78 69 5A 4B 3C 2D 1E 0F 00 11 22 33 44 55 66
k8=F0 E1 D2 C3 B4 A5 96 87 78 69 5A 4B 3C 2D 1E 0F 00 11 22 33 44 55 66 77
```

the corresponding ciphertext is:

```
c1=03 42 9E 83 8C E2 D1 4B      c2=A4 29 9E 27 46 9F F6 7B
c3=AF D5 AE D1 C1 BC 96 A8      c4=10 85 1C 0E 38 58 DA 9F
c5=E6 F5 1E D7 9B 9D B2 1F      c6=64 A6 E1 4A FD 36 B4 6F
c7=80 C7 D7 D4 5A 54 79 AD      c8=05 04 4B 62 FA 52 D0 80
```

In order to use the scheme on files, we need to develop a new Blowfish encryption program (utility).

Building a Blowfish utility to work with files

There are a number of Blowfish implementations available for building a utility. We will use the one developed by Paul Kocher. This implementation comes with two C program files, namely blowfish.c and blowfish.h. Copies of these two programs can be found in a number of search engines or they can be downloaded from the site accompanying this book.

To use the program blowfish.c to encrypt/decrypt data, the following statements are needed:

```
1: BLOWFISH_CTX ctx;
2: unsigned long X,Y;
3: unsigned char *key
4: Blowfish_Init (&ctx,key, n);
5: Blowfish_Encrypt(&ctx, &X, &Y);
6: Blowfish_Decrypt(&ctx, &X, &Y);
```

The first line defines a structure containing arrays `P[18]` and S-boxes `S[4][256]`. The second line declares two 32-bit integers (i.e. unsigned long) `x` and `y` representing the left and right halves of the 64-bit plaintext block. The user input key is defined in line 3 and is a byte string (i.e. unsigned char). Before any encryption or decryption, the initialization function `Blowfish_init()` in line 3 must be called so that all the subkeys are available. The functions in line 5 and 6 perform Blowfish encryption and decryption respectively. A Blowfish utility working on files can be built by the driver program `blowfishdriver.c`.

```
Example: blowfishdriver.c - Blowfish driver program          (Part I)

 1: #include <stdio.h>
 2: #include "blowfish.c"
 3:
 4: #define GET_UINT32(X,b,i)                                  \
 5: {                                                          \
 6:       (X) = ( (unsigned long) (b)[(i)     ] << 24 )        \
 7:           | ( (unsigned long) (b)[(i) + 1] << 16 )        \
 8:           | ( (unsigned long) (b)[(i) + 2] <<  8 )        \
 9:           | ( (unsigned long) (b)[(i) + 3]         );     \
10: }
11:
12: #define PUT_UINT32(X,b,i)                                  \
13: {                                                          \
14:       (b)[(i)     ] = (unsigned char) ( (X) >> 24 );      \
15:       (b)[(i) + 1] = (unsigned char) ( (X) >> 16 );      \
16:       (b)[(i) + 2] = (unsigned char) ( (X) >>  8 );      \
17:       (b)[(i) + 3] = (unsigned char) ( (X)         );      \
18: }
19:
```

This is the first part of the driver program to perform encryption/decryption. The main program `blowfish.c` is included in this interface in line 2. Apart from the two macros in lines 4 and 12, this driver is similar to the driver programs that we have developed before.

The first macro `GET_UNINT32()` in lines 4–10 has three parameters. The main purpose of this macro is to get four bytes from the array `b[]` starting at position `i` and convert them to one 32-bit word stored in `x`. Macro is a feature of the C language that will replace all occurrences of the macro by the statements defining it and therefore will run faster. The second macro is the opposite of the first. It is used to put a 32-bit word back to the byte string `b[]` starting at position `i`.

These two macros are used to compose the left and right halves of the 64-bit plaintext (or ciphertext) blocks and will be used heavily in the program. Consider part II of `blowfishdriver.c`.

Example: Continuation of the C program blowfishdriver.c   (Part II)

```
20: int main(int argc, char *argv[])
21: {
22:  int i, n;
23:  BLOWFISH_CTX ctx;
24:  unsigned char buf[8];
25:  unsigned char kkey1[72];
26:  FILE *inK, *inP, *outF;
27:  unsigned long X,Y;
28:
29:  if (argc!=5) {
30:   printf("Usage:\n blowfishdriver (e)|(d) <infile> <outfile>
            <keyfile>\n");
31:   return 2;
32:  }
33:  for (i=0;i<256;i++) kkey1[i]=0;
34:  for (i=0;i<8;i++)   buf[i]=0;
35:
36:  if((inK=fopen(argv[4],"rb"))==NULL){
37:      printf("\r\nCould not open input file: %s",argv[4]);
38:      return 2;
39:  } else {
40:      n= fread(kkey1,1,256,inK);
41:      fclose(inK);
42:  }
43:   Blowfish_Init (&ctx,kkey1, n);
44:
45:  if((inP=fopen(argv[2],"rb"))==NULL){
46:      printf("\r\nCould not open input file: %s",argv[2]);
47:      return 2;
48:  }
49:  if((outF=fopen(argv[3],"wb"))==NULL){
50:      printf("\r\nCould not open output file: %s",argv[3]);
51:      return 2;
52:  }
53:
54:  if(argv[1][0]=='e') {
55:    while ((n=fread(buf,1,8,inP)) >0) {
56:       if (n < 8) {
57:           for(i=n;i<8;i++) buf[i]=0;
58:       }
59:       GET_UINT32( X, buf, 0 );
60:       GET_UINT32( Y, buf, 4 );
```

```
61:          Blowfish_Encrypt(&ctx, &X, &Y);
62:          PUT_UINT32( X, buf, 0 );
63:          PUT_UINT32( Y, buf, 4 );
64:          if(fwrite(buf,1,8,outF) < 8) {
65:              printf("\r\nError writing to output file\r\n");
66:              return(3);
67:          }
68:      }
69:  }
70:  if(argv[1][0]=='d') {
71:     while ((n=fread(buf,1,8,inP)) >0) {
72:         if (n < 8) {
73:             for(i=n;i<8;i++) buf[i]=0;
74:         }
75:          GET_UINT32( X, buf, 0 );
76:          GET_UINT32( Y, buf, 4 );
77:          Blowfish_Decrypt(&ctx, &X, &Y);
78:          PUT_UINT32( X, buf, 0 );
79:          PUT_UINT32( Y, buf, 4 );
80:          if(fwrite(buf,1,8,outF) < 8) {
81:              printf("\r\nError writing to output file\r\n");
82:              return(3);
83:          }
84:      }
85:  }
86:  fclose(inP); fclose(outF);
87:  return 0;
88: }
```

This program is similar to the interface programs in previous chapters and only
the new statements are highlighted and explained. Line 23 defines a structure to
be used by the program. The arrays to store the message and key are declared in
lines 24 and 25. The length of the key is specified as 72 bytes. After the key is read
into the program in lines 36–42, the function Blowfish_Init() is called in line 43 so
that all the subkeys are set. If encryption is true, the statements in lines 59–63 are
executed. The two macros in lines 59–60 extract eight bytes from plaintext array
buf[] to form two 32-bit words called X and Y. They are the left and right halves
of the 64-bit block to be encrypted by line 61. The result is stored back in X and Y.
The two macros in lines 62–63 combine the two 32-bit words X and Y back to the
array buf[] so that it now contains the ciphertext. The final result is written to the
outfile by the conditional-if statement in lines 64–67. For the decryption process,
the operation is similar. The only difference is that the decryption function in

Fig. 6.8 A utility for Blowfish

```
H:\ch06>gcc -o blowfishdriver blowfishdriver.c
H:\ch06>blowfishdriver
Usage:
 blowfishdriver (e)|(d) <infile> <outfile> <keyfile>

H:\ch06>blowfishdriver e zplain.txt zen.txt zkey.txt
H:\ch06>blowfishdriver d zen.txt zde.txt zkey.txt
H:\ch06>type zde.txt

Meet Me At 2pm Tomorrow

H:\ch06>tohex xen.txt

cc 5d bd 4d 49 7b f8 7e 6e a3 9f c4 6f e9 a1 ea
1c 72 46 26 64 f8 3c 6b

H:\ch06>
```

line 77 is executed instead. A compiling and execution session of this program is captured and shown in Figure 6.8.

You can see that the ciphertext output from the program is the same as the output from the Web page ex06-01.htm.

6.2.3   Generating any digit of π and Blowfish constants

As we mentioned in Section 6.1.1, the starting values for Blowfish subkeys are the fractional digits of π. One of the reasons for using π as a starting value is that its fractional part is infinitely long and is a perfectly random sequence. In fact, you can shuffle the digits and use it for a one-time-pad (OTP). In this section, a detailed discussion on how to generate any digit of π is presented.

Before you can generate and convert the fractional part of π, you need to know how to change the bases (or radix) of a fractional number.

For example, consider the decimal value, $a = 123456.78125$. This value can be changed to hexadecimal by splitting it into integer and fractional parts:

$$\text{int}(123456.78125) \quad = 123456 \quad \text{(dec)}$$
$$\text{fract}(123456.781250) = 0.78125 \quad \text{(dec)}$$

The conversion of the integer part is the usual hex conversion, and we have 123456 (dec) = 1e240 (hex). The conversion of the fractional part can be done by:

■ multiplying the fractional part by 16 and splitting the result into integer and fractional parts;

- converting the integer part to hexadecimal digits;

- continuing the first step until finished.

For example, the hexadecimal representation of 0.78125 (dec) is calculated below.

$$0.78125 \times 16 = 12.5 \qquad \text{convert (12) to hex digit} \rightarrow c$$
$$0.5 \times 16 = 8 \qquad \text{convert (8) to hex digit} \rightarrow 8$$
$$\Rightarrow \quad 0.78125 \text{ (dec)} = c8 \text{ (hex)}$$

That is, the hexadecimal representation of 123456.78125 (dec) is 1e240.c8 (hex).

During the history of π, there have been many methods and formulas to evaluate the constant. Many of them can generate billions of digits. For the Blowfish scheme, only a couple of thousand digits are needed. More precisely, we need $(1024 + 18) \times 8 = 8336$ digits in hexadecimal format. Sometimes, for some small devices, even a thousand digits of π stored in memory may not be feasible. In this case we need to be able to compute each digit of π independently.

In this section, a π formula using a 'binary exponential algorithm' is introduced. It is based on the article 'A Quest for Pi' by Bailey et al. (available as a downloadable pdf; use a search engine to search for the title). The method can generate any digit of π. We will implement this algorithm to generate the starting subkeys for the Blowfish scheme. A direct translation to the C language is also provided so that a complete listing of the Blowfish starting values is available.

The constant π can be calculated by the formula

$$\pi = \sum_{i=0}^{\infty} \frac{1}{16^i} \left(\frac{4}{8i+1} - \frac{2}{8i+4} - \frac{1}{8i+5} - \frac{1}{8i+6} \right)$$

For practical purposes, we will not go through the details of the proof. Obviously, the fractional part of π is the same as the fractional part of the right-hand side of the formula. With some substitutions S_1, S_2, S_3 and S_4, the formula can be written as

$$\pi = \sum_{i=0}^{\infty} (4S_1 - 2S_1 - S_3 - S_4)$$

Now, the fractional part of π can be calculated by the combinations of S_1, S_2, S_3 and S_4. Consider the first term:

$$S_1 = \sum_{i=0}^{\infty} \frac{1}{16^i (8i+1)}$$

The hexadecimal digits of S_1 beginning at position $d+1$ can be obtained by multiplying both sides by 16^d and taking the fractional part, i.e. the fractional part of $(16^d S_1)$. Split the summation into two parts and we have

$$\text{frac}(16^d S_1) = \sum_{i=0}^{d} \frac{16^{d-i} \bmod (8i+1)}{(8i+1)} \bmod 1 + \sum_{i=d+1}^{\infty} \frac{16^{d-i}}{(8i+1)} \bmod 1$$

The numerator of the first part can be computed easily by the binary exponentiation algorithm. With the help of some additional terms from the second part, the fractional part of S_1 can be evaluated effectively. Similarly, all four terms S_1, S_2, S_3 and S_4 can be computed in this way to yield a particular hexadecimal digit of π.

In general, the numerator of the first part above can be written as $a^p \bmod m$. Given a, p and m, the r in '$r = a^p \bmod m$' can be computed by the binary exponentiation algorithm and pseudo-code in ex06-05.txt.

Example: ex06-05.txt – The binary exponentiation algorithm for
r = aᵖ mod m

```
Step1:  Find the largest power of 2 less than or equal to p
        and call it (2ⁱ = pt). Set r=1

Step2:  r can be computed by the following for-loop:
        for (j = 1 ; j <= i ; j++) do
           if (p >= pt) do
              r = a * r mod m
              p = p - pt;
           end-if
           pt = pt * 0.5;
           if ( pt >= 1.0) do
              r = r * r mod m
           end-if
        end-for
        return r;
```

This is an efficient algorithm and all the operations are simple. This method can be traced back to 200 BC (see the article by Bailey et al. for more information). Now, we have everything that we need to compute any hexadecimal digit of π. Consider script ex06-03.js.

Example: ex06-03.js – Finding any digit of pi   **(Part I)**

```
1: function getPiDigit(iP)
2: {
3:    var s1= 0.0, s2= 0.0, s3= 0.0, s4= 0.0, piD= 0.0;
4:       s1 = SS(1, iP);
5:       s2 = SS(4, iP);
6:       s3 = SS(5, iP);
7:       s4 = SS(6, iP);
```

```
 8:     piD = 4.0 * s1 - 2.0 * s2 - s3 - s4;
 9:     piD = piD - Math.floor(piD) + 1.0;
10:     return gethex(piD);
11: }
12:
13: function SS(ii, dd)
14: {
15:    var k = 0,    mm = 0.0;
16:    var p = 0.0, s = 0.0, t = 0.0;
17:    for (k = 0 ; k < dd ; k++) {
18:        mm = 8 * k + ii;
19:        p = dd - k;
20:        t = expm(p, mm);
21:        s = s + t / mm;
22:        s = s - Math.floor(s);
23:    }
24:    for (k = dd ; k <= dd + 10 ; k++) {
25:        mm = 8 * k + ii;
26:        t = Math.pow(16.0,dd-k) / mm;
27:        s = s + t;
28:        s = s - Math.floor(s);
29:    }
30:    return s;
31: }
32:
33: function gethex(x)
34: {
35:    var i = 0,    cPos = 0;
36:    var y = 0.0, retV=0;
37:    var cSt= "0123456789abcdef";
38:    y = Math.abs(x);
39:    cPos = Math.floor(16.0 * (y - Math.floor(y)));
40:    return (cSt.substring(cPos,cPos+1));
41: }
42:
```

This script contains three functions. The first function getPiDigit() takes a parameter iP representing the position of the digit and returns the corresponding π digit in hexadecimal format. Inside the function the four variables s1, s2, s3 and s4 are the terms in the π formula above. Given a position iP, say, lines 4–7 compute the values of s1, s2, s3 and s4. The calculation in lines 8–9 effectively computes the fractional part of π containing the digit required. The function call in line 10 returns the digit in hexadecimal form.

The second function ss() is used to evaluate the corresponding values of s1, s2, s3 and s4. The program codes are line-by-line translations of the algorithm described above. The for-loop in lines 17–23 computes the summation from the π formula up to dd digits. The binary exponentiation algorithm (or function expm()) is used in line 20 to compute the numerator. This function will be described in part II of the script. The for-loop in lines 24–29 computes more terms to ensure that the digit required is accurately included. The third function gethex() is used to compute the hexadecimal of the digit and return to the function caller. The implementation of the binary exponentiation function expm() is in part II of script ex06-03.js.

```
Example: Continuation of ex06-03.js                        (Part II)

43: function expm (p, mm)
44: {
45:    var i  = 1,     j = 0;
46:    var p1 = 0.0,   pt = 1.0, eps= 0.0000000000001;
47:    var r  = 1.0, ntp = 25;
48:
49:    if ( Math.abs(mm - 1.0) < eps ) return 0.0;
50:    for (i = 1 ; i < ntp ; i++) {
51:        pt = 2.0 * pt;
52:        if (pt > p) break;
53:    }
54:    pt = pt / 2.0;
55:
56:    p1 = p; r = 1.0;
57:    for (j = 1 ; j <= i ; j++) {
58:        if (p1 >= pt) {
59:            r = 16.0 * r;
60:            r = r - Math.floor(r/mm) * mm;
61:            p1 = p1 - pt;
62:        }
63:        pt = pt * 0.5;
64:        if ( pt >= 1.0) {
65:            r = r * r;
66:            r = r - Math.floor(r / mm) * mm;
67:        }
68:    }
69:    return r;
70: }
71:
```

Based on the pseudo-code in ex06-05.txt, this script is not difficult to understand. Given values in p and mm, the function expm() is used to compute r where $r=16^p$

mod mm. The for-loop in lines 50–53 is used to find the largest 2 to the power less than or equal to p and call it pt in line 54. The value of r is set to 1 in line 56. Lines 59–60 compute the value r=a*r mod mm with a=16. Similarly, lines 65–66 compute the value r=r*r mod mm. The result is returned to the caller by line 69.

The function getPiDigit() in lines 1–11 can calculate any digit of π. To evaluate the constants used in the Blowfish scheme, we add two more functions in part III of ex06-03.js.

```
Example: Continuation of ex06-03.js                    (Part III)

72: function FindP(inI)
73: {
74:   var i;
75:   var ii;
76:   var retSt = "";
77:   if ((inI < 0) || (inI > 17)) return 0;
78:   ii = inI * 8;
79:   for (i= ii;i<ii+8;i++) {
80:     retSt += getPiDigit(i);
81:   }
82:   return retSt;
83: }
84:
85: function FindSBox(S,inP)
86: {
87:   var i, ii;
88:   var retSt = "";
89:   if ((S   < 0) || (S > 3)) return 0;
90:   if ((inP < 0) || (inP > 255)) return 0;
91:
92:   ii = ((18+ (S) * 256) + inP)*8;
93:   for (i= ii;i<ii+8;i++) {
94:     retSt += getPiDigit(i);
95:   }
96:   return retSt;
97: }
```

The first function in this script fragment is FindP(). It is used to find any of the 18 elements in the subkeys array P[] used by Blowfish. This array starts from 0. The returned value is a string containing eight hexadecimal numbers. Given an input number inI, the starting digit position of π is calculated by line 78. The for-loop in lines 79–80 computes a further eight digits and return it as the constant string. The second function FindSBox() computes the constants of the S-boxes. For example, the first element of the first S-box is computed by `FindSBox(0,0)`. Given the S-box number `S` and element position `inP`, the variable `ii` in line 92 calculates the corresponding digit position of π. The for-loop in lines 93–95 computes a further eight digits and returns it as a string.

To test this script, an example Web page is developed in `ex06-03.htm`.

```
Example: ex06-03.htm - Finding any digit of π and Blowfish constants
                                                              (Part I)

 1: <style>
 2:   .butSt{font-size:16pt;width:250px;height:35px;
 3:            font-weight:bold;background:#dddddd;color:#ff0000}
 4: </style>
 5: <body style="font-family:arial;font-size:24pt;text-align:center;
 6:        background:#000088;color:#ffff00">
 7:   Digits of <span style="font-family:symbol;font-size:32pt">p
 8:   </span>and Blowfish constants<br />
 9:   <img alt="pic" src="line1.gif" height="7" width="620" /><br />
10:
11: <table style="font-size:18pt" align="center" width="600">
12: <tr><td>Finding The Fractional Digits of <span style=
13:         "font-family:symbol;font-size:32pt">p</span> (Hex)</td><tr>
14: <tr><td>
15:   <table style="font-size:18pt" align="center" width="570">
16:   <tr><td width="100"><input type="button" class="butSt"
17:          style="width:80px" value="OK" onclick="pi_fun()" /></td>
18:     <td width="80">Digits [</td>
19:     <td width="140"><input type="text" class="butSt"
            style="width:140px"
20:          maxlength="4" value="0" id="d0" name="d0" /></td>
21:     <td width="40" > ] = </td>
22:     <td colspan="3" style="text-align:left">
23:       <input type="text" size="120" maxlength="20" readonly
24:         style="font-size:16pt;width:60px;height:35px;
25:         font-weight:bold;background:#dddddd;
            color:#ff0000" value="0" id="d1" /></td></tr>
26:   </table></td></tr>
27: <tr><td><br />Finding The Blowfish Constants</td><tr>
28: <tr><td>
29:   <table style="font-size:18pt" align="center" width="570">
30:   <tr><td width="100"><input type="button" onclick="bp_fun()"
31:          class="butSt" style="width:80px" value="OK" /></td>
32:     <td width="30">P [</td>
```

```
33:    <td width="40"><input type="text" class="butSt"
34:        style="width:40px" maxlength="2" value="0"
            id="bp0" /></td>
35:    <td width="100" > ] = </td>
36:    <td colspan="3" style="text-align:left">
37:      <input type="text" size="120" maxlength="20"
          style="font-size:16pt;
38:        width:220px;height:35px;
          font-weight:bold;background:#dddddd;color:
39:        #ff0000" value="00000000" readonly id="bp1" /></td></tr>
40:  </table></td></tr>
41: <tr><td>
42: <table style="font-size:18pt" align="center" width="570">
43:  <tr>
44:    <td width="100"><input type="button" class="butSt"
        style="width:80px"
45:                    value="OK" onclick="bs_fun()" /></td>
46:    <td width="30">S [</td>
47:    <td width="30"><input type="text" class="butSt"
        style="width:30px"
48:                    maxlength="1" value="0" id="bs0" /></td>
49:    <td width="20" > ][</td>
50:    <td width="50"><input type="text" class="butSt"
        style="width:50px"
51:                    maxlength="3" value="0" id="bs1" /></td>
52:    <td width="30" > ] = </td>
53:    <td colspan="3" style="text-align:left">
54:      <input type="text" size="120" maxlength="20"
          style="font-size:16pt;
55:        width:220px;height:35px;
          font-weight:bold;background:#dddddd;color:
56:        #ff0000" value="00000000" readonly id="bs2" /></td></tr>
57:  </table></td></tr>
58: </table>
```

This page fragment contains three sections and computes any digit of π, p[] and S-box values for the Blowfish scheme. The first section in lines 15–25 gets the digit of π from the user. When the user inputs a value in the text box in lines 19–20 and clicks the OK button (lines 16–17), the corresponding digit of π is calculated by the function pi_fun() and will appear in the text box defined in lines 23–25.

The second and third sections defined in lines 29–40 and 42–57 are used to compute the Blowfish constants P[] and S[][] respectively. When the user inputs a value in the text box in lines 33–34 and clicks the OK button (lines 30–31), the corresponding Blowfish constant of P[] is calculated by the function bp_fun() and displayed in the text box in lines 37–39. Similarly, when the values for S-boxes S[][] are input in lines 47–48 and 50–51, the function bs_fun() is used to compute the S-box constant and display it on the screen.

The three functions pi_fun(), bp_fun() and bs_fun() are defined in part II of ex06-03.htm.

```
Example: Continuation of ex06-03.htm                    (Part II)

59: <script src="ex06-03.js"></script>
60: <script>
61: function pi_fun()
62: {
63:    var D0;
64:    D0 = parseInt(document.getElementById("d0").value,10);
65:    document.getElementById("d1").value = getPiDigit(D0);
66: }
67: function bp_fun()
68: {
69:    var D0;
70:    D0 = parseInt(document.getElementById("bp0").value,10);
71:    document.getElementById("bp1").value = FindP(D0);
72: }
73: function bs_fun()
74: {
75:    var D0,D1
76:    D0 = parseInt(document.getElementById("bs0").value,10);
77:    D1 = parseInt(document.getElementById("bs1").value,10);
78:    document.getElementById("bs2").value = FindSBox(D0,D1);
79: }
80: </script>
81: </body>
```

This page fragment contains three simple functions. The first, pi_fun(), computes any digit of π. When the function is called, it will capture the user input value from the statement in line 64. Since the user input value is a string, the function parseInt() will convert it to an integer D0. This D0 is input to the function getPiDigit() in line 65 to compute the digit and display it in the text box identified by the identity id="d1". The second function, bp_fun(), uses the function FindP() in line 71 to calculate the constant in the subkey array P[]. The third function, bs_fun(), in lines 73–79 captures the S-box positions from Web page to variables D0 and D1. These two variables are input to the function FindSBox() in line 78 to find the S-box value. Screenshots of this example are shown in Figures 6.9 and 6.10.

Fig. 6.9   Script `ex06-03.htm`

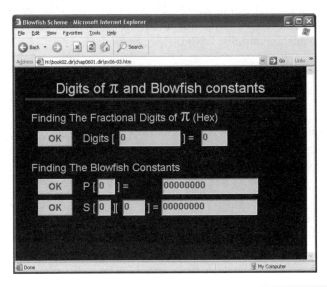

Fig. 6.10   Finding any digit of π

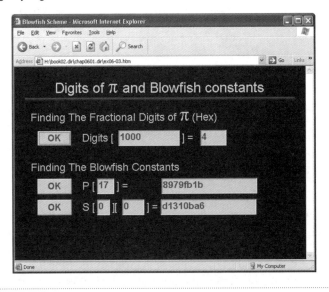

Now we understand how the Blowfish scheme works, let's consider another fully parameterized encryption/decryption scheme known as RC6.

6.3   A fully parameterized block cipher: RC6

6.3.1   The RC6-/w/r/b algorithm

RC6 is another well-known algorithm from Ron Rivest in the crypto-community.
The algorithm was designed in 1998 in response to the AES competition and was
one of the strongest candidates for the AES standard. It is the successor to RC5.
Following the traditions of the RC family of ciphers, the RC6 algorithm is simple,
easy to implement, and has exceptionally high security strength. Many people like
Ron's codes for these reasons.

RC6 is, in fact, not a single cipher. The fully parameterized feature forms a family
of ciphers. RC6 can be characterized by the following three parameters:

- w – the number of bits used in a word;

- r – the number of rounds;

- b – the key length measure in bytes.

By changing these values, different ciphers or versions are obtained. For example,
a typical implementation of RC6 is RC6-/32/20/b meaning that the cipher uses
32-bit words, 20 rounds and can have a variable key length up to 256 bytes
($0 \leq b \leq 255$).

Like many block ciphers, the RC6 algorithm is described by three processes,
namely key schedule, encryption and decryption. The key schedule process,
basically, is to use the user input key to set up a number of subkeys for encryption
and decryption. For RC6, the input key is b bytes and used to generate $2r + 4$ words
stored in array `S[0],...,S[2r+3]`. The subkeys `S[]` are used to encrypt/decrypt
messages.

The RC6-/w/r/b encryption process

RC6 operates with four w-bit words called A, B, C and D containing the plaintext
input. The ciphertext output is also stored in the same four words. The encryption
process is described by the pseudo-code in `ex06-06.txt`.

The entire encryption process can be described by just 15 lines of pseudo-code. The
symbol '<<<-' is the left rotation. The `lgw` is the value of $\log_2 w$. When `w = 32` (or 2^5),
the value of `lgw` is 5. A graphical representation of the RC6 process is presented in
Figure 6.11.

As you can see from `ex06-06.txt` and Figure 6.11, the structure of RC6 encryption
involves only simple operations. The ciphertext block is stored back in A, B, C and D.

Fig. 6.11 The RC6 process

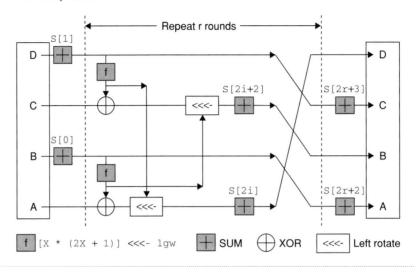

f $[X * (2X + 1)]$ <<<- lgw   ⊞ SUM   ⊕ XOR   [<<<-] Left rotate

---

Example: ex06-06.txt – The RC6-/w/r/b encryption process

```
 1: Input: A, B, C, D :- w-bit words stored the plaintext/ciphertext block
 2:        S[0], ..., S[2r+3] :- array stores the subkeys
 3:
 4: Procedure:
 5:        B = B + S[0];
 6:        D = D + S[1];
 7:        for (i=1; i<=r; r++) do
 8:              t = (B * (2*B+1)) <<<- lgw;
 9:              u = (D * (2*D+1)) <<<- lgw;
10:              A = ((A ^ t) <<<- u) + S[2*i];
11:              C = ((C ^ u) <<<- t) + S[2*i+1];
12:              (A,B,C,D) = (B,C,D,A)
13:        end-for
14:        A = A + S[2*r+2];
15:        C = C + S[2*r+3];
```

The RC6-/w/r/b decryption process

The RC6 decryption process also operates with four w-bit words A, B, C and D. Together with the subkeys S[0],...,S[2r+3], the process can be described by the pseudo-code listed in ex06-07.txt.

```
Example: ex06-07.txt - The RC6-/w/r/b decryption process

 1: Input: A, B, C, D :- w-bit words store the ciphertext/plaintext block
 2:        S[0], ..., S[2r+3] :- array stores the subkeys
 3:
 4: Procedure:
 5:        C = C - S[2r+3];
 6:        A = A - S[2r+2];
 7:        for (i=r; i>=1; r--) do
 8:            (A,B,C,D) = (D,A,B,C)
 9:            u = (D * (2*D+1) <<<- lgw;
10:            t = (B * (2*B+1) <<<- lgw;
11:            C = ((C - S[2i+1]) ->>> t) ^ u ;
12:            A = ((A - S[2i]) ->>> u) ^ t;
13:        end-for
14:        D = D - S[1];
15:        B = B - S[0];
```

As you can see, the decryption process is also simple. The only new operation here is the symbol '->>>' representing the right rotation. After decryption, the plaintext block is stored in A, B, C and D.

Key schedule process

Compared to many other ciphers, the key schedule of RC6 is not complicated. In fact, it is the same as RC5. Given a b-byte key string supplied by the user, this process sets up 2r + 4 subkeys stored in array S[].

First, the b-byte key is preloaded into a w-bit array called L[0],...,L[c-1]. The first byte of the key is stored as the low-order byte of L[0]. For a 32-bit implementation, each element of L[] can store four bytes. The last element L[c-1] is padded with zeros to make it w-bit if necessary.

Together with two magic numbers P and Q, the key schedule can be described by the pseudo-code listed in ex06-08.txt.

As you can see, the key schedule process involves only simple operations and is easy to implement. The for-loop in lines 6–8 initializes the subkey array S[]. The for-loop in lines 12–17 populates the subkeys in S[]. This key schedule process is the same as that for RC5 proposed in the mid 1990s and no security flaw was found. In fact, there is no known efficient attack on either RC5 or RC6, and both are considered to be secure. The magic numbers P and Q used in the scheme depend on the w-bit. For 32-bit implementation, the values are P_{32}=0xb7e15163 and Q_{32}=0x9e3779b9. The values are in hexadecimal format with eight digits forming a 32-bit value each. These magic numbers, and how to generate them for different w bits, will be discussed in Section 6.3.4. Now, let's develop a page for RC6 encryption/decryption.

6.3.2   A Web page for RC6 encryption/decryption

The most popular and typical implementation of RC6 is RC6-/32/20/b. Using 32-bit words, the scheme is suitable for most applications on 32-bit machines, such as PCs. Consider the script ex06-04.js.

```
 6: var oBytes = oBits/8;
 7: var R24 = 2* rounds +4;
 8: var lgw = 5;
 9:
10: function bit32_add(x, y)
11: {
12:   var low = (x & 0xffff) + (y & 0xffff);
13:   var hig = (x >>> 16) + (y >>> 16) + (low >>> 16);
14:   return (hig << 16) | (low & 0xffff);
15: }
16:
17: function bit32_mult(a,b)
18: {
19:   var tmp1,tmp2;
20:
21:   tmp1 = b >>> 16;
22:   tmp2 = (a * tmp1 << 16) & 0xffffffff;
23:   tmp2 += a * (b & 0xffff);
24:   tmp2 = tmp2 & 0xffffffff;
25:   return (tmp2);
26: }
27:
28: function ROTL(x,y) {
29:  return (((x)<<(y&(oBits-1))) |
30:          ((x)>>>(oBits-(y&(oBits-1))))) & 0xffffffff;
31: }
32:
33: function ROTR(x,y) {
34:  return (((x)>>>(y&(oBits-1)))|
35:          ((x)<<(oBits-(y&(oBits-1))))) & 0xffffffff;
36: }
37:
```

This script contains global variables and some functions used by the RC6 scheme. Lines 1–2 define the rounds and bits of the RC6 implementation. It is 32-bit and uses 20 rounds of RC6. The magic numbers are specified in lines 3–4. Based on this information, the number of bytes in a word is oBytes=4. The number of subkeys is R24 = (2*rounds + 4), and the 2 to the power of w-bits $lg_2w=5$ are defined. After the global variables, the functions bit32_add() and bit32_mult() follow for 32-bit additions and multiplications. For example, the function bit32_add(x,y) adds x and y modulo 2^{32}. The left and right rotation instructions are given in lines 28–36. The rotation functions depend on the w-bit of the algorithm. The key schedule process is given in part II of ex06-04.js.

```
38: var S = new Array(R24-1);
39: function rc6_key_setup(inK,b)
40: {
41:   var i, j, s, v, tmp1, tmp2;
42:   var A, B, c;
43:   var oC = Math.floor((32 +oBytes-1)/oBytes);
44:   var L = new Array(oC);
45:
46:   for(i=0;i<R24;i++) S[i] = 0;
47:   for(i=0;i<oC;i++) L[i] = 0;
48:
49:   c = Math.floor((b + oBytes -1)/oBytes);
50:   L[c - 1] = 0;
51:   for (i = b - 1; i >= 0; i--) {
52:      tmp1 = Math.floor(i/oBytes);
53:      tmp2 = (L[tmp1] << 8);
54:      L[tmp1] = bit32_add(tmp2,inK[i]);
55:   }
56:   S[0] = P32;
57:   for (i=1; i<=(2*rounds +3);i++) S[i]=S[i-1] + Q32;
58:
59:   A = B = i = j = 0; v = R24;
60:   if (c > v) v = c;
61:   v *= 3;
62:   for (s = 1; s <= v; s++) {
63:      tmp1 = bit32_add(bit32_add(A,B),S[i]);
64:      tmp2 = ROTL(tmp1,3);
65:      A = tmp2;
66:      S[i] = tmp2;
67:      tmp1 = bit32_add(A,B);
68:      tmp2 = bit32_add(L[j],tmp1);
69:      B = ROTL(tmp2,tmp1);
70:      L[j] = B;
71:      i = (i + 1) % R24;
72:      j = (j + 1) % c;
73:   }
74: }
75:
```

This script fragment contains one function `rc6_key_setup()` with two parameters `inK` and `b`. Variable `inK` is an array containing the byte string of the input key and `b` is the key length. This function is used to set up all the subkeys for the scheme.

After the initialization codes in lines 46–47, the input key `inK` is preloaded into the array `L[]` by the statements in lines 49–55. For a 32-bit implementation, the number of bytes in a word is `oByte = 4`. Lines 52–54 load every four bytes of the key into one element of `L[]`. Lines 56–57 initialize the subkey array `S[]` with the magic numbers P_{32} and Q_{32}. Lines 59–73 populate the subkeys following line-by-line translation of the pseudo-code in `ex06-08.txt`. The encryption/decryption processes are listed in part III of `ex06-04.js`.

```
Example: Continuation of ex06-04.js                        (Part III)

76: function rc6_block_encrypt(ppt)
77: {
78:     var A, B, C, D, t, u, x;
79:     var i, j, tmp1=0;
80:
81:     A = ppt[0]; B = ppt[1]; C = ppt[2]; D = ppt[3];
82:     B += S[0]; D += S[1];
83:     for (i = 2; i <= (2 * rounds); i += 2)
84:     {
85:         tmp1 = bit32_mult(B, bit32_add(bit32_mult(2,B),1));
86:         t = ROTL(tmp1,5);
87:         tmp1= bit32_mult(D, bit32_add(bit32_mult(2,D),1));
88:         u = ROTL(tmp1,5);
89:         tmp1 = ROTL((A ^ t), u);
90:         A = bit32_add(tmp1, S[i]);
91:         tmp1 = ROTL((C ^ u), t);
92:         C = bit32_add(tmp1, S[i + 1]);
93:         x = A; A = B; B = C; C = D; D = x;
94:     }
95:     A= bit32_add(A, S[2 * 20 + 2]);
96:     C= bit32_add(C, S[2 * 20 + 3]);
97:     return Array(A,B,C,D);
98: }
99:
100: function rc6_block_decrypt(cct)
101: {
102:     var A, B, C, D, t, u, x;
103:     var i, j, tmp1;
104:
105:     A = cct[0]; B = cct[1]; C = cct[2]; D = cct[3];
106:     C -= S[(2* rounds) + 3];
107:     A -= S[(2* rounds) + 2];
108:     for (i = 2 * rounds; i >= 2; i -= 2)
```

```
109:    {
110:        x = D; D = C; C = B; B = A; A = x;
111:        tmp1 = bit32_mult(D,bit32_add(1,bit32_mult(2,D)));
112:        u = ROTL(tmp1,5);
113:        tmp1 = bit32_mult(B,bit32_add(1,bit32_mult(2,B)));
114:        t = ROTL(tmp1,5);
115:        C = ROTR(C - S[i + 1], t) ^ u;
116:        A = ROTR(A - S[i], u) ^ t;
117:    }
118:    D -= S[1]; B -= S[0];
119:    return Array(A,B,C,D);
120: }
121:
```

The first function in this script is `rc6_block_encrypt()`. This function takes an array of four elements `ppt[]` as an input block of the message and encrypts it. First, the elements of `ppt[]` are copied to variables A, B, C and D in line 81. Once the values of A, B, C, D and subkeys S[] are available, the encryption operations are carried out by statements in lines 83–97 according to the pseudo-code in `ex06-06.txt`. Note that we have replaced the addition and multiplication with the corresponding 32-bit functions. After the encryption, the results are stored in A, B, C and D and returned as an array by line 97. Similarly, the decryption function `rc6_block_decrypt()` in lines 100–120 takes the message block array `cct[]` and decrypts it. The decrypted results are stored in variables A, B, C, and D and returned as an array by line 119.

In order to use this script effectively, some interface functions are defined in part IV of `ex06-04.js`.

Example: Continuation of ex06-04.js (Part IV)

```
122: function keyStToSubkeys(inKeySt)
123: {
124:    var i, rKeyArr = new Array();
125:    var len = inKeySt.length;
126:    for (i=0; i<len; i++) rKeyArr[i] = inKeySt.charCodeAt(i);
127:    rc6_key_setup(rKeyArr, len);
128: }
129:
130: function rc6(keySt, msgSt, encrypt)
131: {
132:    var m=0, chunk=0, len = msgSt.length;
133:    var i, tResult="", result="";
```

```
134:    var lrArr=new Array(4);
135:
136:    keyStToSubkeys(keySt);
137:    while (m < len) {
138:     lrArr[0]= (msgSt.charCodeAt(m++) << 24)|
                   (msgSt.charCodeAt(m++) << 16)|
139:               (msgSt.charCodeAt(m++) << 8) |
                    msgSt.charCodeAt(m++);
140:     lrArr[1]= (msgSt.charCodeAt(m++) << 24)|
                   (msgSt.charCodeAt(m++) << 16)|
141:               (msgSt.charCodeAt(m++) << 8) |
                    msgSt.charCodeAt(m++);
142:     lrArr[2]= (msgSt.charCodeAt(m++) << 24)|
                   (msgSt.charCodeAt(m++) << 16)|
143:               (msgSt.charCodeAt(m++) << 8) |
                    msgSt.charCodeAt(m++);
144:     lrArr[3]= (msgSt.charCodeAt(m++) << 24)|
                   (msgSt.charCodeAt(m++) << 16)|
145:               (msgSt.charCodeAt(m++) << 8) |
                    msgSt.charCodeAt(m++);
146:
147:    if (encrypt) {
148:         lrArr = rc6_block_encrypt(lrArr);
149:    } else {
150:         lrArr = rc6_block_decrypt(lrArr);
151:    }
152:    tempSt= String.fromCharCode(
153:      ((lrArr[0] >>> 24) & 0xff), ((lrArr[0] >>> 16) & 0xff),
154:      ((lrArr[0] >>>  8) & 0xff), ( lrArr[0]          & 0xff),
155:      ((lrArr[1] >>> 24) & 0xff), ((lrArr[1] >>> 16) & 0xff),
156:      ((lrArr[1] >>>  8) & 0xff), ( lrArr[1]          & 0xff),
157:      ((lrArr[2] >>> 24) & 0xff), ((lrArr[2] >>> 16) & 0xff),
158:      ((lrArr[2] >>>  8) & 0xff), ( lrArr[2]          & 0xff),
159:      ((lrArr[3] >>> 24) & 0xff), ((lrArr[3] >>> 16) & 0xff),
160:      ((lrArr[3] >>>  8) & 0xff), ( lrArr[3]          & 0xff));
161:
162:    tResult += tempSt; chunk += 16;
163:    if (chunk == 512) {
164:       result += tResult; tResult = ""; chunk = 0;
165:     }
166:   }
167:   return result + tResult;
168: }
```

This part of the script contains two simple interface functions to perform RC6 encryption/decryption. They are similar to those developed in previous sections. The first function keyStToSubkeys() converts the input key string into an array of bytes (line 126). Together with the key length len, the function rc6_key_setup() is called in line 127 to set up all the subkeys.

The main interface function rc6() is defined in lines 130–168. The three parameters of this function are the key string keySt, the message string msgSt, and a boolean type variable encrypt. The keySt and msgSt are captured from the associated Web page. The status (true or false) of the variable encrypt determines whether encryption or decryption is executed. First, an array of four elements lrArr[] is declared in 134. It is used to pass the message block to the encryption/decryption engine and store the result back. After the input key keySt is passed to the function keyStToSubkeys() in line 136 to set up all the subkeys, 16 bytes of the message string msgSt are extracted to populate the four elements in array lrArr[]. Note that each element of lrArr[] is a 32-bit value and can store four bytes. When the value of encrypt is true, the function call in line 148

```
lrArr = rc6_block_encrypt(lrArr);
```

is executed to encrypt the message lrArr. When the decryption operation is true, the statement in line 150 will be run instead to decrypt the message. In both cases, the result is in lrArr[]. The single statement in lines 152–160 converts the array lrArr[] into a string tempSt. This string is collected into a large string variable tResult and later returned to the Web page for display purposes.

To test this script, a Web page is required. One simple way to generate such a page is to make a copy of ex06-01.htm and call it ex06-04.htm. Modify the following lines in this new page:

```
 9: RC6 Encryption/Decryption<br />
31: class="butSt" style="width:180px" value="OK" onclick="rc6_fun()" />
44: function rc6_fun()
52:    llst = byteStToHex(rc6(key, message,true))
58:    llst = rc6(key, message,false)
```

As you can see, only five lines need to change. The first line will display the message that we are working with the RC6 scheme. When the OK button is clicked, the function rc6_fun() is called. In line 44, the function rc6_fun() is declared. When encryption is needed, the statement in line 52 calls function rc6() with a true parameter at the end so that encryption is performed. When encryption is false, the statement in line 58 will be executed. Screenshots of this example are shown in Figures 6.12 and 6.13.

Now we have a page for the RC6 scheme. Let's compare some of the standard results and build a utility to work with files.

Fig. 6.12 RC6 encryption

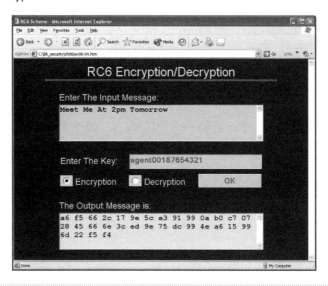

Fig. 6.13 RC6 decryption

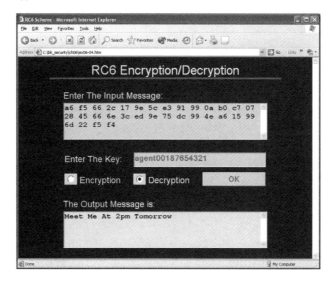

6.3.3 Testing vectors and building a utility

To test our implementation and compare it with others, the following six test vectors are provided.

```
1:  k(16) = {0x00, 0x00, 0x00, 0x00, 0x00, 0x00, 0x00, 0x00,
                   0x00, 0x00, 0x00, 0x00, 0x00, 0x00, 0x00, 0x00}
     p =    {0x00000000, 0x00000000, 0x00000000, 0x00000000}
     c =    {0x36a5c38f, 0x78f7b156, 0x4edf29c1, 0x1ea44898}

2:  k(16) = {0x01, 0x23, 0x45, 0x67, 0x89, 0xab, 0xcd, 0xef,
                   0x01, 0x12, 0x23, 0x34, 0x45, 0x56, 0x67, 0x78}
     p =    {0x35241302, 0x79685746, 0xbdac9b8a, 0xf1e0dfce}
     c =    {0x2f194e52, 0x23c61547, 0x36f6511f, 0x183fa47e}

3:  k(24) = {0x00, 0x00, 0x00, 0x00, 0x00, 0x00, 0x00, 0x00,
                   0x00, 0x00, 0x00, 0x00, 0x00, 0x00, 0x00, 0x00,
                   0x00, 0x00, 0x00, 0x00, 0x00, 0x00, 0x00, 0x00}
     p =    {0x00000000, 0x00000000, 0x00000000, 0x00000000}
     c =    {0xcb1bd66c, 0x38300b19, 0x163f8a4e, 0x82ae9086}

4:  k(24) = {0x01, 0x23, 0x45, 0x67, 0x89, 0xab, 0xcd, 0xef,
                   0x01, 0x12, 0x23, 0x34, 0x45, 0x56, 0x67, 0x78,
                   0x89, 0x9a, 0xab, 0xbc, 0xcd, 0xde, 0xef, 0xf0}
     p =    {0x35241302, 0x79685746, 0xbdac9b8a, 0xf1e0dfce}
     c =    {0xd0298368, 0x0405e519, 0x2ae9521e, 0xd49152f9}

5:  k(32) = {0x00, 0x00, 0x00, 0x00, 0x00, 0x00, 0x00, 0x00,
                   0x00, 0x00, 0x00, 0x00, 0x00, 0x00, 0x00, 0x00,
                   0x00, 0x00, 0x00, 0x00, 0x00, 0x00, 0x00, 0x00,
                   0x00, 0x00, 0x00, 0x00, 0x00, 0x00, 0x00, 0x00},
     p =    {0x00000000, 0x00000000, 0x00000000, 0x00000000}
     c =    {0x05bd5f8f, 0xa85fd110, 0xda3ffa93, 0xc27e856e}

6:  k(32) = {0x01, 0x23, 0x45, 0x67, 0x89, 0xab, 0xcd, 0xef,
                   0x01, 0x12, 0x23, 0x34, 0x45, 0x56, 0x67, 0x78,
                   0x89, 0x9a, 0xab, 0xbc, 0xcd, 0xde, 0xef, 0xf0,
                   0x10, 0x32, 0x54, 0x76, 0x98, 0xba, 0xdc, 0xfe}
     p =    {0x35241302, 0x79685746, 0xbdac9b8a, 0xf1e0dfce}
     c =    {0x161824c8, 0x89e4d7f0, 0xa116ad20, 0x485d4e67}
```

Consider the first vector. The key k(16) consists of 16 bytes and all of them are zero. The plaintext p is a block of four 32-bit words; each of them is zero. The ciphertext c is listed after the plaintext. Since all these test vectors are in hexadecimal format, a page that can read hexadecimal values is needed. To develop such a page is easy. A quick way is to copy ex06-02.htm and call it ex06-05.htm and then modify the following lines:

```
 9:  RC6 Encryption/Decryption (Hex Input)<br />
31:  class="butSt" style="width:180px" value="OK"
     onclick="rc6_hex_fun()" />
41:  <script src="ex06-04.js"></script>
44:  function rc6_hex_fun()
52:      llst = byteStToHex(rc6(key, message,true));
59:      llst = byteStToHex(rc6(key, message,false));
63: var kSt="01 23 45 67 89 ab cd ef 01 12 23 34 45 56 67 78";
64: var pSt="35 24 13 02 79 68 57 46 bd ac 9b 8a f1 e0 df ce";
```

Line 9 is to change the display. Line 41 is to include the RC6 script file `ex06-04.js` so that RC6 functions are available. When the OK button is clicked, the statement in line 31 calls the new function `rc6_hex_fun()`. Inside this function, all you need do is change the function to `rc6()` as highlighted. Finally, a default test vector is declared in lines 63–64. Screenshots are shown in Figures 6.14 and 6.15.

As you can see, the ciphertext is the same as the ciphertext in test vector 2 above.

To develop an RC6 utility to work with files, a public domain program in C language is considered. This program is called `rc6.c` and was developed by Salvo Salasio. A copy of this program can be found and downloaded from a number of search engines or the site accompanying this book. There is a main function 'int main()' in this program to test the result. In order to develop a program driver consistent with all our previous examples, we rename the 'int main()' to 'int main00()' so that only the RC6 functions inside will be called and run. Our driver program is very similar to the Blowfish case in Section 6.2.2. Make

Fig. 6.14 RC6 encryption (hex)

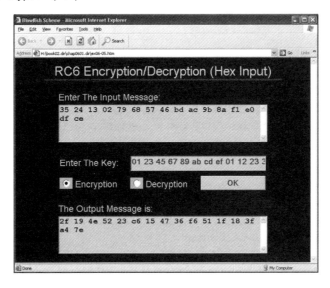

Fig. 6.15 RC6 decryption (hex)

a copy of `blowfishdriver.c` and call it `rc6driver.c`. In this new C program, make the following changes:

```
 2: #include "rc6.c"
23: /** delete this line **/
30:   printf("\nUsage: rc6driver (e)|(d) <infile> <outfile> <keyfile>\n");
43:   rc6_key_setup(kkey1, n);
55:   while ((n=fread(buf,1,16,inP)) >0) {
56:       if (n < 16) {
57:           for(i=n;i<16;i++) buf[i]=0;
58:       }
59:       GET_UINT32( X[0], buf, 0 ); GET_UINT32( X[1], buf, 4 );
60:       GET_UINT32( X[2], buf, 8 ); GET_UINT32( X[3], buf, 12 );
61:       rc6_block_encrypt(X, Y);
62:       PUT_UINT32(Y[0],buf,0); PUT_UINT32(Y[1],buf,4);
63:       PUT_UINT32(Y[2],buf,8); PUT_UINT32(Y[3],buf,12);
71:   while ((n=fread(buf,1,16,inP)) >0) {
72:       if (n < 16) {
73:           for(i=n;i<16;i++) buf[i]=0;
74:       }
75:       GET_UINT32( X[0], buf, 0 ); GET_UINT32( X[1], buf, 4 );
76:       GET_UINT32( X[2], buf, 8 ); GET_UINT32( X[3], buf, 12 );
77:       rc6_block_decrypt(X, Y);
78:       PUT_UINT32(Y[0],buf,0); PUT_UINT32(Y[1],buf,4);
79:       PUT_UINT32(Y[2],buf,8); PUT_UINT32(Y[3],buf,12);
```

Fig. 6.16 RC6 driver program

```
H:\ch06>gcc -o rc6driver rc6driver.c
H:\ch06>rc6driver
Usage:
 rc6driver (e)|(d) <infile> <outfile> <keyfile>

H:\ch06>rc6driver e zplain.txt zen.txt zkey.txt
H:\ch06>rc6driver d zen.txt zde.txt zkey.txt

H:\ch06>type zde.txt
Meet Me At 2pm Tomorrow

H:\ch06>tohex zen.txt

a6 f5 66 2c 17 9e 5c e3 91 99 0a b0 c7 07 28 45
66 6e 3c ed 9e 75 dc 99 4e a6 15 99 6d 22 f5 f4

H:\ch06>
```

Line 2 includes the rc6.c file into the program. Since there is no structure used in the program, the contents of line 23 are deleted. Line 30 changes the display. The function in line 43 sets up all the RC6 subkeys. The changes in the while-loop in lines 55–58 are to make sure that 16 bytes are read at any one time. The statements in lines 59–60 convert the 16 bytes into a 32-bit word and input it into the encryption engine in line 61. The encrypted block is stored in a 32-bit word Y. This Y is converted back to bytes by lines 62–63. The remaining code is for the decryption process and is similar to encryption. The while-loop in lines 71–74 read 16 bytes and then input it to the decryption function in line 77. The result in Y is converted back to bytes by lines 78–79. The final result are saved in the outfile. An operation process is captured and shown in Figure 6.16.

As you can see, the ciphertext is the same as in ex06-04.htm. RC6 is fast: for example, a 5 MB file in Acrobat pdf format can be encrypted and decrypted by a low-end portable PC (2.0 GHZ) in less than half a second.

6.3.4 The magic numbers of RC6

When working with ciphers, you will often come across some strange numbers in the initialization process. Have you ever asked yourself what are they and how they are used? Can we use other numbers, or can we use numbers or set-up process from other ciphers? It is believed that the first step in understanding the mind of cipher designers is to understand why they select these 'magic' numbers. In many cases, the magic numbers can be changed. In fact, if you change the numbers or the initialization process, you may well create a proprietary implementation of the ciphers and cause a major headache for many crypto-experts. For example,

Blowfish uses more than 8000 digits of π to set up the subkeys. Have you tried to use other constants, such as the fractional part of e = 2.71828 . . . (the base of natural logs), as the starting values for the Blowfish scheme?

In the main script `ex06-04.js` of RC6, two magic constants are used. They are declared in lines 3–4 in the script:

```
3: var P32 = 0xB7E15163;   4: var Q32 = 0x9E3779B9;
```

The constant `P32` is, in fact, the fractional part of e = 2.718 . . . In this case, only eight hexadecimal digits (32-bit) are selected since the implementation is 32-bit. For w-bit implementation, w bits should be used. The value of `Q32` comes from the fractional part of the 'golden ratio'. These two important mathematical constants have many properties and are used in many applications. They have the simple formulas below:

$$P = e = \sum_{n=0}^{\infty} \frac{1}{n!} \qquad Q = \tfrac{1}{2}(\sqrt{5} + 1)$$

There are a large number of methods and algorithms for generating the values of these two constants. Many of them produce millions of digits. For the first 60 fractional digits, in decimal format, the values are

P_d = 2.7182818284 5904523536 0287471352 6624977572 4709369995 9574966967
Q_d = 1.6180339887 4989484820 4586834365 6381177203 0917980576 2862135448

In Section 6.2.3, we briefly discussed how to convert the fractional part of a number into hexadecimal format. Basically, given a fractional number x, the algorithm is divided into three steps.

Step 1 $x = x * 16$

Step 2   int(x) $\rightarrow$ Convert to hexadecimal and output

Step 3 x = fract(x) $\rightarrow$ Go back to step 1

For each round, the x in step 1 is multiplied by 16. The integer part of x, i.e. int(x), is converted to a hexadecimal value and output as the digit required (step 2). The fractional part of x, i.e. fract(x), is used to continue the process to obtain the next digit.

Using this algorithm to handle big numbers is not difficult. All you need to do is handle a big number part by part, just like a message. For example, the fractional part can be represented by a character string. Now, let's develop a Web page to do the conversion.

For a stable calculation, avoiding rounding errors of floating point numbers, integer operations are used. Note that integer arithmetic, computing and high precision calculations are subjects beyond the scope of this section. For obvious reasons, only a demonstration program is presented here. Consider script `ex06-06.js`.

Example: ex06-06.js - Fraction decimal to hexadecimal conversion

```
1: var maxD=100;
2: function fractToHex(noHexSt,digitSt)
3: {
4:  var a = new Array(maxD);
5:  var i=0, j=0, m=0;    len =0,   di=0;
6:  var tmp1=0,   tmp2=0, retSt="", runFlag = 1;
7:  var cSt="0123456789abcdef";
8:
9:  for(j=0;j<maxD;j++) a[j]=0;
10:
11:  digitSt += "00000";
12:  len = digitSt.length;
13:  di = parseInt(noHexSt,10);
14:  if (di > maxD ) {
15:    retSt="Error... Max Digit is " + maxD;
16:    runFlag=0;
17:  }
18:  while (i+5 < len){
19:    a[m++] = parseInt(digitSt.substring(i,i+5),10);
20:    i += 5;
21:  }
22:
23:  if (runFlag ==1) {
24:    for (k=0;k< di ;k++)
25:    {
26:      for (i= maxD-1;i > 0;i--)
27:      {
28:        tmp1 = a[i] * 16 + tmp2;
29:        tmp2 = Math.floor(tmp1 * 0.00001);
30:        a[i] = tmp1 - tmp2*100000;
31:      }
32:      tmp1 = a[i] * 16 + tmp2;
33:      tmp2 = Math.floor(tmp1 * 0.00001);
34:      a[i] = tmp1 - tmp2*100000;
35:      if (( tmp2 < 0) || (tmp2 > 15)) {
36:          retSt = "Execution Error...";
37:          break;
38:      }
39:      else retSt += cSt.substring(tmp2,tmp2+1);
40:    }
41:  }
42:  return retSt;
43: }
```

This script contains one function `fractToHex()` and can be used to convert a fractional number represented by a digit string called `digitSt` to hexadecimal digits. The number of digits required is also input as string `noHexSt`. As a demonstration program, the maximum number of digits that you can enter is 100, specified by the variable `maxD` in line 1. This number creates the array `a[]` of 100 elements in line 4.

Basically, the method employed by this script to handle a big number is that each element of `a[]` stores five digits from the input string as an integer. An array of 100 elements, such as `a[]`, can store a total of 500 digits. In each round, the entire array `a[]` is multiplied by 16. For element `a[99]` to `a[0]`, a value having more than five digits will be extracted and added to the previous element as a two digit number. Finally, the value more than five digits in `a[0]` is extracted and converted to a single hexadecimal value and output.

The input fraction string `msgSt` is padded with five zeros in line 11 so that at least five digits are stored in `a[]`. The length of the input string and the number of hexadecimal digits required are captured by lines 12–13. The while-loop in lines 18–21 divides the input string into five digits, and each is stored in `a[]` as an integer. By default, the function `parseInt()` will consider an integer as an octal number when the starting digit is zero. To avoid this confusion, the value 10 at the end of the `parseInt()` function is needed. If everything is OK, the double for-loop in lines 24–41 will compute the required rounds to generate the hexadecimal string. The operation is described in the previous paragraph. The extracted value from `a[0]` is converted to a hexadecimal digit by line 39 and added to the return string `retSt`. When all the digits are generated, `retSt` string is returned to the function caller.

To handle more input digits, you can change the variable `maxD` in line 1. You can also change how many digits of the input are stored in `a[]` as an integer. Note that when representing a fraction in hexadecimal format, you will usually get a repeated cycle of digits, for example:

```
0.1 (dec) = 0.1999999999... (hex)    0.6 (dec) = 0.9999999999... (hex)
0.2 (dec) = 0.3333333333... (hex)    0.7 (dec) = 0.b333333333... (hex)
0.3 (dec) = 0.4cccccccccc... (hex)    0.8 (dec) = 0.cccccccccc... (hex)
0.4 (dec) = 0.6666666666... (hex)    0.9 (dec) = 0.e666666666... (hex)
0.5 (dec) = 0.8            (hex)
```

To test the script, consider the body part of `ex06-06.htm`.

```
Example: ex06-06.htm - Fractional to hexadecimal digits

1:  <style>
2:    .butSt{font-size:16pt;width:250px;height:40px;
3:            font-weight:bold;background:#dddddd;color:#ff0000}
4:  </style>
```

```
 5: <body style="font-family:arial;font-size:26pt;text-align:center;
 6: background:#000088;color:#ffff00">
 7:  Fractional Digits To Hex Digits<br />
 8:  <img alt="pic" src="line1.gif" height="7" width="650" /><br />
 9:
10: <table style="font-size:18pt" align="center">
11:  <tr><td><br />Enter The Fractional Digits (dec): </td></tr>
12:  <tr><td><textarea style="font-size:16pt;width:570px;height:100px;
13:          font-weight:bold;background:#dddddd" rows="5" cols="40"
14:          id="in_mesg">141592653589793238462643383279
           </textarea></td></tr>
15: </table>
16: <form action="">
17: <table style="font-size:18pt" cellspacing="10" align="center">
18:  <tr><td>Number of Hex Digits Desired: </td>
19:      <td style="text-align:center" colspan=2>
20:        <input type="text" id="d_v" size="120" maxlength="2"
21:         style="font-size:16pt;width:60px;height:40px;
          font-weight:bold;
22:         background:#dddddd;color:#ff0000" value="8" /></td>
23:    <td style="width:180px;text-align:left"><input size="20"
                                                type="button"
24:  class="butSt" style="width:180px" value="OK"
     onclick="fractToHex_fun()" />
25: </td></tr>
26: </table>
27: </form>
28: <table style="font-size:18pt" align="center">
29:  <tr><td>The Hexadecimal Digits are: </td></tr>
30:  <tr><td><textarea rows="5" cols="40" id="out_mesg" readonly
31:          style="font-size:16pt;font-weight:bold;width:570px;
32:          height:100px;background:#aaffaa"></textarea></td></tr>
33: </table>
34: <script src="ex06-06.js"></script>
35: <script src="hexlib.js"></script>
36: <script>
37:  function fractToHex_fun()
38:  {
39:   var digSt="",message="",llst="";
40:   digSt = document.getElementById("d_v").value;
41:   message = document.getElementById("in_mesg").value;
42:   llst = fractToHex(digSt,message);
43:   document.getElementById("out_mesg").value = llst;
44:  }
45: </script>
46: </body>
```

This simple page contains two text areas, one text box and one OK button. The first text area in lines 12–14 will allow a user to enter the fractional digits represented as a string. The default value is some of the digits of π (line 14). The text box in lines 20–22 is restricted by `maxlength="2"` so that the maximum value that can be input is 99. When the `OK` button defined in lines 23–24 is clicked, the function `fractToHex_fun()` is activated. The result will be displayed in the `readonly` text area in lines 30–32. The function `fractToHex_fun()` is easy to read. First, the number of digits and fraction are captured by the statements in lines 40–41. The function `fractToHex()` in line 42 calculates all the hexadecimal digits in variable `llst`. This string is output by the statement in line 43. Screenshots are shown in Figures 6.17 and 6.18.

Fig. 6.17 RC6 magic number P (hex)

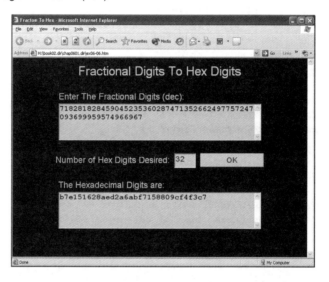

Fig. 6.18 RC6 magic number Q (hex)

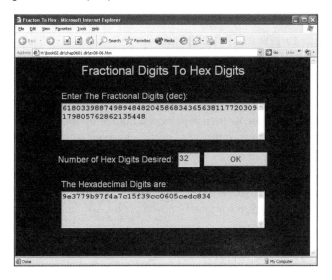

The 32-bit value of P_{32} is rounded up from the output shown in Figure 6.17.

We have studied and implemented a number of ciphers. That should give you confidence to handle one of the most important ciphers, called the 'Advanced Encryption Standard' (AES), promoted by the US government.

6.4 A step-by-step advanced encryption standard

6.4.1 From DES to the AES challenge

Following the request from NBS in 1973 for a data encryption technology, IBM submitted an algorithm that met all the criteria and became the Data Encryption Standard (DES) published as FIPS 46. Since the publication of FIPS 46 in 1977, DES has been used as the primary encryption technology for US government departments and many commercial sectors and has dominated the application side of cryptography.

Twenty years later, in January 1997, the National Institute of Standards and Technology of the US government published a request for attempts to be made to create a new encryption standard known as the Advanced Encryption Standard (AES).

One of the objectives of the AES challenge was to be able to protect sensitive government information in an unclassified manner well into the twenty-first century. Unlike DES, the winner of AES could be composed of more than one algorithm if necessary.

The requirement for an AES submission to meet the challenge was that it should be a symmetric-key block cipher and (at a minimum) support block sizes of 128-bits and key sizes of 128-, 192- and 256-bits. The minimum acceptance and evaluation criteria were:

- the algorithm and design of AES should be publicly defined;
- the key length of AES may be increased as needed;
- the algorithm can be implemented in both hardware and software;
- the specification of AES should either be freely available or available under terms consistent with the American National Standards Institute (ANSI) patent policy.

Algorithms which met the above requirements would be judged based on the following practical or implementation specifications:

- security (i.e. the effort required to crypto-analyze or crack the system);
- computational efficiency;
- memory requirements;
- hardware and software suitability;
- simplicity and flexibility;
- licensing requirements.

Unlike the DES challenge of more than 30 years ago, many algorithms were submitted for the AES competition. In August 1998, NIST announced a group of fifteen finalists. With help from cryptographers, computer security companies and universities around the world, five algorithms were selected for the final. They were:

- MARS (submitted by IBM Corp.);

- RC6 (submitted by RSA Laboratories);

- Rijndael (submitted by Joan Daemen and Vincent Rijmen);

- Serpent (submitted by Ross Anderson, Eli Biham and Lars Knudsen);

- Twofish (submitted by Bruce Schneier, John Kelsey, Doug Whiting, David Wagner, Chris Hall and Niels Ferguson).

After extensive testing, NIST announced in October 2000 that the winner was the Rijndael algorithm. Shortly after the announcement, a draft FIPS specification for the AES was published for review, comment and scrutiny by the public. The Rijndael algorithm became the new AES standard in November 2001 and was called FIPS 197. The following comments are an original quote from NIST's AES homepage.

> 'Rijndael appears to be consistently a very good performer in both hardware and software across a wide range of computing environments regardless of its use in feedback or non-feedback modes. Its key setup time is excellent, and its key agility is good. Rijndael's very low memory requirements make it very well suited for restricted-space environments, in which it also demonstrates excellent performance. Rijndael's operations are among the easiest to defend against power and timing attack . . .'.

Unlike many other block ciphers, the AES algorithm involves more mathematics and may need a stronger mathematical background for understanding. AES encryption and decryption will be discussed in the next section and a more detailed step-by-step demonstration is presented in Section 6.4.3. An optimized implementation is provided in Section 6.5.

6.4.2 The mathematics used by AES

The basic operational element of AES is the byte and each byte is eight bits. Unlike ordinary byte values, the bytes used by AES are represented by polynomials in the so-called Galois field (or finite field) $GF(2^8)$. In general, a byte with binary value $B = b_7 b_6 b_5 b_4 b_3 b_2 b_1 b_0$ in AES has the polynomial form

$$B = b_7 x^7 + b_6 x^6 + b_5 x^5 + b_4 x^4 + b_3 x^3 + b_2 x^2 + b_1 x + b_0$$

That is, the coefficients of the polynomial are the binary digits of the byte. For example, the hexadecimal value 57 has the binary representation

57 (hex) = 1010111 (binary)

This number in AES is represented by the polynomial

$$(1)x^6 + (1)x^4 + (1)x^2 + (1)x + 1$$

The addition of two elements in a finite field is carried out by adding the coefficients of the corresponding powers in the two polynomials. The addition is performed with modulo 2, which is equivalent to the XOR operation represented by the symbol $\oplus$. For example, the addition of 57 and 83 is

$$(x^6 + x^4 + x^2 + x + 1) + (x^7 + x + 1) = x^7 + x^6 + x^4 + x^2 \quad \text{(polynomial)}$$

$$\{01010111\} \oplus \{10000011\} = \{11010100\} \quad \text{(binary)}$$

$$57 \oplus 83 = d4 \quad \text{(hexadecimal)}$$

The multiplication of two polynomials in GF(2^8) is denoted by the symbol $\bullet$. For example the multiplication of 57 and 83 is

$$(x^6 + x^4 + x^2 + x + 1) \bullet (x^7 + x + 1) = x^{13} + x^{11} + x^9 + x^8 + x^7 + x^7 + x^5 + x^3$$
$$+ x^2 + x^7 + x^6 + x^4 + x^2 + x^1 + 1$$

$$= x^{13} + x^{11} + x^9 + x^8 + x^6 + x^5 + x^4 + x^3 + 1$$

In order to make the degree of polynomial less than 8, the multiplication result is modulo with an irreducible polynomial ($x^8 + x^4 + x^3 + x + 1$). We have

$$x^{13} + x^{11} + x^9 + x^8 + x^6 + x^5 + x^4 + x^3 + 1 \quad \text{mod} \quad (x^8 + x^4 + x^3 + x + 1)$$

$$= x^7 + x^6 + 1 = 011000001 \quad \text{(binary)} \quad = \quad c1 \quad \text{(hexadecimal)}$$

Unlike addition, there is no simple operation at the byte level that corresponds to this multiplication. For the AES algorithm this multiplication on the finite field GF(2^8) can be computed efficiently by Tables 6.1 and 6.2.

Table 6.1 L(x, y)

	0	1	2	3	4	5	6	7	8	9	a	b	c	d	e	f
0		00	19	01	32	02	1a	c6	4b	c7	1b	68	33	ee	df	03
1	64	04	e0	0e	34	8d	81	ef	4c	71	08	c8	f8	69	1c	c1
2	7d	c2	1d	b5	f9	b9	27	6a	4d	e4	a6	72	9a	c9	09	78
3	65	2f	8a	05	21	0f	e1	24	12	f0	82	45	35	93	da	8e
4	96	8f	db	bd	36	d0	ce	94	13	5c	d2	f1	40	46	83	38
5	66	dd	fd	30	bf	06	8b	62	b3	25	e2	98	22	88	91	10
6	7e	6e	48	c3	a3	b6	1e	42	3a	6b	28	54	fa	85	3d	ba
7	2b	79	0a	15	9b	9f	5e	ca	4e	d4	ac	e5	f3	73	a7	57
8	af	58	a8	50	f4	ea	d6	74	4f	ae	e9	d5	e7	e6	ad	e8
9	2c	d7	75	7a	eb	16	0b	f5	59	cb	5f	b0	9c	a9	51	a0
a	7f	0c	f6	6f	17	c4	49	ec	d8	43	1f	2d	a4	76	7b	b7
b	cc	bb	3e	5a	fb	60	b1	86	3b	52	a1	6c	aa	55	29	9d
c	97	b2	87	90	61	be	dc	fc	bc	95	cf	cd	37	3f	5b	d1
d	53	39	84	3c	41	a2	6d	47	14	2a	9e	5d	56	f2	d3	ab
e	44	11	92	d9	23	20	2e	89	b4	7c	b8	26	77	99	e3	a5
f	67	4a	ed	de	c5	31	fe	18	0d	63	8c	80	c0	f7	70	07

Table 6.2 $E(x, y)$

	0	1	2	3	4	5	6	7	8	9	a	b	c	d	e	f
0	01	03	05	0f	11	33	55	ff	1a	2e	72	96	a1	f8	13	35
1	5f	e1	38	48	d8	73	95	a4	f7	02	06	0a	1e	22	66	aa
2	e5	34	5c	e4	37	59	eb	26	6a	be	d9	70	90	ab	e6	31
3	53	f5	04	0c	14	3c	44	cc	4f	d1	68	b8	d3	6e	b2	cd
4	4c	d4	67	a9	e0	3b	4d	d7	62	a6	f1	08	18	28	78	88
5	83	9e	b9	d0	6b	bd	dc	7f	81	98	b3	ce	49	db	76	9a
6	b5	c4	57	f9	10	30	50	f0	0b	1d	27	69	bb	d6	61	a3
7	fe	19	2b	7d	87	92	ad	ec	2f	71	93	ae	e9	20	60	a0
8	fb	16	3a	4e	d2	6d	b7	c2	5d	e7	32	56	fa	15	3f	41
9	c3	5e	e2	3d	47	c9	40	c0	5b	ed	2c	74	9c	bf	da	75
a	9f	ba	d5	64	ac	ef	2a	7e	82	9d	bc	df	7a	8e	89	80
b	9b	b6	**c1**	58	e8	23	65	af	ea	25	6f	b1	c8	43	c5	54
c	fc	1f	21	63	a5	f4	07	09	1b	2d	77	99	b0	cb	46	ca
d	45	cf	4a	de	79	8b	86	91	a8	e3	3e	42	c6	51	f3	0e
e	12	36	5a	ee	29	7b	8d	8c	8f	8a	85	94	a7	f2	0d	17
f	39	4b	dd	7c	84	97	a2	fd	1c	24	6c	b4	c7	52	f6	01

For example, the multiplication of 57 and 83 can be carried out by using these two tables

$$57 \bullet 83 = E(L(5, 7) + L(8, 3)) = E(62 + 50)$$

$$= E(b2) = E(b, 2)$$

$$= c1$$

The value 57 in Table 6.1 is $L(5, 7)$, or the value at the 5th row and 7th column. The result is 62. After adding the value 50, the value 112 is converted to hexadecimal value b2. Using the transformation $E(b, 2)$ in Table 6.2, the final result is c1 in hexadecimal format.

If the value before the $E(x, y)$ transformation is bigger than 255 (or ff), the value is subtracted by 255 (or ff). In fact, $L(x, y)$ is the logarithm and $E(x, y)$ is the exponential power for multiplication on the $GF(2^8)$ of AES. That's it! Now, we have everything to study AES encryption and decryption.

6.4.3   The AES encryption/decryption algorithm

AES encryption scheme

The AES encryption scheme is divided into two processes, namely key scheduling and encryption. The key schedule process uses the user input key to set up all the subkeys. Each subkey is used in the 'AddRoundKey' procedure in the encryption process. The encryption process is described in Figure 6.19.

Fig. 6.19 The AES encryption process

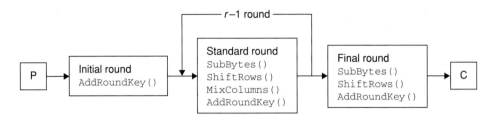

For a plaintext block P, the first round of AES encryption is simply applying AddRoundKey() on the block. For each of the r-1 rounds, standard operations are employed. The process involves four transformations, namely SubBytes(), ShiftRows(), Mixcolumns(), and AddRoundKey(). The final round is similar to the standard round but without the MixColumns() transformation. The output is the ciphertext block c. AES is designed to operate with bytes. For the plaintext block P with size 128 bits, 16 bytes are used. The 16 bytes are organized as a 4×4 matrix (the state matrix). Given the following 16 bytes, the state matrix **B** is

$$B_{00}B_{10}B_{20}B_{30}B_{01}B_{11}B_{21}B_{31}B_{02}B_{12}B_{22}B_{32}B_{03}B_{13}B_{23}B_{33} \rightarrow B = \begin{pmatrix} B_{00} & B_{01} & B_{02} & B_{03} \\ B_{10} & B_{11} & B_{12} & B_{13} \\ B_{20} & B_{21} & B_{22} & B_{23} \\ B_{30} & B_{31} & B_{32} & B_{33} \end{pmatrix}$$

The first column is populated first. If the block size is 192-bit, two more columns are added. Similarly for 256-bit block length, four more columns are required. All AES encryption operations are carried out with this matrix. On 32-bit machines, each column is implemented as a 32-bit word. For a 4×4 matrix, four 32-bit words are used for the implementation. Also, the number of rounds in AES is determined by the number of words as listed in Table 6.3.

Table 6.3 AES key lengths and numbers of rounds

	Key length N_k (32-bit words)	Block size N_b (32 bit words)	Number of rounds N_r
AES-128	4	4	10
AES-192	6	4	12
AES-256	8	4	14

The AES encryption uses four transformations, and they are explained below.

1 AddRoundKey() – this operation XORs each element B_{ij} in matrix **B** with the subkey K_{ij}.

2 SubBytes() – this operation substitutes each byte B_{ij} in matrix **B** with a value from the subBytes() table given as Table 6.4.

Table 6.4 The subBytes() table

	0	1	2	3	4	5	6	7	8	9	a	b	c	d	e	f
0	63	7C	77	7B	F2	6B	6F	C5	30	01	67	2B	FE	D7	AB	76
1	CA	82	C9	7D	FA	59	47	F0	AD	D4	A2	AF	9C	A4	72	C0
2	B7	FD	93	26	36	3F	F7	CC	34	A5	E5	F1	71	D8	31	15
3	04	C7	23	C3	18	96	05	9A	07	12	80	E2	EB	27	B2	75
4	09	83	2C	1A	1B	6E	5A	A0	52	3B	D6	B3	29	E3	2F	84
5	53	D1	00	ED	20	FC	B1	5B	6A	CB	BE	39	4A	4C	58	CF
6	D0	EF	AA	FB	43	4D	33	85	45	F9	02	7F	50	3C	9F	A8
7	51	A3	40	8F	92	9D	38	F5	BC	B6	DA	21	10	FF	F3	D2
8	CD	0C	13	EC	5F	97	44	17	C4	A7	7E	3D	64	5D	19	73
9	60	81	4F	DC	22	2A	90	88	46	EE	B8	14	DE	5E	0B	DB
a	E0	32	3A	0A	49	06	24	5C	C2	D3	AC	62	91	95	E4	79
b	E7	C8	37	6D	8D	D5	4E	A9	6C	56	F4	EA	65	7A	AE	08
c	BA	78	25	2E	1C	A6	B4	C6	E8	DD	74	1F	4B	BD	8B	8A
d	70	3E	B5	66	48	03	F6	0E	61	35	57	B9	86	C1	1D	9E
e	E1	F8	98	11	69	D9	8E	94	9B	1E	87	E9	CE	55	28	DF
f	8C	A1	89	0D	BF	E6	42	68	41	99	2D	0F	B0	54	BB	16

For example, for the value B00 = 01, the result of ByteSub() is

ByteSub(01)=7C   (i.e. the value at the intersection of row 0 and column 1)

3 ShiftRows() – this operation rotates the 2nd, 3rd and 4th rows of matrix **B** left by 1, 2 and 3 elements (or bytes) respectively as highlighted in bold.

$$\begin{pmatrix} B_{00} & B_{01} & B_{02} & B_{03} \\ \boldsymbol{B_{10}} & B_{11} & B_{12} & B_{13} \\ \boldsymbol{B_{20}} & \boldsymbol{B_{21}} & B_{22} & B_{23} \\ \boldsymbol{B_{30}} & \boldsymbol{B_{31}} & \boldsymbol{B_{32}} & B_{33} \end{pmatrix} \rightarrow \begin{pmatrix} B_{00} & B_{01} & B_{02} & B_{03} \\ B_{11} & B_{12} & B_{13} & \boldsymbol{B_{10}} \\ B_{22} & B_{23} & \boldsymbol{B_{20}} & \boldsymbol{B_{21}} \\ B_{33} & \boldsymbol{B_{30}} & \boldsymbol{B_{31}} & \boldsymbol{B_{32}} \end{pmatrix}$$

4 MixColumns() – for each column of matrix **B,** this operation performs the following matrix multiplication:

$$\begin{pmatrix} B'_{0c} \\ B'_{1c} \\ B'_{2c} \\ B'_{3c} \end{pmatrix} = \begin{pmatrix} 02 & 03 & 01 & 01 \\ 01 & 02 & 03 & 01 \\ 01 & 01 & 02 & 03 \\ 03 & 01 & 01 & 02 \end{pmatrix} \begin{pmatrix} B_{0c} \\ B_{1c} \\ B_{2c} \\ B_{3c} \end{pmatrix}$$

where 'c' is the column index. Note that the multiplication and addition are the operations in the finite field GF(2^8) discussed in Section 6.4.2. For example, the first element B'_{0c} is calculated by

$$B'_{0c} = (\{02\} \bullet B_{0c}) \oplus (\{03\} \bullet B_{1c}) \oplus B_{2c} \oplus B_{3c}$$

To complete the encryption, all that remains is the key schedule, or key expansion, procedure.

The key expansion process

This process takes the user input key and generates a total of $N_b(N_r + 1)$ subkeys, where N_b is the block length and N_r is the number of rounds. When the block length is four (32-bit word) and there are ten rounds, the total number of subkeys is 44. Each subkey is a 32-bit (or 4 byte) value stored in an array w[i], where $0 \le i \le N_b(N_r + 1)$. Together with the key length N_k, the key expansion is described in ex06-09.txt.

```
Example: ex06-09.txt - AES key expansion

 1: Input:    Byte key[4*Nk], word w[Nb*(Nr+1)], Nk
 2: Procedure begin
 3:    i=0;
 4:    while (i < Nk)
 5:        w[i] = word(key[4*i], key[4*i+1], key[4*i+2], key[4*i+3]);
 6:        i =i+1;
 7:    end-while
 8:    i = Nk
 9:    while ( i< Nb * (Nr +1))
10:        temp = w[i-1];
11:        if (i mod Nk == 0)
12:            temp = SubWord(RotWord(temp)) XOR Rcon[i/Nk];
13:        else if (Nk > 6 and i mod Nk ==4)
14:            temp = SubWord(temp);
15:        end-if
16:        w[i] = w[i-Nk] XOR temp
17:        i = i+1
18:    end-while
19: end
```

The while-loop in lines 4–7 concatenates the input key array key[] into 32-bit words. In the case of $N_k=4$, the 16 bytes in key[0] to key[15] are stored in elements w[0], w[1], w[2] and w[3]. They are the first four subkeys. The statements in lines 8–18 compute the remaining subkeys. First, the temporary variable temp contains the value w[i-1] (line 10). If the subkey number is a multiple of N_k, the statement in line 12 is executed:

```
temp = SubWord(RotWord(temp)) XOR Rcon[i/Nk];
```

This statement involves two functions. The first is RotWord(), which takes a 4-byte word $[a_0 a_1 a_2 a_3]$ and performs a rotation to $[a_1 a_2 a_3 a_0]$. The second function,

Fig. 6.20 The AES decryption process

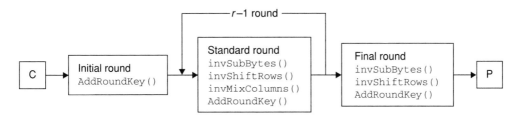

SubWord(), takes a 4-byte word $[a_0 a_1 a_2 a_3]$ and uses Table 6.4 to perform byte substitution to get a new word $[b_0\ b_1\ b_2\ b_3]$. The round constant array is Rcon[i]=$[x^{i-1},00,00,00]$, where x={02}. This x^{i-1} is the power of x in $GF(2^8)$. Since AES uses no more than ten Rcon elements, in practice this array can be pre-computed using Tables 6.1 and 6.2 as

```
RCON = [ 0x01000000, 0x02000000, 0x04000000, 0x08000000, 0x10000000,
         0x20000000, 0x40000000, 0x80000000, 0x1B000000, 0x36000000]
```

The variable temp is then XORed with w[i-Nk] to form the next subkey. It is also important to note that, for AES-256 (Nk=8), the key expansion is slightly different in the 192- and 128-bit cases. For AES-256, when N_k=8 and i-4 is a multiple of N_k, the function SubWord() is applied to temp before the XOR operation (line 14).

The AES decryption scheme

Parallel with Figure 6.19, the decryption process of AES is described in Figure 6.20.

The four procedures, or transformations, of the decryption are explained below.

1 AddRoundKey() – this operation applies the subkey to every element B_{ij} in matrix **B** in reverse order.

2 invSubBytes() – this operation substitutes each byte B_{ij} in matrix **B** with a value from the decryption table shown in Table 6.5.

The values in this table are the reverse transformations in Table 6.5.

3 invShiftRows() – this operation is the inverse of ShiftRows(). That is, it rotates the 2nd, 3rd and 4th rows of the matrix right by 1, 2 and 3 elements (or bytes) respectively:

$$
\begin{pmatrix}
B_{00} & B_{01} & B_{02} & B_{03} \\
B_{10} & B_{11} & B_{12} & B_{13} \\
B_{20} & B_{21} & B_{22} & B_{23} \\
B_{30} & B_{31} & B_{32} & B_{33}
\end{pmatrix}
\rightarrow
\begin{pmatrix}
B_{00} & B_{01} & B_{02} & B_{03} \\
B_{13} & B_{10} & B_{11} & B_{12} \\
B_{22} & B_{23} & B_{20} & B_{21} \\
B_{31} & B_{32} & B_{33} & B_{30}
\end{pmatrix}
$$

Table 6.5 The `invSubBytes()` table

	0	1	2	3	4	5	6	7	8	9	a	b	c	d	e	f
0	52	09	6a	d5	30	36	a5	38	bf	40	a3	9e	81	f3	d7	fb
1	7c	e3	39	82	9b	2f	ff	87	34	8e	43	44	c4	de	e9	cb
2	54	7b	94	32	a6	c2	23	3d	ee	4c	95	0b	42	fa	c3	4e
3	08	2e	a1	66	28	d9	24	b2	76	5b	a2	49	6d	8b	d1	25
4	72	f8	f6	64	86	68	98	16	d4	a4	5c	cc	5d	65	b6	92
5	6c	70	48	50	fd	ed	b9	da	5e	15	46	57	a7	8d	9d	84
6	90	d8	ab	00	8c	bc	d3	0a	f7	e4	58	05	b8	b3	45	06
7	d0	2c	1e	8f	ca	3f	0f	02	c1	af	bd	03	01	13	8a	6b
8	3a	91	11	41	4f	67	dc	ea	97	f2	cf	ce	f0	b4	e6	73
9	96	ac	74	22	e7	ad	35	85	e2	f9	37	e8	1c	75	df	6e
a	47	f1	1a	71	1d	29	c5	89	6f	b7	62	0e	aa	18	be	1b
b	fc	56	3e	4b	c6	d2	79	20	9a	db	c0	fe	78	cd	5a	f4
c	1f	dd	a8	33	88	07	c7	31	b1	12	10	59	27	80	ec	5f
d	60	51	7f	a9	19	b5	4a	0d	2d	e5	7a	9f	93	c9	9c	ef
e	a0	e0	3b	4d	ae	2a	f5	b0	c8	eb	bb	3c	83	53	99	61
f	17	2b	04	7e	ba	77	d6	26	e1	69	14	63	55	21	0c	7d

4 `invMixColumns()` – for each column of matrix **B**, this operation performs the following matrix multiplication:

$$\begin{pmatrix} B'_{0c} \\ B'_{1c} \\ B'_{2c} \\ B'_{3c} \end{pmatrix} = \begin{pmatrix} 0e & 0b & 0d & 09 \\ 09 & 0e & 0b & 0d \\ 0d & 09 & 0e & 0b \\ 0b & 0d & 09 & 0e \end{pmatrix} \begin{pmatrix} B_{0c} \\ B_{1c} \\ B_{2c} \\ B_{3c} \end{pmatrix}$$

where 'c' is the column index. Note that the matrix is the inverse of the matrix used in `MixColumns()`. Also, the multiplication and addition operations are in the finite field GF(2^8).

From Figure 6.20, the decryption, or the inverse cipher, uses the same form as the forward (encryption) cipher. Recognizing the equivalence of these two ciphers is not difficult. First, the order of `SubBytes()` and `ShiftRows()` is not important for the execution of the scheme. `SubBytes()` changes the values of the state matrix without affecting the position, whereas `ShiftRows()` changes the position only. The order of `AddRoundKey()` and `invMixColumns()` can also be changed simply because the column mixing operation is linear and, therefore, we have:

```
invMixColumns( state XOR k) = invMixColumns(state) XOR invMixColumns(k)
```

As you can see, the key k for decryption is slightly different. In addition, the subkeys are applied in reverse order; the decryption subkeys for the standard rounds are also required to mix with the `invMixColumns()` operations. This can be done at the beginning of decryption key expansion, so the decryption design is a direct inverse of the forward cipher.

Now we know how to do AES encryption and decryption. Let's put all this into practice by encrypting some data.

6.4.4 A step-by-step demonstration of AES

Consider the following 16 bytes of input key (i.e. N_k=4):

```
2b 7e 15 16    28 ae d2 a6    ab f7 15 88    09 cf 4f 3c
```

The first thing in the key expansion is to group the key string into four words w[0] to w[3]

```
w[0] = 2b7e1516  w[1] = 28aed2a6  w[2] = abf71588  w[3] = 09cf4f3c
```

To compute w[4] to w[7], this procedure is used:

```
w[4]: temp=09cf4f3c                         (Assign to w[3])
      => RotWord(temp) = cf4f3c09           (By Rotation)
      => SubWord(cf4f3c09)     = 8a84eb01   (Table 6.4)
      => 8a84eb01 XOR 01000000 = 8b84eb01   (XOR Recon[0])
      => 8b84eb01 XOR 2b7e1516 = a0fafe17   (i.e. XOR w[i-4]=w[0])

w[5]: temp=a0fafe17 => a0fafe17 XOR 28aed2a6 = 88542cb1 (i.e. XOR w[1])
w[6]: temp=88542cb1 => 88542cb1 XOR abf71588 = 23a33939 (i.e. XOR w[2])
w[7]: temp=23a33939 => 23a33939 XOR 09cf4f3c = 2a6c7605 (i.e. XOR w[3])
```

Continuing this process generates all the subkeys. All the subkeys, w[4]-w[43], are generated in Table 6.6.

Table 6.6 AES subkey table

w[i]	temp	RotWord( )	SubWord( )	Rcon[i/Nk]	XOR Rcon	W[i-Nk]	W[i] Temp ^ w[i-Nk]
4	09cf4f3c	cf4f3c09	8a84eb01	01000000	8b84eb01	2b7e1516	**a0fafe17**
5	a0fafe17					28aed2a6	**88542cb1**
6	88542cb1					abf71588	**23a33939**
7	23a33939					09cf4f3c	**2a6c7605**
8	2a6c7605	6c76052a	50386be5	02000000	52386be5	a0fafe17	**f2c295f2**
9	f2c295f2					88542cb1	**7a96b943**
10	7a96b943					23a33939	**5935807a**
11	5935807a					2a6c7605	**7359f67f**
12	7359f67f	59f67f73	cb42d28f	04000000	cf42d28f	f2c295f2	**3d80477d**
13	3d80477d					7a96b943	**4716fe3e**
14	4716fe3e					5935807a	**1e237e44**
15	1e237e44					7359f67f	**6d7a883b**
16	6d7a883b	7a883b6d	dac4e23c	08000000	d2c4e23c	3d80477d	**ef44a541**
	. . .	. . .	. . .	. . .	. . .	. . .	
40	575c006e	5c006e57	4a639f5b	36000000	7c639f5b	ac7766f3	**d014f9a8**
41	d014f9a8					19fadc21	**c9ee2589**
42	c9ee2589					28d12941	**e13f0cc8**
43	e13f0cc8					575c006e	**b6630ca6**

The AES subkeys are shown in the last column of Table 6.6. Each subkey is a 4-byte (32-bit) word and can be considered as one column of four elements (1 byte each) of a matrix. In this case, the subkeys w[0]–w[3] form a 4 × 4 matrix. Each subkey is one column with four elements. The subkeys w[4]–w[7] form another matrix. Subkeys w[0]–w[43] can be used to form 11 matrices (or round keys) as listed below.

2b	28	ab	09
7e	ae	f7	cf
15	d2	15	4f
16	a6	88	3c

Round key 0

a0	88	23	2a
fa	54	a3	6c
fe	2c	39	76
17	b1	39	05

Round key 1

f2	7a	59	73
c2	96	35	59
95	b9	80	f6
f2	43	7a	7f

Round key 2

3d	47	1e	6d
80	16	23	7a
47	fe	7e	88
7d	3e	44	3b

Round key 3

ef	a8	b6	db
44	52	71	0b
a5	5b	25	ad
41	7f	3b	00

Round key 4

d4	7c	ca	11
d1	83	f2	f9
c6	9d	b8	15
f8	87	bc	bc

Round key 5

6d	11	db	ca
88	0b	f9	00
a3	3e	86	93
7a	fd	41	fd

Round key 6

4e	5f	84	4e
54	5f	a6	a6
f7	c9	4f	dc
0e	f3	b2	4f

Round key 7

ea	b5	31	7f
d2	8d	2b	8d
73	ba	f5	29
21	d2	60	2f

Round key 8

ac	19	28	57
77	fa	d1	5c
66	dc	29	00
f3	21	41	6e

Round key 9

d0	c9	e1	b6
14	ee	3f	63
f9	25	0c	0c
a8	89	c8	a6

Round key 10

With all the round keys, AES encryption can be performed. For AES-128 ($N_k=4$), the encryption process has one initial round, nine standard rounds and one final round. Consider the plaintext block

32 43 f6 a8 88 5a 30 8d 31 31 98 a2 e0 37 07 34

The initial round simply XORs this plaintext matrix with round key 0:

32	88	31	e0
43	5a	31	37
f6	30	98	07
a8	8d	a2	34

2b	28	ab	09
7e	ae	f7	cf
15	d2	15	4f
16	a6	88	3c

=

19	a0	9a	e9
3d	f4	c6	f8
e3	e2	8d	48
be	2b	2a	08

The result of the initial round is used in the nine standard rounds. Each standard round runs through the transformations SubBytes(), ShiftRows(), MixColumns() and AddRoundKey(). The first round is illustrated below:

SubBytes()					ShiftRows()					MixColumns()						Result block			
d4	e0	b8	1e		d4	e0	b8	1e		04	e0	48	28	XOR with		a4	68	6b	02
27	bf	b4	41		bf	b4	41	27		66	cb	f8	06	Round		9c	9f	5b	6a
11	98	5d	52		5d	52	11	98		81	19	d3	26	key 1 =		7f	35	ea	50
ae	f1	e5	30		30	ae	f1	e5		e5	9a	7a	4c			f2	2b	43	49

The result of this round is carried on for the second round. The ninth round is illustrated in the following:

SubBytes()					ShiftRows()					MixColumns()						Result block			
87	f2	4d	97		87	f2	4d	97		47	40	a3	4c	XOR with		eb	59	8b	1b
ec	6e	4c	90		6e	4c	90	ec		37	d4	70	9f	Round		40	2e	a1	c3
4a	c3	46	e7		46	e7	4a	c3		94	e4	3a	42	key 9 =		f2	38	13	42
8c	d8	95	a6		a6	8c	d8	95		ed	a5	a6	bc			1e	84	e7	d2

The result of this ninth round is used in the final round of the encryption. This involves the transformations SubBytes(), ShiftRows() and AddRoundKey().

Starting Value					SubBytes()					ShiftRows()						Ciphertext			
eb	59	8b	1b		e9	cb	3d	af		e9	cb	3d	af	XOR with		39	02	dc	19
40	2e	a1	c3		09	31	32	2e		31	32	2e	09	Round		25	dc	11	6a
f2	38	13	42		89	07	7d	2c		7d	2c	89	07	key 10 =		84	09	85	0b
1e	84	e7	d2		72	5f	94	65		b5	72	5f	94			1d	fb	97	32

The ciphertext is highlighted in bold above. Now, we have some experience with AES encryption and decryption, it's time to consider some techniques to optimize the execution.

6.5 An optimized implementation of AES

6.5.1 Using optimized table lookup

The efficiency of AES can be enhanced by the following table lookup techniques. First, consider a particular column (e.g. the cth column) of a block under the procedures of a standard round, `SubBytes()`, `ShiftRows()`, `MixColumns()` and `AddRoundKey()`.

After `SubBytes()`:
$$\begin{bmatrix} D_{0c} \\ D_{1c} \\ D_{2c} \\ D_{3c} \end{bmatrix} = \begin{bmatrix} S\,[B_{0c}] \\ S\,[B_{1c}] \\ S\,[B_{2c}] \\ S\,[B_{3c}] \end{bmatrix}$$
where table `S[]` is `SubBytes()` given as Table 6.4 in Section 6.4.3.

After `ShiftRows()`:
$$\begin{bmatrix} D'_{0c} \\ D'_{1c} \\ D'_{2c} \\ D'_{3c} \end{bmatrix} = \begin{bmatrix} S\,[B_{0c(0)}] \\ S\,[B_{1c(1)}] \\ S\,[B_{2c(2)}] \\ S\,[B_{3c(3)}] \end{bmatrix}$$

$h(r, N_c)$		Row (r)		
		1	2	3
	4	1	2	3
N_c	6	1	2	3
	8	1	3	4

where $c(r) = [c + h(r, N_c)] \bmod N_c$, with $c(0) = c$. The function $h(r, N_c)$ is defined by the table above.

After `MixColumns()`:
$$\begin{bmatrix} D''_{0c} \\ D''_{1c} \\ D''_{2c} \\ D''_{3c} \end{bmatrix} = \begin{bmatrix} 02 & 03 & 01 & 01 \\ 01 & 02 & 03 & 01 \\ 01 & 01 & 02 & 03 \\ 03 & 01 & 01 & 02 \end{bmatrix} \begin{bmatrix} S\,[B_{0c(0)}] \\ S\,[B_{1c(1)}] \\ S\,[B_{2c(2)}] \\ S\,[B_{3c(3)}] \end{bmatrix}$$

After `AddRoundKey()`:
$$\begin{bmatrix} B'_{0c} \\ B'_{1c} \\ B'_{2c} \\ B'_{3c} \end{bmatrix} = \begin{bmatrix} 02 & 03 & 01 & 01 \\ 01 & 02 & 03 & 01 \\ 01 & 01 & 02 & 03 \\ 03 & 01 & 01 & 02 \end{bmatrix} \begin{bmatrix} S\,[B_{0c(0)}] \\ S\,[B_{1c(1)}] \\ S\,[B_{2c(2)}] \\ S\,[B_{3c(3)}] \end{bmatrix} \oplus \begin{bmatrix} k_{0c} \\ k_{1c} \\ k_{2c} \\ k_{3c} \end{bmatrix}$$

This final transformation can be written as a single transformation in column form:

$$\begin{bmatrix} B'_{0c} \\ B'_{1c} \\ B'_{2c} \\ B'_{3c} \end{bmatrix} = S[B_{0c(0)}] \bullet \begin{bmatrix} 02 \\ 01 \\ 01 \\ 03 \end{bmatrix} \oplus S[B_{1c(1)}] \bullet \begin{bmatrix} 03 \\ 02 \\ 01 \\ 01 \end{bmatrix} \oplus S[B_{2c(2)}] \bullet \begin{bmatrix} 01 \\ 03 \\ 02 \\ 01 \end{bmatrix} \oplus S[B_{3c(3)}] \bullet \begin{bmatrix} 01 \\ 01 \\ 03 \\ 02 \end{bmatrix} \oplus \begin{bmatrix} k_{0c} \\ k_{1c} \\ k_{2c} \\ k_{3c} \end{bmatrix}$$

where the multiplication is in $GF(2^8)$.

If we define the following four tables:

$$FT_0[x] = \begin{bmatrix} 02 \bullet S[x] \\ S[x] \\ S[x] \\ 03 \bullet S[x] \end{bmatrix}, \ FT_1[x] = \begin{bmatrix} 03 \bullet S[x] \\ 02 \bullet S[x] \\ S[x] \\ S[x] \end{bmatrix}, \ FT_2[x] = \begin{bmatrix} S[x] \\ 03 \bullet S[x] \\ 02 \bullet S[x] \\ S[x] \end{bmatrix}, \ FT_3[x] = \begin{bmatrix} S[x] \\ S[x] \\ 03 \bullet S[x] \\ 02 \bullet S[x] \end{bmatrix}$$

the final transformation can be written as

$$\begin{bmatrix} B'_{0c} \\ B'_{1c} \\ B'_{2c} \\ B'_{3c} \end{bmatrix} = FT_0[B_{0c(0)}] \oplus FT_1[B_{1c(1)}] \oplus FT_2[B_{2c(2)}] \oplus FT_3[B_{3c(3)}] \oplus k_{round,c}$$

If the four tables FT_0, FT_1, FT_2 and FT_3 are pre-computed, the final transformation involves four XOR operations with one word from the key and four words from the tables, indexed by the corresponding bytes. We don't even need to put the $GF(2^8)$ multiplication in the implementation.

Now, let's generate the data in tables FT_0, FT_1, FT_2 and FT_3. Given the SubBytes() table in S[], these tables are just multiplications in $GF(2^8)$ and can be easily computed using $L(x, y)$ and $E(x, y)$ values from Tables 6.1 and 6.2. For example, the ith element in $FT_0[i]$ is

$$FT_0[i] = (02 \bullet S[i] << 24) \mid (S[i] << 16) \mid (S[i] << 8) \mid (03 \bullet S[i])$$

Note that this value is a word and considered to be a column in AES algorithm. To generate all the tables, consider the program listing in ex06-07.htm.

```
Example: ex06-07.htm - Generating AES forward tables FT0, FT1, FT2
and FT3

 1: <body style="font-family:courier;font-size:12pt">
 2: <script src="hexlib.js"></script>
 3: <script>
 4: var lTable = new Array(
 5:    0x00, 0x00, 0x19, 0x01, 0x32, 0x02, 0x1a, 0xc6,
 6:    0x4b, 0xc7, 0x1b, 0x68, 0x33, 0xee, 0xdf, 0x03,
 7:    0x64, 0x04, 0xe0, 0x0e, 0x34, 0x8d, 0x81, 0xef,
       .... .... .....    .... .... .....
       .... .... .....    .... .... .....
37:
38: var eTable = new Array(
39:    0x01, 0x03, 0x05, 0x0f, 0x11, 0x33, 0x55, 0xff,
40:    0x1a, 0x2e, 0x72, 0x96, 0xa1, 0xf8, 0x13, 0x35,
       .... .... .....    .... .... .....
       .... .... .....    .... .... .....
```

```
 71:
 72: var FSb = new Array(
 73:    0x63, 0x7C, 0x77, 0x7B, 0xF2, 0x6B, 0x6F, 0xC5,
 74:    0x30, 0x01, 0x67, 0x2B, 0xFE, 0xD7, 0xAB, 0x76,
        .... .... .....       .... .... .....
        .... .... .....       .... .... .....
104:    0x41, 0x99, 0x2D, 0x0F, 0xB0, 0x54, 0xBB, 0x16 );
105:
106: function multGF(x,y)
107: {
108:    tmp1 = lTable[x] + lTable[y];
109:    if (tmp1 > 255 ) tmp1 -=255;
110:    return (eTable[tmp1] & 0xff);
111: }
112:
113: function genFTbFun()
114: {
115:    var i=0, k=0, m=0;
116:    var tmp1=0;
117:    var SS = new Array(0x2,0x1,0x1,0x3,
118:                       0x3,0x2,0x1,0x1,
119:                       0x1,0x3,0x2,0x1,
120:                       0x1,0x1,0x3,0x2);
121:    for (k=0;k< 16;k+=4) {
122:    document.write("var FT"+m+" = new Array( <br />");
123:    for (i=0;i<256;i++) {
124:     tmp1 = (multGF(SS[k],FSb[i]) << 24)|
               (multGF(SS[k+1],FSb[i]) << 16)
125:          | (multGF(SS[k+2],FSb[i]) << 8)|(multGF(SS[k+3],FSb[i])));
126:     if (i==255) document.write("0x"+byte4ToHex(tmp1)+" );
            <br /><br />");
127:     else    {
128:       if (i % 4 == 0) document.write("<br />    ");
129:       document.write( "0x"+byte4ToHex(tmp1)+",");
130:     }
131:    }
132:    m++;
133:   }
134: }
135: genFTbFun();
136: </script>
137: </body>
```

Fig. 6.21 AES FT tables

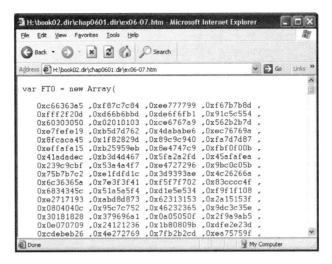

Lines 1–37 and 38–71 define the data of the logarithm (lTable) and exponential (eTable) tables which are used to perform multiplication in GF(2^8). The data of S[] (or the forward S-box) is specified in lines 72–104 as array FSb[]. The function multGF() in lines 106–111 performs the finite field GF(2^8) multiplication. The operation is simple – all you need to do is get the values from the lTable and perform the addition (line 108). The result is another lookup from the eTable (line 110).

The table-generating function genFTbFun() is defined in lines 113–134. The transformation matrix SS[] is specified as an array in lines 117–120. For every row (or four elements) of this matrix SS[], a table is generated by the for-loop in lines 121–133. The main operation is the statement in lines 124–125 to perform the finite field multiplication with the SS[] elements and concatenate the values together to form a 32-bit word. The remaining statements in lines 126–130 are used to format the output as an array in ECMAScript. We can simply copy and paste the data into another script program for the AES encryption. A screenshot of this example is shown in Figure 6.21.

The data in Figure 6.21 is formatted as an array in ECMAScript so that it is easy to copy and paste for encryption. For AES decryption, another set of tables is generated. The tables are RT0, RT1, RT2 and RT3. To generate these tables, all you have to do is use ex06-07.htm and replace the SubBytes() table by the invSubBytes() table. Also, the SS[] array in lines 117–120 is replaced by the following inverse transformation in invMixColumns()

Fig. 6.22 AES RT tables

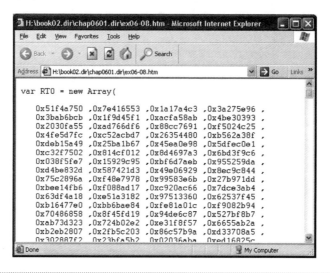

```
117: var SS = new Array(0xe,0x9,0xd,0xb,
118:                     0xb,0xe,0x9,0xd,
119:                     0xd,0xb,0xe,0x9,
120:                     0x9,0xd,0xb,0xe);
```

The modified page is called ex06-08.htm. The execution of this page and the RT tables generated are shown in Figure 6.22. Now we can tackle the implementation of an optimized AES scheme.

6.5.2   Implementation of the AES scheme

AES is a slightly complicated scheme involving some mathematics. This implementation may be a bit longer than others. However, you may be surprised that the execution of the program is extremely efficient and fast, and can compare with many other fast schemes.

The first thing to do to implement AES encryption and decryption is to set up the data used by the scheme. Copy the table data generated by the pages ex06-07.htm and ex06-08.htm into a script called ex06-09.js. At the end of this script file add the following codes starting from S29.

```
 1: var FT0 = new Array (
 2:      0xc66363a5, 0xf87c7c84, 0xee777799, 0xf67b7b8d,
 3:      0xfff2f20d, 0xd66b6bbd, 0xde6f6fb1, 0x91c5c554,
         .... .... .....       .... .... .....

263:     0xb0b0cb7b, 0x5454fca8, 0xbbbbd66d, 0x16163a2c );
264:
265: var RT0 = new Array(
266:     0x51f4a750, 0x7e416553, 0x1a17a4c3, 0x3a275e96,
         .... .... .....       .... .... .....
         .... .... .....       .... .... .....
527:     0xcb84617b, 0x32b670d5, 0x6c5c7448, 0xb85742d0 );
528:
529: var FSb = new Array(
530:     0x63, 0x7C, 0x77, 0x7B, 0xF2, 0x6B, 0x6F, 0xC5,
         .... .... .....       .... .... .....
         .... .... .....       .... .... .....
563: var RSb = new Array(
564:     0x52, 0x09, 0x6A, 0xD5, 0x30, 0x36, 0xA5, 0x38,
565:     0xBF, 0x40, 0xA3, 0x9E, 0x81, 0xF3, 0xD7, 0xFB,
         .... .... .....       .... .... .....
         .... .... .....       .... .... .....
597:
598: var RCON = new Array(
599:     0x01000000, 0x02000000, 0x04000000, 0x08000000,
600:     0x10000000, 0x20000000, 0x40000000, 0x80000000,
601:     0x1B000000, 0x36000000 );
602:
603: var KT_init = 1;
604: var KT0 = new Array(256);
605: var KT1 = new Array(256);
606: var KT2 = new Array(256);
607: var KT3 = new Array(256);
608:
609: var aes_erk = new Array(64);
610: var aes_drk = new Array(64);
611: var aes_nr;
612: var grki =0;
613:
```

Lines 1–263 define tables FT0, FT1, FT2 and FT3 generated by ex06-07.htm.
Lines 265–527 are the tables RT0, RT1, RT2 and RT3 from ex06-08.htm. The

`SubBytes()` data for encryption and decryption is defined in arrays `FSb[]` and `RSb[]` in lines 529–562 and 563–596 respectively. The round constant `RCON[]` is specified in lines 598–601. The arrays `KT0[]`, `KT1[]`, `KT2[]` and `KT3[]` are used to generate the decryption round keys. The final encryption and decryption subkeys are stored in arrays `aes_erk[]` and `aes_drk[]` (lines 609–610). The number of rounds, `aes_nr`, and a global index for the key, `grki`, are declared in line 611 and 612.

The key expansion process for AES encryption is given in part II of `ex06-09.js`.

```
Example: Continuation of ex06-09.js                          (Part II)

614: function get_uint32(b,i)
615: {
616:   var n;
617:   n = ((b[i] & 0xff)    << 24) | ((b[i+1] & 0xff) << 16)
618:      |((b[i+2] & 0xff) << 8)  |  (b[i+3] & 0xff);
619:   return n;
620: }
621:
622: function aes_set_enkey(key,nbits )
623: {
624:   var i,  rki = 0;
625:   switch( nbits )
626:   {
627:      case 128: aes_nr = 10; break;
628:      case 192: aes_nr = 12; break;
629:      case 256: aes_nr = 14; break;
630:      default : return( 1 );
631:   }
632:
633:   rki = 0; grki=0;
634:   for( i = 0; i < (nbits >>> 5); i++ ) {
635:      aes_erk[i] = get_uint32(key, i * 4 );
636:   }
637:   switch( nbits )
638:   {
639:    case 128:
640:      for( i = 0; i < 10; i++, rki += 4 )
641:      {
642:       aes_erk[rki+4] = aes_erk[rki+0]  ^ RCON[i] ^
643:         ( FSb[( aes_erk[rki+3] >>> 16 ) &0xff ] << 24 ) ^
644:         ( FSb[( aes_erk[rki+3] >>>  8 ) &0xff ] << 16 ) ^
645:         ( FSb[( aes_erk[rki+3]         ) &0xff ] <<  8 ) ^
646:         ( FSb[( aes_erk[rki+3] >>> 24 ) &0xff ]          );
647:
```

```
648:      aes_erk[rki+5] = aes_erk[rki+1] ^ aes_erk[rki+4];
649:       aes_erk[rki+6] = aes_erk[rki+2] ^ aes_erk[rki+5];
650:       aes_erk[rki+7] = aes_erk[rki+3] ^ aes_erk[rki+6];
651:       }
652:       break;
653:    case 192:
654:     for( i = 0; i < 8; i++, rki += 6 )
655:     {
656:     aes_erk[rki+6] = aes_erk[rki+0] ^ RCON[i] ^
657:        ( FSb[( aes_erk[rki+5] >>> 16 ) &0xff ] << 24 ) ^
658:        ( FSb[( aes_erk[rki+5] >>>  8 ) &0xff ] << 16 ) ^
659:        ( FSb[( aes_erk[rki+5]         ) &0xff ] <<  8 ) ^
660:        ( FSb[( aes_erk[rki+5] >>> 24 ) &0xff ]          );
661:
662:      aes_erk[rki+7]  = aes_erk[rki+1] ^ aes_erk[rki+6];
663:      aes_erk[rki+8]  = aes_erk[rki+2] ^ aes_erk[rki+7];
664:      aes_erk[rki+9]  = aes_erk[rki+3] ^ aes_erk[rki+8];
665:      aes_erk[rki+10] = aes_erk[rki+4] ^ aes_erk[rki+9];
666:      aes_erk[rki+11] = aes_erk[rki+5] ^ aes_erk[rki+10];
667:       }
668:       break;
```

This script fragment contains the two functions used by the key expansion process. The first function, get_uint32(), is simple. It converts four bytes from array b[], starting at position i, to a 32-bit word n and returns to the function caller.

The function aes_set_enkey() uses the input key key[] and number of bits nbits as parameters to generate all the subkeys used in encryption. First, the number of bits nbits determines the number of rounds aes_nr in lines 625–631. Then the input key, represented as byte array key[], is converted into words and copied to the subkeys aes_erk[] by the for-loop in lines 634–636.

The key expansion also depends on the parameter nbits. If the 128-bit format is used, the statements in lines 640–651 expand the input key to all the subkeys. In fact, apart from the first four subkeys, all others are generated by these lines. The statements in lines 643–646 generate the subkeys in a standard round (a batch multiple of 4) involving the rotation RotWord() followed by SubBytes(). The result is XORed with round constants RECON[] and the previous subkey. Lines 648–650 generate the final round of subkeys and involve simple XOR operations only.

For the AES-192 case, all the subkeys are created by lines 654–667. In this case, the subkeys are a multiple of 6 generated by lines 656–660. Others are generated by simple XOR operations in lines 662–666. With the discussion above, the key expansion for AES-256 (256-bit) listed in part III of ex06-09.js is easy to read and understand.

```
669:  case 256:
670:   for( i = 0; i < 7; i++, rki += 8 )
671:   {
672:    aes_erk[rki+8] = aes_erk[rki+0] ^ RCON[i] ^
673:      ( FSb[( aes_erk[rki+7] >>> 16 ) &0xff ] << 24 ) ^
674:      ( FSb[( aes_erk[rki+7] >>>  8 ) &0xff ] << 16 ) ^
675:      ( FSb[( aes_erk[rki+7]         ) &0xff ] <<  8 ) ^
676:      ( FSb[( aes_erk[rki+7] >>> 24 ) &0xff ]          );
677:    aes_erk[rki+9]  = aes_erk[rki+1] ^ aes_erk[rki+8];
678:    aes_erk[rki+10] = aes_erk[rki+2] ^ aes_erk[rki+9];
679:    aes_erk[rki+11] = aes_erk[rki+3] ^ aes_erk[rki+10];
680:    aes_erk[rki+12] = aes_erk[rki+4] ^
681:      ( FSb[ (aes_erk[rki+11] >>> 24) &0xff]  << 24 ) ^
682:      ( FSb[ (aes_erk[rki+11] >>> 16) &0xff ] << 16 ) ^
683:      ( FSb[ (aes_erk[rki+11] >>>  8) &0xff ] <<  8 ) ^
684:      ( FSb[ (aes_erk[rki+11]        ) &0xff ]          );
685:    aes_erk[rki+13] = aes_erk[rki+5] ^ aes_erk[rki+12];
686:    aes_erk[rki+14] = aes_erk[rki+6] ^ aes_erk[rki+13];
687:    aes_erk[rki+15] = aes_erk[rki+7] ^ aes_erk[rki+14];
688:   }
689:   break;
690:  }
691:  grki = rki;
692: }
693:
```

For the 256-bit case, the statements in lines 672–687 generate eight subkeys and are slightly different from the 128-bit and 192-bit situations. The main difference is in lines 680–684. When the subkey is a multiple of 4, these lines apply another SubBytes() operation on the keys. Note that the SubBytes() operation is equivalent to the table lookup from the array FSb[]. The assignment in line 691 stores the subkey index and will be used in the key schedule for decryption. The key expansion for decryption is listed in part IV of ex06-09.js.

```
694: function aes_set_dekey(key,nbits )
695: {
696:   var ski=0, rki=0;
697:   aes_set_enkey(key,nbits);
698:   if( KT_init ) {
```

```
699:     for( i = 0; i < 256; i++ ) {
700:         KT0[i] = RT0[ FSb[i] ];
701:         KT1[i] = RT1[ FSb[i] ];
702:         KT2[i] = RT2[ FSb[i] ];
703:         KT3[i] = RT3[ FSb[i] ];
704:     }
705:     KT_init = 0;
706: }
707: ski = 0; rki=grki;
708: aes_drk[ski++] = aes_erk[rki++];
709: aes_drk[ski++] = aes_erk[rki++];
710: aes_drk[ski++] = aes_erk[rki++];
711: aes_drk[ski++] = aes_erk[rki++];
712:
713: for( i = 1; i < aes_nr; i++ )
714: {
715:  rki -=8;
716:  aes_drk[ski++] = KT0[(aes_erk[rki] >>> 24 ) & 0xff ] ^
717:                   KT1[(aes_erk[rki] >>> 16 ) & 0xff ] ^
718:                   KT2[(aes_erk[rki] >>>  8 ) & 0xff ] ^
719:                   KT3[(aes_erk[rki]         ) & 0xff ]; rki++;
720:  aes_drk[ski++] = KT0[(aes_erk[rki] >>> 24 ) & 0xff ] ^
721:                   KT1[(aes_erk[rki] >>> 16 ) & 0xff ] ^
722:                   KT2[(aes_erk[rki] >>>  8 ) & 0xff ] ^
723:                   KT3[(aes_erk[rki]         ) & 0xff ]; rki++;
724:  aes_drk[ski++] = KT0[(aes_erk[rki] >>> 24 ) & 0xff ] ^
725:                   KT1[(aes_erk[rki] >>> 16 ) & 0xff ] ^
726:                   KT2[(aes_erk[rki] >>>  8 ) & 0xff ] ^
727:                   KT3[(aes_erk[rki]         ) & 0xff ]; rki++;
728:  aes_drk[ski++] = KT0[(aes_erk[rki] >>> 24 ) & 0xff ] ^
729:                   KT1[(aes_erk[rki] >>> 16 ) & 0xff ] ^
730:                   KT2[(aes_erk[rki] >>>  8 ) & 0xff ] ^
731:                   KT3[(aes_erk[rki]         ) & 0xff ]; rki++;
732: }
733: rki -= 8;
734: aes_drk[ski++] = aes_erk[rki++];
735: aes_drk[ski++] = aes_erk[rki++];
736: aes_drk[ski++] = aes_erk[rki++];
737: aes_drk[ski++] = aes_erk[rki++];
738: }
739:
```

The key schedule for AES decryption is basically the reverse of the encryption subkeys using invMixColumns() operations in the standard rounds. The first thing to do to generate the decryption subkeys is to obtain the encryption subkeys. This is done by the statement in line 697. The invMixColumns() transformation is performed by tables RT0, RT1, RT2 and RT3 with the help of the for-loop in lines 699–704.

To reverse the key order, two variables ski (increase from 0) and rki (decrease from grki) are used. The first four decryption subkeys are the last four subkeys from the encryption key schedule (lines 708–711). The decryption subkeys of the standard round are computed by the for-loop in lines 713–732. The computation method is that from the last subkey; the key index rki is subtracted by 8 in line 715. The statements in lines 716–731 compute four decryption subkeys. The index rki is subtracted by another 8, and another four subkeys are computed. After all the standard rounds, only the last four decryption subkeys remain to be computed. The statements in lines 733–737 subtract the index rki by 8 and then assign the last four decryption subkeys as the first four encryption subkeys.

Since we have put all the SubBytes(), ShiftRows() and MixColumns() procedures into tables FT0, FT1, FT2 and FT3, the standard round for the encryption is simple and is listed in part V of ex06-09.js.

```
Example: Continuation of ex06-09.js                        (Part V)

740: function aes_round(XX,YY,i)
741: {
742:     XX[0] = aes_erk[i+0] ^ FT0[( YY[0] >>> 24 ) & 0xff ]
743:                          ^ FT1[( YY[1] >>> 16 ) & 0xff ]
744:                          ^ FT2[( YY[2] >>>  8 ) & 0xff ]
745:                          ^ FT3[( YY[3]         ) & 0xff ];
746:     XX[1] = aes_erk[i+1] ^ FT0[( YY[1] >>> 24 ) & 0xff ]
747:                          ^ FT1[( YY[2] >>> 16 ) & 0xff ]
748:                          ^ FT2[( YY[3] >>>  8 ) & 0xff ]
749:                          ^ FT3[( YY[0]         ) & 0xff ];
750:     XX[2] = aes_erk[i+2] ^ FT0[( YY[2] >>> 24 ) & 0xff ]
751:                          ^ FT1[( YY[3] >>> 16 ) & 0xff ]
752:                          ^ FT2[( YY[0] >>>  8 ) & 0xff ]
753:                          ^ FT3[( YY[1]         ) & 0xff ];
754:     XX[3] = aes_erk[i+3] ^ FT0[( YY[3] >>> 24 ) & 0xff ]
755:                          ^ FT1[( YY[0] >>> 16 ) & 0xff ]
756:                          ^ FT2[( YY[1] >>>  8 ) & 0xff ]
757:                          ^ FT3[( YY[2]         ) & 0xff ];
758:     return XX;
759: }
760:
761: function aes_deround(XX,YY,i)
762: {
```

```
763:    XX[0] = aes_drk[i+0] ^ RT0[( YY[0] >>> 24 ) & 0xff ]
764:                         ^ RT1[( YY[3] >>> 16 ) & 0xff ]
765:                         ^ RT2[( YY[2] >>>  8 ) & 0xff ]
766:                         ^ RT3[( YY[1]         ) & 0xff ];
767:    XX[1] = aes_drk[i+1] ^ RT0[( YY[1] >>> 24 ) & 0xff ]
768:                         ^ RT1[( YY[0] >>> 16 ) & 0xff ]
769:                         ^ RT2[( YY[3] >>>  8 ) & 0xff ]
770:                         ^ RT3[( YY[2]         ) & 0xff ];
771:    XX[2] = aes_drk[i+2] ^ RT0[( YY[2] >>> 24 ) & 0xff ]
772:                         ^ RT1[( YY[1] >>> 16 ) & 0xff ]
773:                         ^ RT2[( YY[0] >>>  8 ) & 0xff ]
774:                         ^ RT3[( YY[3]         ) & 0xff ];
775:    XX[3] = aes_drk[i+3] ^ RT0[( YY[3] >>> 24 ) & 0xff ]
776:                         ^ RT1[( YY[2] >>> 16 ) & 0xff ]
777:                         ^ RT2[( YY[1] >>>  8 ) & 0xff ]
778:                         ^ RT3[( YY[0]         ) & 0xff ];
779:    return XX;
780: }
781:
```

This script contains two functions for the AES encryption and decryption rounds. The parameters XX[] and YY[] are arrays of four elements. Each element represents one column of the state matrix. It is equivalent to inputting the state matrix YY, and the resulting state matrix is returned by XX. The encryption computation (lines 740–759) is just a table lookup from the FT tables and XOR with the subkeys. The decryption computation (lines 761–780) is similar to encryption. All you need to do is use the decryption subkeys aes_drk[] and the RT tables. There is no multiplication in the finite field GF(2^8) involved.

The AES encryption process is listed in part VI of ex06-09.js.

```
Example: Continuation of ex06-09.js                        (Part VI)

782: function aes_encrypt(input)
783: {
784:     var X = new Array(4), Y = new Array(4), rki=0;
785:     X = input; rki = 0;
786:     X[0] ^= aes_erk[0];
787:     X[1] ^= aes_erk[1];
788:     X[2] ^= aes_erk[2];
789:     X[3] ^= aes_erk[3];
790:
```

```
791:     Y = aes_round( Y, X, rki += 4);
792:     X = aes_round( X, Y, rki += 4);
793:     Y = aes_round( Y, X, rki += 4);
794:     X = aes_round( X, Y, rki += 4);
795:     Y = aes_round( Y, X, rki += 4);
796:     X = aes_round( X, Y, rki += 4);
797:     Y = aes_round( Y, X, rki += 4);
798:     X = aes_round( X, Y, rki += 4);
799:     Y = aes_round( Y, X, rki += 4);
800:
801:     if( aes_nr > 10 ) {
802:         X = aes_round(X,Y,rki +=4);
803:         Y = aes_round(Y,X,rki +=4);
804:     }
805:     if( aes_nr > 12 ) {
806:         X = aes_round(X,Y,rki +=4);
807:         Y = aes_round(Y,X,rki +=4);
808:     }
809:     rki +=4;
810:     X[0]= aes_erk[rki+0] ^ (FSb[(Y[0] >>> 24) & 0xff] << 24 )
811:                          ^ (FSb[(Y[1] >>> 16) & 0xff] << 16 )
812:                          ^ (FSb[(Y[2] >>>  8) & 0xff] <<  8 )
813:                          ^ (FSb[(Y[3]       ) & 0xff]       );
814:     X[1]= aes_erk[rki+1] ^ (FSb[(Y[1] >>> 24) & 0xff] << 24 )
815:                          ^ (FSb[(Y[2] >>> 16) & 0xff] << 16 )
816:                          ^ (FSb[(Y[3] >>>  8) & 0xff] <<  8 )
817:                          ^ (FSb[(Y[0]       ) & 0xff]       );
818:     X[2]= aes_erk[rki+2] ^ (FSb[(Y[2] >>> 24) & 0xff] << 24 )
819:                          ^ (FSb[(Y[3] >>> 16) & 0xff] << 16 )
820:                          ^ (FSb[(Y[0] >>>  8) & 0xff] <<  8 )
821:                          ^ (FSb[(Y[1]       ) & 0xff]       );
822:     X[3]= aes_erk[rki+3] ^ (FSb[(Y[3] >>> 24) & 0xff] << 24 )
823:                          ^ (FSb[(Y[0] >>> 16) & 0xff] << 16 )
824:                          ^ (FSb[(Y[1] >>>  8) & 0xff] <<  8 )
825:                          ^ (FSb[(Y[2]       ) & 0xff]       );
826:  return X;
827: }
828:
```

The AES encryption function aes_encrypt() has one parameter. It is an array of four elements representing the state matrix of the scheme. The array is copied to a local array called X[] in line 785. Each element of X[] is XORed with the encryption subkeys forming the initial round of the algorithm. The next nine standard rounds of the scheme are carried out by lines 791–799. If the number of rounds `aes_nr` is greater than 10, two more standard rounds are executed in lines 802–803. When `aes_nr` is greater than 12, two more rounds are computed by lines 806–807. For the final round of the encryption, the statements in lines 810–825 perform the transformations `SubBytes()`, `ShiftRows()` and `AddRoundKey()`. The result of the state matrix, or the ciphertext, is stored in array `X[]` and returned to the function caller.

The decryption function is similar and is listed in part VII of `ex06-09.js`.

```
Example: Continuation of ex06-09.js                          (Part VII)

829: function aes_decrypt(input)
830: {
831:     var X = new Array(4), Y = new Array(4), rki=0;
832:
833:     rki = 0;
834:     X = input;
835:     X[0] ^= aes_drk[0];
836:     X[1] ^= aes_drk[1];
837:     X[2] ^= aes_drk[2];
838:     X[3] ^= aes_drk[3];
839:     Y = aes_deround( Y, X, rki += 4);
840:     X = aes_deround( X, Y, rki += 4);
841:     Y = aes_deround( Y, X, rki += 4);
842:     X = aes_deround( X, Y, rki += 4);
843:     Y = aes_deround( Y, X, rki += 4);
844:     X = aes_deround( X, Y, rki += 4);
845:     Y = aes_deround( Y, X, rki += 4);
846:     X = aes_deround( X, Y, rki += 4);
847:     Y = aes_deround( Y, X, rki += 4);
848:
849:     if( aes_nr > 10 ) {
850:         X = aes_deround( X, Y, rki +=4);
851:         Y = aes_deround( Y, X, rki +=4);
852:     }
853:     if( aes_nr > 12 ) {
854:         X = aes_deround( X, Y, rki +=4);
855:         Y = aes_deround( Y, X, rki +=4);
856:     }
857:     rki +=4;
858:     X[0] = aes_drk[rki+0] ^ ( RSb[( Y[0] >>> 24 ) & 0xff ] << 24 );
859:                          ^ ( RSb[( Y[3] >>> 16 ) & 0xff ] << 16 )
860:                          ^ ( RSb[( Y[2] >>>  8 ) & 0xff ] <<  8 )
861:                          ^ ( RSb[( Y[1]        ) & 0xff ]         );
```

```
862:      X[1] = aes_drk[rki+1] ^ ( RSb[( Y[1] >>> 24 ) & 0xff ] << 24 )
863:                           ^ ( RSb[( Y[0] >>> 16 ) & 0xff ] << 16 )
864:                           ^ ( RSb[( Y[3] >>>  8 ) & 0xff ] <<  8 )
865:                           ^ ( RSb[( Y[2]          ) & 0xff ]       );
866:      X[2] = aes_drk[rki+2] ^ ( RSb[( Y[2] >>> 24 ) & 0xff ] << 24 )
867:                           ^ ( RSb[( Y[1] >>> 16 ) & 0xff ] << 16 )
868:                           ^ ( RSb[( Y[0] >>>  8 ) & 0xff ] <<  8 )
869:                           ^ ( RSb[( Y[3]          ) & 0xff ]       );
870:      X[3] = aes_drk[rki+3] ^ ( RSb[( Y[3] >>> 24 ) & 0xff ] << 24 )
871:                           ^ ( RSb[( Y[2] >>> 16 ) & 0xff ] << 16 )
872:                           ^ ( RSb[( Y[1] >>>  8 ) & 0xff ] <<  8 )
873:                           ^ ( RSb[( Y[0]          ) & 0xff ]       );
874:   return X;
875: }
876:
```

The operation of decryption is similar to encryption. All you need to do is replace the subkeys by aes_drk[], as illustrated in lines 835–838. The standard rounds are carried out by aes_deround(). For the final round, the tables are replaced by the decryption tables RSb[] (lines 858–873). The decrypted message is returned by line 874.

To test the encryption and decryption functions, some interface functions are needed and these are listed in part VIII of ex06-09.js.

```
Example: Continuation of ex06-09.js                          (Part VIII)

877: function keyStToSubkeys(inKeySt,encrypt)
878: {
879:   var i, rKeyArr = new Array();
880:   var len = inKeySt.length;
881:   var padKey = "\0\0\0\0\0\0\0\0\0\0\0\0\0\0\0\0"
882:   if (len < 16) {
883:       inKeySt = inKeySt +padKey;
884:       inKeySt = inKeySt.substring(0,16);
885:       len = 16;
886:   }
887:   if ((len > 16) && (len < 24)) {
888:       inKeySt += padKey;
889:       inKeySt = inKeySt.substring(0,24);
890:       len = 24;
891:   }
```

```
892:        if (len > 24) {
893:        inKeySt += padKey;
894:        inKeySt = inKeySt.substring(0,32);
895:        len = 32;
896:    }
897:    for (i=0; i<len; i++) rKeyArr[i] = inKeySt.charCodeAt(i);
898:    if (encrypt) {
899:        aes_set_enkey(rKeyArr, len*8);
900:    } else {
901:        aes_set_dekey(rKeyArr, len*8);
902:    }
903: }
904:
```

This is our usual interface function to capture the user key string from a Web page and set up all subkeys accordingly. When the length of the input key is less than 16 (16 bytes), the statements in lines 883–885 pad the key to 16 bytes (128-bit). When the key length is between 17 and 23, the key is padded and expanded to 24 bytes (192-bit) in lines 888–890. When the key length is bigger than 24, it is set to 32 bytes (256-bit) by lines 893–895. If the key length is 16 bytes or 24 bytes, there is no need to set anything. The for-loop in line 897 converts the key string into a byte array and the conditional-if statement in lines 899–902 sets the encryption or decryption subkeys depending on the status of the boolean variable `encrypt`. The main interface function is in part IX of `ex06-09.js`, and this completes the scheme.

```
Example: Continuation of ex06-09.js                          (Part IX)

905: function aes(keySt, msgSt, encrypt)
906: {
907:    var m=0, chunk=0, len = msgSt.length;
908:    var i, tResult="", result="";
909:    var lrArr=new Array(4);
910:
911:    keyStToSubkeys(keySt,encrypt);
912:    while (m < len) {
913:        lrArr[0]=(msgSt.charCodeAt(m++) << 24)|
                     (msgSt.charCodeAt(m++) << 16)|
914:                 (msgSt.charCodeAt(m++) <<  8)|
                      msgSt.charCodeAt(m++);
915:        lrArr[1]=(msgSt.charCodeAt(m++) << 24)|
                     (msgSt.charCodeAt(m++) << 16)|
916:                 (msgSt.charCodeAt(m++) <<  8)|
                      msgSt.charCodeAt(m++);
```

```
917:     lrArr[2]=(msgSt.charCodeAt(m++) << 24)|
                  (msgSt.charCodeAt(m++) << 16)|
918:              (msgSt.charCodeAt(m++) <<  8)|
                  msgSt.charCodeAt(m++);
919:     lrArr[3]=(msgSt.charCodeAt(m++) << 24)|
                  (msgSt.charCodeAt(m++) << 16)|
920:              (msgSt.charCodeAt(m++) <<  8)|
                  msgSt.charCodeAt(m++);
921:
922:     if (encrypt) {
923:          lrArr = aes_encrypt(lrArr);
924:     } else {
925:          lrArr = aes_decrypt(lrArr);
926:     }
927:     tempSt= String.fromCharCode(
928:        ((lrArr[0] >>> 24) & 0xff), ((lrArr[0] >>> 16) & 0xff),
929:        ((lrArr[0] >>>  8) & 0xff), ( lrArr[0]         & 0xff),
930:        ((lrArr[1] >>> 24) & 0xff), ((lrArr[1] >>> 16) & 0xff),
931:        ((lrArr[1] >>>  8) & 0xff), ( lrArr[1]         & 0xff),
932:        ((lrArr[2] >>> 24) & 0xff), ((lrArr[2] >>> 16) & 0xff),
933:        ((lrArr[2] >>>  8) & 0xff), ( lrArr[2]         & 0xff),
934:        ((lrArr[3] >>> 24) & 0xff), ((lrArr[3] >>> 16) & 0xff),
935:        ((lrArr[3] >>>  8) & 0xff), ( lrArr[3]         & 0xff));
936:
937:     tResult += tempSt; chunk += 16;
938:     if (chunk == 512) {
939:        result += tResult; tResult = ""; chunk = 0;
940:     }
941:   }
942:   return result + tResult;
943: }
```

This main interface is straightforward to read. First, the key and message strings captured from the Web page are input into the function as parameters. The function in line 911 is to set up all the subkeys. The while-loop in line 912 processes all the characters of the message. Every 16 bytes of the message are extracted and converted into four 32-bit elements in array lrArr[] (the state matrix). When encryption is true, the function in line 923 is called to encrypt the message. Otherwise, decryption is performed by line 925. The result is stored in array lrArr[]. The single statement in lines 927–935 converts the results back to a character string called tempSt. This is stored in tResult and later returns to the function caller by lines 937–942.

Fig. 6.23 AES encryption

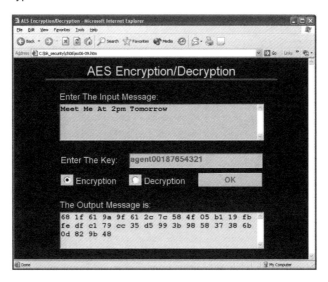

To test this script, make a copy of ex06-05.htm and call it ex06-09.htm. Now, modify the following lines:

```
 9: AES Encryption/Decryption<br />
31:   class="butSt" style="width:180px" value="OK" onclick="aes_fun()" />
44:  function aes_fun()
52:      llst = byteStToHex(aes(key, message,true))
58:      llst = aes(key, message,false)
```

All the modifications just change names. Line 9 changes the display. When the OK button is clicked, the function aes_fun() is called in line 31. This function is defined in lines 44. When encryption is true, the function aes() in line 52 is called to encrypt the message. When decryption is true, the function aes() in line 58, with a false parameter, will decrypt the message. Screenshots of this example are shown in Figures 6.23 and 6.24.

6.5.3 Testing vectors and building an AES utility

There are many test vectors for the AES scheme. To test our implementation, and compare it with others, the following nine testing vectors are provided.

Fig. 6.24 AES decryption

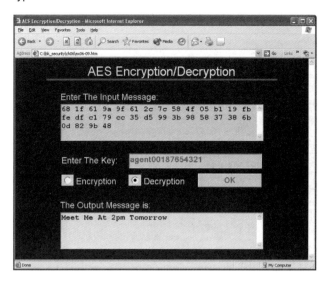

```
KEYSIZE=128

    key=00 01 02 03 05 06 07 08 0a 0b 0c 0d 0f 10 11 12
    pt= 50 68 12 a4 5f 08 c8 89 b9 7f 59 80 03 8b 83 59
    ct= d8 f5 32 53 82 89 ef 7d 06 b5 06 a4 fd 5b e9 c9

    key=14 15 16 17 19 1a 1b 1c 1e 1f 20 21 23 24 25 26
    pt= 5c 6d 71 ca 30 de 8b 8b 00 54 99 84 d2 ec 7d 4b
    ct= 59 ab 30 f4 d4 ee 6e 4f f9 90 7e f6 5b 1f b6 8c

    key=28 29 2a 2b 2d 2e 2f 30 32 33 34 35 37 38 39 3a
    pt= 53 f3 f4 c6 4f 86 16 e4 e7 c5 61 99 f4 8f 21 f6
    ct= bf 1e d2 fc b2 af 3f d4 14 43 b5 6d 85 02 5c b1

KEYSIZE=192

    key=00 01 02 03 05 06 07 08 0a 0b 0c 0d 0f 10 11 12
        14 15 16 17 19 1a 1b 1c
    pt= 2d 33 ee f2 c0 43 0a 8a 9e bf 45 e8 09 c4 0b b6
    ct= df f4 94 5e 03 36 df 4c 1c 56 bc 70 0e ff 83 7f

    key=1e 1f 20 21 23 24 25 26 28 29 2a 2b 2d 2e 2f 30
        32 33 34 35 37 38 39 3a
    pt= 6a a3 75 d1 fa 15 5a 61 fb 72 35 3e 0a 5a 87 56
    ct= b6 fd de f4 75 27 65 e3 47 d5 d2 dc 19 6d 12 52

    key=3c 3d 3e 3f 41 42 43 44 46 47 48 49 4b 4c 4d 4e
        50 51 52 53 55 56 57 58
    pt= bc 37 36 51 8b 94 90 dc b8 ed 60 eb 26 75 8e d4
    ct= d2 36 84 e3 d9 63 b3 af cf 1a 11 4a ca 90 cb d6
```

```
KEYSIZE=256
 key=00 01 02 03 05 06 07 08 0a 0b 0c 0d 0f 10 11 12
     14 15 16 17 19 1a 1b 1c 1e 1f 20 21 23 24 25 26
 pt= 83 4e ad fc ca c7 e1 b3 06 64 b1 ab a4 48 15 ab
 ct= 19 46 da bf 6a 03 a2 a2 c3 d0 b0 50 80 ae d6 fc

 key=28 29 2a 2b 2d 2e 2f 30 32 33 34 35 37 38 39 3a
     3c 3d 3e 3f 41 42 43 44 46 47 48 49 4b 4c 4d 4e
 pt= d9 dc 4d ba 30 21 b0 5d 67 c0 51 8f 72 b6 2b f1
 ct= 5e d3 01 d7 47 d3 cc 71 54 45 eb de c6 2f 2f b4

 key=50 51 52 53 55 56 57 58 5a 5b 5c 5d 5f 60 61 62
     64 65 66 67 69 6a 6b 6c 6e 6f 70 71 73 74 75 76
 pt= a2 91 d8 63 01 a4 a7 39 f7 39 21 73 aa 3c 60 4c
 ct= 65 85 c8 f4 3d 13 a6 be ab 64 19 fc 59 35 b9 d0
```

Since all these vectors are in hexadecimal format, a page that can read hexadecimal values is required for the testing. A quick way is to copy ex06-05.htm and call it ex06-010.htm. Modifying the following lines:

```
 9: AES Encryption/Decryption (Hex Input)<br />
31: class="butSt" style="width:180px" value="OK"
    onclick="aes_hex_fun()" />
41: <script src="ex06-09.js"></script>
44: function rc6_hex_fun()
52:     l1st = byteStToHex(aes(key, message,true));
59:     l1st = byteStToHex(aes(key, message,false));
63: var kSt="2b 7e 15 16 28 ae d2 a6 ab f7 15 88 09 cf 4f 3c ";
64: var pSt="32 43 f6 a8 88 5a 30 8d 31 31 98 a2 e0 37 07 34 ";
```

Line 9 changes the display. Line 41 includes the AES script file ex06-09.js so that its AES functions are available. When the OK button is clicked, the statement in line 31 calls the new function aes_hex_fun(). This new function is defined in line 44. For lines 52–59, all you need to do is change the function to aes(). Finally, a default test vector is declared in lines 63–64. This default test vector is the same as the one used in Section 6.4.4. Screenshots are shown in Figures 6.25 and 6.26.

As you can see from Figure 6.25, the ciphertext is the same as that in Section 6.4.4.

To build a utility to use the AES scheme on files, we consider a public domain program developed by Christophe Devine. The program has two C files aes.c and aes.h. A copy of these program files can be found in a number of search engines or downloaded from the site accompanying this book. To use the program, you may need to develop the following codes:

```
aes_context ctx;
aes_set_key( &ctx, key, nbit);
aes_encrypt( &ctx, buf, buf );
aes_decrypt( &ctx, buf, buf );
```

Fig. 6.25 AES encryption (hex)

Fig. 6.26 AES decryption (hex)

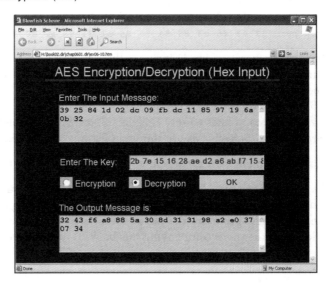

The first line defines a structure in the C language to accommodate the encryption and decryption subkeys. The second statement sets up all the AES subkeys in the structure `ctx`. The function in the third line encrypts the message in the byte array `buf[]` and outputs the result in the same array. The last statement performs decryption on the message in `buf[]`. To develop a driver utility to use AES on files, consider the C program `aesdriver.c`.

Example: aesdriver.c - The AES encryption/decryption driver

```
 1: #include <stdio.h>
 2: #include "aes.c"
 3: int main(int argc, char *argv[])
 4: {
 5:  int i, n;
 6:  unsigned char buf[16];
 7:  unsigned char kkey1[32];
 8:  FILE *inK, *inP, *outF;
 9:  aes_context ctx;
10:
11:  if (argc!=5) {
12:   printf("\nUsage: \n aesdriver (e)|(d) <infile> <outfile>
            <keyfile>\n");
13:   return 2;
14:  }
15:  for (i=0;i<32;i++) kkey1[i]=0;
16:  for (i=0;i<16;i++) buf[i]=0;
17:
18:  if((inK=fopen(argv[4],"rb"))==NULL){
19:     printf("\r\nCould not open input file: %s",argv[4]);
20:     return 2;
21:  } else {
22:     n= fread(kkey1,1,32,inK);
23:     fclose(inK);
24:  }
25:  if ( n < 16)              n = 16;
26:  if ((n > 16) && (n < 24)) n = 24;
27:  if ( n > 24)              n = 32;
28:  aes_set_key( &ctx, kkey1, n*8);
29:
30:  if((inP=fopen(argv[2],"rb"))==NULL){
31:     printf("\r\nCould not open input file: %s",argv[2]);
32:     return 2;
33:  }
```

```
34:  if((outF=fopen(argv[3],"wb"))==NULL){
35:        printf("\r\nCould not open output file: %s",argv[3]);
36:        return 2;
37:  }
38:
39:  if(argv[1][0]=='e') {
40:    while ((n=fread(buf,1,16,inP)) >0) {
41:        if (n < 16) {
42:            for(i=n;i<16;i++) buf[i]=0;
43:        }
44:        aes_encrypt( &ctx, buf, buf );
45:        if(fwrite(buf,1,16,outF) < 16) {
46:            printf("\r\nError writing to output file\r\n");
47:            return(3);
48:        }
49:    }
50:  }
51:  if(argv[1][0]=='d') {
52:    while ((n=fread(buf,1,16,inP)) >0) {
53:        if (n < 16) {
54:            for(i=n;i<16;i++) buf[i]=0;
55:        }
56:        aes_decrypt( &ctx, buf, buf );
57:        if(fwrite(buf,1,16,outF) < 16) {
58:            printf("\r\nError writing to output file\r\n");
59:            return(3);
60:        }
61:    }
62:  }
63:  fclose(inP); fclose(outF);
64:  return 0;
65: }
```

This driver program is similar to many of those we developed in previous sections. The new statements are highlighted and explained. Line 2 includes the program aes.c in the program. Line 22 reads in the user input key. The key is specified as maximum 32 bytes (256-bit). The number of rounds is determined by lines 25–27. All the AES subkeys are set by the execution of the function in line 28. When encryption is true, the statement in line 44 encrypts the message in buf[]. The resulting ciphertext is stored back in buf[] and saved to the outfile specified by the user. When decryption is true, the function in line 56 is executed and the result buf[] (plaintext) is saved to the outfile. A compiling and execution session of this driver program with a gcc C compiler is captured and shown in Figure 6.27.

Fig. 6.27   An AES encryption/decryption utility

```
H:\ch06>gcc -o aesdriver aesdriver.c
H:\ch06>aesdriver

Usage:
aesdriver (e)|(d) <infile> <outfile> <keyfile>

H:\ch06>aesdriver e zplain.txt zen.txt zkey.txt
H:\ch06>aesdriver d zen.txt zde.txt zkey.txt

H:\ch06>type zde.txt
Meet Me At 2pm Tomorrow

H:\ch06>tohex zen.txt
68 1f 61 9a 9f 61 2c 7c 58 4f 05 b1 19 fb fe df
c1 79 cc 35 d5 99 3b 98 58 37 38 6b 0d 82 9b 48

H:\ch06>
```

From this you can see that the ciphertext result is the same as that in Figure 6.23. Also, despite the complexity of the scheme, AES is extremely fast. For example, a 5MB Acrobat pdf file can be encrypted and decrypted by this driver program in less than half a second.

Now that we have a substantial experience of ciphers it's time to see some of the practical applications of them. Let's see how to use them on the so-called Common Gateway Interface (CGI) and Web databases providing security to users.

7

Encryption and server skills for Web page protection

7.1 Encryption skills for Web page protection

7.1.1 Protecting web pages with encryption

One of the great features of the World Wide Web is that documents (or Web pages) written in the HTML/XHTML language can be displayed by any machine on the Internet equipped with a Web browser such as IE, NS or Opera. Whether for business or personal use, the Web is an ideal place to publicize and exchange information reaching the global network population with a public protocol – HyperText Transport Protocol (HTTP). However, if pages can be read by any computer with a browser, the information they contain can no longer be considered to be safe. This creates one of the biggest security problems on the Web. Not many companies would like to post sensitive business information on a Web page without proper protection. Even for personal use, would you post family information on a Web page?

Fig. 7.1 Protecting Web pages with encryption

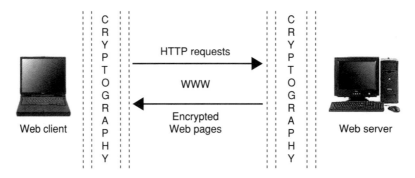

Providing a solution and protecting your own pages is not difficult. All you need to do is encrypt your page with one of the encryption processes described in previous chapters. Basically, when you request a page from the server, it returns an encrypted page to your browser and asks for a password. The password is used to decrypt the page contents and display it on the browser. Since decryption is done at the browser level and only encrypted information is transmitted on the Web, security is maintained to a certain degree.

Encryption offers data which can be transmitted safely over the insecure Internet and Web environment. Only authorized personnel, with passwords, can decrypt and obtain original messages back. Consider the simple example in ex07-01.htm.

Example: ex07-01.htm - A simple page to be encrypted

```
1:  <html><head><title></title></head>
2:  <body style="font-family:arial;font-size:18pt;
3:    color:#000000;background:#eeeeff">
4:    Dear Daddy <br />
5:    This is the picture I took yesterday!
6:  <image src="06_img.jpg">
7:  <script>window.resizeTo(750,700)</script>
8:  </body></html>
```

This is a simple HTML page to post a family photo on the Web. One of the easiest ways to encrypt this page is to use, for example, the AES encryption in ex06-09.htm. When you copy this page onto the input box and enter a key, a series of hexadecimal values is obtained, as shown in Figure 7.2.

As you can see, the page is encrypted with the password 'agent00187654321'. The next step is to write a page to incorporate the password and the encrypted message. One example is shown in ex07-02.htm.

Example: ex07-02.htm - Protecting Web page contents

```
1:  <head><title>Protecting Web Page Contents -
       ex07-02.htm </title></head>
2:  <style>
3:    .butSt{background-color:#aaffaa;font-family:arial;
           font-weight:bold;
4:          font-size:18pt;color:#880000;width:250px;height:35px}
5:    .txtSt{font-family:arial;font-weight:bold; text-align:left;
6:          font-size:18pt;color:#ffff00}</style>
7:  <body style="background:#000088">
8:  <table style="position:absolute;left:60px;top:30px" class="txtSt">
```

Fig. 7.2 Encrypting a Web page

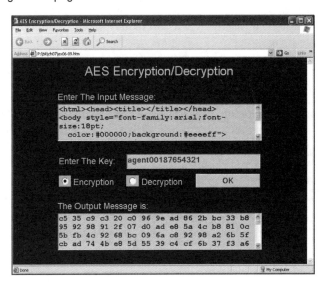

```
 9:    <tr><td colspan="2" >
10:      Private Site<br /> Enter Name & Password<br /><br/></td></tr>
11:    <tr><td>Name:</td>
12:        <td><input type="text" name="userId" id="userId"
13:            class="butSt" value="johnsmith"></td></tr>
14:    <tr><td>Password:</td>
15:        <td><input type="password" name="passId" id="passId"
16:            class="butSt" value="agent00187654321"></td></tr>
17:    <tr><td colspan="2">
18:        <input type="button" onclick="sub_fun()" class="butSt"
19:         style="width:150px;background:#dddddd"
               value="O.K."></td></tr>
20: </table>
21: <script src="hexlib.js"></script>
22: <script src="ex06-09.js"></script>
23: <script>
24: window.resizeTo(600,500);
25: function sub_fun()
26: {
27:  var enData=
28:   "c5 35 c9 c3 20 c0 96 9e ad 86 2b bc 33 b8 95 92 98 91 2f "+
29:   "07 d0 ad e8 5a 4c b8 81 0c 5b fb 4c 92 68 bc 09 6a c8 92 "+
```

```
30:     "98 a2 6b 5f cb ad 74 4b e8 5d 55 39 c4 cf 6b 37 f3 a6 75 "+
31:     "52 e0 24 a9 ee d2 17 6a ff 3e 6f ab a4 c4 95 51 f8 9a 5a "+
32:     "94 aa ea a6 a1 35 fd f6 4f 69 c7 4d ee 40 3f 62 96 c7 72 "+
33:     "27 44 d0 52 1f ca 69 bd ed c3 e7 4b d7 75 84 ae 19 4c 4d "+
34:     "95 58 23 56 2c 24 31 c7 b0 5f 98 52 8b 3c 0f d3 82 c8 7b "+
35:     "a3 7e fa ee 06 e8 7b bd 84 50 7d 94 41 11 fd d7 c0 7d b5 "+
36:     "46 d3 b7 30 df 73 83 19 0e 72 98 3a 2b 2b 82 65 7d 50 8d "+
37:     "ee df 41 ee c4 6b b9 e5 c3 29 60 01 bd 72 e5 13 8f dd e6 "+
38:     "32 79 88 dd 74 11 86 e5 94 c9 34 bc 6e 2c a0 c5 62 b4 90 "+
39:     "a8 77 f0 2e 0d c0 05 58 e5 25 86 c4 d5 cd 56 ed db 17 31 "+
40:     "cd ca 26 4f 27 2e f1 0f 57 13 46 5d 54 11 57 05 ea fe 19 "+
41:     "19 a4 8c ab c5 aa c8 77 23 54 0d a9 53 61 01 46 12 5d a6 "+
42:     "22 de f6 e8 b2 71 ";
43:     var key = document.getElementById("passId").value;
44:     var message = hexStToByteSt(enData);
45:     var llst = aes(key, message,false);
46:     document.write(llst);
47: }
48: </script>
49: </body>
```

This is the main part of a simple page to transmit encrypted information to a
browser. The table structure in lines 8–20 constructs two text boxes so that
the user can enter a name and password. When the OK button is pressed, the
function sub_fun() in lines 25–47 is executed. The first variable of this function
is enData containing the encrypted data of the Web page ex07-01.htm from
Figure 7.2. The input password is captured by the statement in line 43. This
password is used to decrypt the encrypted page using the AES scheme specified
in line 45. In fact, any of the encryption/decryption schemes in previous
chapters can be used. Since the AES scheme is used, the AES associated files are
included in lines 21–22. The decrypted page is then output to the screen by the
document.write() function in line 46. Screenshots of this example in action are
shown in Figures 7.3 and 7.4.

One of the characteristics of this example is that the main page is protected by AES
encryption and only the encrypted data of the page is transmitted over the Internet.
The password is entered locally and used to decrypt the page at the browser level.
Even if the transmission is captured by an intruder they still need to guess the
password in order to crack the encryption code.

A page like this is safe but not very practical. The reason is that the encrypted data
in lines 27–42 is hard-coded by hand. For a more practical tool, let's consider how
to construct a page to generate encrypted Web pages automatically.

Fig. 7.3 `ex07-02.htm`

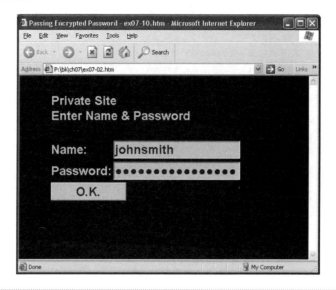

Fig. 7.4 The decrypted page

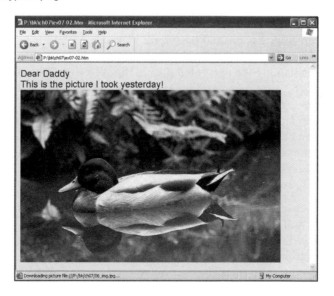

7.1.2 Generating encrypted Web pages

The basic idea behind generating an encrypted page is simple. The first step is to get an encryption scheme introduced in previous chapters and modify it to generate a page similar to ex07-02.htm. Consider the newly modified page (ex07-03.htm).

Example: ex07-03.htm – Generating an encrypted Web page (Part I)

```
 1: <head><title>Generating Encrypted Web Page</title></head>
 2: <style>
 3:   .butSt{font-size:12pt;width:250px;height:40px;
 4:          font-weight:bold;background:#dddddd;color:#ff0000}
 5: </style>
 6: <body style="font-family:arial;font-size:16pt;text-align:center;
 7:        background:#eeeeff;color:#000000">
 8:  Generating Encrypted Web Pages<br />
 9:  <img alt="pic" src="line1.gif" height="7" width="650" /><br />
10:
11: <table style="font-size:14pt" align="center">
12:  <tr><td><br />Enter The Input Message: </td></tr>
13:  <tr><td><textarea style="font-size:12pt;width:650px;height:150px;
14:         font-weight:bold;background:#dddddd" rows="5" cols="40"
15:         id="in_mesg">Meet Me At 2pm Tomorrow</textarea></td></tr>
16: </table>
17:
18: <form action="">
19: <table style="font-size:14pt" cellspacing="10" align="center">
20:  <tr><td>Enter Your Password: </td>
21:    <td><input type="password" id="key_v" size="32" maxlength="32"
22:        style="font-size:12pt;width:200px;height:30px;
23:        font-weight:bold;background:#dddddd;color:#ff0000"
            value="agent00187654321" /></td>
24:    <td style="width:180px;text-align:left"><input size="20"
25:    type="button" class="butSt" style="width:80px" value="OK"
       onclick="gen_fun()" />
26:    </td></tr>
27: </table>
28: </form>
29:
30: <table style="font-size:14pt" align="center">
31:  <tr><td>The Encrypted Page Is: </td></tr>
32:  <tr><td><textarea rows="5" cols="40" id="out_mesg" readonly
33:         style="font-size:12pt;font-weight:bold;width:650px;
34:         height:150px;background:#aaffaa"></textarea></td></tr>
35: </table>
```

This page fragment contains two text areas, one text box and one OK button. The page, or data, you want to encrypt should be pasted in the first text area specified in lines 13–15. The password is entered in the text box in lines 21–23. When the OK button is clicked, the function gen_fun() is activated and an entire new page is generated, similar to ex07-02.htm. This new page contains the encrypted page using the specified password. The driving force function gen_fun() is listed in part II of ex07-03.htm.

```
Example: Continuation of ex07-03.htm                    (Part II)

36:  <script src="hexlib.js"></script>
37:  <script src="ex06-09.js"></script>
38:  <script>
39:   function gen_fun()
40:   {
41:    var key="", message="",llst="";llstV="";
42:    var indexS=0, indexE=indexS +51;
43:
44:    document.getElementById("out_mesg").value = llst;
45:    key = document.getElementById("key_v").value;
46:    message = document.getElementById("in_mesg").value;
47:    llst = byteStToHex(aes(key, message,true));
48:
49:    llstV = " \""+llst.substring(indexS, indexE)+"\"+ \n";
50:    indexS=indexE; indexE=indexS +51;
51:
52:    while (indexE < llst.length) {
53:      llstV += " \""+llst.substring(indexS, indexE)+"\"+ \n"
54:      indexS=indexE; indexE=indexS +51;
55:    }
56:    llstV += " \""+llst.substring(indexS, llst.length)+"\"; \n"
57:
58:    var htmlSt00 =
59:    '<html><head><title></title></head> \n' +
60:    '<style> \n' +
61:    '  .butSt{background-color:#aaffaa;font-family:arial; \n' +
62:    '     font-weight:bold;font-size:18pt;color:#880000; \n' +
63:    '     width:250px;height:35px} \n' +
64:    '  .txtSt{font-family:arial;font-weight:bold; \n' +
65:    '     text-align:left;font-size:18pt;color:#ffff00}</style> \n' +
66:    '<body style="background:#000088"> \n' +
67:    '<table style="position:absolute;left:60px;top:30px"
             class="txtSt"> \n'+
68:    '  <tr><td colspan="2" >Private Site<br /> \n' +
```

```
69:  '          Enter Name & Password<br /><br/></td></tr> \n' +
70:  '   <tr><td>Name:</td> \n' +
71:  '        <td><input type="text" name="userId" id="userId" \n' +
72:  '            class="butSt" value="johnsmith"></td></tr> \n' +
73:  '   <tr><td>Password:</td> \n' +
74:  '        <td><input type="password" name="passId" id="passId" \n' +
75:  '            class="butSt" value="agent00187654321"></td></tr>
                \n' +
76:  '   <tr><td colspan="2"><input type="button" \n' +
77:  '           onclick="sub_fun()" class="butSt"
                style="width:150px; \n' +
78:  '           background:#dddddd" value="O.K."></td></tr> \n' +
79:  '</table> \n' +
80:  '<script src="hexlib.js"><\/script> \n' +
81:  '<script src="ex06-09.js"><\/script> \n' +
82:  '<script> \n' +
83:  'window.resizeTo(600,500); \n' +
84:  ' function sub_fun()\n'+
85:  ' { '+
86:  '    var enData=\n' + llstV + '\n'+
87:  '    var key = document.getElementById("passId").value;\n'+
88:  '    var message = hexStToByteSt(enData); \n'+
89:  '    var llst = aes(key, message,false); \n'+
90:  '    document.write(llst); \n'+
91:  ' } \n'+
92:  ' <\/script> \n'+
93:  '</body></html> ';
94:   document.getElementById("out_mesg").value = htmlSt00;
95:  }
96: </script>
97: </body>
```

The two statements in lines 36–37 include the AES scheme in the page so that AES encryption and decryption are available. The password and page contents from part I of ex07-03.htm are captured by lines 45–46. The entire content is encrypted by the statement in line 47 and stored in variable llst. Since llst can be a long string depending on the input, statements in lines 49–56 are used to break it into smaller sections. Each section is 52 characters controlled by the variables indexS and indexE. Line 49 gets the first section, and the variables indexS and indexE are updated by line 50. The while-loop in lines 52–55 continues through the sections and appends them to variable llstV. The last section is extracted and added into llstV in line 56.

Now, a page similar to ex07-02.htm is constructed (lines 58–93) and stored in variable htmlSt00. Note that the encrypted data llstV is inserted into htmlSt00 at

Fig. 7.5 Generating an encrypted page

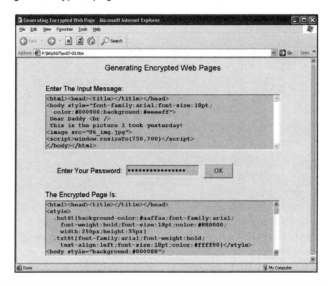

line 86 so that the variable html St00 is actually a generated Web page containing the encrypted data. This page is output to the second text area by the statement in line 94. A screenshot is shown in Figure 7.5.

From this, we can see that ex07-01.htm is input into the first text area. After the password is entered and the OK button pressed, a page similar to ex07-02.htm is generated in the second text area. This page can then be cut and pasted as a new page or application. When this page is called, you will see the result as in Figures 7.3 and 7.4. The line break symbols '\n' in lines 49–83 are used to generate line breaks in Figure 7.5 so that the page can be read more easily. The page will still work without them.

To protect a page using encryption against unauthorized users is important and effective against intruders. However, when the page is decrypted and run successfully, the source code of the script is generally obtainable through the 'View|Source' option of the browser. The next problem to tackle is protecting the intellectual property rights (IPR) of a script and/or page designs against the openness of the World Wide Web.

7.1.3   Protecting intellectual property rights

Suppose you have developed some valuable Web pages and/or software, such as some of the encryption programs in Chapters 3–6. Do you want to protect the source code against the View|Source option of a capable browser?

Encryption is only good at preventing unauthorized users. It offers little protection to intellectual property rights (IPR), particularly for Web pages and software. The openness of the World Wide Web makes all HTML/XHTML and script (ECMAScript) source codes visible, or obtainable so that they can be run properly. For this reason, it is not easy to secure the source code from authorized users. In fact, many people don't believe that you can protect the sources of HTML/XHTML pages and scripts. However, we can make the source of an HTML/XHTML object difficult or impossible to read and modify. This process is generally known as 'obfuscation'.

In many cases, making a page or script program hard to read has the same effect as protecting the IPR. From a functional point of view, obfuscation has no effect on the execution – all functions and features remain the same.

One of the early pieces of obfuscation software (obfuscator) is Microsoft's 'Script Encoder'. You can download this software through the download center and search engine at the Microsoft website. This program can make the script inside a page difficult to read. The encoding program is called `screnc.exe`, and one of the best ways to demonstrate how to use it is by example. Suppose you have a page `ex07-04.htm`.

```
Example: ex07-04.htm - A test page for Windows Script Encoder

 1:  <html>
 2:  <head><title>Script Encoder Sample Page</title></head>
 3:  <body style="font-family:arial;font-size:22pt;
 4:     font-weight:bold;background:#000088;color:#ffff00">
 5:  <script>
 6:     //**Start Encode**
 7:     function myTest()
 8:     {
 9:      var st = "This is a testing Page Protected<br />"+
10:              "by Ms Windows Script Encoder <br />"
11:     document.write(st);
12:     }
13:     myTest()
14:  </script>
15:  </body></html>
```

This page is easy to read. The only interesting statement is line 4, i.e. `//**Start Encode**`. This statement will instruct the script encoder `screnc.exe` to start the encoding process on the next line. If you issue the command

```
screnc ex07-04.htm ex07-04en.htm
```

the page will be obfuscated and the result is shown in a new page `ex07-04en.htm`. When you edit the encoded page, the source code will be seen as shown in Figure 7.6.

Fig. 7.6 Obfuscated page

```
<html>
<head><title>Script Encoder Sample
Page</title></head>
<body style="font-family:arial;font-size:22pt;
  font-
weight:bold;background:#000088;color:#ffff00">
<script language = JScript.Encode>
  //**Start Encode**#@~^wwAAAA==@#@&P~6E
        mYbW
        ~:HKn/D`b@#@&PPP@#@&,PP7C.PkY,'~JP4b/~kk~1
,YndDkxL~hlL+,KMWO▯mD+N@!4M~z@*JQ@#@&P~~,PP,~P,PPr
8zPt/,▯rx[GS/~?1.kaY~3
        mW[nMP@!4M~J@*E@#@&,PP9W1;:▯xORSDrO▯`/Dbi@
#@&P,N@#@&,PsXP+dOv#@#@&/jEAAA==^#~@</script>
</body></html>
```

As you can see, the script is encoded and difficult to read. However, the encoder is easily reversible and provides little security to the source code of the script. A number of decoders for `screnc.exe` are available. One of the most popular is called 'Windows Script Decoder' (`scrdec14.exe`) and it can be downloaded by using a search engine and searching for 'Windows Script Decoder'. The C source code `scrdec14.c` is also available. To compile this C program, you can use the command

```
gcc -o scrdec14.exe scrdec14.c
```

The executable program `scrdec14.exe` will be stored in your local directory. To decode the page `ex07-04en.htm`, you can use

```
scrdec14 ex07-04en.htm ex07-04de.htm
```

The decoded page `ex07-04de.htm` is exactly the same as the original `ex07-04.htm`. From the security point of view, Windows Script Encoder doesn't provide secure obfuscation.

To better protect source code and IPR against theft, one solution is to use a one-way obfuscator. The reason is simple. If there is no way (or it is very hard) to obtain the original, the obfuscating result will remain difficult to read for everyone. This will apply to all hackers, including the original designer as well. One such free obfuscator is called Javascript Chaos Engine (JCE) developed by Syntropy Development.

The JCE engine is, in fact, a program called `jce.jar`. When this program is launched, a JCE window is opened. To obfuscate a script you can use the 'open' option to load it into the window. For example, the obfuscation of the RC4 encryption script (i.e. `ex05-08.js`) is shown in Figure 7.7. Basically, the engine replaces all function and variable names by long numeric names, making the script

Fig. 7.7 Obfuscating `ex05-08.js`

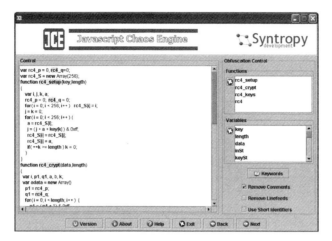

difficult to read. On the right-hand side of the JCE window, there are two boxes listing the function and variable names. You can use these boxes to control which functions or variables you don't want to obfuscate. For example, there are four functions listed in the top box for you to use in Figure 7.7.

From Chapter 5 we know that the RC4 page contains three files, namely `ex05-08.htm`, `ex05-08.js` and `hexlib.js`. The main page calls the function `rc4()` inside the script `ex05-08.js`. Therefore, we don't want to obfuscate the name of function `rc4()`. In this case, we delete this function name from the top box and click the `Next` button – the obfuscated result is shown in Figure 7.8.

Fig. 7.8 The obfuscated result

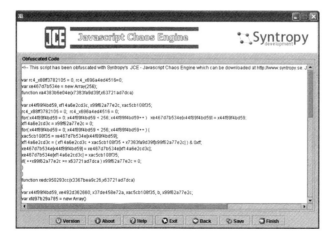

The obfuscated result can be copied (or saved) and run as a normal script. For a comparison, the listings of the original and obfuscated functions rc4() are given in Figures 7.9 and 7.10.

Fig. 7.9 The original rc4()

```
function rc4(keySt, msgSt)
{
  var len = msgSt.length;
  var i, tempSt="";
  var msgArr = new Array(), outArr = new Array();
  for (i=0;i<256;i++) rc4_S[i]=0;
  rc4_p1=0; rc_q1=0;

  rc4_keys(keySt,keySt.length);

  for (i=0;i< len;i++) msgArr[i] = msgSt.charCodeAt(i) & 0xff;
  outArr = rc4_crypt(msgArr,len);

  tempSt = "";
  for (i=0;i< len;i++) {
    tempSt += String.fromCharCode(outArr[i] & 0xff);
  }
  return tempSt;
}
```

Fig. 7.10 The obfuscated rc4()

```
function rc4(xb63150f1cf4, xb2a61a951a3)
{
var x63721ad7dca = xb2a61a951a3.length;
var x44f89f4bd59, x77ee165a60a="";
var x1e2583fc348 = new Array(), x6f362991efa = new Array();
for (x44f89f4bd59=0;x44f89f4bd59<256;x44f89f4bd59++)
xe467d7b534e[x44f89f4bd59]=0;
rc4_xe492d362660=0; rc_x37de458e72a=0;
x5fa3728fdb3(xb63150f1cf4,xb63150f1cf4.length);
for (x44f89f4bd59=0;x44f89f4bd59< x63721ad7dca;x44f89f4bd59++)
x1e2583fc348[x44f89f4bd59] =
xb2a61a951a3.charCodeAt(x44f89f4bd59) & 0xff;
x6f362991efa = xedc95Q293cc(x1e2583fc348,x63721ad7dca);
x77ee165a60a = "";
for (x44f89f4bd59=0;x44f89f4bd59< x63721ad7dca;x44f89f4bd59++) {
x77ee165a60a += String.fromCharCode(x6f362991efa[x44f89f4bd59] &
0xff);
}
return x77ee165a60a;
}
```

As you can see from Figure 7.10, all the variables of `rc4()` are changed, making it difficult to read, modify or reuse. If you have a large and complicated script or program, the effect of the obfuscation will became more significant. Also, the JCE engine produces a new set of names every time you run the program. The operation is one-way, providing enhanced security for the source code and IPR. Some people may not consider obfuscation as an encryption technique because there is no password involved and the obfuscated result is basically same as the original. In Chapter 1, we refer to encryption as a process to transform readable text into unreadable gibberish. Under this broadened definition, obfuscation is an encryption technique.

By combining obfuscation and encryption, both the source code (or IPR) and accessibility to the Web software can be protected at same time. For example, you can combine the main page of RC4, `ex05-08.htm`, and the obfuscated file, `ex05-08.js`, to form a page called `ex07-05.htm`. This page is, in fact, Web software to perform RC4 encryption/decryption. Also the RC4 part of the page is obfuscated – the source code and IPR are protected.

To further protect the RC4 software against unauthorized use, you can encrypt the RC4 page `ex07-05.htm` by using `ex07-03.htm`. For example, when you insert `ex07-05.htm` into the input window of `ex07-03.htm` and click the OK button, the encrypted page is generated in the lower box (see Figure 7.11). Let's call the encrypted page `ex07-05en.htm`. When you run this page, you will see a window asking for a username and password. The password is used to decrypt the page and the result is shown in Figure 7.12.

Fig. 7.11 Encrypting the RC4 scheme

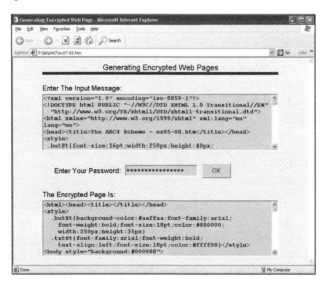

Fig. 7.12 Running the RC4 scheme

Obfuscation is an interesting technique for protecting software at source level. When combined with encryption, such as ex07-03.htm, a powerful security tool is generated.

One of the drawbacks of encryption page ex07-03.htm is that it cannot be shared with many people. Users have to use the same password to gain access to the encrypted page. Another idea for protecting your page, or downloadable software, such that it can be shared with many people is using 'activation code'.

7.1.4 Licensing your Web page with activation code

Suppose you have developed some valuable Web software, such as the RC4 scheme in Section 7.1.2. Do you want to both protect the software and license it to many users at the same time? In fact, this does not just apply to Web software; you will find that many companies offer valuable Web information such as shares and investments, horse racing tips, premium jobs and downloadable songs to their members or customers.

Much of this Web software and information is protected by the so-called 'activation code' process. Once you have paid for and registered the software, the associated company will email you with an activation code. Only when you enter the activation code into the software or page, will it run and be displayed properly by the browser. This kind of online business is sometimes regarded as information licensing.

Some readers may already have figured out that the basic idea behind activation code is encryption. In fact, the licensing process can be described by the following steps.

1   Preparing the encrypted page or software

- Select a secret key (or license code) for the page or software to be licensed.

- Encrypt the page or software using the secret key.

2   Generating the activation code

- Get the registered information, such as the name of the user.

- Use the name to encrypt the secret code obtaining the activation code.

- Email the activation code to the registered user.

3   Decrypting the encrypted page

- Develop a page incorporating the encrypted page and ask for the username and activation code.

- Decrypt the activation code using the registered name to obtain the secret key.

- Use the secret key to decrypt the page for the browser.

The RC4 encryption page in Section 7.1.3 is a bit too long for demonstration purposes. To illustrate the activation code idea, consider the simple page presented as `ex07-06.htm`.

```
Example: ex07-06.htm - A page to be licensed

1:  <html><head><title></title></head>
2:  <body style="font-family:arial;font-size:22pt;
3:    color:#ffff00;background:#000088">
4:   Unbeatable Shares and Investments<br />
5:   Great Tips For Horse Racing <br />
6:   Premium Job Information <br />
7:   Free Downloadable Music & Songs<br />
8:  </body></html>
```

Suppose this page can provide valuable information to your members. The next step is to select a secret password for the encryption. For this example, we use the

Fig. 7.13 Generating an encrypted page

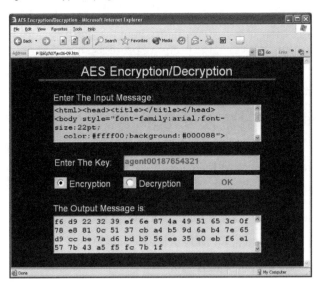

secret key 'agent00187654321'. Using this password, page `ex07-06.htm` can be encrypted by the AES scheme `ex06-09.htm` in Chapter 6. The encrypted result is shown in Figure 7.13.

Now we have the encrypted Web page, in hexadecimal format, the next step is to generate the activation code for a particular user. Suppose the registered user is called 'johnsmith'. The activation code for 'johnsmith' can be obtained by encrypting the secret key (or license code) 'agent00187654321' using the password 'johnsmith'. The process is demonstrated in Figure 7.14.

Figure 7.14 shows that the activation code for 'johnsmith' is `91 8f b1 be 4b 1a aa de 47 b1 db c5 59 47 a8 11`, which is a sequence of hexadecimal values generated by the AES program `ex06-09.htm`. Other data formats and encryption schemes described in previous chapters can also be applied. The activation code can now be sent to the user.

The central idea of the activation code is that when the code is decrypted using the username, the secret key is obtained. This secret key is used to decrypt the protected page and render it at the browser level. This arrangement allows each user to have a different activation code, thus providing a basic solution to the sharing problem (see Figure 7.15).

As with the username/password case above, we can develop a page asking for a username/activation pair. An example page is provided in `ex07-07.htm`.

Fig. 7.14 Generating an activation code

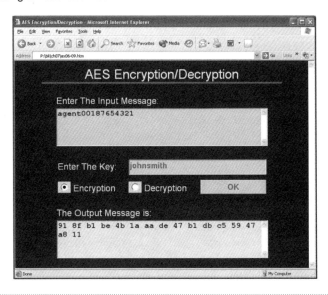

Fig. 7.15 The use of activation codes for Web software

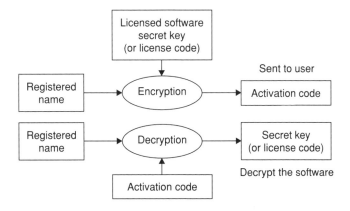

Example: ex07-07.htm – Software licensing and activation codes

```
 1: <head><title>Protecting Page With Activation Code</title></head>
 2: <style>
 3:    .butSt{background-color:#aaffaa;font-family:arial;
           font-weight:bold;
 4:           font-size:18pt;color:#880000;width:250px;height:35px}
 5:    .txtSt{font-family:arial;font-weight:bold; text-align:left;
 6:           font-size:18pt;color:#ffff00}</style>
 7: <body style="background:#000088">
 8: <table style="position:absolute;left:60px;top:30px" class="txtSt">
 9:    <tr><td colspan="2" >Licensed Page/Software<br />
10:         Enter Name & Activation code<br /><br/></td></tr>
11:    <tr><td>Name:</td>
12:       <td><input type="text" name="userId" id="userId"
13:          class="butSt" value="johnsmith"></td></tr>
14:    <tr><td colspan="2">Activation Code:</td></tr>
15:    <tr><td colspan="2"><input type="text" name="passId" id="passId"
16:          class="butSt" style="width:450px" value=></td></tr>
17:    <tr><td colspan="2">
18:       <input type="button" onclick="sub_fun()" class="butSt"
19:        style="width:150px;background:#dddddd"
           value="O.K."></td></tr>
20: </table>
21: <script src="hexlib.js"></script>
22: <script src="ex06-09.js"></script>
23: <script>
24: window.resizeTo(600,500);
25: function sub_fun()
26: {
27: var enData=
28:    "c5 35 c9 c3 20 c0 96 9e ad 86 2b bc 33 b8 95 92 98 91 2f 07 "+
29:    "d0 ad e8 5a 4c b8 81 0c 5b fb 4c 92 68 bc 09 6a c8 92 98 a2 "+
30:    "6b 5f cb ad 74 4b e8 5d 55 39 c4 cf 6b 37 f3 a6 75 52 e0 24 "+
31:    "a9 ee d2 17 e0 ac 88 27 d3 a0 9f 41 7a 7e 0b 92 a2 f3 6d 5b "+
32:    "00 cf 03 ca 28 59 ee f1 3e 8b 8c 6e 18 87 d0 69 4c f6 6b cb "+
33:    "62 a9 9c 24 ff 3f 67 a2 1f ce b4 50 c8 1e 9c 27 80 7a eb f7 "+
34:    "b8 ce 3e 67 28 55 0f fa ff 2a 1f 30 67 8d 7a d7 37 54 0e 73 "+
35:    "02 6c 43 09 bc c5 53 cf e4 46 e6 31 c6 3b 50 c4 05 76 44 83 "+
36:    "ef 98 a4 10 e2 b5 fc 94 d2 a1 30 b3 0d 7b 81 0d 6f 2a 66 a8 "+
37:    "0c 8a c6 f8 59 12 85 bb 83 b3 49 d9 1b c1 b7 8d 6a 8d ce 07 "+
38:    "6f 82 92 1a 06 fb 5c 0e d8 92 ee 55 ed 51 5e ab a4 1e ce 67 "+
39:    "fc cd 7c 1e cc a2 ab 47 02 ad 9d 82 79 6a 20 59 98 c4 f6 d9 "+
40:    "22 32 39 ef 6e 87 4a 49 51 65 3c 0f 78 e8 81 0c 51 37 cb a4 "+
41:    "b5 9d 6a b4 7e 65 d9 cc be 7a d6 bd b9 56 ee 35 e0 eb f6 e1 "+
42:    "57 7b 43 a5 f5 fc 7b 1f ";
```

```
43:    var tmpSt = hexStToByteSt(document.getElementById("passId").value);
44:    var key0 = document.getElementById("userId").value;
45:    var message = hexStToByteSt(enData);
46:    var key = aes(key0,tmpSt,false);
47:    var llst = aes(key, message,false);
48:    document.write(llst);
49: }
50: </script>
51: </body>
```

If you compare this page with ex07-02.htm, you will find that they are similar. For the XHTML part, the only lines modified are 9 and 10 reflecting the changes of use. This page will ask for a username and the activation code to activate the page. When the OK button is pressed, the function sub_fun() is run and the encrypted page is decrypted and displayed. The function sub_fun() is listed in lines 25–49.

First, the encrypted data are stored in variable enData (lines 28–42). The activation code and username are captured by the statement in lines 43–44. The activation code is then decrypted by the username, as illustrated in line 46. The result is the secret key stored in variable key. This secret key is used to decrypt the encrypted page data in line 47. The document.write() function in line 48 displays the result in the browser window. Screenshots are shown in Figures 7.16 and 7.17.

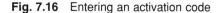

Fig. 7.16 Entering an activation code

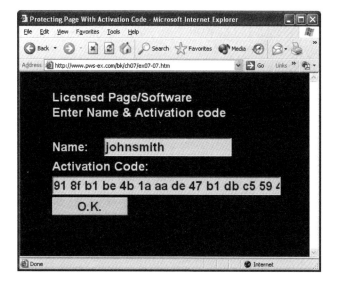

Fig. 7.17 Displaying the decrypted page

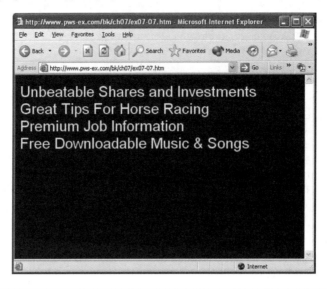

This example demonstrates how to protect licensed software or pages. For each registered user, a separate activation code is issued. The code is used to gain access to the page information. Almost anything acceptable by the browser, including multimedia pages, movies clips and games, can be protected in this way. Encrypted pages like this can also be changed easily, weekly or even daily depending on the requirement. Some readers may find that having to enter an activation code every time could be tedious. Even if people can store the code in a file and paste it into the page, it may discourage many customers. A solution to this problem is provided by the idea of 'cookies'.

7.1.5 Using cookies for security

A cookie is a small piece of information stored in the client machine by a Web page. Netscape stores its cookies in a file called `cookies.txt`. Internet Explorer uses a whole directory (under the window directory) called `cookies`. Cookies, or cookie information, can be accessed and manipulated using the script feature `document.cookie`.

The original idea of cookies was to make it easier for surfers to access their favourite Web sites. For example, when you visit a site for the first time, you may be asked to enter your name and perhaps your email address and other information to identify yourself. The site will then place a cookie containing this information on your system. When you return next time, the site will request information based on the cookie in your machine to determine who you are, and perhaps whether you have authorization to access the site.

Since cookie messages are unprotected and hidden from users, they create serious security issues that affect most Web users. Let's take a look at how a Web site (e.g. www.pws-ex.com) can set cookies in your local machine. Consider the following script fragment:

```
1: <script>
2:  var expDate = new Date ()
3:  expDate.setTime(expDate.getTime() + (1000 * 60 * 60 * 24))
4:  document.cookie="Username=JohnSmith;
      expires="+expDate.toGMTString()
5:  document.cookie="Email=JohnSmith@pws-ex.com;
      expires="+expDate.toGMTString()
6: </script>
```

This script will set two cookies on your machine, namely `Username` and `Email`.

Basically, every cookie consists of three parts – cookie name, cookie value and an expiry date. The cookie name and value can be any character string representing the information that you want to store. The expiry date determines the lifespan of the cookie. If the date is before the current time, the cookie is deleted immediately. If no expiry date is set, the cookie will be deleted soon after your Web session. As illustrated in lines 2–3 above, the lifespan of the cookie is set by the two procedures below:

- get the current time;

- add a counting number in terms of thousandths of a second.

The counting number `1000*60*60*24` in line 3 represent a lifespan of one day. If you want the cookie to last for a year, you use the counting number `1000*60*60*24*365`. The general format for setting a cookie in a client machine is (line 4)

```
document.cookie="cookieName=cookieValue; expires=expirationDate"
```

The three variables `cookieName`, `cookieValue` and `expirationDate` are user-defined. They form the basic components of a cookie. All cookie transactions between browser and server are normally transparent to users.

When you visit the site www.pws-ex.com again, your browser will search for cookies from it and return them as a string in `document.cookie`. This is why information can be stored as cookies and retrieved later. Cookies are ideal places to store, for example, the activation code described in Section 7.1.3.

Now let's develop some basic cookie functions which will be used later in this chapter. Consider the script file `cookie.js`.

Example: cookie.js - ECMAScript for cookie functions

```
 1: function setCookie(cookieName, cookieValue, expDate)
 2: {
 3:   var cookieSt = cookieName + "=" + escape(cookieValue) +
 4:     ((expDate) ? "; expires=" + expDate.toGMTString() : "");
 5:   document.cookie = cookieSt;
 6: }
 7:
 8: function getCookie(cookieName)
 9: {
10:   var cookieItem = document.cookie.split("; ");
11:   for (var ii=0; ii< cookieItem.length; ii++) {
12:    if (cookieName == cookieItem[ii].split("=")[0])
13:     return unescape(cookieItem[ii].split("=")[1]);
14:   }
15:   return 0;
16: }
17:
18: function setACode(activeCode)
19: {
20:   expDate = new Date();
21:   expDate.setTime(expDate.getTime() + (1000 * 60 * 60 * 24*30));
22:   setCookie("actCode",activeCode,expDate);
23: }
24:
25: function setUsrName(nameV)
26: {
27:   expDate = new Date();
28:   expDate.setTime(expDate.getTime() + (1000 * 60 * 60 * 24*30));
29:   setCookie("usrName",nameV,expDate);
30: }
31:
32: function deleteACode()
33: {
34:   aCode="";
35:   expDate = new Date();
36:   expDate.setTime(expDate.getTime() - (1000 * 60 * 60 * 24));
37:   setCookie("actCode",aCode,expDate)
38: }
```

This script file contains five cookie functions. The first two are general functions. The function setCookie() in lines 1–6 has three arguments. The first two parameters are strings representing the cookie name and value. The third parameter is the expiry date. When this function is executed, the corresponding cookie will be planted on your system. Once you have a cookie on your machine, you can use the getCookie() function to obtain the value of a particular cookie. The remaining three functions are specifically for the activation code. For example, the function setACode() sets a cookie with the following properties:

Cookie name: actCode

Cookie value: activeCode   (determined by function call)

Expiry date: one month from the current time

Similarly, the function setUsrName sets a cookie related to the username. When the deleteACode() function is called, the activation cookie will be deleted. Now, we can develop a page to use cookies for activation code. Consider ex07-08.htm.

Example: ex07-08.htm – Security with cookies   **(Part I)**

```
 1: <head><title>Security Using Cookies</title></head>
 2: <style>
 3:   .butSt{background-color:#aaffaa;font-family:arial;
            font-weight:bold;
 4:          font-size:18pt;color:#880000;width:250px;height:35px}
 5:   .txtSt{font-family:arial;font-weight:bold; text-align:left;
 6:          font-size:18pt;color:#ffff00}</style>
 7: <body style="font-family:arial;font-size:22pt;color:#ffff00;
 8:     background:#000088">
 9: <script src="hexlib.js"></script>
10: <script src="ex06-09.js"></script>
11: <script src="cookie.js"></script>
12: <script>
13:  var htmlSt00 =
14:   '<table style="position:absolute;left:60px;top:30px"
        class="txtSt"> '+
15:  '   <tr><td colspan="2" >Licensed Page/Software<br /> '+
16:  '         Enter Name & Activation code<br /><br/></td></tr>'+
17:  '   <tr><td>Name:</td>'+
18:  '       <td><input type="text" name="userId" id="userId" '+
19:  '            class="butSt" value="johnsmith"></td></tr>'+
20:  '   <tr><td colspan="2">Activation Code:</td></tr> '+
21:  '   <tr><td colspan="2"><input type="text" name="passId"
                id="passId" '+
22:  '            class="butSt" style="width:450px" value=></td></tr>'+
23:  '   <tr><td colspan="2">'+
24:  '      <input type="button" onclick="sub_fun()" class="butSt" '+
25:  '        style="width:150px;background:#dddddd"
              value="O.K."></td></tr>'+
26:  '</table>'+
```

```
27:    '<script src="cookie.js"><\/script> '+
28:    '<script> '+
29:    'function sub_fun() '+
30:    '{'+
31:    '  var aCode = document.getElementById("passId").value; '+
32:    '  var uName = document.getElementById("userId").value; '+
33:    '  setACode(aCode);'+
34:    '  setUsrName(uName);'+
35:    '  location.href="ex07-06.htm" '+
36:    '} '+
37:    '<\/script> ';
38:
```

Apart from the AES engine and cookie functions in lines 9–11, this page fragment contains only one variable htmlst00. In fact, it is a Web page. When there is no activation cookie in the local machine, this page will be displayed asking for username and activation code. After the OK button is clicked, the function sub_fun() in lines 29–36 is activated. This function uses the input information to set the activation code and username as cookies (lines 31–34). The statement in line 35 redirects control to the same page with the cookies installed.

The next step is to make sure that when this page is run with the cookies in place, the encrypted (valuable) page will be decrypted and displayed by the browser. This function is listed in part II of ex07-08.htm.

```
Example: Continuation of ex07-08.htm                         (Part II)
39:  function decrypt_page(usrV,acV)
40:  {
41:   var enData=
42:   "c5 35 c9 c3 20 c0 96 9e ad 86 2b bc 33 b8 95 92 98 91 2f 07 "+
43:   "d0 ad e8 5a 4c b8 81 0c 5b fb 4c 92 68 bc 09 6a c8 92 98 a2 "+
44:   "6b 5f cb ad 74 4b e8 5d 55 39 c4 cf 6b 37 f3 a6 75 52 e0 24 "+
45:   "a9 ee d2 17 e0 ac 88 27 d3 a0 9f 41 7a 7e 0b 92 a2 f3 6d 5b "+
46:   "00 cf 03 ca 28 59 ee f1 3e 8b 8c 6e 18 87 d0 69 4c f6 6b cb "+
47:   "62 a9 9c 24 ff 3f 67 a2 1f ce b4 50 c8 1e 9c 27 80 7a eb f7 "+
48:   "b8 ce 3e 67 28 55 0f fa ff 2a 1f 30 67 8d 7a d7 37 54 0e 73 "+
49:   "02 6c 43 09 bc c5 53 cf e4 46 e6 31 c6 3b 50 c4 05 76 44 83 "+
50:   "ef 98 a4 10 e2 b5 fc 94 d2 a1 30 b3 0d 7b 81 0d 6f 2a 66 a8 "+
51:   "0c 8a c6 f8 59 12 85 bb 83 b3 49 d9 1b c1 b7 8d 6a 8d ce 07 "+
52:   "6f 82 92 1a 06 fb 5c 0e d8 92 ee 55 ed 51 5e ab a4 1e ce 67 "+
53:   "fc cd 7c 1e cc a2 ab 47 02 ad 9d 82 79 6a 20 59 98 c4 f6 d9 "+
54:   "22 32 39 ef 6e 87 4a 49 51 65 3c 0f 78 e8 81 0c 51 37 cb a4 "+
55:   "b5 9d 6a b4 7e 65 d9 cc be 7a d6 bd b9 56 ee 35 e0 eb f6 e1 "+
56:   "57 7b 43 a5 f5 fc 7b 1f ";
```

```
57:
58:    window.resizeTo(600,500);
59:    var tmpSt = hexStToByteSt(acV);
60:    var key0 = usrV;
61:    var message = hexStToByteSt(enData);
62:    var key = aes(key0,tmpSt,false);
63:    var llst = aes(key, message,false);
64:    document.write(llst);
65: }
66:
67: function checkActCode()
68: {
69:    var aaC = getCookie("actCode");
70:    var uuN = getCookie("usrName");
71:    if ((aaC ==0)||(aaC =="undefined")||(uuN ==0)||
       (uuN =="undefined")) {
72:      document.write(htmlSt00);
73:    } else {
74:      decrypt_page(uuN,aaC);
75:    }
76: }
77:
78: //deleteACode();
79: checkActCode();
80: </script>
81: </body>
```

When this page is run with the activation code installed, the function
decrypt_page() is executed (lines 39–65). This function has two parameters, usrV
(username) and acV (activation code). The variable usrV is used to decrypt the
string acV to obtain the secret key for the encrypted page stored in enData.
Finally, the decrypted page stored in llst (lines 62–63) is displayed by the
document.write() function in line 64. The structure of this function is similar to
ex07-02.htm.

The function checkActCode() in lines 67–76 is used to check whether the activation
cookie exists and to perform actions accordingly. First, the values of the cookies
usrName and actCode are obtained by the statements in lines 69–70. If one of the
cookies is empty or not defined, the login window stored in variable htmlSt00 is
displayed (line 72). In this case, the username and activation code will be asked
for and put into cookies. Otherwise, the decrypt_page() function is run for the
decryption. The execution results are the same as shown in Figures 7.16 and 7.17
except that there is no need to input the activation code every time. Provided that

Fig. 7.18 Internet Options window

the machine you are working on is accessible by only you and is not connected to the Internet all the time, storing cookies on your machine poses little security threat.

For better Web security, it is recommended that you never allow unwanted cookies to be stored in your machine. Check your machine regularly and instruct your favourite browser to always ask before storing a cookie. If you are using IE, this can be done by going to `Tools|Internet Options` and opening the `Internet Options` window (Figure 7.18). From this window go to `Privacy` and click the `Advance` button to open the `Advanced Privacy Setting` window. Now, select the `Override automatic cookie handling` and check both the `Prompt` radio buttons as illustrated in Figure 7.19.

Also, remember to delete cookies regularly. This can be done by clicking the 'Delete Cookies' button from the 'Internet Options' window.

Example `ex07-08.htm` demonstrates how to license Web pages to people in a protective way. The structure is flexible, convenient and you can make changes

Fig. 7.19 Handling cookies

on the encrypted page on a regular basis. You don't need any server knowledge to operate this. However, you have no control over the users. There is no record of users who access the encrypted information. You may not even know whether the access is legitimate. For deeper user control or authentication you need the help of a server, or server technologies.

7.2 Server technologies and security

7.2.1 An introduction to server technologies and CGI

From a user's point of view, Web browsers, such as IE, NS and Opera, are the most important tools on the Internet. With a simple click, information or documents around the world can be displayed on the browser window instantly. Therefore, server knowledge is not generally needed for many Web users. For Web programmers, a solid background of server software, such as Apache, and server technologies, such as Practical Extraction and Report Language (Perl), Active Server Page (ASP) and PHP: Hypertext Preprocessor (PHP), is essential for handling various Web problems.

Also, the functionalities of browsers are nowadays far beyond the original design for displaying HTML/XHTML documents and for running scripts in the ECMAScript Language, i.e. client-side activities. A capable basic browser should also act as interface for the following server-side activities:

■ trigger and execute programs in server;

■ work with other server technologies such as Perl, ASP and PHP;

■ communicate with databases in remote sites;

■ safeguard the network and perform security encryptions and business transactions.

Actions inside a Web server are generally called 'server technologies'. Since a server is a machine connected to the Internet and running all the time, actions on server are more reliable and permanent. If you want a permanent record of an order or a transaction, or just reliable date and time information for your business, you may have no choice but to use one or more server techniques. In fact, server skills are vital to most online businesses. From online shopping, ordering and confirmation to checkout, payment and transactions, almost all online businesses require actions from a server. With a simple click, the browser can trigger and run a program on the server to perform all kinds of business activities. In particular, security checks can be performed before sending the associated HTML/XHTML documents back to the browser.

As a simple example, if you have an executable program such as `mycgi` (or `mycgi.exe` for Microsoft systems) on a server such as www.pws-ex.com, you can run it by issuing the following HTTP command in the address bar of the browser:

```
http://www.pws-ex.com/mycgi.exe
```

If the executable program generates an HTML/XHTML document back to the calling browser via the standard input/output (I/O) channel, the browser can process and display the document as if it was a proper HTML/XHTML document.

This process is generally regarded as the Common Gateway Interface (CGI) process. In particular, if a program resides on a server and generates an HTML/XHTML document on the standard output (or the console window) when executed, the browser can catch the document and display it as if it had been returned by the server. In this case, the program is called a CGI program. Before developing some CGI programs, let's have a reminder of the browser–server dialog from Chapter 1.

When you request the document from your favourite browser, such as

```
http://www.pws-ex.com/ex07-01.htm
```

your browser sends a request to the server e.g. www.pws-ex.com for the file ex07-01.htm. This process is known as the client–server dialog. In a normal circumstance, the server sends back a message as defined in lx07-01.txt.

```
Example: lx07-01.txt - Server CGI response

 1: HTTP/1.1 200 OK
 2: Date: Monday, 09-May-2005 13:04:12 GMT
 3: Server: www.pws-ex.com
 4: MIME-version: 1.0
 5: Last-modified: Wednesday, 13-Oct-2004 11:33:16 GMT
 6: Content-type: text/html
 7: Content-length: 195
 8:     * a blank line *
 9: <html><head><title>Example: ex01-01.htm</title></head>
10: <body style="font-family:arial;font-size:28pt;text-align:center">
11:    I Know How The Web <br /> Works Now</body></html>
```

In line 1 the Web server agrees to use HTTP for communication, and the status 200 identifier indicates the successful completion of the whole request. After some HTTP system variables, the statement Content-type: text/html in line 6 confirms that the document returned will indeed be an HTML document (or page). From this dialog, you can see that the entire HTML page (i.e. ex01-01.htm) is transmitted to the browser after the 'blank line' in line 8. This style and transmission format is specified by the so-called HTTP protocol. The browser will now be able to interpret the page and display it.

In fact, the important statements for this communication are lines 1, 3, 6 and 8, which are known as a CGI header. After the blank line in line 8, the entire HTML/XHTML document is sent. A program can print out these four statements to a standard output, such as screen, together with an HTML/XHTML document generally referred to as a CGI program. If the proper CGI header is sent, the generated page will be displayed by the browser. As an example, consider a CGI program written in the C language (ex07-09.c).

```
Example: ex07-09.c - A C/C++ program for CGI

 1: #include "stdio.h"
 2: int main()
 3: {
 4:   printf("HTTP/1.0 200 OK \n");
 5:   printf("Server:www.pwt-ex.com\nMIME-Version:1.0\n");
 6:   printf("Content-type: text/html\n\n");
 7:
 8:   printf("<?xml version=\"1.0\" encoding=\"iso-8859-1\"?> \n");
 9:   printf("<!DOCTYPE html PUBLIC \"-//W3C//DTD XHTML 1.0 \n");
10:   printf("  Transitional//EN\" \n
              http://www.w3.org/TR/xhtml1/DTD/ \n");
11:   printf("  xhtml1-transitional.dtd\"> \n");
12:   printf("<html xmlns=\"http://www.w3.org/1999/xhtml\" \n");
13:   printf("  xml:lang=\"en\" lang=\"en\">\n");
14:
15:   printf("<head><title></title></head> \n");
16:   printf("<body style=\"background:#000088;color:#ffff00;\n");
17:   printf("  font-weight:bold;\n font-family:arial;
              font-size:22pt;");
18:   printf("  text-align:center\"> \n");
19:   printf(" <br /><br /> \n This page was generated by \n");
20:   printf(" a C program <br /> \n");
21:   printf(" and run as a CGI script \n</body>\n</html>\n");
22:   return 0;
23: }
```

From this C/C++ program, we can see that only one function printf() is used.
This function is a popular statement in C to output a string to screen. For example,
the statement in line 4

```
printf("HTTP/1.0 200 OK \n");
```

will output the string 'HTTP/1.0 200 OK' with a line break on the screen. In fact,
lines 4–6 output the necessary CGI header to the screen. Note that the double
line breaks '\n\n' at the end of line 6 generate a blank line. The remaining lines
(lines 9–22) return a simple XHTML page that can be displayed by a browser.

If you issue the command 'gcc -o ex07-01.exe ex07-01.c' to compile the C
program, you should have an executable program ex07-01.exe on your machine.
For many systems, including NT and UNIX/LINUX, CGI programs are usually
stored in a default directory called cgi-bin. Other systems may have a different
default directory. If the program ex07-01.exe is inside a default directory, such as
/book/chap07 of www.pws-ex.com, you can run this program directly from the
browser by issuing the HTTP command

```
http://www.pws-ex.com/book/chap07/ex07-01.exe
```

By executing this command, the browser requests the document `ex07-01.exe` from the site www.pws-ex.com and directory `/book/chap07`. Since the document is an executable program, the server will run the program first. The execution result is a CGI header and a XHTML document, and therefore can be displayed on the browser window.

A screenshot of this example is shown in Figure 7.20. If you activate `View` and then `Source` from the browser menu, the source code of the page will be seen to be the same as the output from the executable program `ex07-01.exe` (except for the CGI header). The output of the executable program on a console window is shown in Figure 7.21.

For UNIX/LINUX systems, you may have a different name for the executable program and may need to change the program status to `executable` so that it can be run by server.

Note that the minimum requirement for a CGI program to work is the simple CGI magic string listed below:

```
Content-type: text/html\n\n
```

That is, the content type plus a blank new line. This statement will instruct the browser to listen for an HTML/XHTML document. CGI programs can be considered to be special applications on servers generating HTML/XHTML documents and communicating with browsers. For this reason, a general

Fig. 7.20   `ex07-09.exe`

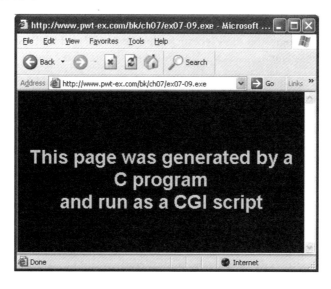

Fig. 7.21 Source generated by program `ex07-09.exe`

```
<?xml version="1.0" encoding="iso-8859-1"?>
<!DOCTYPE html PUBLIC "-//W3C//DTD XHTML 1.0
  Transitional//EN"
  http://www.w3.org/TR/xhtml1/DTD/
  xhtml1-transitional.dtd">
<html xmlns="http://www.w3.org/1999/xhtml"
  xml:lang="en" lang="en">
<head><title></title></head>
<body style="background:#000088;color:#ffff00;
  font-weight:bold;
  font-family:arial;font-size:22pt;  text-
align:center">
  <br /><br />
  This page was generated by
  a C program <br />
  and run as a CGI script
</body>
</html>
```

computing language, such as C/C++, is not suitable for the task. More dedicated programming languages are needed.

7.2.2   CGI technologies and preprocessors

Any program or application that generates the CGI magic string 'Content-type: text/html' plus a blank line and returning an HTML/XHTML document generally qualifies as a CGI application. This idea is the origin of almost all server technologies on the Web, including Perl, ASP and PHP. Since most CGI technologies generate XHTML documents, they are also called CGI preprocessors.

There are two kinds of CGI preprocessor. One is 'non-embedded' and the other is 'embedded'. A non-embedded CGI preprocessor is a language or technology that does not include HTML/XHTML as part of the technology. For example, the C language can be used for CGI applications but XHTML is not a part of the C language. One popular non-embedded CGI technology is Perl. When HTML/XHTML statements can be used or considered to be part of the CGI application, the CGI technology said to be embedded. For example, ASP and PHP are embedded CGI preprocessors. That is, you can use XHTML statements inside ASP or PHP programs.

CGI is a big subject on the Web, and even a brief discussion is well beyond the scope of this chapter. For this reason, only selected topics on Perl and PHP will be discussed. Also, only those techniques directly related to security application will be presented. In particular, we will focus on how to handle encrypted data between browser and server.

Now, let's have a look at some CGI preprocessors, namely Perl and PHP.

The Perl preprocessor

For Web applications, the searching and extraction power of the Perl language make it an ideal choice for handling CGI applications. In general, the Perl package contains an executable program, or preprocessor, called `perl` to process documents written in the Perl language (or Perl script).

Basically, the `perl` program reads in a file called a Perl script and produces a CGI header and an XHTML document. When these two values are sent to a browser, such as IE, NS or Opera, the XHTML document is displayed. Since the Perl language has many more Web features than C languages, Perl is more suitable for Web programming. Some advantages of using Perl are:

- the system is independent and easy to understand;

- it is a powerful alternative to C/C++ or any other programming languages;

- the ability to call system commands and functions;

- its strong text-processing functions, such as pattern matching.

If you have a UNIX/LINUX system up and running, you may already have the `perl` preprocessor installed. If you are using Windows XP, 2000, 9.x and/or NT, a `perl` preprocessor package called `ActivePerl` can be downloaded from www.activestate.com. Basically, `perl` is free and available to everyone. Sending an XHTML document from browser to server using `perl` is simple – consider the framework listed in `ex07-10.pl`.

Example: ex07-10.pl – A framework for converting XHTML to Perl

```
 1: #! /usr/bin/perl
 2: print ("Content-type: text/html\n\n");
 3: my $timeV = scalar(localtime());
 4: print << "mypage";
 5: <html><head><title></title></head>
 6: <body style="font-family:arial;font-weight:bold;
 7:    font-size:24pt;color:#000000;background:#eeeeee">
 8:   This is a page generated by<br /> a Perl program<br />
 9:   Now is the time: <br />$timeV
10: </body></html>
11: mypage
```

This is a Perl file to be interpreted by the `perl` program in generating a simple XHTML page. After the location of the `perl` program (line 1), the statement in line 2 outputs the 'magic' string 'Content-type: text/html' and a blank line to the standard output (screen). This is the minimum requirement to instruct the browser to listen for an HTML/XHTML document. The Perl statement in line 3 obtains the date and time from the server and stores it in variable `$timeV`. Note that local variables in Perl are declared with keyword `my`. The `print<<"mypage"` command in line 4 specifies a 'here-document' and is used to output all the messages in lines 5–10 to the screen as an HTML page. Now, the variable `$timeV` containing the time is also a part of the page (line 9).

If you have the `perl` program installed, you can activate it from a shell window (or MSDOS window). One such command is

```
shell> perl ex07-10.pl
```

If you run `ex07-08.pl` as a CGI application, you can use

```
http://www.pws-ex.com/chap07/ex07-10.pl
```

from the browser. In this case, the Perl file is assumed to be in the `/chap07` directory. The result is shown in Figure 7.22. The purpose of this example is not the display but to understand the basic nature of CGI applications, the Perl preprocessor (`perl`), the Perl source file and the relationship with the Web browsers. When you use `Tools|View` to see the page, you will see the display shown in Figure 7.23.

Fig. 7.22   Running a Perl script

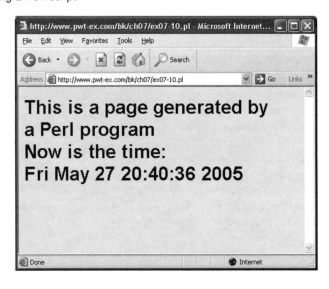

Fig. 7.23 The generated Web page

```
<html><head><title></title></head>
<body style="font-family:arial;
font-weight:bold;fontsize:24pt;
color:#000000;background:#eeeeee">

This is a page generated by<br />
a Perl program<br />
Now is the time: <br />
Fri May 27 20:40:36 2005

</body></html>
```

For non-embedded CGI preprocessors, all HTML/XHTML statements need to be output by the print() or similar function before they can be displayed by the browser. In other words, Perl statements cannot be mixed with HTML/XHTML statements. As an example of an embedded CGI preprocessor, we consider PHP.

The PHP preprocessor

A popular embedded CGI preprocessor on the Web is the PHP:HyperText Preprocessor (PHP). The PHP software is a program called 'php'. Perl and PHP are Web technologies that can be used to develop platform-independent CGI applications. They both work in a similar fashion in that a CGI header and an XHTML document are output to the browser via the standard output device.

Unlike Perl, XHTML documents or statements can be embedded into a PHP program. To understand how PHP works, consider a date and time example using PHP script as listed in ex07-11.php.

```
Example: ex07-11.php - Generating XHTML with PHP

1: <?PHP echo"<?";?>xml version="1.0"
     encoding="iso-8859-1"<?PHP echo"?>";?>
2: <!DOCTYPE html PUBLIC "-//W3C//DTD XHTML 1.0 Transitional//EN"
3:     "http://www.w3.org/TR/xhtml1/DTD/xhtml1-transitional.dtd">
4: <html xmlns="http://www.w3.org/1999/xhtml" xml:lang="en" lang="en">
5: <head><title>Getting Date & Time Using PHP --
     ex14-03.php</title></head>
6: <body style="background:#000088;text-align:center;
     font-family:arial;
7:   font-size:16pt;color:#ffff00"> Getting Today's
     Date Using PHP <br /><br />
```

```
 8: <?PHP    $today = getdate();
 9:          $month = $today['month'];
10:          $mday = $today['mday'];
11:          $year = $today['year'];
12:          $hours = $today['hours'];
13:          $minutes = $today['minutes'];
14:          $seconds = $today['seconds'];
15: ?>
16: <script>
17:   document.write("Today Is <br />")
18:   document.write("The Current Day = <?PHP echo "$mday"; ?> <br />")
19:   document.write("The Current Month = <?PHP echo "$month"; ?> <br />")
20:   document.write("The Current Year = <?PHP echo "$year"; ?>
                     <br /><br />")
21:   document.write("And The Time Is <br />")
22:   document.write("The Current Hours = <?PHP echo "$hours"; ?> <br />")
23:   document.write("The Current Minutes= <?PHP echo
                     "$minutes"; ?> <br />")
24:   document.write("The Current Seconds = <?PHP echo
                     "$seconds"; ?> <br />")
25: </script>
26: </body> 27: </html>
```

Any statements between the PHP bracket pair `<?PHP` and `?>` will be processed
by the PHP preprocessor in the server before sending them back to the browser.
The PHP `echo 'xxx'` function prints out the string to the screen. For example, the
command in line 1

```
<?PHP echo"<?";?>
```

outputs the string '`<?`', which is the first two characters for an XHTML page. Also,
all PHP variables are prefixed with a '$' symbol. The statement in line 8 gets the
date and time in variable `$today`. Lines 9–14 extract the corresponding values
for month, weekday, year, hours, minutes and seconds. These values are used
to construct a Web page in lines 18–24. As a result, a valid XHTML page is
constructed and sent back to browser.

Provided you have a proper installation of PHP, you can run this PHP script with
the command

```
shell>php ex07-11.php
```

where `shell>` is the command prompt in the associated console window. The
processing result is shown in Figure 7.24. From this you can see that the first three
lines are similar to:

```
X-Powered-By:PHP/xx.xx.xx
Content-type: text/html
xxxx a Blank Line xxxx
```

The first statement is the identity of the PHP preprocessor. The second and third lines are the 'magic' CGI header to the browser. If the following HTTP command is issued from the browser:

```
http://www.pws-ex.com/chap07/ex07-11.php
```

the XHTML document is rendered and displayed as shown in Figure 7.25.

Now you have some idea how CGI technologies such as Perl and PHP work. Before you can use them effectively for CGI applications, a basic understanding of how they communicate with Web pages is needed.

Fig. 7.24 Output from PHP

```
P:\bk\ch07>o:\php\php ex07-11.php
X-Powered-By: PHP/4.0.6
Content-type: text/html

<?xml version="1.0" encoding="iso-8859-1"?>
<!DOCTYPE html PUBLIC "-//W3C//DTD XH TML 1.0
   Transitional//EN" "http://www.w3.org/TR/
   xhtml1/DTD/xhtml1-transitional.dtd">
<html xmlns="http://www.w3.org/1999/xhtml"
xml:lang="en" lang="en">
<head><title>Getting Date & Time Using PHP -ex07-11.php
</title></head>
<body style="background:#000088;text-align:center;
   font-family:arial;font-size:18pt;color:#ffff00">
Getting Today's Date Using PHP <br /><br />
<script>
   document.write("Today Is <br />")
   document.write("The Current Day = 27 <br />")
   document.write("The Current Month = May <br />")
   document.write("The Current Year = 2005 <br /><br />")
   document.write("And The Time Is <br />")
   document.write("The Current Hours = 21 <br />")
   document.write("The Current  Minutes = 30 <br />")
   document.write("The Current Seconds = 26 <br />")
</script>
</body>
</html>
```

Fig. 7.25 ex07-11.php

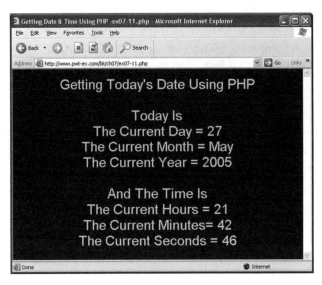

7.2.3 Passing password information to servers

Pages written by server technologies such as Perl and PHP are called server pages. Server pages, in general, can be called or activated by the XHTML form element <form>. This specifies a form for a user to fill out. Commonly, they are used to get user input and trigger a page on a server. More than one form can be specified in a single page, and they can be nested, i.e. forms can be inside a form. The general format for a form is illustrated in ex07-02.txt.

```
Example: ex07-02.txt - HTML/XHTML form element
1: <form action ="url" method="xxx" style="xxx" id="xx" name="xx">
2:  ...
3:  ... Any Sensible XHTML Elements
4:  ... Such as Text, Buttons, Radio Boxes, Checkboxes, and TextAreas
5:  ...
6:  <input type="submit" value="Submit" style="xxx" name="xxx"
    id="xxx" />
7: </form>
```

The input element in line 6 is a button-like structure called submit, which is associated with the form. When this button is pressed, the entire form is submitted to the server application, or server page, specified by the form action and URL location in line 1. All well-defined XHTML elements associated with the form are submitted at the same time.

The `action` attribute usually specifies a CGI page on a server to be run with the submitted data. If this attribute is absent, then the current document URL is used. The `method` attribute determines how the data, parameters or form contents are to be submitted. In normal circumstance, two choices are available:

- `get` – causes the form contents to be appended to the URL as if they were a normal query;

- `post` – causes the form contents to be sent to the server as a data body rather than as part of the URL.

As soon as the `Submit` button of a form is pressed, every element with a `name` attribute between `<form>` and `</form>` is passed to the CGI application specified by the form `action`. Consider the following form declaration.

```
<form action="my_perl.pl" method="get">
  Enter Your Name:
  <input type="text" name="nameId" id="nameId" value=""><br />
  Enter Password:
  <input type="text" name="passId" id="passId" value=""><br />
  <input type="submit" value="Submit">
</form>
```

This is an example of using the form element in HTML/XHTML to pass a username and password to the server. In this case, the `get` CGI communication method is used. When the `method` attribute is absent, the `get` method is the default. If the user enters

```
Enter Your Name: JohnSmith
Enter Password:  john199
```

to the form and presses the `Submit` button, an HTTP request (client–server interaction) from the client would look something like the listing in `ex07-03.txt`.

```
Example: ex07-03.txt - Client-server communication with the get method

1: GET my_perl.pl?nameId=JohnSmith&passed=john011
2: Accept: www/source
3: Accept: text/html
4: Accept: image/gif
5: Accept: image/jpg
6: User Agent: xxxx
7: From: xxxx
8:    *** a blank line ***
```

As you can see from this message, the form contents are assembled into a query URL to the server as directed by line 1

```
GET my_perl.pl?nameId=JohnSmith&paddId=john199
```

After the keyword GET is the name of the document to be activated. It can be a C program or any server page, such as ASP or PHP. In this case, a Perl program my_perl.pl is requested. The string after the first question mark '?' is called the 'query string'. In this example, the query string passes two name/value pairs to the program my_perl.pl. They are

```
nameId=JohnSmith&passId=john199
```

The left-hand side is the name specified by the name attribute of the form and the right-hand side is the value. Each name/value pair is separated by an ampersand symbol '&'. That is, there are two name/value pairs passed to the server. Note that the password 'john199' is not encrypted (not yet!). Some general rules for the query string are:

- Strange characters in any of the name or value strings will be escaped: this includes '=', '&' and punctuation – the space character is replaced by a '+' sign.

- For text and password entry fields the user input will be the value of the field – if the user didn't type anything, the value would be empty but the name= part of the query string would still be present.

How the name/value pairs are separated, and obtaining the user input data, is application dependent. If the action is referenced to a C program, say, you may need to parse the name and value yourself. If you are using server technology such as Perl, ASP or PHP, these languages have built-in functions to extract the name and value pairs.

When the get method is used, the query string is attached to the requesting URL and will appear in the address bar of your browser. If the post method is used, the query string will be passed to the server at the end of the client–server dialog. Consider the following name and password example fragment:

```
<form action="my_perl.pl" method="post">
  Enter Your Name:
  <input type="text" name="nameId" id="nameId" value=""><br />
  Enter Password:
  <input type="text" name="passId" id="passId" value=""><br />
  <input type="submit" value="Submit">
</form>
```

This is a form application using the post method. When the form is filled out as

```
Enter Your Name: Mr. John JohnSmith
Enter Password:  john199
```

and submitted to the server, the client–server dialog in `ex07-04.txt` is sent to server by the browser.

```
Example: ex07-04.txt - An HTTP message from the client: post method

 1: POST /my_perl.pl HTTP/1.0
 2: Accept: www/source
 3: Accept: text/html
 4: Accept: image/gif
 5: Accept: image/jpg
 6: User Agent: xxxx
 7: From: xxxxxx
 8: Content-type: application/x-www-form-urlencoded
 9: Content-length: 30
10:    *** a blank line ***
11: usrName=Mr.+John+JohnSmith&tel=john011
```

Sometimes, the `post` method is also called the post-query. This post-query requests the file `my_perl.pl` from the root directory of the server (line 1). In this case, the file is a Perl script and, in fact, can be any CGI application acceptable to the CGI protocol.

For most CGI applications, the `Content-type` is the key word `text/html` to indicate that the application is an XHTML document. The `Content-type` in this case is the MIME-type specified as `application/x-www-form-urlencoded` (line 8). This means that the variable name/value pairs will be encoded the same way as a URL is encoded. The total length of data (lines 11) is 30 and stored in `Content-length` (line 9). After the blank new line in line 10, the query string is attached.

With client–server interaction and CGI data communication in mind, you will have a basic idea of how CGI works. In fact, surfing on the Web can be considered as a special case of CGI application where the server sends back an HTML/XHTML document without any preprocessing. Again, CGI is a big subject and only selected topics directly related to security are presented in the following sections.

7.2.4 Verifying encrypted passwords using Perl script

To use CGI for security application, we first consider how to pass encrypted (or hashed) passwords to the server page. The encrypted password can be used to perform user authentication using CGI techniques such as Perl and PHP. Consider the interface page shown in `ex07-12.htm`.

```
Example: ex07-12.htm - An HTML/XHTML password page

 1: <head><title>Passing Encrypted Password -
    ex07-12.htm </title></head>
 2: <style>
 3:   .butSt{background-color:#aaffaa;font-family:arial;
            font-weight:bold;
 4:           font-size:18pt;color:#880000;width:250px;height:35px}
 5:   .txtSt{font-family:arial;font-weight:bold; text-align:left;
 6:           font-size:18pt;color:#ffff00}</style>
 7: <body style="background:#000088">
 8: <form action="ex07-12.pl" method="get" id="formId">
 9:   <table style="position:absolute;left:60px;top:30px" class="txtSt">
10:    <tr><td colspan="2" style="text-align:center">
11:      Private Site<br /> Enter Name & Password<br /><br/></td></tr>
12:    <tr><td>Name:</td><td><input type="text" name="userId" id="userId"
13:      class="butSt" value="johnsmith"></td></tr>
14:    <tr><td>Password:</td><td><input type="password" name="passId"
15:      id="passId" class="butSt" value="john199"></td></tr>
16:    <tr><td><input type="button" class="butSt" value="O.K."
17:      onclick="sub_fun()" style="width:150px;background:
       #dddddd"></td></tr>
18:    </table>
19: </form>
20: <script src="ex03-05.js"></script>
21: <script>
22:  function sub_fun()
23:  {
24:    var tmp = document.getElementById("passId").value;
25:    document.getElementById("passId").value = md5(tmp);
26:    document.getElementById("formId").submit();
27:  }
28: </script>
29: </body>
```

This page contains one text area and one password box. When these boxes are filled and the OK button is clicked, the ECMAScript function sub_fun() in lines 22–27 is activated. First, the input password is captured by the statement in line 24 and stored in variable tmp. To perform encryption on the password, the message digest function md5(tmp) is used. Details of the md5() codes are specified in ex03-05.js (Chapter 3) and included in this page in line 20. The encrypted password is put back to the password box as illustrated in line 25. The submit() function in line 26 submits the entire form data to the CGI application, in this case the Perl script ex07-12.pl, for processing. Since the get method is used in line 8, the following query string is passed to the Perl program:

```
userId=johnsmith&passId=3e69ae5dcdb81d1e625c5d7a0218fc1d
```

In particular, the encrypted password will be used to perform the login operation. The details of `ex07-12.pl` are given below.

Example: ex07-12.pl

```perl
 1: #! /usr/bin/perl
 2: use warnings;
 3: use CGI qw( :standard );
 4: print ("Content-type: text/html\n\n");
 5:
 6: my $username = param("userId");
 7: my $password = param("passId");
 8: my $matchuser=0;
 9: my $matchpass=0;
10:
11: my @name = ("johnsmith","Robinson","Brown");
12: my @pass = ("3e69ae5dcdb81d1e625c5d7a0218fc1d",
13:             "f1de84639d427c7e9d2da7e6c40f5bfb",
14:             "ce968ccb0c284596e6b4c5ec126b81f7");
15: foreach my $ii (0...2) {
16:    if($name[$ii] eq $username) {
17:       $matchuser = 1;
18:       if ($pass[$ii] eq $password) {
19:          $matchpass = 1;
20:       }
21:    }
22: }
23: print << "myDoc";
24:    <?xml version="1.0" encoding="iso-8859-1"?>
25:    <!DOCTYPE html PUBLIC "-//W3C//DTD XHTML 1.0 Transitional//EN"
26:    "http://www.w3.org/TR/xhtml1/DTD/xhtml1-transitional.dtd">
27:    <html xmlns="http://www.w3.org/1999/xhtml" xml:lang="en"
          lang="en">
28:    <head><title>Perl Example: ex07-05.pl</title></head>
29:    <body style="background:#000088;font-family:arial;font-size:18pt;
30:    color:#ffff00;font-weight:bold">
31: myDoc
32:
33: if ($matchuser && $matchpass) {
34:    print "Thank you! $username.<br />";
35:    print "You have logged on successfully.";
36: } elsif ($matchuser && !$matchpass) {
```

```
37:     print "Sorry! $username.<br />";
38:     print "Wrong password.";
39: } else {
40:     print "Sorry! Access Denied.";
41: }
42: print "</body></html>"
```

This is a Perl script on the server and will be called by `ex07-12.htm`. After the CGI header in line 4, two `param()` functions are used to get the username (`userId`) and password (`passId`) data from the query string into the script. Two local variables `$matchuser` and `$matchpass` are also declared in lines 8–9. They are used to indicate whether the username and/or password are matched or not. In lines 11–14, two arrays `name` and `pass` are defined. These arrays store the list of usernames and encrypted passwords. These encrypted passwords are the corresponding MD5 values and are listed below:

```
md5(john199)="3e69ae5dcdb81d1e625c5d7a0218fc1d"
md5(tom110) ="f1de84639d427c7e9d2da7e6c40f5bfb"
md5(may213) ="ce968ccb0c284596e6b4c5ec126b81f7"
```

The MD5 values can be obtained by using `ex03-05.htm` in Chapter 3. As a simple demonstration, only three names and passwords are included. For a more professional approach, data from a file or storage media should be used – this will be discussed in Section 7.3. Before that, we just want to hard-code the usernames and passwords as array elements.

The main operation of this password program is the for-loop in lines 15–22. The loop variable `$ii` runs through 0 to 2. That is, for each name in the array `$name[]` a comparison test takes place against the username variable `$username`. If they match, the variable `$matchuser` is set to `true`. The comparison test carries on to test the password. If a match is found, the variable `$matchpass` is also set to `true`. The conditions of `$matchuser` and `$matchpass` are used to determine whether the user is allowed to gain access to the system. If both `$matchuser` and `$matchpass` are `true`, access is granted to use the system and a welcome message is displayed. If `$matchuser` is `true` but not `$matchpass`, then we have a wrong password case, as illustrated in lines 36–38. If the username is wrong, login is denied and a message is displayed as in line 40. This script will be revisited in Chapter 8 to build a proper password program. Screenshots are shown in Figures 7.26 and 7.27.

One characteristic of this example is that the plaintext password is encrypted by the browser. Only the encrypted password is transmitted to the server so that the original password will not be compromised even if the communication and/or the server has been hacked by an intruder. Note that the communication method of this example is `get`. In this case, the following entire query string including the encrypted password appears in the address bar as shown in Figure 7.27.

Fig. 7.26 The GET method

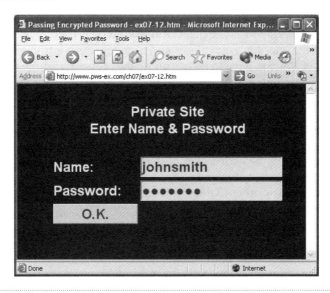

Fig. 7.27 Logon successful

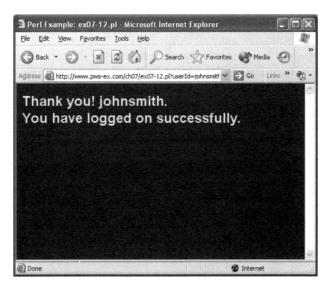

```
http://www.pws-ex.com/ch07/ex07-12.pl?
userId=johnsmith&passId=3e69ae5dcdb81d1e625c5d7a0218fc1d
```

In this example, the message digest function md5() is used to encrypt the password.
In fact, all the one-way encryptions and hash functions introduced in Chapter 3
can be used. All you have to do is include the proper script file and call the
associated function. Also, if you modify line 8 of ex07-12.htm as

```
8:  <form action="ex07-12.pl" method="post" id="formId">
```

the page will use the post method for communication. In this case, the query
string is passed as part of the client–server dialog and therefore the query string
will not appear in the address bar of the browser. This example performs user
authentication using a non-embedded CGI application Perl. In order to gain more
confidence on how other CGI technologies can be used for security applications,
let's convert this example to PHP.

7.2.5   Verifying passwords using PHP

Modifying example ex07-12.htm to be used by PHP is quite straightforward and
can be done using line-by-line translations. We will use the same user interface to
obtain the username and encrypted password. Make a copy of ex07-12.htm and
call it ex07-13.htm. Modify the following line:

```
8:  <form action="ex07-13.php" method="get" id="formId">
```

Now, the form will call the PHP page ex07-13.php to perform authentication.
When ex07-13.htm is executed by browser, the display will be as in Figure 7.26
asking for a username and password. The password will be encrypted by the same
md5() function. When the OK button is pressed, the input data will be passed to the
PHP page ex07-13.php and executed by the server.

```
Example: ex07-13.php - User authentication using PHP

 1: <?php echo"<?";?>xml version="1.0" encoding="iso-8859-1"
    <?php echo"?>";?>
 2: <!DOCTYPE html PUBLIC "-//W3C//DTD XHTML 1.0 Transitional//EN"
 3:  "http://www.w3.org/TR/xhtml11/DTD/xhtml11-transitional.dtd">
 4: <html xmlns="http://www.w3.org/1999/xhtml" xml:lang="en" lang="en">
 5: <head><title>Perl Example: ex07-13.pl</title></head>
 6: <body style="background:#000088;font-family:arial;font-size:18pt;
 7: color:#ffff00;font-weight:bold">
 8: <?php
 9:    $username = $userId;
10:    $password = $passId;
11:    $matchuser=0;
12:    $matchpass=0;
```

```
13:
14:   $name = array("johnsmith","Robinson","Brown");
15:   $pass = array("3e69ae5dcdb81d1e625c5d7a0218fc1d",
16:                 "f1de84639d427c7e9d2da7e6c40f5bfb",
17:                 "ce968ccb0c284596e6b4c5ec126b81f7");
18:   for ($ii=0; $ii<3; $ii++) {
19:     if($name[$ii] == $username) {
20:       $matchuser = 1;
21:       if ($pass[$ii] == $password) {
22:         $matchpass = 1;
23:       }
24:     }
25:   }
26:   if ($matchuser && $matchpass) {
27:       printf("Thank you! %s <br />",$username);
28:       printf("You have logged on successfully.");
29:   } else if ($matchuser && ! $matchpass) {
30:       printf("Sorry! %s .<br />",$username);
31:       printf("Wrong password.");
32:   } else {
33:       printf("Sorry! Access Denied.");
34:   }
35:   printf("</body></html>");
36: ?>
```

The logic of this PHP script is similar to the Perl case. Recall that everything
between the delimiters `<?php` and `?>` will be processed by the PHP preprocessor
in the server. Also remember that PHP variables are prefixed with the symbol `$`.
After the XHTML header in lines 1–7, the remaining PHP statements from line 8 to
36 are used to complete the XHTML page. First, the username and password from
`ex07-13.htm` are passed to this PHP page as variables `$userId` and `$passId`. These
two variables are assigned to `$username` and `$password` respectively in lines 9–10.
As in the Perl case, two arrays `$name` and `$pass` are declared in lines 14–17 to store
the username and encrypted password. The for-loop in lines 18–25 performs the
comparison looking for a match of username and/or password. The conditional-if
statement in lines 26–34 composes the matched result as an XHTML statement and
returns it to the browser. For PHP, the function `printf()` is used to output a string
to the standard output. This function is similar to the `printf()` in the C/C++
language. Consider the statement in line 27:

```
printf("Thank you! %s <br />",$username);
```

This statement will output the string 'Thank you!' together with the string stored in
variable `$username`. The symbol `%s` is the string directive and is used to output the
string value in a variable. Screenshots of this example in action are shown in
Figures 7.28 and 7.29.

Fig. 7.28 ex07-13.htm

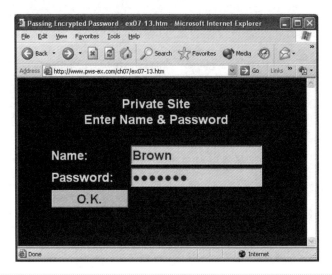

Fig. 7.29 Logon successful

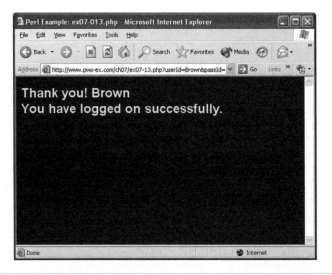

Now, you should have the confidence to handle CGI applications and use Perl and PHP to pass encrypted passwords. However, hard-coding the usernames and encrypted passwords inside server pages is not ideal. In particular, if you have a large number of users for your page, the administration work will become a nightmare. To solve this problem, using file storage in the server is recommended.

7.3 Using server storage for security

7.3.1 Access file storage using Perl and PHP

Accessing server storage is a valuable feature for many CGI applications. File storage creates a permanent and reliable record for your Web activity, which in many cases is vital for many applications. From a simple page counter or database to money transaction business, the ability to use server storage is critical. When used properly, files can be used to store encrypted passwords or other any sensitive data, providing secure and private storage for your applications.

File access using Perl script

To open a file using Perl script, the following open statement is often used:

```
open (filehandle, "<myfile");
```

This `open` command opens the file 'myfile'. The symbol '<' is the file mode, which indicates that the file is opened for reading. In this case, the contents of the file will be read and controlled by the variable `filehandle`. To enhance security against intruders and to guard against the openness of the Web, all opened files are recommended to be in a protected area (not accessible by the HTTP protocol).

Suppose we have a page `ex07-06.htm` and want to protect it against general HTTP access from the site www.pws-ex.com. One simple way to do this is to put `ex07-06.htm` into a non-accessible directory, for example the parent directory of your Web site. In normal circumstances, the parent of the root directory of a site cannot be accessed by Web surfing and, therefore, the page is protected. The next step is to develop a Web page similar to `ex07-14.html`.

```
Example: ex07-14.htm - Using file storage with Perl

1: <head><title>File Access Using Perl - ex07-14.htm </title></head>
2: <style>
3:    .butSt{background-color:#aaffaa;font-family:arial;
            font-weight:bold;
4:            font-size:18pt;color:#880000;width:250px;height:35px}
5:    .txtSt{font-family:arial;font-weight:bold; text-align:left;
6:            font-size:18pt;color:#ffff00}</style>
7: <body style="background:#000088">
8: <form action="ex07-14.pl" method="post" id="formId">
9:  <table style="position:absolute;left:60px;top:30px" class="txtSt">
10:   <tr><td colspan="2" style="text-align:center">
11:     Private Site<br /> Enter Name & Page You
       Want<br /><br/></td></tr>
```

```
12:    <tr><td>Name:</td><td><input type="text" name="userId" id="userId"
13:      class="butSt" value="johnsmith"></td></tr>
14:    <tr><td>Page:</td><td><input type="text" name="pageId"
15:      id="pageId" class="butSt" value="ex07-06.htm"></td></tr>
16:    <tr><td><input type="submit" class="butSt" value="submit"
17:      style="width:150px;background:#dddddd"></td></tr>
18:    </table>
19: </form>
20: </body>
```

This page contains two text boxes asking for the username and password when the page is requested. When the Submit button is clicked, the Perl script ex07-14.pl specified in line 8 is activated. This script displays the file specified by the user in the parent of the root directory. The details of this script are listed in ex07-14.pl.

```
Example: ex07-14.pl - The Perl script used by ex07-14.htm

 1: #! /usr/bin/perl
 2: use warnings;
 3: use CGI qw( :standard );
 4: print ("Content-type: text/html\n\n");
 5:
 6: my $username = param("userId");
 7: my $pathV = "../" . param("pageId");
 8:
 9: open(filehandle,"$pathV")
10:    or die("Cannot open message.dat for reading");
11: while (my $st = <filehandle>)
12: {
13:    print("$st");
14: }
15: close(filehandle);
```

This Perl script is simple. After the CGI header in line 4, the username and page, stored in userId and passId respectively, are captured by the param() function in lines 6–7. If you enter 'ex07-06.htm' for the page you want, the variable param("pageId") contains this value. The statement in line 7 turns out to be

```
"../" . param("pageId");  ==>  ../ex07-06.htm
```

In the Perl language, the full stop symbol '.' is used to concatenate two strings. The result is that the variable $pathV contains the location of page ex07-06.htm,

which is the parent of the current directory. If the current directory is the root of your Web site, the page cannot be accessed by a normal URL. The statement in line 9 opens the file ex07-06.htm for reading. If not successful, the die statement displays a message and terminates the program. If the file operation is successful, a while-loop in lines 11–14 is used to display the contents of the file. The statement

```
$st = <filehandle>
```

reads a string from the filehandle (or the file). The print command in line 13 outputs the string to the browser as a CGI application. Since the file is an XHTML document, it can be displayed by the browser. Finally, for good programming practice, don't forget to close the file with the close() command as illustrated in line 15. Screenshots of this example are shown in Figures 7.30 and 7.31.

Putting Web documents in an inaccessible or protected directories is a basic protection against ordinary Web users. Depending on your system and operating environment, a capable hacker can still hack into the server to obtain the document. For this reason, if you have a more sensitive document, you should protect it further using the encryption skills described in Section 7.1.

Example ex07-14.pl demonstrates file access with reading mode. Some other file-accessing modes are listed in Table 7.1. Note that the file access mode is applied at the front of the filename. When there is no mode specified, the reading mode is assumed as default.

Fig. 7.30   ex07-14.htm

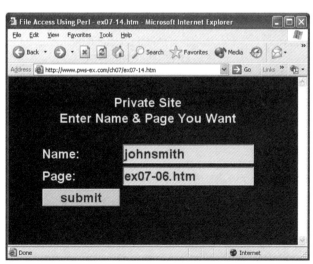

Fig. 7.31 Accessing file `ex07-06.htm`

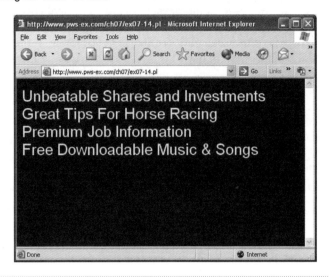

Table 7.1 File access modes of Perl

Mode	Operation	Description and example
<	Read	Open a file for reading. E.g. `open (filehandle, "<filename");`
>	Write	Create a file for writing. If the file already exists, discard the contents. E.g. `open (filehandle, ">filename");`
>>	Append	Open or create a file for writing. If the file exists, writing is at the end of the file. E.g. `open (filehandle, ">>filename");`
+>	Update	Create a file for update. If the file exists, discard the contents. E.g. `open (filehandle, "+>filename");`
+<	Read & write	Open the file for update (i.e. reading and writing). Keep the contents of the file. E.g. `open (filehandle, "+<filename");`
+>>	Update & append	Open or create a file for updating. Writing is at the end of the file E.g. `open (filehandle, "+>>filename");`

Now, let's consider how to use file storage with PHP.

File access using PHP script

The PHP language is similar to C in many ways. For example, the following statement is used to open page `ex07-06.htm`.

```
$fp = fopen("../ex07-06.htm", "r");
```

Similar to C, the `fopen()` function opens the file '../ex07-06.htm' for reading.
If the file is opened successfully, the file handle `$fp` can be used to access the
contents. To construct a PHP program to protect and access the file, make a copy
of `ex07-14.htm` and call it `ex07-15.htm`. Modify the following line:

```
8: <form action="ex07-15.php" method="post" id="formId">
```

This page display two text boxes and one submit button. When the button is
pressed, the PHP program `ex07-15.php` is executed. This program opens the file
specified in the parent directory of the root and returns it to the browser. The
listing of `ex07-15.php` is given below.

```
Example: ex07-15.php - Using file storage with PHP

 1: <?php
 2:   $username = $userId;
 3:   $pathV = "../" . $pageId;
 4:   $handle = fopen($pathV, "r");
 5:   while (!feof($handle)) {
 6:     $buffer = fgets($handle,4096);
 7:     echo ($buffer);
 8:   }
 9:   fclose($handle);
10: ?>
```

Yes! This PHP program has only ten lines. The user and file names are captured
by lines 2–3 and stored in variables `$username` and `$pathv` respectively. Remember
that the full stop symbol '.' in line 3 is used to concatenate two strings. In this case,
the variable `$pathv` stores the path of the file as the parent of the current directory.
If the current directory is the root of your Web site, the parent directory will not be
accessible from the Web and therefore is protected.

The statement in line 4 opens the file for reading. If the file is opened successfully,
`$handle` is used to access the contents. The `fgets()` function in line 6 reads one
string with maximum 4096 characters to variable `$buffer`. The `echo()` function in
line 7 outputs the string `$buffer` to the browser. The while-loop in lines 5–8 makes
sure that every line of the file is read until the end of file. The statement in line 9
closes the file before the program terminated. Screenshots of this example are the
same as those in Figures 7.30 and 7.31.

For faster and more efficient file handling, PHP provides the `fread()` function,
which can be used to read the entire file in one step. For example, `ex07-15.php` can
be replaced by the following PHP script:

```php
<?php
  $username = $userId;
  $pathV = "../" . $pageId;
  $handle = fopen($pathV, "r");

  $contents = fread($handle, filesize($pageId));
  echo($contents);
  fclose($handle);
?>
```

This script shows that the while-loop in `ex07-15.php` can be replaced by a single `fread()` function so that the entire file is read in one step, and therefore provides more efficient coding. This example demonstrates how to use PHP to open a file for reading. Table 7.2 gives other file-accessing operations (or modes).

Table 7.2 The file access modes of PHP

Mode	Operation	Description and example
r	Read	Open a file for reading. E.g. `$fp = fopen("filename", "r");`
w	Write	Create a file for writing. If the file already exists, discard the contents. E.g. `$fp = fopen("filename", "w");`
a	Append	Open or create a file for writing. If the file exists, writing is at the end of the file. E.g. `$fp = fopen("filename", "a");`
r+	Read & write	Open the file for updating (i.e. reading and writing). Keep the contents of the file. E.g. `$fp = fopen("filename", "w+");`
w+	Read & write	Create a file for updating. If the file exists, discard the contents. E.g. `$fp = fopen("filename", "r+");`
a+	Update & append	Open or create a file for updating. Writing is at the end of the file E.g. `$fp = fopen("filename", "a+");`

If you compare Tables 7.1 and 7.2, you will find that the structure and features of the file modes are the same. In fact, almost all programming structures, including file operations, have the same, or similar, logical and computational structures no matter which language is used for programming. The algorithms, in general, can be considered to be a logical and computational representation of them all in an abstract manner.

In order to allow a group of people to have their own individual passwords and have access to the same Web resources or pages, you may need to use file storage to establish an encrypted password file.

7.3.2   User authentication using password files

In this section, we consider how to use file storage to construct password files and put it to use for user authentication. First, suppose we have the following username and password pairs stored in a file.

Username	Password
Paul	paul123321
John	john199330
Peter	p2341558
Mary	mary2001482
Tom	tom213556

Username	Password
Joe	joe900187
Anna	anna230977
Emma	emma411212
JohnSmith	jk123008
Sue	sue334112

Since this password file is not protected, it could be disastrous if this file is stolen by a hacker. To protect it, you can run through all passwords with any of the one-way encryption programs given in Chapter 3. For example, the corresponding new password file with SHA-1 encryption (or hash) is given in listing ex07-05.txt.

```
Example: ex07-05.txt - SHA-1 hashed password file: password.txt

 1: Paul,bc73bb5aeb45d1c5ec2d312040f3001ac7c12b8f
 2: John,70aa9c67d4f5079db7398cbbd98f2674a6d043af
 3: Peter,4abd1f3ad992c6caeaffde1777b87b45b4d4d9fd
 4: Mary,d2740cfbf11473253110b223cbfd9a9604a448dc
 5: Tom,ce0be0684f5a1d4b6748c8bf922c948449edcb0e
 6: Joe,2a36faf4cb32f5bb4bf243a748e2d7ffdc540847
 7: Anna,d3a1f4ce51528815c849ef2ef831b86db98771b5
 8: Emma,18ebde6104f91710f80157f98d25ceb500de79a9
 9: JohnSmith,35e87f12a60ad90a0c4afb910a131b663d844841
10: Sue,6b2337d6d54f65698f91dda05d87cc16558693d0
```

These values can be obtained using ex03-08.htm in Chapter 3. For example, the passwords for Paul and John are captured in Figures 7.32 and 7.33.

The next step is developing an XHTML page to collect the username and password for comparison against the password file. Again, we will provide both Perl and PHP versions.

User authentication using password files and Perl

A quick way to start this page is to make a copy of the username/password page (ex07-12.htm) and call it ex07-16.htm. In this new page, modify the following lines:

Fig. 7.32 SHA password for Paul

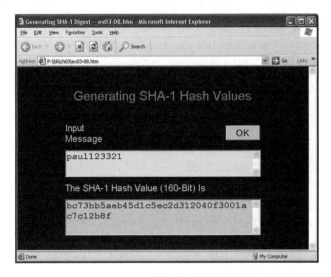

Fig. 7.33 SHA password for John

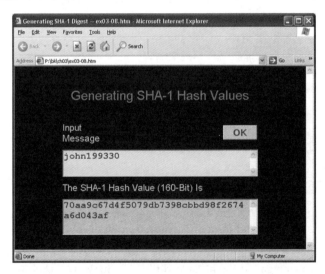

```
 8: <form action="ex07-16.pl" method="get" id="formId">
20: <script src="ex03-08.js"></script>
25:     document.getElementById("passId").value = sha1(tmp);
```

This XHTML page displays two text boxes asking for the username and password. When the Submit button is pressed, the Perl script ex07-16.pl is run as illustrated in line 8. Since we want to use SHA-1 one-way encryption, the SHA-1 engine `ex03-08.js` is included in line 20. Finally, the encryption function `sha1()` is called at line 25. The process engine is listed in `ex07-16.pl`.

```
Example: ex07-16.pl - The Perl script for ex07-16.htm

 1: #!usr/bin/perl
 2: use CGI qw (:standard);
 3: my $userF=0;
 4: my $passwordF=0;
 5: my $username = param(userId);
 6: my $password = param(passId);
 7: print "Content-type: text/html\n\n";
 8:
 9: open(filehandle, "password.txt") or
10:  die "Error.. Program Terminated...";
11:
12: while(my $st = <filehandle>) {
13:    $st =~ s/\n//g;
14:    ($name, $pass) = split(/,/, $st);
15:
16:    if($name eq "$username") {
17:       $userF = 1;
18:       if ($pass eq "$password") {
19:          $passwordF = 1;
20:       }
21:    }
22:  }
23: close(filehandle);
24:
25: if ($userF && $passwordF) {
26:     open(fhandle,"../ex07-06.htm")
27:        or die("Error.. Program Terminated..");
28:     while (my $sst = <fhandle>) {
29:        print("$sst");
30:     }
31:     close(fhandle);
32: } elsif ($userF && !$passwordF) {
33:     print ("Sorry, Wrong Password !!");
34: } else {
35:     print ("Sorry, Access Denied !!");
36: }
```

This Perl script will be called by ex07-16.htm to perform the following tasks:

- capture the username and password pair from ex07-16.htm;
- open the password file password.txt;
- compare the username/password pair against the pairs in the password file;
- if a match is found the page '../ex07-06.htm' is displayed. Otherwise the message 'Access Denied' is displayed.

The username and encrypted password from the interface ex07-16.htm are captured by the variables $username and $password defined in lines 5–6. The Perl statements in lines 9–10 open the password file password.txt. Once the file is opened successfully, a while-loop (lines 12–21) is employed to read through the username/password contents to variable pair $name/$pass. Since the file records are sequential with a carriage return and/or a new line, the statement in line 13 is used to chop off the carriage return symbol. The split() function in line 14 splits the record into $name and $password.

The conditional-if statement in lines 17–21 performs the username and password matching. If $username equals $name then we have a match on username. In this case, the value of the username flag $userF is set to 1. If the input password $password equals the password in the file $pass, a match is found on password. In this case, the value of the password flag $passwordF is set to 1.

To interpret the comparison results, a series of if statements (lines 25–36) are used. If both username and password are matched, the print statement in lines 26–31 will be executed, and hence the page '../ex07-04.htm' is read and returned to the browser. If the username is matched but not the password, the 'Sorry, Wrong Password' message is output. If the username is not matched, the 'Sorry, Access Denied' message defined in line 35 is displayed. Screenshots of this example are shown in Figures 7.34 and 7.35.

Now, let's see how to convert this program into PHP script.

User authentication using password files and PHP

To construct a PHP program for user authentication with a password file, make a copy of ex07-16.htm and call it ex07-17.htm. In the new page, modify the following line:

```
8: <form action="ex07-17.php" method="post" id="formId">
```

This page has the same display as ex07-16.htm, containing two text boxes and one submit button.

When the Submit button is pressed, the PHP program ex07-17.php is executed. This program will open the password file password.txt and perform user authentication based on the username/password records.

Fig. 7.34 `ex07-16.htm`

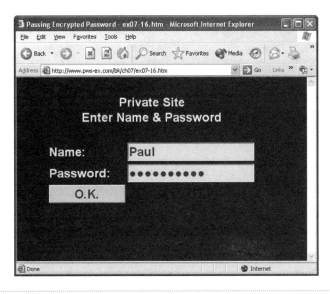

Fig. 7.35 User authentication

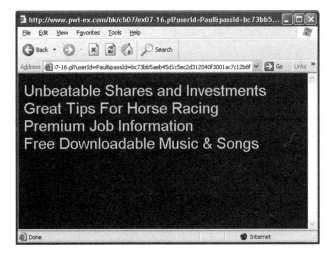

```php
1:  <?php
2:  $userF=0;
3:  $passwordF=0;
4:  $username = $userId;
5:  $password = $passId;
6:
7:  $handle = fopen("password.txt", "r");
8:  while (!feof($handle)) {
9:      $st = fgets($handle,4096);
10:     $st = chop($st);
11:     list($name, $pass) = split(",", $st);
12:     if($name == $username) {
13:         $userF = 1;
14:         if ($pass == $password) {
15:             $passwordF = 1;
16:         }
17:     }
18: }
19: fclose($handle);
20: $pageId = "../ex07-06.htm";
21: if ($userF && $passwordF) {
22:         $fhandle = fopen($pageId, "r");
23:         $contents = fread($fhandle, filesize($pageId));
24:         echo($contents);
25:         fclose($fhandle);
26: } else if ($userF && ! $passwordF) {
27:         printf("Sorry! %s .<br />",$username);
28:         printf("Wrong password.");
29: } else {
30:         printf("Sorry! Access Denied.");
31: }
32: ?>
```

This PHP program is a line-by-line translation from the Perl script ex07-16.pl. The username and encrypted password from ex07-17.htm are captured by variables $username and $password in lines 4–5. Line 7 opens the password file. The while-loop in lines 8–18 reads all the records, looking for a match with $username and $password. Note that the chop() function in line 10 is to chop off the carriage return symbol at the end of the string $st so that accurate matching can be performed. The string $st contains the username and password separated with a comma ','. The split() function in line 11 is used to split the string $st at the ',' symbol into variables $name and $password so that comparison can be done in lines 12–17.

When both username and password are matched, the statements in lines 22–25 are executed. In this case, the page '../ex07-06.htm' is read and returned to the browser. The execution results of this example are the same as those in Figures 7.34 and 7.35.

One advantage of this authentication is that only the SHA-1 encrypted data is transmitted on the Internet. The original password will not be compromised even when both the Web transmission and server are hacked by an intruder.

For a successful business site, you also need to develop a page which allows your users to sign up for membership with confidence.

7.3.3 Setting up new password accounts

In this section, we are going to develop a sign-up utility to allow someone to join the membership of a group. This page will display two boxes asking for the username/password pair. The password will be encrypted using SHA-1 encryption. Both the username and password will then be appended into the associated password file. Also, if the username has already been used by someone, the utility will let you know and ask you to sign up again with a new username.

Consider Perl script ex07-18.pl.

```
Example: ex07-18.pl - Setting up a password account using Perl (Part I)

 1: #!usr/bin/perl
 2: use CGI qw (:standard);
 3: print "Content-type: text/html\n\n";
 4: print << "myDoc";
 5:   <?xml version="1.0" encoding="iso-8859-1"?>
 6:   <!DOCTYPE html PUBLIC "-//W3C//DTD XHTML 1.0 Transitional//EN"
 7:   "http://www.w3.org/TR/xhtml1/DTD/xhtml1-transitional.dtd">
 8:   <html xmlns="http://www.w3.org/1999/xhtml"
        xml:lang="en" lang="en">
 9:   <head><title>Set Up New Password Accounts -
        ex07-18.php</title></head>
10:   <style>
11:     .butSt{background-color:#aaffaa;font-family:arial;
          font-weight:bold;
12:       font-size:18pt;color:#880000;width:250px;height:35px}
13:     .butSt2{background-color:#dddddd;font-family:arial;
          font-weight:bold;
14:       font-size:18pt;color:#880000;width:150px;height:35px}
15:     .txtSt{font-family:arial;font-weight:bold; text-align:left;
16:       font-size:18pt;color:#ffff00}</style>
```

```
17:    <body style="font-family:arial;font-size:18pt;
18:        background:#000088" class="txtSt">
19: myDoc
20: my $llst = 'Enter Your Username and Password To Join Member' .
21:    ' <form action="ex07-18.pl" method="post" id="formId">'.
22:    ' <table class="txtSt"><tr>' .
23:    '    <td>Username:</td><td>' .
24:    ' <input type="text" name="userId" id="userId"
            class="butSt" /></td>'.
25:    ' </tr><tr>' .
26:    '    <td>Password:</td><td>' .
27:    ' <input type="password" name="passId" id="passId"
            class="butSt" />' .
28:    ' </td></tr><tr><td colspan="2"
            style="text-align:center"><br />' .
29:    ' <input type="button" class="butSt2" value="O.K." '.
30:    '    onclick="sub_fun()" />' .
31:    ' <input type="reset" value="Clear"
            class="butSt2" /></td></tr>' .
32:    ' </table>' .
33:    ' </form> ' .
34:    ' <script src="ex03-08.js"></script>' .
35:    ' <script>' .
36:    ' function sub_fun()' .
37:    ' {' .
38:    '   var tmp = document.getElementById("passId").value;' .
39:    '   document.getElementById("passId").value = sha1(tmp);' .
40:    '   document.getElementById("formId").submit();' .
41:    ' }' .
42:    ' </script>' ;
```

This Perl script fragment is the first part of the example and is not difficult to
understand. First, the standard CGI magic string is output to the browser in line 3.
Lines 4–19 return the header and body of an XHTML page. Next, a string $llst is
defined. This variable is a long string occupying lines 20–42. In fact, it contains one
XHTML form and two script blocks.

When variable $llst is output to the browser, it displays two text boxes and
two push buttons asking for the username and password. When the OK button
is clicked, the function sub_fun() in lines 36–41 is run. This function encrypts
the password using SHA-1 encryption and submits the entire form to itself
(i.e. ex07-18.pl). The actual operation of the example is defined in part II of
ex07-18.pl.

```perl
43: my $userF=0;
44: my $passwordF=0;
45: my $username = param(userId);
46: my $password = param(passId);
47:
48: if ($username && $password) {
49:     open(filehandle, "password.txt") or
50:         die "Error... Program Terminated...";
51:
52:     while(my $st = <filehandle>) {
53:         $st =~ s/\n//g;
54:         ($name, $pass) = split(/,/, $st);
55:
56:         if($name eq "$username") {
57:             $userF = 1;
58:             if ($pass eq "$password") {
59:                 $passwordF = 1;
60:             }
61:         }
62:     }
63:     close(filehandle);
64:
65:     if ($userF) {
66:         print ("The User Name You Picked Has Been <br />" .
67:                 "Used By Someone. Please Try again! <br /><br />");
68:         print($llst);
69:     } else {
70:         open(fhandle,">>password.txt")
71:             or die("Error.. Program Terminated..");
72:         print (fhandle "$username,$password\n");
73:         close(fhandle);
74:         print("A New Account Has Been Set Up <br /><br />" .
75:                 "Username = $username <br />" .
76:                 "Encrypted Password = <br />$password <br />");
77:     }
78: } else {
79:     print($llst);
80: }
81: print("<img src=\"line1.gif\" width=\"550\"
            height=\"6\" alt=\"pic\" />" .
82:          "<br /><br /></body></html>");
```

First, the statements in lines 45–46 capture the username and password. If both of the values are not empty, the statements in lines 49–77 will be executed. If one of the values is empty, the variable $llst is output to the browser in line 79. In this case, the same interface window will be displayed asking for the username and password again.

When both username and password are not empty, lines 49–63 open the password file password.txt to perform authentication. The matching results are stored in variables $userF and $passwordF. If the username has already been registered by another member, the message in lines 66–67 is displayed. The statement in line 68 outputs the string $llst so that the user can try again with a new username. If the entered username is new to the system, the password file is opened again by line 70. The new username/password pair is appended at the end of the password file by line 72. Finally, a message is printed to show that a new password account has been set up and is ready to use (lines 74–76).

In this example, we have put everything into this Perl program. Therefore there is no need to set up another Web page to call this script. You can call this Perl script ex07-18.pl using http://. Screenshots of this example in action are shown in Figures 7.36 and 7.37.

For the PHP equivalent of ex07-18.pl, consider the PHP page ex07-19.php.

Fig. 7.36   ex07-18.pl

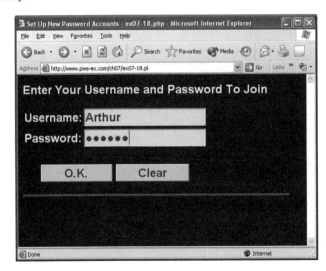

Fig. 7.37 Set up a new account

```
Example: ex07-19.php - Setting up a password account using PHP (Part I)

 1: <?PHP echo"<?";?>xml version="1.0"
      encoding="iso-8859-1"<?PHP echo"?>";?>
 2: <!DOCTYPE html PUBLIC "-//W3C//DTD XHTML 1.0 Transitional//EN"
 3:      "http://www.w3.org/TR/xhtml1/DTD/xhtml1-transitional.dtd">
 4: <html xmlns="http://www.w3.org/1999/xhtml" xml:lang="en" lang="en">
 5: <head><title>Encrypted Password in Database -
      ex19-05.php</title></head>
 6: <style>
 7:    .butSt{background-color:#aaffaa;font-family:arial;
         font-weight:bold;
 8:         font-size:18pt;color:#880000;width:250px;height:35px}
 9:    .butSt2{background-color:#eeeeee;font-family:arial;
         font-weight:bold;
10:         font-size:18pt;color:#880000;width:150px;height:35px}
11:    .txtSt{font-family:arial;font-weight:bold; text-align:left;
12:         font-size:18pt;color:#ffff00}</style>
13: <body style="background:#000088" class="txtSt">
14: <?php
15:  Global $llst, $userId, $passId;
16:  $llst = 'Enter Your Username and Password To Join ' .
17:     ' <form action="ex07-19.php" method="post" id="formId">'.
18:     ' <table class="txtSt"><tr>' .
```

```
19:  '    <td>Username:</td><td>' .
20:  ' <input type="text" name="userId" id="userId"
         class="butSt" /></td>' .
21:  '    </tr><tr>' .
22:  '    <td>Password:</td><td>' .
23:  ' <input type="password" name="passId" id="passId"
         class="butSt" />' .
24:  '    </td></tr><tr><td colspan="2"
         style="text-align:center"><br />' .
25:  '    <input type="button" class="butSt2" value="O.K." ' .
26:  '       onclick="sub_fun()" />' .
27:  '    <input type="reset" value="Clear"
         class="butSt2" /></td></tr>' .
28:  ' </table>' .
29:  ' </form> ' .
30:  ' <script src="ex03-08.js"></script>' .
31:  ' <script>' .
32:  ' function sub_fun()' .
33:  ' {' .
34:  '    var tmp = document.getElementById("passId").value;' .
35:  '    document.getElementById("passId").value = sha1(tmp);' .
36:  '    document.getElementById("formId").submit();' .
37:  ' }' .
38:  ' </script>' ;
```

This PHP page is the equivalent to part I of ex07-18.pl. After the XHTML header, the variable $11st in lines 16–38 stores the XHTML code for an input window. When this variable is rendered by a browser, an interface window asking for a username and password appears. Like the Perl case, the actual operation of the page is defined in part II of ex07-19.php.

Example: Continuation of ex07-19.php   (Part II)

```
39:  $userF=0; $passwordF=0;
40:  $username = $userId;
41:  $password = $passId;
42:  if ($username && $password) {
43:
44:    $handle = fopen("password.txt", "r");
45:    while (!feof($handle)) {
46:      $st = fgets($handle,4096);
47:      $st = chop($st);
```

```
48:        if ($st) {
49:            list($name,$pass) = split(",",$st);
50:            if($name == $username) {
51:                $userF = 1;
52:                if ($pass == $password) {
53:                    $passwordF = 1;
54:                }
55:            }
56:        }
57:    }
58:    fclose($handle);
59:
60:    if ($userF) {
61:        echo("The User Name You Picked Has Been <br />" .
62:            "Used By Someone. Please Try again! <br /><br />");
63:        echo($llst);
64:    } else {
65:        $fhandle = fopen("password.txt", "a");
66:        fputs($fhandle,"$username,$password\n");
67:        fclose($fhandle);
68:        echo("A New Account Has Been Set Up <br /><br />" .
69:            "Username = $username <br />" .
70:            "Encrypted Password = <br />$password <br />");
71:    }
72:    } else {
73:    echo "$llst";
74: }
75: ?>
76: <img src="line1.gif" width="550" height="6" alt="pic" />
77: </body> </html>
```

This page fragment also has one to one correspondence with part II of ex07-18.pl, so only a brief explanation is given. When either of the username or password values is empty, the variable $llst is printed in line 73, asking for the username/ password pair from the user again. When both values are not empty, lines 42–72 are run looking for a match. First, the password file password.txt is opened and comparison is carried out against the file records (lines 44–58). If the input username has already been used by someone, lines 61–63 are executed so that string $llst is rendered and the user can try again. If the username is new, the statements in lines 65–70 are carried out. As a result, a new username and password are appended at the end of the password file (line 66). The execution of this example is the same as the Perl case, and the screenshoots would look the same as Figures 7.36 and 7.37.

Since all passwords are encrypted at the browser level, transmitting them to the server is considerably safer. Although most CGI technologies, such as Perl and PHP, have encryption functions built in, the process of transmitting a plaintext password and encrypting it in a server for authentication is not recommended.

Now we have some experience of handling CGI applications with Perl and PHP, it's time to move on to consider some security applications using Web databases.

7.4 Handling password accounts with MySQL

7.4.1 Creating an encrypted password table in MySQL

If your Web site or business has a large number of members, storing encrypted passwords in a file may not be efficient and could be difficult to maintain. Also, putting users and their passwords into a database can have all the benefits of a database application. For example, the following tasks can be handled more effectively by using a database with structured query language (SQL) statements:

- searching for passwords and performing user authentication;
- adding and deleting new member accounts;
- updating or changing passwords or records.

We will show you how to develop Web pages to perform these database functionalities in the remaining sections of this chapter. For demonstration purposes, a database product called MySQL is introduced.

Supporting more than ten different operating systems, the database product MySQL became one of the most popular, and free, database packages available. From Microsoft Windows through Mac OS to UNIX/LINUX and Solaris, it is quite likely that you will find a MySQL distribution suitable for your machine and operating environment. Also, since all source codes related to the product are freely available, you have total freedom to modify the product to suit your need.

In this section, we assume that a version of MySQL is installed on the www.pws-ex.com server and that you can access it. Also, the MySQL client program mysql should be available on your local machine so that you can connect to the database server. Normally, you will need a hostname, username and password to make the connection properly. Suppose you have the following information from your database administrator:

- Hostname (MySQL): www.pws-ex.com
- Username (MySQL): johnsmith
- Password (MySQL): johnsmith

The connection to MySQL server can be done by using the program mysql:

```
C:\>mysql -h www.pws-ex.com -u johnsmith -p
Enter Password: ********
```

where www.pws-ex.com is the address of the site running the MySQL server. The directive -p instructs MySQL to display the prompt for you to enter your password. Your password will appear as a sequence of asterisks. If you are using the host machine, you can ignore the -h directive and host name. If the connection is successful, you will see some introductory information followed by a 'mysql>'

prompt. When you see this, your MySQL is ready for action. The operations are illustrated in Figures 7.38 and 7.39.

Figure 7.38 shows the connection to the MySQL database server by user 'johnsmith'. The SHOW DATABASES command will show all databases available to him. In Figure 7.39 two databases, namely testDB and passwordDB, are created by using the CREATE DATABASE command. As a convention, MySQL system commands

Fig. 7.38 Using MySQL database I

```
C:\mysql\bin>mysql -ujohnsmith -p
Enter password: ********
Welcome to the MySQL monitor.
  Commands end with ; or \g.
Your MySQL connection id is 12 to
  server version: 3.23.43-nt
Type 'help;' or '\h' for help.
Type '\c' to clear the buffer.

mysql> SHOW DATABASES;
+----------+
| Database |
+----------+
| mysql    |
+----------+
1 row in set (0.00 sec)
mysql>
```

Fig. 7.39 Using MySQL database II

```
mysql> CREATE DATABASE testDB;
 Query OK, 1 row affected (0.00 sec)
mysql> CREATE DATABASE passwordDB;
 Query OK, 1 row affected (0.02 sec)
mysql> SHOW DATABASES;
+------------+
| Database   |
+------------+
| mysql      |
| passwordDB |
| testDB     |
+------------+
 3 rows in set (0.00 sec)
mysql> DROP DATABASE testDB;
 Query OK, 0 rows affected (0.01 sec)
mysql>
```

are usually represented as capital letters. You can delete a database by using the DROP DATABASE command as illustrated at the end of Figure 7.39.

Elements inside a MySQL database are called tables – a database without any tables would not be very useful. For security applications, the next step is to create a password table inside database passwordDB. For simplicity, our password table contains only three fields:

- id   – is a number to store the identity or index of each row;

- name   – character string (max. 30) to store the username;

- password – character string (max. 60) to store the encrypted password.

To generate this password table the text file ex07-06.txt is used.

```
Example: ex07-06.txt - Password data file for MySQL: password2.txt

 1: NULL,Paul,bc73bb5aeb45d1c5ec2d312040f3001ac7c12b8f
 2: NULL,John,70aa9c67d4f5079db7398cbbd98f2674a6d043af
 3: NULL,Peter,4abd1f3ad992c6caeaffde1777b87b45b4d4d9fd
 4: NULL,Mary,d2740cfbf11473253110b223cbfd9a9604a448dc
 5: NULL,Tom,ce0be0684f5a1d4b6748c8bf922c948449edcb0e
 6: NULL,Joe,2a36faf4cb32f5bb4bf243a748e2d7ffdc540847
 7: NULL,Anna,d3a1f4ce51528815c849ef2ef831b86db98771b5
 8: NULL,Emma,18ebde6104f91710f80157f98d25ceb500de79a9
 9: NULL,JohnSmith,35e87f12a60ad90a0c4afb910a131b663d844841
10: NULL,Sue,6b2337d6d54f65698f91dda05d87cc16558693d0
```

This data file contains three fields, namely id, name and password, separated by commas. The passwords are encrypted with the SHA-1 scheme. In fact, this file is similar to the password.txt file in previous sections. The next step is to create the password table in database passwordDB. You can do that by issuing the CREATE TABLE command with the definition of each field. An example is given in listing ex07-07.txt.

```
Example: ex07-07.txt - Creating the table password

1: mysql> CREATE TABLE password (
2:     ->    id SMALLINT UNSIGNED NOT NULL AUTO_INCREMENT,
3:     ->    name VARCHAR(30),
4:     ->    password VARCHAR(60),
5:     ->    PRIMARY KEY (id)
6:     -> );
```

The first line instructs mySQL to create a table called 'password' in the database. This table contains three fields. The first is called id, which is a positive small number, cannot be empty, and will be incremented by 1 automatically (line 2). The name field is defined in line 3 with the key word VARCHAR(30). This means that the name is a character string with maximum 30 characters. Similarly the maximum number of characters for the password is 60. The statement in line 5 instructs MySQL to use the id field as primary key. If the command in lines 1–6 is successful, the database password table will be created and the 'Query OK' message returned.

Once you have the table, you can load the data file password2.txt into this password table by the LOAD DATA command. An example of this operation is shown in listing ex07-08.txt.

```
Example: ex07-08.txt - Load data from password2.txt into password table

1: mysql> LOAD DATA INFILE 'password2.txt'
2:    ->    INTO TABLE password
3:    ->    FIELDS TERMINATED BY ','
4:    ->    LINES TERMINATED BY '\r\n';
```

You can verify the password data in the table by issuing the SQL statement 'SELECT * FROM password;' This command will select everything from the password table. A sample of this operation is shown in Figures 7.40 and 7.41.

Fig. 7.40 Loading data to table

```
mysql> USE passwordDB;
Database changed
mysql> CREATE TABLE password (
  -> id SMALLINT UNSIGNED NOT NULL AUTO_INCREMENT,
  -> name VARCHAR(30),
  -> password VARCHAR(60),
  -> PRIMARY KEY (id)
  -> );
 Query OK, 0 rows affected (0.04 sec)
mysql> SHOW TABLES;
+---------------------+
| Tables_in_passwordDB |
+---------------------+
| password            |
+---------------------+
 1 row in set (0.00 sec)
mysql> LOAD DATA INFILE 'password3.txt'
  -> INTO TABLE password
  -> FIELDS TERMINATED BY ','
  -> LINES TERMINATED BY '\r\n';
 Query OK, 10 rows affected (0.00 sec)
```

Fig. 7.41 Verifying table data

```
mysql> SELECT * FROM password;
+----+-----------+------------------------------------------+
| id | name      | password                                 |
+----+-----------+------------------------------------------+
|  1 | Paul      | bc73bb5aeb45d1c5ec2d312040f3001ac7c12b8f |
|  2 | John      | 70aa9c67d4f5079db7398cbbd98f2674a6d043af |
|  3 | Peter     | 4abd1f3ad992c6caeaffde1777b87b45b4d4d9fd |
|  4 | Mary      | d2740cfbf11473253110b223cbfd9a9604a448dc |
|  5 | Tom       | ce0be0684f5a1d4b6748c8bf922c948449edcb0e |
|  6 | Joe       | 2a36faf4cb32f5bb4bf243a748e2d7ffdc540847 |
|  7 | Anna      | d3a1f4ce51528815c849ef2ef831b86db98771b5 |
|  8 | Emma      | 18ebde6104f91710f80157f98d25ceb500de79a9 |
|  9 | JohnSmith | 35e87f12a60ad90a0c4afb910a131b663d844841 |
| 10 | Sue       | 6b2337d6d54f65698f91dda05d87cc16558693d0 |
+----+-----------+------------------------------------------+
 10 rows in set (0.00 sec)

mysql> SELECT * FROM password WHERE name="John";
+----+------+------------------------------------------+
| id | name | password                                 |
+----+------+------------------------------------------+
|  2 | John | 70aa9c67d4f5079db7398cbbd98f2674a6d043af |
+----+------+------------------------------------------+
 1 row in set (0.00 sec)
```

In Figure 7.40, the USE command in the first line changes the current database to
passwordDB. The remaining statements create and load data into the password
table. When the SELECT command is issued in Figure 7.41, the entire table is
displayed. The SQL command

```
SELECT * FROM password WHERE name="John";
```

displays the record in the password table where the name is equal to 'John'. The
record is, in fact, the encrypted password. Now, we have a password table in the
MySQL database passwordDB. One application of this password table is to use it to
identify a user using Web pages.

7.4.2 User authentication using MySQL database and ODBC

There are a number of ways you can access a MySQL database from your local
machine or Web browser. One popular technique is to use PHP and Microsoft's
Open DataBase Connectivity (ODBC). Perhaps the most important reason for the
success of PHP is the support of a wide range of databases. PHP has built-in
functions that directly support more than 20 database products, including MySQL.
For the remainder of this chapter, PHP is the default language for handling
databases.

ODBC is a product from Microsoft for providing a unified interface for different database types. ODBC has existed since the early days of Windows and has become the de facto standard for database applications across different vendors and platforms. Once you have registered your database with ODBC, you can access your remote data with browsers. Whether you have Microsoft Access, dBase, FoxPro, Oracle or MySQL you can control it using the same type of programming and coding.

Before you can use the MySQL database on a remote site, you first need to register a database with ODBC on your local machine. The driver for handling MySQL databases is called MyODBC and is available from the official site of MySQL. Basically, there are two versions of MyODBC – one is for Windows and the other is for UNIX/LINUX operating systems.

To install the Windows version, you can unzip the downloaded file myodbc-x.xx.xx-nt.zip into an empty directory and run the setup program setup.exe. You will see a Setup dialog window as shown in Figure 7.42. If you press the Continue button, the install drivers dialog box will appear as shown in Figure 7.43. Highlight the MySQL driver and click the OK button. Once MyODBC is installed, you are ready to register your remote MySQL databases with ODBC.

Assume that you have a MySQL database passwordDB located in a server called www.pws-ex.com. The procedure for registering this database on a client machine running Windows XP is as follows.

- Activate Start|Control Panel and click Administrative Tools (Figure 7.44).

- Click the Data Source (ODBC) icon to open the Administrator window (Figure 7.45).

Fig. 7.42 MyODBC installation

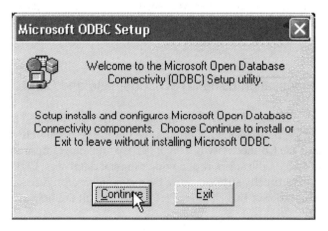

Fig. 7.43 MySQL driver for ODBC

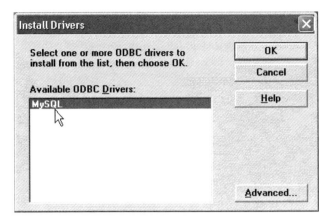

Fig. 7.44 MyODBC installation

- Click the `System DSN` tab and press the `Add` button.

- The `Create New Data Source` window is shown. Highlight the `MySQL` option and click the `Finish` button (Figure 7.46).

- The MySQL driver default configuration screen appears (Figure 7.47). For a basic configuration with `hostname`, `username` and `password`, fill in the following fields and click the `OK` button:

Fig. 7.45 System DSN

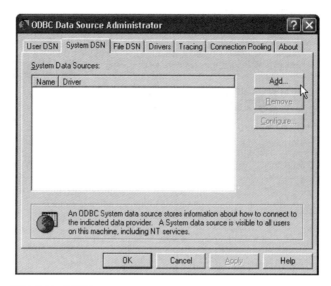

Fig. 7.46 Create new data source

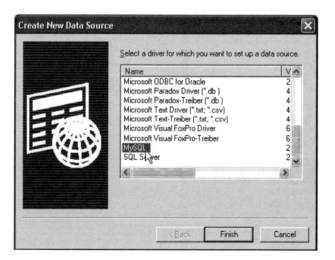

Windows DSN name: passwordDB
MySQL host(name or IP): www.pws-ex.com
MySql database name: passwordDB
User: johnsmith
Password: *********

Fig. 7.47 MySQL driver configuration

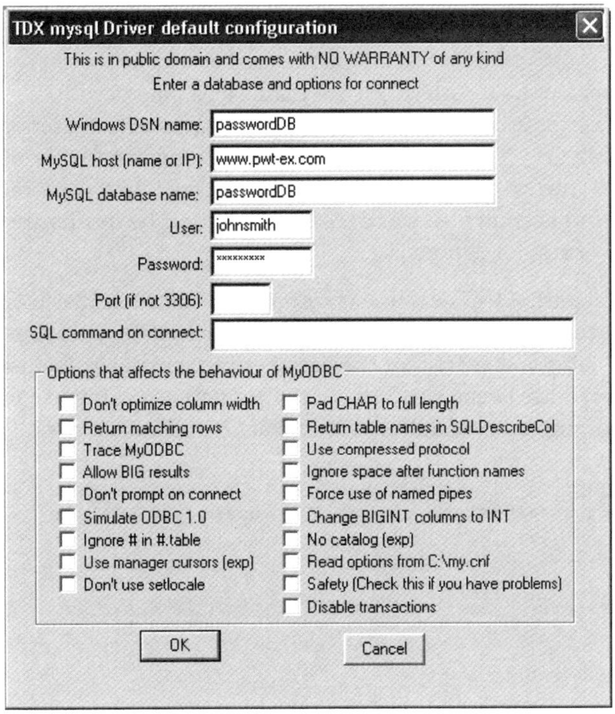

The values in these fields will be used as the defaults when you attempt to make a connection. Now you have a remote MySQL database called `passwordDB` registered in your local machine under ODBC. One way to test your MyODBC driver and MySQL system is to develop a Web page to access the remote database with browsers.

As a quick reminder, the information you need to build a MySQL database application is:

■ Hostname (MySQL): `www.pws-ex.com`

■ Username (MySQL): `johnsmith`

■ Password (MySQL): `john654321`

■ Database name: `passwordDB`

■ Table name: `password`

For this database page, we would like to use PHP for the development. The interface part of this example is almost the same as part I of `ex07-19.php`, which will display a window asking for a username and password. Make a copy of part I of ex07-19.php and call it ex07-20.php. In this new PHP script, modify this line:

```
16: $llst = 'Enter Your Username and Password <br /> To Log On ' .
```

This line tells users to enter their username and password to log on to the system. The main purpose of this PHP page fragment is to define a string $llst. When this variable $llst is echoed or printed to the browser, two text boxes appear for the user to enter a username and password. Also, when you press the OK button, the password is encrypted by SHA-1 encryption. The results are then passed to the same PHP script for processing.

The second part of this example is responsible for all database operations and password comparisons. First it will contact the MySQL database, locate the password table and search for the password that matches the username. Once the password has been extracted from the database, a simple comparison against the user input password is performed. Part II of the example is listed below.

```
Example: Continuation of the PHP script ex07-20.php          (Part II)
39: if ($passId && $userId)
40: {
41:     $handle = fopen("../mysql_pass.txt", "r");
42:     $st = fgets($handle,4096);
43:     $st = chop($st);
44:     list($mysql_name, $mysql_pass) = split(",", $st);
45:     fclose($handle);
46:
47:     $db = mysql_connect("www.pws-ex.com",$mysql_name,$mysql_pass);
48:     mysql_select_db("passwordDB",$db);
49:
50:     $query = "SELECT * FROM password WHERE name='$userId'";
51:     $result = mysql_query ($query) or die ("SQL Query Error...");
52:
53:     $row = mysql_fetch_array ($result);
54:
55:     if ($passId == $row['password']) {
56:         echo"Thank You $userId! <br /> Enjoy Your Visit<br /><br />";
57:     } else {
58:         echo "$llst";
59:     }
60:     mysql_free_result ($result);
61: } else {
62:     echo "$llst";
63: }
64: ?>
65: </body>
66: </html>
```

The conditional-if statement in line 39 performs a test to find out if both the username and password are not empty. If one of the fields is not filled, the echo statement in line 62 is executed and the user has to log on again. If both the username and password are not empty, the statements in lines 41–60 are executed. First, the MySQL username and password are read from a remote location and stored in variables `$mysql_name` and `$mysql_pass` respectively. These values are needed to access the MySQL database and are usually provided by your database manager or administrator.

The function `mysql_connnect()` in line 47 is used to make a connection to the MySQL database server. The statement in line 48 selects `passwordDB` as the current database. For user authentication, the following SQL statement is defined (line 50):

```
SELECT * FROM password WHERE name='$userId'
```

Since the variable `$userId` contains the input username, this SQL statement will return the record (name and password) where the name equals `$userId`. To execute this SQL statement, the `mysql_query()` function is called and the result is stored in variable `$result`.

The `mysql_fetch_array()` function in line 53 extracts the record and puts it into an array variable called `$row`. A simple comparison of `$passId` against the variable `$row['password']`, as illustrated in line 55, will determine whether a match on the encrypted password is found. If there is a match, a simple welcome message is displayed. If the two passwords are different, the echo statement in line 58 will display `$llst` asking the user to try again.

This example is a framework for demonstrating how to put encrypted passwords into a database. In a real application, you should put your Web page, or even encrypted document, inside the line 56. Screenshots of this example are shown in Figures 7.48 and 7.49.

By using a database, a large number of users or members can be handled effectively. Even with a very low-end computer, thousands of records can be searched in a fraction of a second. Also, you can develop pages to add new accounts easily.

7.4.3 Adding a new password account to a database

In this section, we are going to develop a sign-up page to allow someone to join a membership group. This page is similar to `ex07-19.php` except that a database is involved. First, the page will display a window so that the user can enter a username and password. The password is encrypted by the SHA-1 scheme and then submitted to the same page for processing. The input username is searched against all records in the database. If there is no existing member with the same name, a new record is added. If the name has already been used by someone, a window appears for the user to try again.

Fig. 7.48 ex07-20.php

Fig. 7.49 Sign on successfully

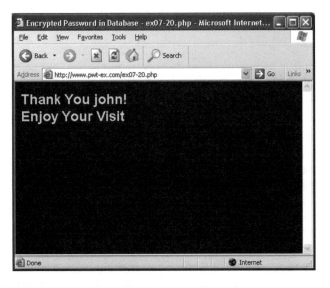

The interface part of this example is the same as part I of ex07-19.php, and there is no need to change anything. All you have to do is to copy part I of ex07-19.php and call it ex07-21.php. At the end of this PHP script, you also need to insert the $userId (username) and $passId (password) into the database if the username is new. To do this, you execute the following SQL statement:

```
INSERT INTO password (id,name,password)
    VALUES (NULL,'$userId','$passId');
```

The second part of the PHP program is listed below.

```
Example: Continuation of the PHP script ex07-21.php          (Part II)
39: if ($passId && $userId)
40: {
41:     $handle = fopen("../mysql_pass.txt", "r");
42:     $st = fgets($handle,4096);
43:     $st = chop($st);
44:     list($mysql_name, $mysql_pass) = split(",", $st);
45:     fclose($handle);
46:
47:     $db = mysql_connect("www.pws-ex.com",$mysql_name,$mysql_pass);
48:     mysql_select_db("passwordDB",$db);
49:
50:     $query = "SELECT * FROM password WHERE name='$userId'";
51:     $result = mysql_query ($query) or die ("SQL Query Error...");
52:     $row = mysql_fetch_array ($result);
53:     if ($userId != $row['name'])
54:     {
55:         $sql = "INSERT INTO password (id,name,password)
56:                 VALUES (NULL,'$userId','$passId')";
57:         $result = mysql_query($sql) or die ("SQL Query Error...");
58:
59:         echo "A New Account Has Been Set Up <br /><br />";
60:         echo "Username = $userId <br />";
61:         echo "Encrypted Password = <br />$passId <br />";
62:     } else {
63:         echo "The User Name You Picked <br />Has Been " .
64:              "Used By Someone.<br /> Please Try again! <br />";
65:         echo($llst);
66:     }
67: } else {
68:     echo "$llst";
69: }
70: ?>
71: <br /><img src="line1.gif" width="500" height="6" alt="pic" />
72: <br /><br />
73: </body>
74: </html>
```

The connecting process to the database is the same as in `ex07-20.php`. Lines 41–45 get the connection name and password from the file `mysql_pass.txt`. The values are used to make connection in line 47. Then the following SQL statement is run, searching for the existence of `$userId`.

```
SELECT * FROM password WHERE name='$userId';
```

If the username exists in the database then the `echo` statements in lines 63–65 output the variable `$llst` so that the user can try again. If the username is new, the SQL `INSERT` statement is executed to add the username and encrypted password into the database as a new record (lines 55–61):

```
INSERT INTO password (id,name,password)
        VALUES (NULL,'$userId','$passId');
```

This SQL statement inserts the values (or fields) `NULL`, $userId and $passId at the end of the database password table. Screenshots of this example are shown in Figures 7.50 and 7.51.

To see the entire password table, you can issue the command `SELECT * FROM password` from the MySQL monitor program `mysql`. You will see `name` and `password` records as in Figure 7.52.

As you can see, the newly created account 'Arthur' appears at the end of the database password table.

If you search the Internet, you will find that many companies and sites offer utilities to join membership. However, not many of them have a friendly facility to

Fig. 7.50 `ex07-21.php`

Fig. 7.51 Adding a new password account

Fig. 7.52 Adding a new password account

```
mysql> SELECT * FROM password;
+----+-----------+------------------------------------------+
| id | name      | password                                 |
+----+-----------+------------------------------------------+
|  1 | Paul      | bc73bb5aeb45d1c5ec2d312040f3001ac7c12b8f |
|  2 | John      | 70aa9c67d4f5079db7398cbbd98f2674a6d043af |
|  3 | Peter     | 4abd1f3ad992c6caeaffde1777b87b45b4d4d9fd |
|  4 | Mary      | d2740cfbf11473253110b223cbfd9a9604a448dc |
|  5 | Tom       | ce0be0684f5a1d4b6748c8bf922c948449edcb0e |
|  6 | Joe       | 2a36faf4cb32f5bb4bf243a748e2d7ffdc540847 |
|  7 | Anna      | d3a1f4ce51528815c849ef2ef831b86db98771b5 |
|  8 | Emma      | 18ebde6104f91710f80157f98d25ceb500de79a9 |
|  9 | JohnSmith | 35e87f12a60ad90a0c4afb910a131b663d844841 |
| 10 | Sue       | 6b2337d6d54f65698f91dda05d87cc16558693d0 |
| 12 | Arthur    | 7f02de9df74dfd7faedde73934969ad49191b44c |
+----+-----------+------------------------------------------+
11 rows in set (0.00 sec)

mysql>
```

allow you to change the account information or password. By using databases, this can be done easily.

7.4.4   Updating and changing password accounts

One of the commonest security measures against intruders is to change your password regularly. This basic process has still not been implemented on a large scale. Although many Web sites still haven't provided utilities to allow members to change their account passwords, developing a page to do that online is simple. Basically, all you have to do is to get the following information from the user:

- username;

- current password;

- new password;

- confirm password.

When the username and current password match the information in the database, and the new password is the same as the 'confirm' password, you have consistent data. In this case, a simple SQL update statement can be employed to update the data in the database.

One the other hand, if either the username or current password does not match the data in the database, or the new password is not the same as the 'confirm' password, you have inconsistent data. In this case, all operations should stop and the user should try again. Consider part I of the PHP script ex07-22.php.

```
Example: ex07-22.php Updating and changing a password account (Part I)
 1: <?PHP echo"<?";?>xml version="1.0"
       encoding="iso-8859-1"<?PHP echo"?>";?>
 2: <!DOCTYPE html PUBLIC "-//W3C//DTD XHTML 1.0 Transitional//EN"
 3:      "http://www.w3.org/TR/xhtml1/DTD/xhtml1-transitional.dtd">
 4: <html xmlns="http://www.w3.org/1999/xhtml" xml:lang="en" lang="en">
 5: <head><title>A Page To Change Password - ex07-22.php</title></head>
 6: <style>
 7:   .butSt{background-color:#aaffaa;font-family:arial;
          font-weight:bold;
 8:        font-size:18pt;color:#880000;width:250px;height:35px}
 9:   .butSt2{background-color:#eeeeee;font-family:arial;
          font-weight:bold;
10:        font-size:18pt;color:#880000;width:150px;height:35px}
11:   .txtSt{font-family:arial;font-weight:bold; text-align:left;
```

```
12: font-size:18pt;color:#ffff00}</style>
13: <body style="background:#000088" class="txtSt">
14: <?php
15:   Global $llst,$userId,$passId,$newId,$confId;
16:   $llst = 'Change Your Password<br /> ' .
17:   ' Please Enter All Information Below:<br /><br />' .
18:   ' <form action="ex07-22.php" method="post" id="formId">'.
19:   ' <table class="txtSt"><tr><td>' .
20:   '  Username:</td><td>' .
21:   ' <input type="text" name="userId" id="userId"
               class="butSt" />' .
22:   '      </td></tr><tr><td>' .
23:   '  Current Password:</td><td>' .
24:   ' <input type="password" name="passId" id="passId"
               class="butSt" />' .
25:   '      </td></tr><tr><td> ' .
26:   '  New Password:</td><td>' .
27:   ' <input type="password" name="newId" id="newId"
               class="butSt" />' .
28:   '      </td></tr><tr><td> ' .
29:   '  Confirm Your Password:</td><td>' .
30:   ' <input type="password" name="confId" id="confId"
               class="butSt" />' .
31:   '      </td></tr><tr><td> ' .
32:   ' <input type="button" class="butSt2" value="O.K." '.
33:   '       onclick="sub_fun()" /> </td><td>' .
34:   ' <input type="reset" value="Clear" class="butSt2" />' .
35:   '      </td></tr></table>' .
36:   ' </form> ' .
37:   ' <script src="ex03-08.js"></script>' .
38:   ' <script>' .
39:   ' function sub_fun()' .
40:   ' {' .
41:   ' var tmp; '.
42:   ' tmp = document.getElementById("passId").value;' .
43:   ' document.getElementById("passId").value = sha1(tmp);' .
44:   ' tmp = document.getElementById("newId").value;' .
45:   ' document.getElementById("newId").value = sha1(tmp);' .
46:   ' tmp = document.getElementById("confId").value;' .
47:   ' document.getElementById("confId").value = sha1(tmp);'.
48:   ' document.getElementById("formId").submit();'.
49:   ' }'.
50:   ' </script>';
```

Again, the main feature of this PHP program fragment is the string $llst defined in lines 16–50. This string contains XHTML coding to generate four input text fields, namely Username, Current Password, New Password and Confirm Password. When $llst is printed by the function echo(), the text boxes will be displayed by the browser. When the OK button is clicked, the function sub_fun() is activated. In this case the current password, new password and confirm password are encrypted by the SHA-1 method (lines 42–47) before being submitted to the same PHP page ex07-22.php.

The driving force for the password update is listed in part II of script ex07-22.php.

```
Example: Continuation of ex07-22.php                          (Part II)

51: if ($passId && $userId && $newId && $confId)
52: {
53:     $handle = fopen("../mysql_pass.txt", "r");
54:     $st = fgets($handle,4096);
55:     $st = chop($st);
56:     list($mysql_name, $mysql_pass) = split(",", $st);
57:     fclose($handle);
58:
59:     $db = mysql_connect("localhost",$mysql_name,$mysql_pass);
60:     mysql_select_db("passwordDB",$db);
61:
62:     $query = "SELECT * FROM password WHERE name='$userId'";
63:     $result = mysql_query ($query) or die ("SQL Query Error...");
64:     $row = mysql_fetch_array ($result);
65:     $id = $row['id'];
66:
67:     if (($userId == $row['name']) && ($passId == $row['password']) &&
68:         ($newId == $confId))
69:     {
70:         $sql = "UPDATE password SET name='$userId',
71:         password='$newId' WHERE id='$id'";
72:         $result = mysql_query($sql) or die ("SQL Query Error...");
73:         echo "Thank you! $userId <br /><br />";
74:         echo "Your Password Has Been Updated <br />";
75:         echo "Encrypted Password Is <br />$newId <br />";
76:     } else {
77:         echo "Your Information Is Not Consistent: <br />".
78:             "Please Check The Following:<br /><br />" .
79:             "  Spelling Of Your Username <br />".
80:             "  Double Check Your Current Password <br />".
81:             "  Your New Password May Not Match Your<br />".
```

```
82:                    "  Confirm Password <br /><br />".
83:                    "Please Try Again!<br />";
84:    }
85: } else {
86:    echo "$llst";
87: }
88: ?>
89: <img src="line1.gif" width="550" height="6" alt="pic" />
90: <br /><br />
91: </body>
92: </html>
```

This program fragment begins with a detection process to see whether all four fields are filled with data. If not, the echo statement in line 86 will generate the fields and the user can try again. If all the fields are filled, the program starts a process to connect to the database. The process is the same as in ex07-20.php and ex07-21.php. All the information, including id, name and password of the user, are extracted and stored in variables $row['id'], $row['name'] and $row['password'] respectively. Now, we want to perform a data consistency test. In other words, we want to see if:

- the input username matches the username in the database;

- the input password (encrypted) matches the password in the database;

- the new password is the same as the 'confirm' password.

These tasks can be performed as a single if statement as illustrated in lines 67–68. If the data fails the consistency test, the echo statement in lines 77–83 is executed to suggest a possible reason. If the data is well defined, the following simple SQL update statement is served:

```
UPDATE password SET name='$userId',
    password='$newId' WHERE id='$id';
```

This statement updates the record in the database based on the id number. Screenshots of this example in action are shown in Figures 7.53–7.56.

Fig. 7.53 ex07-22.php

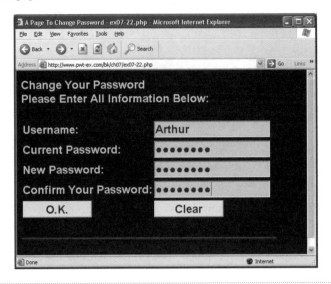

Fig. 7.54 Changing a password successfully

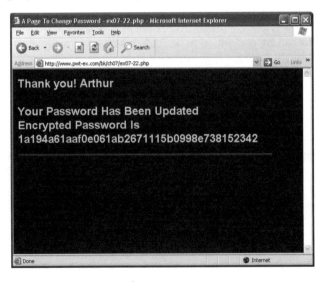

Fig. 7.55 Checking password data

```
mysql> SELECT * FROM password;
+----+-----------+------------------------------------------+
| id | name      | password                                 |
+----+-----------+------------------------------------------+
|  1 | Paul      | bc73bb5aeb45d1c5ec2d312040f3001ac7c12b8f |
|  2 | John      | 70aa9c67d4f5079db7398cbbd98f2674a6d043af |
|  3 | Peter     | 4abd1f3ad992c6caeaffde1777b87b45b4d4d9fd |
|  4 | Mary      | d2740cfbf11473253110b223cbfd9a9604a448dc |
|  5 | Tom       | ce0be0684f5a1d4b6748c8bf922c948449edcb0e |
|  6 | Joe       | 2a36faf4cb32f5bb4bf243a748e2d7ffdc540847 |
|  7 | Anna      | d3a1f4ce51528815c849ef2ef831b86db98771b5 |
|  8 | Emma      | 18ebde6104f91710f80157f98d25ceb500de79a9 |
|  9 | JohnSmith | 35e87f12a60ad90a0c4afb910a131b663d844841 |
| 10 | Sue       | 6b2337d6d54f65698f91dda05d87cc16558693d0 |
| 14 | Arthur    | 1a194a61aaf0e061ab2671115b0998e738152342 |
+----+-----------+------------------------------------------+
11 rows in set (0.00 sec)
```

Fig. 7.56 Input data not consistent

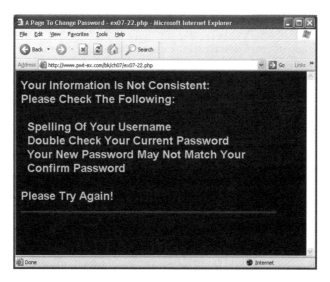

8

Practical public-key security and digital signatures

8.1 Security with public-key technology

8.1.1 Key distribution problems and public-key encryption

Conventional encryption methods, such as symmetric key, use only one key for encryption and decryption. The sender encrypts the message or document with this key and sends it to the receiver. In order to decrypt this document, the receiver has to have the same key. The advantage of these types of algorithms is that they are fast, efficient and computationally safe.

If you want to share the encrypted message with someone, you may have to give up the secrecy of your password (or key) so that your message can be properly decoded by the person you trust. This may create the so-called 'key distribution' problems and compromise data security. If the encrypted message is shared with only one or two parties, exchanging passwords or keys can be done in a strictly private manner and may not be a problem. The key distribution problem would soon turn out to be a nightmare when more parties, say 40, are involved.

The major problem of symmetric-key encryption is that if somebody else does have the key then the entire security will be compromised. The use of so-called 'public keys' can provide a solution to this problem. Instead of using one key, a public key is a concept where two keys are involved. One key is called the public key, which can be obtained by anyone. Many people suggest that a public-key server should be involved in distributing them. The other key is called the secret key (or private key) and should be kept secret by the owner permanently. Any good public-key encryption scheme should be make it computationally infeasible (or difficult) to derive the secret key from the public key or vice versa.

The public-key scheme operation is simple. When a message is encrypted with one key, the other key must be used to decrypt the message. An example is demonstrated in Figure 8.1.

Fig. 8.1 Public-key encryption/decryption scheme

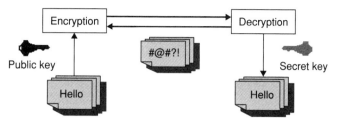

Suppose you want to send a sensitive message to Bob, who has a public key called 'Bob_P'. All you have to do is to obtain this key. You then apply this key to encrypt the message you want to send. The result is an encrypted message which can only be decrypted by using Bob's secret key, such as 'Bob_S'. If the keys Bob_P and Bob_S are totally different, and one cannot be obtained by the other, the key distribution problem is solved. This is because Bob doesn't need to distribute his secret key at all.

When used properly, this public-key structure can generate trust such that dedicated messages can be read only by the intended recipient. In fact public-key technology (or infrastructure) not only solves the key distribution problem, it creates an entire new chapter of security applications, forming a solid foundation for modern cryptography.

8.1.2   Data integrity, digital signature and non-repudiation

Conventional encryption using one key is not easy to perform with data integrity and verification. For example, how can your partner identity that a message was really sent by you? As a simple example, if you send a message to your bank, how does the bank manager determine that the message was really sent by you? How does the bank know that the message sent by you hasn't been attacked by a hacker to transfer money to another account? Even if you know how to protect the integrity of your message using the hash functions discussed in Chapter 3, a capable hacker can hack your message – change it, produce a new hash value, and deliver these to your bank manager. Apart from message confidentiality, public-key techniques also provide solutions to these security problems, namely:

- digital signature – proof of data and/or entity identification;

- non-repudiation – protection against falsely denying;

- data integrity   – making sure no alteration can be made.

One of the great features of the public-key technique is that it can be used to identify the message sender. This process is generally referred to as the digital signature.

For example, suppose the public–private key pairs of Bob and Sue are (Bob_P, Bob_S) and (Sue_P, Sue_S) respectively. When Sue wants to send Bob an important message, she can encrypt the message using her private key first and then Bob's public key. The result is a double-encrypted message ready to send to Bob. When Bob gets the message, he can use his own private key and then Sue's public key to decrypt it. When the message is successfully decrypted by Sue's public key, the message must be sent by Sue herself. When Sue encrypts the message using her private key, it is like to sign the message with her signature, and therefore the process is called digital signature. This process is demonstrated in Figure 8.2.

In fact, Sue doesn't need to encrypt the entire message using her private key. She can encrypt part of the message, or some personal information to identify her, with the private key instead. This process can also be used for non-repudiation. In other words, it will stop the fraudulent claim from Sue that she didn't send the message.

Another problem is how to maintain the integrity of the data that you have sent. In other words, how can you verify that the messages you send to the bank haven't been modified or replaced (cut and paste attack) by an intruder? Even if you generate the hash value (or hash) of the document, a capable hacker can also replace yours with his generated hash. An unprotected hash is a dangerous thing. However, when combined with public-key encryption, data integrity is greatly enhanced. The data integrity verification process is illustrated in Figure 8.3.

Chapter 3 pointed out that hash functions can produce a summary, called a hash, of a message representing a signature good only for that particular message. When the hash of a document is protected by public-key encryption, data integrity of the document is maintained.

Suppose Sue wants to send Bob an important message and protect the contents against alterations at the same time. She can:

■ obtain the hash value of the message;

■ encrypt the hash with Sue's secret key, Sue_S;

■ encrypt the message using Bob's public key, Bob_P.

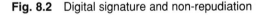

Fig. 8.2 Digital signature and non-repudiation

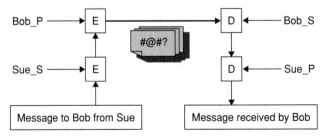

Fig. 8.3 Data integrity verification

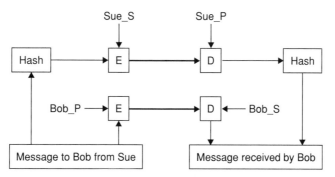

The results are sent to Bob separately. When Bob gets the encrypted message and hash, he can obtain the originals by decryption and perform a data integrity test as follows:

- use the key Sue_P to get the hash of the message;

- use the key Bob_S to obtain the message;

- use the hash to verify the integrity of the message.

If the received message produces the same hash, the data integrity of the message is intact. In fact, the data integrity verification process is similar to verifying the signature (secret key) of the message.

Since the first version of a public-key commercial product called Pretty Good Privacy (PGP) at the beginning of the 1990s, public-key encryption technologies have been very popular. In fact, we have a standard for it. It is called the IETF RFC 2440 and is known as Open Pretty Good Privacy (OpenPGP). Based on this standard specification, a freely available public-key security product called Gnu Privacy Guard (GnuPG) is developed for anyone who wants to use it. Both PGP and GnuPG will be discussed in Chapter 9 in detail. In particular we will discuss how to use these two products to protect information communication over the World Wide Web and/or Internet. To enhance our background on public-key security, let's consider some popular public-key encryption/decryption algorithms.

8.2 The Diffie–Hellman key exchange scheme

8.2.1 The Diffie–Hellman key exchange

One of the current public-key concepts is from the Diffie–Hellman (DH) key exchange created by Whitfield Diffie and Martin Hellman in the middle of the 1970s. The DH key exchange scheme allows two people to share a secret key over an open or unsecure channel such as the Internet or Web. The scheme is based on elementary number theory.

Let p be a prime number: the set $Z_p = \{0, 1, 2, \ldots, p-1\}$ is a finite field. This set can be considered as the remainders of any integer divided by p. The non-zero elements Z_p^* of Z_p form a group under multiplication modulo p, i.e.

$$Z_p^* = \{1, 2, \ldots, p-1\}$$

This set has $p - 1$ elements. An element g ($1 < g < p$) is said to be the generator of Z_p^* if Z_p^* can be generated by the powers of g, i.e.

$$Z_p^* = \{1, g^2, g^3, \ldots, g^{p-2}\} \bmod p$$

For example, if $p = 11$, we have $Z_{11}^* = \{1, 2, \ldots, 10\}$. Also, it is easy to see that 2 is a generator of Z_{11}^*:

$$Z_{11}^* = \{1, 2, 2^2, \ldots, 2^9\} \bmod 11 = \{1, 2, 4, 8, 5, 10, 9, 7, 3, 6\}$$

In other words, the number 2 generates the complete set of Z_p^*. Other numbers, such as 3, 4 and 5, are not generators. Numbers 6 and 7 are again generators. Generators are sometimes called primitive roots of Z_p^* and can be used to construct many security applications related to Z_p^*.

Given an integer a, the smallest integer n such that

$$1 = a^n \bmod p$$

is called the order of a (mod p). If the order of 'a (mod p)' is $p - 1$, then integer a is a generator of Z_p^*. With this mathematical background, the DH key exchange can be described as follows.

The DH key exchange scheme

Suppose Bob and Sue want to share a secret key 'K' using the DH key exchange. The process is as follows.

- Select a 'large' prime number p and a generator $1 < g < p - 1$ of Z_p^*.

- Bob picks a random secret integer x, $1 < x < p - 1$, and the following result is computed:

$$X = g^x \bmod p.$$

- The secret key is x and the public key is (X, g, p), i.e.

$$\text{Bob\_S} = x; \text{Bob\_P} = (X, g, p).$$

- Sue selects a secret number y, $1 < y < p - 1$, and the following result is computed:

$$Y = g^y \bmod p.$$

- The secret key for Sue is y and the public key is (Y, g, p)

$$\text{Sue\_S} = y; \text{Sue\_P} = (Y, g, p).$$

- When Sue receives Bob's public key Bob_P = (X, g, p), the shared secret key can be computed by using Sue's secret key y:

$$K = X^y \bmod p = (g^x)^y \bmod p.$$

- When Bob receives Sue's public key Sue_P = (Y, g, p), the shared secret key can be computed by using Bob's secret key x:

$$K = Y^x \bmod p = (g^y)^x \bmod p.$$

In this case, the shared key is K. In other words, key K is shared for communication by Bob and Sue over an insecure environment (see Figure 8.4).

For example, consider a small prime $p = 73699$ with generator $g = 2$. Bob chooses $x = 137$ for his secret key. The public key is computed by

$$g^x = 2^{137} \bmod 73699$$
$$= 174224571863520493293247799005065324265472 \bmod 73699$$
$$= 31072 \bmod 73699$$
$$\Rightarrow \text{Bob\_P} = [X, g, p] = [31072, 2, 73699)$$

Sue picks $y = 193$ as her secret key and the public key is

$$g^y = 2^{193} \bmod 73699$$
$$= 12554203470773361527671578846415332832204710888928069025792 \bmod 73699$$
$$= 19048 \bmod 73699$$
$$\Rightarrow \text{Sue\_P} = [Y, g, p] = [19048, 2, 73699]$$

Fig. 8.4 Diffie–Hellman key exchange algorithm

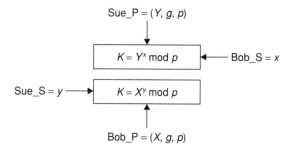

If Sue wants to send a secret message to Bob, she can compute the key K by

$$K = 31072^{193} \bmod 73699$$
$$= 61344 \bmod 73699$$

When Bob receives the message encrypted by K from Sue, he can compute the key K by

$$K = (19048)^{137} \bmod 73699$$
$$= 61344 \bmod 73699$$

The shared key can be used to decrypt the message. One of the interesting features of this key exchange setting is that the algorithm is expandable. To see this in action, suppose that Mary wants to join the shared-key scheme with Bob and Sue. All she needs to do is pick her secret key and calculate her public key:

$$\text{Mary\_S} = 167 \text{ (say)}$$
$$2^{167} \bmod 73699 = 70188 \bmod 73699$$
$$\text{Mary\_P} = [70188, 2, 73699]$$

The combination of all the shared keys is shown in Table 8.1.

The first row and column give the DH keys of Bob, Sue and Mary. The remaining cells show the corresponding shared keys among them. From this example we can see that the shared keys between any two people are different. Also, the scheme is fully expandable. In other words, new members can be added easily.

The implementation of the algorithm may look straightforward, involving a simple power modulo operation '$a^x \bmod p$'. For a small x and prime p the operation is trivial. For a big integer x and a large prime p the operation can be troublesome. For example, consider the number of digits in the following numbers:

$$2^{137} \text{ has 42 digits} \qquad 2^{167} \text{ has 51 digits} \qquad 2^{193} \text{ has 59 digits}$$

Not many computer systems can handle these big numbers directly. In normal circumstances, the largest number in the memory of a 32-bit computer is $2^{32} = 4294967296$ (10 digits). Anything more needs additional treatment. It is also

Table 8.1 Combination of shared keys of Bob, Sue and Mary

The DH key exchange scheme	Bob_S = (137) Bob_P = (31072, 2, 73699)	Sue_S = (193) Sue_P = (19048, 2, 73699)	Mary_S = 167 Mary_P = (70188, 2, 73699)
Bob_S = (137) Bob_P = (31072, 2, 73699)	9314 mod 73699	61344 mod 73699	71352 mod 73699
Sue_S = (193) Sue_P = (19048, 2, 73699)	61344 mod 73699	66969 mod 73699	65763 mod 73699
Mary_S = 167 Mary_P = (70188, 2, 73699)	71352 mod 73699	65763 mod 73699	59364 mod 73699

obvious that, for a secure scheme, the prime p must be big enough to discourage brute-force attackers.

In order to handle big numbers, or the precision implementation problems, a software package such as arbitrary precision mathematics (APM) is needed.

8.2.2 Using arbitrary precision mathematics packages

In this section, we consider how to use an APM package to implement the DH scheme. The package is called 'Big Integer Library'. It is a script-based library (`BigInt.js`) and is freely available to everyone. A copy can be downloaded from the site accompanying this book or any search engine with keyword 'BigInt.js'.

From the operational point of view, the Diffie–Hellman scheme has two parts. The first is to generate and publish the public key. The second part is to compute the shared key for encryption/decryption. Generating the DH public key is simple, all you have to do is:

- select a prime p and a generator g;

- pick a random number y as your secret key;

- compute and publish the public key (Y, g, p), where $Y = g^y \bmod p$.

Since we are going to use an APM package, the calculation of $a^y \bmod p$ is no longer an implementation problem. Consider the listing in ex08-01.htm.

```
Example: ex08-01.htm - Generating the Diffie-Hellman public key

 1: <head><title>The DH Key Exchange Scheme</title></head>
 2: <style>
 3:   .butSt{font-size:16pt;width:70px;height:35px;
 4:          font-weight:bold;background:#ddffdd;color:#ff0000}
 5:   .txtSt{font-size:14pt;width:240px;height:35px;font-weight:bold;
 6:          background:#dddddd;color:#ff0000}
 7: </style>
 8: <body style="font-family:arial;font-size:20pt;text-align:center;
 9:        background:#000088;color:#ffff00">
10:  Generating Diffie-Hellman Public-Key <br />
        Y =(g) <sup>y</sup> mod p
11: <br /><img alt="pic" src="line1.gif" height="7" width="650" /><br />
12: <form action="">
13: <table style="font-size:16pt;width:560px" cellspacing="5"
       align="center">
14:  <tr><td>The Secret-Key: y</td><td >
15:          <input type="text" id="sec_y" size="32" maxlength="32"
16:             class="txtSt" value="137" /></td></tr>
```

```
17:              <tr><td>The Generator g: </td><td >
18:          <input type="text" id="gen_g" size="32" maxlength="32"
19:          class="txtSt" value="2" /></td></tr>
20:   <tr><td>The Prime p: </td><td>
21:          <input type="text" id="pri_p" size="32" maxlength="32"
22:          class="txtSt" value="73699" /></td></tr>
23:   <tr><td>The Public-Key (Y,a,p): </td><td>
24:          <input type="text" id="result" size="32"
25:           maxlength="32" readonly class="txtSt" value="" />
26:          <input type="button" class="butSt" value="OK"
27:          onclick="dh_key()" /></td></tr>
28: </table></form>
29: <script src="BigInt.js"></script>
30: <script>
31:   function dh_key()
32:   {
33:     var secret_y, public_Y,gen_g,prime_p;
34:     ty = document.getElementById("sec_y").value;
35:     tg = document.getElementById("gen_g").value;
36:     tp = document.getElementById("pri_p").value
37:     secret_y = str2bigInt(ty,10,0);
38:     gen_g    = str2bigInt(tg,10,0);
39:     prime_p  = str2bigInt(tp,10,0);
40:
41:     powMod(gen_g,secret_y,prime_p);
42:     llst = bigInt2str(gen_g,10)+","+tg+","+tp;
43:     document.getElementById("result").value = llst;
44:   }
45: </script>
46: </body>
```

This page contains four text boxes and one push button. The first text box in lines 15–16 is to get the user-specified secret key y. The next two boxes are for the generator g and prime p. When the OK button in line 27 is clicked, the function dh_key() is executed. This function computes the public key (Y, g, p) and displays it in the fourth text box (lines 24–25).

To use the APM library, the script file BigInt.js is included in the page at line 29. The values of secret key y, generator g and the prime p are captured by the statements in lines 34–36. Since these values are base 10 format and are represented as strings, the function str2bigInt() is used to convert them into big numbers. Now, variables secret_y, gen_g, and prime_p are big numbers in APM format. Consider the function in line 41

```
powMod(gen_g,secret_y,prime_p);
```

Fig. 8.5 The DH public key

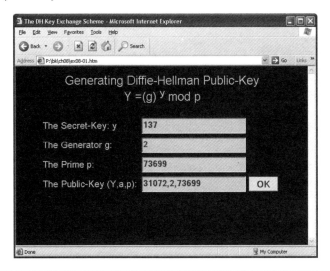

This function computes the value $(gen\_g)^{secret\_y}$ mod $(prime\_p)$, which is the component of the DH public key. The result is stored back to the first variable gen_g. Variable gen_g is a big number and therefore the function bigInt2str() in line 42 is needed to a convert it to a string. When all the public-key components (Y, g, p) are composed to variable llst in line 42, this variable is displayed to the fourth text box by the statement in line 43. A screenshot of this example is shown in Figure 8.5.

The second part of the DH scheme computes the shared key K. This key is used to perform encryption/decryption. The value of K is determined by

- my secret key y;
- shared key formula: $K = Y^x \bmod p$;
- someone's public key (Y, g, p).

With the APM package BigInt.js, the shared-key formula can be calculated easily. Consider ex08-02.htm.

Example: ex08-02.htm – Computing the DH shared key

```
1:  <head><title>compute The DH Key Shared-Key</title></head>
2:  <style>
3:    .butSt{font-size:16pt;width:70px;height:35px;
4:          font-weight:bold;background:#ddffdd;color:#ff0000}
```

```
 5:    .txtSt{font-size:14pt;width:240px;height:35px;font-weight:bold;
 6:          background:#dddddd;color:#ff0000}
 7:  </style>
 8:  <body style="font-family:arial;font-size:20pt;text-align:center;
 9:        background:#000088;color:#ffff00">
10:   The Diffie-Hellman Shared-Key <br /> K =(Y) <sup>y</sup> mod p
11:  <br /><img alt="pic" src="line1.gif" height="7" width="650" /><br />
12:  <form action="">
13:  <table style="font-size:16pt;width:560px" cellspacing="5"
      align="center">
14:  <tr><td>The Secret-Key: y</td><td >
15:           <input type="text" id="sec_y" size="32" maxlength="32"
16:            class="txtSt" value="137" /></td></tr>
17:  <tr><td>The Public-Key Y</td><td>
18:           <input type="text" id="pub_Y" size="32" maxlength="32"
19:            class="txtSt" value="19048" /></td></tr>
20:  <tr><td>The Generator g: </td><td >
21:           <input type="text" id="gen_g" size="32" maxlength="32"
22:            class="txtSt" value="2" /></td></tr>
23:  <tr><td>The Prime p: </td><td>
24:           <input type="text" id="pri_p" size="32" maxlength="32"
25:            class="txtSt" value="73699" /></td></tr>
26:  <tr><td>The Shared-Key K: </td><td>
27:           <input type="text" id="result" size="32"
28:            maxlength="32" readonly class="txtSt" value="" />
29:           <input type="button" class="butSt" value="OK"
30:            onclick="sh_key()" /></td></tr>
31:  </table></form>
32:  <script src="BigInt.js"></script>
33:  <script>
34:  function sh_key()
35:  {
36:    var secret_y, public_Y,gen_g,prime_p;
37:    secret_y = str2bigInt(document.getElementById
                            ("sec_y").value,10,0);
38:    public_Y = str2bigInt(document.getElementById
                            ("pub_Y").value,10,0);
39:    gen_g = str2bigInt(document.getElementById
                            ("gen_g").value,10,0);
40:    prime_p = str2bigInt(document.getElementById
                            ("pri_p").value,10,0);
41:    powMod(public_Y,secret_y,prime_p);
42:    llst = bigInt2str(public_Y,10);
43:    document.getElementById("result").value = llst;
44:  }
45:  </script>
46:  </body>
```

Fig. 8.6 The shared key

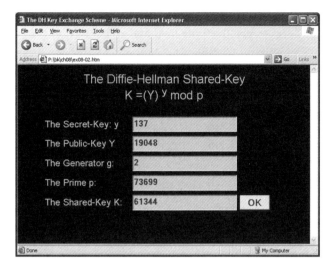

This page contains five text boxes and one OK button. The first four text boxes are used to get the secret key y, public-key component Y, generator g, and the prime p. When the OK button at line 30 is clicked, the function sh_key() is activated. This function computes the shared key K and displays it in the fifth text box in lines 28–30.

First, the function sh_key() in lines 34–44 captures the strings y, Y, g and p. These strings are converted into big numbers secret_y, public_Y, gen_g and prime_p respectively. The statement in line 41

```
powMod(public_Y,secret_x,prime_p);
```

is equivalent to computing the value Y^y mod p, which is the shared key K. Since this value is a big number, the function bigInt2str() is used to convert it to string llst. This llst is output by the statement in line 43. A screenshot of this example is shown in Figure 8.6.

Now we know how to perform Diffie–Hellman key exchange. The next question is: how safe is this scheme? In other words, can someone get the secret key y when all the public-key components (Y, g, p) are available?

8.2.3 The discrete logarithm problem and brute-force attack

It is well known that the security of the Diffie–Hellman algorithm is equivalent to the so-called 'discrete logarithm problem'. If you can solve this problem effectively, the DH scheme can be cracked.

The discrete logarithm problem

Let p be a prime and a be an arbitrary integer such that $1 < a < p - 1$. Let the set $Z_p = \{0, 1, 2, \ldots, p - 1\}$ be the finite field and Z_p^* be the non-zero elements of Z_p. The following power modulo mapping,

$$e_a(n) = a^n \bmod p = N \quad (n \geq 0)$$

maps any non-negative integer n (i.e. $n \geq 0$) to an element N in Z_p^*. When this map is an onto function, the element a is a primitive root (or generator).

Given integer values (n, a, p) it is easy to compute the number N. However, given values (N, a, p) it is not that easy to compute the integer value n.

For the floating point (or real) number situation, the mapping above may look like the exponential function $y = a^x$. Given the ordered pair (a, x) it is easy to compute y. For values (y, a), x can be computed by the logarithm function, i.e. $y = x \log a$. If you have a calculator, you can obtain the approximate value instantly. It is because there is a Taylor series approximation and this converges rapidly inside your calculator circuitry. However, it doesn't make sense to have an approximation to an integer n. The discrete logarithm problem can be described by the following statement:

given an element N in Z_p^*, if $e_a(n) = N$ holds for some integer n, then find n.

If such $n > 0$ exists, the smallest n is called the 'discrete log of N to base a mod p'. From the definition of generator, we know that the solution n (or the discrete log of N) exists when a is a generator of Z_p^*. However, there is no 'fast' algorithm to compute the integer n from values (N, a, p).

In terms of the DH scheme, the secret key y is protected by the discrete logarithm problem even if the public key (Y, g, p) is known. In fact, the security of a number of cryptographic schemes depends on the assumption that the discrete logarithm problem is hard to solve.

Next, we consider how to perform a simple brute-force attack on the Diffie–Hellman secret key.

Brute-force attack on the DH secret key

Performing a brute-force attack on the DH scheme is simple. Given the public-key component (Y, g, p), the secret key y can be obtained using the equation $Y = g^y \bmod p$. Solving this equation may be hard, but we can apply brute force to search all y in $1 < y < p - 1$ for a match to Y. The pseudo-code for the attack is:

```
ii=1
while(ii>0) {
   if (ii != p-2) {
      tmp = g^ii mod p;
```

```
        if (tmp == Y) {
            ii=0; output "ii as the secret-key";
        } else ii++;
    } else {
       ii=0; output "No Solution Found";
    }
}
```

To convert this pseudo-code into an implementation is not difficult. Consider the listing in ex08-03.htm.

Example: ex08-03.htm – Brute-force attack on the DH key exchange scheme

```
 1: <head><title>Brute-Force Attack On DH Scheme</title></head>
 2: <style>
 3:  .butSt{font-size:16pt;width:70px;height:35px;
 4:         font-weight:bold;background:#ddffdd;color:#ff0000}
 5:  .txtSt{font-size:14pt;width:240px;height:35px;font-weight:bold;
 6:         background:#dddddd;color:#ff0000}
 7: </style>
 8: <body style="font-family:arial;font-size:20pt;text-align:center;
 9:        background:#000088;color:#ffff00">
10:  Brute-Force Attack On the <br /> Diffie-Hellman Secret-Key
11: <br /><img alt="pic" src="line1.gif" height="7" width="650" /><br />
12: <form action="">
13: <table style="font-size:16pt;width:560px" cellspacing="5"
    align="center">
14:  <tr><td>The Public-Key Y</td><td>
15:        <input type="text" id="pub_Y" size="32" maxlength="32"
16:         class="txtSt" value="19048" /></td></tr>
17:  <tr><td>The Generator g: </td><td >
18:        <input type="text" id="gen_g" size="32" maxlength="32"
19:         class="txtSt" value="2" /></td></tr>
20:  <tr><td>The Prime p: </td><td>
21:        <input type="text" id="pri_p" size="32" maxlength="32"
22:         class="txtSt" value="73699" /></td></tr>
23:  <tr><td>The secret-key y: </td><td>
24:        <input type="text" id="result" size="32"
25:         maxlength="32" readonly class="txtSt" value="" />
26:        <input type="button" class="butSt" value="OK"
27:         onclick="bt_skey()" /></td></tr>
28: </table></form>
29: <script src="BigInt.js"></script>
```

```
30:   <script>
31:   function bt_skey()
32:   {
33:     var secret_y, public_Y,gen_g,prime_p, llst="";
34:     var ii=1,bii;
35:     tY = str2bigInt(document.getElementById("pub_Y").value,10,0);
36:     tg = str2bigInt(document.getElementById("gen_g").value,10,0);
37:     tp = str2bigInt(document.getElementById("pri_p").value,10,0);
38:
39:     p2 = dup(tp); p1 = int2bigInt(2,1,1); sub(p2,p1);
40:
41:     bii = int2bigInt(1,1,1);
42:     while (ii > 0) {
43:       copyInt(bii,ii);
44:       ttg = dup(tg); ttp = dup(tp);
45:       if ( !equals(p2,bii) ) {
46:         powMod(ttg,bii,ttp);
47:         if (equals(ttg,tY)) {
48:             ii=0;
49:             llst = bigInt2str(bii,10);
50:         } else ii++;
51:       } else {
52:           ii=0;
53:           llst = "No solution Found";
54:       }
55:     }
56:     document.getElementById("result").value = llst;
57:   }
58:   </script>
59:   </body>
```

The XHTML code of this page contains four text boxes and one OK button. The first three boxes are used to obtain the DH public-key information (Y, g, p). When the OK button is clicked, the function bt_skey() is run to search the secret key using brute-force attack. Apart from the big integer manipulation, the entire process is the same as the pseudo-code above. First, the public-key values (Y,g,p) are captured and converted into big integers (tY,tg,tp) by lines 35–37. Since they are big integers, ordinary operations such as addition and subtraction will not work properly. For example, to subtract the prime by 2, the statements in line 39 are used:

```
p2 = dup(tp); p1 = int2bigInt(2,1,1); sub(p2,p1);
```

The dup() function duplicates a copy of the prime tp to another big integer p2. The second function int2bigInt(2,1,1) converts number 2 into big integer p1 with minimum 1 bit and 1 array. The sub() function finally performs the p2-p1 operation and stores the result back into p2. Line 41 generates a big integer bii with value 1. The while-loop in line 42–55 performs the brute-force search for the secret key.

The search process starts by making a copy of the generator tg and prime tp into variables ttg and ttp (line 44). When the search is not exhausted, the power modulo g^{ii} mod p is calculated at line 46. The result is then compared with the public-key component tY. If a match is found, the secret key is obtained by variable bii. In this case, the setting ii=0 terminates the search and the value bii (or secret key) is output by the statement in line 49. Otherwise, the search continues until the while-loop is exhausted. A screenshot of this example is given in Figure 8.7.

For a small prime, $p = 73699$, this brute-force search is effective. For example, the search is completed in less than 0.1 second on a low-end portable PC – a small prime and secret-key value provide no security for the Diffie–Hellman scheme. It will be harder to find the secret key y if, for example, the following public-key information (Y, g, p) is chosen:

- prime $p = 2741966908132111069327034363307379$

- Generator $g = 5$

- public key $Y = 225226783730824783911298547035868$69

The secret key, in this case, is $y = 1000003$. As we mentioned in Section 8.2.3, the security of the Diffie–Hellman scheme is equivalent to the discrete logarithm problem and therefore is called the discrete log-based crypto-system. Another widely used discrete log crypto-system is ElGamal.

Fig. 8.7 Brute-force attack on the Diffie–Hellman scheme

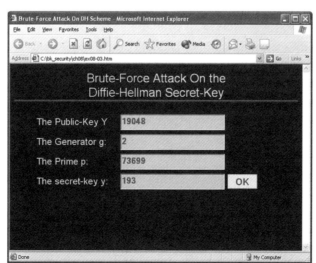

8.3 The ElGamal public-key algorithm and digital signatures

8.3.1 The ElGamal public-key algorithm

Unlike the Diffie-Hellman key exchange, the ElGamal algorithm is designed for public-key encryption/decryption based on discrete logarithms. It was created by Taher ElGamal and promoted by many big organizations on the Internet. For example, the ElGamal algorithm is used in the free GNU Privacy Guard (GnuPG) software, which is an implementation of a standard called Open Pretty Good Privacy (PGP). Many other crypto-systems use it too. It can be used for message encryption/decryption directly, and also for digital signatures. NSA's digital signature algorithm is based on ElGamal.

Given a prime p and a generator g, the ElGamal encryption/decryption algorithm works as follows.

- Bob selects his secret key y, and computes the public-key component (Y, g, p), where $Y = g^y \bmod p$.

- If Sue wants to send a message to Bob, she first converts the message into a number m.

- Sue then generates a random integer k and computes the number pair (c, d) and sends it to Bob, where

$$c = g^k \bmod p \quad \text{and} \quad d = m\,(Y^k) \bmod p$$

- Bob can then reconstruct the message m using his secret key y to calculate $\dfrac{d}{c^y}$,

$$\text{where} \quad \frac{d}{c^y} = \frac{m(Y^k)}{(g^k)^y} = \frac{m(g^{yk})}{g^{ky}} = m.$$

- In practice, the message m can be split into multiple values m_i. In this case, the encrypted result is the number c together with a sequence of d_i, i.e. $\{c, d_1, d_2, \ldots, d_n\}$.

This encryption/decryption process is demonstrated in Figure 8.8.

To understand the operation of the ElGamal scheme better, let's consider a step-by-step example.

An ElGamal encryption/decryption example

Suppose Bob and Sue want to communicate messages using the ElGamal encrytion scheme. Bob's secret and public key components are

$$\text{Bob\_S} = 520 \qquad \text{Bob\_P} = (65079, 5, 170003).$$

Fig. 8.8 ElGamal encryption/decryption

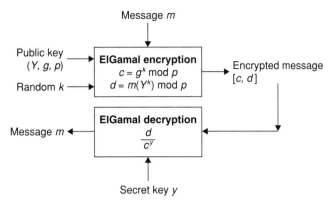

Note that $65079 = 5^{520}$ mod 170003. When Sue wants to send Bob a message $m =$ 'Hello Bob', say, the first thing is to convert this message into an array of numbers. For simplicity, we use ASCII code below:

$m = $ {Hello Bob} = {072 101 108 108 111 032 066 111 098}

Note that we have used decimal ASCII code, and that each code has three digits. As one single number, this message may be a bit too long. It can be grouped into five numbers. Each number represents two characters:

$m = $ {072101, 108108, 111032, 066111, 098}

The next step is that Sue picks a random number k (e.g. $k = 429$) and uses it to encrypt the message m. The first constant c is computed by g^k mod p.

$c = g^k$ mod $p = 5^{429}$ mod $170003 = 47049$

For each element of the message array $m[\ ]$, the following encryption formula is used to compute the elements d_i as an array $d[\ ]$:

$d_i = ((Y^k$ mod $p)* m[i])$ mod p (for $i = 1$ to 5)
   $= $ {26751, 91891, 127714, 145578, 151087}

The values c and d_i are sent to Bob. When Bob receives the following encrypted message

{$c, d[1], d[2], \ldots , d[5]$} = {47049, 26751, 91891, 127714, 145578, 151087},

the original plaintext message can be obtained by Bob's secret key y and the formula

$$m[i] = \frac{d[i]}{c^y} \bmod p$$

For example, the element $m[1]$ is obtained by

$$m[1] = \frac{26751}{47079^{429}} \bmod 170003 = 72101$$

This number represents the first two characters of the plaintext {072, 101} = {He}. When all the plaintext characters are recovered, we have

$$\begin{aligned} m[i] &= \{72101, 108108, 111032, 66111, 98\} \\ &= \{072, 101, 108, 108, 111, 032, 066, 111, 098\} \\ &= \{\text{Hello Bob}\} \end{aligned}$$

It is easy to see that the security of the ElGamal algorithm depends on the discrete logarithm problem, so that the security strength is similar to that of Diffie–Hellman. Now, let's see how to implement this ElGamal encryption/encryption scheme.

8.3.2   ElGamal encryption/decryption with APM

From the previous section we know that the ElGamal encryption algorithm depends on the following information:

- plaintext message m;

- public-key information (Y, g, p);

- a selected encryption number k.

Given a plaintext m, the encrypted message is a pair of numbers, namely (c, d). The formulae to compute c and d are

$$c = g^k \bmod p \qquad \text{and} \qquad d = m* (Y^k \bmod p) \bmod p$$

These (c, d) values are sent to the recipient. With our arbitrary precision mathematics package `BigInt.js`, the implementation of these formulae is quite straight forward. Consider listing `ex08-04.htm`.

```
Example: ex08-04.htm - The ElGamal encryption algorithm

1:  <head><title>The ElGamal Encryption</title></head>
2:  <style>
3:  .butSt{font-size:16pt;width:70px;height:35px;
4:          font-weight:bold;background:#ddffdd;color:#ff0000}
5:  .txtSt{font-size:14pt;width:240px;height:35px;font-weight:bold;
6:          background:#dddddd;color:#ff0000}
7:  </style>
8:  <body style="font-family:arial;font-size:20pt;text-align:center;
9:          background:#000088;color:#ffff00">
```

```
10:  The ElGamal Encryption [c,d]
       <br /><span style="font-size:16pt"><br />
11:  c = g <sup>k</sup> mod p     &    
12:  d = m*(Y<sup>k</sup> mod p) mod p </span>
13: <form action="">
14: <table style="font-size:16pt;width:580px" cellspacing="5"
    align="center">
15:  <tr><td>Plaintext Number m</td><td>
16:         <input type="text" id="tm" size="32" maxlength="32"
17:          class="txtSt" value="072101" /></td></tr>
18:  <tr><td>Encryption number k:</td><td >
19:         <input type="text" id="tk" size="32" maxlength="32"
20:           class="txtSt" value="429" /></td></tr>
21:  <tr><td>The Public-Key Y: </td><td >
22:         <input type="text" id="tY" size="32" maxlength="32"
23:          class="txtSt" value="65079" /></td></tr>
24:  <tr><td>The generator g: </td><td >
25:         <input type="text" id="tg" size="32" maxlength="32"
26:          class="txtSt" value="5" /></td></tr>
27:  <tr><td>The Prime p: </td><td>
28:         <input type="text" id="tp" size="32" maxlength="32"
29:          class="txtSt" value="170003" /></td></tr>
30:  <tr><td>Encrypted Numbers [c,d] </td><td>
31:         <input type="text" id="result" size="32"
32:          maxlength="32" readonly class="txtSt" value="" />
33:         <input type="button" class="butSt" value="OK"
34:         onclick="elgamal_en()" /></td></tr>
35: </table></form>
36: <script src="BigInt.js"></script>
37: <script>
38:  function elgamal_en()
39:  {
40:   var ttm,ttk,ttY,ttg,ttp;
41:   ttm = str2bigInt(document.getElementById("tm").value,10,0);
42:   ttk = str2bigInt(document.getElementById("tk").value,10,0);
43:   ttY = str2bigInt(document.getElementById("tY").value,10,0);
44:   ttg = str2bigInt(document.getElementById("tg").value,10,0);
45:   ttp = str2bigInt(document.getElementById("tp").value,10,0);
46:
47:   tmp01 = dup(ttg);
48:   powMod(tmp01,ttk,ttp);
49:   tmp02 = dup(ttY);
50:   powMod(tmp02,ttk,ttp);
```

```
51:     multMod(tmp02,ttm,ttp);
52:     llst = "[ "+bigInt2str(tmp01,10)+" ,  "+bigInt2str(tmp02,10)+" ]";
53:     document.getElementById("result").value = llst;
54: }
55: </script>
56: </body>
```

For simplicity, only two numbers [c, d] are considered in this example. This page implements the ElGamal encryption algorithm. The XHTML code in lines 14–35 generates six text boxes and one OK button. The first two boxes are used to obtain the plaintext number m and encryption number k. The next three boxes get the public-key information (Y, g, p) of the recipient. When the OK button is clicked, the encryption function elgamal_en() is activated. The encrypted numbers [c,d] are displayed in the last text box. The details of the function elgamal_en() is given in lines 38–54.

First, the information concerning m, k, Y, g and p is captured and converted into big integers by the statements in lines 41–45. The two statements in lines 47–48 compute the constant c, stored in variable tmp01. Lines 50–51 calculate the constant d, stored in tmp02. These two values are then converted to strings and output in the [c,d] format (line 52). A screenshot of this example is given in Figure 8.9.

Compared to encryption, the input information for decryption is relatively simple. The decryption depends on

Fig. 8.9 ElGamal encryption

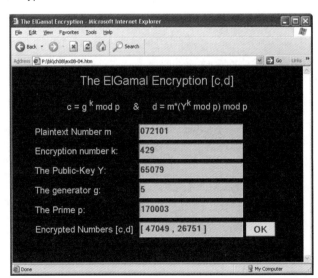

- the encrypted numbers [*c*, *d*];

- the secret key for the recipient *y*.

The plaintext number *m* can be computed by '$m = (d/c^y) \bmod p$.' A simple implementation of this decryption scheme is given in ex08-05.htm.

```
Example: ex08-05.htm - The ElGamal decryption algorithm

 1: <head><title>The ElGamal Decryption</title></head>
 2: <style>
 3:  .butSt{font-size:16pt;width:70px;height:35px;
 4:         font-weight:bold;background:#ddffdd;color:#ff0000}
 5:  .txtSt{font-size:14pt;width:240px;height:35px;font-weight:bold;
 6:         background:#dddddd;color:#ff0000}
 7: </style>
 8: <body style="font-family:arial;font-size:20pt;text-align:center;
 9:         background:#000088;color:#ffff00">
10:  The ElGamal Decryption<br /> m = [ d / c <sup>y</sup> ] mod p
11:
12: <form action="">
13: <table style="font-size:16pt;width:560px" cellspacing="5"
     align="center">
14:  <tr><td>The Constant d</td><td>
15:         <input type="text" id="td" size="32" maxlength="32"
16:          class="txtSt" value="26751" /></td></tr>
17:  <tr><td>The Constant c: </td><td >
18:         <input type="text" id="tc" size="32" maxlength="32"
19:          class="txtSt" value="47049" /></td></tr>
20:  <tr><td>The Prime p: </td><td>
21:         <input type="text" id="tp" size="32" maxlength="32"
22:          class="txtSt" value="170003" /></td></tr>
23:  <tr><td>The Secret-Key: y</td><td >
24:         <input type="text" id="ty" size="32" maxlength="32"
25:          class="txtSt" value="520" /></td></tr>
26:  <tr><td>The Plaintext m: </td><td>
27:         <input type="text" id="result" size="32"
28:          maxlength="32" readonly class="txtSt" value="" />
29:         <input type="button" class="butSt" value="OK"
30:          onclick="elgamal_de()" /></td></tr>
31: </table></form>
32: <script src="BigInt.js"></script>
33: <script>
34:  function elgamal_de()
35:  {
```

```
36:    var secret_y, public_Y,gen_g,prime_p;
37:    ttd = str2bigInt(document.getElementById("td").value,10,0);
38:    ttc = str2bigInt(document.getElementById("tc").value,10,0);
39:    tty = str2bigInt(document.getElementById("ty").value,10,0);
40:    ttp = str2bigInt(document.getElementById("tp").value,10,0);
41:
42:    tmp01 = dup(ttc);
43:    powMod(tmp01,tty,ttp);
44:    inverseMod(tmp01,ttp);
45:    multMod(tmp01,ttd,ttp);
46:    llst = bigInt2str(tmp01,10);
47:    document.getElementById("result").value = llst;
48:  }
49: </script>
50: </body>
```

The XHTML code in lines 13–31 generates five text boxes and one OK button. The first two boxes allow a user to input the ElGamal encryption numbers c and d. The next two boxes are for the prime p and secret-key y. When the OK button is pressed, the plaintext number m will be computed and displayed in the last text box. The decryption engine is the function elgamal_de() defined in lines 34–48.

The decryption information d, c, y and p is captured and converted to big integers by the statements in lines 37–40. Line 43 computes the value c^y mod p. The inverseMod() function is used to calculate $1/c^y$ mod p. Finally, the multiplication modulo function multMod() in line 45 finishes the computation of d/c^y mod p, which is the ElGamal decryption formula. The result is a big integer tmp01 representing the plaintext number m. After converting into string in line 46, the result is output to the last text box by line 47. A screenshot of the decryption is shown in Figure 8.10.

If you enter the encryption numbers c and d obtained from Figure 8.9, you will have the plaintext $m = 72101$. This number is, in fact, the two ASCII codes {072, 101} representing the two characters {He} in the example discussed in Section 8.2.4.

Now we know how to implement the ElGamal encryption/decryption algorithm with an APM package. The next step is to extend the implementation for general message encryption.

8.3.3   Implementing message encryption/decryption

In examples ex08-04.htm and ex08-05.htm, we saw that ElGamal encryption works with big numbers. By grouping two ASCII codes together, a number representing two characters is generated for the encryption process. In fact, there are a number

Fig. 8.10 ElGamal decryption

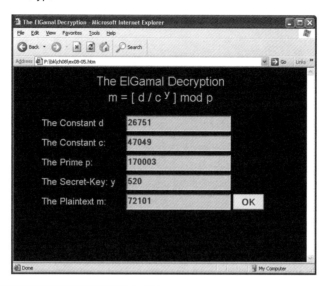

of methods of converting message characters into numbers for ElGamal encryption. Another is to use the following mapping before the character grouping:

$$01 \to \text{'a'}, \qquad 02 \to \text{'b'}, \ldots, \qquad 26 \to \text{'z'}$$

This method produces smaller plaintext numbers, but cannot handle other non-English characters or languages easily. In this section, a technique for converting messages into sequences of numbers is presented. This method is particularly efficient for 32-bit computers and systems.

Given a message string `msgSt[]` as an array of characters, a big number `lrArr` can easily be constructed by grouping every four characters together with their corresponding ASCII codes. This process is illustrated by the while-loop below.

```
m=0;
while ( m < msgSt.length) {
  lrArr= (msgSt.charCodeAt(m++) << 24)|(msgSt.charCodeAt(m++) << 16)|
         (msgSt.charCodeAt(m++) << 8) | msgSt.charCodeAt(m++);
  //- Perform ElGamal encryption on number lrArr here -//
}
```

This while-loop groups every four characters from the string `msgSt[]` to form a 32-bit integer `lrArr`, which is particularly handy for 32-bit computer platforms. In order to perform ElGamal encryption, the public-key information [Y, g, p] and a random number k are needed, as described in Section 8.3.2. Now, consider the encryption page shown in `ex08-06.htm`.

```
 1: <head><title>ElGamal Message Encryption</title></head>
 2: <style>
 3:   .butSt{font-size:14pt;width:250px;height:30px;
 4:          font-weight:bold;background:#dddddd;color:#ff0000}
 5: </style>
 6: <body style="font-family:arial;font-size:22pt;text-align:center;
 7:       background:#000088;color:#ffff00">
 8:   Message Encryption Using<br />ElGamal Public-Key Scheme
 9: <form action="">
10: <table style="font-size:14pt;width:750px" align="center"
    cellspacing=10>
11:   <tr><td colspan="2">Enter The Input Message: </td></tr>
12:   <tr><td colspan="2"><textarea style="font-size:14pt;width:700px;
13:     height:150px;font-weight:bold;background:#dddddd" rows="5"
14:     cols="40" id="in_mesg">Meet Me At 2pm
      Tomorrow</textarea></td></tr>
15:   <tr><td >Key Info: [ k Y g p ] </td>
16:     <td><input type="text" id="key_v" size="100" maxlength="100"
17:     style="font-size:14pt;width:440px;height:35px;font-weight:bold;
18:     background:#dddddd;color:#ff0000"
19:     value="5218523 927268357353 5 2684702861777" /></td></tr>
20:   <tr><td style="height:40px;width:250px" valign=middle>
21:     The Output Message is: </td>
22:     <td><input size="20" type="button" class="butSt"
            style="width:180px"
23:       value="OK" onclick="encrypt_fun()" /> </td>
24:   <tr><td colspan="2"><textarea rows="5" cols="40"
      id="out_mesg" readonly
25:          style="font-size:14pt;font-weight:bold;width:700px;
26:          height:150px;background:#aaffaa"></textarea></td></tr>
27: </tbody></table>
28: </form>
```

This page fragment is the interface part of the example containing two text areas, one text box and one OK button. The first text area in lines 12–14 allows a user to enter a plaintext message in character form. The default message for this page is 'Meet Me At 2pm Tomorrow' as illustrated in line 14. The text box defined in lines 16–19 is used to obtain the public-key information [k, Y, g, p]. For demonstration purposes, the default values are

$$[k \; Y \; g \; p] = [5218523 \; 927268357353 \; 5 \; 2684702861777]$$

Note that k is a random number selected by the user and $[Y, g, p]$ is the ElGamal public key of some other persons. Note also that if you group four characters into one 32-bit integer, the prime p that you are using should be bigger than 32-bit.

When the OK button is clicked, the function encrypt_fun() is run (lines 22–23). This function will encrypt the plaintext and display the result in the second text area specified in lines 24–26. The function encrypt_fun() is defined in part II of ex08-06.htm.

Example: Continuation of ex08-06.htm   (Part II)

```
29: <script src="hexlib.js"></script>
30: <script src="BigInt.js"></script>
31: <script>
32:  function encrypt_fun()
33:  {
34:    var keySt="",message="",llst="", keyV;
35:    document.getElementById("out_mesg").value = llst;
36:    key = document.getElementById("key_v").value;
37:    message = document.getElementById("in_mesg").value;
38:
39:    llst = elgamal_en(key, message);
40:    document.getElementById("out_mesg").value = llst;
41:  }
42:
43:  function elgamal_en(keySt, msgSt)
44:  {
45:    var m=0,len = msgSt.length;
46:    var ii, ttc="", ttd="",ttk,ttY,ttg,ttp;
47:    var lrArr, keyV, tmp01, tmp02;
48:
49:    keyV = myParseSt(keySt);
50:    ttk = str2bigInt(keyV[0],10,5);
51:    ttY = str2bigInt(keyV[1],10,5);
52:    ttg = str2bigInt(keyV[2],10,5);
53:    ttp = str2bigInt(keyV[3],10,5);
54:    tmp01 = dup(ttg);
55:    powMod(tmp01,ttk,ttp);
56:    ttc = bigInt2str(tmp01,10);
57:
58:    while (m < len) {
59:      lrArr= (msgSt.charCodeAt(m++) << 24)|
                (msgSt.charCodeAt(m++) << 16)|
60:             (msgSt.charCodeAt(m++) << 8) |
                 msgSt.charCodeAt(m++);
```

```
61:        ttm = int2bigInt(lrArr,10,5);
62:        tmp02 = dup(ttY);
63:        powMod(tmp02,ttk,ttp);
64:        multMod(tmp02,ttm,ttp);
65:        ttd += bigInt2str(tmp02,10) +" ";
66:    }
67:  return ttc+" "+ttd;
68:  }
69: </script>
70: </body>
```

This page contains two functions. The first function, encrypt_fun(), in lines 32–41 controls the entire encryption process. In lines 36–37, the public-key information [k, Y, g, p] and the plaintext message are captured and stored in the variables key and message respectively. These values are used as input to call the function elgamal_en() for the encryption. The result is returned to variable llst and displayed by the statement in line 40.

The main encryption engine of this example is the function elgamal_en() in lines 43–68. This function takes two input strings, namely keySt and msgSt, representing the public key and plaintext message information. It will use the keySt information to encrypt the plaintext msgSt producing the encrypted message {c,d[1],d[2],...,d[n]}

First, the information inside keySt is parsed by the function myParseSt() in line 49 to obtain the individual strings k, Y, g and p. These values are stored in array keyV[] in that order: that is, k is stored in the first element of array keyV[] (keyV[0]). The statement in line 50 converts this keyV[0] string into a big integer called ttk, where ttk is a base 10 number with minimum element size 5 (see the instructions for the APM package BigInt.js). Similarly, the public-key values [Y, g, p] are obtained and converted to big integers ttY, ttg and ttp respectively.

Lines 54–56 use the encryption formula '$c = g^k$ mod p' to compute the constant c stored in variable ttc. The while-loop in lines 58–66 groups every four characters from the plaintext msgSt into a number lrArr. This number is converted to a big integer variable called ttm and then uses it to compute the encrypted message d_i using the formula

$$ttd = d[i] = ((Y^k \bmod p) * ttm_i) \bmod p$$

The encrypted message [ttc,ttd] is returned to the caller function by the statement in line 67. A screenshot of this example is given in Figure 8.11.

As you can see from Figure 8.11, the ElGamal encrypted results are big integers. The first one is c and the remaining elements are d[i]. These values are used in the decryption process to recover the plaintext.

Fig. 8.11 ElGamal message encryption

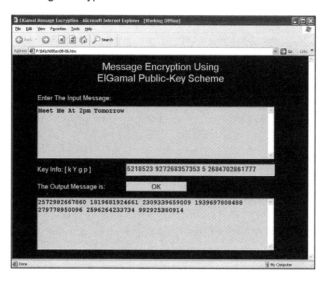

To perform ElGamal decryption, make a copy of part I of ex08-06.htm and call it ex08-07.htm. Modify the following lines:

```
 8: Message Decryption Using<br />ElGamal Public-Key Scheme
15: <tr><td>Secret-Key Info: [ y p ] </td>
23:     value="OK" onclick="decrypt_fun()" /> </td>
```

Line 8 changes the title of the page to indicate that the program is for decryption. For decryption, the secret key of the user is required and is illustrated in line 15. In this case, the secret-key value [y,p] is expected. Finally, when the OK button is clicked, the statement in line 23 executes the function decrypt_fun() to perform the decryption. The interface structure of ex08-07.htm is the same as that of ex08-06.htm. The decryption engine decrypt_fun() is defined in part II of ex08-07.htm.

```
Example: ex08-07.htm - Continuation of ex08-07.htm          (Part II)

29: <script src="hexlib.js"></script>
30: <script src="BigInt.js"></script>
31: <script>
32:  function decrypt_fun()
33:  {
34:    var keySt="",message="",llst="", keyV;
35:    document.getElementById("out_mesg").value = llst
36:    key = document.getElementById("key_v").value
37:    message = document.getElementById("in_mesg").value
```

```
38:
39:    llst = elgamal_de(key, message);
40:    document.getElementById("out_mesg").value = llst;
41:  }
42:
43:  function elgamal_de(keySt, msgSt)
44:  {
45:   var ii, tResult="", result="", llst="";
46:   var lrArr, keyV, tmp01, tmp02;
47:
48:   keyV = myParseSt(keySt);
49:   tty = str2bigInt(keyV[0],10,5);
50:   ttp = str2bigInt(keyV[1],10,5);
51:
52:   lrArr = myParseSt(msgSt);
53:   ttc = str2bigInt(lrArr[0],10,5);
54:   for (ii=0; ii < lrArr.length -1; ii++) {
55:     tmp01 = dup(ttc);
56:     powMod(tmp01,tty,ttp);
57:     inverseMod(tmp01,ttp);
58:     ttd = str2bigInt(lrArr[ii+1],10,5);
59:     multMod(tmp01,ttd,ttp);
60:     result = bigInt2str(tmp01,10);
61:     tresult = parseInt(result,10);
62:
63:     tempSt= String.fromCharCode(
64:       ((tresult >>> 24) & 0xff), ((tresult >>> 16) & 0xff),
65:       ((tresult >>>  8) & 0xff), ( tresult        & 0xff));
66:     llst += tempSt;
67:   }
68:   return llst;
69:  }
70: var testSt = "2572982667860 1819681924661 2309339659009 "+
71:        "1939697808488 279778950096 2596264233734 992925380914";
72: document.getElementById("in_mesg").value=testSt;
73: </script>
74: </body>
```

This page contains two functions, namely decrypt_fun() and elgamal_de().
The first controls the operation of the decryption and is basically the same as the
encryption encrypt_fun() in ex08-06.htm. The only difference is that the ElGamal
decryption function elgamal_de() is called in line 39. When elgamal_de() is
executed with the secret key and ciphertext information, decryption is performed.

First, the secret-key information stored in variable keySt is parsed into individual strings and converted to big integers [tty, ttp] (lines 48–50). Also, the encrypted message in msgSt is parsed into an array of strings lrArr[]. The first element of lrArr[0] contains the value of the decryption constant c and is, therefore, extracted into big integer ttc in line 53. The for-loop in lines 54–67 extracts each remaining element lrArr[ii] and converts it to a decryption constant d[ii]. The statements in lines 55–59 are used to perform the decryption

$$m[i] = \frac{d[ii]}{c^y} \mod p$$

The result is stored in variable tmp01 in line 59. The next thing is to convert this big number format tmp01 (or m[ii]) into ordinary number 32-bit format. Finally, the statements in lines 63–68 convert this 32-bit integer back to characters, append them to llst and return to the function caller. As a result the decrypted message appears in the second text area of the page.

For demonstration purposes, a test encryption string is included in lines 70–72. This string is copied from the result of ex08-06.htm so that the plaintext can be obtained in this ex08-07.htm example. A screenshot is shown in Figure 8.12.

If you have a big prime p, say more than 100 digits, you can group more characters into one big integer. In this case, you may need to replace the following statement with the appropriate routines from the APM package BigInt.js.

```
lrArr= (msgSt.charCodeAt(m++) << 24)|(msgSt.charCodeAt(m++) << 16)|
       (msgSt.charCodeAt(m++) << 8)  | msgSt.charCodeAt(m++);
```

Fig. 8.12 ElGamal message decryption

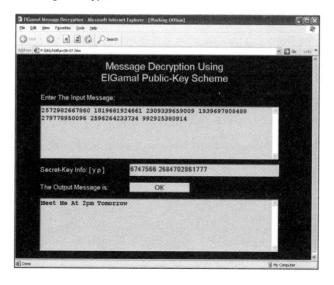

As well as the privacy or confidentiality of message, another essential application of public-key schemes is the digital signature and data integrity, which will be discussed in the next section.

8.3.4   Using the ElGamal scheme for digital signatures and data integrity

The idea of the digital signature is simple – it is similar to that on a piece of paper. The main difference is that the 'paper' is in electronic document form. When you sign a paper or contract, the purpose is to make something unique and binding. A legal process can then use the signature to identify you, and hence trust can be built within legal systems covering all business activities.

The basic principle of encryption is that you don't want the document to be readable by other than trusted people. The digital signature process is different. Basically, you want to construct a way in which the recipient can identify the document sender. One of the natural ways of doing that is to sign the document with your secret key.

The ElGamal digital signature and data integrity

Suppose the public and private keys of Bob are (Y, g, p) and y respectively. The following procedure is used to perform an ElGamal digital signature:

■ Let the message be m.

■ Pick a random number k relatively prime to $(p - 1)$.

■ Compute the ElGamal signature constants s_1 and s_2:

$$s_1 = g^k \bmod p; \qquad s_2 = \frac{m - s_1 y}{k} \bmod (p - 1).$$

The constant s_2 is similar to signing the message m with the secret key y.

■ Send the information $\{m, s_1, s_2\}$ to the recipient.

■ The recipient can verify the sender by computing the constants r_1 and r_2

$$r_1 = g^m \bmod p; \qquad r_2 = Y^{s_1} s_1^{s_2} \bmod p.$$

■ If $r_1 = r_2$, the message m must have been sent by the owner of (Y, g, p) and y.

Consider the constant r_2. If you substitute the definitions of Y, s_1 and s_2 into r_2, you have

$$r_2 = Y^{s_1} s_1^{s_2} \bmod p$$

$$= (g^y)^{s_1} (g^k)^{\frac{m - y s_1}{k}} \bmod p$$

$$= g^m \bmod p$$

This result is the constant r_1. In other words, the signed document $\{m, s_1, s_2\}$ can be verified by the public-key information (Y, g, p) by computing the constants r_1 and r_2. If they are equal, the signed document $\{m, s_1, s_2\}$, in an ideal case, must have been sent by the owner of the public key $\{Y, g, p\}$.

In practice, the message m is usually the hash value (or digest) of a document. By signing the hash value using the secret key, the digest of the document is protected by public-key encryption. In this case no alteration can be made and, therefore, data integrity is maintained.

The numbers s_1 and s_2 can be considered to be the signature of the owner of keys (Y, g, p, y) signing on the document m. This digital signature process is illustrated in Figure 8.13.

Consider a practical example. Suppose the public and secret keys of Bob are

$$(Y, g, p) = (65079, 5, 170003) \qquad y = 520$$

Let the message $m = 72101$ and the selected number k relatively prime to $(p - 1)$ be $k = 70001$.

$$s_1 = 5^{70001} \bmod 170003 \qquad s_2 = \frac{72101 - 520(119060)}{70001} \bmod 170002$$

$$= 119060; \qquad\qquad\qquad = 122563$$

The signed document is therefore $\{72101, 119060, 122563\}$. These values can be sent to the recipient for verification. To verify the signature, the constants r_1 and r_2 are computed as follows:

$$r_1 = 5^{72101} \bmod 170003 = 135849$$

$$r_2 = (65079^{119060} \bmod 170003)(119060^{122563} \bmod 170003) \bmod 170003$$
$$= 135849$$

Fig. 8.13 ElGamal digital signature and data integrity

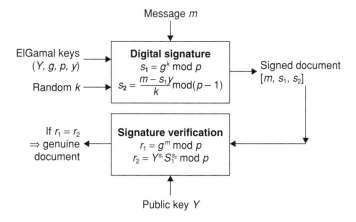

8.3 The ElGamal public-key algorithm and digital signatures **599**

From this example, we know that the signed document {72101, 119060, 122563}, in an ideal case, must have been sent by the owner of the public key (65079, 5, 170003)

8.3.5   Implementation of the digital signature scheme

The ElGamal digital signature process has two parts. The first is to generate the signature value pair $[s_1, s_2]$ of a plaintext number m. In practice, the number m is usually the hash value (or digest) of a document. The formulae governing the values of s_1 and s_2 are provided in Figure 8.13. Therefore, the implementation of an ElGamal signature is simply a process of programming these two formulae into a Web page. Consider the example given in ex08-08.htm.

```
Example: ex08-08.htm - The ElGamal digital signature           (Part I)

 1:  <head><title>The ElGamal Digital Signature</title></head>
 2:  <style>
 3:  .butSt{font-size:16pt;width:70px;height:35px;
 4:          font-weight:bold;background:#ddffdd;color:#ff0000}
 5:  .txtSt{font-size:14pt;width:240px;height:35px;font-weight:bold;
 6:          background:#dddddd;color:#ff0000}
 7:  </style>
 8:  <body style="font-family:arial;font-size:20pt;text-align:center;
 9:          background:#000088;color:#ffff00">
10:  The ElGamal Digital Signature [s1,s2] <br />
11:  <span style="font-size:16pt"><br />
12:  s1 = g <sup>k</sup> mod p     &    
13:  s2 = ( m - y*s1 ) / k    mod (p-1) </span>
14:  <form action="">
15:  <table style="font-size:16pt;width:620px" cellspacing="5"
     align="center">
16:  <tr><td>Plaintext Number m</td><td>
17:          <input type="text" id="tm" size="32" maxlength="32"
18:          class="txtSt" value="072101" /></td></tr>
19:  <tr><td>Signature number k:</td><td >
20:          <input type="text" id="tk" size="32" maxlength="32"
21:          class="txtSt" value="70001" /></td></tr>
22:  <tr><td>The Public-Key Y: </td><td >
23:          <input type="text" id="tY" size="32" maxlength="32"
24:          class="txtSt" value="65079" /></td></tr>
25:  <tr><td>The generator g: </td><td >
26:          <input type="text" id="tg" size="32" maxlength="32"
27:          class="txtSt" value="5" /></td></tr>
28:  <tr><td>The Prime p: </td><td>
```

```
29:            <input type="text" id="tp" size="32" maxlength="32"
30:             class="txtSt" value="170003" /></td></tr>
31:  <tr><td>The secret-key y: </td><td>
32:            <input type="text" id="tyy" size="32" maxlength="32"
33:             class="txtSt" value="520" /></td></tr>
34:  <tr><td>Encrypted Numbers [s1,s2] </td><td>
35:            <input type="text" id="result" size="32"
36:             maxlength="32" class="txtSt" value="" />
37:            <input type="button" class="butSt" value="OK"
38:             onclick="elgamal_sig()" /></td></tr>
39:  </table></form>
```

This XHTML code generates seven text boxes and one OK button. The first six boxes are used to get the information [*m*, *k*, *Y*, *g*, *p*, *y*] respectively. When the OK button is clicked, the function `elgamal_sig()` in line 38 is run and the signature pair `[s1,s2]` is generated in the last text box. The details of the function `elgamal_sig()` are given in part II of `ex08-08.htm`.

```
Example: Continuation of ex08-08.htm                    (Part II)

40: <script src="BigInt.js"></script>
41: <script>
42:  function elgamal_sig()
43:  {
44:    var ttm,ttk,ttY,ttg,ttp,tty,tmp01,tmp02,s1,s2;
45:    ttm = str2bigInt(document.getElementById("tm").value,10,0);
46:    ttk = str2bigInt(document.getElementById("tk").value,10,0);
47:    ttY = str2bigInt(document.getElementById("tY").value,10,0);
48:    ttg = str2bigInt(document.getElementById("tg").value,10,0);
49:    ttp = str2bigInt(document.getElementById("tp").value,10,0);
50:    tty = str2bigInt(document.getElementById("tyy").value,10,0);
51:
52:    s1 = dup(ttg);              powMod(s1,ttk,ttp);
53:    oneInt = int2bigInt(1,1,1);  sub(ttp,oneInt);
54:    tmp01 = dup(tty);            mult(tmp01,s1);
55:    tmp02 = dup(ttm);
56:    if (greater(tmp02,tmp01)) {
57:        sub(tmp02,tmp01);
58:        tmp03 = tmp02; sflag = 0;
59:    } else {
60:        sub(tmp01,tmp02);
61:        tmp03 = tmp01; sflag = 1;
62:    }
```

```
63:        s2 = dup(ttk);
64:        inverseMod(s2,ttp);
65:        multMod(s2,tmp03,ttp);
66:        if (sflag ==1) {
67:            ts2 = dup(ttp);
68:            sub(ts2,s2); s2=dup(ts2);
69:        }
70:        llst = "[ "+bigInt2str(s1,10)+" , "+bigInt2str(s2,10)+" ]";
71:        document.getElementById("result").value = llst;
72:    }
73: </script>
74: </body>
```

Line 40 includes the APM package BigInt.js into the page so that precision computations are available. The statements in lines 45–50 get the information $[m, k, Y, g, p, y]$ from the XHTML interface. The first signature constant s_1 is calculated by line 52 using the formula

$$s_1 = g^k \bmod p$$

Line 53 computes the value $(p - 1)$. It generates the number 1 in big integer format and then subtracts the prime (i.e. ttp) by 1. The remaining statements are used to compute the second signature constant s_2 using

$$s_2 = \frac{m - s_1 y}{k} \bmod (p - 1)$$

First, the values of m and $s_1 y$ are computed. In order to avoid negative numbers, a comparison statement is used in lines 56–62. This determines if m is greater than $s_1 y$ and performs the non-negative subtraction $|m - s_1 y|$. If the result, stored in variable tmp03, is a negative number, the flag sflag is set to 1. Lines 64–65 perform the computation

$$\frac{\left| m - s_1 y \right|}{k} \bmod (p - 1)$$

If this number is supposed to be negative then sflag is 1. In this case, lines 67–68 subtract this value by the prime ttp to produce the result of s_2. Both s_1 and s_2 are output by the statement in lines 70–71. The document m and the signature $[s_1, s_2]$ are then sent to the recipient for verification. A screenshot of this example is shown in Figure 8.14.

The values $[s_1, s_2]$ are generally regarded as the signature of the message m. In practice, the message m and the signature are sent to the recipient. When the recipient receives the signature of the document in the format $\{m, s_1, s_2\}$, they can perform the verification process to identify the sender of the document. Consider the Web page listed in ex08-09.htm.

Fig. 8.14   ElGamal digital signature

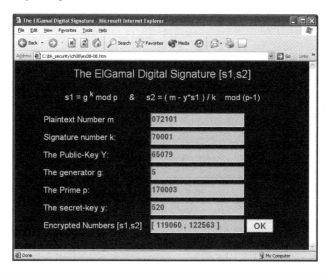

The ElGamal Digital Signature [s1,s2]

$$s1 = g^k \bmod p \quad \& \quad s2 = (m - y \cdot s1)/k \bmod (p-1)$$

Plaintext Number m	072101
Signature number k:	70001
The Public-Key Y:	65079
The generator g:	5
The Prime p:	170003
The secret-key y:	520
Encrypted Numbers [s1,s2]	[119060 , 122563] OK

```
Example: ex08-09.htm - Digital signature verification        (Part I)

 1: <head><title>The ElGamal Signature Verification</title></head>
 2: <style>
 3:   .butSt{font-size:16pt;width:70px;height:35px;
 4:          font-weight:bold;background:#ddffdd;color:#ff0000}
 5:   .txtSt{font-size:14pt;width:240px;height:35px;font-weight:bold;
 6:          background:#dddddd;color:#ff0000}
 7: </style>
 8: <body style="font-family:arial;font-size:20pt;text-align:center;
 9:        background:#000088;color:#ffff00">
10:   The ElGamal Signature Verfication [r1,r2] <br />
11:   <span style="font-size:16pt"><br />
12:   r1 = g <sup>m</sup> mod p     &    
13:   r2 = ( Y <sup>s1</sup> s1<sup>s2</sup> )  
          mod p<|span></span>
14: <form action="">
15: <table style="font-size:16pt;width:620px" cellspacing="5"
     align="center">
16:   <tr><td>Plaintext Number m</td><td>
17:          <input type="text" id="tm" size="32" maxlength="32"
18:           class="txtSt" value="072101" /></td></tr>
19:   <tr><td>Signature Constant s1: </td><td>
20:          <input type="text" id="ts1" size="32" maxlength="32"
```

```
21:            class="txtSt" value="119060" /></td></tr>
22:  <tr><td>Signature Constant s2: </td><td>
23:            <input type="text" id="ts2" size="32" maxlength="32"
24:            class="txtSt" value="122563" /></td></tr>
25:  <tr><td>The Public-Key Y: </td><td >
26:            <input type="text" id="tY" size="32" maxlength="32"
27:            class="txtSt" value="65079" /></td></tr>
28:  <tr><td>The generator g: </td><td >
29:            <input type="text" id="tg" size="32" maxlength="32"
30:            class="txtSt" value="5" /></td></tr>
31:  <tr><td>The Prime p: </td><td>
32:            <input type="text" id="tp" size="32" maxlength="32"
33:            class="txtSt" value="170003" /></td></tr>
34:  <tr><td>Verification Numbers [r1,r2] </td><td>
35:            <input type="text" id="result" size="32"
36:            maxlength="32" class="txtSt" value="" />
37:            <input type="button" class="butSt" value="OK"
38:            onclick="elgamal_sig2()" /></td></tr>
39: </table></form>
```

This XHTML code acts as an interface for the ElGamal signature verification process. It generates seven text boxes and one OK button. The first six boxes are used to obtain the information $\{m, s_1, s_2, Y, g, p\}$ respectively. When the OK button is clicked, the function elgamal_sig2() in line 38 is activated to perform signature verification. The verification constants $[r_1, r_2]$ will be displayed in the last text box declared in lines 35–36. The details of this function are given in part II of ex08-09.htm.

```
Example: Continuation of ex08-09.htm                          (Part II)

40: <script src="BigInt.js"></script>
41: <script>
42:  function elgamal_sig2()
43:  {
44:    var ttm,tts1,tts2,ttY,ttg,ttp,tmp01,tmp02,r1,r2;
45:    ttm = str2bigInt(document.getElementById("tm").value,10,0);
46:    tts1 = str2bigInt(document.getElementById("ts1").value,10,0);
47:    tts2 = str2bigInt(document.getElementById("ts2").value,10,0);
48:    ttY = str2bigInt(document.getElementById("tY").value,10,0);
49:    ttg = str2bigInt(document.getElementById("tg").value,10,0);
50:    ttp = str2bigInt(document.getElementById("tp").value,10,0);
51:
52:    powMod(ttg,ttm,ttp);          r1 = dup(ttg);
```

```
53:     tmp01 = dup(ttY);
54:     powMod(tmp01,tts1,ttp);
55:     tmp02 = dup(tts1);
56:     powMod(tmp02,tts2,ttp);
57:     multMod(tmp01,tmp02,ttp);   r2 = dup(tmp01);
58:
59:     llst = "[ "+bigInt2str(r1,10)+" , "+bigInt2str(r1,10)+" ]";
60:     document.getElementById("result").value = llst;
61:  }
62: </script>
63: </body>
```

First, the information $\{m, s_1, s_2, Y, g, p\}$ is captured and converted into big integers in lines 45–50. The statement in line 52 calculates the first verification constant r_1:

$$r_1 = g^m \bmod p$$

The statements in lines 53–57 compute the second verification constant r_2:

$$r_2 = Y^{s_1} s_1^{s_2} \bmod p$$

These two values are displayed by lines 59–60 as the $[r_1, r_2]$ pair. When $r_1 = r_2$, we know that the message m was really sent by the owner of the public key $\{Y, g, p\}$. A screenshot is shown in Figure 8.15.

Fig. 8.15 Signature verification

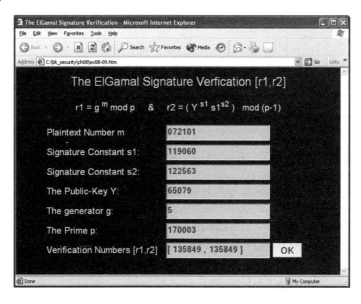

8.4 The RSA scheme, digital signature and hybrid encryption

8.4.1 The RSA public-key algorithm and challenge

RSA is another popular public-key encryption/decryption scheme. It was invented in 1977 by Ron Rivest, Adi Shamir and Leonard Adleman. The scheme works by generating a public key and a secret key. Both keys can be used to encrypt messages. When one key is used to encrypt, the other one must be applied for the decryption. The purpose of the public key is to make it available to anyone. In an ideal case, only the owner of the secret key is able to decrypt the ciphertext.

As with many other public-key technologies, RSA public-key infrastructures and algorithms consist of three parts:

- generating the keys;

- message encryption and decryption;

- digital signatures and authentications.

We will discuss them individually in this section. First, let's consider how to generate RSA keys.

Generating RSA public and secret keys

The operation of the scheme is described by the following steps.

- Select two large primes, p and q.

- Compute the values $n = pq$, and $\phi = (p - 1)(q - 1)$.

- Choose a number, $e < n$, such that e and $(p - 1)(q - 1)$ have no common factors except 1, i.e.

$$\gcd (e, (p - 1)(q - 1)) = 1$$

where gcd is the 'greatest common divisor'. In practice, [e, n] is the public key.

- Compute another number d such that

$$d = \frac{1}{e} \bmod (p - 1)(q - 1) \quad \text{or} \quad ed - 1 = k(p - 1)(q - 1),$$

In other words $(ed - 1)$ is divisible by $(p - 1)(q - 1)$. The existence of d is guaranteed by the Chinese Remainder Theorem. The value [d, n] is the secret key.

Given an arbitrary integer $m \neq 0 \bmod n$, and using Fermat's Little Theorem, we have the encryption/decryption formula:

$$m^{(p-1)(q-1)} = 1 \bmod n \quad \Rightarrow \quad (m^e)^d = m \bmod n.$$

As long as the prime factors p and q are not known, or n cannot be factorized easily, the scheme is secure. In other words, it may not be easy to derive the secret key [d, n] from knowledge of the public key [e, n], or vice versa. For this reason, the prime factors p and q are usually either kept with the secret key or destroyed.

The security strength of RSA algorithm lies in the fact that factorization of a big number n into two primes p and q is not easy. If one could factor n into p and q, then the secret key [d, n] could be obtained from the public-key information [e, n].

RSA encryption/decryption

One of the best ways to demonstrate how to perform encryption/decryption with RSA keys is by example. Suppose Bob and Sue have the following RSA public and secret keys:

Bob_P = [e_b, n_b]   Sue_P = [e_s, n_s]

Bob_S = [d_b, n_b]   Sue_S = [d_s, n_s]

When Bob wants to send a message m to Sue, Bob creates the ciphertext c_s by applying the public key Sue_P and the formula

$$c_s = m^{e_s} \bmod n_s$$

When the ciphertext arrives, Sue uses her secret key Sue_S and the formula below to decrypt the message:

$$m = c_s^{d_s} \bmod n_s$$

The chosen relationship between e and d in the encryption formula ensures that Sue correctly recovers m. In an ideal case, Sue is the sole owner of the secret key d and only Sue can decrypt it.

RSA digital signatures and authentications

Suppose Bob wants to send a message m to Sue in such a way that the identity of the sender, Bob in this case, could be verified by Sue. To do that, Bob can sign the message m using his secret key [d_b, n_b]. The signing process is done by the formula

$$s_b = m^{d_b} \bmod n_b$$

Bob sends both the message m and the signature s_b to Sue. The authentication process can be checked by Sue using Bob's public key [e_b, n_b] and the formula

$$m = s_b^{e_b} \bmod n_b$$

If the plaintext m is recovered, it must have been sent by Bob.

As you can see from this process, authentication takes place without any sharing of private keys. In other words, the security of the private keys is not compromised.

Each person uses only another person's public key and his or her own private key. Anyone can send an encrypted message to the one intended. To verify a signed message, only the public key of the sender is needed.

RSA challenges and attacks

One of the nightmares for most public-key algorithms is that an attacker will discover the private key corresponding to a given public key. This would enable the attacker to read all messages encrypted with the public key. Even worse, the attacker could forge signatures and the entire security of authentication and data integrity would be compromised. Two of these attacks on the RSA scheme are summarized below.

- Factorizing the public modulo n to primes p and q – if the public modulo can be factorized into primes p and q, the attacker can easily get d, the private-key exponent from the public-key exponent. The RSA scheme is based on the assumption that factoring n is difficult.

- Finding the eth roots mod n – this method finds a technique to compute the eth roots mod n. That is, to solve the following equation for the plaintext m:

$$c = m^e \bmod n$$

This is a direct method and would allow someone to recover plaintext messages. Similarly, by solving the digital signature equation

$$m = s^e \bmod n$$

forging signatures can be done without even knowing the private key. This attack is believed to be not related to the factorization of n. However, there is no known effective algorithm to find the eth roots of mod n.

Now, let's see how to generate RSA public and secret keys and, more importantly, how to use them to perform encryption/decryption on messages.

8.4.2   Generating RSA public and secret keys

The basic construction of RSA public and secret keys is simple. Basically, you need two prime numbers p and q, and a selected public-key component e. The secret key d is generated by the inverse modulo formula

$$d = \frac{1}{e} \bmod (p-1)(q-1)$$

The public key and secret key are $[e, n]$ and $[d, n]$, where $n = pq$. The security of the algorithm relies on the difficulty of factoring n. In order to have high security strength, the primes p and q must be big enough to discourage attackers using prime factorization attacks.

For example, consider a 29-digit number n = 83729636702158658998761175349. This number can be factorized into two primes in less than half a second on a low-end portable PC. The result is two 15 digit primes p and q,

n = 83729636702158658998761175349
= (976746753830539)*(85722974121791)

In the real world, any prime number with less than 20 digits (~70-bit) used with RSA algorithms is trivially easy to crack. A prime number with 100 digits (~300-bit) can provide only very limited security under attack. For realistic protection, the prime number must have more than 200 digits (~700-bit). By using the APM package `BigInt.js`, a random 70-bit prime number can be obtained by the function calls

```
prime_p = int2bigInt(0,70,0);
randTruePrime(prime_p,70)
```

The first statement converts the number 0 into a big integer called `prime_p` with at least 70 bits. This is necessary simply to make sure that the variable `prime_p` is big enough to store the prime number of 70-bit length. The second statement generates a random true prime to `prime_p`. Knowing the bit length, the RSA keys can be described by the algorithm:

- given bit length b, generate the random primes p and q of b bit length;

- given public key e, compute the secret key d using the formula above.

Consider the script listed in `ex08-10.htm`.

```
Example: ex08-10.htm – Generating RSA public and secret keys (Part I)

 1: <head><title>Generating RSA Keys</title></head>
 2: <style>
 3:   .butSt{font-size:16pt;width:70px;height:35px;
 4:          font-weight:bold;background:#ddffdd;color:#ff0000}
 5:   .txtSt{font-size:14pt;width:500px;height:35px;font-weight:bold;
 6:          background:#eeeeee;color:#ff0000}
 7: </style>
 8: <body style="font-family:arial;font-size:20pt;text-align:center;
 9:        background:#000088;color:#ffff00">
10:  Generating The RSA Public and Secret Keys<br />
11:  <span style="font-size:16pt"><br />d = 1 / e    
12:        mod    (p-1)(q-1)</span><br /><br/>
13: <form action="">
14: <table style="font-size:16pt;width:660px" cellspacing="5"
      align="center">
15:  <tr><td>The bit-length b</td><td>
```

```
16:              <input type="text" id="tb" size="32" maxlength="32"
17:               class="txtSt" style="width:50px" value="70" /></td>
18:        <td>Public-Key e</td><td>
19:              <input type="text" id="te" size="32" maxlength="32"
20:               class="txtSt" style="width:280px" value="65537" />
21: </table><br />
22: <table style="font-size:16pt;width:660px" cellspacing="5"
     align="center">
23: <tr><td colspan="2"> Generate the RSA Secret-Key:   
24:        <input type="button" class="butSt" value="OK"
25:         onclick="rsa_keys()" /></td></tr>
26: <tr><td>Prime p</td><td>
27:        <input type="text" id="tp" size="32" maxlength="32" readonly
28:         class="txtSt" style="color:#008800" value="" /></td></tr>
29: <tr><td>Prime q</td><td >
30:        <input type="text" id="tq" size="32" maxlength="32" readonly
31:         class="txtSt" style="color:#008800" value="" /></td></tr>
32: <tr><td>n = pq</td><td >
33:        <input type="text" id="tn" size="32" maxlength="42" readonly
34:         class="txtSt" style="color:#008800" value="" /></td></tr>
35: <tr><td>Secret-Key d</td><td>
36:        <input type="text" id="td" size="32" maxlength="42" readonly
37:         class="txtSt" style="color:#008800" value="" /></td></tr>
38: </table></form>
```

This XHTML code contains two input boxes, one OK button and four output boxes. The two input boxes in lines 16–17 and 19–20 allow a user to fill in the bit length b and the public key e. When the OK button in lines 24–25 is clicked, the function rsa_keys() is executed. As a result, the random primes p and q, the product $n = pq$, and the secret key d are displayed in the last four read-only output boxes.

Details of the function rsa_keys() are given in part II of ex08-10.htm.

```
Example: Continuation of ex08-10.htm                    (Part II)

39: <script src="BigInt.js"></script>
40: <script>
41: var rsa_b, rsa_e, rsa_p, rsa_q, rsa_n;
42: function rsa_keys()
43: {
44:    rsa_b = parseInt(document.getElementById("tb").value);
45:
46:    if (rsa_b < 5) alert("Bit Length Cannot Less Than 5");
```

```
47:    else {
48:       rsa_p=int2bigInt(0,rsa_b,0);
49:       rsa_q=int2bigInt(0,rsa_b,0);
50:       rsa_e = str2bigInt(document.getElementById("te").value,10,0);
51:       rsa_primes();
52:       rsa_n();
53:       rsa_d();
54:    }
55: }
```

The function `rsa_keys()` in lines 42–55 controls the key generation process. First, a number of global variables are declared. They are

    rsa_b, rsa_e, rsa_p, rsa_q, and rsa_n

They are used to store the corresponding values of b, e, p, q and n in the RSA public and secret key formula. Line 44 captures the b bit length as variable `rsa_b`. To avoid some computational short-circuit behaviour, a bit length less than 5 is not allowed. If `rsa_b` is more than or equal to 5, the statements in lines 48–53 are executed. Lines 48–49 create `rsa_b`-bit integers `rsa_p1` and `rsa_q1`. They are used to store the two random primes. The public-key information is captured and converted to big integer `rsa_e`. Once `rsa_b` and `rsa_e` are available, the following functions are run:

- `rsa_primes()` – generates two random primes p and q of b bit length;

- `rsa_n()`   – computes the modulus $n = p * q$;

- `rsa_d()`   – computes the secret key d.

These three functions are defined in part III of `ex08-10.htm`.

Example: Continuation of ex08-10.htm   **(Part III)**

```
56: function rsa_primes()
57: {
58:   var tmp;
59:   while (1) {
60:      randTruePrime(rsa_p,rsa_b);
61:      tmp=dup(rsa_p);
62:      mod(tmp,rsa_e,0);
63:      if (!equalsInt(tmp,1))
64:      break;
65:   }
66:   document.getElementById("tp").value=bigInt2str(rsa_p,10);
67:   while(1) {
68:      randTruePrime(rsa_q,rsa_b);
```

```
69:        tmp=dup(rsa_q);
70:        mod(tmp,rsa_e,0);
71:        if (!equals(rsa_p,rsa_q) && !equalsInt(tmp,1))
72:          break;
73:      }
74:      document.getElementById("tq").value=bigInt2str(rsa_q,10);
75:  }
76:  function rsa_n()
77:  {
78:      var s = rsa_p.length + rsa_q.length-1;
79:      var tmp1;
80:      tmp1=int2bigInt(0,10,s)
81:      copy(tmp1,rsa_p);
82:      mult(tmp1,rsa_q);
83:      document.getElementById("tn").value=bigInt2str(tmp1,10);
84:  }
85:  function rsa_d()
86:  {
87:      var tmp1, tmq1, phi;
88:      var errorSt="Public-key e not invertible. Try a different prime";
89:      var s = rsa_p.length + rsa_q.length-1;
90:      phi=int2bigInt(0,10,s)
91:      tmpe = int2bigInt(0,10,s)
92:      tmp1 = dup(rsa_p); tmq1 = dup(rsa_q);
93:      addInt(tmp1,-1); addInt(tmq1,-1);
94:      copy(phi,tmp1)
95:      mult(phi,tmq1);
96:      copy(tmpe,rsa_e);
97:      s=inverseMod(tmpe,phi);
98:      if (!s)
99:        document.getElementById("td").value=errorSt;
100:     else
101:        document.getElementById("td").value=bigInt2str(tmpe,10);
102:   }
103: </script>
104: </body>
```

The function rsa_primes() generates the two primes p and q with b bit length. In order to satisfy the greatest common divisor criterion

$$\gcd(e, (p-1)(q-1)) = 1,$$

lines 61–62 computes the value '$p \bmod e$'. If this value is 1, the value $(p-1)$ is divisible by e. In this case, the gcd condition above is not satisfied. The prime p is rejected and a new one is needed, as illustrated by the while-loop in lines 59–65. The search is continued until a proper prime p is found. The prime is then output to the first display box by line 66. Note that variables in this example are prefixed with 'rsa': for example, p is represented by `rsa_p`.

The while-loop in 67–73 searches for another random prime q using the same argument as prime p. In addition to the gcd criterion, prime q should not be equal to prime p. When these two conditions are satisfied, this prime q is output to the second display box by line 74.

The function `rsa_n()` computes the product of p and q. Before the actual multiplication, the statement in line 78 computes the necessary bit length to hold the product. The result, $n = pq$, is output to the third display box by line 83.

The secret key is computed by the function `rsa_d()` in lines 85–102 using the formula

$$d = \frac{1}{e} \bmod (p-1)(q-1)$$

Lines 92–93 compute the values $p-1$, and $q-1$. The product $(p-1)(q-1)$ is calculated by lines 94–96 and stored in variable `phi`. The function in 97 computes the inverse of e mod ϕ. The result is d stored in variable `tmpe`. The variable `s` contains the operation status. If there is an error, the error message `errorSt` is printed to indicate that the value e is not invertible. If there is no error, the value of d is output to the last text box by line 101. A screenshot of this example is shown in Figure 8.16.

Fig. 8.16 Generating RSA keys

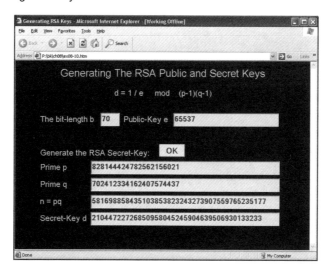

You can see that the 70-bit primes p and q have 21 digits and that the values of $n = pq$ and $\phi = (p - 1)(q - 1)$ have 42 digits. In order to prevent prime factorization of n, both the primes should be more than 70 bits. For secure public-key encryptions, you do need big numbers.

8.4.3 Message encryption/decryption using the RSA scheme

Given the public key and secret key pair

public key = $[e, n]$;   secret key = $[d, n]$

the message encryption and decryption are governed by the formula

$$c = m^e \bmod n \qquad m = c^d \bmod n$$

where m is the plaintext message operated on as a number. To perform real message encryption/decryption, we follow the approach as described for the ElGamal situation. A long message is grouped into elements of four characters. Each element is represented by a 32-bit integer m so that the first equation above can be applied to encrypt the data.

To build a simple demonstration page, the XHTML interface listed in ex08-11.htm is used.

```
Example: ex08-11.htm - Message encryption using the RSA scheme (Part I)

 1: <head><title>RSA Message Encryption</title></head>
 2: <style>
 3:   .butSt{font-size:14pt;width:250px;height:30px;
 4:           font-weight:bold;background:#dddddd;color:#ff0000}
 5: </style>
 6: <body style="font-family:arial;font-size:22pt;text-align:center;
 7:         background:#000088;color:#ffff00">
 8: Message Encryption Using <br />RSA Public-Key Scheme
 9: <form action="">
10: <table style="font-size:14pt;width:720px"
     align="center" cellspacing=5>
11: <tr><td>Input Message: </td></tr>
12: <tr><td><textarea rows="5" cols="40" id="in_mesg"
13:        style="font-size:14pt;width:700px;height:150px;
            font-weight:bold;
14:        background:#dddddd" >Meet Me At 2pm
            Tomorrow</textarea></td></tr>
15: <tr><td ><br />Enter RSA Keys (Public-Key or
     Secret-Key)</td></tr>
```

```
16:  <tr><td><input type="text" id="key_v" size="100" maxlength="100"
17:        style="font-size:14pt;width:700px;height:35px;
        font-weight:bold;
18:        background:#dddddd;color:#ff0000" value="" /></td></tr>
19:  <tr><td ><br />Encrypt The Message    
20:        <input size="20" type="button" class="butSt"
        style="width:180px"
21:        value="OK" onclick="rsa_en()" /></td></tr>
22:  <tr><td><textarea rows="5" cols="40" id="out_mesg" readonly
23:        style="font-size:14pt;font-weight:bold;width:700px;
24:        height:150px;background:#aaffaa"></textarea></td></tr>
25:  </tbody></table>
26:  </form>
```

This XHTML code displays a simple interface for message encryption containing two text areas, one text box and one OK button. The plaintext is input in the first text area defined in lines 12–14. Since you can use either the public key $[c, n]$ or secret key $[d, n]$ for encryption, the key is input into the text box (lines 16–17). When the OK button is pressed, the function rsa_en() in line 21 is run and the encrypted message appears in the text area at the bottom of the browser window. The construction of the function rsa_en() is given in part II of ex08-11.htm.

```
Example: Continuation of ex08-11.htm                          (Part II)

27:  <script src="hexlib.js"></script>
28:  <script src="BigInt.js"></script>
29:  <script>
30:   var kSt="65537 5816988584351038538232432739075597652351 77";
31:   document.getElementById("key_v").value = kSt;
32:
33:   function rsa_en()
34:   {
35:     var keySt="",message="",llst="", keyV;
36:     document.getElementById("out_mesg").value = llst;
37:     key = document.getElementById("key_v").value;
38:     message = document.getElementById("in_mesg").value;
39:     llst = rsa_enf(key, message);
40:     document.getElementById("out_mesg").value = llst;
41:   }
42:
```

```
43:   function rsa_enf(keySt, msgSt)
44:   {
45:     var m=0,len = msgSt.length;
46:     var ret="", ttm, lrArr, keyV, tmp;
47:     keyV = myParseSt(keySt);
48:     tte = str2bigInt(keyV[0],10,keyV[0].length);
49:     ttn = str2bigInt(keyV[1],10,keyV[1].length);
50:     tmp = int2bigInt(0,10,keyV[1].length);
51:     while (m < len) {
52:       lrArr= (msgSt.charCodeAt(m++) << 24)|
                 (msgSt.charCodeAt(m++) << 16)|
53:               (msgSt.charCodeAt(m++) << 8) |
                msgSt.charCodeAt(m++);
54:       ttm = int2bigInt(lrArr,10,0);
55:       copy(tmp,ttm);
56:       powMod(tmp,tte,ttn);
57:       ret += bigInt2str(tmp,10) +" ";
58:     }
59:    return ret;
60:   }
61: </script>
62: </body>
```

First, a test key is defined in lines 30–31 and put into the input box for the key.

```
public-key [c,n] = [65537 58169885843510385382324327390755976525177]
```

This key is the public key generated by ex08-10.htm. The controlling function rsa_en() captures the key and plaintext in lines 37–38 and calls the encryption engine rsa_enf() to encrypt the data. The result is returned to variable llst and displayed by the statement in line 40.

The encryption engine rsa_enf() in line 43 takes the key (keySt) and plaintext (msgSt) as input. The contents of the key are extracted by lines 47–50 into components [tte,ttn]. For every four characters of the plaintext, the statements in lines 52–53 are used to group them into one 32-bit integer in variable lrArr. This value is converted to a big integer ttm (lines 54–55). The powerMod() function in line 56 computes the ciphertext stored in variable tmp. This ciphertext value is converted to a string, appended to the result, and returned to the function caller at the end. A screenshot is shown in Figure 8.17.

Figure 8.17 shows that the plaintext 'Meet Me At 2pm Tomorrow' contains 23 characters. This string is grouped into six elements and each is a 32-bit integer.

Fig. 8.17 RSA message encryption

After the encryption, the first element representing the word 'Meet' turns out to be

457032209851124051311256138534184044126257

This is a big integer of 42 digits. It is easy to see that the size of the output depends on the size of the modulo $n = pq$. Since the modulus n has 42 digits, you would expect the encryption results for each element normally to have 42 digits as well. For more secure encryption, or longer n, the ciphertext will become bigger. This is one of the disadvantages for many public-key encryptions. Also, bigger numbers will complicate and slow down the computation. One compensation technique may be to group more characters into one bigger element using an APM package.

For a decryption page, we use the same XHTML interface as part I of ex08-11.htm. Make a copy of this XHTML code and call it ex08-12.htm. Modify the following lines:

```
 8: Message Decryption Using <br />RSA Public-Key Scheme
21:        value="OK" onclick="rsa_de()" /></td></tr>
```

The first modification is for display information only. When the OK button is clicked, the function rsa_de() in line 21 will be called to perform decryption. The details of this function are given in part II of ex08-12.htm.

Example: ex08-12.htm - Message decryption using the RSA scheme   (Part II)

```
27:  <script src="hexlib.js"></script>
28:  <script src="BigInt.js"></script>
29:  <script>
30:  var msgSt="4570322098511240513112561385341840441 26257 "+
31:            "4912229648689108652512199720717579826 60736 "+
32:            "2858663757507114918189369109597489351 00656 "+
33:            "4771227577663080856603120034860584180 63318 "+
34:            "8047894279141856200154427119177936934 1457 "+
35:            "2332511878788986896499536430168599680 45350 ";
36:  document.getElementById("in_mesg").value = msgSt;
37:  var kSt ="21044722726850958045245904639506930133233 "+
38:           "5816988584351038538232432739075597652 35177";
39:  document.getElementById("key_v").value = kSt;
40:
41:  function rsa_de()
42:  {
43:    var keySt="",message="",llst="", keyV;
44:    document.getElementById("out_mesg").value = llst;
45:    key = document.getElementById("key_v").value;
46:    message = document.getElementById("in_mesg").value;
47:    llst = rsa_def(key, message);
48:    document.getElementById("out_mesg").value = llst;
49:  }
50:
51:  function rsa_def(keySt, msgSt)
52:  {
53:    var m=0,len = msgSt.length;
54:    var ii,ttc="",ttd,ttn,ret="",tempSt,result,tresult,lrArr;
55:    keyV = myParseSt(keySt);
56:    ttd = str2bigInt(keyV[0],10,keyV[0].length);
57:    ttn = str2bigInt(keyV[1],10,keyV[1].length);
58:    lrArr = myParseSt(msgSt);
59:    for (ii=0; ii < lrArr.length; ii++) {
60:      ttc = str2bigInt(lrArr[ii],10,lrArr[ii].length);
61:      powMod(ttc,ttd,ttn);
62:      result = bigInt2str(ttc,10);
63:      tresult = parseInt(result,10);
64:      tempSt= String.fromCharCode(
65:        ((tresult >>> 24) & 0xff), ((tresult >>> 16) & 0xff),
66:        ((tresult >>>  8) & 0xff), ( tresult        & 0xff));
67:      ret += tempSt;
68:    }
69:   return ret;
70:  }
71:  </script>
72:  </body>
```

Lines 30–35 define a test ciphertext and put it into the first text box by the statement in line 36. This ciphertext is obtained from ex08-11.htm. A test secret key is also provided in lines 37–39:

```
[d,n] = [ 210447227268509580452459046395069300133233
          581698858435103853823243273907559765235177 ]
```

This key is the corresponding secret key used in example ex08-11.htm so that the following original plaintext is expected:

'Meet Me At 2pm Tomorrow'

The statements in lines 45–46 inside function rsa_de() capture the input and key strings. Then the decryption engine rsa_def() is called. The decrypted result is displayed at the bottom of the text area defined by line 48.

The decryption engine rsa_def() is defined in lines 51–70. This function takes the key and message strings as input. The decryption key components [d,n] are extracted from the key string by lines 55–57. Each big number in the input ciphertext is parsed into a big integer variable ttc. The power modulo function powMod() in line 61 performs the decryption. Although the result is a big integer, we know that it is a 32-bit integer and can be converted into a string of four characters by the statements in lines 64–66. This string is added into the variable ret and returned to the function called by line 69. A screenshot of this example is shown in Figure 8.18.

Fig. 8.18 RSA message decryption

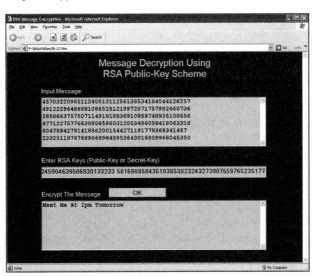

Note that the RSA encryption and decryption formulas are symmetric. In other words, both the public and secret keys can be used for encryption. If you use one key for encryption, the other key must be used for decryption. This feature is the foundation of the digital signature and creates a new application chapter for security applications. From now on, remember that both keys can be used for encryption.

8.4.4 Sending and receiving secure messages with RSA digital signatures

In this section, we consider how to use the RSA scheme to construct a system for sending and receiving secure message with signatures. The main idea is described as follows. To send a secure message with a digital signature:

■ encrypt the document using the sender's secret key (signing the document);

■ encrypt the document again using the receiver's public key.

To receive the secure message:

■ decrypt the document using the receiver's secret key;

■ decrypt the document again using the sender's public key (equivalent to verifying the sender's digital signature).

Given the RSA public key = [e, n] and secret key = [d, n], the encryption and decryption of message m are governed by the equations

$$\text{encryption: } c = m^e \bmod n; \qquad \text{decryption: } m = c^d \bmod n$$

Remember that both keys can be used for encryption. If you use one key for encryption, the other key must be used for decryption. To build the page, we first use the XHTML interface listed in ex08-13.htm.

Example: ex08-13.htm – Sending secure messages with signatures

(Part I)

```
1: <head><title>Sending RSA Secure Message</title></head>
2: <style>
3:   .butSt{font-size:14pt;width:250px;height:30px;
4:            font-weight:bold;background:#dddddd;color:#ff0000}
5: </style>
6: <body style="font-family:arial;font-size:22pt;text-align:center;
7:        background:#000088;color:#ffff00">
8: Sending RSA Secure Message with <br />Digital Signature
```

```
 9:  <form action="">
10:  <table style="font-size:14pt;width:720px;text-align:left"
     align=center>
11:  <tr><td>Input Message: </td></tr>
12:  <tr><td><textarea rows="5" cols="40" id="in_mesg"
13:      style="font-size:14pt;width:700px;height:150px;
         font-weight:bold;
14:      background:#dddddd" >Meet Me At 2pm
         Tomorrow</textarea></td></tr>
15:  <tr><td ><br />Sender's RSA Secret-Key -- Signing Document</td></tr>
16:  <tr><td><input type="text" id="s_key" size="100" maxlength="100"
17:      style="font-size:14pt;width:700px;height:35px;font-
         weight:bold;
18:      background:#dddddd;color:#ff0000" value="" /></td></tr>
19:  <tr><td >Reciever's RSA Public-Key -- Intended Receiver</td></tr>
20:  <tr><td><input type="text" id="p_key" size="100" maxlength="100"
21:      style="font-size:14pt;width:700px;height:35px;font-
         weight:bold;
22:      background:#dddddd;color:#ff0000" value="" /></td></tr>
23:  <tr><td ><br />Encrypt The Message    
24:      <input size="20" type="button" class="butSt"
           style="width:180px"
25:      value="OK" onclick="rsa_en()" /></td></tr>
26:  <tr><td><textarea rows="5" cols="40" id="out_mesg" readonly
27:      style="font-size:14pt;font-weight:bold;width:700px;
28:      height:150px;background:#aaffaa"></textarea></td></tr>
29:  </table>
30:  </form>
```

This interface contains two text areas, two text boxes and one OK button. The first text area allows the sender to input a message. The first text box is for the sender's secret key so that the message can be signed. The second text box is for the receiver's public key so that the signed message can be encrypted and directed only to the intended receiver. Once the OK button is clicked, the message will be signed and encrypted for that particular receiver. In an ideal situation, only the intended receiver can decrypt the message and use the public key of the sender to identify the signature.

The processing engine is the function rsa_en() (line 25). This function is given in part II of ex08-13.htm.

Example: Continuation of ex08-13.htm   **(Part II)**

```
31: <script src="hexlib.js"></script>
32: <script src="BigInt.js"></script>
33: <script>
34:  var skSt="42440281951699 210327467686187";
35:  var pkSt="3830539 3296694054529433";
36:  document.getElementById("s_key").value = skSt;
37:  document.getElementById("p_key").value = pkSt;
38:
39:  function rsa_en()
40:  {
41:   var skey="",pkey="",message="",llst="";
42:   document.getElementById("out_mesg").value = llst;
43:   skey = document.getElementById("s_key").value;
44:   pkey = document.getElementById("p_key").value;
45:   message = document.getElementById("in_mesg").value;
46:   llst = rsa_enf(skey,pkey,message);
47:   document.getElementById("out_mesg").value = llst;
48:  }
49:  function rsa_enf(skeySt,pkeySt,msgSt)
50:  {
51:   var m=0,len = msgSt.length,ttm,tts,ttp,ttns,ttnp;
52:   var ret="",lrArr,pkeyV,skeyV,tmp;
53:   skeyV = myParseSt(skeySt);
54:      tts = str2bigInt(skeyV[0],10,skeyV[0].length);
55:      ttns = str2bigInt(skeyV[1],10,skeyV[1].length);
56:   pkeyV = myParseSt(pkeySt);
57:      ttp = str2bigInt(pkeyV[0],10,pkeyV[0].length);
58:      ttnp = str2bigInt(pkeyV[1],10,pkeyV[1].length);
59:   tmp = int2bigInt(0,10,pkeyV[1].length);
60:   while (m < len) {
61:    lrArr= (msgSt.charCodeAt(m++) << 24)|
                (msgSt.charCodeAt(m++) << 16)|
62:              (msgSt.charCodeAt(m++) << 8) | msgSt.charCodeAt(m++);
63:    ttm = int2bigInt(lrArr,10,5);
64:    copy(tmp,ttm);
65:    powMod(tmp,tts,ttns);
66:    powMod(tmp,ttp,ttnp);
67:    ret += bigInt2str(tmp,10) +" ";
68:   }
69:   return ret;
70:  }
71: </script>
72: </body>
```

To create a test sample for this page, lines 34–35 store the secret key of the sender and the public key of the receiver. These two keys are put into the text boxes by lines 36–37. When the OK button is pressed, the rsa_en() function is run. The secret key, public key and message are captured by lines 43–45. These strings are input to the function rsa_enf() for the signing and encryption processes. The result is returned to variable llst and printed to the text area at the bottom of the screen.

Inside the function rsa_enf(), the components of the sender's secret key [d, n] are extracted to variables tts and ttns (lines 53–55). The components of the receiver's public key [e, n] are extracted to variables ttp and ttnp (lines 56–58). The while-loop is used for processing every four characters of the plaintext into a 32-bit integer. This integer is converted to a big integer ttm by lines 63–64. The first power modulo function in line 65 is equivalent to signing the message using the secret key of the sender. The next power modulo function (line 66) performs encryption on the signed message so that only the intended person can decrypt and read it. The result is converted into a string, added into variable ret and returned to the function caller at line 69.

Suppose you have a sensitive letter to be sent to a specific person: you can sign and encrypt it as shown in Figure 8.19.

For decryption and verification of the signature process, a similar page is needed. To construct this page, first make a copy of part I of ex08-13.htm and call it ex08-14.htm. Modify the following lines:

Fig. 8.19 Sending a secure message with a digital signature

```
 8: Receiving RSA Secure Message with <br />Digital Signature
15:   <tr><td ><br />Sender's RSA Public-Key -- Evaluate
          Signature</td></tr>
16:   <tr><td><input type="text" id="p_key" size="100" maxlength="100"
19:   <tr><td >Reciever's RSA secret-Key -- Intended Receiver</td></tr>
20:   <tr><td><input type="text" id="s_key" size="100" maxlength="100"
25:       value="OK" onclick="rsa_de()" /></td></tr>
```

Line 8 changes the displayed title. Lines 15–16 ask the user to input the sender's public key so that the signature of the sender can be identified properly. Lines 19–20 are for the user's (or receiver's) secret key so that the message can be decrypted. When the OK button is clicked, the function rsa_de() is run for the entire process. This function is given in part II of ex08-14.htm.

```
Example: Continuation of ex08-14.htm                        (Part II)

31: <script src="hexlib.js"></script>
32: <script src="BigInt.js"></script>
33: <script>
34:  var pkSt="3073699 210327467686187";
35:  var skSt="3249322896629023 3296694054529433";
36:  var cSt = "117609435150577 261542301093665 118076629232528 "+
37:           "1793254257998247 1709547461124399 1542346838415894 ";
38:  document.getElementById("p_key").value = pkSt;
39:  document.getElementById("s_key").value = skSt;
40:  document.getElementById("in_mesg").value = cSt;
41:
42:  function rsa_de()
43:  {
44:   var skey="",pkey="",message="",llst="";
45:   document.getElementById("out_mesg").value = llst;
46:   skey = document.getElementById("s_key").value;
47:   pkey = document.getElementById("p_key").value;
48:   message = document.getElementById("in_mesg").value;
49:   llst = rsa_def(skey,pkey,message);
50:   document.getElementById("out_mesg").value = llst;
51: }
52: function rsa_def(skeySt,pkeySt,msgSt)
53: {
54:  var m=0,len = msgSt.length,ttc,tts,ttns,ttp,ttnp,ttn;
55:  var ii,ret="",tempSt,result,tresult,lrArr;
56:  skeyV = myParseSt(skeySt);
57:    tts = str2bigInt(skeyV[0],10,skeyV[0].length);
58:    ttns = str2bigInt(skeyV[1],10,skeyV[1].length);
```

```
59:  pkeyV = myParseSt(pkeySt);
60:    ttp = str2bigInt(pkeyV[0],10,pkeyV[0].length);
61:    ttnp = str2bigInt(pkeyV[1],10,pkeyV[1].length);
62:  lrArr = myParseSt(msgSt);
63:  for (ii=0; ii < lrArr.length; ii++) {
64:    ttc = str2bigInt(lrArr[ii],10,lrArr[0].length);
65:    powMod(ttc,tts,ttns);
66:    powMod(ttc,ttp,ttnp);
67:    result = bigInt2str(ttc,10);
68:    tresult = parseInt(result,10);
69:    tempSt= String.fromCharCode(
70:       ((tresult >>> 24) & 0xff), ((tresult >>> 16) & 0xff),
71:       ((tresult >>>  8) & 0xff), ( tresult        & 0xff));
72:    ret += tempSt;
73:  }
74:  return ret;
75: }
76: </script>
77: </body>
```

For a test sample, lines 34–37 store the sender's public key, the receiver's secret key and a sample of ciphertext. These values are put into the appropriate text area and boxes. When the OK button is pressed, the function rsa_de() is run. This function captures the keys and ciphertext into variables skey, pkey and msgSt respectively. The function call rsa_def() in line 49 performs the entire process. The result is returned to variable llst and output to the text area at the bottom of the browser window.

The function rsa_def() extracts the sender's public-key components [e, n] into variables tts and ttns. Similarly, the receiver's secret-key components [d, n] are extracted into variables ttp and ttnp respectively. The for-loop in lines 63–73 will process each big number in the ciphertext. The first power modulo function in line 65 decrypts the message using the receiver's secret key. After the decryption, the sender's public key is used to identify the signature. The result is the plaintext in big number format. The statements in lines 68–72 convert the big number into character format and add this into variable ret. After the entire process, the plaintext is stored in ret and returned to the function caller at line 74 for display purposes.

Using this example, the decryption and signature verification of ex08-13.htm is shown in Figure 8.20. As you can see, the original sensitive letter is displayed in the text area at the bottom of the browser window.

Fig. 8.20 Receiving a secure message with a digital signature

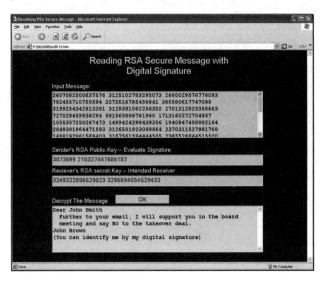

8.4.5 Building a hybrid encryption scheme: RSA + AES

Since the invention of public-key schemes in the early 1970s, public-key encryptions have provided a solution to a number of difficult problems, such as key exchange and digital signatures, involving modern cryptology and information security. However, from the experience of the previous few sections, there are some obvious disadvantages of public-key schemes:

- calculations, in general, involve big numbers – even if you have good APM package the computations are slow;

- encrypted messages are bigger than those using conventional symmetric-key encryption;

- the security of public-key schemes is generally weaker than with convention encryption.

These disadvantages make it neither ideal nor efficient to encrypt even small documents. Together with lower security strength, the applications of public-key schemes are restricted. To compensate for this problem, the idea of 'hybrid encryption' was established.

Generally speaking, hybrid encryption is a combination of conventional symmetric-key and public-key schemes. The main purpose is to use the advantages of both crypto-systems to solve security problems.

A popular applications of hybrid encryption is described below:

- perform message encryption/decryption using symmetric-key methods;

- protect and transmit the symmetric-key password using public-key encryption.

In this case, the plaintext message is protected by a much tougher symmetric-key encryption. If you want to transmit the encrypted message to someone, all you need to do is encrypt the password using the public-key of the receiver.

A hybrid encryption is developed in this section using the MD5, AES and RSA schemes. The structure is simple. Given a character message m, a password or key is constructed by the command

```
key = md5(m +Date()+Math.random())
```

This will combine the message m, the date and a random number together. After the md5() function, a message digest value (128-bit) is obtained as key. This key is used as the password to encrypt the message m with the AES scheme, i.e.

```
c0 = AES(m,key)
```

When you want to send the ciphertext c0 to someone such as Bob, you can encrypt the key with Bob's public key Bob_P, i.e.

```
c1 = RSA(key,Bob_P)
```

After concatenating c1 and c0, the result is sent to Bob for decryption. Consider ex08-15.htm below.

```
Example: ex08-15.htm - Message encryption with a hybrid scheme (Part I)

 1: <head><title>Hybrid Message Encryption</title></head>
 2: <style>
 3:   .butSt{font-size:14pt;width:250px;height:30px;
 4:        font-weight:bold;background:#dddddd;color:#ff0000}
 5:   .txtArea{font-size:14pt;width:780px;height:130px;
 6:            font-weight:bold;background:#dddddd}
 7: </style>
 8: <body style="font-family:arial;font-size:22pt;text-align:center;
 9:        background:#000088;color:#ffff00">
10: Message Encryption Using <br />A Hybrid Scheme: (RSA + MD5 + AES)
11: <form action="">
12: <table style="font-size:14pt;width:800px" align="center"
       cellspacing=5>
13: <tr><td>Input Message: </td></tr>
14: <tr><td><textarea rows="5" cols="40" id="in_mesg"
15:        class="txtArea">Meet Me At 2pm Tomorrow</textarea></td></tr>
16: <tr><td>Enter RSA Keys (Public-Key or Secret-Key)</td></tr>
```

```
17:   <tr><td><textarea rows="5" cols="40" id="key_v" class="txtArea"
18:       style="height:60px"></textarea></td></tr>
19:   <tr><td >Encrypt The Message    
20:       <input size="20" type="button" class="butSt"
          style="width:180px"
21:       value="OK" onclick="hyb_en()" /></td></tr>
22:   <tr><td><textarea rows="5" cols="40" id="out_mesg" class="txtArea"
23:       readonly style="background:#00ee00"></textarea></td></tr>
24: </tbody></table>
25: </form>
```

The XHTML codes in this page generate three text areas. The first is for the plaintext. The second text area allows a user to input the RSA public-key [*e*, *n*] of the recipient. When the OK button is clicked at line 21, the function hyb_en() is run. As a result, a session key combining the MD5 hash, plaintext message, date and a random number is generated. This key is used to encrypt the plaintext using the AES scheme. The encrypted result is displayed in the text area at the bottom of the browser window. The function hyb_en() is given in part II of ex08-15.htm.

Example: Continuation of ex08-15.htm   **(Part II)**

```
26: <script src="hexlib.js"></script>
27: <script src="ex06-09.js"></script>
28: <script src="ex03-05.js"></script>
29: <script src="BigInt.js"></script>
30: <script>
31: var kSt="531007548716379717949070709 "+
32:        "349309920095549615294937187063756384577";
33: document.getElementById("key_v").value = kSt;
34:
35: function hyb_en()
36: {
37:   var keySt="",message="",llst="", keyV;
38:   document.getElementById("out_mesg").value = llst;
39:   key = document.getElementById("key_v").value;
40:   message = document.getElementById("in_mesg").value;
41:   llst = hyb_enf(key, message);
42:   document.getElementById("out_mesg").value = llst;
43: }
44: function hyb_enf(keySt, msgSt)
45: {
46:   var m=0,len = msgSt.length;
```

```
47:     var ret="", ttm, lrArr, keyV, tmp;
48:     keyV = myParseSt(keySt);
49:       tte = str2bigInt(keyV[0],10,keyV[0].length);
50:       ttn = str2bigInt(keyV[1],10,keyV[1].length);
51:     tmp = int2bigInt(0,10,keyV[1].length+1);
52:     sessionKey = md5(msgSt + Date() + Math.random());
53:
54:     sessB = str2bigInt(sessionKey,16,sessionKey.length);
55:     if (greater(sessB,ttn)) mod(sessB,ttn);
56:
57:     keySt = bigInt2str(sessB,16);
58:     sessionKey = keySt.toLowerCase();
59:
60:     lst = byteStToHex(aes(sessionKey, msgSt,true));
61:     tmp = str2bigInt(sessionKey,16,sessionKey.length);
62:     powMod(tmp,tte,ttn);
63:     otmpSt = bigInt2str(tmp,16);
64:     otmpSt = otmpSt.toLowerCase();
65:     ret = byteToHex(otmpSt.length)+" "+otmpSt+" "+lst;
66:     return ret;
67:   }
68: </script>
69: </body>
```

First, the MD5 and AES codes are included in the page in lines 27–28. Lines 31–33 store values of a test public key [e, n] – this key will be put into the interface page and used to encrypt a session key generated by the program. When the OK button is clicked, the function hyb_en() run. First, this function captures the plaintext and the encryption key information into variables message and key respectively. These values are input to the encryption engine hyb_enf() in line 41. This function is defined in lines 44–67.

First, the information [e, n] of the key string keySt is extracted by lines 48–50 into variables tte and ttn. The next step is to build a session key (line 52):

```
sessionKey = md5(msgSt + Date() + Math.random());
```

This key is an MD5 hash value combining the plaintext, the current date and a random number. The hash is a 128-bit value in hexadecimal character format. When this value is converted into number sessB, by line 54, it can be bigger than the modulus of the public key ttn. The conditional-if statement in line 55 makes sure that sessB is smaller than ttn. Once this value is available, it is converted into a string (lower case string) and used to encrypt the plaintext with the AES scheme (line 60). Now, the remaining task is to encrypt the session key with the RSA public-key [e, n]. The encryption result is stored in variable otmpSt. This otmpSt and the AES encryption lst are returned to the function caller by line 65 so that all the

Fig. 8.21 Hybrid encryption

information is included in the ciphertext. In practice, this may not be an ideal situation since an intruder can extract the session key from the ciphertext. This may compromise the security of the scheme. Under the Kerckhoff principle, the secrecy of any scheme should not be assumed. The design here is intended for demonstration and educational purposes. A screenshot of this hybrid encryption is shown in Figure 8.21.

For the decryption, the same interface is used. Make a copy of part I of ex08-15.htm and call it ex08-16.htm. Modify the following two lines:

```
10: Message Decryption Using <br />A Hybrid Scheme: (RSA + MD5 + AES)
21:        value="OK" onclick="hyb_de()" /></td></tr>
```

Line 10 changes the display title. When the OK button is clicked, the decryption function hyb_de() is called at line 21 instead. This function is given in part II of ex08-16.htm.

Lines 30–37 store values of a test ciphertext and secret key [d, n] of the receiver. When the OK button is clicked, the function hyb_de() captures the plaintext and key (lines 43–44) and performs the decryption by calling the engine hyb_def() at line 45.

The decryption engine hyb_def() is defined in lines 49–67. First, the information of the decryption key [d, n] is extracted into variables ttd and ttn respectively. The encrypted session key is extracted by lines 56–57. After the RSA decryption process in lines 58–61, the session key is obtained in variable sessionKey. The AES encrypted message is extracted by line 63. This ciphertext is decrypted by

Example: ex08-16.htm - Message encryption with a hybrid scheme

```
26: <script src="hexlib.js"></script>
27: <script src="ex06-09.js"></script>
28: <script src="BigInt.js"></script>
29: <script>
30:  var msgSt="20 bb4fc4dc69258c71575137bd5b1a9022 "+
31:            "95 2b a5 05 46 ce d0 f3 8a 77 20 f1 37 80 ae "+
32:            "74 24 df 17 bd b7 cf 5a 6f 16 83 e0 "+
33:            "c5 20 a1 91 c9 ";
34:  document.getElementById("in_mesg").value = msgSt;
35:  var kSt ="26199974519428187073376512691501922 5025 "+
36:           "3493099200955496152949371870637563845 77";
37:  document.getElementById("key_v").value = kSt;
38:
39:  function hyb_de()
40:  {
41:    var keySt="",message="",llst="", keyV;
42:    document.getElementById("out_mesg").value = llst;
43:    key = document.getElementById("key_v").value;
44:    message = document.getElementById("in_mesg").value;
45:    llst = hyb_def(key, message);
46:    document.getElementById("out_mesg").value = llst;
47:  }
48:
49:  function hyb_def(keySt, msgSt)
50:  {
51:    var m=0,len = msgSt.length;
52:    var ii,ttc="",ttd,ttn,ret="",tempSt,result,tresult,lrArr;
53:    keyV = myParseSt(keySt);
54:      ttd = str2bigInt(keyV[0],10,keyV[0].length);
55:      ttn = str2bigInt(keyV[1],10,keyV[1].length);
56:    ind = parseInt(msgSt.substring(0,2),16);
57:    sessionKey = msgSt.substring(3,3+ind);
58:    ttc = str2bigInt(sessionKey,16,sessionKey.length);
59:    powMod(ttc,ttd,ttn);
60:    sessionKey = bigInt2str(ttc,16);
61:    sessionKey = sessionKey.toLowerCase();
62:
63:    msgSt = msgSt.substring(3+ind,msgSt.length);
64:    message = hexStToByteSt(msgSt)
65:    ret = aes(sessionKey, message, false);
66:   return ret;
67:  }
68: </script>
69: </body>
```

Fig. 8.22 Hybrid decryption

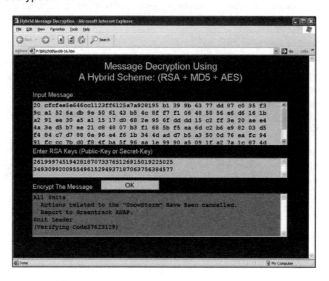

sessionKey in line 65. The result, the plaintext, is stored in variable `ret` and returned to the function caller for display purposes. A screenshot of this example in action is shown in Figure 8.22. From this you can see that the plaintext shown in Figure 8.21 appears in the decryption box in Figure 8.22.

The public-key schemes discussed so far are all based on the number theory and factorization over Galois Fields (GF). The next popular public key that we are going to introduce is slightly different. It depends on a special kind of curve called an elliptic curve.

8.5 Elliptic curves and public-key encryption/decryption

8.5.1 What are elliptic curves?

An elliptic curve is the set of solutions (x, y) to an equation of the form

$$y^2 = x^3 + ax + b,$$

where a and b are constants. Note that the right-hand side is a special cubic polynomial. The left-hand side is a quadratic term. In order to prevent repeated roots on the right-hand side, the constants a and b are restricted by

$$4a^3 + 27b^2 \neq 0.$$

Despite their simple form, elliptic curves have been studied for many years and have many significant applications in mathematics. Maybe one of the most interesting results related to the application of elliptic curves is that they are used to prove Fermat's Last Theorem. Elliptic curve encryption/decryption, or cryptography, was proposed and studied by Victor Miller and Neal Koblitz in the mid 1980s and quickly became a popular subject in cryptology.

In general, public-key encryption/decryption with elliptic curves, can provide faster algorithms, smaller keys, and the same level of security. We will discuss this shortly. First, let's examine some elliptic curves. Four are shown in Figures 8.23–8.26.

Fig. 8.23 $y^2 = x^3 - 7$

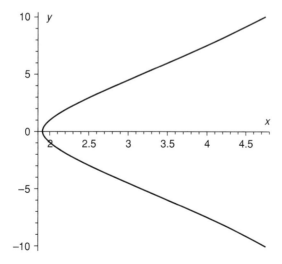

Fig. 8.24 $y^2 = x^3 - 4x$

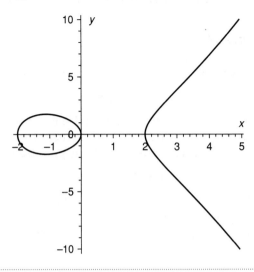

Fig. 8.25 $y^2 = x^3 - 3x + 3$

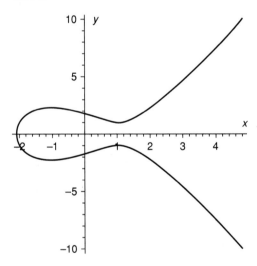

One of the interesting and powerful features of elliptic curves is that by using a special 'add' operation, any two points added together will result in a third point on the same curve.

Fig. 8.26 $y^2 = x^3 - 10x - 7$

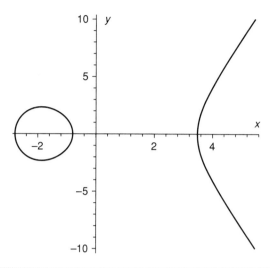

Adding points on an elliptic curve

Given two points $u = (x_1, y_1)$ and $v = (x_2, y_2)$ on the elliptic curve (see Figure 8.27), the point $u + v$ is calculated by:

- drawing a straight line through u and v and finding the third intersecting point w;

- drawing a vertical line through w (and O) and finding the third intersecting point $u + v$.

To make this rule work we assume the following.

- An extra imaginary point O on the curve, also known as the identity element or the point at infinity. It has no specific (x, y) coordinates, but one might imagine that its location is infinitely high above the curve where all vertical lines converge.

- A line tangent to a point on the curve is said to intersect the point twice. Think of the tangent as the limit of a line through two distinct points as the points approach each other.

If we consider O as the identity element, the addition of two points on an elliptic curve will result in a point on the same curve.

Based on elliptic curve addition, scalar multiplications can also be defined. Given a scalar integer s and a point u on an elliptic curve, scalar multiplication is defined by the addition

$$(s)u = \underbrace{u + u + \ldots + u}_{(s\ \text{times})}$$

Fig. 8.27 Adding two points on an elliptic curve

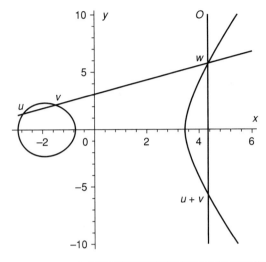

Now, let's consider how to compute the addition of two points on an elliptic curve. Suppose $u = (x_1, y_1)$ and $v = (x_2, y_2)$ are two points on an elliptic curve. The addition result is another point, $r = (x_3, y_3)$, on the same curve calculated by the addition formulae

$$x_3 = \lambda^2 - x_1 - x_2$$

$$\lambda = \begin{cases} \dfrac{y_2 - y_1}{x_2 - x_1} & \text{for } x_1 \neq x_2 \\[2mm] \dfrac{3x_1^2 + a}{2y_1} & \text{for } x_1 = x_2 \end{cases}$$

$$y_3 = \lambda (x_1 - x_3) - y_1$$

For encryption and decryption we always need integer operations, and therefore only elliptic curves over finite fields are considered. The most popular finite fields for this are integers modulo a prime number p. With this formula, the computations are carried out simply with $a \pmod p$ operation. Now, let's see how to use elliptic curves to perform encryption and decryption.

8.5.2 Elliptic curve cryptography

Using elliptic curves for encryption/decryption is called 'elliptic curve cryptography' (ECC). For this purpose, all points on an elliptic curve are considered as integers over a finite field, or more precisely a field generated by a large prime number. Instead of real (or floating point) numbers, computations (or additions) are performed with modulus of a prime number p. The use of elliptic curves over finite fields as a basis for encryption/decryption was first suggested by Koblitz.

Given a prime number p, the elliptic curve E over the finite field GF(p) is given by

$$E: y^2 = x^3 + ax + b \quad \mathrm{mod}\ p$$

where x, y, a and b are elements of $\{1, 2, 3, \ldots, p-1\}$. In computational form, an elliptic curve in GF(p) is uniquely defined by elements $[a, b, p]$ and therefore is represented by $E: [a, b, p]$.

In general, ECC schemes are public-key based. In other words, a public key and a secret key are generated. Normally, the public key is used for encryption and the secret key for decryption.

Generating the public and secret keys of an ECC scheme

To generate ECC public and secret keys, the following steps are required.

- Select a base point called B on the curve.

- Pick a random integer, k (secret key) and kept secret.

- Compute the point K (public key) by the scalar multiplication $K = k * B$.

The public and secret keys of the elliptic curve system are

secret key: $[k, B, a, b, p]$ and public key: $[K, B, a, b, p]$

Note that the secret key k is a value whereas the public key K is a point with x-y coordinates. In practice, and in terms of x-y coordinate values, we have:

secret key: $[k, Bx, By, a, b, p]$ and public key: $[Kx, Ky, Bx, By, a, b, p]$

All values are computed against modulo p (or mod p). The difficulty in obtaining the private key from the public key is based on the discrete log problem (DLP) for elliptic curves. The DLP states that, given a point K and a base point B, it is difficult to find an integer k such that

$$K = k * B \quad \mathrm{mod}\ p$$

To compare the security strength, NIST and ANSI X9 recommend the following key sizes for RSA, ECC and symmetric key.

Encryption scheme	Minimum key size
RSA public key	1024 bits
Elliptic public key	160 bits
Symmetric key	80 bits

From this table, we can see that for the same, or similar, encryption strength, the RSA, elliptic and symmetric-key key lengths are 1024, 160 and 80 bits respectively. In other words, elliptic encryption is much stronger than RSA since the key required for elliptic encryption is significantly shorter.

Encryption and decryption on elliptic curves

Suppose Sue wants to send a sensitive message to Bob with the following public and secret keys:

Bob's public key: $[K, B, a, b, p]$ and   Bob's secret key: $[k, B, a, b, p]$

Suppose the message is represented as a point M on the elliptic curve E: $[a, b, p]$. Sue can use Bob's public key to encrypt the message M as follows:

- select a random integer, r, and compute the ciphertext pair $[c0\ c1]$, where

$$c0 = r * B \quad \text{and} \quad c1 = M + r * K;$$

- send the ciphertext $[c0\ c1]$ to Bob;

- to decrypt the ciphertext, Bob multiplies the first component by his secret key k, and subtracts from the second component,

$$c1 - k * c0 = (M + r * K) - k * (r * B) = M + r * (k * B) - k * (r * B) = M$$

From these steps, we can see that both the encryption and decryption operations rely on the addition and scalar multiplication of points on the elliptic curve.

8.5.3 Adding two points on an elliptic curve

Suppose we have an elliptic curve E defined by the equation over a finite field GF(p):

$$E: y^2 = x^3 + ax + b \bmod p, \quad \text{where} \quad 4a^3 + 27b^2 \neq 0$$

Computationally, this curve is uniquely defined by the values E: $[a, b, p]$. For security strength, the value p is assumed to be a big prime number.

From Section 8.5.2, we know that the calculation of the public and secret keys of an ECC system depends on the scalar multiplication of points on an elliptic curve. Also, the scalar multiplication is carried out by the addition formula demonstrated in Figure 8.27. To implement this addition formula, consider example ex08-17.htm.

```
Example: ex08-17.htm - Adding two points on an elliptic curve (Part I)

1:  <head><title>Adding Two Points On An Elliptic Curve</title></head>
2:  <style>
3:  .butSt{font-size:16pt;width:70px;height:35px;
4:          font-weight:bold;background:#ddffdd;color:#ff0000}
5:  .txtSt{font-size:14pt;width:500px;height:35px;font-weight:bold;
6:          background:#eeeeee;color:#ff0000}
7:  .txtArea{font-size:14pt;width:630px;height:100px;
            font-weight:bold;
```

```
 8:          background:#aaffaa}
 9: </style>
10: <body style="font-family:arial;font-size:20pt;text-align:center;
11:        background:#000088;color:#ffff00">
12:  Adding Two Points P[x y] and Q[x y] <br />On An Elliptic
                                                Curve<br />
13:  <span style="font-size:16pt"><br />E: º   y<sup>2</sup>
14:       = x<sup>3</sup> + ax +b     mod    p
15:  </span><br /><br/>
16: <form action="">
17: <table style="font-size:16pt;width:680px" cellspacing="5"
      align="center">
18:  <tr><td style="width:130px">Point P:[x y]</td><td>
19:       <input type="text" id="tp" size="132" maxlength="132"
20:         class="txtSt" style="color:#008800" value="0 18" /></td></tr>
21:  <tr><td>Point Q:[x y]</td><td >
22:       <input type="text" id="tq" size="132" maxlength="132"
23:         class="txtSt" style="color:#008800" value="18 11" /></td></tr>
24:  <tr><td>E: [a b p]</td><td >
25:       <input type="text" id="te" size="132" maxlength="142"
26:         class="txtSt" style="color:#008800"
               value="4 14 31" /></td></tr>
27:  <tr><td colspan="2"> Calculating (P+Q)[x y] on Curve E   
28:       <input type="button" class="butSt" value="OK"
29:         onclick="add_fun()" /></td></tr>
30:  <tr><td colspan="2"><textarea rows="5" cols="40" id="out_mesg"
31:         class="txtArea" readonly ></textarea></td></tr>
32: </table></form>
33: <script src="BigInt.js"></script>
34: <script src="hexlib.js"></script>
35: <script src="elliptic.js"></script>
```

This XHTML code is the interface part of the example. It generates three text boxes, one push button and one text area. The three text boxes are designed to obtain the points *P*, *Q* and the elliptic curve *E* from the user. When the OK button is clicked, the function add_fun() is run (line 29). This function performs the addition of points *P* and *Q*. The resulting point is displayed in the text area at the bottom of the browser window.

In addition to the usual script files BigInt.js and hexlib.js, a new script called elliptic.js (defined shortly) is included in line 35. This file contains all the functions needed to handle elliptic curves for the rest of this chapter.

The function add_fun() is provided in part II of ex08-17.htm.

```
36: <script>
37:    pSt = "1773056069879938 1092467599646463";
38:    qSt = "1773056069879938 1092467599646463";
39:    eSt = "589758509 280934777552806 2237171265681283";
40:    document.getElementById("tp").value = pSt;
41:    document.getElementById("tq").value = qSt;
42:    document.getElementById("te").value = eSt;
43: function add_fun()
44: {
45:    var tmpSt,ta,tb,tp,tPx,tPy,tQx,tQy,tRx,tRy,lDigits=10;
46:    ta  = int2bigInt(0,10,lDigits); tb  = int2bigInt(0,10,lDigits);
47:    tp  = int2bigInt(0,10,lDigits);
48:    tPx = int2bigInt(0,10,lDigits); tPy = int2bigInt(0,10,lDigits);
49:    tQx = int2bigInt(0,10,lDigits); tQy = int2bigInt(0,10,lDigits);
50:    tRx = int2bigInt(0,10,lDigits); tRy = int2bigInt(0,10,lDigits);
51:
52:    tmpSt = document.getElementById("te").value;
53:    eleV=myParseSt(tmpSt); ta=str2bigInt(eleV[0],10,lDigits);
54:    tb=str2bigInt(eleV[1],10,lDigits);
       tp=str2bigInt(eleV[2],10,lDigits);
55:    while (negative(ta)) add(ta,tp); while (negative(tb)) add(tb,tp);
56:
57:    tmpSt=document.getElementById("tp").value;
58:    eleV1=myParseSt(tmpSt);
59:    tPx=str2bigInt(eleV1[0],10,lDigits);
       tPy=str2bigInt(eleV1[1],10,lDigits);
60:
61:    tmpSt=document.getElementById("tq").value;
62:    eleV2=myParseSt(tmpSt);
63:    tQx=str2bigInt(eleV2[0],10,lDigits);
       tQy=str2bigInt(eleV2[1],10,lDigits);
64
65:    elliptic_add(tPx,tPy,tQx,tQy,ta,tb,tp,tRx,tRy);
66:    document.getElementById("out_mesg").value =
67:      bigInt2str(tRx,10) +" "+ bigInt2str(tRy,lDigits);
68: }
69: </script>
70: </body>
```

To test this page, two sample points and an elliptic curve are provided in lines 37–39. For example, the string pSt in line 37 representing the point *P* contains the *x-y* coordinates of the point *P*:

$P[x\ y] = [1773056069879938\ 1092467599646463]$

In general, we will use this $P\ [x\ y]$ convention to represent points on an elliptic curve down to the x-y coordinate level. The elliptic curve E is defined by the $[a, b, p]$ values given in line 39:

$E[a, b, p] = [589758509\ 280934777552806\ 2237171265681283]$

The strings P, Q and E are put into the necessary text boxes given in the XHTML code in part I. When the OK button is clicked, the function add_fun() in lines 43–68 is run. Since we are dealing with big integers, all variables are defined in big integer format (lines 45–50).

The values of the elliptic curve E are obtained and extracted into variables ta, tb and tp in lines 52–55. The while-loops in lines 55 are used to handle negative value cases. The coordinates of point P are obtained and extracted into variables tPx and tPy in lines57–59. Similarly, the coordinates of point Q are obtained and stored in variables tQx and tQy (lines 61–63). The function call in line 65 performs the actual point addition of points P: [tPx tPy] and Q: [tQx tQy] on curve E [ta, tb, tp]:

```
elliptic_add(tPx,tPy,tQx,tQy,ta,tb,tp,tRx,tRy);
```

The result is another point R on the curve represented by the x-y coordinates tRx and tRy. This function is given by the script file elliptic.js.

```
Example: ECMAScript file elliptic.js for elliptic curves      (Part I)

 1: function elliptic_add(ttPx,ttPy,ttQx,ttQy,tta,ttb,ttp,ttRx,ttRy)
 2: {
 3:  var dPxQx,dPyQy,aPxQx,dQxRx,tQx,idPxQx,slop,idQ2y,gDigits=10;
 4:  dPxQx  = int2bigInt(0,10,gDigits); dPyQy = int2bigInt(0,10,gDigits);
 5:  aPxQx  = int2bigInt(0,10,gDigits); dQxRx = int2bigInt(0,10,gDigits);
 6:  tQx    = int2bigInt(0,10,gDigits); slop  = int2bigInt(0,10,gDigits);
 7:  idPxQx = int2bigInt(0,10,gDigits); iQ2y  = int2bigInt(0,10,gDigits);
 8:  Rx     = int2bigInt(0,10,gDigits); Ry    = int2bigInt(0,10,gDigits);
 9:  if (!equals(ttPx,ttQx) && !equals(ttPy,ttQy))
10:  {
11:    copy(dPxQx,ttPx);    //Px - Qx
12:    sub(dPxQx,ttQx);     while (negative(dPxQx)) add(dPxQx,ttp);
13:    copy(dPyQy,ttPy);    //Py - Qy
14:    sub(dPyQy,ttQy);     while (negative(dPyQy)) add(dPyQy,ttp);
15:
16:    copy(idPxQx,dPxQx); inverseMod(idPxQx,ttp);    // 1/(Px-Qx) mod p
17:    copy(aPxQx,ttPx);    add(aPxQx,ttQx);          //Px + Qx
18:    copy(slop,dPyQy);    multMod(slop,idPxQx,ttp); //(py-Qy)/(Px-Qx)
19:
20:    copy(Rx,slop);       multMod(Rx,Rx,ttp);
```

```
21:     sub(Rx,aPxQx);        while (negative(Rx)) add(Rx,ttp);
22:     mod(Rx,ttp);
23:     copy(dQxRx,ttQx);
24:     sub(dQxRx,Rx);        while (negative(dQxRx)) add(dQxRx,ttp);
25:
26:     multMod(dQxRx,slop,ttp); copy(Ry,dQxRx);
27:     sub(Ry,ttQy);         while (negative(Ry)) add(Ry,ttp);
28:     mod(Ry,ttp);
29: }
30: if (equals(ttPx,ttQx) && equals(ttPy,ttQy))
31: {
32:     var two = int2bigInt(2,10,gDigits);
           three = int2bigInt(3,10,gDigits);
33:     copy(iQ2y,ttQy); multMod(iQ2y,two,ttp); inverseMod(iQ2y,ttp);
34:
35:     copy(Rx,ttQx);    multMod(Rx,Rx,ttp);    multMod(Rx,three,ttp);
36:     add(Rx,tta);      multMod(Rx,iQ2y,ttp);  copy(Ry,Rx);
37:     multMod(Rx,Rx,ttp);
38:
39:     copy(tQx,ttQx);   multMod(tQx,two,ttp);
40:     sub(Rx,tQx);      while (negative(Rx)) add(Rx,ttp);
41:
42:     copy(dQxRx,ttQx);
43:     sub(dQxRx,Rx);    while (negative(dQxRx)) add(dQxRx,ttp);
44:     multMod(Ry,dQxRx,ttp);
45:     sub(Ry,ttQy);     while (negative(Ry)) add(Ry,ttp);
46:     mod(Ry,ttp);
47: }
48: copy(ttRx,Rx); copy(ttRy,Ry);
49: }
50:
```

This script implements the following addition formulae of two points P and Q on elliptic curve E. The result is a third point R: $[x\ y]$ on curve E.

$$R_x = \lambda^2 - P_x - Q_x \qquad\qquad \lambda = \begin{cases} \dfrac{P_y - Q_y}{P_x - Q_x} & \text{for } P \neq Q \\[2ex] \dfrac{3Q_x^2 + a}{2Q_y} & \text{for } P = Q \end{cases}$$

$$R_y = \lambda(Q_x - R_x) - Q_y$$

The implementation is carried out using the routines for big integers. Lines 9–29 handle the situation when $P \neq Q$. First, the value λ is computed by lines 11–18 and

Fig. 8.28 Adding two points on an elliptic curve

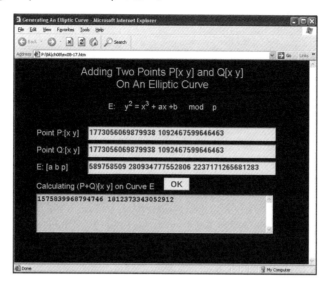

stored in variable `slop`. Lines 20–24 calculate the *x*-coordinate of point *R* (R_x). The statements in lines 26–28 compute the *y*-coordinate of *R*(R_y). Similarly, lines 30–49 calculate the *x-y* coordinates of the point *R* when *P* = *Q*.

Note that the implementation above has been kept simple. In particular, there is no code to handle the situation where the *x*-coordinates of *P* and *Q* are equal. In this case, the function should return infinity (or point *O*). Also, there is no arrangement for points at infinity. In a more professional approach, all points on the elliptic curve should have a status indicating whether it is an infinity point. A screenshot of this example in action is shown in Figure 8.28.

Scalar multiplication on elliptic curves is implemented in the next section. As a result, both the secret key and the public key of an ECC system are generated.

8.5.4 Scalar multiplication and generating the keys for ECC

Given a point *P*[*x y*] on an elliptic curve *E*[*a, b, p*], the scalar multiplication of *P* by an integer *s* is computed by the following addition formulae on an elliptic curve:

$$(s)P_x = \underbrace{P_x + P_x + \ldots + P_x}_{(s \text{ times})} \qquad (s)P_y = \underbrace{P_y + P_y + \ldots + P_y}_{(s \text{ times})}$$

There are a number of ways of implementing a series of additions. The simplest is using a for-loop and calling the addition routine in previous section. However, this will be too slow for many ECC applications. For a faster implementation, we use the algorithm and pseudo-code below.

```
Example: Pseudo-code for scalar multiplication on an elliptic curve

1:  Function elliptic_mult(s, P, E, W)
2:  {
3:      var T1, T2, d, r;               //T1 & T2 variables for points
4:      T2=P;                           //Assign point P to variable T2
5:      d = integer(s/2); r = s%2;      //Quotient (d) and remainder (r)
6:      while (d > 0) {                 //While-loop
7:          T1 = T2; T2 = elliptic_add(T1,T1); //T2 is point P in power of 2
8:          if (r==1) W = elliptic_add(W,T1);  //Adding T1 to point W
9:          if (d==1) W = elliptic_add(W,T2);  //Adding T2 to point W
10:         d = integer(s/2); r = s%2;  //New d, r and continue while-loop
11:     }
12: }
```

This algorithm may not be the fastest. It is easy to read – given a point P on an elliptic curve E, this pseudo-code is used to calculate the scalar multiplication of s and P (i.e. $s * P$). The result is another point W on the same curve E. The speed of this algorithm is the power of 2 – instead of adding P to P s times, s is converted into its equivalent to the power 2 first.

To implement this scalar multiplication, make a copy of part I of ex08-17.htm and call it ex08-18.htm. Modify the following lines:

```
12: Scalar Multiplication of A Point P[x y]<br/>On An Elliptic Curve<br/>
18: <tr><td style="width:130px">Integer s:</td><td >
19:     <input type="text" id="ts" size="132" maxlength="132"
27: <tr><td colspan="2"> Calculating The Point: (s*Q)[x y]   
29:         onclick="mult_fun()" /></td></tr>
```

The first four lines above are used to change the display. When the OK button is clicked, the function mult_fun() is run to perform the scalar multiplication on an elliptic curve. This function is defined in part II of ex08-18.htm.

```
Example: ex08-18.htm – Scalar multiplication on an elliptic curve
                                                          (Part II)

36: <script>
37:     sSt = "87654321";
38:     qSt ="471297869785160 1168237617386861";
39:     eSt = "589758509 280934777552806 2237171265681283";
```

```
40:    document.getElementById("ts").value = sSt;
41:    document.getElementById("tq").value = qSt;
42:    document.getElementById("te").value = eSt;
43: function mult_fun()
44: {
45:    var tmpSt,ta,tb,tp,tx,tPx,tPy,tRx,tRy,lDigits=10;
46:    ta  = int2bigInt(0,10,lDigits);  tb  = int2bigInt(0,10,lDigits);
47:    tp  = int2bigInt(0,10,lDigits);  ts  = int2bigInt(0,10,lDigits);
48:    tQx = int2bigInt(0,10,lDigits);  tQy = int2bigInt(0,10,lDigits);
49:    tRx = int2bigInt(0,10,lDigits);  tRy = int2bigInt(0,10,lDigits);
50:
51:    tmpSt = document.getElementById("te").value;
52:    eleV = myParseSt(tmpSt);            ta = str2bigInt(eleV[0],10,10);
53:    tb = str2bigInt(eleV[1],10,10);  tp = str2bigInt(eleV[2],10,10);
54:    while (negative(ta)) add(ta,tp); while (negative(tb)) add(tb,tp);
55:
56:    tmpSt = document.getElementById("tq").value;
57:    eleV1 = myParseSt(tmpSt);
58:    tQx = str2bigInt(eleV1[0],10,10);
       tQy = str2bigInt(eleV1[1],10,10);
59:
60:    tmpSt = document.getElementById("ts").value;
61:    ts = str2bigInt(tmpSt,10,0);
62
63:    elliptic_mult(ts,tQx,tQy,ta,tb,tp,tRx,tRy);
64:    document.getElementById("out_mesg").value =
65:      bigInt2str(tRx,10) +" "+ bigInt2str(tRy,10);
66: }
67: </script>
68: </body>
```

Lines 37–42 provide a test sample for the scalar multiplication. The function `mult_fun()` is defined in lines 43–66. The values of the elliptic curve E are obtained and extracted into variables `ta`, `tb` and `tp` (lines 51–54). The x-y coordinates of the point Q are extracted into variables `tQx` and `tQy` (lines 56–58). The scalar s is obtained by lines 60–61. The function call in line 63

```
elliptic_mult(ts,tQx,tQy,ta,tb,tp,tRx,tRy);
```

performs the scalar multiplication of s on the point $Q[x\ y]$. The result is another point R on E with x-y coordinates $R[$`tRx` `tRy`$]$. The scalar multiplication function `elliptic_mult()` is given in part II of the script file `elliptic.js`.

Example: ECMAScript file elliptic.js for elliptic curves   (Part II)

```
51: function elliptic_mult(tts,ttPx,ttPy,tta,ttb,ttp,ttRx,ttRy)
52: {
53:   var r1x,r1y,r2x,r2y,wx,wy,d,r,zero,one,two,tm0,tm1,gDigits=10;
54:   r1x = int2bigInt(0,10,gDigits); r1y = int2bigInt(0,10,gDigits);
55:   r2x = int2bigInt(0,10,gDigits); r2y = int2bigInt(0,10,gDigits);
56:   wx  = int2bigInt(0,10,gDigits); wy  = int2bigInt(0,10,gDigits);
57:   d   = int2bigInt(0,10,gDigits); r   = int2bigInt(0,10,gDigits);
58:   zero= int2bigInt(0,10,gDigits); one = int2bigInt(1,10,gDigits);
59:   two = int2bigInt(2,10,gDigits);
60:   tm0 = int2bigInt(0,10,gDigits); tm1 = int2bigInt(0,10,gDigits);
61:   Rx  = int2bigInt(0,10,gDigits); Ry  = int2bigInt(0,10,gDigits);
62:
63:   copy(r2x,ttPx); copy(r2y,ttPy); sub(wx,one); sub(wy,one);
64:   copy(tm0,tts); divide(tm0,two,d,r);
65:   while( greater(d,zero)) {
66:     copy(r1x,r2x);            copy(r1y,r2y);
67:     elliptic_add(r1x,r1y,r1x,r1y,tta,ttb,ttp,ttRx,ttRy);
68:     copy(r2x,ttRx);           copy(r2y,ttRy);
69:     if( equals(r,one)) {
70:       if ( negative(wx) && negative(wy)) {
71:           copy(wx,r1x);       copy(wy,r1y);
72:       } else {
73:           elliptic_add(wx,wy,r1x,r1y,tta,ttb,ttp,ttRx,ttRy);
74:           copy(wx,ttRx);      copy(wy,ttRy);
75:       }
76:     }
77:     if( equals(d,one)) {
78:       if ( negative(wx) && negative(wy)) {
79:           copy(wx,r2x);       copy(wy,r2y);
80:       } else {
81:           elliptic_add(wx,wy,r2x,r2y,tta,ttb,ttp,ttRx,ttRy);
82:           copy(wx,ttRx);      copy(wy,ttRy);
83:       }
84:     }
85:     copy(tm0,d);              divide(tm0,two,d,r);
86:   }
87:   copy(ttRx,wx); copy(ttRy,wy);
88: }
```

The script function `elliptic_mult()` in lines 51–88 is a direct implementation of the pseudo-code for scalar multiplication. The *x-y* coordinates of point P[tPx tPy] are copied to variables R2[r2x r2y] in line 63. Also, the point W[wx wy] is assigned

Fig. 8.29 Scalar multiplication on an elliptic curve

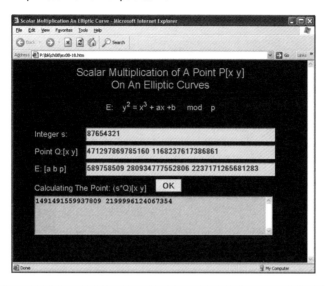

an initial value −1. After the scalar `tts` is copied to variable `tm0`, the quotient and remainder of `tm0/2` are obtained as `d` and `r` respectively (line 64). While `d` is bigger than zero, the point `R1[r1x r1y]` is set to the value of point `R2[r2x r2y]`. The point `R2` is then calculated as elliptic addition `R1+R1` by lines 67–68. If the remainder `r` is 1, the point `R1` is added into point `w` (lines 69–76). If the quotient `d` is 1, the point `R2` is added into point `w` in lines 77–84. The statements in line 85 compute the quotient `d` and remainder `r` again for the while-loop. When the while-loop is exhausted (i.e. `d = 0`), the scalar product (or resulting) point `w[wx wy]` is copied to point `R[ttRx ttRy]` and returned to the function caller. A screenshot of this example is shown in Figure 8.29.

Given a random integer *k* (secret key) and a base point *B[x y]* on the elliptic curve *E[a b p]*, the public key *K* of the ECC is generated by *K = k * B*, which is simply a scalar multiplication. Therefore, developing a page to generate ECC secret and public keys is simple. All you have to do is to make a complete copy of `ex08-18.htm`, call it `ex08-19.htm`, and modify the following lines:

```
12: Generating The Public-Key K[x y]<br/>For An ECC System<br/>
13: <span style="font-size:16pt"><br />
14:    K[x y] = (k *B)[x y]
18: <tr><td style="width:130px">Secret-Key k:</td><td >
21: <tr><td>Point B:[x y]</td><td>
27: <tr><td colspan="2"> Generating The Public-Key
        K[x y]    
```

Fig. 8.30   Generating a public key

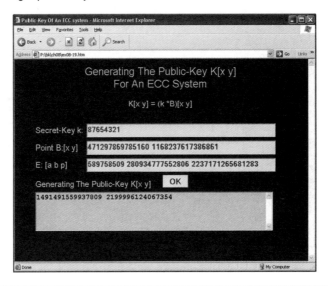

Yes! All you have to do is to change six lines. In fact, they are for display purposes only and have no impact on the calculation. A screenshot of this example is shown in Figure 8.30.

With the secret key and public key generated, it's time to consider how to perform encryption/decryption for an ECC system.

8.5.5   Encryption/decryption using elliptic curves

Suppose we have the public-key and secret-key information below:

public key: $[K, B, a, b, p]$ and   secret key $[k, B, a, b, p]$

The encryption of a message M represented as a point on the elliptic curve $E[a, b, p]$ is given by

$$c0 = r * B \qquad c1 = M + r * K \qquad \text{(ECC encryption)}$$

where r is a random integer. From the addition and scalar multiplication of elliptic curves, the ciphertext pair $[c0, c1]$ are, in fact, two points on the curve $E[a, b, p]$.

To perform the decryption and obtain the plaintext M back, the following formula is used:

$$c1 - k * c0 = M \qquad \text{(ECC decryption)}$$

Note that the integer r in the encryption process plays no part in the decryption process. To implement the ECC encryption, consider ex08-20.htm.

Example: ex08-20.htm – Elliptic curve encryption   **(Part I)**

```
 1: <head><title>ECC Encryption</title></head>
 2: <style>
 3:   .butSt{font-size:16pt;width:70px;height:35px;
 4:         font-weight:bold;background:#ddffdd;color:#ff0000}
 5:   .txtSt{font-size:14pt;width:500px;height:35px;font-weight:bold;
 6:         background:#eeeeee;color:#ff0000}
 7:   .txtArea{font-size:14pt;width:630px;height:100px;
 8:         font-weight:bold;background:#aaffaa}
 9: </style>
10: <body style="font-family:arial;font-size:20pt;text-align:center;
11:         background:#000088;color:#ffff00">
12:   Encryption Using Elliptic Curves<br />
13:   <span style="font-size:16pt"><br />
14:   c0 = (r*B)[x y]      c1= (M + r * K)[x y]
15:   </span><br /><br/>
16: <form action="">
17: <table style="font-size:16pt;width:700px" cellspacing="5"
    align="center">
18:   <tr><td>Message M:[x y]</td><td>
19:       <input type="text" id="tm" size="132" maxlength="132"
20:         class="txtSt" style="color:#008800" value="" /></td></tr>
21:   <tr><td>Integer r:</td><td >
22:       <input type="text" id="tr" size="132" maxlength="132"
23:         class="txtSt" style="color:#008800" value="" /></td></tr>
24:   <tr><td>Public-Key K[x y]</td><td>
25:       <input type="text" id="tk" size="132" maxlength="132"
26:         class="txtSt" style="color:#008800" value="" /></td></tr>
27:   <tr><td>Point B:[x y]</td><td>
28:       <input type="text" id="tb" size="132" maxlength="132"
29:         class="txtSt" style="color:#008800" value="" /></td></tr>
30:   <tr><td>E: [a b p]</td><td >
31:       <input type="text" id="te" size="132" maxlength="142"
32:         class="txtSt" style="color:#008800" value="" /></td></tr>
33:   <tr><td colspan="2"> Generating The Public-Key  
34:       <input type="button" class="butSt" value="OK"
35:         onclick="en_fun()" /></td></tr>
36:   <tr><td colspan="2"><textarea rows="5" cols="40" id="out_mesg"
37:         class="txtArea" readonly ></textarea></td></tr>
38: </table></form>
39: <script src="BigInt.js"></script>
40: <script src="hexlib.js"></script>
41: <script src="elliptic.js"></script>
```

This page fragment is the interface part of the example, and it contains five text boxes, one OK button and one text area. The first two text boxes are for the plaintext *M* and an arbitrary integer *r*. The remaining three text boxes are for the public key *K*, base point *B* and elliptic curve *E*[*a*, *b*, *p*]. Once the OK button is clicked, the function en_fun() is run (line 35) and the ciphertext values c0 and c1 are displayed in the text area at the bottom of the browser window. The encryption function en_fun() is given in part II of ex08-20.htm.

```
Example: Continuation of ex08-20.htm                        (Part II)

42: <script>
43:   mSt = "1435965740019437 530943628671512";
44:   eSt = "589758509 280934777552806 2237171265681283";
45:   rSt = "7561",
46:   bSt = "471297869785160 1168237617386861";
47:   kSt = "2127814482883134 2049972171869118"; //Secret-Key: 1568
48:   document.getElementById("tm").value = mSt;
49:   document.getElementById("tr").value = rSt;
50:   document.getElementById("tk").value = kSt;
51:   document.getElementById("tb").value = bSt;
52:   document.getElementById("te").value = eSt;
53:
54: function en_fun()
55: {
56:   var tmpSt,ta,tb,tp,tBx,tBy,tQx,tQy,outSt="",lDigits=10;
57:   ta  = int2bigInt(0,10,lDigits);  tb  = int2bigInt(0,10,lDigits);
58:   tp  = int2bigInt(0,10,lDigits);  tr  = int2bigInt(0,10,lDigits);
59:   tMx = int2bigInt(0,10,lDigits);  tMy = int2bigInt(0,10,lDigits);
60:   tBx = int2bigInt(0,10,lDigits);  tBy = int2bigInt(0,10,lDigits);
61:   tKx = int2bigInt(0,10,lDigits);  tKy = int2bigInt(0,10,lDigits);
62:   tmx = int2bigInt(0,10,lDigits);  tmy = int2bigInt(0,10,lDigits);
63:   tRx = int2bigInt(0,10,lDigits);  tRy = int2bigInt(0,10,lDigits);
64:
65:   tmpSt = document.getElementById("te").value;
66:   eleV = myParseSt(tmpSt);              ta = str2bigInt(eleV[0],10,10);
67:   tb = str2bigInt(eleV[1],10,10);   tp = str2bigInt(eleV[2],10,10);
68:   while (negative(ta)) add(ta,tp); while (negative(tb)) add(tb,tp);
69:
70:   tmpSt = document.getElementById("tb").value;
71:   eleV1 = myParseSt(tmpSt);
72:   tBx = str2bigInt(eleV1[0],10,10); tBy = str2bigInt(eleV1[1],10,10);
73:
74:   tmpSt = document.getElementById("tr").value;
```

```
75:    tr = str2bigInt(tmpSt,10,0);
76:    elliptic_mult(tr,tBx,tBy,ta,tb,tp,tRx,tRy);
77:    outSt="Ciphertext c0=\n"+bigInt2str(tRx,10)+"
                          "+bigInt2str(tRy,10)+"\n";
78:
79:    tmpSt = document.getElementById("tm").value;
80:    eleV1 = myParseSt(tmpSt);
81:    tMx = str2bigInt(eleV1[0],10,10); tMy = str2bigInt(eleV1[1],10,10);
82:
83:    tmpSt = document.getElementById("tk").value;
84:    eleV1 = myParseSt(tmpSt);
85:    tKx = str2bigInt(eleV1[0],10,10); tKy = str2bigInt(eleV1[1],10,10);
86:
87:    elliptic_mult(tr,tKx,tKy,ta,tb,tp,tRx,tRy);
88:      copy(tmx,tRx);        copy(tmy,tRy);
89:    elliptic_add(tMx,tMy,tmx,tmy,ta,tb,tp,tRx,tRy);
90:
91:    outSt+="Ciphertext c1=\n"+bigInt2str(tRx,10)+"
                          "+bigInt2str(tRy,10)+"\n";
92:    document.getElementById("out_mesg").value = outSt;
93: }
94: </script>
95: </body>
```

Lines 43–52 provide a test sample of plaintext M, an arbitrary integer r, and the public-key information $\{K, B, E[a, b, p]\}$. Once the OK button is pressed, the function en_fun() in lines 54–93 is activated to encrypt the plaintext. Lines 65–68 obtain the information of the elliptic curve $E[a, b, p]$. The statements in lines 70–72 get the x-y coordinates of the base point $B[x\ y]$. The arbitrary integer r is obtained by lines 74–75. As soon as this information is available, the function in line 76 computes the first ciphertext point $c0[x\ y] = (r * B)[x\ y]$ on $E[a, b, p]$, i.e.

```
elliptic_mult(tr,tBx,tBy,ta,tb,tp,tRx,tRy);
```

Since $c0$ is a point on E, the x-y coordinates are stored in [tRx, tRy]. This point $c0$ is appended to the string variable outSt at line 77 for display purposes.

The x-y coordinates of plaintext $M[x\ y]$ are captured by lines 79–81. Together with the public key $K[x\ y]$, the scalar multiplication in line 87 computes the x-y coordinates of $(r * K)[x\ y]$. By adding the plaintext M in line 89, the second ciphertext $c1$ is obtained, i.e.

$$c1[x\ y] = (M + r * K)[x\ y]$$

Fig. 8.31 ECC encryption

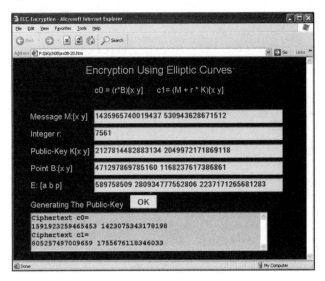

This point $c1$ is appended into string variable `outst` at line 91 and displayed at the bottom of the browser window by the statement in line 92. A screenshot of this example is shown in Figure 8.31.

For ECC decryption, we use a very similar interface to that described in `ex08-20.htm`. Make a copy of part I of `ex08-20.htm` and call it `ex08-21.htm`, modifying the following lines:

```
12: Decryption Using Elliptic Curves<br />
14:   M[x y] = (c1 - k*c0)[x y] = (M + r*k*B - k*r*B)[x y]
18: <tr><td>c0:    [x y] </td><td>
19:     <input type="text" id="c0" size="132" maxlength="132"
21: <tr><td>c1:    [x,y] </td><td >
22:     <input type="text" id="c1" size="132" maxlength="132"
27: <tr style="visibility:hidden"><td>Point B:[x y]</td><td>
35:         onclick="de_fun()" /></td></tr>
```

The first two lines change the display text. Lines 18–19 generate a text box for the first ciphertext $c0[x\ y]$. Similarly, lines 21–22 generate a text box for the second ciphertext $c1[x\ y]$. For decryption, the base point B is not needed. By putting the attribute `visibility:hidden` in line 27, the entire row of the base point will disappear. When the OK button is clicked, the function `de_fun()` in line 35 is activated to perform decryption on $c0$ and $c1$. This decryption function `de_fun()` is defined in part II of `ex08-21.htm`.

```
42: <script>
43:   c0St = "1591923259465453 1423075343178198";
44:   c1St = "805257497009659 1755676118346033";
45:   kSt = "1568";       // K[x y]="2127814482883134 2049972171869118"
46:   eSt = "589758509 280934777552806 2237171265681283";
47:   document.getElementById("c0").value = c0St;
48:   document.getElementById("c1").value = c1St;
49:   document.getElementById("tk").value = kSt;
50:   document.getElementById("te").value = eSt;
51:
52: function de_fun()
53: {
54:   var tmpSt,ta,tb,tp,c0x,c0y,c1x,c1y,tk,outSt="",elev1,lDigits=10;
55:   ta  = int2bigInt(0,10,lDigits); tb  = int2bigInt(0,10,lDigits);
56:   tp  = int2bigInt(0,10,lDigits); tk  = int2bigInt(0,10,lDigits);
57:   c0x = int2bigInt(0,10,lDigits); c0y = int2bigInt(0,10,lDigits);
58:   c1x = int2bigInt(0,10,lDigits); c1y = int2bigInt(0,10,lDigits);
59:   tRx = int2bigInt(0,10,lDigits); tRy = int2bigInt(0,10,lDigits);
60:
61:   tmpSt = document.getElementById("te").value;
62:   eleV1 = myParseSt(tmpSt);
63:   ta=str2bigInt(eleV1[0],10,lDigits);
      tb=str2bigInt(eleV1[1],10,lDigits);
64:   tp=str2bigInt(eleV1[2],10,lDigits);
65:   while (negative(ta)) add(ta,tp); while (negative(tb)) add(tb,tp);
66:
67:   tmpSt = document.getElementById("c0").value;
68:   eleV1 = myParseSt(tmpSt);
69:   c0x=str2bigInt(eleV1[0],10,lDigits);
      c0y=str2bigInt(eleV1[1],10,lDigits);
70:
71:   tmpSt = document.getElementById("c1").value;
72:   eleV1 = myParseSt(tmpSt);
73:   c1x=str2bigInt(eleV1[0],10,lDigits);
      c1y=str2bigInt(eleV1[1],10,lDigits);
74:
75:   tmpSt = document.getElementById("tk").value;
76:   tk = str2bigInt(tmpSt,10,lDigits);
77:
78:   elliptic_mult(tk,c0x,c0y,ta,tb,tp,tRx,tRy);
79:
80:   multInt(tRy,-1); if (negative(tRy)) add(tRy,tp);
         //Finding minus point
81:   copy(c0x,tRx); copy(c0y,tRy);
```

```
82:     elliptic_add(c1x,c1y,c0x,c0y,ta,tb,tp,tRx,tRy);
83:
84:     outSt+= "Plaintext (M)= \n"+
85:         bigInt2str(tRx,10) + " "+ bigInt2str(tRy,10) +"\n";
86:     document.getElementById("out_mesg").value = outSt;
87: }
88: </script>
89: </body>
```

Lines 43–50 provide a test sample for the decryption. The elliptic curve information is captured by lines 61–65. The ciphertext pair $c0[x\ y]$ and $c1[x\ y]$ are obtained by lines 67–73. Together with the secret key k, the function in line 78 computes the value

$$(k * c0\ )[x\ y]$$

To invert the sign of this point, we need to multiply -1 onto the y-coordinate as illustrated in line 80. Therefore, the function `elliptic_add()` in line 82 effectively adds the points $c1$ and $-(k * c0)$ together to get the plaintext M, i.e.

$$M[x\ y] = (c1 - k * c0\ )[x\ y]$$

A screenshot of this example in action is shown in Figure 8.32. From this you can see that if the ciphertext $c0$ and $c1$ in `ex08-20.htm` is used, the same plaintext $M[x\ y]$ is obtained.

Fig. 8.32 ECC decryption

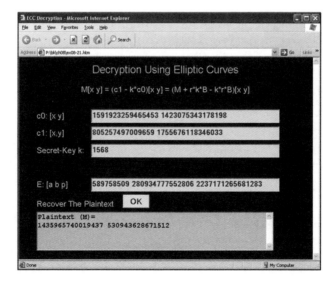

9

Security applications with GnuPG, WinPT and server techniques

9.1 An introduction to Gnu Privacy Guard

9.1.1 What are PGP, OpenPGP and GnuPG?

In Chapter 8, we discussed a number of public-key schemes and their applications to digital signatures and signing documents. In this chapter some popular and professional packages, including PGP and OpenPGP, are considered. With the algorithm and implementation knowledge gained from Chapter 8 the operations and theory behind these industrial packages can be understood more deeply.

Compared to public-key schemes, conventional symmetric-key encryption provides more efficient and safer protection against intruders. For this reason, most advanced crypto-systems nowadays implement hybrid schemes to take advantage of both methods.

The implementation of a hybrid scheme involves:

- generating a session key at run time (with date and serial information);
- using a public-key method to encrypt the session key, forming an encrypted key;
- encrypting the plaintext M with the session key to produce the ciphertext C;
- sending both the encrypted key and the ciphertext to the recipient;
- the recipient using their secret key on the encrypted key to obtain the session key;
- using the session key to decrypt the ciphtertext C to obtain the plaintext M.

In Section 8.4, we implemented a hybrid scheme which was a combination of RSA, MD5 and AES (see `ex08-15.htm` and `ex08-16.htm`). The structure is a direct

Fig. 9.1 A symmetric-key and public-key hybrid scheme

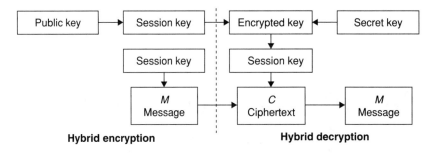

implementation of Figure 9.1. In fact the structure of many popular commercial and industrial security packages is similar to that in Figure 9.1.

The first industrial product of public-key technology and hybrid methods was Pretty Good Privacy (PGP) developed by Philip Zimmermann. Based on this product, an IETF standard known as RFC 2440 (or OpenPGP) was established in November 1998. As a compliant of the standard, a freely available implementation of OpenPGP was developed by GNU. It is called Gnu Privacy Guard (GnuPG).

PGP and the US export law

The original PGP program was developed by Phil Zimmermann in the early 1990s to provide strong encryption for email transmission or electronic message exchange. It is believed that the primary purpose of the development was in response to the US Senate Bill 266, which was designed to force manufacturers to build a 'trap door' into every secure communication so that the US government would be able to intercept and decrypt those communications.

It seems that the government at that time wanted to control the public use of encryption, and encryption technology was declared as a type of 'munitions'. When the source code of PGP was released and made freely available around the world, Zimmermann was charged by the government for 'exporting munitions'. The charge was finally dropped in 1996 and version 5 of PGP was released. In 1999, the US encryption export law was relaxed so that sophisticated encryptions could be exported anywhere except those countries classified as arch enemies, such as Iraq, Iran and Cuba.

As you may imagine, PGP uses a hybrid scheme for encryption. As shown in Figure 9.1, the email message is encrypted using a symmetric-key algorithm with a key normally of 128 bits. That key is then encrypted using a public-key scheme with a key usually of 2048 bits. The entire message is then sent to the recipient. The recipient uses their secret key to obtain the symmetric key and finally decrypt the ciphertext. There are a number of symmetric-key algorithms used in PGP, such as

Blowfish, Triple-DES, CAST and IDEA. The main public-key algorithms in PGP are RSA and Diffie-Hellman.

Despite all the odds, including lack of funding and government persecution, PGP became the most widely used email encryption software in the world. After the US government dropped its charges against Zimmermann, PGP Inc. was formed in 1996. One year later, Network Associates Inc. (NAI) bought PGP and released version 6, which is still free for non-commercial use. A graphical interface was written for the Windows and Mac versions. In 2002, NAI discontinued PGP development and sold the rights to a new company called PGP Corporation. Now PGP has gone through version 8 and is owned by PGP Corporation (www.pgp.com). A limited version of PGP is still free for personal use.

The standardization of OpenPGP

After leaving NAI in January 2001, Zimmermann started the OpenPGP Alliance, involving the standardization of PGP. OpenPGP is, in fact, an open standard protocol based on PGP. The OpenPGP working group is working hard to found it as an Internet standard via the role of IETF. The official standardization document, or specification, of OpenPGP is called RFC 2440.

RFC 2440 is a long document, well over 65 pages, with the title *OpenPGP Message Format*. This document provides implementation and operational details of PGP. It covers the following topics:

- confidentiality via encryption;

- compression;

- authentication via digital signatures;

- conversion to radix-64 encoding.

The confidentiality section describes a hybrid encryption scheme similar to that in Figure 9.1. The authentication process of PGP is equivalent to signing a document using the concept of the digital signature. In PGP, compression is also employed to reduce the size of a file if necessary. The output of PGP is a radix-64 encoding.

Due to the popularity of the PGP program and the legal restrictions of the IDEA and RSA schemes in the original design of PGP, a group of open-source programmers related to the GNU project developed the so-called Gnu Privacy Guard, which is free software conforming to the OpenPGP standards.

The Gnu Privacy Guard

The GNU Privacy Guard (GnuPG) is a free software package available to everyone from the Internet. It is a standard implementation of the specification known as IETF standard RFC 2440 (or OpenPGP). Since it is completely free and the source code is available with no legal restrictions, early sections of this chapter are dedicated to this package and how to use it for security applications.

Basically, GnuPG is a complicated program offering many command line arguments. The main program is called gpg. This contains more than 30 commands and another 30+ options. We will cover some of the most popular uses of the program from a practical point of view. Examples related to GnuPG will have the file extension .gpg in this chapter.

Before we consider the application of GnuPG, you will need to install and set up the package.

9.1.2   The installation and set-up of GnuPG

A copy of the OpenPG software package can be downloaded from the official site www.gnupg.org. GnuPG has a number of versions dedicated to various platforms and operating systems. If you want to start from scratch, you can download the following full version, including the source code, and compile the software yourself:

```
gnupg-xxxx.tar.gz
```

If you are using a UNIX/LINUX system you are particularly encouraged to compile and install the software yourself. The version number of the package is represented by the string xxxx of the downloaded file. At the time of this writing, the latest and recommended version is gnupg-1.2.4.tar.gz. The compilation and installation of the software for a typical Redhat LINUX system is summarized under the following steps.

- Unpack the package by executing the following commands:

  gunzip gnupg-1.2.4.tar.gz to extract the tar file gnupg-1.2.4.tar;

  tar -xzvf gnupg-1.2.4.tar to extract all files into the gnupg-1.2.4 directory.

- Go to the default directory, such as gnupg-1.2.4, and issue the command ./configure.

- Now build the package by executing the make utility, such as make.

- Finally, install the software by typing the command make install.

If you want to build the software to be used on a Microsoft Windows system, the details are in the readme.w32 file.

It is strongly recommended that you double-check whether you have unmodified software before you install it on your system. One simple way of checking the integrity of the software is the MD5 string. According to the official site of GnuPG, the MD5 string of the file gnupg-1.2.4.tar.gz is

```
md5(gnupg-1.2.4.tar.gz) = adfab529010ba55533c8e538c0b042a2
```

You can use the MD5 utility mddriver.exe (see Chapter 3) to verify the integrity of the software. If you don't want to start GnuPG from the source code, you can download the binary version for your machine. For Microsoft Windows systems, the binary version and MD5 string are

```
gnupg-w32cli-1.2.4.zip
md5(gnupg-w32cli-1.2.4.zip) = bb568fe26abbe045d91f95ae0324eab2
```

Installing this binary version for Microsoft Windows is simple. All you need to do is unzip the package and store everything in a directory such as `c:\gnupg`. To install GnuPG into another directory, you may need to add a string to the Windows registry. In this case, you may want to read the `readme.w32` file for more details.

When you have installed the software on your system successfully, you can start to use it for data security and protection. Basically, GnuPG is a command line package and the main program is `gpg`. To use `gpg`, you may need to open a shell window (or a DOS window if you are using Windows) and issue commands inside it. For a general introduction to all commands and related options, you can issue the following command inside a shell window

```
gpg --help
```

If you see an output similar to that in Figure 9.2 there is a good chance that you have installed and set up GnuPG properly.

From the help window, you can see that GnuPG uses many different encryption schemes, classified as 'supported algorithms'. Interestingly, most of the algorithms and their implementations are covered in Chapters 3–6 and 8 of this book.

Now, let's see how to use GnuPG for security applications.

Fig. 9.2 GnuPG help option

```
C:\gnupg>gpg --help
gpg (GnuPG) 1.2.4
Copyright (C) 2003 Free Software Foundation, Inc.
This program comes with ABSOLUTELY NO WARRANTY.
This is free software, and you are welcome to redistribute it
under certain conditions. See the file COPYING for details.

Home: c:/gnupg
Supported algorithms:
Pubkey: RSA, RSA-E, RSA-S, ELG-E, DSA, ELG
Cipher: 3DES, CAST5, BLOWFISH, AES, AES192,
 AES256, TWOFISH
Hash: MD5, SHA1, RIPEMD160, SHA256
Compression: Uncompressed, ZIP, ZLIB

Syntax: gpg [options] [files]
sign, check, encrypt or decrypt
default operation depends on the input data
Commands:
```

9.2 Using GnuPG for security applications

9.2.1 Generating and handling public and secret keys

In order to use GnuPG effectively, you are advised to consult the handbook, manual, guide and/or how-to documents related to the software. The following is just a quick discussion with simple demonstrations on how to use GnuPG for data security. In addition to the package, applications and examples on key generation, deletion, key management, encryption and decryption are provided.

The first thing to do when using a public-key security package such as GnuPG is to generate keys. For security reasons, it is recommended that you:

- only generate keys on a machine for which you have complete control and direct access;

- never generate keys over a network.

When you are ready, you generate the public/secret keys by opening a shell window (or MS-DOS Window) and issue the command:

```
gpg --gen-key
```

When you use this command, you will be asked a number of questions so that the key pair (public/secret) can be generated successfully. For most, you can press the Enter key to accept the default. The questions and the information that GnuPG requires are as follows.

- Which algorithm to use to generate the key pairs (the default is DSA/ElGamal)?

- What key length do you want to use (the default is 1024-bit)?

- The life of the key pairs (the default is never expire).

- What is your real name (to identify you e.g. johnsmith)?

- What is your email address (e.g. johnsmith@pws-ex.com)?

- Enter a comment (can be anything e.g. gnupg).

- Enter a passphrase (to protect the secret key).

- Confirm your passphrase (retype your passphrase).

After you have confirmed the passphrase, you will be given the opportunity to change the information entered before the key pair is generated. If you enter OK at this point, the key pair will be generated. A complete dialog of this process is shown in example ex09-01.gpg – the user response to the questions is emboldened. Also, we have assumed that GnuPG is installed in the c:\gnupg directory if you are using Microsoft Windows. From now on, all GnuPG commands are issued from the shell window.

Example: ex09-01.gpg - Generating a public/secret key Pair on GnuPG

```
 1: shell>gpg --gen-key
 2: gpg (GnuPG) 1.2.4; Copyright (C) 2003 Free Software Foundation, Inc.
 3: This program comes with ABSOLUTELY NO WARRANTY.
 4: This is free software, and you are welcome to redistribute it
 5: under certain conditions. See the file COPYING for details.
 6:
 7: Please select what kind of key you want:
 8:    (1) DSA and ElGamal (default)
 9:    (2) DSA (sign only)
10:    (4) ElGamal (sign and encrypt)
11: Your selection?                      -----(Just Press Enter Key Here)
12:
13: DSA keypair will have 1024 bits.
14: About to generate a new ELG-E keypair.
15:              minimum keysize is 768 bits
16:              default keysize is 1024 bits
17:     highest suggested keysize is 2048 bits
18: What keysize do you want? (1024) -----(Just Press Enter Key Here)
19:
20: Requested keysize is 1024 bits
21: Please specify how long the key should be valid.
22:        0 = key does not expire
23:      <n>  = key expires in n days
24:      <n>w = key expires in n weeks
25:      <n>m = key expires in n months
26:      <n>y = key expires in n years
27: Key is valid for? (0)                -----(Just Press Enter Key Here)
28:
29: Key does not expire at all
30:
31: Is this correct (y/n)? y
32:
33: You need a User-ID to identify your key; the software constructs the
34: user id from Real Name, Comment and Email Address in this form:
35:    "Heinrich Heine (Der Dichter) <heinrichh@duesseldorf.de>"
36:
37: Real name: johnsmith
38:
39: Email address: johnsmith@pws-ex.com
40:
41: Comment: gnupg
42:
```

```
43: You selected this USER-ID:
44:     "johnsmith (gnupg) <johnsmith@pws-ex.com>"
45:
46: Change (N)ame, (C)omment, (E)mail or (O)kay/(Q)uit? O
47:
48: You need a Passphrase to protect your secret key.
49:
50: Enter passphrase: have a nice day ---(You will not see this string)
51: Repeat passphrase: have a nice day ---(You will not see this string)
52:
53: We need to generate a lot of random bytes. It is a good idea to perform
54: some other action (type on the keyboard, move the mouse, utilize the
55: disks) during the prime generation; this gives the random number
56: generator a better chance to gain enough entropy.
57: +++++++++++++++++++++++.++++++++++..+++++++++++++++.+++++
58: ...++++++++++.+++++++++++++++++++++++++++++++++++++++>+++++..+++++
59:
60: gpg: c:/gnupg\trustdb.gpg: trustdb created
61: public and secret key created and signed.
62: key marked as ultimately trusted.
63:
64: pub 1024D/DBE5FF7D 2005-07-01 JohnSmith
        (gnupg) <johnsmith@pws-ex.com>
65:     Key fingerprint = 578C 02B0 504E A2AF 9650
           7E5D 7C31 7C12 DBE5 FF7D
66: sub 1024g/AD44B809 2005-07-01
67:
```

By picking the default key type in line 11, two key pairs are generated. The first optional key pair is the DSA type. One of the important applications of this key pair is to sign a document. The second key pair is the ElGamal type called 'ElGamal subordinate keys'. This key pair is responsible for encryption/decryption. The 'real name' and 'email address' are used to identify you. If you don't want to use your real name, you may enter any unique name to identify yourself. The comment in line 41 can be any string. The question in line 46 offers you the chance to make any changes before generating the key pairs.

To help safeguard the secret key, the software saves all secret keys in an encrypted format protected by a symmetric (or conventional) encryption. The key for this symmetric encryption is the passphrase that you supply in lines 50–51. You will need this passphrase every time you want to use your secret key. The DSA and ElGamal public keys are shown in lines 64–66.

Inside GnuPG, there are two key rings. One is called the public-key ring containing all public keys in the system. The other is called the secret-key ring. Key rings are used to maintain and/or perform administrations on keys. To see the public keys in the public-key ring, you can use the command `gpg --list-keys` inside the shell window (see `ex09-02.gpg`).

```
Example: ex09-02.gpg - Displaying keys in the public-key ring

1: shell>gpg --list-keys
2:
3: c:/gnupg\pubring.gpg
4: --------------------
5: pub  1024D/DBE5FF7D 2005-07-01 JohnSmith
     (gnupg) <johnsmith@pws-ex.com>
6: sub  1024g/AD44B809 2005-07-01
```

In this case, the public-key ring file is `pubring.gpg` located in the `c:\gnupg` directory. The DSA public key is shown in line 5. The ElGamal subordinate public key is shown in line 6.

If you want to delete the key pair of 'johnsmith', you need to delete the secret key from the secret-key ring first and then delete the public key from the public-key ring. The commands to delete the key pairs are:

```
gpg --delete-secret-key johnsmith@pws-ex.com
gpg --delete-key johnsmith@pws-ex.com
```

In this example, the email address is used to identify the user in GnuPG. A processing dialog is shown in `ex09-03.gpg`.

```
Example: ex09-03.gpg - Deleting the personal primary key pairs

 1: shell>gpg --delete-secret-key johnsmith@pws-ex.com
 2:
 3: gpg (GnuPG) 1.2.4; Copyright (C) 2003 Free Software Foundation, Inc.
 4: This program comes with ABSOLUTELY NO WARRANTY.
 5: This is free software, and you are welcome to redistribute it
 6: under certain conditions. See the file COPYING for details.
 7:
 8: sec  1024D/DBE5FF7D 2005-07-01 JohnSmith
    (gnupg) <johnsmith@pws-ex.com>
 9:
10: Delete this key from the keyring? y
11: This is a secret key! - really delete? y
12:
13:
14: shell>gpg --delete-key johnsmith@pws-ex.com
```

```
15:
16: gpg (GnuPG) 1.2.4; Copyright (C) 2003 Free Software Foundation, Inc.
17: This program comes with ABSOLUTELY NO WARRANTY.
18: This is free software, and you are welcome to redistribute it
19: under certain conditions. See the file COPYING for details.
20:
21: pub  1024D/DBE5FF7D 2005-07-01 JohnSmith
        (gnupg) <johnsmith@pws-ex.com>
22:
23: Delete this key from the keyring? y
24:
25: shell>gpg --list-keys
26: shell>
```

The secret key of johnsmith@pws-ex.com is deleted by the statement in line 1. The symbol sec in line 8 indicates that the information is indeed a secret key. After double confirmations in lines 10–11, the key is deleted from the secret-key ring. The command in line 14 is used to delete the public key. If you have a secret key in the key ring, you may need to delete the secret key first before you can delete the public key.

Before anyone can send you an encrypted message using GnuPG, you need to export your public key to others. Similarly, you may need to import the corresponding public keys from others so that two-way communication can be established.

9.2.2   Exporting and importing public keys

Suppose you (John Smith) have a business partner called Mary Anderson. You want to carryout secure communication with Mary using GnuPG. The first thing you should do is to export your public key to Mary, and Mary should export her public key to you.

Exporting public keys using GnuPG

If you have a public key in your GnuPG system, you can export it into a ASCII (or text) file by the command

```
gpg --armor --output "johnsmith.key" --export "johnsmith"
```

where the command arguments have the following meaning:

--armor – output the key as ASCII code

--output – output the key into a file

--export – export whose key

This command has no return message on the screen. In this case, the public key identified by the real name 'johnsmith' is output to the file johnsmith.key in ASCII code. An example of the 1024-bit public key is shown in example ex09-04.gpg.

```
Example: ex09-04.gpg - The public key of johnsmith
(file: johnsmith.key)

 1: -----BEGIN PGP PUBLIC KEY BLOCK-----
 2: Version: GnuPG v1.2.4 (MingW32)
 3:
 4: mQGiBEDkkCgRBAC3KactYhEMudXDNhL1SUzJASTokZ3qYQGneuFD0Gl8pPs/x1+7
 5: ONzaekmyyBSIki/ntfZBa2WF1YRaGUmt/1CG7BvKruE1q9wmdzzBMqBz+j2Coq5u
 6: iZobgqkJUbph98prE/0TGySpJnzkWXLoIlJtPSKN8W2087wX+QfLLSKxWwCg6vxw
 7: c1NlOByiS51m12O3pQTxOlUD/iAUiukmZJPZesSUYSinS32aGmgRVouPmw5GJfdy
 8: /SJ7baiUZ4Au35Pm03d6bhoShAjtA5EM2D3nF7TrvwdfJWkUFagitzU3Mh4uJWCo
 9: PsHmKYkOOZpz/36MzinduLroGhbf+8YumhfEHVuLT9lWoV8OfSB8AAAIySX/16T5
10: E5JPA/496eX3HSUJWA8ugDYJ3/7hJ2HEcP1rUCcQXNNqqLfcreMleV3nEmc7WiGU
11: cVwKF5Ep7tKSiW509wuUhkDPXVfgE2eom57u3PrelvHvGod5zsw8eJtz8xVfMW8v
12: T3wbHcTBOKooa0GRQ0nGBDCHGt0jzXpHlGoe6+wxieU0+30gN7Qoam9obnNtaXRo
13: IChnbnVwZykgPGpvaG5zbWl0aEBwd3MtT.ntZXguY29tPoheBBMRAgAeBQJA5JAoAhsD
14: BgsJCAcDAgMVAgMDFgIBAh4BAheAAAoJELiszIsDS9XZHlsAnR2lNyVZofXPZ6Pc
15: sZG/fAQgfKfEAKDCYoSpXoFLmpEhB9PE3U+Hz1PLGrkBDQRA5JApEAQAu3GV99Oj
16: AAeMaQWTsSHahEkZeb0ZsofJy2xivH7F2oRrgR1PjwcANSOP2AxjD+D8o3lyfLzY
17: 0XQEp9G8db6HydXYB0N64maR1cwQSgUva6i9gvqwS1Zg53n+iRL+Ajs6hz/mq3iq
18: munp0ANK8XjepxU36bHJb9CyqR94W6Ks4HsAAwYEAK7NOSpcrxSICRTFfLQI6yln
19: AqftZ/TrLa7yRpkGV/QfnYOog6XsSuFUqierP6n+EN+bRov6G0PnDwk0ZDI+QTxJ
20: Y/hPGrXIipANJq75zzQnzofe7DamQQ7LmTGfHc9hNR3GhJh76N41ceGFu/HsF07r
21: 9HqNxv5aHkg+uffC+/KxiEkEGBECAAkFAkDkkCkCGwwACgkQuKzMiwNL1dnqUACb
22: BVDnOCTdtHDD26uNywE949kPxEIAoJQ+AxEE9CUUihDMHEuveBFBVJiX
23: =5DWd
24: -----END PGP PUBLIC KEY BLOCK-----
```

Now, you can send this public-key file to Mary by email so that she can use it to send encrypted messages to you. Similarly, Mary can email her public key to you. Once you receive this from Mary, you can import the key into your public-key ring.

Importing a public key into a GnuPG key ring

Suppose the public-key file of Mary is called mary_key. You can import Mary's public key into your key ring by the command

```
gpg --import mary.key
```

This statement will import the public key stored in file mary.key into your GnuPG public-key ring. The dialog and process are shown in example ex09-05.gpg.

```
Example: ex09-05.gpg - Importing a public key

1: shell>gpg --import mary.key
2: gpg: key D5427275: public key "Mary Anderson <mary@aabbccdd.com>"
       imported
3: gpg: Total number processed: 1
4: gpg:                imported: 1
```

As you can see from this example, the real name and email address of the key owner are also displayed. After the key is imported, the following command provides a complete listing of all keys in the public-key ring, gpg --list-keys (see ex09-06.gpg).

```
Example: ex09-06.gpg - List all public keys

1: shell>gpg --list-keys
2: c:/gnupg\pubring.gpg
3: --------------------
4: pub  1024D/034BD5D9 2005-07-01 johnsmith
     (gnupg) <johnsmith@pws-ex.com>
5: sub  1024g/A235EC47 2005-07-01
6:
7: pub  1024D/D5427275 2005-07-01 Mary Anderson <mary@aabbccdd.com>
8: sub  1024g/83D53A20 2005-07-01
```

When you have a new public key in your key ring, the key should be validated, signed and a level of trust issued. This process can be done by extracting the fingerprint of the public key. For example, you can extract the fingerprint of Mary's public key and telephone her to verify the key. To extract the fingerprint, you can use the edit-key command

```
gpg --edit-key mary@aabbccdd.com
```

In this case, the identity of Mary is identified by her email address. This command will show the public key of mary@aabbccdd.com and display a command prompt

```
command>
```

This command prompt is used for further input. If you enter the subcommand frp, the program will display a fingerprint of Mary's key. The fingerprint of Mary's public key is a numeric string in hexadecimal, similar to a message digest string (line 14 of ex09-07.gpg). This fingerprint can be verified with Mary for consistency by telephone or some other means. After the verifying process, you can validate the key by signing it with the subcommand sign (line 16). Such a processing dialog is shown in ex09-07.gpg.

Example: ex09-07.gpg - Validating and signing an imported key

```
 1: shell>gpg --edit-key mary@aabbccdd.com
 2:
 3: gpg (GnuPG) 1.2.4; Copyright (C) 2003 Free Software Foundation, Inc.
 4: This program comes with ABSOLUTELY NO WARRANTY.
 5: This is free software, and you are welcome to redistribute it
 6: under certain conditions. See the file COPYING for details.
 7:
 8: pub  1024D/D5427275 created: 2005-07-01 expires: never trust: -/-
 9: sub  1024g/83D53A20 created: 2005-07-01 expires: never
10: (1). Mary Anderson <mary@aabbccdd.com>
11:
12: Command> fpr
13: pub  1024D/D5427275 2005-07-01 Mary Anderson <mary@aabbccdd.com>
14: Primary key fingerprint: 3C90 0076 A853 DE99 20B5 D878 3AAE B1EE
       D542 7275
15:
16: Command> sign
17:
18: pub  1024D/D5427275 created: 2005-07-01 expires: never trust: -/-
19: Primary key fingerprint: 3C90 0076 A853 DE99 20B5 D878 3AAE B1EE
       D542 7275
20:
21:     Mary Anderson <mary@aabbccdd.com>
22:
23: How carefully have you verified the key you are about to sign actually
24: belongs to the person named above? If you don't know what to answer,
25: enter "0".
26:
27:    (0) I will not answer. (default)
28:    (1) I have not checked at all.
29:    (2) I have done casual checking.
30:    (3) I have done very careful checking.
31:
32: Your selection? (enter '?' for more information): 3
33: Are you really sure that you want to sign this key
34: with your key: "johnsmith (gnupg) <johnsmith@pws-ex.com>" (034BD5D9)
35: I have checked this key very carefully.
36:
37:
38: Really sign? y
39:
40: You need a passphrase to unlock the secret key for
41: user: "johnsmith (gnupg) <johnsmith@pws-ex.com>"
```

```
42: 1024-bit DSA key, ID 034BD5D9, created 2005-07-01
43:
44: Enter passphrase: have a nice day
45: Command> quit
46: Save Changes? y
```

This process also provides a trust level for the imported key in lines 27–30. Once you have verified the key with Mary, you can give it a trust level '3', as illustrated in line 32. After the confirmation line 38, the imported key is signed.

Now, we have everything ready to perform message encryption and decryption using GnuPG.

9.2.3   Message encryption and decryption using GnuPG

GnuPG is a powerful cryptographic package. It can perform both public-key and symmetric-key encryptions on messages.

Public-key encryption/decryption

Compared to other activities, encryption and decryption are relatively easy. For example, suppose you (or 'johnsmith') want to encrypt and send the following message to Mary.

```
Example: ex09-08.txt - Sample important file: mary.txt

1: Dear Mary
2:
3: Your executive promotion will be
4: discussed in the board meeting
5: tomorrow.
6:
7: Regards
8:
9: John Smith
```

To encrypt this text file with Mary's public key, all you have to do is to execute the command

```
gpg --output mary.gpg --armor --encrypt --recipient "Mary Anderson"
    mary.txt
```

This command encrypts the file mary.txt using the public key of 'Mary Anderson' and produces an ASCII output ciphertext (or encrypted message) which is stored in file mary.gpg. This encrypted file is listed in ex09-09.gpg.

```
Example: ex09-09.gpg - The encrypted message file: mary.gpg

-----BEGIN PGP MESSAGE-----
Version: GnuPG v1.2.4 (MingW32)

hQEOAwkz2cGD1TogEAP/QEHyDkY5wcBoN3u34xzPJebCGP6dfRkITCALhpokbveV
Oi8r59OXzyDcxQRoGnq7IiXR2vea6mZKq1NzQ4xQuPQ94qic4fVy7glqJpihUPn+
EehU7WYIEDGpkAXOd0LhRIsuVCMutcpi0wUJo+TT/zwVqOw/uZimgmA9WsB243kD
/1E6Hkf1Tq7ZnnF80HfeCQc6/SM0f6F69LwmV1HQ8hyJvjJEfO+qDeNZWPW6Ufab
egCSGqTPFjLiTXVw12KUQkrMOnP0JAeqUcy2bqjSaLHVkx6PxNgp9wmRtvA3bUly
vsgOoOEAC666YQBrM01IfEfTeCfWMk0j6xLZVII7XrlC0q0B0iEMvWmhI3gKYeXW
a/C/F8bcI/+1+OIuvFA/sO0E6BjLVU5SJ+mdKGLc/L9MvjQg33YDVCXTDw4wRcei
pFC1gdqzk7oTcFYKrG/Kt67uRUyLRFMZv4FXk83shwpqpcjh1LCwBsBoskylkSa7
nOQCQ7jWugpdZvQaO7h1f7U37i00LedPahuhzUGg2fZChXcVQIfPaBxmGqWfOZgA
RzhH7B5sfbpcU5xvr19Erg==
=9jsN
-----END PGP MESSAGE-----
```

You can transmit or email this file as an attachment to Mary, and only Mary, or the owner of Mary's secret key, can decrypt it. When Mary receives the file, she can decrypt it using the command

```
gpg --output message.txt --decrypt mary.gpg
```

In this case, the file `mary.gpg` will be decrypted by Mary's secret key and the result output to a file called `message.txt`. Since all secret keys in GnuPG are protected by passphrases, Mary may need to provide her passphrase to complete the decryption. A typical processing dialog is shown in `ex09-10.gpg`.

```
Example: ex09-10.gpg - Decryption using GnuPG

 1: shell>gpg --output message.txt --decrypt mary.gpg
 2:
 3: You need a passphrase to unlock the secret key for
 4: user: "Mary Anderson <mary@aabbccdd.com>"
 5: 1024-bit ELG-E key, ID 83D53A20, created 2005-07-01
    (main key ID D5427275)
 6:
 7: Enter passphrase: see you later -----(You will not see this string)
 8:
 9: gpg: encrypted with 1024-bit ELG-E key, ID 83D53A20,
         created 2005-07-01
10:     "Mary Anderson <mary@aabbccdd.com>"
11:
```

In this case, the decrypted message is stored in file `message.txt`. This file will be the same as the plaintext given in `ex09-08.txt`.

Symmetric-key encryption/decryption

As we mentioned earlier in this chapter, GnuPG basically is a hybrid encryption scheme. The actual message encryption is done by a symmetric-key algorithm. Therefore, GnuPG can also offer symmetric encryption/decryption. For example, Mary can activate the symmetric encryption on GnuPG by issuing the command

```
gpg -output en_mesg.gpg -armor -symmetric mymesg.txt
```

This command uses the symmetric method to encrypt the file `mymesg.txt`. The encrypted result is stored in file `en_mesg.gpg`. Since symmetric-key encryption is used, the same key should be used for decryption. To decrypt `en_mesg.gpg`, the following command is used:

```
gpg -output message --decrypt en_mesg.gpg
```

A typical processing dialog is shown in `ex09-11.gpg`.

```
Example: ex09-11.gpg - Symmetric encryption/decryption using GnuPG

1: shell> gpg --output en_mesg.gpg --symmetric mymesg.txt
2:
3: Enter passphrase: see you later -----(You will not see this string)
4: Repeat passphrase: see you later-----(You will not see this string)
5: shell>
6:
7: shell> gpg --output message.txt --decrypt en_mesg.gpg
8: Enter passphrase: see you later  -----(You will not see this string)
9: shell>
```

This symmetric-key encryption is a handy tool for protecting the messages and files of the secret key owner. Since the secret key is protected by a passphrase, you will be asked for this whenever the secret key is used.

9.2.4 Digital signatures and signing documents using GnuPG

In Chapter 8 we discussed digital signatures in some detail. Basically, a digital signature certifies an electronic document with a timestamp. In an ideal situation, it can also be used like a hand-signed signature on paper. All digital signatures can be checked, one way or another, for verification purposes. When you sign a document using a digital signature, any later modifications will be discovered immediately. Also, on the other hand, it is difficult to deny the signature once you have signed it. The distribution of the source code of GnuPG, for example, is signed by a digital signature so that you can verify the integrity of the package against alteration.

Generating digital signatures and signing documents is slightly different from the encryption/decryption process. Usually, a signature is created using your secret key. Signing a document is similar to encrypting the document with your secret key. If the recipient can use your public key for decryption, in an ideal case the document must have been sent by you.

In GnuPG there are three methods of signing documents, and they are discussed separately, with examples, in the following sub-sections.

Signing documents in binary form

This is the most common process for signing electronic documents and is illustrated by the following example.

Suppose John Smith has an important legal document to send to Mary Anderson, as shown in Figure 9.3. The document is called `smith212.doc` and is in Microsoft Word format. Before John delivers the document to Mary by email, the document is signed by the GnuPG command

```
gpg --output smith212.sig --sign smith212.doc
```

Fig. 9.3 A legal document

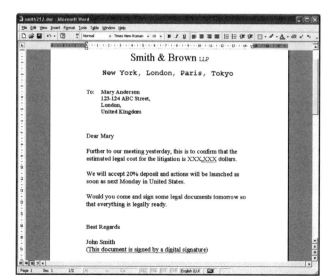

Fig. 9.4   Signing a document

```
shell>gpg --output smith212.sig --sign smith212.doc

You need a passphrase to unlock the secret key for
user: "johnsmith (gnupg) <johnsmith@pws-ex.com>"
1024-bit DSA key, ID 034BD5D9, created 2005-07-01

Enter passphrase:

user: "johnsmith (gnupg) <johnsmith@pws-ex.com>"
1024-bit DSA key, ID 034BD5D9, created 2005-07-01
```

In this case, the command line option `--sign` is used to generate a digital signature. The document to be signed is `smith212.doc`, and the output signed document is `smith212.sig`. The dialog for this process is shown in Figure 9.4.

Since the default secret key in the system is 'John Smith', the process in Figure 9.4 is equivalent to John Smith signing the document himself.

In GnuPG, the document `smith212.doc` is compressed before being signed, and the output is in binary format.

When Mary Anderson receives the signed message, she has two options. She can either check the signature, or check the signature and decrypt the document at the same time. To check the document she can use the command

```
gpg --verify smith212.sig
```

This statement uses John Smith's public key inside Mary's public-key ring to verify the signature. If the signature is good, Mary would see something like the statements below (also see Figure 9.5):

```
gpg: Signature made 07/02/05 12:15:26 using DSA key ID 034BD5D9
gpg: Good signature from "johnsmith (gnupg) <johnsmith@pws-ex.com>"
```

Fig. 9.5   Verification and decryption

```
shell>gpg --verify smith212.sig
gpg: Signature made 07/02/05 12:15:26 using
DSA key ID 034BD5D9
gpg: Good signature from "johnsmith
(gnupg) <johnsmith@pws-ex.com>"

shell>gpg --output smith212.doc --decrypt smith212.sig
gpg: Signature made 07/02/05 12:15:26 using
DSA key ID 034BD5D9
gpg: Good signature from "johnsmith
(gnupg) <johnsmith@pws-ex.com>"
```

The first statement identifies the signature in the document. The second verifies that the signature actually came from John Smith. When Mary is satisfied with the verification process, she can issue the following command to decrypt it:

```
gpg --output smith212.doc --decrypt smith212.sig
```

If the signature is good, this command verifies and decrypts the document. This command produces the same output as for the `--verify` case.

Now, Mary should have the document `smith212.doc` in her local directory. This document is the same as that shown in Figure 9.3. Sometimes, binary format may not be ideal for application. GnuPG also provides a signing process in text mode called 'clearsigning'.

Clearsigned documents: the --clearsign option

For text files, GnuPG offers a process called 'clearsigned document' so that documents can be signed in ASCII mode. Suppose John Smith has a text message as shown in Figure 9.6 stored in `smith212.txt`. He can use the following command to sign the text file in ASCII mode:

```
shell>gpg --clearsign smith212.txt
```

This statement reads the text file `smith212.txt` and generates a clearsigned document called `smith212.asc` (ASCII mode) in the local directory. Since the signing process involves the secret key of the signer, GnuPG will ask for a passphrase, and the process dialog is shown below:

```
You need a passphrase to unlock the secret key for
user: "johnsmith (gnupg) <johnsmith@pws-ex.com>"
1024-bit DSA key, ID 034BD5D9, created 2005-07-01
Enter passphrase:have a nice day   (This string will not display)
```

Fig. 9.6   Text file: `smith212.txt`

Dear Mary

Further to our meeting yesterday, this is to confirm
that the estimated legal cost for the litigation
is XXX,XXX dollars.

We will accept 20% deposit and actions will be
launched as soon as next Monday in United States.
Would you come and sign some legal documents tomorrow
so that everything is legally ready.

Best Regards
John Smith
(This document is signed by a digital signature)

Fig. 9.7 Clearsigned document

```
-----BEGIN PGP SIGNED MESSAGE-----
Hash: SHA1

Dear Mary

Further to our meeting yesterday, this is to confirm
that the estimated legal cost for the litigation
is XXX,XXX dollars.

We will accept 20% deposit and actions will be
launched as soon as next Monday in United States.
Would you come and sign some legal documents tomorrow
so that everything is legally ready.

Best Regards
John Smith
(This document is signed by a digital signature)
-----BEGIN PGP SIGNATURE-----
Version: GnuPG v1.2.4 (MingW32)

iD8DBQFA5U3UuKzMiwNL1dkRAi8dAJ9sNeXKV1XxkP8qjPapUSh8jf
1SwCg0cnL
+U3nURTdbHyMKbqmfMM9tII=
=GZKO
-----END PGP SIGNATURE-----
```

If you edit the clearsigned file `smith212.asc`, you will see a display similar to that in Figure 9.7.

GnuPG employs SHA-1 for the signing process. For example, notice the string 'Hash: SHA1' on the second line of Figure 9.7. The SHA algorithm and SHA-1 implementation have been studied in detail in Section 3.5. It is a 160-bit hash string acting as a digest of the document. The actual hash value appears at the bottom of the document (Figure 9.7). To verify the signature, you can use the usual `--verify` option on the clearsigned document, e.g.

```
gpg --verify smith212.asc
```

Sometimes, having a digital signature inside a document may not be convenient for the application. For this reason, GnuPG provides a third signing process called 'detached signature'.

Detached signatures: the `--detach-sig` option

A detached signature is generated by the `--detach-sig` option. The purpose of this signing process is to separate the original document and the signature itself. Unlike previous signing methods, for which you may need to perform decryption or editing to get the original document back, the detached signature will be produced in a separate file. For example, the following command will process the document `smith212.txt` and generate a detached signature in a separate file:

```
gpg --output smith212_det.sig –detach-sig smith212.txt

You need a passphrase to unlock the secret-key for
user: "johnsmith (gnupg) <johnsmith@pws-ex.com>"
1024-bit DSA key, ID 034BD5D9, created 2005-07-01
Enter passphrase:
```

In this case, the detached signature is generated in file `smith212_det.sig`. In order to verify this signature, you may need to input both the document and the signature files into GnuPG. For example, the `--verify` option now should have two inputs:

```
gpg --verify smith212_det.sig smith212.txt

gpg: Signature made 07/02/05 12:15:26 using DSA key ID 034BD5D9
gpg: Good signature from "johnsmith (gnupg) <johnsmith@pws-ex.com>"
```

Combining many practical encryptions together, it is easy to see that GnuPG is a useful package for transmitting and receiving secure messages. However, the package itself is designed as a command line program and may not be very convenient for a beginner. To make it more practical, either a graphical interface or integration with other programs is necessary.

9.3 A graphical GnuPG interface for Windows: WinPT

9.3.1 The installation and set-up of WinPT

One of the original ideas for developing GnuPG was that it could be used for sending and receiving encrypted emails and as a complete replacement of PGP. In order to do that, GnuPG must be user-friendly and fully integrated with email programs, such as Microsoft Outlook Express (OE). An integrated piece of software (plug-in) of GnuPG and OE called GPGOE is born. Imagine that by clicking a button, all your daily emails can be encrypted, decrypted and signed by GnuPG encryption schemes inside Outlook Express.

More than that – by combining a number of applications, including GPGOE, a fully integrated package called 'Windows Privacy Tools' (WinPT) is developed.

WinPT is a collection of security tools to help you protect your privacy in Microsoft Windows systems. It is GnuPG-based and compatible with the standard OpenPGP (RFC 2440). The main objective of WinPT is to ease installation, integration and use of GnuPG for Windows users. It provides encryption, decryption and signing functionalities on any data available through the Windows system including the clipboard, the current window, files, emails and instant messaging.

Like all GNU projects, the entire WinPT package, with the source code, is free for both commercial and non-commercial use.

Installing and setting up WinPT

There are two ways to install and set up WinPT. The first is to download the entire package, including the installer, from the official site www.winpt.org. This will give you the following executable file:

```
winpt-install-1.0rc2.exe
```

When you run this program, it will allow you to choose exactly what tools you want to install. The current available applications are:

- GnuPG – the official release;

- WinPT-GUI – a general graphical interface for use on Windows;

- WinPT Explorer Extensions – a tool providing file security and wiping functions for IE;

- WinPT Outlook Express plug-in – a tool providing secure emailing;

- WinPT Passphrase Agent – a component to cache passphrases used by GnuPG.

In addition to these applications, the package also provides shortcuts to important online information, a copy of the WinPT handbook in pdf format, a shortcut to GnuPG command line access, and other information.

The second installation method is to download the individual applications and install them yourself. This method may be more suitable for more experienced users, or by anyone wanting to upgrade one of the tools.

A step-by-step installation of the WinPT package on a Windows XP system is provided below.

■ Run the program `winpt-install-1.0rc2.exe` and select your language (Figure 9.8).

■ The WinPT set-up wizard will guide you through the installation process (Figure 9.9).

Fig. 9.8 Select a language

Fig. 9.9 The setup wizard

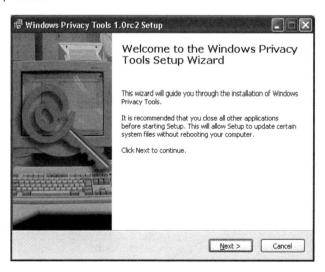

- First, you may need to click the `I agree` button in the 'License Agreement' (Figure 9.10).
- A window appears to allow you to select the installation location. In this case, the default location is `\Program Files\Windows Privacy Tools` (Figure 9.11).

Fig. 9.10 The license agreement

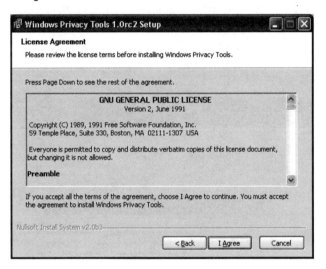

Fig. 9.11 Installation location

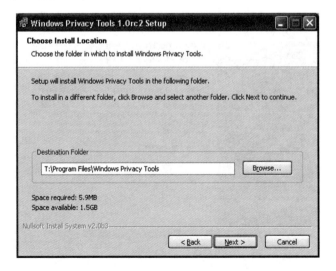

Fig. 9.12   Choose components

Fig. 9.13   Start menu folder

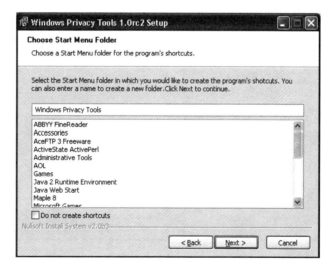

■ A 'Choose Components' window pops up to allow you to select the installation components (Figure 9.12).

■ After this choice has been made you may need to choose a start menu folder. In this case, the folder is 'Windows Privacy Tools' (Figure 9.13).

Fig. 9.14 Select additional tasks I

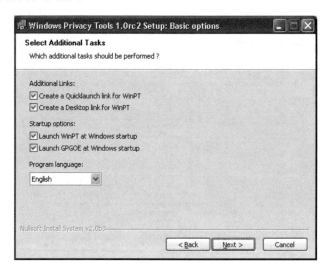

Fig. 9.15 Select additional tasks II

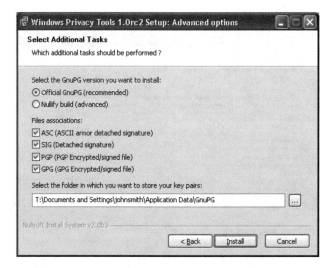

- After selecting the menu folder, the 'Select Additional Tasks' window appears to allow you to customize 'Additional Links' and 'Startup Options' (Figure 9.14).

- Next, another 'Select Additional Tasks' window appears to allow you select the version of the GnuPG you require and any file associations. Also, you can select the folder to store your public and secret key-pairs (Figure 9.15).

Fig. 9.16 The finish window

Fig. 9.17 WinPT in the System Tray

- Now the installation begins by copying all necessary files into the appropriate directories. After that a finish window appears and you can select whether you want to run WinPT or not (Figure 9.16).

- If you check the run box and click the Finish button (as in Figure 9.16), the installation process is completed and WinPT will run immediately. You will see the WinPT icon appear in the system tray as shown in Figure 9.17.

Fig. 9.18 Documentation for WinPT

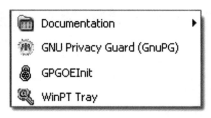

If you hover over the WinPT icon in the system tray with your mouse, the WinPT menu will appear, as shown in Figure 9.17. This menu provides instant security functions for your Windows system. Now you have finished the installation and are ready to use WinPT. If you go to `Start|All Programs|Windows Privacy Tools`, you will find the documentation of the package, as shown in Figure 9.18.

Although the documentation is still under development, it provides useful information on how to use WinPT effectively. If you activate the second option, GnuPG, a DOS window will open so that you can use GnuPG in the command line. 'GPGOEInit' option is plug-in software to allow you to use GnuPG inside Outlook Express. If you activate the final option in Figure 9.18, the WinPT icon will appear in the system tray as shown in Figure 9.17.

Now, let's see how to use WinPT to perform some basic security operations. You may be surprised at how easily and smoothly the package can be used.

9.3.2 Generating keys and key management with WinPT

Obviously, before any encryption or decryption can be performed, one of the basic security tasks is to generate the public and secret key pair.

Generating the public and secret key pair

Generating the public and secret key pair using WinPT is easy. First, you go to the system tray and activate the key manager as illustrated in Figure 9.19. The key manager window will show up as in Figure 9.20.

Inside the key manager window, go to the `Key|Generate` option to open the key generation window. In this window, complete the key generation form as illustrated in Figure 9.21. You need to enter the user name, email address and a passphrase to generate the key. Note that the information style is the same as

Fig. 9.19 The key manager

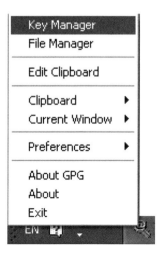

Fig. 9.20 The key manager window

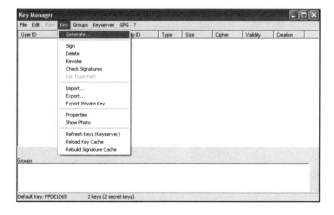

GnuPG since WinPT uses this to perform its actions. Once the `start` button is clicked, the key generation dialog begins as shown in Figure 9.22.

When both the public and secret keys have been generated, a GnuPG status dialog box is displayed to tell you that the generation process is completed (Figure 9.23). When you hit the `ok` button, a warning dialog box (Figure 9.24) is displayed to prompt you to back up the newly generated keys and key rings.

Fig. 9.21 Key generation

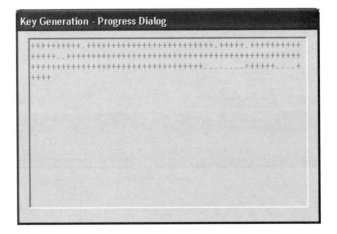

Fig. 9.22 Key generation dialog

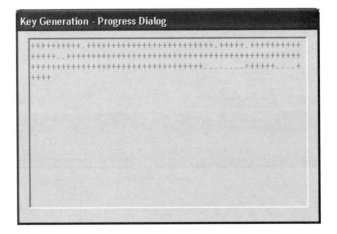

If you click the `Yes` button, both the public- and secret-key rings will be saved in files `pubring.gpg` and `secring.gpg` respectively (see Figures 9.25 and 9.26).

In order to see the newly generated keys, WinPT will ask you to reload the `keycache` (see Figure 9.27). Once you hit the `Yes` button, the generated keys are displayed inside the key manager window, as illustrated in Figure 9.28.

Fig. 9.23   Key generation completed

Fig. 9.24   Backing up the keys

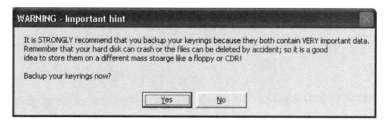

Fig. 9.25   Saving the public-key ring

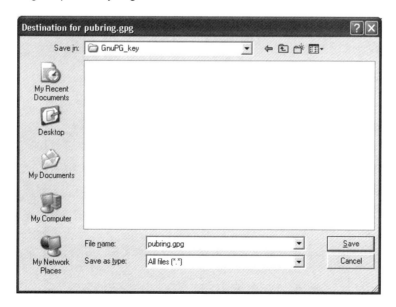

Fig. 9.26   Saving the secret-key ring

Fig. 9.27   Reload keycache

Fig. 9.28   Keys in key manager

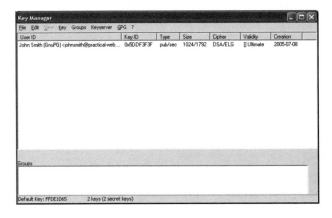

Now we have one key pair inside WinPT, it's time to import more keys into the system.

Importing keys into WinPT

Importing keys into WinPT is also simple. You can go to the `Key|Import` option, as shown in Figure 9.29, to open a dialog box called `Choose Name of the Key File`. You double click the key file that you want to import, as illustrated in Figure 9.30.

Fig. 9.29 Importing keys

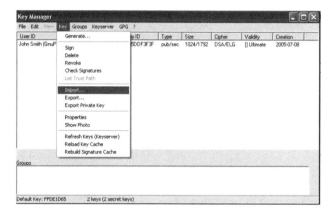

Fig. 9.30 Selecting a key to import

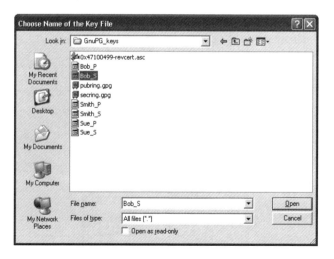

The selected key is displayed in the `File Import` dialog box (Figure 9.31). If you press the `Import` button, the key is imported into the system and a set of statistics is shown, as in Figure 9.32.

After importing Bob's public and secret keys, the key manager shows the results, as in Figure 9.33. If Bob wants to send Sue a secure email, he also needs to import Sue's public key (see Figure 9.34).

If you have a very limited number of keys, say fewer than ten, you might not have problems handling them manually using GnuPG. As your network of

Fig. 9.31 The imported key

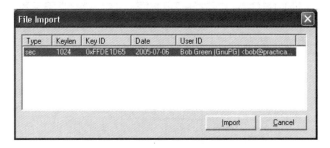

Fig. 9.32 Statistics concerning the imported key

Fig. 9.33 Bob's public and secret keys

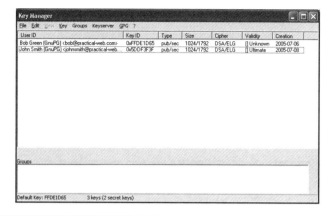

Fig. 9.34 Sue's public key

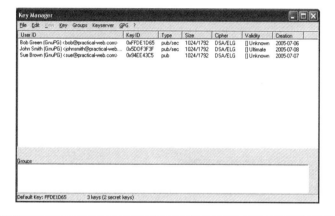

communication grows (e.g. more than 50 keys) the administration of keys soon turns out to be a nightmare. Continuing to use the command line GnuPG may not even be an option.

As you can see from Figures 9.33 and 9.34, all keys (or key pairs) are displayed in the key manager window of WinPT interactively. The visibility of keys provides a significant advantage in performing key management compared to the traditional command line GnuPG.

Key management with WinPT

Using WinPT, most key management operations can be done smoothly and effortlessly. For example, you can use your left mouse-button to highlight a key in the key manager window and click the right mouse-button to activate the key management menu, as in Figure 9.35. This menu allows you to perform many actions on the selected key.

Apart from the usual key management, such as key copying and deletion, important key information can also be extracted instantly by a mouse click. For example, if you activate the `Key Attributes` submenu, you can make a copy of the user ID, key ID and fingerprint to the clipboard for your applications (see Figure 9.36).

Fig. 9.35 Key management menu

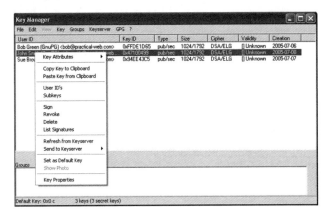

Fig. 9.36 Key management submenu

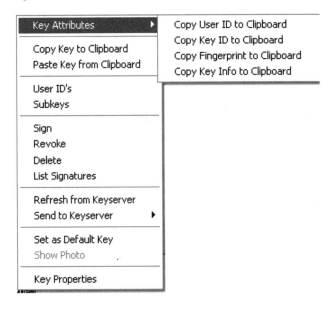

Fig. 9.37 Sending a key to a keyserver

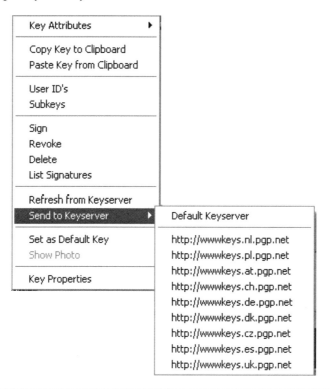

You can also send the selected key to a public-key server on the Web. This sending action and some available key servers are shown in Figure 9.37. By clicking on the `Key Property` option, you can edit the properties of a key directly (Figure 9.38). Editing key properties directly can have some undesirable effects, so be careful.

Now, let's see how to perform encryption and decryption on data in a Windows system.

9.3.3 Encryption/decryption with files, clipboard and current window

By using WinPT, there are a number of ways to encrypt/decrypt a file in a Windows system. The first method uses File Manager.

Using File Manager

The File Manager window can be activated from the WinPT icon in the system tray (see Figure 9.39). If you want to encrypt a file, you can drag and drop it from the system tray to the File Manager window.

Fig. 9.38 Editing key properties

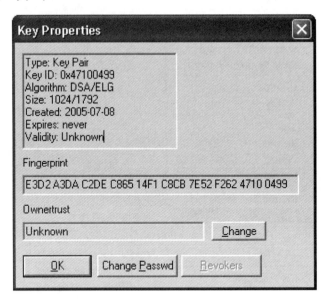

Fig. 9.39 Activating File Manager

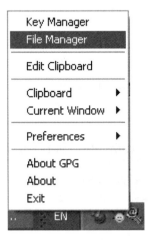

As an example, a file called `chap0821.pdf` is dragged and dropped into the File Manager window, as shown in Figure 9.40. The next step is to click the `Encrypt` option to open the `File Encrypt` window (see Figure 9.41). To perform the encryption, you will be asked to choose a key from the file encrypt window. You also have options to select `Text Output` and `Wipe Original` by checking the boxes at the bottom of the window (see Figure 9.41).

Now, WinPT encrypts the file `chap0821.pdf` and produces the ciphertext in file `chap0821.pdf.gpg`. If everything is OK, the words 'ENCRYPTED' and 'SUCCESS' will be displayed inside the File Manager window, as shown in Figure 9.42.

In addition to encryption, you can perform decryption, signing and verification operations (see Figure 9.40). All these operations are carried out in a similar way to the encryption process.

Encryption/decryption in the clipboard

Using the clipboard for encryption and decryption is also simple. First you need to copy data into the clipboard. Suppose you have typed a paragraph of text in

Fig. 9.40   Encrypting using File Manager

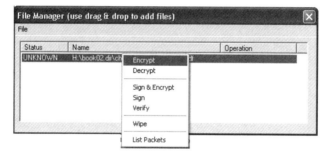

Fig. 9.41   Choosing a key for encryption

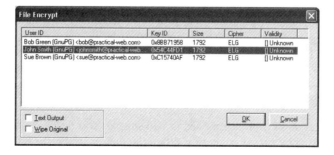

Fig. 9.42 Encryption successful

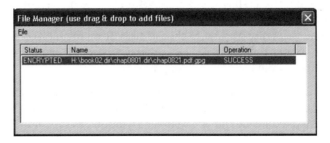

Fig. 9.43 Copying text to the clipboard

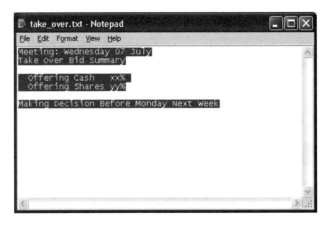

Notepad (see Figure 9.43). You highlight the text and then press Crtl+c (i.e. control and the character c together) and the text is copied to the clipboard.

To perform encryption on this data, you activate the main WinPT menu in the system tray and select the clipboard submenu, as illustrated in Figure 9.44. In the submenu, there are a number of ways of encrypting the data. If you select symmetric-key encryption, you will be prompted for a passphrase as shown in Figure 9.45. Once you have entered the passphrase, you will be asked to enter it again for confirmation. If the two passphrases are consistent, the data in the clipboard is encrypted. In this case, the ciphertext is also stored in the clipboard. You can copy the data from the clipboard to your editor, such as Notepad, by pressing Crtl+v (i.e. control and the character v together). For example, the ciphertext is copied to Notepad in Figure 9.46.

To do decryption in the clipboard is also simple. You first copy the ciphertext into the clipboard by pressing Crtl+c. When the data is in the clipboard, you activate

Fig. 9.44 Encrypting the contents of the clipboard

Fig. 9.45 Entering passphrases

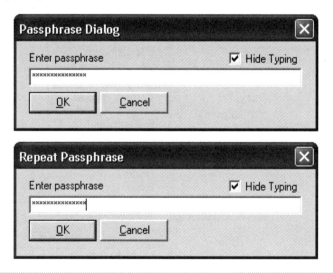

the main WinPT menu from the system tray and select the Clipboard submenu. In this submenu, you pick the option Decrypt/Verify as shown in Figure 9.47.

A decryption window, as shown in Figure 9.48, appears asking for the decryption passphrase. If you enter the passphrase correctly and press the OK button, the

Fig. 9.46 Ciphertext copied from the clipboard to Notepad

Fig. 9.47 Decryption in the clipboard

ciphertext in the clipboard will be decrypted. The result is the original message stored in the clipboard. You can copy the data from the clipboard to your application using Crtl+v.

Sometimes, using the WinPT menu in the system tray may not be the most efficient way of performing encryption/decryption in the clipboard. For this reason, WinPT provides a series of hotkeys to do the same tasks. The hotkeys are listed below.

Fig. 9.48 The decryption window

Fig. 9.49 A piece of text to be encrypted

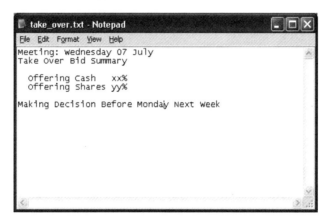

- encrypt clipboard: Ctrl+Alt+e
- decrypt/verify clipboard: Ctrl+Alt+d
- sign clipboard: Ctrl+Alt+s
- export clipboard: Ctrl+Alt+x
- import clipboard: Ctrl+Alt+i

Encryption/decryption in the current window

WinPT also supports encryption, decryption and signing functions inside the active window (or current window). The only restriction with the current WinPT version is that the contents of the window must be text-based. As well as using the options in the WinPT main menu in the system tray, an effective alternative is using hot keys as before:

- encrypt current window: `Alt+Shift+e`
- decrypt/verify current window: `Alt+Shift+d`
- sign current window: `Alt+Shift+s`

As a demonstration, consider the piece of text in Notepad as shown in Figure 9.49. When you press `Alt+Shift+e`, the text will be marked and an encryption window displayed (see Figure 9.50). In this, you can select the key for encryption.

Once the OK button is clicked, the encrypted message will be inserted back in the Notepad window as illustrated in Figure 9.51.

To perform decryption and verification in the current window, the key stroke `Alt+Shift+d` is executed. In this case, the decryption window appears asking for a passphrase to release the secret key. Once the correct passphrase is entered, as in Figure 9.52, the ciphertext is decrypted and the original message inserted back in Notepad, as in Figure 9.49.

One of the original ideas for developing PGP, OpenPGP and GnuPG was to provide a privacy tool for secure email communication. WinPT, as a result, can be considered to be an integrated security package for Windows.

Fig. 9.50 Encryption window

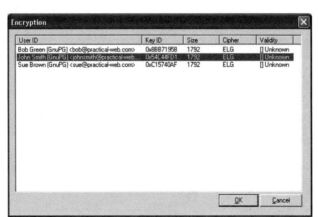

Fig. 9.51 A piece of encrypted text

Fig. 9.52 The decryption window

9.3.4 Sending and receiving secure emails with Outlook Express

As part of the integrated package, WinPT also includes some plug-in software for Outlook Express (OE), called GPGOE, to handle secure email transmission. If you install the entire package, GPGOE will be installed automatically in your system. For example, if you go to `Start|All Programs` and select Windows Privacy Tools, you will see the start up program `GPGOEInit` (Figure 9.53) for GPGOE. When you

Fig. 9.53 GPGOEInit

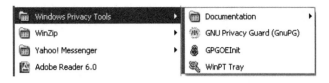

Fig. 9.54 GPGOE in the system tray

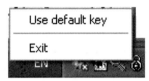

run this program, the GPGOE icon will appear in the system tray as shown in Figure 9.54.

Now, you can use GPGOE with Outlook Express. If you haven't installed GPGOE from WinPT, or want to upgrade a newer version, you may want to download the program from www.gpgoe.org and install it yourself.

Installing GPGOE as stand-alone software

Basically, the GPGOE package consists of two zip files:

`gpgoe-0.4.0-src.zip`   and   `gpgoe-0.4.1-dll.zip`

The first file contains the source code and the second is the compiled (or binary) version of the software. The current development version is 0.4, as illustrated in the `zip` files. If you don't want to compile the software yourself, you can use the compiled one directly. The package can be installed in two simple steps:

- unzip the file `gpgoe-0.4.1-dll.zip` to a temporary location;

- copy `GPGOE.dll` and `GPGOEInit.exe` to a directory such as `c:\gnupg` (it is important that these two files are in the same directory).

In fact, you can install and use GPGOE without WinPT. The only requirement for GPGOE to work is that a working version of GnuPG for Windows is running on your system. If you install GPGOE as stand-alone software, you may need to register it in the Windows Registry so that GPGOE knows where GnuPG is located. For this purpose, a Windows registration file called `gnupg-w32.reg` is provided. The contents of this file may look like:

```
1: REGEDIT4
2:
3: [HKEY_CURRENT_USER\Software\GNU\GNUPG]
4: "HomeDir"="C:\\GnuPG"
5: "gpgProgram"="C:\\GnuPG\\gpg.exe"
```

In this case, the GnuPG package and the main program `gpg.exe` are assumed to be in the directory `c:\GnuPG`. If you have installed GnuPG to a different location, you should modify the path in lines 3–4 accordingly. When you double-click this file, your Windows system will put a record into the Registry to identify the location so that the GPGOE plug-in can use this information to run GnuPG.

If you execute the initialization program `GPGOEInit`, Windows will register the file `GPGOE.dll`, and produce an icon in your system tray to show that GPGOE is installed and active. If you can see this icon, the GPGOE plug-in is properly set up for Outlook Express. To terminate the program and to unload the GPGOE plug-in you can run the `Exit` option from the icon, as shown in Figure 9.54. Now, we are ready to use Outlook Express to send and receive encrypted emails.

Sending encrypted emails with GPGOE and Outlook Express

Suppose Bob and Sue are colleagues and want to use Outlook Express to communicate encrypted emails. They both have WinPT and GPGOE installed, and Sue's public key has been imported to Bob's WinPT system.

When Bob wants to send a sensitive email (see Figure 9.55) to Sue he clicks the `Create Mail` button and the `New Message` window appears. This window has two special buttons on the toolbar. One is `Encrypt` and the other is `Sign`. The `Encrypt` button is used to encrypt the email using GnuPG public-key encryption. These two buttons are standard buttons from OE. If you cannot see them, you may need to add them by using `View|Toolbars|Customize...`

Now Bob can click the `Encrypt` button to instruct GPGOE to encrypt the email before sending it. Notice that there is a small encryption icon on the right-hand side of the `From` field.

Once the `Send` button is clicked, the email will be encrypted by Sue's public key, identified by her email address. The encrypted email will be put into the Outbox of OE as shown in Figure 9.56.

You can see that the style of the encrypted email is the same as generated by GnuPG and, in fact, is compliant with the OpenPGP (RFC 2440) standard. The versions of GnuPG and GPGOE are displayed in the second line. The actual encrypted data is displayed after a blank line.

When the `Send/Recv` button is clicked by Bob, the email is sent. Let's see how Sue can receive and decrypt the message.

Fig. 9.55 Sending an encrypted email

Fig. 9.56 The encrypted email

Fig. 9.57 Receiving an encrypted email

Receiving and decrypting an encrypted email

When Sue checks her email using OE, she will see that the message from bob@practical-web.com appears in the Inbox as shown in Figure 9.57. The contents of the email will be in encrypted form. Provided that GnuPG is installed on the system with Sue's secret key and that the plug-in software GPGOE is activated, she can double-click the email in OE to decrypt it.

Since all secret keys in GnuPG are protected by a passphrase, a `GPG Plug-in Decrypt` window appears (see Figure 9.58). This window identifies Sue's secret key and asks for a passphrase from the user. Once the correct passphrase is entered and the `OK` button clicked, the encrypted email will be decrypted and displayed in a separate window called `Message Viewer` (see Figure 9.59).

This is one way of decrypting the email from Bob. Sue could also make a copy of the encrypted email (Figure 9.57) into a text file and then decrypt it using GnuPG. Suppose the encrypted message is stored in the text file `bob_to_sue.en`. The following GnuPG command can be used for decryption:

```
gpg --output bob_to_sue.de --decrypt bob_to_sue.en
```

Again, GnuPG will ask for the passphrase before the secret key is used. The decrypted message, in this case, is output to the text file `bob_to_sue.de`. Sue can edit or just display the decrypted file using the corresponding system commands. An example of this decrypting process is shown in Figure 9.60.

Fig. 9.58 Asking for a passphrase

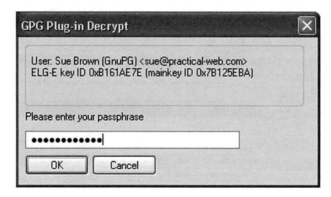

Fig. 9.59 The decrypted email

Signing emails with Outlook Express

One of the best ways of showing how to use OE to sign an email is by example. Suppose Bob has composed the email as shown in Figure 9.61. He can click the Sign button to create a small sign icon on the right-hand side of the From field to indicate that the email will be signed before being sent. When the Send button is clicked, a signing window appears so that a signature can be chosen (see Figure 9.62). Then a 'GPG Plug-in Sign' will appear asking for a passphrase.

After the correct passphrase is entered, the email will be put into the Outbox and sent to Sue.

When Sue receives the email in her Inbox (see Figure 9.63), she can double-click the message to verify the signature of the sender. Since the public key of Bob is inside

Fig. 9.60   Alternative decryption

```
Shell >gpg --output bob_to_sue.de --decrypt bob_to_sue.en

You need a passphrase to unlock the secret key for
user: "Sue Brown (GnuPG) <sue@practical-web.com>"
1792-bit ELG-E key, ID 7B125EBA, created 2005-06-15
(main key ID B161AE7E)

gpg: encrypted with 1792-bit ELG-E key, ID 7B125EBA,
created 2005-06-15 "Sue Brown (GnuPG)
<sue@practical-web.com>"

Shell >type bob_to_sue.de
Dear Sue

You are invited to take part the company
re-form meeting at 2:pm next Wednesday.

Best

Bob Green
```

Fig. 9.61   Signing an email

the GnuPG system, a verification window shows that the signature was, indeed, that of Bob Green (see Figure 9.64).

The original `Encrypt` and `Sign` buttons in Outlook Express are designed for another secure email protocol known as S/MINE. They use a different kind of digital key and are not compatible with GnuPG.

Fig. 9.62 Choosing a signature and entering a passphrase

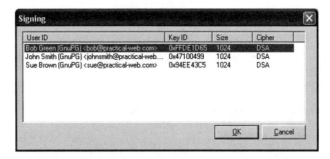

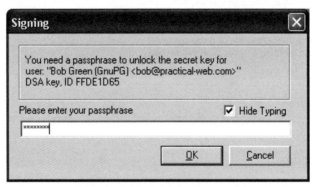

Fig. 9.63 A signed email

Fig. 9.64 Verification window

Fig. 9.65 Preparing to decrypt

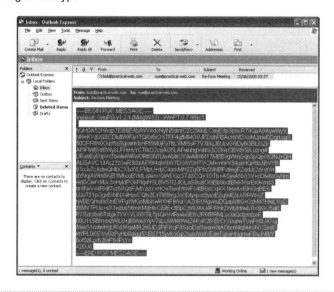

For more direct and rapid action, hotkeys are available to perform encryption and signing. For example, when Bob finishes a letter to Sue, he can use the following key strokes to sign and encrypt the letter in the clipboard. He then copies the letter from the clipboard to OE and sends it to Sue.

    sign clipboard: `Ctrl+Alt+s`
    encrypt clipboard: `Ctrl+Alt+e`

When Sue receives the message from OE, she can highlight and copy the data into the clipboard (see Figure 9.65). Then she can use the key stroke below to decrypt it in the clipboard:

    decrypt/verify clipboard: `Ctrl+Alt+d`

Fig. 9.66 Requesting a passphrase

A decryption window will pop up asking for Sue Brown's passphrase, as shown in Figure 9.66.

When the OK button is clicked, the message in the clipboard is decrypted. The result is a signed message as shown in Figure 9.67. If Sue presses Ctrl+Alt+d again, the signed message will be verified. If the public key of Bob is in Sue's system, a verify

Fig. 9.67 A signed document

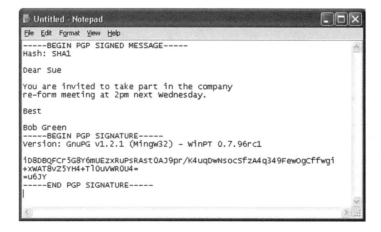

Fig. 9.68 The verification window

window will appear with the message 'The signature is good', as shown in Figure 9.68.

Based on the discussion above, we know that GnuPG, WinPT and GPGOE are fully compatible with each other, and any combination can be used to provide security applications for Windows systems.

All the security applications discussed in this chapter so far are locally based. In other words, the programs are run locally in your PC or system. Client-side (or local) applications are important since they can provide higher security strength against intruders and hacking. No intruder can hack into a system which is not networked or online via the Internet. On the other hand, client-side applications sometimes may not be practically convenient.

For example, you cannot send a secure email to someone without their public key. For the same reason, your friends or customers cannot send you sensitive emails or orders without your public key online. Publishing your public key in a keyserver may solve the distribution problem partially. Nothing is more effective than publishing your public key inside your own Web site so that any visitor can send you a secure message using your own public key. If your Web site has facilities for emailing or online ordering, secure messages or orders can reach you directly. For this reason, we need to establish GnuPG security with server technologies.

9.4 Secure emailing with server technologies

9.4.1 Calling GnuPG functions using Perl

In Chapter 7, we examined Perl scripts as CGI server techniques and their security applications for passwords, Web site protection and MySQL databases. In this section, we will concentrate on how Perl can be used with GnuPG to provide public-key technologies for email communications.

As a quick reminder about using Perl, the first two lines of a Perl script are

```
#!/usr/bin/perl
print "Content-type: text/html \n\n";
```

The first line is a classical header for a Perl script in a UNIX/LINUX environment. The purpose is to locate the Perl interpreter. In this case, the Perl interpreter `perl` is assumed to be stored in the directory `/usr/bin`. If your Perl interpreter is located in another directory, you may need to change the header to reflect the location. If you are using a Microsoft system with an IIS server and a Perl interpreter, you may use the line above as it is. For Microsoft systems with an Apache server, you may need to include the drive and location of the interpreter. The second line outputs the CGI magic string to the browser so that Web page or HTML/XHTML documents can be displayed correctly.

Perl is a powerful general programming language. It allows you to call and run system functions, commands and even other scripts. For example, you can run a command and send the result to screen by

```
print `command`;
```

where the command inside the quotation marks is the name of the executable command or program to be run by the Perl script. Note that the symbol ` above is not the normal single quotation mark. Usually it is the key above the `Tab` key on your keyboard.

For example, `ex09-12.php` is a complete Perl script to display the current date and time by calling the system (UNIX/LINUX) command date.

```
Example: ex09-12.pl

1: #!/usr/bin/perl
2: print "Content-type: text/html \n\n";
3: print "The Date and Time is =";
4: print `/bin/date`;
```

If this Perl page is stored in a Web server, such as www.pws-ex.com it can be run directly by a browser using the HTTP command:

```
http://www.pws-ex.com/ex09-12.pl
```

In a UNIX/LINUX system, the date function is usually located in the directory `/bin/date`. The function `date` returns the current date and time to the browser window. If you are using Windows, you can replace line 4 by the following two lines:

```
print `date /T`;
print `time /T`;
```

where `date /T` is a DOS command to display the current date. In order to use system function calls, you need to know what kind of system is on the server and what kinds of system functions are available. Obviously, you cannot call Windows functions or commands inside a UNIX/LINUX server system or vice versa.

For our purposes one of the important reasons for calling system functions is to call GnuPG functions so that public-key security can be achieved at the CGI or server level. Consider the simple page listed in `ex09-13.pl`.

Example: ex09-13.pl

```
 1: #! /usr/bin/perl
 2: print ("Content-type: text/html\n\n");
 3:
 4: print << "mypage";
 5: <?xml version="1.0" encoding="iso-8859-1"?>
 6: <!DOCTYPE html PUBLIC "-//W3C//DTD XHTML 1.0 Transitional//EN"
 7: "http://www.w3.org/TR/xhtml1/DTD/xhtml1-transitional.dtd">
 8: <html xmlns="http://www.w3.org/1999/xhtml" xml:lang="en" lang="en">
 9: <head><title>Example: ex09-13.pl</title></head>
10: <style>.txtSt{font-size:14pt;color:#ffff00;
                  font-family:arial}</style>
11: <body style="background:#000088;color:#ffff00;font-family:arial;
12:  font-size:22pt;font-weight:bold;text-align:center">
13: Calling GnuPG Functions With Perl Script <br /><br />
14: <pre style="font-size:16pt;font-weight:bold;text-align:left">
15: mypage
16:
17: print `gpg --help`;
18: print "</pre></bod></html>";
```

This demonstrates how easy it is to call GnuPG functions using a Perl script. After the Perl header and CGI magic string in lines 1–2, a complete XHTML page is sent to the browser for rendering (lines 4–18). The main statement of this page is the print function in line 17:

```
print `gpg --help`;
```

Fig. 9.69 Using GnuPG with Perl I

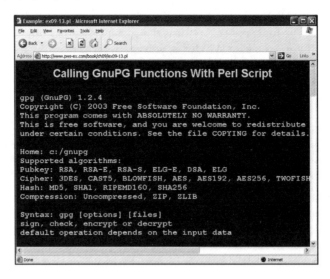

It calls the GnuPG program `gpg` with the argument `--help`. As a result, a listing of options and explanations of `gpg` are returned and displayed by the browser. A screenshot of this example is shown in Figure 9.69. If you change line 17 to

```
print `gpg -list-key`;
```

you display all the public keys of the GnuPG system in the Web server (see Figure 9.70).

Now we know how to call GnuPG functions using Perl. Before we can use it to encrypt and sign emails, a basic knowledge of sending email using Perl is necessary.

9.4.2 Using `sendmail` and SMTP with Perl

Basically, there are two popular ways of sending emails using Perl. The first is to use a mailing agent called `sendmail` and the second is to use a Simple Mail Transfer Protocol (SMTP) mail server. The application `sendmail` is a popular mail program available in almost all UNIX/LINUX environments. Some books are dedicated entirely to this program. Using SMTP to send email is more platform-independent. The requirement is the address of the SMTP server.

Using `sendmail` with Perl

Suppose the program `sendmail` is located in the `/usr/lib` directory. To call `sendmail` from Perl the following program framework in `ex09-14.pl` is frequently used.

Fig. 9.70 Using GnuPG with Perl II

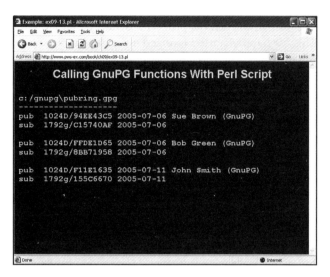

Example: ex09-14.pl – An email framework with Perl

```perl
 1: #!/usr/bin/perl
 2: use warnings;
 3: use CGI qw(:standard);
 4:
 5: print "Content-type:text/html\n\n";
 6: open (USRMAIL, "| /usr/sbin/sendmail -oi -n -t" );
 7:
 8: print USRMAIL << "usr_message";
 9: To: johnbrown\@practical-web.com
10: From: johnsmith\@practical-web.com
11: Subject:Sending Email with Perl
12:
13: Dear John:
14:
15: This is testing Email from johnsmith@practical-web.com to
16: johnbrown@practical-web.com using Perl.
17:
18: JohnSmith
19: usr_message
20: close USRMAIL;
```

After the usual CGI and Perl headers, the `open` statement in line 6 activates the `sendmail` program located in the `/usr/sbin` directory. The parameters associated with `sendmail` are used to convert the program as a file handle (or stream) with the name `USRMAIL`. This file handle is used to insert an entire email message by using the `here` document feature of Perl. The `close` statement in line 20 terminates the file handle.

The information in the `To` and `From` fields can be any acceptable email address. The forward slash before @ in line 9 is a requirement in order to generate a proper @ symbol.

In this example, all the email data are hard-coded into the Perl script, and this arrangement is not very practical. For a more practical emailing page, consider `ex09-15.htm`.

```
Example: ex09-15.htm - A generating page to send email with Perl
 1: <head><title>ex09-15.pl</title></head>
 2: <style>
 3:  .tx01{font-size:14pt;color:#ffff00;font-weight:bold}
 4:  .tx02{font-family:arial;font-size:14pt;background:#ffffff;
 5:       color:#000000;width:400px}
 6:  .butSt{background-color:#aaffaa;font-family:arial;
             font-weight:bold;
 7:          font-size:14pt;color:#008800;width:120px;height:30px}
 8: </style>
 9: <body style="background:#000088;font-family:arial;color:#ffff00">
10: <div align="center" style="font-size:18pt;font-weight:bold">
11: Sending An Email with <br />Perl Script
12: <form method="post" action="ex09-15.pl">
13: <table class="tx01">
14:  <tr><td>From:</td>
15:     <td><input class="tx02" type="text" name="from" id="from"
16:      value="johnsmith\@practical-web.com"></td></tr>
17:  <tr><td>To:</td>
18:     <td><input class="tx02" type="text" name="to" id="to"
19:      value="sue\@practical-web.com"></td></tr>
20:  <tr><td>Subject:</td>
21:     <td><input class="tx02" type="text" name="subject" id="subject"
22:      value="A Testing Email"></td></tr>
23:  <tr><td valign="top">Message:</td>
24:     <td><textarea name="message" id="message" class="tx02"
25:         rows="6" cols="40" wrap="yes">This is a
                test</textarea></td></tr>
26:  <tr><td><input class="butSt" type="submit" value="Submit"></td>
27:     <td><input class="butSt" type="reset" value="Reset"></td></tr>
28: </table>
29: </form>
30: </div></body>
```

This is a simple interface to get information for emailing. The page contains three text boxes and one text area. The text boxes (lines 14–22) are used to get the information for the `From`, `To` and `Subject` fields. The text area defined in lines 24–25 obtains the contents of the email.

Once the `Submit` button is clicked, the associated Perl script `ex09-15.pl` is run (line 12). This script will capture all the data and deliver the email using the mail program `sendmail`.

```
Example: ex09-15.pl - Perl script for ex09-15.htm

 1: #!/usr/local/bin/perl
 2: use CGI qw( :standard );
 3:
 4: $from = param( "from" );
 5: $to = param( "to" );
 6: $subject = param( "subject" );
 7: $message = param( "message" );
 8:
 9: print ("Content-type: text/html\n\n");
10: open (USRMAIL, "| /usr/sbin/sendmail -oi -n -t" );
11:
12: print USRMAIL << "usr_message";
13: To: $to
14: From: $from
15: Subject: $subject
16:
17: $message
18:
19: usr_message
20: close USRMAIL;
21:
22: print << "mypage";
23:    <?xml version="1.0" encoding="iso-8859-1"?>
24:    <!DOCTYPE html PUBLIC "-//W3C//DTD XHTML 1.0 Transitional//EN"
25:       "http://www.w3.org/TR/xhtml1/DTD/xhtml1-transitional.dtd">
26:    <html xmlns="http://www.w3.org/1999/xhtml" xml:lang="en" lang="en">
27:    <head><title>Sending Email Using Sendmail </title></head>
28:    <body style="background:#000088">
29:    <div style="font-family:arial;font-size:18pt;color:#ffff00">
30:        Your Email has been sent to <br />$to
31:    </div></body></html>
32: mypage
```

Fig. 9.71 Sending an email with Perl

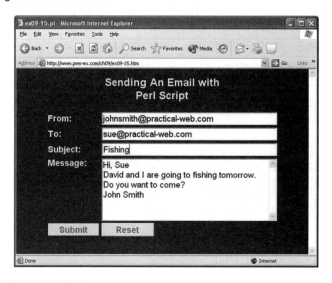

After the Perl header in lines 1–2, the email information `From`, `To`, `Subject` and `Message` are captured into variables `$from`, `$to`, `$subject` and `$message` respectively (lines 4–7). Line 10 activates the mail program `sendmail` and opens a file handle called `USRMAIL`. The entire email is passed to `USRMAIL` in lines 13–18 and sent to the recipient specified by the variable `$from`. After the email is sent, a small Web page is generated in lines 22–32. This page will be displayed by the local browser to state that the email has been delivered to the recipient. This Perl script can be considered as a general page for sending email, and screenshots are shown in Figures 9.71 and 9.72. The screenshot of the received email in Outlook Express is provided in Figure 9.73.

If for any reason the `sendmail` program is not available, you can still use Perl to send your email if the name of your SMTP server is known.

Sending email with SMTP

SMTP is a popular protocol for sending email messages between servers. The machine running SMTP is usually called an SMTP server. Your network administrator or ISP should be able to provide you with the identity (or IP address) of the SMTP server. You need this information to set up a mail client, such as Outlook Express, before you can use it for emailing.

One of the quickest ways of developing a page to perform emailing using an SMTP server is to make a copy of `ex09-15.htm` calling it `ex09-16.htm`. In the new file, modify the following line:

```
12: <form method="post" action="ex09-16.pl">
```

Fig. 9.72 The acknowledgement

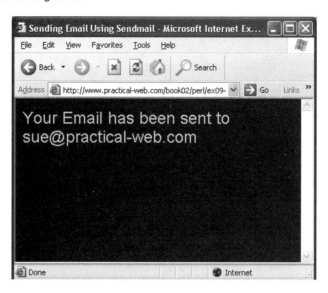

Fig. 9.73 The received email

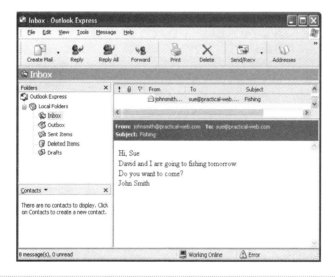

The modified statement in line 12 above makes sure that the program `ex09-16.pl` is run once the `Submit` button is clicked. This is the main engine of this example. It will collect the email information and pass it to the specified SMTP server for the actual delivery.

Example: ex09-16.pl – Sending email using an SMTP server

```perl
 1: #!/usr/local/bin/perl
 2:
 3: use warnings;
 4: use Net::SMTP;
 5: use CGI qw( :standard );
 6:
 7: my $from = param( "from" );
 8: my $to = param( "to" );
 9: my $subject = param( "subject" );
10: my $message = param( "message" );
11:
12: print ("Content-type: text/html\n\n");
13: my $smtp = Net::SMTP->new ("mail.practical-web.com")
14:    or die("Cannot connect to SMTP server: $!");
15:
16: $smtp->mail( "$from" );
17: $smtp->to( "$to" );
18: .
19: $smtp->data();
20: $smtp->datasend( "From: $from\n" );
21: $smtp->datasend( "To: $to\n" );
22: $smtp->datasend( "Subject: $subject\n\n" );
23: $smtp->datasend( "$message\n" );
24: $smtp->dataend();
25: $smtp->quit();
26:
27: print << "mypage";
28:    <?xml version="1.0" encoding="iso-8859-1"?>
29:    <!DOCTYPE html PUBLIC "-//W3C//DTD XHTML 1.0 Transitional//EN"
30:       "http://www.w3.org/TR/xhtml1/DTD/xhtml1-transitional.dtd">
31:    <html xmlns="http://www.w3.org/1999/xhtml" xml:lang="en" lang="en">
32:    <head><title>Sending Email Using SMTP Server</title></head>
33:    <body style="background:#000088">
34:    <div style="font-family:arial;font-size:18pt;color:#ffff00">
35:       Your Email has been sent to $to
36:    </div></body></html>
37: mypage
```

In order to connect to an SMTP server, you need an external module called NET::SMTP (line 4), which can be found inside a library called libnet. Most Perl implementations will have this package installed. For some systems, you may need to install it yourself. Suppose the identity of an SMTP server that you can use is mail.practical-web.com.

After the collection of data from the interface (lines 7–10), a connection to the server (line 13–14) is made and the connection object is assigned to a local variable $smtp. Since $smtp is an object, you can call all its member functions directly. The first function associated with $smtp is $smtp->mail("$from"). This function tells the server who is the sender of the email. The function $smtp->to("$to") identifies the recipient. The remaining series of function calls (lines 19–25) are used to create a data section and fill in the necessary To, From, Subject and Message fields of an email. The function dataend() terminates the data section and quit() disconnects the SMTP server. The screenshots of this example are very similar to those in Figures 9.71 to 9.73.

If you have GnuPG installed in your Web server, you can use it, together with the Perl script discussed above, to encrypt the email that you are going to send.

9.4.3 Sending encrypted emails using GnuPG and Perl

Suppose a working version of GnuPG is installed in your server system and you know the location of the GnuPG program gpg. (Your network administrator or ISP should be able to provide you with the information.) There follows an example showing how anyone can send you email encrypted by your GnuPG public key.

First, an XHTML interface is needed to collect information about the sender. This page is listed in ex09-17.htm.

```
Example: ex09-17.htm – Sending public-key encrypted email with Perl

 1: <head><title>Sending Encrypted Email ex09-17.htm</title></head>
 2: <style>
 3:  .tx01{font-size:14pt;color:#ffff00;font-weight:bold}
 4:  .tx02{font-family:arial;font-size:14pt;background:#ffffff;
 5:       color:#000000;width:400px}
 6:  .butSt{background-color:#aaffaa;font-family:arial;
            font-weight:bold;
 7:       font-size:14pt;color:#008800;width:120px;height:30px}
 8: </style>
 9: <body style="background:#000088;font-family:arial;color:#ffff00">
10: <div align="center" style="font-size:18pt;font-weight:bold">
11:  Encrypted Email To John Smith <br /> GnuPG Public-Key
12:  <form method="post" action="ex09-17.pl">
13:  <table class="tx01">
14:   <tr><td>From:</td>
15:      <td><input class="tx02" type="text" name="from" id="from"
16:         value="sue@practical-web.com"></td></tr>
17:   <tr><td>Subject:</td>
```

```
18:        <td><input class="tx02" type="text" name="subject" id="subject"
19:          value="Secret Message"></td></tr>
20:    <tr><td valign="top">Message:</td>
21:        <td><textarea name="message" id="message" class="tx02" rows="6"
22:          cols="40" wrap="yes">Dear John
23: The business is not good and
24: we need to talk.
25: Sue Brown</textarea></td></tr>
26:    <tr><td><input class="butSt" type="submit" value="Submit"></td>
27:        <td><input class="butSt" type="reset" value="Reset"></td></tr>
28:    </table>
29:    </form>
30: </div></body>
```

Again, this is a simple Web page containing two text boxes, one text area and two action buttons. The first text box defined in lines 15–16 is to get the information (or email address) of the sender. The second text box is to get the subject of the email. The text area specified in lines 21–25 allows you to type in a message. In order to test this example, a test message is included.

Since this page is designed to send you (John Smith) an encrypted email with John Smith's GnuPG public key automatically there is no need for the user to enter the email address. Once the Submit button is clicked, all data are submitted to the Perl script called ex09-17.pl. The functions of this are:

- capture and store the message content into a file (e.g. ex09-17.txt);

- encrypt the file ex09-17.txt using John Smith's public key;

- send the encrypted result (stored in file ex09-17.gpg) to John Smith using Perl;

- display an acknowledgement after the email is sent.

After the Perl header and CGI magic string in lines 1–2, the information concerning the From, Subject and Message fields is captured by lines 6–8. Note that the email address of the recipient, John Smith, is hard-coded as illustrated at line 5 – you should replace the address by where you want to send the email.

The statements in lines 10–13 of ex09-17.pl open the file ex09-17.txt and the contents of the email are written into it. Line 15 composes an encryption command using GnuPG:

```
gpg -a -o -e --batch --yes ex09-17.gpg -r $to ex09-17.txt
```

This command will encrypt the file ex09-17.txt using the public key of the recipient stored in variable $to (i.e. johnsmith@practical-web.com). The encryption result is stored in file ex09-17.gpg as specified by the options -a -o. We have assumed that the GnuPG program gpg is located or is accessible in the default path.

```
Example: ex09-17.pl - Sending encrypted email using GnuPG and Perl
                                                            (Part I)

 1: #!/usr/bin/perl
 2: use CGI qw( :standard );
 3: print ("Content-type: text/html\n\n");
 4: use CGI qw( :standard );
 5: $to      = "johnsmith\@practical-web.com"; ##Should be your address
 6: $from    = param( "from" );
 7: $subject = param( "subject" );
 8: $message = param( "message" );
 9:
10: open(outfile, ">ex09-17.txt")
11:    or die("Cannot Open File.. Error");
12: print(outfile $message);
13: close(outfile);
14:
15: $commSt = "gpg -a -e --batch --yes -o ex09-17.gpg -r $to ex09-17.txt";
16: print '$commSt';
```

If your gpg program is stored in another directory, you should include the path in front of the gpg program. The options --batch --yes instruct the gpg never to ask questions and to take 'yes' for an answers. The statement in line 16 executes this GnuPG command.

Now we have the encrypted email in file ex09-17.gpg. The next step is to read it back using a Perl script and send it to the recipient, johnsmith@practical-web.com.

Opening a file for reading and writing using Perl is not difficult and has been discussed in Section 7.3.1. Sending an email with Perl was covered in Section 9.4.2. By combining these two processes, a process for sending an encrypted email is established. Consider part II of ex09-17.pl.

Lines 17–18 define two variables $message and $dMessage. Variable $message will be used to store the contents of the encrypted email. In this case, it will be sent to johnsmith@practical-web.com. The variable $dMessage stores the encrypted email in displayable format so that it can be displayed by the browser as an acknowledgement.

The open statement in line 19 opens the file ex09-17.gpg for reading. The while-loop will read the file line by line into variable $st. This string $st is added to the message variable $message at line 22, so that $message effectively contains the full content of the encrypted email. Each $st is also added to $dMessage with a line break <br /> in line 23 so that $dMessage can be displayed by a browser. Lines 27–35 send the encrypted email stored in $message to the recipient $to (i.e. johnsmith@practical-web.com).

```
17: $message ="";
18: $dMessage="";
19: open(infile, "<ex09-17.gpg")
20:   or die("Cannot Open File.. Error");
21: while( my $st =<infile>) {
22:   $message .= $st;
23:   $dMessage .= $st . "<br />";
24: }
25: close(infile);
26:
27: open (USRMAIL, "| /usr/sbin/sendmail -oi -n -t" );
28: print USRMAIL << "usr_message";
29: To: $to
30: From: $from
31: Subject: $subject
32:
33: $message
34: usr_message
35: close USRMAIL;
36:
```

Part III of this example displays an acknowledgement so that we know that the
encrypted email has been sent. The Perl script is shown below.

Example: Continuation of ex09-17.pl   (Part III)

```
37: print << "mypage";
38: <?xml version="1.0" encoding="iso-8859-1"?>
39: <!DOCTYPE html PUBLIC "-//W3C//DTD XHTML 1.0 Transitional//EN"
40:    "http://www.w3.org/TR/xhtml1/DTD/xhtml1-transitional.dtd">
41: <html xmlns="http://www.w3.org/1999/xhtml" xml:lang="en" lang="en">
42: <head><title>Sending Email Using Sendmail </title></head>
43: <body style="font-family:'courier new';font-size:18pt;
44:        font-weight:bold;text-align:center">
45:   Your Encrypted Email Has Been Sent To <br /><br />
46: <div style="font-size:12pt;text-align:left">
47:   To: $to <br />
48:   From: $from <br />
49:   Subject: $subject <br /><br />
50:   $dMessage
51: </div></body></html>
52: mypage
```

This script fragment is, in fact, a simple Web page to display the information $to, $from, $subject and $message on the browser window. Screenshots of this example in action are shown in Figures 9.74 and 9.75.

Once you have filled in the form, as in Figure 9.74, and the Submit button is clicked, the email will be encrypted and sent. An acknowledgement, together with the encrypted email, is displayed (see Figure 9.75).

Fig. 9.74   Sending encrypted email I

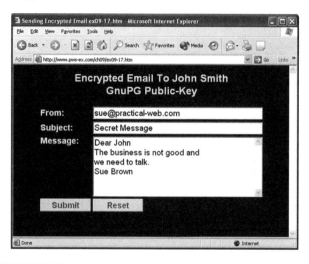

Fig. 9.75   Sending encrypted email II

When John Smith turns on his computer and checks his email, this encrypted email from sue@practical-web.com will appear in the Inbox inside Outlook Express as illustrated in Figure 9.76.

To decrypt this email, John Smith can copy and paste it into an editor such as Notepad (see Figure 9.77). If WinPT is installed on John Smith's system, the decryption can be performed by simply pressing the hotkey sequence

```
Alt+Shift+d
```

Fig. 9.76   Receiving encrypted email

Fig. 9.77   Encrypted email in an active window

Recall that this command performs decryption on the current window. The decryption requires the secret key of John smith. Since every GnuPG secret key is protected by a passphrase, a decryption window will pop up asking for the passphrase (see Figure 9.78). When the correct passphrase is entered and the OK button clicked, the email will be decrypted by the secret key. The result is put back into the current window, as shown in Figure 9.79).

Example ex09-17.pl is a framework for sending encrypted email using GnuPG. The coding is for demonstration purposes. Some of you may realize that both the original and encrypted emails are not deleted after use. From a security point of view, this may cause a major risk. Also, if two users access ex09-17.pl at the same

Fig. 9.78 Asking for a passphrase

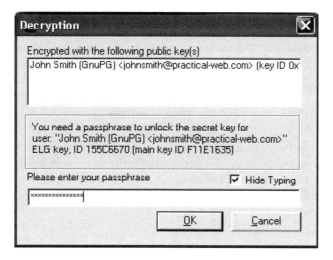

Fig. 9.79 The decrypted email

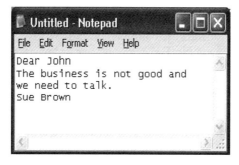

time, the files `ex09-17.txt` and `ex09-17.gpg` may be corrupted or confused. For a more professional approach, these two problems should be fixed.

In general, the process for sending secure emails can be summarized as follows.

- Develop an interface to get the email information (such as From, To, Message) from the user.

- Save the message into a file.

- Call the GnuPG `gpg` program to encrypt the message file producing the encrypted file.

- Read the encrypted file back as a secure message.

- Send the email with the secure message.

If you are using a Windows system, the mailer program `sendmail` may not be available to you. In this case, you may need to use SMTP to deliver secure email. Using example `ex09-16.pl`, this can be done with some simple modifications.

Now we know how to handle encrypted emails using Perl. Next we want to do similar things with PHP script.

9.4.4 Using GnuPG and PHP for secure emailing

Compared to Perl, the emailing mechanism of PHP is simpler. You don't need any additional software. In other words, whether your mailing agent is `sendmail` or SMTP, the installation of PHP includes instructions to configure them correctly. Thanks to the PHP development group, emailing became one of the standard language features of PHP.

Sending emails with PHP

The PHP language provides a standard command to make the process of sending email easy. This command is called `mail` and has the calling syntax

```
bool mail (string $to, string $subject, string $message
    [, string $additional_headers ])
```

The first three parameters are compulsory and are used to specify the To, Subject and Message fields. For example, one of the simplest ways to use the function `mail()` is

```
mail("johnsmith@practical-web.com","sue@practical-web.com",
  "Hi, Sue \nDo you want to go fishing tomorrow? \nJohn Smith");
```

The simplicity of this `mail()` function provides a powerful tool for programming and handling email in your applications directly. If the optional fourth string argument in `mail()` is presented, this is inserted at the end of the header. This is used to add extra headers, and many advanced applications are based on this structure. In fact, we will use this interesting feature to develop an email page to deliver attachments in Section 9.5.3.

The `mail()` function returns `true` if the email has been sent successfully, otherwise a `false` value is returned. This `mail()` function is generally regarded as the basic PHP framework for sending email. Let's consider how to use `mail()` to deliver encrypted emails.

Sending encrypted emails with GnuPG and PHP

In order to send an encrypted email, it is important that a working copy of GnuPG is installed on your server system and that the location of the GnuPG program `gpg` is available. The next step is to develop an interface page to obtain the sender's information. For simplicity, we use the same structure as in Web page `ex09-17.htm`. Make a copy of this and call it `ex09-18.htm`, modifying the following line:

```
12: <form method="post" action="ex09-18.php">
```

This statement will make sure that the PHP script `ex09-18.php` is run when the OK button is clicked. Like the Perl case, the functions of this PHP script are:

- capture and store the message content in a file (e.g. `ex09-18.txt`)

- encrypt the file `ex09-18.txt` using John Smith's public key;

- send the encrypted result (stored in file `ex09-18.gpg`) to John Smith using PHP;

- display an acknowledgement after the email is sent.

Compared to the Perl case, the PHP script `ex09-18.php` is simpler.

First, any codes between the bracket pair `<?php` and `?>` will be processed by the PHP pre-processor in the server before reaching the browser. The main script block of this program is defined in lines 8–36. Also, another feature of PHP is that all CGI variables (i.e. variables or data submitted by a form) are converted to PHP variables automatically. In other words, when the OK button in the Web page `ex09-18.htm` is clicked, the form data of the page is submitted together with the following variables defined:

```
$from,    $subject,    and    $message
```

These variables can be used directly inside the PHP script `ex09-18.php`. Therefore, only the `$to` field is defined in line 9 to specify the recipient. Lines 10–11 specify two file names into variables `$fileOr` and `$fileEn` representing the original and encrypted files. The file operations in lines 13–15 write the contents of the original email into file `$fileOr`. The main encryption statement is in line 17:

```
system("gpg -e -a --batch --yes -o $fileEn -r $to $fileOr");
```

Example: ex09-18.php - PHP script for page ex09-18.htm

```php
 1: <?PHP echo"<?";?>xml version="1.0"
    encoding="iso-8859-1"<?PHP echo"?>";?>
 2: <!DOCTYPE html PUBLIC "-//W3C//DTD XHTML 1.0 Transitional//EN"
 3:     "http://www.w3.org/TR/xhtml1/DTD/xhtml1-transitional.dtd">
 4: <html xmlns="http://www.w3.org/1999/xhtml"
    xml:lang="en" lang="en">
 5: <head><title>Sending Encrypted Email With PHP</title></head>
 6: <body style="text-align:center;font-family:'courier
    new';font-size:18pt;
 7:  font-weight:bold">
 8: <?php
 9: $to = "johnsmith@practical-web.com";
10: $fileOr = "ex09-18.txt";
11: $fileEn = "ex09-18.gpg";
12:
13: $fp = fopen($fileOr, "w");
14: fputs($fp, $message);
15: fclose($fp);
16:
17: system("gpg -e -a --batch --yes -o $fileEn -r $to $fileOr");
18:
19: $fd = fopen($fileEn, "r");
20: $mailEn = fread($fd, filesize($fileEn));
21: fclose($fd);
22:
23: $mailheaders = "From: $from\n";
24: mail($to,$subject,$mailEn,$mailheaders);
25:
26: echo "Your Encrypted Email Has Been Sent To <br />
27: <pre style='font-size:12pt;font-weight:bold;text-align:left'>
28: To: $to
29: From: $from
30: Subject: $subject
31:
32: $mailEn</pre>";
33:
34: unlink($fileOr);
35: unlink($fileEn);
36: ?>
37: </body>
38: </html>
```

This command calls the GnuPG program `gpg` to encrypt file `$fileOr` and output the encryption result to file `$fileEn` using the public key specified by the recipient `$to`. The `system()` function is a general command in PHP to call an external program, and this is an ideal situation to use it. After the email is encrypted, lines 19–21 open and read the contents of the encrypted file into variable `$mailEn`. Together with the `$to`, `$subject` and `$mailheaders`, an email is sent to recipient `$to` by the execution of the `mail()` function in lines 23–24. After the email is sent, an acknowledgement is displayed on the browser screen by the statements in lines 26–32. Finally, for security reasons, the files `$fileOr` and `$fileEn` are deleted in lines 34–35. Screenshots are shown in Figures 9.80 and 9.81.

Note that the details of the encrypted message in Figure 9.81 are different from those in Figure 9.75. This is because the program `gpg` produces different results for every encryption, even if the input plaintext is the same. When John Smith checks his email, the encrypted email from Sue will appear in the Inbox in Outlook Express as illustrated in Figure 9.82.

If John Smith has WinPT installed on his machine, there are a number of ways of decrypting the message. For example he can copy and paste the message into Notepad and press the hotkey sequence

```
Alt+Shift+d
```

Fig. 9.80 Encrypted email with PHP

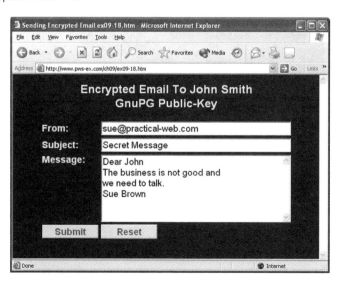

Fig. 9.81 The encrypted email

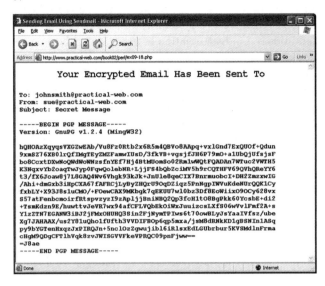

This hotkey command will perform decryption on the current window. The decryption requires the secret key and passphrase from John, and a decryption window will pop up asking for it (see Figure 9.83). When the correct passphrase is entered and the OK button clicked, the email will be

Fig. 9.82 Receiving encrypted email

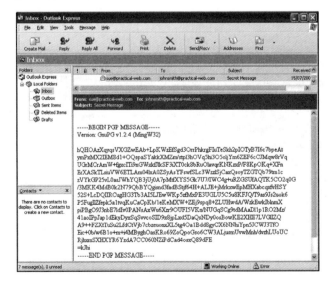

Fig. 9.83 Asking for a passphrase

Fig. 9.84 The decrypted email

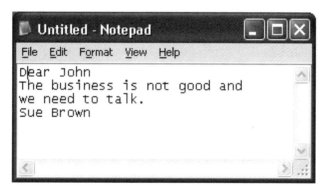

decrypted. The result is put back into the current window as shown in Figure 9.84.

Now we know how to encrypt email in text form, but in order to have a completely secure email system the ability to encrypt attachments is needed.

9.5 Sending secure attachments with server technologies

9.5.1 MIME format: the construction of attachments

There is no doubt that the attachment is a crucial component of many email systems. In addition to text messages, attachments allow binary files including Microsoft Office documents, photos, music and movies to be transmitted over the Internet and Web. Before we can discuss attachment encryption, let's see how attachments work in an email system.

To incorporate attachments into email, you need the so-called 'Multiple Internet Mail Extension' (MIME) format. MIME is an important aspect of email and is a subject in its own right. It was first introduced in 1996 to specify a standard for Internet messaging known as RFC 2045. The specification was soon widely adopted by all email systems. Generally speaking, it is a protocol for determining the structure, style and transmission of emails. For obvious reasons, details of the MIME specifications are beyond the scope of this book, and only a brief description of MIME and how to use it for attachments is discussed. One of the best ways to understand the MIME format is to examine the structure of an email.

The MIME format of an email

Whether you are using `sendmail`, SMTP or the PHP `mail()` function, the style and structure of an email are basically the same. For example, consider the following PHP `mail()` function:

```
mail( "sue@practical-web.com",
      "Hello",
      "Hi, John \n How are you today? \n
      John Smith",
      "From: johnsmith@practical-web.com")
```

It is easy to see that this command delivers a text email from John Smith to Sue. Depending on the mailer you are using, the format of this email will contain a header and a body similar to that shown below.

```
Example: Standard email

1: To:      sue@practical-web.com
2: From:    johnsmith@practical-web.com
3: Subject: Hello
4: Content-type: text/plain; charset="iso-8859-1"
5: Content-transfer-encoding: 7bit
6:
7: Hi, John
8: How are you today?
9: JohnSmith
10:
```

Lines 1–5 are the headers. Apart from the `To`, `From` and `Subject` fields, the header statement in line 4 specifies the email as a plain text document using a character set the same as US ASCII code. The statement in line 5 instructs the mailer to transfer the email with 7-bit encoding. Lines 7–9 are the contents of the body – they are separated by one blank line. The header of this email determines the structure, style and transmission and is generally called the MIME format. Now, let's see what happens if this email carries an attachment.

The MIME format with a text file as an attachment

In fact, MIME is just a set of rules for defining mail headers and boundary lines within your mail message, so that a MIME-compliant mail-reader can view the various portions accordingly. Suppose the email above carries a text file as an attachment, called `text.txt`. The raw structure and format of the email is similar to that listed below.

```
Example: email with MIME type

 1: To: johnsmith@practical-web.com
 2: From: sue@practical-web.com
 3: Subject: Hello
 4: MIME-Version: 1.0
 5: Content-type: multipart/mixed;
 6: boundary="my.boundary_string.754821478"
 7:
 8: This is a MIME encoded message.
 9:
10: --my.boundary_string.754821478
11: Content-type:text/plain; charset="iso-8859-1"
12: Content-transfer-encoding: 7bit
13:
14: Hi, John
15: How are you today?
16: JohnSmith
17: (PS) I have attached a document for you.
18:
19: --my.boundary_string.754821478
20: Content-Type: application/octet-stream; name="mytext"
21: Content-Disposition: attachment; filename="text.txt"
22: Content-Transfer-Encoding: 7bit
23:
24: This text is the contents of attached file text.txt
25:
26: --my.boundary_string.754821478-
```

Lines 1–6 are the headers in MIME format. After the usual email fields To, From and Subject, the version of the MIME format is specified in line 4. The Content-type of this email is multipart/mixed so that applications and attachments, as well as text messages, can be mixed together. In order to separate different content, a boundary string such as my.boundary_string.754821478 is specified in line 6. This boundary string can be any string to identify the boundary. You can also specify a comment for the header, as illustrated in lines 7–9. Now the email body can have multiple sections, each being separated by the boundary string.

The email body of this example consists of two parts. The first (lines 10–18) is a normal text message. The second (lines 20–26) contains the data of an application. The name of the application is mytext. In fact, it is a file attachment and the file name is text.txt. This attachment is transmitted as a stream of octet data in ASCII (7-bit) encoding. After one blank line in line 23, the actual file data of text.txt is read in and displayed. If you want to attach another file or attachment, you can issue a blank line and the boundary string again. To terminate the attachment, you should issue the boundary string with a hyphen at the end, as illustrated in line 26. Now, if you send this email to a MIME-compliant mail reader, the message and attachment will show up in your chosen mail client, such as Outlook Express.

This example demonstrates the MIME format for an email with a text file as an attachment. Attaching a text file may not be very useful since text files can be read and displayed in the email body directly. The real power of the attachment is that it can be used to deliver binary files including Word documents, images, photos, music, movies and many more.

The MIME format with a binary file as an attachment

Suppose the email to John Smith contains a Microsoft Word document called proposal.doc. Since the document is a binary file, the format in the previous example will not work. To attach a binary file, the file must be encoded in a displayable style, such as Base64. Consider the following example.

```
Example: email with an attachment

 1: To: johnsmith@practical-web.com
 2: From: sue@practical-web.com
 3: Subject: Hello
 4: MIME-Version: 1.0
 5: Content-type: multipart/mixed;
 6: boundary="another.boundary.87654321"
 7:
 8: This is a MIME encoded message.
 9:
10: --another.boundary.87654321
```

```
11: Content-type:text/plain; charset="iso-8859-1"
12: Content-transfer-encoding: 7bit
13:
14: Hi, John
15: How are you today?
16: JohnSmith
17: (PS) I have attached a document for you.
18:
19: --another.boundary.87654321
20: Content-type:application/octet-stream;name=proposal
21: Content-Disposition: attachment; filename="proposal.doc"
22: Content-transfer-encoding:base64
23:
24:   #### File Data ####
25:     ### ### ### ###
26:   #### File Data ####
27:
28: --another.boundary.87654321-
```

Lines 1–6 are the headers in MIME format. After the usual email fields, the version of the MIME format is specified in line 4. The `Content-type` of this email is `multipart/mixed` so that applications, attachments and text messages can be mixed together. As before, a boundary is defined in line 6. Lines 7–9 are a comment for the mailer.

The email body consists of two parts separated by the boundary string `another.boundary.87654321`. The first part (lines 10–19) is a normal text message. The second part (lines 20–27) contains the data of an application. The name of the application is `proposal` and it is transmitted as a stream of octet data in Base64 encoding. After one blank line, the actual file data appears. Note that the file data now should be Base64 encoded, as specified by line 22. After the file data, the attachment is terminated by the statement in line 28. If you send this email to a MIME-compliant mail reader, you will see the message and will be able to download the binary attachment.

You may remember that the `Content-type: text/html` string or keyword is used in CGI applications. In fact, CGI applications use MIME format to make sure that the returned document is indeed an HTML/XHTML page. Also, browsers such as IE, NS and Opera use MIME format (or `Content-type`) to determine the document type so that proper action can be taken accordingly. Some popular options for `Content-type` are listed below:

- `text/plain` for text;

- `text/html` for HTML/XHTML pages;

- application/octet-stream; multipart/mixed for attachments;

- application/msword for Microsoft Word files;

- application/vnd.ms-excel for Microsoft Excel files;

- application/pdf for pdf files;

- image/gif, image/jpeg and image/png for GIF, JPEG and PNG files respectively;

- audio/mpeg for MP3 files, video/mpeg for MPEG movies, video/quicktime for Quicktime (.mov) files.

To program and send emails with attachments, all you need to do is generate the email in MIME format as shown in the second and third examples above. The basic idea behind sending a secure attachment is to encrypt it before submitting it to the mail program.

9.5.2 Sending secure attachments with Perl

In theory, all you need to do to send an attachment is to create a message, such as the final two examples in the previous section, and send it. If you encrypt the attachment using GnuPG before composing the MIME format, you have effectively constructed a mechanism to deliver a secure attachment. Both symmetric-key and public-key encryption techniques discussed in previous chapters can be used. You can also sign the attachment before sending it.

In practice, however, many UNIX/LINUX mail clients, including sendmail, do not allow you to create the necessary MIME-version and Content-type headers as in the earlier examples. Therefore ordinary emailing methods will not work. The reason is that the mail client inserts a blank line automatically after the header block it creates. All your extensions and additional headers are treated as message text rather than headers.

One way of solving this problem is to use the standard input to the mail client. For example, you can input the text content in file page.txt to the sendmail program directly by:

```
/usr/lib/sendmail johnsmith@practical-web.com < page.txt
```

There are a number of third-party UNIX/LINUX mail clients which are MIME-compliant and can send and receive attachments. Also, there are many attachment-capable mail clients for Windows systems. However, most of them are commercial products. In fact, programming attachments yourself is not difficult. Some examples are provided below.

A page to send a secure attachment using Perl

In example ex09-16.htm and ex09-16.pl, a Perl program using SMTP to send email was constructed. Now we are going to modify this example to deliver a secure attachment. First, we will use the interface page `ex09-19.htm` to get the necessary email information from the user.

```
Example: ex09-19.htm - Email with MIME type

 1: <?xml version="1.0" encoding="iso-8859-1"?>
 2: <!DOCTYPE html PUBLIC "-//W3C//DTD XHTML 1.0 Transitional//EN"
 3:     "http://www.w3.org/TR/xhtml1/DTD/xhtml1-transitional.dtd">
 4: <html xmlns="http://www.w3.org/1999/xhtml"
    xml:lang="en" lang="en">
 5: <head><title> Email With MIME Type - ex09-19.htm</title></head>
 6: <style>
 7:  .tx01{font-size:14pt;color:#ffff00;font-weight:bold}
 8:  .tx02{font-family:arial;
          font-size:14pt;background:#ffffff;color:#000000}
 9:  .butSt{background-color:#aaffaa;font-family:arial;
          font-weight:bold;
10:        font-size:14pt;color:#008800;width:80px;height:30px}
11:  .butSt2{background-color:#aaffaa;font-family:arial;
           font-weight:bold;
12:        font-size:14pt;color:#008800;width:320px;height:30px}
13: </style>
14: <body style="background:#000088;font-family:arial;color:#00ee00">
15: <div align="center" style="font-size:24pt;font-weight:bold">
16: A Page To Send Email<br /><br />
17: <form method="post" action="ex09-19.pl">
18:
19: <table class="tx01">
20: <tr><td>From: (Email Add.)</td>
21:   <td><input class="tx02" type="text" name="from"
                  id="from"></td></tr>
22:  <tr><td>To: (Email Add.)</td>
23:   <td><input class="tx02" type="text" name="to" id="to"></td></tr>
24:  <tr><td>Subject:</td>
25:  <td><input class="tx02" type="text" name="subject"
                  id="subject"></td>
26:  <tr><td>Attachment Name: </td>
27: <td><input class="tx02" type="text" name="attname"
                id="attname"></td></tr>
28:  <tr><td>Attachment File:</td>
29: <td><input type="file" class="butSt2" name="attfile"
                id="attfile"></td>
30:   </TR>
31:   </tr><tr><td valign="top">Message:</td>
```

```
32:       <td><textarea name="message" id="message" class="tx02"
33:           rows="6" cols="40" wrap="yes"></textarea></td></tr><tr><td>
34:         <input class="butSt" type="submit" value="Send"></td>
35:       <td><input class="butSt" type="reset" value="Reset"></td></tr>
36:       </table>
37:       </form>
38:       </div>
39: </body>
40: </html>
```

This page is a form application used to obtain the From, To, Subject and Attachment Name information from the user. The only new feature is the input statement given in lines 28–29. Consider line 29:

```
<input type="file" class="butSt2" name="attfile" id="attfile">
```

This statement generates an open-file window so that the attachment file (attfile) can be picked up by using a mouse click. Once the Send button in line 34 is pressed, the corresponding Perl program ex09-19.pl (line 17) is called to encrypt the attachment file and send it to the recipient. Now, consider part I of ex09-19.pl.

Example: ex09-19.pl – The Perl script for ex09-19.htm　　　　**(Part I)**

```
 1: #!/usr/bin/perl
 2: use CGI qw( :standard );
 3: print ("Content-type: text/html\n\n");
 4:
 5: use MIME::Lite;
 6: use Net::SMTP;
 7:
 8: my $from = param("from");
 9: my $to = param("to");
10: my $subject = param("subject");
12: my $message = param("message");
11: my $mime_type = 'TEXT';
13:
14: my $mime_msg = MIME::Lite->new(
15:     From => $from,
16:     To => $to,
17:     Subject => $subject,
18:     Type => $mime_type,
19:     Data => $message
```

```
20:   )
21:   or die "Error creating MIME body: $!\n";
22:
23: my $filename = param('attfile');
24: my $fileEn = $filename . ".gpg";
25:
26: print `gpg -a --batch --yes -o $fileEn -e -r $to $filename`;
27:
28: my $recommended_filename = param('attname') . ".gpg";
29: $mime_msg->attach(
30:     Type => 'application/octet-stream',
31:     Path => $fileEn,
32:     Filename => $recommended_filename
33:     )
34:   or die "Error attaching test file: $!\n";
35:
36: my $msg_body = $mime_msg->body_as_string();
37:
```

Since we need to handle MIME format in this Perl script, a module called
MIME::Lite is included in line 5. This module will provide all the necessary
functions to generate an attachment in MIME format. The module NeT::SMTP is
used to send emails using an SMTP server. First, the email information From, To,
Subject and Message from ex09-19.htm is captured into variables $from, $to,
$subject and $message respectively. Together with the MIME type declaration
in line 11, an object called $mime_msg is created with MIME::Lite (lines 14–20).
Before the attachment is added into this MIME object $mime_msg, it must be
encrypted using GnuPG.

For the encryption, the attachment file name is captured and stored in
variable $filename (line 23). The statement in line 24 makes sure that the
encrypted file name (or variable $fileEn) will have the extension .gpg. The
statement in line 26 calls the GnuPG program gpg to perform encryption on
$filename producing an ASCII file stored in $fileEn using the public key of the
recipient ($to). Once we have the encrypted file $fileEn, the statements in lines
29–33 use the attach() function to generate the MIME format of the attachment
and store it in $mime_msg. In order to convert this object into a string for SMTP
emailing, the statement in line 36 is used. The result is a string called $msg_body
which contains the attachment settings in MIME format and is ready to be sent
using SMTP.

The actual sending process is given in part II of ex09-19.pl.

```
38: my $ServerName = "mail.practical-web.com";
39: $smtp = Net::SMTP->new($ServerName) or
40:    die "Couldn't connect to server";
41:
42: $smtp->mail($from);
43: $smtp->to($to);
44:
45: $smtp->data();
46: $smtp->datasend($mail_body);
47: $smtp->dataend();
48: $smtp->quit();
49:
50: print << "mypage";
51:   <?xml version="1.0" encoding="iso-8859-1"?>
52:   <!DOCTYPE html PUBLIC "-//W3C//DTD XHTML 1.0 Transitional//EN"
53:      "http://www.w3.org/TR/xhtml1/DTD/xhtml1-transitional.dtd">
54:   <html xmlns="http://www.w3.org/1999/xhtml" xml:lang="en"
        lang="en">
55:   <head><title>Sending Secure Attachment</title></head>
56:   <body style="background:#000088">
57:   <div style="font-family:arial;font-size:22pt;color:#ffff00">
58:       Your Email has been sent to <br />$to <br /><br />
59:       The Encrypted Attachment File is <br />$fileEn
60:   </div></body></html>
61: mypage
```

Lines 38–40 specify the SMTP server and make a connection to it through the variable $smtp. The statements in lines 42–43 define the sender and recipient. Lines 45–47 send the MIME string stored in variable $mail_body. The process is terminated by the statement in line 48 and an acknowledgement page is displayed in lines 50–61. Screenshots are shown in Figures 9.85 and 9.86.

When John Smith turns on his computer and checks his email, he will see an email with an attachment called proposal from Sue Brown, as shown in Figure 9.87.

In this case, John Smith can download and save the encrypted attachment file proposal.doc.gpg in his machine. To decrypt the encrypted file, the following GnuPG command line is used:

```
gpg -o proposal.de.doc -d proposal.doc.gpg
```

Fig. 9.85   Selecting and sending an attachment file

Fig. 9.86   Acknowledgement

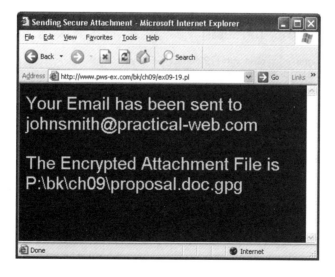

Fig. 9.87 Receiving an encrypted attachment

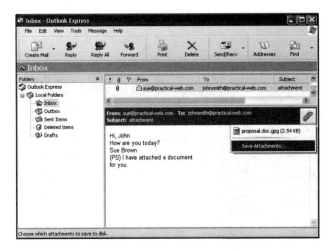

Fig. 9.88 Decrypting the attachment

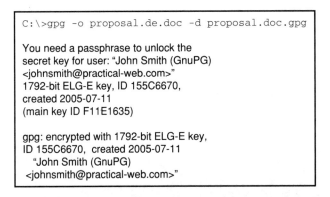

```
C:\>gpg -o proposal.de.doc -d proposal.doc.gpg

You need a passphrase to unlock the
secret key for user: "John Smith (GnuPG)
<johnsmith@practical-web.com>"
1792-bit ELG-E key, ID 155C6670,
created 2005-07-11
(main key ID F11E1635)

gpg: encrypted with 1792-bit ELG-E key,
ID 155C6670, created 2005-07-11
  "John Smith (GnuPG)
<johnsmith@practical-web.com>"
```

This command will decrypt the file `proposal.doc.gpg` using the default secret key of John Smith and producing the ciphertext in file `proposal.de.doc`. Since a secret key is required, GnuPG will ask for the passphrase. When the correct passphrase is entered, the decryption result is generated. The execution dialog is shown in Figure 9.88. After decryption, John Smith can read this Microsoft Word document in the usual way (see Figure 9.89).

This example demonstrates how to send encrypted attachments using the MIME format relying heavily on the Perl module `MIME::Lite` to generate a MIME message.

In order to understand attachments fully, let's consider how to generate MIME messages and send secure attachments from scratch using PHP.

Fig. 9.89   Displaying the attachment

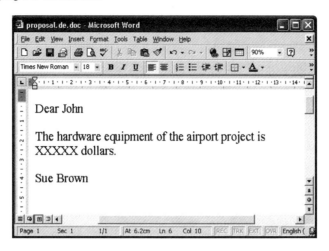

9.5.3   Programming the MIME format and secure attachments with PHP

In general, the basic idea behind programming and sending a secure attachment is to encrypt and incorporate the attachment data into the email body. The attachment file can then be sent later via the MIME format. If you want to do it from the very beginning, this involves the following tasks:

■   get the email and attachment information from the user;

■   encrypt the attachment using GnuPG;

■   read the encrypted attachment;

■   convert the attachment into Base64 encoding;

■   generate the MIME headers for the attachment;

■   send the secure attachment to the recipient.

Recall that the following program fragment can be used to open and read a file using PHP:

```
$fHandle = fopen("myfile", "r");
$fData = fread($fHandle, filesize("datafile"));
```

The first statement is to open a data file `myfile` for reading and to create a file handle called `$fHandle`. Using this file handle, you can read the entire file into a variable `$fData` (file data) with the PHP function `fread()`. We will use this function later to perform efficient file reading.

In order to produce the same interface as for the Perl case, make a copy of ex09-19.htm and call it ex09-20.htm. Modify the following line:

```
17: <form method="post" action="ex09-20.php">
```

When this file is rendered by the browser, the same interface as shown in Figure 9.85 appears so that the user can fill in the email information From, To, Subject and Message. The Browse button in the interface will allow you to select a file as an attachment. Now, if the Send button is clicked, line 17 above will make sure that the PHP program ex09-20.php is run. This program executes all the tasks above and delivers the encrypted attachment to the recipient.

```
Example: ex09-20.php - A PHP program for ex09-20.htm

 1: <?PHP echo"<?";?>xml version="1.0"
      encoding="iso-8859-1"<?PHP echo"?>";?>
 2: <!DOCTYPE html PUBLIC "-//W3C//DTD XHTML 1.0 Transitional//EN"
 3:     "http://www.w3.org/TR/xhtml1/DTD/xhtml1-transitional.dtd">
 4: <html xmlns="http://www.w3.org/1999/xhtml"
      xml:lang="en" lang="en">
 5: <body style="background:#000088;text-align:center;
      font-family:arial">
 6: <div align="left" style="font-size:18pt;color:#ffff00"><br />
 7: <?php
 8:   global $vFrom, $vTo, $vSubject, $vBody;
 9:   global $vAttName, $vAtt, $vAttSize, $vHeaders;
10:
11:   $vFrom =$from;
12:   $vTo =$to;
13:   $vSubject =$subject;
14:   $vBody = $message;
15:   $vAttName = $attname . ".gpg";
16:
17:   $vAtt = $attfile . ".gpg";
18:   system("gpg -a --batch --yes -o $vAtt -r $vFrom -e $attfile");
19:   $vAttSize = filesize($vAtt);
20:
21:   $vHeaders="From: $vFrom\n";
22:
23:   include "ex09-20.inc";
24:
25:   if (!empty($vAttName) && ($vAttSize >0) )
26:   {
27:      myAttachment();
```

```
28:  } else {
29:     $vHeaders .= "Content-type: text/plain;
          charset=\"iso-8859-1\" \n";
30:     $vHeaders .= "Content-transfer-encoding: 7bit \n\n";
31:  }
32:
33:  if (mail($vTo,$vSubject,$vBody,$vHeaders))
34:  {
35:      echo "<br />Thankyou! $vFrom <br /><br />";
36:      echo "An Email Has Been Sent To $vTo Successfully";
37:  } else {
38:      echo "<br />Sorry! $vFrom <br /><br />";
39:      echo " Unable To Send Your Email To $vTo .";
40:  }
41: ?>
42: </div></body>
43: </html>
```

The first part of this PHP program (lines 1–14) is to get the email data From, To, Subject and Message from Web page ex09-20.htm. The selected attachment file from the Web page is stored in variable $attfile. Similar to the Perl case, the statement in line 18 calls the GnuPG program gpg to perform encryption on $attfile using the secret key of the sender ($vTo.). The encryption result is stored in variable $vAtt. In order to read this encrypted file, the file size is obtained by the statement in line 19.

If the encrypted attachment name is not empty and the corresponding file size is bigger than zero (line 25), we know that the encrypted attachment is well defined. The function myAttachment() is called to generate the necessary MIME format. This function is defined in the external PHP module ex09-20.inc as an included file of ex09-20.php (line 23). If the encrypted attachment does not exist or is not defined, the usual text headers are generated in lines 29–30. This arrangement makes sure that the mail() function in line 33 can deliver the email correctly in both cases. If the encrypted attachment is sent successfully, the message in lines 35–36 is displayed. Otherwise an error message is displayed (lines 38–39).

The details of the included file ex09-20.inc are listed below.

Example: ex09-20.inc – An included file for ex09-20.php

```
1: <?php
2: function myAttachment()
3: {
4:  global $vBody;
```

```
 5:    global $vAttName, $vAtt, $vHeaders;
 6:
 7:    $fileHandle = fopen($vAtt, "r");
 8:    $fileData = fread($fileHandle, filesize($vAtt));
 9:    $fileData = chunk_split(base64_encode($fileData));
10:
11:    $vBoundaryString = md5(uniqid(time()));
12:    $lHeaders = $vHeaders;
13:    $lHeaders .= "MIME-Version: 1.0\n";
14:    $lHeaders .= "Content-type: multipart/mixed;
15:    boundary=\"$vBoundaryString\" \n\n";
16:    $lHeaders .= "This is a MIME encoded message. \n\n";
17:    $lBody = "--$vBoundaryString\n";
18:    $lBody .= "Content-type: text/plain; charset=\"iso-8859-1\" \n";
19:    $lBody .= "Content-transfer-encoding: 7bit \n\n";
20:    $lBody .= "$vBody \n";
21:    $lBody .= "--$vBoundaryString\n";
22:    $lBody .= "Content-type: application/octet-stream;
         name=$vAttName \n";
23:    $lBody .= "Content-transfer-encoding: base64 \n\n";
24:    $lBody .= $fileData . "\n\n";
25:    $lBody .= "--$vBoundaryString-";
26:    $vBody = $lBody;
27:    $vHeaders = $lHeaders;
28: }
29: ?>
```

Global variables are used in this page to simplify passing variables. Soon after
the variable declarations, the encrypted attachment is opened and the data read in
line 8. The data are then split into chunks of Base64 encoded stream. The stream
is represented by the variable $fileData.

The next step is to define the boundary string $vBounddaryString (line 11). In order
to have a unique string, we call the UNIX time function time(), convert it into a
unique identifier and finally call the md5() function to transform it to a 32-character
string (or hash). From the properties of MD5, we know that there is virtually no
chance of a repeated boundary string.

The remaining task is to construct the header and the body in MIME format. A
local variable $lHeaders is used to generate and store the header (lines 12–14).
Another local variable $lBody is used to generate the email body. Since we have
designated one message and one attachment only, $lBody has two parts separated
by the boundary string $vBoundaryString. The first part (lines 18–20) is the email
message, and the content is stored in variable $vBody. The second part is the
attachment, and the file data is copied into $lBody as shown in line 24. Finally,

the header and body are copied back to the global variables $vHeader and $vBody. Now the necessary MIME format for an attachment has been generated and we are ready to deliver the email with the attachment (encrypted) by making the mail() function call below (see also line 33 of ex09-20.php):

```
mail($vTo,$vSubject,$vBody,$vHeaders)
```

The screen shots of this example are the same as those generated in the Perl case. When the Web page ex09-20.htm is rendered by a browser, the interface and operation to deliver a secure attachment are the same as those in Figures 9.85 and 9.86. When John Smith checks his email, he will see the message and the encrypted attachment proposal.doc.gpg in his mail client, such as Outlook Express (see Figure 9.87). After he has downloaded the attachment, the following command can be used to perform decryption producing the decrypted file proposal.de.doc.

```
gpg -o proposal.de.doc -d proposal.doc.gpg
```

The operation of this command is shown in Figure 9.88. After decryption, the file proposal.de.doc can be displayed by Microsoft Word (see Figure 9.89) or a Word-compliant program.

This example demonstrates how an encrypted attachment can be generated and sent using GnuPG, emailing and PHP techniques. By using the MIME format, even the simple mail() function can perform complicated email and attachment operations.

10

SSL security, applications and XML contracts

10.1 Digital certificates and contracts

10.1.1 The legal status of digital contracts

In June 2000, the US government granted legal status to electronic signatures through the Electronic Signatures in Global and National Commerce Act, known as the 'E-sign' law. Roughly speaking, this act states that documents signed by an electronic signature will have the same legal rights as paper contracts with handwritten signatures.

An electronic signature is defined as any electronic symbol, or process attached to or logically associated with a record, and executed or adopted by a person with the intent of signing an electronic document or record.

One interesting characteristic of this E-sign law is that it is technologically neutral and does not specify any technical specifications or verification procedures. In fact, by permitting a wide range of electronic techniques as signatures the federal E-sign law has technically established the following basic principles and characteristics of digital contracts so that they can be challenged on the same legal grounds as a traditional written signature or contract:

- Authenticity – is the electronically signed document a forgery or otherwise unauthorized?

- Integrity – was the message received in the same form as it was originally sent?

Since the E-sign law contains no technical details, companies can decide for themselves how to implement electronic signatures and how to verify the authenticity and integrity of signed electronic documents. In general, we consider any document signed with an electronic signature to be regarded as a digital contract.

This basic principle provides a general specification for digital contracts. In particular, all the digital signatures discussed in Chapter 8 are included as a specific type of electronic signature which uses encryption technology to sign messages with a secure code and which are verifiable via a digital process. Therefore, documents signed by any digital signature discussed in Chapter 8 are legally valid.

Under the same principle, even a simple mouse-click may generate a legal electronic signature and constitute the so-called 'click-through' contract providing a legal basis for many online business and electronic transactions. In practice, courts in many countries have consistently upheld the legal rights of electronic signatures obtained with the click-through contract promoting businesses in a truly international and global manner.

For example, before you install some new software, you will often be presented with an electronic agreement. After viewing all the terms and conditions, a simple mouse-click on the `I agree` button generates an electronic signature and legally binds you to the contract. In January 2002, a legal endorsement of the Act stated that click-through terms may prevail over written terms.

Click-through agreement is a low-cost and highly effective way to implement business contracts for one-off electronic transactions. For higher-value or repetitive business-to-business transactions, it is often required by law that written permission or authorization is necessary. In this situation, it is important to implement a more secure way of protecting against fraud and ensuring the authenticity and integrity of electronic signatures. One popular technique, promoted by the US government and the W3C consortium, is to use 'certificates' administrated by 'certification authorities'.

10.1.2 Certificates and certification authorities

In Chapters 8 and 9, we discussed some basic implementations and applications of public-key technology. By using two keys (namely a public key and a private key), digital signature, authentication and verification can be implemented effectively.

Basically, when a signer signs a document using a private key, the result is similar to a digital signature. To verify the digital signature, the verifier must obtain the corresponding public key and make sure that this public key matches the signer's private key. This is the easy part. A more difficult problem to solve is that, even when the public and private key pair match, there is no mechanism to associate them with any person. The keys are simply a pair of numbers. The association between a particular person and a key pair must be made by trust. How to establish and implement this trust in a scientific way is not an easy task.

One obvious solution to generating trust and proof of genuine identity is that the prospective document signer can issue a statement or certificate like this:

I will take full responsibility of all documents signed with my digital signature verifiable by the following public key . . .

One advantage of this method is that the statement and the associated record or certificate can be used again and again for multiple transactions over a period of time. However, the credibility of a certificate like this is rather low. People doing business with the signer may well be unwilling to take the signer's own word for its identification being verifiable by the signer's public key. This is particularly true when business transactions are conducted within a network environment such as the World Wide Web, rather than face to face. The reason for this is that a third party would run a great risk in dealing with a phantom that is only identifiable by a number (public key).

In order to establish trust between two parties in a digital environment, a trusted third party must be presented. The job of this third party is to ensure that the signer does exist, is responsible and has a proper identity. This third party is called the 'certification authority' (CA). More precise definitions of certificate and certification authority are given below.

- A certification authority is a trusted third party that verifies the identity of an applicant registering for a digital certificate. Once a CA is satisfied with the identity and authentication method of an applicant, it issues a digital certificate to the applicant binding their identity to a public key.

- A digital signature certificate is a computer-generated record. It contains the identity of the certificate holder, the public key which is digitally signed by the CA. The digital signature certificate is associated with both a public key and a private key.

Certificates can be signed by any certified CA. In order to establish trust, it is recommended that parties should exchange their corresponding certificates while signing the contract. For example, certificates can be used independently or imported into a browser such as IE, NS or Opera for the signing process. An imported certificate in IE is shown in Figure 10.1. From this, you can see that the certificate is issued to 'johnsmith' by a CA called 'MyCA'. This CA is, obviously, not real and will be generated in Section 10.3.2. In a real-world application, the certificate should be signed by a responsible CA.

The certificate in Figure 10.1 also includes a starting and expiring date. When your browser connects to a so-called 'secure site', the certificates of your browser and the site will be exchanged to build the trust and complete the connection. This process is specified by the HTTPS (HTTP with Security) protocol and will be discussed in Section 10.4.

There are a number of ways of generating certificates and getting them signed by a CA. The most popular and widely used on the Web is called Secure Socket Layer (SSL). Basically, SSL uses the idea of certificates to establish secure communications on the Web and will be discussed in some detail in Section 10.1.3. For example, if

Fig. 10.1 A certificate in Internet Explorer

John Smith wants to generate a certificate such as that in Figure 10.1, he can use SSL to generate a certificate signing request (CSR) file, such as `johnsmith.csr`, in the system. The next step is to send this CSR file to a CA for signing. The result is a real certificate that can be used in applications. In many cases, certificates created by SSL can be imported into browsers such as IE, NS and Opera directly.

There are several commercial CAs on the Web ready to sign CSRs. Two of them are

- VeriSign at http://digitalid.verisign.com

- Thawte Consulting at http://www.thawte.com

To get your CSR file signed by a CA, you may need to complete a form in their Web site and post your CSR. They will digitally sign your CSR and return a signed certificate to you. The signed certificate is normally a file with the file extension `crt`, such as `johnsmith.crt`. Before further details of certificates and signing processes are discussed, a basic understanding of SSL and SSL security is needed.

10.1.3　SSL security and HTTPS protocol

SSL is a communication protocol layer which provides protection between your TCP/IP and client-server communications. In particular, it is designed to intercept and monitor your Web traffic, to establish trust and provide security for browser and server communication using the idea of certificates. If you have a certificate installed in your favourite browser, such as IE or NS, this can be used to identify you, and the encryptions employed by SSL guarantee that communication over the Web is protected. More importantly, all security operations are hidden from the user under SSL security.

The first practical SSL protocol, known as SSL v2.0, was implemented by Netscape and supported by products such as NS 1.x/2.x and IE 3.x browsers. This early version of SSL was mainly vendor specific and had limited features, but it opened up a new security concept for Web businesses and their users. The next version of SSL (SSL v3.0) attracted much more attention and is widely supported by the Web community today.

Thanks to the wide acceptance of online businesses and commercial applications, almost all browsers, including IE, NS and Opera, support security in a strong cryptography sense. For example, they all support 128-bit encryption as a minimum standard. For SSL type security, they support the RSA key exchange, SSL v1.0/v2.0, and the SSL successor Transport Layer Security (TLS v1.0) from the IETF standard. All major browsers also extend cryptography support to a wider area beyond HTTP (Web) covering NNTP (news), POP and SMTP (email). In general, all capable browsers can nowadays provide security through encryption/decryption, generating private and public keys and responding to certificate (in the SSL sense) requests.

Due to the popularity and usefulness of SSL, an open source implementation called OpenSSL has been developed and is freely available from the Open Source Initiative (OSI). In addition to encryption/decryption, the following main applications of OpenSSL are also implemented:

- generating and handling certificates;
- integrating with server software to build a secure site.

OpenSSL can be used to integrate with server software such as Apache, IIS and other Web servers with little effort. The result is a secure site practising HTTPS protocol and communications. Therefore, secure Web servers or add-on transmission packages are no longer costly proprietary products. In fact, the latest implementation of OpenSSL meets almost all cryptography standards including both SSL v2.0/v3.0 and TLS v1.0. Now we can say that SSL security for Web businesses and users is here, free, and is widely available for all.

In fact OpenSSL is similar to GnuPG in the sense that both are cryptology toolkits. More precisely, OpenSSL is a collection of functions organized in a library structure controlled by a command line program called `openssl`. The package implements the SSL v2.0/v3.0 and TLS v1.0 network protocols and many other related cryptography standards. Apart from the traditional encryption, certificates generated by OpenSSL can be imported into your favourite browser directly. When you request a Web document from a secure (or SSL secure) Web server, the certificate will be used for authentication.

We will show you how to install OpenSSL and how to use it for basic security applications in Section 10.2. Generating and handling certificates will be introduced in Section 10.3. In Section 10.4 we will show you how to set up a secure Web site with the HTTPS protocol. In the final section, OpenSSL will be used to establish XML signatures and contracts. XML signatures can be embedded and verified in the World Wide Web environment more effectively. Examples related to SSL will have the extension `.ssl` in this chapter.

As a starting point, a brief introduction to SSL will be helpful. Basically, SSL works by establishing mutual trust between browser and server. This mutual trust is controlled by SSL record protocol with handshake sequences. The handshake contains three layers:

- SSL handshake protocol: exchanging certificates;

- SSL change cipher specification: employing encryption;

- SSL alert protocol: launching alerts.

These sequences are used to establish an SSL session. When an SSL session is identified and established, secure connection and transmission take place. In normal circumstances, there will be some kind of certificate exchange and an agreed cipher suite used for the transmission. This means that both the client and server have the chance to identify themselves and request authentication from each other via certificate requests. When this initial handshake is established, an agreed cipher (encryption) is used to protect the privacy of the transmission. If something goes wrong during the connection or SSL session, the SSL alert protocol is used to convey SSL error messages between client and server. A typical SSL session is shown in Figure 10.2.

The central idea behind SSL is certificate administration. A certificate in SSL is a special piece of information associated with a public key and the real identity of the object concerned, which may include an individual, a server or some other entity. Any SSL implementation should be able to generate certificates for you and/or your applications. The public key can be used to decrypt the message you send to the receiver. In order to increase the credibility of the certificate, it should be signed by a trusted CA, as mentioned in Section 10.1.2.

In a normal situation, a Web server equipped with SSL security is regarded as a secure server. Secure Web servers can be surfed using a special protocol known as HTTP with security (or HTTPS),

```
https://www.pws-ex.com
```

Fig. 10.2 A typical SSL session between browser and server

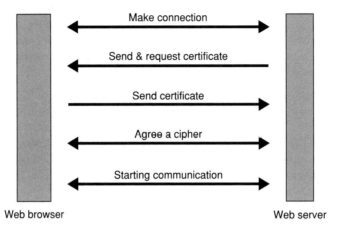

This command requests the default document from domain www.pws-ex.com in security mode. After some form of certificate exchange, encryptions are employed to protect the Web traffic and communication against intruders. The HTTPS command `https://` can also be embedded into an anchor element such as

```
<a href="https://www.pws-ex.com"> This is a secure link</a>
```

When your browser surfs the Web with HTTPS, you see an alert window. The alert windows for IE, NS and Opera are shown in Figures 10.3 to 10.5.

Fig. 10.3 IE6.x security alert window

Fig. 10.4 NS6.x security alert window

Fig. 10.5 Opera security alert window

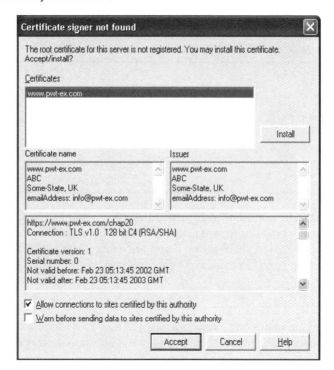

Also, when you terminate the security connection via HTTPS protocol and return to ordinary HTTP mode, a similar alert window will appear to let you know the status.

Now let's consider how to install the SSL package OpenSSL and how to use it to perform some basic security applications.

10.2 Basic security applications with OpenSSL

10.2.1 Installing OpenSSL

OpenSSL is a software package from Open Source Initiative (OSI). It is free and you can use it for commercial or non-commercial purposes. You can download a copy of the software from the official site www.openssl.org. The distribution of OpenSSL software is via the tarball file

```
openssl-x.x.x.tar.gz
```

The string x.x.x represents the version of the package. The version used in this chapter is 0.9.7d. It is recommended that you should always download the latest version of OpenSSL. Unlike many other software packages, this file contains everything you may need to install OpenSSL for the following platforms.

Operating system	Installation file
UNIX/LINUX	INSTALL
OpenVMS	INSTALL.VMS
OS2	INSTALL.OS2
MacOS	INSTALL.MacOS
Windows	INSTALL.W32 INSTALL.DJPP INSTALL.WCE

For each operating system, a corresponding file is used to provide the installation details. The OpenSSL software team has done a good job in covering all these environments in one distribution. If you are using UNIX/LINUX, you can use the following commands to extract the files and subdirectories into your machine:

```
gzip -d openssl-x.x.x.tar.gz
tar -xvf openssl-x.x.x.tar
```

These two commands will extract all files and associated subdirectories into a default directory called openssl-0.9.7d. Sometimes, you can use one process command

```
tar -zxvf openssl-x.x.x.tar.gz
```

to do the job. For Windows users, you can use WinZip to extract all files to the destination directory in one process. After extracting all the files, you should have a directory something like openssl-0.9.7d.

Installing OpenSSL on UNIX/LINUX systems

To build the OpenSSL package on a UNIX/LINUX system, you may also need the following additional packages up and running:

- Perl 5;

- an ANSI C compiler, such as `gcc` or `cc`, with a development environment (e.g. make, libraries and header files).

Suppose you are using a UNIX/LINUX system and you are already inside the OpenSSL file directory (e.g. `openssl-0.9.7d`). You can use the following two commands to build and install the package into your system temporarily:

```
$./config
$make
```

This will build the OpenSSL libraries (`libcrypto.a` and `libssl.a`) and the OpenSSL command line program `openssl`. The command line program is stored in the subdirectory called `apps`. When the package is built, you should test it before installing it to your system permanently. You can test the libraries using the command

```
$make test
```

OpenSSL is a complicated software package – even the test printout is well over two full pages. Basically, the test covers the functionalities of the libraries, such as generating RSA keys and performing various client–server authentications. If everything is in working order, you will see 'passed all tests' at the end of the screen output. In this case, you can perform the following command to install the package:

```
$make install
```

This will build and install OpenSSL in the default location, which is (for historical reasons) `/usr/local/ssl`. If you want to specify your own installation directory, run `config` like this:

```
./config --prefix=/usr/local --openssldir=/usr/local/openssl
```

Among other things, the installation process creates the following subdirectories under the target directory `openssl-0.9.7d`:

- `certs`   Initially empty, this is the default location for certificate files.
- `private`   Initially empty, this is the default location for private keys.
- `bin`   Contains the `openssl` binary and a few other utility programs.
- `include/openssl`   Contains the header files needed if you want to compile programs with the `libcrypto` or `libssl` libraries.
- `lib`   Contains the OpenSSL library files themselves.
- `man/man1`   Manual pages for the `openssl` command line tool.
- `man/man3`   Manual pages for the libraries.
- `misc`   Various scripts.

For most users, the command line program `openssl` and the certificates are the essential tools to make SSL work. For programmers, the header files in the `include/openssl` directory and the libraries are important components in building SSL applications.

If you are using a Windows system, a default subdirectory or folder called `ms` under the folder `openssl-0.9.7d` is available for you to build OpenSSL. To compile OpenSSL under Windows, a Perl package for Win32 is required. Such a package is available from the official site www.activestate.com. Also, you may need at least one of the following compilers:

- Visual C++ (VC++);

- Borland C;

- GNU C (Mingw32 or CygWin32).

Installing OpenSSL on Windows with the Visual C++ compiler

Suppose all the files of the OpenSSL package are extracted under the `openssl-0.9.7d` (or `openssl`) directory and a Visual C++ compiler is up and running. Inside the directory `openssl`, the following Perl command will configure OpenSSL for Visual C++ compiler:

```
perl Configure VC-WIN32
```

The next step is to build the `makefile`, dedicated for Visual C++, by the command

```
ms\do_ms
```

This command runs the batch file `do_ms.bat` under the `ms` directory and subsequently builds all the make files for Visual C++. Now you can compile the software using the `nmake` utility:

```
nmake -f ms\ntdll.mak
```

Again, we assume that all commands were typed under the default `openssl-0.9.7d` directory. If all goes well it will build all dynamic linked libraries (DLLs) and executables in the `out32dll` directory. Now, you can run OpenSSL inside `out32dll`, or put this directory into your path. For example, you can test the libraries and software by

```
cd out32dll
..\ms\test
```

Installing OpenSSL on Windows with the GCC compiler

All files are assumed to be in the default directory. Also both the GCC MingW compiler (`gcc.exe`) and Perl interpreter (`perl.exe`) are assumed to be in the current path. The simple command below will compile the package:

```
ms\mingw32
```

This will create the library and binaries in the out directory. If you have problems, try the following command (without assembler) instead:

```
ms\mingw32 no-asm
```

After compilation, the OpenSSL package is installed in the out directory. To test the package, you can use the command

```
cd out
..\ms\test
```

A brief summary of the test results is listed in ex10-01.ssl.

```
Example: ex10-01.ssl - Testing the OpenSSL package

 1: rsa_test
 2: PKCS #1 v1.5 encryption/decryption ok
 3: OAEP encryption/decryption ok
 4: PKCS #1 v1.5 encryption/decryption ok
 5: OAEP encryption/decryption ok
 6: PKCS #1 v1.5 encryption/decryption ok
 7: OAEP encryption/decryption ok
 8: destest
 9: Doing cbcm
10: Doing ecb
11: Doing ede ecb
12: Doing cbc
13: Doing desx cbc
14: Doing ede cbc
15: Doing pcbc
************************************************************************
************************************************************************
320: TLSv1, cipher TLSv1/SSLv3 EDH-RSA-DES-CBC3-SHA, 512 bit RSA
321: test sslv2/sslv3 with server authentication
322: TLSv1, cipher TLSv1/SSLv3 EDH-RSA-DES-CBC3-SHA, 512 bit RSA
323: test sslv2/sslv3 with client authentication via BIO pair
324: TLSv1, cipher TLSv1/SSLv3 EDH-RSA-DES-CBC3-SHA, 512 bit RSA
325: test sslv2/sslv3 with both client and server authentication via
        BIO pair
326: TLSv1, cipher TLSv1/SSLv3 EDH-RSA-DES-CBC3-SHA, 512 bit RSA
327: passed all tests
```

This is a lengthy test spanning well over 300 lines covering many of the encryption/ decryption or cryptographic features introduced in this book. If you see the phrase 'passed all tests' at the end, it is likely that you have a valid OpenSSL build.

Now we have OpenSSL installed, let's consider some security applications. The first is to use it to generate hash values or one-way encryptions.

10.2.2   Generating passwords and hash values

Most SSL applications can be performed via the command line program `openssl`. This program is similar to the `gpg` of GnuPG in the sense that it is a command line tool for executing functions in the OpenSSL library. The program `openssl` (`openssl.exe`) must be run inside a shell window or DOS window if you are using a Windows system.

OpenSSL is a big package covering most of the encryption/decryption and cryptographic features discussed in this book. Even at a basic level, it can be used for:

- calculating hash values (or one-way encryption);
- symmetric-key encryption and decryption;
- public-key encryption and decryption;
- generating RSA, DH and DSA digital keys and administrations.

The `openssl` program offers well over 100 commands and options. Many of them can be grouped under three categories:

- standard commands;
- message digest commands;
- cipher commands.

Each category contains a rich set of operational commands. Some of them are complicated in that they have many arguments and options. There is a help utility inside `openssl` so that a summary of all commands is available at any time. If the program doesn't understand a command or statement, a command summary is displayed to provide help. A sample session of the command summary is shown in `ex10-02.ssl`.

As a basic introduction to the OpenSSL package, we introduce the use of four standard commands step by step:

```
passwd    dgst    enc    genrsa
```

These commands are emboldened in `ex10-02.ssl`. The first command `passwd` is used to generate some commonly used passwords, including the UNIX `Crypt` and Apache `apr1` (or `md5Crypt`) mentioned in Chapter 3. The `dgst` option generates various message digest (or hash) values. When used with the cipher commands, in lines 17–28, the `enc` option is use to perform encryption/decryption operations. To generate digital keys, the `genrsa` command is used. The RSA keys will be used as a

```
Example: ex10-02.ssl - The command summary of OpenSSL

 1: E:\openssl>openssl help
 2:
 3: Standard commands
 4:  asn1parse    ca           ciphers      crl          crl2pkcs7
 5:  dgst         dh           dhparam      dsa          dsaparam
 6:  enc          engine       errstr       gendh        gendsa
 7:  genrsa       nseq         ocsp         passwd       pkcs12
 8:  pkcs7        pkcs8        rand         req          rsa
 9:  rsautl       s_client     s_server     s_time       sess_id
10:  smime        speed        spkac        verify       version
11:  x509
12:
13: Message Digest commands (see the 'dgst' command for more details)
14:  md2          md4          md5          mdc2         rmd160
15:  sha          sha1
16:
17: Cipher commands (see the 'enc' command for more details)
18:  aes-128-cbc aes-128-ecb aes-192-cbc  aes-192-ecb  aes-256-cbc
19:  aes-256-ecb base64      bf           bf-cbc       bf-cfb
20:  bf-ecb      bf-ofb      cast         cast-cbc     cast5-cbc
21:  cast5-cfb   cast5-ecb   cast5-ofb    des          des-cbc
22:  des-cfb     des-ecb     des-ede      des-ede-cbc  des-ede-cfb
23:  des-ede-ofb des-ede3    des-ede3-cbc des-ede3-cfb des-ede3-ofb
24:  des-ofb     des3        desx         idea         idea-cbc
25:  idea-cfb    idea-ecb    idea-ofb     rc2          rc2-40-cbc
26:  rc2-64-cbc  rc2-cbc     rc2-cfb      rc2-ecb      rc2-ofb
27:  rc4         rc4-40      rc5          rc5-cbc      rc5-cfb
28:  rc5-ecb     rc5-ofb
```

starting point for generating digital certificates and will be discussed in detail in
Section 10.3.

Generating passwords with OpenSSL

In Chapter 3, some popular password algorithms including the standard UNIX
Crypt (see ex03-04.htm) and Apache md5Crypt (ex03-07.htm) were introduced.
These passwords can be used to perform user authentication providing protection
for Web applications against intruders. If you have OpenSSL installed, these
passwords can be obtained easily using the passwd command.

Using `passwd` is straightforward. The main idea is to activate the main program `openssl` together with the `passwd` subcommand and its associated options. The available options for `passwd` are:

- `-crypt`   standard Unix password algorithm (default);
- `-1`   MD5-based password algorithm;
- `-apr1`   MD5-based password algorithm, Apache variant;
- `-salt string`   use provided salt;
- `-in file`   read passwords from file;
- `-stdin`   read passwords from `stdin`;
- `-noverify`   never verify when reading password from terminal;
- `-quiet`   no warnings;
- `-table`   format output as table;
- `-reverse`   switch table columns.

Note that an option in OpenSSL is prefixed with a hyphen. If you want to see all the options for a particular command, you can use the `-help` directive. For example, you will see the options above using the following command (see Figure 10.6):

```
openssl passwd -help
```

If you want to generate the UNIX `crypt` password, you can use the command below:

```
openssl passwd -crypt -salt mr peter
```

Fig. 10.6 The options for `passwd`

```
E:\openssl\bin>openssl passwd -help
Usage: passwd [options] [passwords]
where options are
-crypt          standard Unix password
                algorithm (default)
-1              MD5-based password algorithm
-apr1           MD5-based password algorithm,
                Apache variant
-salt string    use provided salt
-in file        read passwords from file
-stdin          read passwords from stdin
-noverify       never verify when reading
                password from terminal
-quiet          no warnings
-table          format output as table
-reverse        switch table columns
```

Fig. 10.7 Passwords with OpenSSL

```
E:\openssl>openssl passwd -crypt
               -salt mr peter
  mrnJiQG5dGt/I

E:\openssl>openssl passwd -apr1
               -salt mr...... peter
  $apr1$mr......$2Dlj.UdnGAOGS3IDfonFG.

E:\openssl>openssl passwd -apr1
               -salt mr...... peter mary
  $apr1$mr......$2Dlj.UdnGAOGS3IDfonFG.
  $apr1$mr......$38mLHzhmtxN6NuuZTAfaE/

E:\openssl>openssl passwd -apr1 peter mary
  $apr1$it/X31Dc$kWx5j3w7k5o2Df8WpLTLk0
  $apr1$cw2bpiNl$2zPoDTFIInK1nUN7BKiKv1
```

This first option -crypt instructs the OpenSSL package to generate the standard UNIX crypt password. The input original password is 'peter' and the two character salt is 'mr'. Similarly, you can use the command below to generate an Apache md5 password:

```
openssl passwd -apr1 -salt mr...... peter
```

In this case, the input original is 'peter' and the salt value is an eight character string 'mr......'. With OpenSSL, you can generate multiple passwords easily. For example, the following command will generate the md5Crypt passwords for 'peter' and 'mary':

```
openssl passwd -apr1 peter mary
```

If you don't specify the salt value, a random salt will be used. Some execution results are shown in Figure 10.7.

To verify the UNIX crypt result, you can, for example, activate the Web page ex03-04.htm that we developed in Chapter 3. To see the Apache md5Crypt password, the example ex03-07.htm is used. Screenshots are shown in Figures 10.8 and 10.9.

Generating message digest or hash values

To produce a message digest or hash value, the command dgst is used. One of the best ways to show how to use dgst is by example. By default, the dgst command is designed to work with files. If you have a file called johnsmith.txt that contains only one word 'johnsmith', you can obtain the message digest (MD5) string (e.g. md5) of 'johnsmith' by

```
openssl dgst -md5 johnsmith.txt
```

Fig. 10.8 Example `ex03-04.htm`

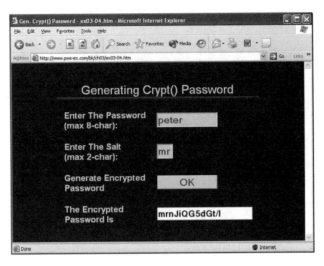

Fig. 10.9 Example `ex03-07.htm`

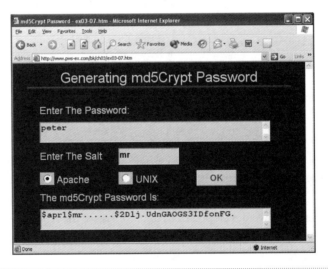

This statement will digest the contents of the file `johnsmith.txt` and output the md5 string to screen. To output the md5 string to a file, you can use

```
openssl dgst -out out.txt -md5 johnsmith.txt
```

If the main program `openssl` cannot understand a command or one of the arguments or options, it will display a help screen with a summary of the arguments and options. For example, you can produce a help screen for `dgst` by using the command `openssl dgst -h` (see `ex10-03.ssl`).

```
Example: ex10-03.ssl - Using message digest with OpenSSL

 1: E:\openssl>openssl dgst -h
 2: unknown option '-h'
 3: options are
 4: -c              to output the digest with separating colons
 5: -d              to output debug info
 6: -hex            output as hex dump
 7: -binary         output in binary form
 8: -sign file      sign digest using private key in file
 9: -verify file    verify a signature using public key in file
10: -prverify file  verify a signature using private key in file
11: -signature file signature to verify
12: -binary         output in binary form
13: -md5 to use the md5 message digest algorithm (default)
14: -md4 to use the md4 message digest algorithm
15: -md2 to use the md2 message digest algorithm
16: -sha1 to use the sha1 message digest algorithm
17: -sha to use the sha message digest algorithm
18: -mdc2 to use the mdc2 message digest algorithm
19: -ripemd160 to use the ripemd160 message digest algorithm
```

To produce the SHA (or SHA-1) hash, you can use the command

```
openssl dgst -sha1 johnsmith.txt
```

The hash value will be displayed on the screen, as shown in Figure 10.10. If you activate the Web page `ex03-08.htm` (Chapter 3) for the string 'johnsmith', you will see an identical hash value, as illustrated in Figure 10.11.

Now, let's see how to use OpenSSL for encryption and decryption.

Fig. 10.10 Using `dgst` in OpenSSL

```
E:\ch10>openssl dgst -md5 johnsmith.txt
MD5(johnsmith.txt)=
cd4388c0c62e65ac8b99e3ec49fd9409

E:\ch10>openssl dgst -sha1 johnsmith.txt
SHA1(johnsmith.txt)=
3b842bcd6faab4047ab49f9a99fa0704b9c9d2d7
```

Fig. 10.11 SHA-1 from `ex03-08.htm`

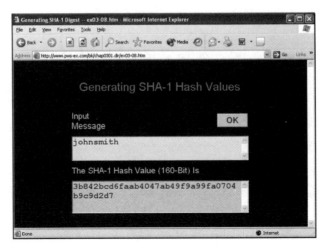

10.2.3 Encryption and decryption

The encryption and decryption processes in OpenSSL are controlled by the standard command `enc`. Similar to the `dgst` situation, this `enc` command has many options. Some of them are listed below:

- `-in <file>` input file;

- `-out <file>` output file;

- `-e` encrypt;

- `-d` decrypt;

- `-a/-base64` Base64 encode/decode, depending on the encryption flag;

- `-k` key is the next argument.

Together with all the cipher options, as in `ex10-02.ssl`, `enc` can be used to perform a number of different kinds of encryption and decryption. Suppose we have a sensitive message stored in a text file called `message.txt`. The following is an example of activating AES encryption on `message.txt`.

```
openssl enc -e -base64 -k johnsmith -aes-256-ecb
         -in message.txt -out message.enc
```

This command will perform AES encryption in ECB mode, specified by the options `-e` and `-aes-256-ecb`. The password key, in this case, is 'johnsmith'. The input file is `message.txt` and the output file `message.enc` is in Base64 encoding. If everything is OK, you will have the encrypted file `message.enc` in your system. Since this file is Base64 encoded, you can display it on your screen as illustrated in Figure 10.12.

Fig. 10.12 AES encryption with OpenSSL

```
E:\openssl>openssl enc -e -aes-256-ecb
  -base64 -k johnsmith
  -in message.txt -out message.enc

E:\openssl>type message.enc

E:\openssl\bin>type message.enc
U2FsdGVkX18qKdwtt9b8LXOMKjVeiG
lmA5Oijfqgexapw9xmUFicz8e1rPP6dPMo
goqDA0g1H08Nyxg/CHJVUGzpMEJ/1bIr
uVMvVQso6oI8UP4Bk0BFD+Qkd9zAZLCy
0e/W7FpkaA2npWsK9p+CndvVqd0y9aE
OZleXxyLWq7FInC5Gqo01t7x7ZREQTl7S
AsN2/7KUHmBZ/rqXUAsp2g==
```

To decrypt the encrypted file `message.enc`, you use the command

```
openssl enc -d -base64 -k johnsmith -aes-256-ecb
        -in message.enc -out message.dec
```

By changing the option to -d, decryption is performed and the output is written to file `message.dec`. This file should be the same as the original `message.txt` (see Figure 10.13).

To build a more practical application, let's consider a page designed to perform different types of encryption and decryption. The basic principle of this application is simple. First, an XHTML page is developed to get the following information and associated actions:

Fig. 10.13 AES decryption with OpenSSL

```
E:\openssl>openssl enc -d -aes-256-ecb
  -base64 -k johnsmith
  -in message.enc -out message.dec

E:\openssl>type message.dec
sue@practical-web.com
Re-form Meeting
```

Dear Sue

You are invited to the company
re-form meeting at 2:pm next
Wednesday.

John Smith

- original plaintext;

- password key;

- select an algorithm;

- perform encryption or decryption.

Once this is completed, a server page is developed to execute the responding OpenSSL processing command. Finally, the result is captured and displayed as another Web page. To simplify the operation, only the following six algorithms are considered:

```
AES-256-ECB    DES-ECB    BlowFish-ECB
AES-256-CBC    DES-CBC    BlowFish-CBC
```

Consider the following body part of ex10-04.htm.

```
Example: ex10-04.htm - Encryption/decryption with OpenSSL

 1: <head><title>Enc/Dec With OpenSSL - ex10-04.htm</title></head>
 2: <style>
 3:   .butSt{background:#aaffaa;width:250px;
 4:         font-family:arial;font-weight:bold;
              font-size:16pt;color:#880000}
 5:   .butSt2{background:#aaffaa;width:30px;height:30px;
 6:          font-family:arial;font-weight:bold;
              font-size:16pt;color:#880000}
 7:   .txtSt{width:200px;background:#000088;
 8:         font-family:arial;font-size:16pt;color:#ffff00}
 9: </style>
10: <body style="background:#000088;font-family:arial;font-size:18pt;
11:    color:#ffff00;font-weight:bold">
12: <div style="font-size:22pt;font-weight:bold;text-align:center">
13:    Encryption/Decryption With OpenSSL</div>
14:
15: <form action="ex10-04.pl" style="text-align:center"
16:    method="post" target="_blank">
17:
18: <table style="font-size:16pt" align="center" width="680">
19:  <tr><td><br />Enter The Input Message: </td></tr>
20:  <tr><td><textarea style="font-size:16pt;width:640px;height:130px;
21:        font-weight:bold;background:#dddddd"
              id="inMesg" name="inMesg"
22:        rows="5" cols="40">Meet Me At 2pm
              Tomorrow</textarea></td></tr>
23: </table><br />
24:
```

```
25: <table style="font-size:16pt" align="center" width="680">
26:  <tr><td style="text-align:left" class="txtSt"
27:      colspan="6">Algorithm</td></tr>
28:  <tr><td><input type="radio" name="br" id="br"
          class="butSt2" checked
29:      value="-aes-256-ecb" /></td><td class="txtSt">AES 256
          ECB</td>
30:    <td><input type="radio" name="br" id="br" class="butSt2"
31:      value="-des-ecb" /></td><td class="txtSt">DES ECB</td>
32:    <td><input type="radio" name="br" id="br" class="butSt2"
33:      value="-bf-ecb" /></td><td class="txtSt">BlowFish
          ECB</td></tr>
34:  <tr><td><input type="radio" name="br" id="br" class="butSt2"
35:      value="-aes-256-cbc" /></td><td class="txtSt">AES 256
          CBC</td>
36:    <td><input type="radio" name="br" id="br" class="butSt2"
37:      value="-des-cbc" /></td><td class="txtSt">DES CBC</td>
38:    <td><input type="radio" name="br" id="br" class="butSt2"
39:      value="-bfcbc" /></td><td class="txtSt">BlowFish
          CBC</td></tr>
40: </table><br />
41:
42: <table style="font-size:16pt" align="center" width="680">
43: <tr><td>Enter The Key: </td>
44:   <td style="text-align:left" colspan=2>
45:     <input type="text" id="keyV" name="keyV" size="32"
        maxlength="32"
46: style="font-size:16pt;width:450px;height:36px;font-weight:bold;
47: background:#dddddd;color:#ff0000"
    value="agent00187654321" /></td></tr>
48: <tr><td style="width:180px;text-align:left"><input type="radio"
          checked
49:      id="b_rad" name="br2" class="butSt2" value="-e" />
          Encryption</td>
50:    <td style="width:230px;text-align:left"><input type="radio"
51:      id="b_rad" name="br2" class="butSt2" value="-d" />
          Decryption</td>
52:    <td style="width:230px;text-align:left"><input size="20"
          type="button"
53:      class="butSt" style="width:210px" value="OK"
          onclick="submit()" />
54:    </td></tr>
55: </table>
56: </form>
57: </body>
```

Fig. 10.14 Encryption with OpenSSL

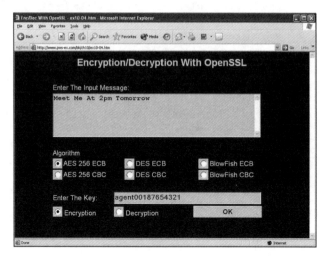

This is a simple page containing one text area, six radio buttons, one text box, another two radio buttons, and one OK button. The text area in lines 20–22 gets the original plaintext. The six radio buttons defined in lines 28–39 are user selectable. Each of them represents one encryption/decryption algorithm. The textbox in lines 45–47 is used to get the input key. Then another two radio buttons are defined (lines 48–51) so that both encryption and decryption can be performed in this page. A screenshot is shown in Figure 10.14.

Once the OK button in lines 52–53 is clicked, all the data in the page is submitted as form elements to the server page ex10-04.pl for encryption and decryption (lines 15–16). Since the attribute target="_blank" is used in line 16, the Perl script ex10-04.pl will be displayed as a blank new page.

As you can see, the length of the entire script rc10-04.pl is fewer than 35 lines. After the header and the CGI magic string in lines 1–3, the submitted data are captured by variables:

- $inM – store the input plaintext;
- $br1 – store the selected encryption algorithm;
- $br2 – store the encryption (-e) or decryption (-d) operation;
- $kV – store the user input key.

Lines 10–18 generate the proper header for the XHTML page. The print functions in lines 19–23 output the title, date and time and other information relating to the example. After that, the three statements in lines 25–27 open the file usr.dat and

```
Example: ex10-04.pl - Perl script for ex10-04.htm

 1: #! /usr/bin/perl
 2: use CGI qw (:standard);
 3: print ("Content-type:text/html\n\n");
 4:
 5: $inM = param("inMesg");
 6: $br1 = param("br");
 7: $br2 = param("br2");
 8: $kV = param("keyV");
 9:
10: print << "myDoc";
11: <?xml version="1.0" encoding="iso-8859-1"?>
12: <!DOCTYPE html PUBLIC "-//W3C//DTD XHTML 1.0 Transitional//EN"
13:   "http://www.w3.org/TR/xhtml1/DTD/xhtml1-transitional.dtd">
14:   <html xmlns="http://www.w3.org/1999/xhtml"
        xml:lang="en" lang="en">
15:   <head><title>Perl Example: ex10-04.pl</title></head>
16:   <body style="background:#000088;font-family:arial;
          font-size:18pt;
17:     color:#ffff00;font-weight:bold">
18: myDoc
19:   print "Encryption/Decryption With OpenSSL: <br />";
20:   print "Time : ",scalar(localtime());
21:   print "<br />Algorithm = $br1 <br />";
22:   print "Encryption/Decryption = $br2 <br /><br />";
23:   print "The Processing Results Are: <br />";
24:
25:   open(filehandle,">usr.dat") or die("Cannot Open File... Error");
26:   print (filehandle "$inM");
27:   close(filehandle);
28:
29:   $enM = `openssl.exe enc $br1 $br2 -base64 -k $kV -in usr.dat`;
30:   print "<textarea style='font-size:14pt;width:750px;height:130px;
31:         font-weight:bold;background:#dddddd' rows='5'
32:         cols='40'>$enM</textarea><br />";
33:   print "</body></html>";
```

store the input plaintext in it. The main operational statement of this example is in line 29. If the selected variables $br1, $br2 and $kV represent the strings '-aes-256-ecb', '-e', and 'agent001' respectively, the command in line 29 turns out to be

```
openssl.exe enc -aes-256-ecb -e -base64 -k agent001 -in usr.dat
```

Fig. 10.15 The encryption results

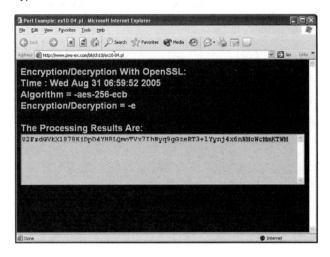

This statement will activate the OpenSSL main program openssl to perform the aes-256-ecb encryption on the file usr.dat using the key 'agent001'. The encrypted result is stored in variable $enM, as illustrated at the beginning of line 29. The print function in lines 30–32 generates a text area to display the encryption result stored in variable $enM. A screenshot is shown in Figure 10.15.

Since all the operations are executed by the openssl program, this page can be considered as a general page for running openssl. In fact, almost all functionalities can be included. For example, if you copy and paste the encrypted string in Figure 10.15 into the input window and select the decryption radio button, as illustrated in Figure 10.16, the variable $br2 will store the string '-d'. In this case, the statement in line 29 turns out to be

```
openssl.exe enc –aes-256-ecb –d –base64 –k agent001 –in usr.dat
```

This statement will, obviously, perform decryption on the newly created file usr.dat, and the decrypted result is displayed in a blank new page (see Figure 10.17).

Using OpenSSL as an engine in the background, encryption or decryption server pages can be developed easily.

Now you have some experience of how to perform encryption/decryption using OpenSSL, but before we continue to investigate certificates, you need to know how to generate digital keys with OpenSSL.

Fig. 10.16 Decryption with OpenSSL

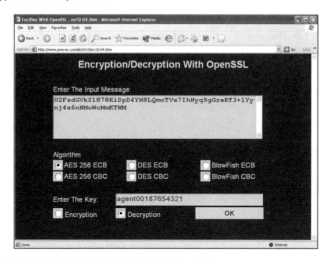

Fig. 10.17 The decryption results

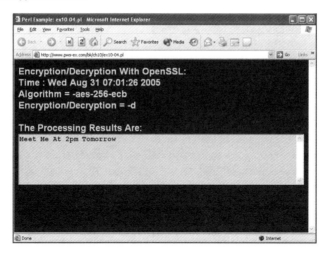

10.2.4   Generating digital keys with OpenSSL

In general, you can use the following two commands to generate digital keys:

    openssl genrsa   or   openssl gendsa

For example, if you want to generate an RSA private key, you can use the command and option

```
openssl genrsa -des3 -out johnsmith.key 1024
```

The option `-des3` (line 24 of `ex10-02.ssl`) specifies the encryption method for protecting the private key. It means that the generated private key is encrypted by the `des3` method with a passphrase.

The program `openssl` will ask you to input the passphrase. Once this is entered, the private key is output to the file `johnsmith.key`. A session showing this command in action is shown in `ex10-05.ssl`.

Example: ex10-05.ssl - Generating an RSA private key using OpenSSL

```
 1: E:\openssl>openssl genrsa -des3 -out johnsmith.key 1024
 2: Loading 'screen' into random state - done
 4: Generating RSA private key, 1024 bit long modulus
 5: .....++++++
 6: ...........................++++++
 7: e is 65537 (0x10001)
 8: Enter pass phrase for johnsmith.key: johnsmith <---- (Not Display)
 9: Verifying - Enter pass phrase for johnsmith.key:
                                        johnsmith <-(Not Display)
10:
11: E:\openssl>type johnsmith.key
12: -----BEGIN RSA PRIVATE KEY-----
13: Proc-Type: 4,ENCRYPTED
14: DEK-Info: DES-EDE3-CBC,929A7CE14A2FF8E5
15:
16: IQ/sgRGNgg1MDqiUh3aour+rxnphWcbGVkTgana0BPzAa38p88QYZdHT1tccr29p
17: 2joCWOEYobe7TQrnUcBHfJQDctEy9Wn6sosnyI0tfow1nhVo3pzJNcPByf5KSI7X
18: ax6RrBD11jU04bzli2P4WlfbdpvFoLfX+4f8X3U5nbOVF3nAI/gso18BNs0WaIwt
19: tdzoQgo1FbO8FhYteZh8pjXwpTzGGdwb2rDvHOHWzUzD5BU5K9Gma3jPBqdPSp4O
20: TxQ5yT4RxCGGSKSvNNdwQjLstRFW8YZLgYtYUYMdP+wi5ObyGN/kNxwCr1SKfsdk
21: X4md+FXJPGu3zzit+ksX1LI5YGG8NdIL/OWxEeHSRqx63xTj1sv3Jn2AJJXsh0OY
22: DenhjhWHpCPh4xwWBm4r0UmDXIkDJmU1YlgYqO7S6Py1mXUqriUNu7gp8QnmDQ55
23: 9vcm/Y8p5icxypwLhLlIBJoHh0czZoBBrhr7NvZ+ktrQ+KbGjgOYnLIy1m5GdR9E
24: 5iMOgp/xWqc59KbtcXSrSpaG5cO1N1tHMeFny2Pb37qyxDnl4XqVQG21AZB5Wtzr
25: zit/jQ+8LVrA1Mv5Ct4kQy4+EDjFu9EpSNXGFayLtxyRnNUoUgZdDKJo/xy9bi27
26: Br7T/z2V16AwZv9dQUoMSpOQHA51mETeFyMWrysSFI9VJLH0zr+L7J3oFpFk/LM1
27: DcEhGOmkRMeGBrDPqhxZ0jQ0/ihgxxoTG5Ccpjn1VVU71XBfsiI7CKwAbXXAfLig
28: 6n1Pzd6L1AY0CVzvwNE/kaqgjZKRKzfqeiQ9wjNSH2ZmQvlprHVosw==
29: -----END RSA PRIVATE KEY-----
30:
```

The `type` command in line 11 is a general system command of DOS windows to display the contents of a file. Lines 13–14 indicate that the key is protected by

DES-EDE3-CBC (des3) encryption with a passphrase. You can see the details of your private key using

```
Openssl rsa -noout -text -in johnsmith.key
```

This statement displays a detailed report about the private key johnsmith.key on the screen. If you just want to store the unprotected private key, you can issue the command

```
openssl rsa -in johnsmith.key -out johnsmith.unprotected
```

After asking for the passphrase, the unprotected private key is output into the file johnsmith.unprotected. Now we can generate certificates using OpenSSL.

10.3 Generating and signing certificates with OpenSSL

10.3.1 Certificate and certificate signing request

To generate a certificate, you need to go through the following two processes:

■ generate a certificate signing request (CSR);

■ get the CSR signed by a certification authority (CA) or yourself.

The CSR is, basically, a digital form for identifying you. Usually, you generate a CSR with your private key. For example, 'johnsmith' can use his private key `johnsmith.key` to generate a CSR form with the command

```
openssl req -new -key johnsmith.key -out johnsmith.csr
```

This command generates a new CSR form in the local directory using the default configuration file `openssl.cnf`. If this configuration file is in other directory, you should include the `-config` option:

```
openssl req -new -key johnsmith.key -out johnsmith.csr -config
./openssl.cnf
```

This statement uses the OpenSSL configuration file `openssl.cnf` in the local directory.

In order to identify yourself, the `openssl` program will ask you a series of questions. You can answer most of them by just hitting the return key. A typical dialog is shown in `ex10-06.ssl`.

Now you have a CSR file, such as `johnsmith.csr`, in your system. The next step is to send this to an authorized CA for signing. The result is a real certificate that can be used for applications. There are several popular commercial CAs on the Web. Two of them are:

■ Verisign at http://digitalid.verisign.com;

■ Thawte Consulting at http://www.thawte.com.

Usually, you need to complete a form in their Web site posting your CSR. They will digitally sign your CSR and return a signed certificate to you. The signed certificate is normally a file with an extension `crt` or `pem`, such as `johnsmith.crt` or `johnsmith.pem`, depending on the file format you have chosen.

For a testing or for a very lightweight application, you can sign your CSR yourself. For example, you can sign the CSR file `johnsmith.csr` by using your own private key as follows:

```
openssl x509 -req -in johnsmith.csr -out johnsmith.crt
       -signkey johnsmith.key -days 365
```

```
Example: ex10-06.ssl - Generating a certificate signing request

 1: E:\openssl>openssl req -new -key johnsmith.key -out johnsmith.csr
 2:           -config ./openssl.cnf
 3: Enter passphrase for johnsmith.key:johnsmith <--(Not Display)
 4: You are about to be asked to enter information that will be
      incorporated
 5: into your certificate request.
 6: What you are about to enter is what is called a Distinguished
      Name or a DN.
 7: There are quite a few fields but you can leave some blank
 8: For some fields there will be a default value,
 9: If you enter '.', the field will be left blank.
10: -----
11: Country Name (2 letter code) [AU]:UK
12: State or Province Name (full name) [Some-State]: (Just Press Return)
13: Locality Name (eg, city) []:                    (Just Press Return)
14: Organization Name (eg, company) [Internet Widgits Pty Ltd]:ABC
15: Organizational Unit Name (eg, section) []:www.pws-ex.com
16: Common Name (eg, YOUR name) []:johnsmith
17: Email Address []:johnsmith@pws-ex.com
18:
19: Please enter the following 'extra' attributes
20: to be sent with your certificate request
21: A challenge password []:johnsmith
22: An optional company name []:              (Just Press Return)
```

This command signs the CSR file using the signing key `johnsmith.key` and outputs the signed certificate using the X509 standard format. The final certificate is output to a file called `johnsmith.crt`. The certificate itself is an encrypted file similar to the key file `johnsmith.key` listed in `ex10-05.ssl`. To convert the file into meaningful text, you can use the command

```
openssl x509 -noout -text -in johnsmith.crt
```

A dialog session using the two statements above is shown in `ex10-07.ssl`.

```
Example: ex10-07.ssl - Signing a CSR with your own private key

 1: E:\openssl>openssl x509 -req -in johnsmith.csr
 2:           -out johnsmith.crt -signkey johnsmith.key -days 365
 3: Loading 'screen' into random state - done
 4: Signature ok
```

```
 5: subject=/C=UK/ST=Some-State/O=ABC/OU=www.pws-ex.com/CN=
 6: johnsmith/emailAddress=jo
 7: hnsmith@pws-ex.com
 8: Getting Private key
 9: Enter passphrase for johnsmith.key:10: johnsmith <--(Not Display)
10:
11: E:\openssl>openssl x509 -noout -text -in johnsmith.crt
12: Certificate:
13:     Data:
14:         Version: 1 (0x0)
15:         Serial Number: 0 (0x0)
16:         Signature Algorithm: md5WithRSAEncryption
17:         Issuer: C=UK, ST=Some-State, O=ABC, OU=www.pws-ex.com,
18:             CN=johnsmith/emailAddress=johnsmith@pws-ex.com
19:         Validity
20:             Not Before: Aug 11 22:57:27 2005 GMT
21:             Not After : Aug 11 22:57:27 2006 GMT
22:         Subject: C=UK, ST=Some-State, O=ABC, OU=www.pws-ex.com,
23:             CN=johnsmith/emailAddress=johnsmith@pws-ex.com
24:         Subject Public Key Info:
25:             Public Key Algorithm: rsaEncryption
26:             RSA Public Key: (1024 bit)
27:                 Modulus (1024 bit):
28:                     00:f0:71:1f:5a:6e:aa:cf:27:ff:41:dc:d1:f4:02:
29:                     4f:00:c6:5a:5a:0f:b2:b9:d5:f4:06:59:73:45:86:
30:                     05:c1:aa:8f:37:35:f9:32:92:a1:e6:2b:05:2d:81:
31:                     85:71:c3:f7:ac:5e:c4:33:a8:ad:6a:6a:bd:1e:ea:
32:                     b5:d8:5b:bf:50:71:bd:d8:d5:a4:bf:46:6a:99:c2:
33:                     c0:11:4a:13:39:58:80:04:5f:6d:dc:f3:7a:72:34:
34:                     bc:11:85:9c:e3:7a:f8:52:aa:7a:39:56:07:2e:14:
35:                     70:e7:96:b0:9b:d3:8b:e6:8e:af:49:6e:7f:fa:bc:
36:                     19:9e:c1:17:83:20:fd:94:7f
37:                 Exponent: 65537 (0x10001)
38:     Signature Algorithm: md5WithRSAEncryption
39:         2a:09:e7:56:53:62:d7:d1:ef:5a:fd:ac:e0:c2:3a:23:22:2b:
40:         3f:ea:c9:ff:8f:75:d9:34:f3:10:19:bb:bb:71:92:cb:16:79:
41:         5d:1f:9c:7e:74:99:20:90:e1:3e:9d:f8:d9:46:d2:68:cd:30:
42:         35:8b:c0:19:c0:ba:a8:dd:ee:f5:39:b3:6d:bf:3f:ca:a9:ed:
43:         0a:21:20:19:98:ca:81:7d:66:35:44:4a:3a:0a:87:bc:97:e6:
44:         1a:f2:85:cd:e5:b0:90:81:a1:42:e8:97:a8:2a:21:1e:72:dc:
45:         c2:85:a3:de:c2:f2:cd:3a:fd:9c:32:90:9e:88:ec:6d:5b:9e:
46:         52:84
47:
```

The command in lines 1–2 is used to generate the signed certificate johnsmith.crt. In order to get the private key, the openssl program asks you to input the passphrase in line 9. The command in line 11 is used to generate meaningful text output from the certificate. From this example, you can see that a certificate contains three sections:

- a validity section to specify the life of the certificate (lines 19–21);

- a public-key section to store the public key (lines 25–37);

- a signature section (lines 38–46).

The information above is vital for any secure communication using certificate exchange. For some real applications, certificates must be signed by a CA. With OpenSSL, we can create our own CA and sign certificates.

10.3.2 Signing certificates as a CA with OpenSSL

To create a CA of your own, you may need to deal with the command

```
openssl ca ... ...
```

This command is one of the most complicated commands in OpenSSL. The full syntax and options are listed below:

```
openssl ca [-verbose] [-config filename] [-name section] [-gencrl]
    [-revoke file] [-subj arg] [-crldays days] [-crlhours hours]
    [-crlexts section] [-startdate date] [-enddate date] [-days arg]
    [-md arg] [-policy arg] [-keyfile arg] [-key arg] [-passin arg]
    [-cert file] [-in file] [-out file] [-notext] [-outdir dir]
    [-infiles][-spkac file] [-ss_cert file] [-preserveDN] [-noemailDN]
    [-batch][-msie_hack] [-extensions section] [-extfile section]
```

Because of some strange arrangement of the configuration file openssl, it doesn't allow one to use this 'openssl ca' easily. For this reason, the distribution of OpenSSL includes a Perl script file called CA.pl in the apps directory to help.

Basically, this Perl script creates an environment such that using the command openssl ca is easier. To take its simplest form, the following command will create a CA certificate and private key:

```
CA.pl -newca
```

The CA signed certificate (cacert.pem) and private key (cakey.pem) are stored in the directories apps/demoCA and apps/demoCA/private respectively. A dialog session is shown in ex10-08.ssl.

If your Perl script CA.pl is in another directory, you may need to include the path such as

```
C:\openssl-0.9.7d\out32dll>perl..\apps\CA.pl -newca
```

```
Example: ex10-08.ssl - Generating a CA certificate and private key

 1: E:\openssl\bin>perl CA.pl -newca
 2: CA certificate filename (or enter to create) <--(Just Press Return)
 3:
 4: Making CA certificate ...
 5: Loading 'screen' into random state - done
 6: Generating a 1024 bit RSA private key
 7: ...++++++
 8: ..........++++++
 9: writing new private key to './demoCA/private/cakey.pem'
10: Enter PEM passphrase: myca <------------------ (Will Not Display)
11: Verifying - Enter PEM passphrase: myca <------ (Will Not Display)
12: -----
13: You are about to be asked to enter information that will be
    incorporated
14: into your certificate request.
15: What you are about to enter is what is called a Distinguished
    Name or a DN.
16: There are quite a few fields but you can leave some blank
17: For some fields there will be a default value,
18: If you enter '.', the field will be left blank.
19: -----
20: Country Name (2 letter code) [AU]:UK
21: State or Province Name (full name) [Some-State]:
                            <--------------- (Just Press Return)
22: Locality Name (eg, city) []:<--------------- (Just Press Return)
23: Organization Name (eg, company) [Internet Widgits Pty Ltd]:MyCA
24: Organizational Unit Name (eg, section) []:<-- (Just Press Return)
25: Common Name (eg, YOUR name) []:<------------- (Just Press Return)
26: Email Address []:<------------------------- (Just Press Return)
```

Please note that you may also need to delete the existing `cacert.pem` and
`cakey.pem` files to make this example work. Now you can use this new CA
certificate and private key to sign the CSR form. One of the simplest ways of
doing this is to rename the `johnsmith.csr` file to `newreq.pem` file and then call the
`CA.pl` script as:

```
CA.pl -sign
```

This command will sign the CSR file `newreq.pem` using the CA generated by
`ex10-08.ssl`. The signed certificate is called `newcert.pem`. This file can be renamed
to `johnsmith.crt` or `johnsmith.pem` later as a real certificate. A dialog session is
shown in example `ex10-09.ssl`.

Example: ex10-09.ssl – Signing a certificate with your own CA

```
 1: E:\openssl\bin>perl CA.pl -sign
 2: Using configuration from ./openssl.cnf
 3: Loading 'screen' into random state - done
 4: 912:error:0E06D06C:configuration file
    routines:NCONF_get_string:no
 5:  value:.\crypto\conf\conf_lib.c:329:group=CA_default
 6:  name=unique_subject
 7: Enter passphrase for ./demoCA/private/cakey.pem:
                                        myca <--- (Not Display)
 8: Check that the request matches the signature
 9: Signature ok
10: Certificate Details:
11:   Serial Number: 1 (0x1)
12:   Validity
13:     Not Before: Aug 13 00:40:16 2005 GMT
14:     Not After : Aug 13 00:40:16 2006 GMT
15:   Subject:
16:     countryName              = UK
17:     stateOrProvinceName      = Some-State
18:     organizationName         = ABC
19:     organizationalUnitName   = www.pws-ex.com
20:     commonName               = johnsmith
21:     emailAddress             = johnsmith@pws-ex.com
22:   X509v3 extensions:
23:     X509v3 Basic Constraints:
24:         CA:FALSE
25:     Netscape Comment:
26:         OpenSSL Generated Certificate
27:     X509v3 Subject Key Identifier:
28:         2A:2F:19:56:CE:7E:AF:BE:B8:66:69:34:82:EB:DF:A8:85:C6:B0:93
29:     X509v3 Authority Key Identifier:
30:         keyid:06:50:03:3B:A4:39:2A:CC:5B:C5:5A:FF:31:2F:E7:D0:85:
            2E:24:31
31:     DirName:/C=UK/ST=Some-State/O=MyCA
32:     serial:00
33:
34: Certificate is to be certified until Aug 13 00:40:16 2006 GMT
    (365 days)
35: Sign the certificate? [y/n]:y
36:
37: 1 out of 1 certificate requests certified, commit? [y/n]y
38: Write out database with 1 new entries
39: Data Base Updated
40: Signed certificate is in newcert.pem
```

You may notice that the certificate file has the extension `.pem`. This is the default certificate format, known as privacy enhanced mail (PEM) encoding, used by OpenSSL. For Web applications some other formats may be used.

10.3.3   Certificate formats: X509 and PKCS#12

By default, the structure of the certificate used in OpenSSL is called X509. This is an authentication certificate scheme recommended by the International Telecommunication Union (ITU-T) and supported by the SSL/TLS standard.

The signed certificate generated by OpenSSL in `ex10-08.ssl` is in the form of Base64 PEM encoding. This is why a number of authors and articles use the file extension `.pem` for certificates generated by OpenSSL. To see this certificate in printable form, the following command can be used:

```
openssl x509 -noout -text -in johnsmith.crt
```

A session of the operation is listed in `ex10-10.ssl`.

```
Example: ex10-10.ssl - The default X509 certificate format

 1: E:\openssl\bin>openssl x509 -noout -text -in johnsmith.crt
 2: Certificate:
 3:   Data:
 4:     Version: 3 (0x2)
 5:     Serial Number: 1 (0x1)
 6:     Signature Algorithm: md5WithRSAEncryption
 7:     Issuer: C=UK, ST=Some-State, O=MyCA
 8:     Validity
 9:         Not Before: Aug 13 00:40:16 2005 GMT
10:         Not After : Aug 13 00:40:16 2006 GMT
11:     Subject: C=UK, ST=Some-State, O=ABC, OU=www.pws-ex.com,
12:             CN=johnsmith/emailAddress=johnsmith@pws-ex.com
13:     Subject Public Key Info:
14:       Public Key Algorithm: rsaEncryption
15:       RSA Public Key: (1024 bit)
16:         Modulus (1024 bit):
17:             00:f0:71:1f:5a:6e:aa:cf:27:ff:41:dc:d1:f4:02:
18:             4f:00:c6:5a:5a:0f:b2:b9:d5:f4:06:59:73:45:86:
19:             05:c1:aa:8f:37:35:f9:32:92:a1:e6:2b:05:2d:81:
20:             85:71:c3:f7:ac:5e:c4:33:a8:ad:6a:6a:bd:1e:ea:
21:             b5:d8:5b:bf:50:71:bd:d8:d5:a4:bf:46:6a:99:c2:
22:             c0:11:4a:13:39:58:80:04:5f:6d:dc:f3:7a:72:34:
23:             bc:11:85:9c:e3:7a:f8:52:aa:7a:39:56:07:2e:14:
```

```
24:                70:e7:96:b0:9b:d3:8b:e6:8e:af:49:6e:7f:fa:bc:
25:                19:9e:c1:17:83:20:fd:94:7f
26:          Exponent: 65537 (0x10001)
27:          X509v3 extensions:
28:            X509v3 Basic Constraints:
29:              CA:FALSE
30:            Netscape Comment:
31:              OpenSSL Generated Certificate
32:            X509v3 Subject Key Identifier:
33:              2A:2F:19:56:CE:7E:AF:BE:B8:66:69:34:82:EB:DF:A8:
                  85:C6:B0:93
34:            X509v3 Authority Key Identifier:
35:              keyid:06:50:03:3B:A4:39:2A:CC:5B:C5:5A:FF:31:2F:E7:
                  D0:85:2E:24:31
36:              DirName:/C=UK/ST=Some-State/O=MyCA
37:              serial:00
38:
39:     Signature Algorithm: md5WithRSAEncryption
40:        b7:3b:9f:e8:f1:9e:29:f5:25:81:c0:bf:00:81:4e:39:bd:72:
41:        6f:14:c5:5e:81:f1:ff:07:8a:f8:32:d8:84:aa:c6:5f:99:9c:
42:        c3:6d:ae:56:38:16:ac:aa:c8:45:b5:ce:f5:ab:37:32:ae:72:
43:        35:42:87:b8:4e:47:36:3d:f0:39:1c:be:2b:6d:33:79:96:20:
44:        3d:af:e0:c3:b3:1c:d8:f7:11:74:ce:89:8f:2c:1c:da:a3:32:
45:        a6:91:39:4e:76:f3:d8:59:e3:c0:be:c2:00:ab:be:81:ff:21:
46:        77:a8:54:9a:0e:3d:3b:06:f9:9a:00:79:54:17:d5:de:64:9e:
47:        c6:66
48:
```

In addition to this PEM structure, another popular certificate format known as PKCS#12 is widely supported by many browsers. It is a format for storing private keys and certificates at the same time. Some characteristics of this format are:

- it is supported by most Web browsers, including IE, NS, Opera;

- by integrating private keys and certificates, only one file is needed for import and export;

- it is probably the only way of accessing the private keys of other certificates.

Using OpenSSL to generate a PKCS#12 file from a standard .pem file is not difficult. For example, you can generate the PKCS#12 file johnsmith.p12 corresponding to johnsmith.key and johnsmith.crt using the command

```
openssl pkcs12 -export -in johnsmith.crt -inkey johnsmith.key
    -certfile cacert.pem -name "johnsmith" -out johnsmith.p12
```

This command takes `johnsmith.crt`, `johnsmith.key` and `cacert.pem` as input arguments. The output file is `johnsmith.p12` in PKCS#12 format. A dialog session of this process is shown in `ex10-11.ssl`.

```
Example: ex10-11.ssl - Creating PKCS#12 certificates

1: openssl-0.9.7d\apps>openssl pkcs12 -export -in johnsmith.crt
2:                     -inkey johnsmith.key -certfile newcert.pem
3:                     -name "johnsmith" -out johnsmith.p12
4:
5: Loading 'screen' into random state - done
6: Enter PEM passphrase:johnsmith  <------------- (Will Not Display)
7: Enter Export Password: anything <------------- (Will Not Display)
8: Verifying password - Enter Export Password: anything
                                        <--- (Will Not Display)
9:
```

Now you have a certificate in PKCS#12 format ready to be imported into your favourite browser on the World Wide Web.

10.3.4   Importing and exporting certificates with browsers

By installing a certificate into a browser, you have given your favourite browser the capability of identifying yourself. This is important when your browser communicates with a Web server in secure mode. Your browser can respond to a server request by sending the certificate over. This process is called 'client authentication'. Together with server authentication, mutual trust can be built and security serves its purpose.

If you are using IE5+ or IE6+, you can use the following procedures to import the certificate authority `MyCA` and certificate `johnsmith.p12`.

Importing a certificate authority into Internet Explorer

To import the newly generated CA `cacert.pem` into IE, the following procedure is used.

- Activate the IE browser.

- From the menu, choose `Tools|Internet Options|Content|Certificates`.

- Click the `Certificate` button to activate the Certificates window and select 'Trusted Root Certification Authorities' (see Figure 10.18).

Fig. 10.18 Certificates window

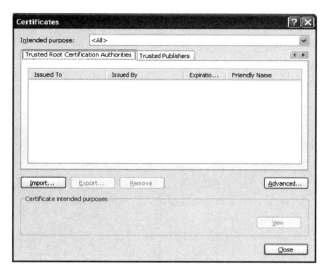

■ Click the Import button to launch the Certificate Import Wizard and then click the Next button to import the file 'cacert.pem' (Figure 10.19). You may use the Browse button to locate files in other folders.

Fig. 10.19 Select the import file

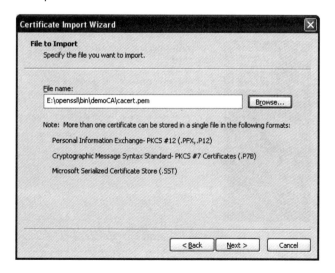

- In the Certificate Import Wizard window, click the Next button to put the CA certificate into 'Trusted Root Certificate Authorities' (see Figure 10.20). When the Next button is hit, the settings of the imported certificate will be displayed (see Figure 10.21).

Fig. 10.20 Confirming the store

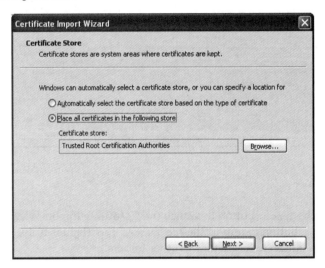

Fig. 10.21 Import file settings

Fig. 10.22 Certificate stored

■ When you click the `Finish` button to confirm the storage of the certificate, the certificate `MyCA` is imported and stored, as illustrated in Figure 10.22.

■ If you highlight the certificate and hit the `View` button, the details of the certificate are displayed (see Figure 10.23).

Now, we have installed the CA certificate `MyCA` into IE. This certificate will be used to verify any certificate issued by MyCA. For example, the certificate `johnsmith.p12` in `ex10-09.ssl` is signed by `MyCA`. When `johnsmith.p12` is imported into IE, the installed `MyCA` certificate will be used to verify it automatically.

Importing a personal certificate into Internet Explorer

To import the personal certificate `johnsmith.p12` into IE, the following procedure is used.

■ Activate the Certificates windows as described in the first three steps in the previous section (see Figure 10.24).

■ Click the `Import` button to launch the Certificate Import Wizard and select the `Personal` option. Now, click the `Next` button to import the certificate file `johnsmith.p12` (Figure 10.25). You may use the Browse button to locate files in other folders.

Fig. 10.23   Certificate summary

Fig. 10.24   Certificates window

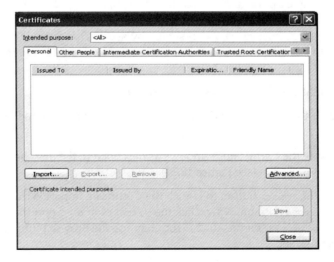

Fig. 10.25   Select the import file

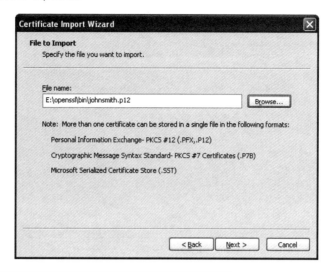

When you click the Next button in Figure 10.25, a Password window appears to allow you to enter a password for the private key (Figure 10.26). Also, you have the chance to increase security by checking the 'strong private key protection' option.

Fig. 10.26   Password for your private key

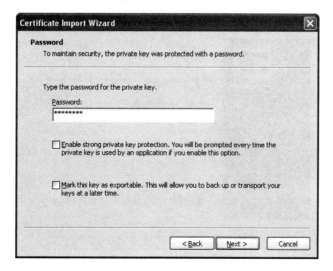

Fig. 10.27 The certificate store

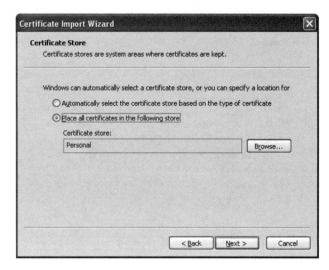

- Clicking the `Next` button activates the Certificate Store window (Figure 10.27). If you want a different certificate store, you can change it by clicking the `Browse` button.

- Next you see a summary of your import certificate settings, as illustrated in Figure 10.28. When the `Finish` button is clicked, an 'import successful' message is displayed (Figure 10.29).

Fig. 10.28 Certificate settings

Fig. 10.29 Import successful

- Finally, the certificate is installed and it is listed in the Certificates window (see Figure 10.30).

- When you highlight the certificate in the Certificates window and hit the `View` button, the details of the certificate are displayed, as shown in Figure 10.31.

Now the newly generated PKCS#12 certificate is installed in the IE browser and is ready for SSL authentication. If you are using NS or Opera, certificates can be imported along similar lines. In addition to importing, an installed certificate can be exported as well.

Fig. 10.30 Certificate installed

Fig. 10.31 Certificate summary

Exporting certificates from browsers

One of the best ways of demonstrating how to export a certificate from a browser is by example. Consider the process below.

- In the Certificates window, highlight the certificate `johnsmith` and click the `Import` button to activate the Certificate Export Wizard as illustrated in Figures 10.32 and 10.33.

- Before the certificate is exported, you have an opportunity to select whether or not you want to export the private key associated with `johnsmith.p12` (see Figure 10.34).

- When the `Next` button in Figure 10.34 is clicked, you can select the output format for the certificate. For this example, the selected format is 'Base64 encoded X.509', as illustrated in Figure 10.35.

- When the `Next` button is pressed, you will be asked for the output filename (see Figure 10.36).

Fig. 10.32 Selecting the certificate

Fig. 10.33 Certificate Export Wizard

Fig. 10.34 Export the private key

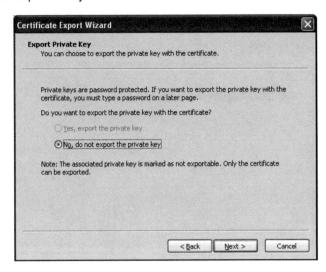

Fig. 10.35 Export format

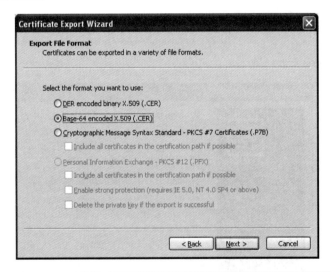

- After two more `Next` buttons, the certificate is exported successfully, as demonstrated in Figures 10.37 and 10.38.

Now you have some experience of handling certificates, it's time to consider how to use these to build a secure site with HTTPS protocol.

Fig. 10.36 Export certificate file name

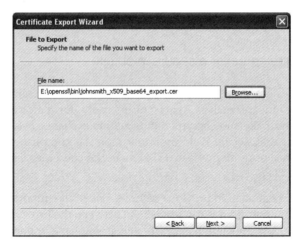

Fig. 10.37 Export file settings

Fig. 10.38 Export successful

10.4 Integrating OpenSSL and Apache to build a secure HTTPS site

10.4.1 Basic requirements for a secure Web site

The basic idea behind setting up a secure Web site is to integrate SSL with Web server software, such as Apache or Internet Information Services. SSL provides handshake and encrypted information exchange between browser and server. As a result, secure Web communication is accomplished. HTTP over a secure channel, or more precisely HTTP over SSL, becomes a new standard known as HTTPS.

As we have mentioned in previous sections, one of the important tasks in securing communication is the handshake between the browser and the server via authentication and certificate exchange. If you have imported certificates into browser for client authentication, you have completed half the job. Together with server authentication, mutual trust is built so that a cipher (encryption method) is employed to protect the desired secure Web communication.

In fact, in many secure Web communications client authentication is optional, depending on the settings of the server software. You can turn off the client authentication requirement. In this case, there will be no client certificate request from the server. However, server authentication is a compulsory requirement for standard HTTPS protocol on the Web.

Apart from security issues, the main difference between HTTP and HTTPS is that they use different ports. By default, an ordinary Web server use port 80. A secure Web server listens via port 443. For example, the following protocols are used to contact normal and secure Web sites:

- `http://www.pws-ex.com` – normal Web communication using port 80

- `https://www.pws-ex.com` – secure Web communication using port 443

With a capable Web server, it is possible to set up a Web site listening to the two protocols above. In this case, all security operations are almost completely hidden from the end users.

In normal circumstances, a secure Web site is a machine running Web server software with SSL functionalities. In this case Web communication can be secured by SSL encryption. Since secure Web sites involve SSL, the basic requirements to build one include:

- Web server software;

- an SSL software implementation or package;

- a software patch to integrate them.

The main reason for selecting these packages is that they are popular and have freely available source code. That means you can build the final software from scratch and use it for both commercial and non-commercial applications.

We covered how to compile and set up OpenSSL in Section 10.2. Although Apache is an important piece of server software and widely used by the Web community, on both UNIX/LINUX and Windows systems, only simple information related to security will be presented here.

Another software package used here is `Mod_SSL` (or `mod_ssl` from the official site). This is a software patch or, more accurately, an Apache interface to OpenSSL. The software can be downloaded from the official site www.modssl.org. The `mod_ssl` package is based on particular versions of Apache. For example, consider the downloaded package

```
mod_ssl-x.x.x-y.y.y.tar.gz
```

The string `x.x.x` represents the version of `mod_ssl`, and the string `y.y.y` is the version of Apache it is designed for. The `mod_ssl` package we are going to use is 'mod_ssl-2.8.19-1.3.31.tar.gz' and is dedicated for Apache version 1.3.31. If you are using other versions of Apache you may need to download the module suitable for your requirement. To make `mod_ssl` work you also need the Apache source code so that they can be compiled together. The version of Apache we are going to use is

```
apache_1.3.31.tar.gz or
apache_1.3.31-win32-x86-src.msi
```

The Microsoft Installer (`msi`) version is for the Windows environment. Both Apache packages are available from www.apache.org. When you extract or unpack Apache, `OpenSSL` and `Mod_SSL` files, you should have the following subdirectories:

- `apache_1.3.31;`

- `mod_ssl-2.8.19-1.3.31;`

- `openssl-0.9.7d.`

We assume that the `OpenSSL` package has already been installed on your system and that the directory `openssl-0.9.7d` is located alongside the others. Now, let's proceed to perform the integration of Apache and OpenSSL.

10.4.2   Integrating Apache and OpenSSL using Mod_SSL

In this section, we will show you how to integrate Apache and OpenSSL using Mod_SSL. By default, the Mod_SSL (Apache interface to OpenSSL) package supports the UNIX/LINUX platform, or platforms of similar type. Therefore, to integrate Apache and OpenSSL on a UNIX/LINUX machine is much simpler. Believe it or not, the entire compilation, installation and configuration process can be done by just a few lines of code, as illustrated in example `ex10-12.ssl`.

```
Example: ex10-12.ssl - Integrating Apache and OpenSSL with Mod_SSL

 1: $ cd mod_ssl-2.8.19-1.3.31
 2: $ ./configure \
 3:    --with-apache=.../apache_1.3.31 \
 4:    --with-ssl=.../openssl-0.9.7d \
 5:    --prefix=/usr/local/apache
 6: $ cd ..
 7: $ cd apache_1.3.31
 8: $ make
 9: $ make certificate
10: $ make install
```

Line 1 is to set a path to the Mod_SSL directory `mod_ssl-2.8.19-1.3.31`. Inside this directory, configuration program is run with parameters (lines 2–5)

```
--with-apache=../apache_1.3.31
--with-ssl=../openssl-0.9.7d
--prefix=/usr/local/apache
```

The first parameter sets the name and location of the Apache source directory. The second parameter in line 4 sets the name and location of the OpenSSL source directory. The `prefix` parameter tells Mod_SSL where to find the installed Apache executables, libraries and binaries. In this case, we have assumed that the installed Apache software is located in `/usr/local/apache`. If your default directory for Apache is not `/usr/local/apache`, you will need to change the `prefix` parameter.

The main function of the configuration program is to set up and prepare an SSL-aware Apache ready for recompilation. Lines 6–7 set the current directory as `apache_1.3.31`. By issuing the `make` command in line 8, the Apache software will be recompiled with SSL features.

Before Apache can be used for server authentication, you need to generate a certificate and import it into the server. The `make` command in line 9 is doing just that. More precisely, this command generates a private key together with a server certificate and installs them into the configuration file `httpd.conf` of Apache. Finally, the `make` statement in line 10 installs the new Apache package to the target install directory `/usr/local/apache`.

In order to make this new Apache server work, you need to activate it with SSL. This can be done using the following command if you are using a UNIX/LINUX system:

```
$ /usr/local/apache/bin/httpd -DSSL
```

If your newly created secure site is called www.pws-ex.com, you can test it with the command

```
https://www.pws-ex.com
```

You will see an alert window (Figure 10.39) telling you that you are about to enter a secure Web environment. If you click the OK button, you will see a welcome message form Mod_SSL, as illustrated in Figure 10.40.

Fig. 10.39 Security alert window

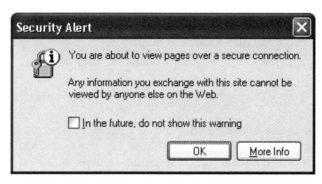

Fig. 10.40 An SSL-aware site

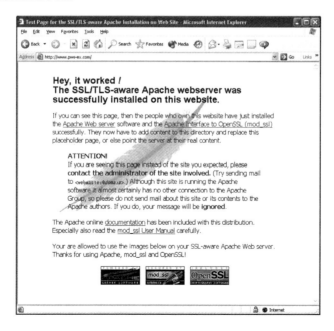

If you are using a Microsoft Windows system, you may need to do it from scratch by yourself. The first step is to get the following packages:

- `apache_1.3.31-win32-x86-src.msi`;

- `mod_ssl-2.8.19-1.3.31.tar.gz`;

- `openssl-0.9.7d.tar.gz`.

If you have a Microsoft installer, you can install the Apache package `apache_1.3.31-win32-x86-src.msi` by double-clicking this file. If you don't have an installer, a copy can be downloaded from the official download centre of www.microsoft.com. Next, you can use the WinZip utility to unzip and extract files from the other two packages. Suppose all three packages are located in the following drive and directories:

- `o:\apache_1.3.31`;

- `o:\mod_ssl-2.8.6-1.3.31`;

- `o:\openssl-0.9.7d`.

In this case we have assumed that the default drive is `o:\`. Please make sure that all three source directories are side by side. Otherwise, you may need to change the following three compilation and configuration steps.

Step 1 Configuring and building the OpenSSL package

This step is similar to the one used to compile OpenSSL in Section 10.2.1. In order to compile and configure OpenSSL, you need Perl and a Visual C/C++ compiler up and running in your system. The entire building process is illustrated in `ex10-13.ssl`.

```
Example: ex10-13.ssl - Configure and build the OpenSSL package
 1: cd openssl-0.9.7d
 2: perl Configure VC-WIN32 --prefix=o:/openssl
 3: ms\do_ms
 4: nmake /f ms\ntdll.mak
 5: md   o:\openssl
 6: md   o:\openssl\bin
 7: md   o:\openssl\lib
 8: md   o:\openssl\include
 9: md   o:\openssl\include\openssl
10: copy /b inc32\*                 o:\openssl\include\openssl
11: copy /b out32dll\ssleay32.lib   o:\openssl\lib
12: copy /b out32dll\libeay32.lib   o:\openssl\lib
13: copy /b out32dll\ssleay32.dll   o:\openssl\bin
14: copy /b out32dll\libeay32.dll   o:\openssl\bin
15: copy /b out32dll\openssl.exe    o:\openssl\bin
16: cd ..
```

The first four lines are used to compile the package with a Visual C/C++ compiler. Please note that we have defined an installation directory for OpenSSL by the parameter `-- prefix = o:/openssl` (line 2). This directory will be used by the compilation process of Apache. Before that, you need to create the following directories for the OpenSSL executables, libraries and binaries (lines 5–9):

- `o:\openssl;`
- `o:\openssl\bin;`
- `o:\openssl\lib;`
- `o:\openssl\include;`
- `o:\openssl\include\openssl.`

By default, all executables, libraries and binaries of the Win32 version of OpenSSL are stored in the `out32dll` directory; a series of copy procedures are employed to copy them into the target directories (lines 10–15). Make sure that the directory `o:\openssl\bin` is in your path.

Step 2 Configuring Mod_SSL for Apache

Now, you can configure the Mod_SSL package for Apache. The configuration process is illustrated in `ex10-14.ssl`.

```
Example: ex10-14.ssl - Configure Mod_SSL for Apache

1: cd mod_ssl-2.8.19-1.3.31
2: configure.bat --with-apache=..\apache_1.3.31 --with-ssl=o:\openssl
3: cd ..
```

Step 3 Building the SSL-aware Apache

To compile Apache, you may need a Visual C/C++ compiler. The actual compilation procedure is incredibly simple, as illustrated in `ex10-15.ssl`.

```
Example: ex10-15.ssl - Building the SSL-aware Apache

1: cd apache_1.3.31\src
2: nmake /f Makefile.win
3: nmake /f Makefile.win installr
```

Line 1 is to go to the Apache source code directory. Then, by calling the `make` utility of Visual C/C++ `nmake` in line 2, the Apache software will be compiled. Another call to the `nmake` utility in line 3 is to install the package in the directory `o:\apache`.

Now, you should have an SSL-aware Apache installed. However, you cannot use SSL features such as HTTPS. The reason is that you still need to configure Apache yourself.

10.4.3 Configuring Apache to use SSL

The information in this section is applicable to Windows users. However, the general techniques for configuring the Apache server are similar for other platforms. After the installation of Apache, you should have the main program `apache.exe` and the following directories under the directory `o:\apache`:

```
bin cgi-bin   conf   htdocs    icons     include
lib libexec   logs   modules   openssl   proxy
```

You still need to configure Apache by:

- creating a certificate and importing it to Apache;

- changing the port setting from 80 to 443 so that secure Web communication can happen.

Before any configuration, we recommend you to do some testing to make sure you have the Apache software properly built. The first test would be to activate the program `apache.exe` with a command line option such as

```
apache -h
```

If you can see all the options as listed in `ex10-16.ssl`, the program is working.

```
Example: ex10-16.ssl - Testing Apache - apache -h

 1: O:\Apache>apache -h
 2: Usage: apache [-D name] [-d directory] [-f file] [-n service]
 3:               [-C "directive"] [-c "directive"] [-k signal]
 4:               [-v] [-V] [-h] [-l] [-L] [-S] [-t] [-T]
 5: -D name        : define a name for use in <IfDefine name> directives
 6: -d directory   : specify an alternate initial ServerRoot
 7: -f file        : specify an alternate ServerConfigFile
 8: -C "directive" : process directive before reading config files
 9: -c "directive" : process directive after reading config files
10: -v             : show version number
11: -V             : show compile settings
12: -h             : list available command line options (this page)
13: -l             : list compiled-in modules
14: -L             : list available configuration directives
15: -S             : show parsed settings (currently only vhost settings)
```

```
16: -t              : run syntax check for config files (with docroot check)
17: -T              : run syntax check for config files (without docroot
                      check)
18: -n name         : name the Apache service for -k options below;
19: -k stop|shutdown : tell running Apache to shutdown
20: -k restart      : tell running Apache to do a graceful restart
21: -k start        : tell Apache to start
22: -k install  | -I : install an Apache service
23: -k config       : reconfigure an installed Apache service
24: -k uninstall | -u : uninstall an Apache service
25: -W service      : after -k config|install; Apache starts after
                      'service'
26: -w              : holds the window open for 30 seconds for
                      fatal errors.
```

Next, you should also perform a test on the server capability to make sure that everything is fine before configuration. Apache with SSL can be run on Windows 98, ME, NT, 2000 and XP. As recommended by the Apache authority, Apache will run better if it is installed as a service (net service) on Windows NT, 2000 and XP. To install and start Apache as a service on Windows XP, the following commands are used:

```
apache -k install
net start apache
```

If your system already has Apache running, you may need to stop it first using the command

```
net stop apache
```

Once you have Apache up and running, you can use your favourite browser to test it. Try the command

```
http://localhost
```

You may want to change the address to some sites you know. If you can see something similar to Figure 10.41, your Apache is properly installed.

Figure 10.41 may also lead you to think that you have also properly set up SSL/LTS-aware Apache. No, you haven't, at least not yet! The reason is that you have used the HTTP protocol, which has no SSL involved. Also, Apache is still listening to port 80. However, you do know that the new Apache is working properly and you can concentrate on its configuration.

Now, backup a copy of the Apache configuration file `httpd.conf` from the default directory `apache\conf`. Edit this file with your favourite editor implementing the following configuration steps.

Fig. 10.41 `http://localhost`

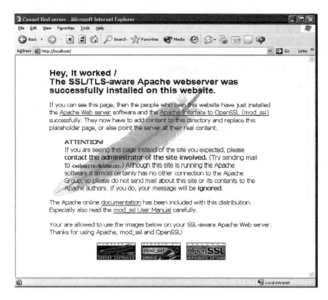

Step 1 Configure the port

- Locate the string 'Port 80' and comment it out as '#Port 80'.

- Locate the string 'Listen' and change it to 'Listen 443'.

- Locate the string 'ServerName' and change it to the real server name of your system. For example: 'ServerName `www.pws-ex.com`'.

Although the SSL feature is still not functioning, you should be able to call your site www.pws-ex.com using port 443. Try the following command on a browser:

```
http://www.pws-ex.com:443
```

If you can see a page like that shown in Figure 10.41, the configuration of the port 443 is OK. Now you can generate a certificate for Apache.

Step 2 Generating a certificate for an Apache server

Go to the subdirectory `openssl` and make sure you have the OpenSSL main program `openssl` there. Open a DOS window and perform the commands listed in `ex10-17.ssl`.

```
Example: ex10-17.ssl - Generating a certificate for an Apache server
1: cd openssl
2: openssl req openssl.cnf -new -out server.csr -config
3: openssl rsa -in privkey.pem -out server.key
4: openssl x509 -in server.csr -out server.crt -req
5:          -signkey server.key -days 365
```

Line 1 gets into the `openssl` directory. Line 2 generates a CSR with a private key called `private.pem`. This certificate will be used to identify your Apache server. Therefore, when `openssl` asks for a common name, you should input the real hostname name of the server, such as www.pws-ex.com. This is necessary because when a browser requests a secure connection such as

```
https://www.pws-ex.com
```

the server will send this certificate to the browser. The browser will complain if the common name of the certificate does not match the server's URL.

Line 3 removes the passphrase from the private key `privkey.pem` and generates a `server.key`. This is used to sign the CSR `server.csr` and output the signed certificate as `server.crt` (lines 4–5). This process is the same as that given in `ex10-15.ssl`.

Please note that the self-signed certificate should be used on a temporary basis or for testing purposes. In real applications, you should replace the self-signed certificate by a real one signed by a CA, or at least signed by a CA created by you.

Now, let's create an `apache/conf/ssl` directory and move both `server.key` and `server.crt` into it. Once you have the server key and certificate, you can insert them into a virtual host of Apache by

```
SSLCertificateFile        conf/ssl/server.crt
SSLCertificateKeyFile     conf/ssl/server.key
```

for certificate exchange. More details will be discussed later. Now, you may want to generate the certificate as a DER-encoded form so that your users can import them into their browser. To generate a DER-encoded certificate, you can use

```
openssl x509 -in server.crt -out server.der.crt -outform DER
```

You can now send this `server.der.crt` file to your staff, users or members so that they can import the certificate into the certificate storage area of their browser.

Step 3 Configuring Apache to use SSL

To use SSL in Windows, the first thing to do is copy the dynamic linked libraries

```
ssleay32.dll  and  libeay32.dll
```

from the `apache\openssl\lib` directory to `WINDOWS\system32`. If you are using NT, the directory should be `WINNT\system32`. Next, you copy all the files necessary to make `openssl` work, such as executables, libraries and binaries, into the Apache directory (e.g. `o:\apache`).

Edit the Apache configuration file `httpd.conf`, locating the string

```
LoadModule ssl_module modules/mod_ssl.so
```

If this statement is commented, you need to uncomment it by removing all the hash symbols in front of it. In this case Apache can load the SSL module `ssl_module`. Make sure that the module `mod_ssl.so` is located inside the directory `apache/modules` or in the path of your system.

In order to make the SSL module functionable, you also need to locate the string

```
AddModule mod_ssl.c
```

and uncomment this statement. Finally, you need to set up an Apache virtual host to use the secure site. An example is given below. You can simple copy the `ex10-18.ssl` example fragment to the end of the configuration file.

```
Example: ex10-18.ssl - Setting configuration

 1: SSLMutex sem
 2: SSLRandomSeed startup builtin
 3: SSLSessionCache none
 4:
 5: SSLLog logs/SSL.log
 6: SSLLogLevel info
 7:
 8: <VirtualHost www.pws-ex.com:443>
 9:    SSLEngine On
10:    SSLCertificateFile conf/ssl/server.crt
11:    SSLCertificateKeyFile conf/ssl/server.key
12: </VirtualHost>
```

Lines 1–6 are the standard routines for initializing SSL so that the SSL powered by OpenSSL is ready for action. If anything goes wrong, you can debug via the log file `SSL.log` located in the `apache/logs` directory. Since the error and log file system of Apache and Mod_SSL are so efficient, some online SSL authors may refuse to answer any of your questions if you haven't read the log file first.

Now you have a new Apache configuration file `httpd.conf`. The next step is to save this file and relaunch Apache to use the new settings. Open a DOS window and issue the following commands:

```
net stop apache
apache -k uninstall
apache -k install
net start apache
```

The first two commands are used to stop the Apache service and then uninstall it from the system. The third command installs the Apache server again with the new configuration settings. The final command starts Apache as a service. You may want to test it by issuing the secure HTTP command

```
https://www.pws-ex.com
```

You should see a page similar to that shown in Figure 10.41. From this page, if you click the underlined text 'documentation', the full documentation of Apache is displayed (see Figure 10.42). If you click the underlined text 'mod_ssl User Manual', the user manual of Mod_SSL is displayed (see Figure 10.43).

As we have mentioned on a number of occasions, one of the differences between the HTTP and HTTPS protocols is the use of ports. They use different ports and therefore are not compatible by default. For example, suppose the site www.pws-ex.com is configured as a secure site. If you use the following command on a browser:

```
http://www.pws-ex.com
```

Fig. 10.42 Apache manual

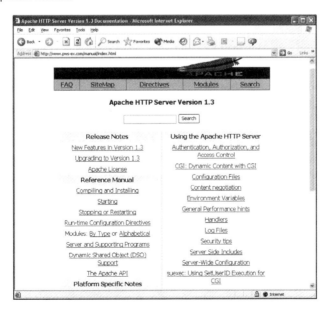

Fig. 10.43 Mod_SSL manual

and the system does not crash, you will get an error message. The reason is that you are using port 80 to talk to a server which can only listen via port 443.

With the elegance of Apache's virtual hosts, it is possible to set up a Web site which listens to both ports 80 and 443.

10.4.4   Configuring Apache for secure and insecure connections

As mentioned in Section 10.4.3, you should backup a copy of the configuration file httpd.conf before any modification is made. Suppose the file httpd.conf is configured for a secure situation. In order to modify it to accept both secure and insecure connections, you need to change it back to the insecure case first. Edit the file httpd.conf with your favourite editor, effecting the following changes.

Step 1   Configure the port

■ Locate the string '#Port 80' and uncomment it out as 'Port 80' so that Apache can use port 80.

■ Locate the string 'Listen 443' and change it to 'Listen 80'.

Step 2   Delete the secure virtual host setting

- Locate the secure virtual host settings as in example `ex10-18.ssl`.

- Delete the entire virtual host settings

Now, your Apache server is set to handle insecure connections. The HTTP protocol is working via port 80. To add secure connection into this `httpd.conf` file, all you need to do is create a virtual host that can activate SSL and listen to port 443. You can do that by copying the code fragment given in `ex10-19.ssl` and pasting it at the end of the configuration file.

```
Example: ex10-19.ssl - Virtual host listens to port 443

 1: SSLMutex sem
 2: SSLRandomSeed startup builtin
 3: SSLSessionCache none
 4:
 5: SSLLog logs/SSL.log
 6: SSLLogLevel info
 7:
 8: <IfDefine HAVE_SSL>
 9: Listen 443
10:   <VirtualHost www.pws-ex.com:443>
11:     SSLEngine On
12:     SSLCertificateFile    conf/ssl/server.crt
13:     SSLCertificateKeyFile conf/ssl/server.key
14:   </VirtualHost>
15: </IfDefine>
```

Yes! That is it. Changing everything back to port 80 means that all normal communication with HTTP will be handled in the usual way. This is because Apache is listening to port 80 by default. All requested documents with `http://` are searched from the `DocumentRoot` location specified in `httpd.conf`. Now, if you activate the following command from your browser:

```
http://www.pws-ex.com
```

the Apache server will search for the default document, such as `index.html`, from the `DocumentRoot` directory and return it to the browser. Note that we have used the root directory as the default URL.

The if-define directive '`<IfDefine HAVE_SSL>`' in lines 8–15 means that if `HAVE_SSL` is defined, Apache will listen to port 443. If the browser requests the virtual host www.pws-ex.com with secure mode (i.e. `www.pws-ex.com:443`), the certificate and key are available from the location specified in lines 12–13. Therefore, when you issue the command

```
https://www.pws-ex.com
```

the Apache server will use this secure virtual host to handle security and connection. Since this virtual host has the same name as the ServerName setting. Apache will search the default document (e.g. `index.html`) from the same directory as specified by HTTP.

In order to use the new settings of this `httpd.conf` file, you may need to relaunch Apache using the following commands:

```
net stop apache
apache -k uninstall
apache -k install -D SSL -D HAVE_SSL
net start apache
```

The third command installs Apache with the variables `SSL` and `HAVE_SSL` defined so that the if-define directive can take effect. Virtual host is a powerful feature of Apache and you can use it to set up different sites at different or identical locations. Each virtual host has its own settings and is treated as an independent site. For more details, the Apache documentation is recommended. Now let's consider some examples showing how to use secure communication on the Web.

10.4.5   Some examples of using the secure site

Using the site you have built in the previous section is easy. All you have to do is put all your Web pages (both secure and insecure) into the directory specified by the variable `DocumentRoot` of Apache. In our case, the directory is `o:\apache\htdocs`.

To call a page in secure mode, all you need to do is change `http` to `https` in all URL situations. For example, you can use `https` in the anchor or button element as

```
<a href="https://www.pws-ex.com/abc.htm">Secure Connection</a>
<input onclick='location.href="https://www.pws-ex.com/abc.htm"'
       type="button" value="Secure Connection" />
```

In the button case, when the `Secure Connection` button is clicked, the `onclick` event will activate the statement

```
https://www.pws-ex.com/abc.htm
```

In this case, the browser is requesting the `abc.htm` page from the Web site www.pws-ex.com using secure mode.

As a simple test example, let's consider writing some donation pages for a charity organization. For security reasons, and also the privacy of donors, we are going to develop a page using both secure and insecure (normal) channels for the donation. Consider the simple XHTML page shown in `ex10-20.htm`.

```
Example: ex10-20.htm - A page to get donation for charity

 1: <?xml version="1.0" encoding="iso-8859-1"?>
 2: <!DOCTYPE html PUBLIC "-//W3C//DTD XHTML 1.0 Transitional//EN"
 3:     "http://www.w3.org/TR/xhtml11/DTD/xhtml1-transitional.dtd">
 4: <html xmlns="http://www.w3.org/1999/xhtml"
     xml:lang="en" lang="en">
 5: <head><title>Secure & Normal Web Connection -
     ex10-20.htm</title></head>
 6: <style>
 7:  .tx01{background-color:#000088;font-family:arial;font-size:22pt;
 8:     font-weight:bold;color:#ffff00;text-align:left}
 9:  .tx03{font-size:18pt;color:#00ff00}
10:  .butSt{background-color:#aaffaa;font-family:arial;
     font-weight:bold;
11:     font-size:14pt;color:#880000;width:250px;height:35px}
12: </style>
13: <body class="tx01" style="text-align:center">
14:   Welcome To ABC Charity Site<br /><br />
15: <div class="tx03">
16:   Your Privacy Is Our Top Priority <br />
17:   You Have A Choice To Use <br />
18:   Secure Or Normal<br />
19:   Channel To Make Your Donation.
20: </div><br />
21:   <input type="button" class="butSt" value="Secure Connection"
     onclick=
22:  'location.href="https://www.pws-ex.com/bk/ch10/ex10-21.htm"'/>
     <br/><br />
23:   <input type="button" class="butSt" value="Normal Connection"
     onclick=
24:  'location.href="http://www.pws-ex.com/bk/ch10/ex10-21.htm "' />
      <br />
25: </body>
26: </html>
```

This is a simple XHTML page containing two buttons offering either secure or normal communication for the charity donors. When the first button (lines 21–22) is clicked, the following command is activated:

```
https://www.pws-ex.com/bk/ch10/ex10-20.htm
```

This command requests the document ex10-20.htm from the server www.pws-ex.com over a secure channel. Normally, the browser would display a security alert window when entering the secure mode. Screenshots of this are shown in Figures 10.44 and 10.45.

Fig. 10.44 `ex10-20.htm`

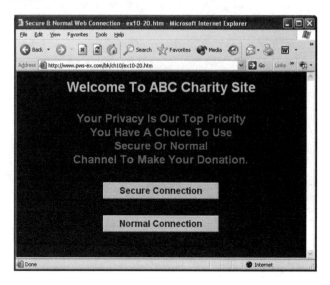

Fig. 10.45 Alert window

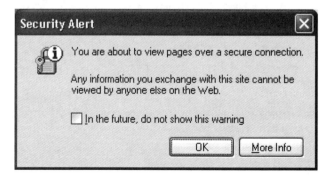

When the OK button in Figure 10.45 is clicked, the XHTML page `ex10-21.htm` is displayed with SSL protection (see Figure 10.46). This is a very simple page to collect the following message from the donor:

■ name;

■ address;

■ telephone;

■ amount.

```
Example: ex10-21.htm - A simple page to accept donation

 1: <?xml version="1.0" encoding="iso-8859-1"?>
 2: <!DOCTYPE html PUBLIC "-//W3C//DTD XHTML 1.0 Transitional//EN"
 3:     "http://www.w3.org/TR/xhtml1/DTD/xhtml1-transitional.dtd">
 4: <html xmlns="http://www.w3.org/1999/xhtml"
     xml:lang="en" lang="en">
 5: <head><title>A Page For Charity Donation -
     ex10-21.htm</title></head>
 6: <style>
 7:   .butSt{background-color:#aaffaa;font-family:arial;
       font-weight:bold;
 8:       font-size:14pt;color:#880000;width:200px;height:28px}
 9:   .txtSt{font-family:arial;font-weight:bold; text-align:center;
10:       font-size:14pt;color:#ffff00}
11:   .txtSt2{font-family:arial;font-weight:bold; text-align:center;
12:       font-size:20pt;color:#00ff00}
13: </style>
14: <body style="background:#000088;text-align:center" class="txtSt">
15: <div class="txtSt" style="font-size:18pt;text-align:center">
16:   Donation This Month:<br />
17:   Disabled Children In The Third World
18:   </div><br /><br />
19:
20: <table border="0" width="400" class="txtSt">
21:   <tr><td >Name</td><td>
22:       <input type="text" name="name" class="butSt"></td><tr>
23:   <tr><td >Address</td><td>
24:       <input type="text" name="add" class="butSt"></td><tr>
25:   <tr><td >Telephone</td><td>
26:       <input type="text" name="phone" class="butSt"></td><tr>
27:   <tr><td >Amount</td><td>
28:       <input type="text" name="amount" class="butSt"></td><tr>
29: </table><br />
30: <a href="ex10-21.htm" class="txtSt2">Back</a><body></html>
```

This page should be easy to understand. The main purpose of this example is
to shown how both a secure and a normal Web communication can be set up
together.

When the donor has completed all the fields and presses the Back button, example
ex10-20.htm is activated with the normal HTTP channel. An alert window is
usually displayed for confirmation when you enter from a secure page into an
ordinary Web page (see Figures 10.46 and 10.47).

Fig. 10.46 `ex10-21.htm`

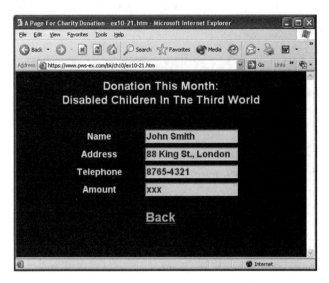

Fig. 10.47 Alert window

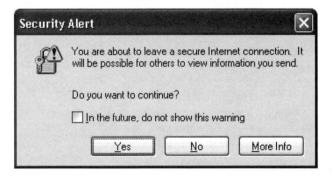

Secure Web pages are very popular in the business community. For example, most e-commerce sites have some links or connections in secure mode. Consider the alert window in Figure 10.45 again. If you press the OK button and if the server's certificate is not a trusted certificate in your browser, you will see a security alert window as shown in Figure 10.48. This window will tell you that the server certificate is not in your trusted list and ask whether you want to proceed. If you press the Yes button, then the `ex10-21.htm` page is displayed in secure mode as shown in Figure 10.46.

Alternatively, if you press the View Certificate button, the details of the certificate are displayed as shown Figure 10.49. You can see that the certificate is

Fig. 10.48 Further security alert

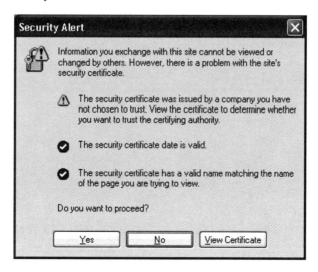

Fig. 10.49 Certificate details

Fig. 10.50 Store the certificate

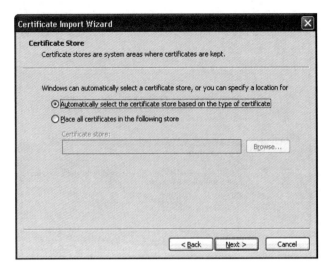

issued to johnsmith by MyCA. Now, you have the opportunity to install the certificate into the trust storage. If you press the `Install Certificate` button, the Certificate Import Wizard is launched. Next, you will be asked whether you want to store the certificate into a location depending on its type.

Next, the system will select the storage area for your certificate and ask for confirmation (see Figure 10.50). If you say yes by pressing the `Next` button, the server certificate is stored in the Root Store. If you go to `Tools|Internet Options|Content|Certificates` from your IE browser and click the 'Trusted Root Certification Authority' tag, you will see the imported certificate as illustrated in Figure 10.51.

Fig. 10.51   Certificates in the trusted root certification authority area

Now you have some experience of OpenSSL security and how to use it to
establish a secure Web site. In fact, OpenSSL can also be used to provide security
on a more general data structure, namely XML. In particular, it can be used to
generate so-called XML signatures and digital contracts.

10.5 XML security and XML digital contracts

10.5.1 An introduction to XML

Before we discuss XML signatures and contracts, an elementary introduction to XML will be given in this section. XML is a big subject by any standard and is well beyond the scope of this section, or even this book. For our Web security applications, we will concentrate only on how to implement security on XML pages and develop XML signatures and contracts with the OpenSSL style.

XML is similar to XHTML and is used to develop documents or pages for the World Wide Web. They share the same structure and the main components of the languages are elements. Unlike XHTML, which is designed for formatting and displaying a document, the main purpose of an XML page (or document) is to describe the data structure and relationships of the elements involved. Hence, XML is more abstract, general and powerful in the sense that it is extensible. Because there is no formatting structure, you can create your own elements and attributes in an XML document. In fact when you develop an XML page you have no choice but to create your own choices of elements and attributes. More interestingly, attributes can be reformulated by the relationships of child elements in a more general way. The flexibility and diversity of XML make it a truly extensible language.

A well-defined (or well-formed) XML document follows the rules below.

- It must begin with an XML declaration, e.g.
  ```
  <?xml version="1.0" encoding="iso-8859-1"?>.
  ```
- It must have one unique root element e.g. `<root>`.
- All start tags must match end-tags, e.g. `<contents></contents>`.
- XML tags must be case sensitive.
- All elements must be closed.
- All elements must be properly nested.
- All attribute values must be quoted, e.g. `<contents from="www.pws-ex.com">`.
- XML entities must be used for special characters, e.g. `&lt; &gt;  `.

These rules are the same as those for XHTML mentioned in Section 1.2.4 because XHTML documents are technically XML pages. Consider example `ex10-22.xml`.

```
Example: ex05-22.xml - My first XML page

1: <?xml version="1.0" encoding="iso-8859-1"?>
2: <message>
3:   <contents>My First XML Page</contents>
4:   <from>www.pws-ex.com</from>
5: </message>
```

By default, all XML pages in this chapter will have file extension `xml`. The first line in `ex10-22.xml` specifies that the document is in XML version 1.0 with character set Latin-1/Western European. Basically, this is the only requirement for a well-formed XML page. You may notice that this line is the same as the first line of all XHTML pages in this book. The reason is simple – all XHTML pages conform to the XML standard and they are all XML well-formed documents.

The rest of the page defines a message element `<message>`. This contains two child elements, `<contents>` and `<from>`. The values of these two elements are also defined. Unlike XHTML, all white spaces in XML are recognized. As a result, this page describes a relationship of elements `<contents>`, `<from>` and `<message>`. Lines 2–4 could also be formulated

```
<message>
   <contents from="www.pws-ex.com">My First XML Page</contents>
</message>
```

In this case, the `from` attribute is considered to be an attribute of `<contents>`. You can rewrite both `contents` and `from` as attributes in the `<message>` if you prefer. Also, all the names of XML elements are user-defined.

Since there is no predefined element in XML, you cannot expect an ordinary browser, such as IE, NS or Opera, to be able to display the page with formatting properties. For example, if you request the document `ex10-22.xml` by using

```
http://www.pws-ex.com/bk/ch10/ex10-22.xml
```

you will see a display like that shown in Figure 10.52.

Fig. 10.52   `ex10-22.xml`

One of the popular applications of XML is to describe a sequence of information which falls in the same structure. Consider example `ex10-22a.xml`.

```
Example: ex10-22a.xml - XML page with simple XSLT transformation

 1: <?xml version="1.0" encoding="ISO-8859-1"?>
 2:
 3: <street>
 4:   <profile>
 5:     <name>Charlie</name>
 6:     <job>Engineer</job>
 7:     <sex>male</sex>
 8:     <phone>123456789</phone>
 9:     <location>England</location>
10:     <address>No.10 Richmond Road, West Yorkshire, England</address>
11:      <age>20</age>
12:   </profile>
13:   <profile>
14:     <name>Peter</name>
15:     <job>Clerk</job>
16:     <sex>male</sex>
17:     <phone>223224225</phone>
18:     <age>25</age>
19:     <location>England</location>
20:     <address>No.11 Richmond Road, West Yorkshire, England</address>
21:   </profile>
22:   <profile>
23:     <name>Mary</name>
24:     <job>Secretary</job>
25:     <sex>female</sex>
26:     <phone>88834421</phone>
27:     <age>19</age>
28:     <location>England</location>
29:     <address>No.12 Richmond Road, West Yorkshire,
          England</address>
30:   </profile>
31: </street>
```

This is an XML page containing information about people living in the same street. For simplicity, only three profiles are listed. Each house in a street and its owner are described as a `<profile>` element. Under each `<profile>` element, detailed information about the owner is presented. XML uses markup elements to describe information in a structural way. If you activate this page in IE you will see Figure 10.53.

Fig. 10.53 `ex10-22a.xml`

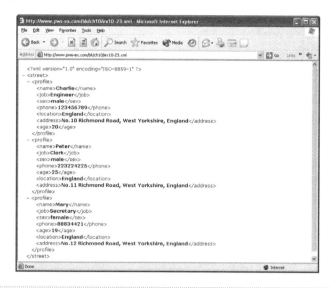

As you have seen from Figures 10.52 and 10.53, XML does not display well in ordinary browsers such as IE and NS. The reason is that XML doesn't contain any formatting elements or attributes. Browsers simply don't know how to display the document.

You may well ask: if XML contains no formatting property or element then how can we display the page on the Web or browser? Where are all those `font-family`, `font-size`, `colors`, `images` and `tables` in XHTML?

The answer lies in the beauty of XML. Since the structure of XML is abstract but technically simple, XML pages can be transformed to other software or device languages relatively easy. For this reason, XML is a markup language for many devices including browsers, chips or even mobile phones. To display an XML page directly on your chosen device, all you need is a proper transformation. For our applications, we will concentrate on how to convert XML into an XHTML page and display it on the Web with a browser. In particularly, we will show you how to use XSLT and an XML parser to display XML pages.

10.5.2 Using XSLT and a parser on XML documents

One of the most popular ways of converting an XML document into the XHTML style is the XML Style Sheet Language Transformation (XSLT).

XHTML uses predefined elements, which can be displayed on a browser directly. The Cascading Style Sheet (CSS) for XHTML can be considered as a more structured way of organizing the formatting layout so that reusability and structure are enhanced.

For XML, the style sheet is called XSL (XML Style Sheet). Since there are no predefined elements in XML, traditional XHTML elements, such as `<div>`, `<p>` and `<table>`, no longer have meanings. The role of XSL is more abstract and far more powerful than CSS in the HTML/XHTML case. On the whole XSL is a language or a mechanism for describing how XML documents should be displayed. One of the most important parts of XSL is the XSL transformation (XSLT), which can be used to transform an XML page into an other format. Consider example `ex10-23.xml`.

Example: ex10-23.xml – My first XML page with XSLT

```
1:  <?xml version="1.0"?>
2:  <?xml-stylesheet type="text/xsl" href="ex10-23.xsl" ?>
3:  <message>
4:    <contents>My First XML Page With XSLT</contents>
5:    <from>www.pws-ex.com</from>
6:  </message>
```

If you compare this page with `ex10-22.xml`, you will find that the main difference is in line 2. This line

```
<?xml-stylesheet type="text/xsl" href="ex10-23.xsl" ?>
```

defines a transformation method for the page. The transform is based on XSL with `text/xsl` type so that XSL files are usually have extension `.xsl`. The detailed XSL transformation and specifications are defined in `ex10-23.xsl`.

Example: ex10-23.xsl – The XSLT transformation file for ex10-23.xml

```
1:  <?xml version="1.0" encoding="iso-8859-1"?>
2:  <xsl:stylesheet version="1.0"
3:    xmlns:xsl="http://www.w3.org/1999/XSL/Transform">
4:
5:  <xsl:template match="/">
6:
7:    <html xmlns="http://www.w3.org/1999/xhtml" xml:lang="en"
        lang="en">
8:    <head><title>My First XSLT Transform</title></head>
9:    <body style="background:#000088;color:#ffff00;
10:               font-family:arial;font-size:24pt;
                   font-weight:bold;text-align:center">
11:   <div style="text-align:center"><br /><br />
```

```
12:     <xsl:value-of select="message/contents" /> <br /><br />
13:     <xsl:value-of select="message/from" /> <br />
14:   </div>
15: </body>
16: </html>
17:
18: </xsl:template>
19: </xsl:stylesheet>
```

Line 1 is the header for an XML page indicating that XSLT files are basically XML pages. Lines 2–3 define the header for XSLT. Whoever calls this XML document will use this style sheet for the transformation.

Line 5 defines an XSL template. The attribute `match="/"` means that this template is used to transform the entire XML page. The actual template is defined in lines 7–16 and is an XHTML document. The function of XSLT, in effect, is to transform the calling document into an XHTML document, which can be displayed on a browser directly.

Inside the XHTML template, the interesting part is the XSL element (line 12):

```
<xsl:value-of select="message/contents" />
```

This element gets the value of the original XML page. In this case, the value is the string under the root element `<message>` and the first child element `<contents>`. The string is 'My First XML Page With XSLT' located in line 4 of `ex10-23.xml`.

When you request this XML page with

```
http://www.pws-ex.com/bk/ch10/ch10-23.xml
```

you will see the transformation in action as illustrated in Figure 10.54. Now, let's consider one more XSLT example.

Consider the example `ex10-22a.xml`. If you want to convert this XML page to XHTML, all you have to do is to develop a proper XSL file. First, make a copy of `ex10-22a.xml` and call it `ex10-24.xml`. In this new page, insert the following statement at line 2:

```
2: <?xml-stylesheet type="text/xsl" href="ex10-24.xsl" ?>
```

This statement will use the XSL page `ex10-24.xsl` for transformation and display purposes. From example `ex10-23.xsl`, we know how to use the XSLT element `<xsl:value-of>` to obtain values from a XML file. For example, consider

```
<xsl:value-of select="street/profile/name" />
```

This element obtains the value stored in the `<name>` element from `ex10-24.xml`. However, we have three sets of information in `ex10-24.xml`. In order to display

Fig. 10.54 My first XSLT page

all the data, a loop is needed. To generate a loop, the XSL for-each element
`<xsl:for-each>` can be used. This element has the general form

```
<xsl:for-each select="street/profile">
   xxx
   xxx
</xsl:for-each>
```

This statement can sequentially read all the children of the `<profile>` element
specified by the calling XML page. Consider the XSLT transformation file
`ex10-24.xsl`.

Line 1 of `ex10-24.xsl` declares that this document is an XML page. Lines 2–3
specify that the document is an XSL transformation converting the calling page
into a displayable format. After the template in line 4, the rest of this document is
an XHTML page with one table. The first row of this table (lines 16–20) defines the
headings `Name`, `Job`, `Sex`, `Age`, `Phone`, `Location` and `Address`.

The for-each element `<xsl:for-each select=xxx>` is defined in lines 21–31. As a
result, it works like a simple for-loop generating a series of statements between the
loops. It will generate a number of table rows for the XHTML table. Also, we have
added some CSS style settings to show that XSL transformation takes care of CSS
properties as well. A screenshot of this example is shown in Figure 10.55.

The XSL language also provides a number of conditional elements so that
conditional testing can be carried out. For example, consider the following `choose`
structure:

Example: ex10-24.xsl - Generating loops

```
 1: <?xml version="1.0" encoding="ISO-8859-1"?>
 2: <xsl:stylesheet version="1.0"
 3: xmlns:xsl="http://www.w3.org/1999/XSL/Transform">
 4: <xsl:template match="/">
 5: <html xmlns="http://www.w3.org/1999/xhtml" xml:lang="en" lang="en">
 6:  <head><title>ex05-12.xsl</title>
 7:  <style>
 8:    .txtSt {font-family:arial;font-size:19pt;font-weight:bold}
 9:  </style>
10: </head>
11: <body class="txtSt" style="color:#000088">
12:    Household Records Of Richmond Road <br />
13:    West Yorkshire <br /><br />
14:    <table border="1" style="background:#888888;
15:       color:#ffffff;font-family:arial;font-size:14pt">
16:       <tr>
17:          <th>Name</th> <th>Job</th>
18:          <th>Sex</th> <th>Age</th>
19:          <th>Phone</th> <th>Location</th> <th>Address</th>
20:       </tr>
21:       <xsl:for-each select="street/profile">
22:       <tr>
23:          <td><xsl:value-of select="name"/></td>
24:          <td><xsl:value-of select="job"/></td>
25:          <td><xsl:value-of select="sex"/></td>
26:          <td><xsl:value-of select="age"/></td>
27:          <td><xsl:value-of select="phone"/></td>
28:          <td><xsl:value-of select="location"/></td>
29:          <td><xsl:value-of select="address"/></td>
30:       </tr>
31:       </xsl:for-each>
32:     </table>
33:  </body>
34:  </html>
35: </xsl:template>
36: </xsl:stylesheet>
```

```
<xsl:choose>
   <xsl:when test="name='Peter'">
          ... ... ... ...
          ... ... ... ...
   </xsl:when>
</xsl:choose>
```

Fig. 10.55 XSLT of `ex10-24.xml`

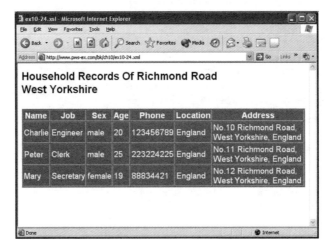

When this structure is used, only those elements with the name 'Peter' will get through. Make a copy of `ex10-24.xsl` and call it `ex10-25.xsl`. In this new example, insert the `<xsl:choose>` element at line 22 as shown below.

```
Example: ex10-25.xsl

21:    <xsl:for-each select="street/profile">
22:       <xsl:choose>
23:          <xsl:when test="name='Peter'">
24:            <tr>
25:              <td><xsl:value-of select="name"/></td>
26:              <td><xsl:value-of select="job"/></td>
27:              <td><xsl:value-of select="sex"/></td>
28:              <td><xsl:value-of select="age"/></td>
29:              <td><xsl:value-of select="phone"/></td>
30:              <td><xsl:value-of select="location"/></td>
31:              <td><xsl:value-of select="address"/></td>
32:            </tr>
33:          </xsl:when>
34:       </xsl:choose>
35:    </xsl:for-each>
36:    </table>
37:  </body>
38:  </html>
39: </xsl:template>
40: </xsl:stylesheet>
```

When this XSLT is called, only those profiles with name='Peter' will be displayed.

XSL is a powerful language providing many sorting and querying functionalities that are beyond the scope of this chapter.

Now you have some basic understanding of the XML element structure and how to display it using XSLT. Again, XSLT is a big subject and even a simple description of every element would be well beyond the scope of this chapter. The techniques introduced here will be used to display XML digital contracts in Section 10.5. Another popular XML transformation is to use the parser.

Using a parser on XML pages

One of the important features of the XML parser is that the elements of an XML page can be located and accessed via a tree structure known as a document object model (DOM). It provides a structure for markup languages, including HTML/XHTML and XML. To see how the parser and DOM work, let's consider the XML page listed in ex10-26.xml.

```
Example: ex10-26.xml - Accessing XML elements with a parser

 1: <?xml version="1.0" encoding="ISO-8859-1"?>
 2: <?xml-stylesheet type="text/css" href="ex05-20.css"?>
 3: <admin>
 4:    <person>
 5:       <name>Michael</name>
 6:       <birth>1950-12-18</birth>
 7:       <sex>M</sex>
 8:       <location>London</location>
 9:       <salary>30000</salary>
10:    </person>
11:    <person>
12:       <name>Mary</name>
13:       <birth>1980-6-22</birth>
14:       <sex>F</sex>
15:       <location>Paris</location>
16:       <salary>23000</salary>
17:    </person>
18: </admin>
```

This page contains one main element <admin>. Inside this there are two child elements called <person>. Each of these contains five child elements called <name>, <birth>, <sex>, <location> and <salary>.

Using the parser and DOM, the contents of the <admin> element can be accessed by the statement

```
xmlDoc.documentElement.firstChild
```

The object `xmlDoc.documentElement` represents the entire structure of the page, and the first child of this page is, therefore, the `<admin>` element. Since there is only one child in this outermost level, the statement

```
xmlDoc.documentElement.lastChild
```

represents the same `<admin>` element. A collection of all the children of this outermost level is represented by the statement

```
prinodes = xmlDoc.documentElement.childNodes
```

Now, all the children nodes of the outermost level are assigned to the user-defined object `prinodes` (primary nodes). This object has two elements and they are

```
prinodes.item(0)
```
 – the first `<person>` element
```
prinodes.item(1)
```
 – the second `<person>` element

The `prinodes.item(0)` object represents the first `<person>` element. The data and information about this person can be collected by the statement

```
nodes = prinodes.item(0).childNodes
```

Now, all children nodes of the first `<person>` element are assigned to another object called `nodes`. Therefore, the data of the first person in `ex10-26.xml` is:

```
nodes.item(0).text
```
 – Michael
```
nodes.item(1).text
```
 – 1950-12-18
```
nodes.item(2).text
```
 – M
```
nodes.item(3).text
```
 – London
```
nodes.item(4).text
```
 – 30000

With these in mind, we can develop an XHTML page to gain access to all the elements of an XML page using the parser. Consider the XHTML page `ex10-26.htm`.

Example: ex10-26.htm – Accessing XML element with a parser

```
 1: <?xml version="1.0" encoding="UTF-8"?>
 2: <!DOCTYPE html
 3:      PUBLIC "-//W3C//DTD XHTML 1.0 Transitional//EN"
 4:      "http://www.w3.org/TR/xhtml1/DTD/xhtml1-transitional.dtd">
 5: <html xmlns="http://www.w3.org/1999/xhtml" xml:lang="en" lang="en">
 6: <head><title>Example: ex10-26.htm </title>
 7: <script>
 8:   function xml_dom()
 9:   {
10:     var xmlDoc=new ActiveXObject("Microsoft.XMLDOM")
11:     xmlDoc.async="false"
12:     xmlDoc.load("ex10-26.xml")
```

```
13:
14:     prinodes=xmlDoc.documentElement.childNodes
15:     for (jj=0;jj< prinodes.length;jj++)
16:     {
17:         nodes = prinodes.item(jj).childNodes
18:         for (ii=0;ii< nodes.length -1 ;ii++)
19:         {
20:           document.write( nodes.item(ii).text + ", ")
21:         }
22:         document.write( nodes.item(ii).text)
23:         document.write("<br />")
24:     }
25:   }
26: </script>
27: <body style="background:#000088;color:#ffff00;text-align:center;
28:       font-family:arial;font-size:18pt;font-weight:bold">
29: <br />Access XML Elements With Parser<br /><br />
30:
31: <script>xml_dom()</script>
32: </body>
33: </html>
```

This is an XHTML page containing one Javascript (or ECMAScript) function called
xml_dom(). After the usual body definition (lines 27–29), the Javascript function is
called by the statement below (see line 31):

```
<script>xml_dom()</script>
```

The detailed definition of this function is given in lines 8–25. The first three lines of
this function (lines 10–12) load the Microsoft XML parser. After that, a collection of
children nodes of the outermost level are assigned to the object prinodes (line 14).
The number of elements inside this prinodes is stored in the property

```
prinodes.length
```

Since there are only two persons in ex10-26.xml, this value is 2. A simple for-loop
on variable jj to prinodes.length will gain access to all <person> elements
(lines 15–24). For each <person> element, all children nodes are assigned to the
object nodes by

```
nodes = prinodes.item(jj).childNodes
```

A simple for-loop on variable ii to value nodes.length-1 (lines 18–24) provides
all the data and information of the associated person in ex10-26.xml. The output
statement in line 20:

```
document.write( nodes.item(ii).text + ", ")
```

Fig. 10.56 XML with parser

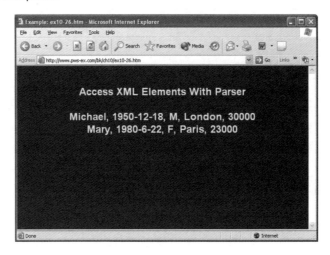

prints the individuals' data name, birthday, sex and location separated by commas. When the last item is reached, the statement in line 22 is used to output the data without commas. A screenshot of this example is shown in Figure 10.56.

Note that example ex10-26.htm is a general page for displaying an XML page using a parser and is independent of the elements used inside. Now, let's consider how to introduce security for XML pages.

10.5.3   The XML security library: adding OpenSSL to XML

A popular way of providing security for XML pages is to use the XML Security Library (XMLSEC). It is a free package developed by Aleksey Sanin written in the C language. The package is a combination of a number of libraries and can be downloaded from the addresses below:

- XMLSec – http://www.aleksey.com

- LibXML2 – http://xmlsoft.org

- LibXSLT – http://xmlsoft.org/XSLT

- OpenSSL – http://www.openssl.org

The main purpose of XMLSEC is to provide encryption and digital signature functionalities to XML pages conforming to the W3C recommendations. The encryption and digital signature standards for XML are specified by the W3C authority via the following documents:

- *XML encryption syntax and processing* (http://www.w3.org/TR/xmlenc-core)

- *XML signature syntax and processing* (http://www.w3.org/TR/xmldsig-core)

In fact, all encryption and digital signature functions of XMLSEC are powered by the OpenSSL package. Therefore, if you know how OpenSSL works, XMLSEC is easy to follow.

Like the OpenSSL situation, most XMLSEC applications can be performed by the command line program `xmlsec`. This program is similar to `openssl` of OpenSSL in the sense that it is a command line tool to execute functions inside the XMLSEC library. The program `xmlsec` (or `xmlsec.exe`) must be run inside a shell window, or DOS window if you are using a Windows system.

To obtain this command line program, you can download all the packages above and compile them. If you are using Windows, you can download the following binary versions from the corresponding sites:

- `libxmlsec-1.2.5+.win32.zip;`

- `libxml2-2.6.11.win32.zip;`

- `libxslt-1.1.8.win32.zip;`

- `iconv-1.9.1.win32.zip;`

- `zlib-1.1.4.win32.zip.`

The installation process simply involves extracting them into the location you want. For example, if you unzip the package `libxmlsec-1.2.5+.win32.zip`, the directory `libxmlsec-1.2.5.win32` will be created on your machine. Under this directory, you will find the following subdirectories:

```
include    lib    util
```

The program `xmlsec` is located inside the `util` directory. If you go into the `util` directory and run the command 'xmlsec', it will not work. The reason is that the program needs the following dynamic link libraries to run:

- `libxmlsec-1.2.5+.win32.zip:`   `libxmlsec.dll`
  `libxmlsec-openssl.dll`
  `libxmlsec-mscrypto.dll`

- `libxml2-2.6.11.win32.zip:`   `libxml2.dll`

- `libxslt-1.1.8.win32.zip:`   `libexslt.dll`
  `libxslt.dll`

- `iconv-1.9.1.win32.zip:`   `iconv.dll`

- `zlib-1.1.4.win32.zip:`   `zlib.dll`

- OpenSSL package: `ssleay32.dll`
  `libeay32.dll`

In order to run the program `xmlsec`, you also need to make sure that these dlls (from the associated packages) are available from the path of your system.

If you have set up XMLSEC on your machine correctly, the command `xmlsec` will display a help screen similar to that generated by `ex10-27.txt`.

```
Example ex10-27.txt - The help screen of the XMLSEC library

 1: E:\libxmlsec-1.2.5.win32\util>xmlsec
 2: Usage: xmlsec <command> [<options>] [<file>]
 3:
 4: xmlsec is a command line tool for signing, verifying, encrypting and
 5: decrypting XML documents. The allowed <command> values are:
 6:   --help        display this help information and exit
 7:   --help-all    display help information for all commands/options
                    and exit
 8:   --help-<cmd>  display help information for command <cmd> and exit
 9:   --version     print version information and exit
10:   --keys        keys XML file manipulation
11:   --sign        sign data and output XML document
12:   --verify      verify signed document
13:   --sign-tmpl   create and sign dynamically generated signature
                    template
14:   --encrypt     encrypt data and output XML document
15:   --decrypt     decrypt data from XML document
16:   --xkms-server-request       process data as XKMS server request
17:
18:
19: Report bugs to http://www.aleksey.com/xmlsec/bugs.html
20:
21: Written by Aleksey Sanin <aleksey@aleksey.com>.
22:
23: Copyright (C) 2002-2003 Aleksey Sanin.
24: This is free software: see the source for copying information.
```

Basically, the XMLSEC library is used to provide OpenSSL security for XML pages. The first set of security functions are obviously, for encryption and decryption.

10.5.4 XML encryption and decryption

The main idea behind XML encryption and decryption is specified in the W3C document *XML encryption syntax and processing* (from www.w3.org/TR/2002/RE-xmlenc-core-20021210).

Without going into every technical detail, this document provides a standard procedure for encrypting data and representing the results in XML. The input data, basically, can be anything from arbitrary data to an XML element, or XML element content. The encrypted result is usually an XML encryption element containing the cipher data. The encrypted XML page can be decrypted effectively across all platforms.

In this section, we are going to show how to perform standard XML encryption using the XMLSEC library. In order to display the input and output documents, XSLT pages are also constructed.

Consider the XML page listed in ex10-28.xml.

```
Example: ex10-28.xml - Input XML page For XML encryption

 1:  <?xml version="1.0" encoding="UTF-8"?>
 2:  <?xml-stylesheet type="text/xsl" href="ex10-28.xsl" ?>
 3:  <Envelope>
 4:    <Head>Encrypt</Head>
 5:    <Data>
 6:      The XMLSEC library can be used to provide
 7:      OpenSSL security features to XML pages including
 8:      encryption, decryption, signing and verifying
 9:      processes related to digital signature.
10:    </Data>
11:  </Envelope>
```

After the XML and XSLT declarations in lines 1–2 is the root element `<Envelope>`. Under this root element, there are two elements, namely `<Head>` and `<Data>`. It is the content of this `<Data>` element that is going to be encrypted.

To encrypt, or decrypt, this XML page using XMLSEC, the following subcommands are used:

encrypt and decrypt

Despite their simple description in ex10-27.txt, each of these subcommands contains many options. For example, if you activate the help information by the command

xmlsec --help-encrypt

you will see more than 40 options covering a whole range of encryption services.

Basically, to perform the XML encryption on ex10-28.xml, you need the following:

■ an input XML page, such as ex10-28.xml;

■ a key corresponding to the encryption method stored in file;

■ an XML template so that the encryption can be perform according to your specification.

Suppose you have an XML template file called `ex10-28_tp.xml`. The DES encryption on `ex10-28.xml` can be performed by the command

```
xmlsec encrypt --deskey johnsmith.txt --xml-data ex10-28.xml
   ex10-28_tp.xml
```

The first option `--deskey` indicates that the encryption method is DES and the key is stored in file `johnsmith.txt`. The option `--xml-data` specifies an XML page to be encrypted – in this case, the input page is `ex10-28.xml`.

For a simple XML template, consider `ex10-28_tp.xml`.

Example: ex10-28_tp.xml – A simple XML encryption template

```
 1: <?xml version="1.0"?>
 2:
 3: <EncryptedData xmlns="http://www.w3.org/2001/04/xmlenc#"
 4:       Type="http://www.w3.org/2001/04/xmlenc#Element">
 5:   <EncryptionMethod
 6:       Algorithm="http://www.w3.org/2001/04/xmlenc#tripledes-cbc"/>
 7:
 8:   <KeyInfo xmlns="http://www.w3.org/2000/09/xmldsig#">
 9:       <KeyName></KeyName>
10:   </KeyInfo>
11:   <CipherData>
12:       <CipherValue>
13:       </CipherValue>
14:   </CipherData>
15: </EncryptedData>
```

The page contains an `<EncryptedData>` element. Under this element, the following three elements are defined:

```
<EncryptedMethod>    <KeyInfo>    <CipherData>
```

The `<EncryptedMethod>` element should contain the `Algorithm` attribute to describe the encryption algorithm to be used. In this case, the encryption method is `tripledes-cbc`. Inside the `<CipherData>` element, an element called `<CipherValue>` is specified as illustrated in lines 12–13. The encrypted result will be inserted into this element.

By default, the encryption command above will output all results on the screen. To output the result in a file such as `ex10-28_enc.xml`, you can use the `--output` option as follows:

```
xmlsec encrypt --deskey johnsmith.txt --xml-data ex10-28.xml
              --output ex10-28_enc.xml ex10-28_tp.xml
```

Example: ex10-28_enc.xml - The Encrypted XML Page

```
 1: <?xml version="1.0" encoding="UTF-8"?>
 2: <?xml-stylesheet type="text/xsl" href="ex10-28.xsl" ?>
 3: <EncryptedData xmlns="http://www.w3.org/2001/04/xmlenc#"
 4:    Type="http://www.w3.org/2001/04/xmlenc#Element">
 5:    <EncryptionMethod
 6:        Algorithm="http://www.w3.org/2001/04/xmlenc#tripledes-cbc"/>
 7:
 8:    <KeyInfo xmlns="http://www.w3.org/2000/09/xmldsig#">
 9:        <KeyName/>
10:    </KeyInfo>
11:    <CipherData>
12:        <CipherValue>
13:            Lrv2aKrWC3P+kUb72Ah4b2ICgKwnVGRb3WmW9kBlLqyXlPxzwWq+jsRJa
14:            P5oJbZA8ZuaE0+QoLy84B6HjbRRfaxKC5ZVzovQBaHQXkDqxqKTqFrxly
15:            5NmpYO2wpJw46nGb6AmbhhyKxdf56jvdvc+MAgCizW7a0Hr8PjhYjHUZq
16:            j5qDX4C41IetJD6XRiaxO+0tPnL23orwC6wSV7C3n2vrssXc0tQrRzdvm
17:            ITSBXonm1Hj84K6deUTHCTdesqnAjW8CRsTiSyxWgOqVITFwMZq/h5H/G
18:            ZtD1RK+V57wJq270h9511jAhRs/Yx/CTdO+wgbhj1Ucom1As3p1hqHQLA
                Q8LgZpKI+2JNRNjbIXuXs=</CipherValue>
19:    </CipherData>
20: </EncryptedData>
```

As you can see from `ex10-28_enc.xml`, the encrypted result of the page `ex10-28.xml` is ouput to the `<CipherData>` element.

To decrypt this page, the following command is used:

```
xmlsec decrypt --deskey johnsmith.txt ex10-28_enc.xml
```

This command will decrypt the page `ex10-28_enc.xml` and the result is displayed on the screen directly. The execution of this command is shown in Figure 10.57.

The decrypted XML page in Figure 10.57 is the same as in `ex10-28.xml`. In order to display both the plaintext and ciphertext pages, an XSLT page called `ex10-28.xsl` is developed.

This is a simple XSLT page to display the pages `ex10-28.xml` and `ex10-28_enc.xml`. In order to detect the original XML page `ex10-28.xml`, the `<xsl:choose>` is employed in line 13. The `<xsl:when>` element in line 14 performs a test on the content of the `<Head>` element. If the content is 'Encrypt', the input page is a plaintext. In this case, encryption is performed and the data is displayed inside the `<textarea>` element in lines 19–21.

Fig. 10.57 XML Decryption

```
E:\ch10>xmlsec decrypt --deskey
      johnsmith.txt ex10-28_enc.xml

<?xml version="1.0" encoding="UTF-8"?>
<?xml-stylesheet type="text/xsl"
 href="ex10-28.xsl" ?>
<Envelope>
 <Head>Encrypt</Head>
 <Data>
  The XMLSEC library can be used to provide
  OpenSSL security features to XML pages including
  encryption, decryption, signing and verifying
  processes related to digital signature.
 </Data>
</Envelope>
```

Example: ex10-28.xsl - XSLT For ex10-28.xml and ex10-28_enc.xml

```
 1: <?xml version="1.0" encoding="iso-8859-1"?>
 2: <xsl:stylesheet version="1.0"
 3: xmlns:xsl="http://www.w3.org/1999/XSL/Transform">
 4:
 5: <xsl:template match="/">
 6:
 7: <html xmlns="http://www.w3.org/1999/xhtml" xml:lang="en" lang="en">
 8: <head><title> XML Encryption</title></head>
 9: <body style="background:#dddddd;color:#000000;font-family:arial;
10:     font-size:24pt;font-weight:bold;text-align:center">
11: <div style="text-align:center"><br />
12:
13: <xsl:choose>
14:  <xsl:when test="Envelope/Head='Encrypt'">
15:   <table style="font-size:18pt;text-align:center;
16:    font-weight:bold;width:680px" border="2">
17:     <tr><td>The XML Encryption Plaintext Is:</td></tr>
18:     <tr><td style="font-size:12pt;text-align:left"
              readonly="true"><br />
19:        <textarea style="font-size:12pt;width:680px;height:160px" >
20:        <xsl:value-of select="Envelope/Data" />
21:        </textarea></td></tr>
22:   </table>
23: </xsl:when>
24:
```

```
25:    <xsl:otherwise>
26:     <table style="font-size:18pt;text-align:center;font-weight:bold;
27:      width:680px" border="2">
28:       <tr><td>The XML Encryption Ciphertext Is:</td></tr>
29:       <tr><td style="font-size:12pt;text-align:left"
                   readonly="true"><br />
30:          <textarea style="font-size:12pt;width:680px;height:160px" >
31:            <xsl:value-of select="/" />
32:          </textarea></td></tr>
33:     </table>
34:    </xsl:otherwise>
35:   </xsl:choose> <br /><br />
36:  </div> </body> </html>
37: </xsl:template>
38: </xsl:stylesheet>
```

If the content of the <Head> element is not 'Encrypt', the input page is a ciphertext (i.e. ex10-28_enc.xml). In this case, the statements inside the <xsl:otherwise> element will be executed for decryption (lines 26–33). The encrypted data will be displayed inside the <textarea> defined in lines 30–32.

With this XSLT page, you can display both pages ex10-28.xml and ex10-28_enc.xml by

```
http://www.pws-ex.com/ch10/ex10-28.xml
http://www.pws-ex.com/ch10/ex10-28_enc.xml
```

The technique shown here is simply a conditional-if statement. Screenshots are shown in Figures 10.58 and 10.59.

If you want to perform AES encryption, all you need to do is modify the XML template file ex10-28_tp.xml. For example, you can make a copy of ex10-28.xml and ex10-28_tp.xml and call them ex10-29.xml and ex10-29_tp.xml respectively. In the new template, modify the following line:

```
6: Algorithm="http://www.w3.org/2001/04/xmlenc#aes256-cbc"/>
```

Now you can issue the following command for encryption:

```
xmlsec encrypt --aeskey johnsmith.txt --xml-data ex10-29.xml
               --output ex10-29_enc.xml ex10-29_tp.xml
```

This command will use the key in the file johnsmith.txt and the template ex10-29_tp.txt to perform the aes-256-cbc encryption on file ex10-29.xml. The result is output to file ex10-29_enc.xml. A screenshot of the encrypted page is shown in Figure 10.60.

Fig. 10.58 The XML plaintext

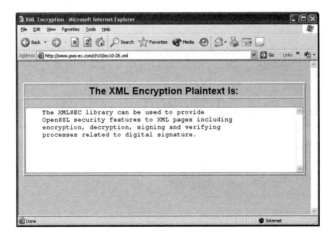

Fig. 10.59 DES encrypted XML

To perform AES decryption on this page, the following command is used:

```
xmlsec decrypt --aeskey johnsmith.txt ex10-29_enc.xml
```

The decryption result will be displayed in the browser window. The execution dialog is shown in Figure 10.61. Now, let's see how XML signatures and contracts are generated and verified.

Fig. 10.60   AES encrypted XML

Fig. 10.61   AES decryption

```
E:\ch10>xmlsec decrypt --aeskey johnsmith.txt
      ex10-29_enc.xml

<?xml version="1.0" encoding="UTF-8"?>
<?xml-stylesheet type="text/xsl" href="ex10-28.xsl" ?>
<Envelope>
 <Head>Encrypt</Head>
 <Data>
  The XMLSEC library can be used to provide
  OpenSSL security features to XML pages including
  encryption, decryption, signing and verifying
  processes related to digital signature.
 </Data>
</Envelope>
```

10.5.5   XML signatures and contracts

Like XML encryption, the standard XML signature is specified by the W3C
document *XML signature syntax and processing* from www.w3.org/TR/2002/REC-
xmldsig-core-20020212.

Without going into every technical detail, this document specifies XML signature
(or XML digital signature) processing rules, methods and application syntax. XML
signatures provide the following security features for XML pages across any
compatible platforms:

- XML signature data integrity – by using hashes or digest values;

- signer authentication – by public and private keys (or digital signatures).

In this section, we show how to perform some standard XML signature applications using the XMLSEC library. In addition to the standard digital signature signing and verifying process, one of our ultimate aims is to design and develop the 'XML digital contract'. The examples provided in this section may be simple but the same principles can be applied to many commercial and non-commercial applications.

XML digital signatures

If you have a well-defined XML document and key file, you can sign and verify the page by using the XMLSEC commands

```
sign   and   verify
```

As with encryption, each of these commands contains more than 40 options covering a whole range of signing and verifying services.

To sign an XML page, you need:

- an input XML template page containing both the data and the signing information;

- a key (or password) corresponding to the signing method stored in file.

For a simple example, consider the XML template `ex10-29_tp.xml`.

To sign an XML page, the corresponding template should contain data and signature sections under the root element, i.e.

```
<Data>   and   <Signature>
```

Basically, the `<data>` element contains user-defined information or, more precisely, the information to be encrypted (lines 4–22). The `<Signature>` element specified by the XML signature standard should contain the elements of signature method, digest method, digest value and signature value. In this case, the information is (see `ex10-29_tp.xml`):

- signature method – `rsa-sha1` (line 9)

- digest method   – `sha1`   (line 14)

- digest value   – store the `digest value`   (line 15)

- signature value – store the `signature value` (line 18)

If you have a private key, such as `rsakey.pem`, you can sign this XML document by the command

```
xmlsec sign --privkey rsakey.pem --output ex10-29_signed.xml
    ex10-29_tp.xml
```

```
Example: ex10-29_tp.xml - A simple XML template for XML signatures

 1: <?xml version="1.0" encoding="UTF-8"?>
 2: <Envelope>
 3:  <Data> Hello, World! </Data>
 4:  <Signature xmlns="http://www.w3.org/2000/09/xmldsig#">
 5:   <SignedInfo>
 6:    <CanonicalizationMethod
 7:       Algorithm="http://www.w3.org/TR/2001/REC-xml-c14n-20010315" />
 8:     <SignatureMethod
 9:        Algorithm="http://www.w3.org/2000/09/xmldsig#rsa-sha1" />
10:      <Reference URI="">
11:       <Transforms><Transform
12:        Algorithm="http://www.w3.org/2000/09/xmldsig#enveloped-
             signature" />
13:       </Transforms>
14:       <DigestMethod Algorithm="http://www.w3.org/2000/09/
             xmldsig#sha1" />
15:       <DigestValue></DigestValue>
16:      </Reference>
17:     </SignedInfo>
18:    <SignatureValue></SignatureValue>
19:    <KeyInfo>
20:        <KeyName></KeyName>
21:    </KeyInfo>
22:  </Signature>
23: </Envelope>
```

The signed XML document is output to the page `ex10-29_signed.xml`.

As you can see from the signed page `ex10-29_signed.xml`, the digest and signature values are inserted in line 15 and lines 19–24. The digest value is designed for data integrity. The signature value can be used for signature verification.

Provided you have an associated public key, such as `rsapub.pem`, you can verify this signed page by issuing the command

```
xmlsec verify --pubkey rsapub.pem ex10-29_signed.xml
```

If the signature verification process is successful, you will see the 'OK' string on your screen. Otherwise, an error message such as 'Error: signature failed' will appear. The execution of this example is captured in Figure 10.62.

Now you know how to sign and verify an XML page by an XML signature, the next step is to modify the `<Data>` element in `ex10-29_tp.xml` to construct an XML digital contract.

```
Example: ex10-29_signed.xml - A simple signed XML page

1:  <?xml version="1.0" encoding="UTF-8"?>
2:  <Envelope>
3:   <Data> Hello, World! </Data>
4:   <Signature xmlns="http://www.w3.org/2000/09/xmldsig#">
5:    <SignedInfo>
6:     <CanonicalizationMethod
7:      Algorithm="http://www.w3.org/TR/2001/REC-xml-c14n-20010315"/>
8:     <SignatureMethod
9:      Algorithm="http://www.w3.org/2000/09/xmldsig#rsa-sha1"/>
10:     <Reference URI="">
11:      <Transforms><Transform
12:   Algorithm="http://www.w3.org/2000/09/xmldsig#enveloped-signature"/>
13:      </Transforms>
14:      <DigestMethod Algorithm="http://www.w3.org/2000/09/
         xmldsig#sha1"/>
15:      <DigestValue>TU8k+474R/P//8OlyLIlNABVTDI=</DigestValue>
16:     </Reference>
17:    </SignedInfo>
18:    <SignatureValue>
19:     Wm+czGqK1/a39u5cBBUT4p2zIJfWj/LCNwIhrlk9vIXDOkuiQergeN6Soh0NtKbM
20:     OuwYe5yHjUzJZHr/RqZ6MxpJoeflLQF1etgrsQFJjvXtfpmQp6ZJ6SymQhWr7VJ8
21:     k0LKq63L41WJpzzdxW0wlfAhpbPBCs32KkvZZjJSuaYpSW9CyqG5iZ3fYbx6coJH
22:     Xhr8LEy2YSQUJgLANBOLZ22HdUL6J8C56na3YNlT0fIThFS+Eoxi2vhvSElAmzyc
23:     Xu4/1XMpEoG/B7pP157mn7SXJQVc7vHcrbJzFOiWuKCYsGcKaJGDlCeACwtyq3er
24:     1NakV4lDp3w+qIz3BWw0oQ==</SignatureValue>
25:    <KeyInfo><KeyName/></KeyInfo>
26:   </Signature>
27:  </Envelope>
```

Fig. 10.62 XML signing and verification

```
E:\ch10>xmlsec sign --privkey rsakey.pem
        --output ex10-29_signed.
        xml ex10-29_tp.xml

E:\ch10>xmlsec verify --pubkey rsapub.pem
        ex10-29_signed.xml

OK
SignedInfo References (ok/all): 1/1
Manifests References (ok/all): 0/0
```

XML digital contracts

As a simple example, make a copy of the XML template ex10-29_tp.xml and call it ex10-30_tp.xml. In this new template, replace the <Data> element by the following.

```
Example: ex10-30_tp.xml - The XML digital contract <Data> element

 1: <Data>
 2:   <Contract_head>
 3:    <head01>Sender and Signer: </head01>
 4:    <head01_Name>XXX Company Limited - Online Service Department
 5:    </head01_Name>
 6:    <head02>Issue To: </head02>
 7:    <head02_Name>Mr. John Smith</head02_Name>
 8:    <head03>Date</head03>
 9:    <head03_Name>5 September 2005</head03_Name>
10:   </Contract_head>
11:
12:   <Contents>
13:    <cont01>Contents:</cont01>
14:    <cont02> This is to confirm that the on-site warranty of the
15:             Washing Machine DJ51200 bought by Mr. John Smith
16:             is extended to 5 years from the date of this contract.
17:    </cont02>
18:   </Contents>
19: </Data>
```

Now, the new XML template ex10-30_tp.xml contains a more appropriate <Data> element for a digital contract. Inside this <Data> element, we have the contract header and contents represented by elements <Contract_head> and <Contents> respectively. Since the <Data> element is the data section of the contract, this template can be signed by the same signing command:

```
xmlsec sign --privkey rsakey.pem --output ex10-30_signed.xml
ex10-30_tp.xml
```

In this case, the signed XML page is ex10-30_signed.xml. The digest and signature values are stored in the same location as in ex10-29_signed.xml. To verify this page, you can use the command

```
xmlsec verify --pubkey rsapub.pem ex10-30_signed.xml
```

The verifying result is the same as that shown in Figure 10.62.

In order to display the signed XML page, we use the parse method. Consider the HTML/XHTML page listing ex10-30.htm.

Example: ex10-30.htm – Displaying an XML contract using a parser

(Part I)

```
 1: <?xml version="1.0" encoding="UTF-8"?>
 2: <!DOCTYPE html
 3: PUBLIC "-//W3C//DTD XHTML 1.0 Transitional//EN"
 4: "http://www.w3.org/TR/xhtml1/DTD/xhtml1-transitional.dtd">
 5: <html xmlns="http://www.w3.org/1999/xhtml" xml:lang="en" lang="en">
 6: <head><title>Example: ex10-31.htm </title>
 7: <body style="background:#ffffff;color:#000000;text-align:center;
 8:    font-size:20pt;font-weight:bold">
 9: <div>Electronic Signed Document<br />(XML Digital
                                        Contract)</div><br />
10:
11: <script>
12: function xml_dom()
13: {
14:  var xmlDoc=new ActiveXObject("Microsoft.XMLDOM");
15:  xmlDoc.async="false";
16:  xmlDoc.load("ex10-30_signed.xml");
17:
18:  tSt="<table style='font-size:14pt;width:700px' cellspacing='10'>";
19:                      //---------------------- contract Header
20: prinodes=xmlDoc.documentElement.childNodes;
21: data = prinodes.item(0).childNodes;
22: nodes = data.item(0).childNodes;
23: document.write(tSt);
24: for (ii=0;ii< nodes.length;ii=ii+2) {
25:   document.write("<tr><td style='width:160px'>"+nodes.item(ii).text +
26:      "</td><td>"+nodes.item(ii+1).text + "</td></tr>");
27: }
28: document.write("</table><br />");
29:                      //--------------------- contract Contents
30: prinodes=xmlDoc.documentElement.childNodes;
31: data = prinodes.item(0).childNodes;
32: nodes = data.item(1).childNodes;
33:
34: document.write(tSt);
35: for (ii=0;ii< nodes.length;ii++) {
36:   document.write("<tr><td>"+nodes.item(ii).text + "</td></tr>");
37: }
38: document.write("</table><br /><br />");
```

Lines 1–9 are XHTML headers and statements. The script block after line 11 defines a function called `xml_dom()`. When this function is called, the signed XML page `ex10-30_signed.xml` will be loaded into the parser (lines 14–16) and displayed on screen. Line 18 defines an XHTML table element stored in variable `tSt`. Lines 20–22 get the node of the contract header. The statement in line 23 and the for-loop in lines 24–28 are used to construct an XHTML table and output all contents of the XML contract header into it.

In fact, the statements in lines 30–32 get the node of the contract contents and the statements in lines 34–38 output all the contract contents into another table. Therefore, all the information in the XML `<Data>` element will be displayed.

The next step is to display the XML signature information. Consider part II of `ex10-30.htm`.

```
Example: Continuation of ex10-30.htm                      (Part II)

39:                                   //------------- Signature Info
40:   prinodes=xmlDoc.documentElement.childNodes
41:   document.write(tSt);
42:   nodes = prinodes.item(1).childNodes
43:                                   //------------- Digest Value
44:   document.write("<tr><td style='width:300px'>Digest Value</td>"+
45:              "<td style='font-family:courier;font-size:14pt'>"+
46:                         nodes.item(0).text + "</td></tr>")
47:                            //----------------------- Verifying Key
48:   document.write("<tr><td>Verifying key can be obtained at: </td>"+
49:              "<td style='font-family:courier;font-size:14pt'>"+
50:                         "http://www.xxx.com/2005</td></tr>")
51:                            //----------------------- XML Signature
52:   document.write("<tr><td colspan=2>Company's Digital
                   Signature:</td></tr>")
53:   document.write("<tr><td colspan=2>"+
54:     "<textarea style='font-size:12pt;width:680px;height:130px'
55:       readonly>"+ nodes.item(1).text + "</textarea></td></tr>");
56:
57:   document.write("</table><br />");
58: }
59: xml_dom();
60: </script>
61: </body></html>
```

The second part of the example is also straightforward. Lines 40–42 obtain the node of the `<Signature>` element. The statements in lines 44–46 output the digest value stored in the element `<DigestValue>`. The actual data in the parser is denoted by

```
nodes.item(0).text
```

Lines 48–50 output the information as to how to obtain the verifying key (public key). This information may be helpful if users want to verify the contract. Finally, the signature value is output to the XHTML text area defined in lines 54–55. Note that the signature value in the `<SignatureValue>` element is represented by the notation `nodes.item(1).text`.

When the function `xml_dom()` is called at line 59, the XML digital contract is displayed. A screenshot of this example is shown in Figure 10.63.

If you have a certificate issued by a trusted party (or CA) such as `rsacert.pem`, you can build the certificate information into the contract. The certificate information is represented by the element `<X509Data>` in the `<KeyInfo>` element. Make a copy of the template `ex10-30_tp.xml` and call it `ex10-31_tp.xml`. In this new template, locate the element `<KeyInfo>` and replace it with the following elements:

```
<KeyInfo>
  <KeyName></KeyName>
  <X509Data></X509Data>
</KeyInfo>
```

Fig. 10.63 A digital contract

All we have done is to add the `<X509Data>` element below the `<KeyName>`. Now, if you sign this template using the command

```
xmlsec    --privkey rsakey.pem,rsacert.pem
          --output ex10-31_signed.xml ex10-31_tp.xml
```

the certification information of `rsacert.pem` will be built into the signed page `ex10-31_signed.xml`. This signed page can be verified by using the certificate of the trusted party. Suppose the certificate of the trusted party is `rootcert.pem`, the verifying command should be

```
xmlsec verify --trusted rootcert.pem ex10-31_signed.xml
```

In order to display this signed page, make a copy of `ex10-30.htm` and call it `ex10-31.htm`. Inside `ex10-31.htm`, modify line 16 to load the signed page `ex10-31_signed.xml`. The next step is to modify part II of the XHTML page as follows.

```
Example: ex10-31.htm - XML digital contract with X509 certificate
                                                          (Part II)
39:                         //----------------------- Signature Info
40:   prinodes=xmlDoc.documentElement.childNodes
41:   document.write(tSt);
42:   nodes = prinodes.item(1).childNodes
43:                         //------------------------- Digest Value
44:   document.write("<tr><td style='width:300px'>Digest Value</td>"+
45:               "<td style='font-family:courier;font-size:14pt'>"+
46:                         nodes.item(0).text + "</td></tr>")
47:                         //----------------------- XML Signature
48:   docUMent.write("<tr><td colspan=2>Company's Digital
                   Signature:</td></tr>")
49:   document.write("<tr><td colspan=2>"+
50:      "<textarea style='font-size:12pt;width:680px;height:130px'
51:      readonly>"+ nodes.item(1).text + "</textarea></td></tr>");
52:                         //--------------------- X509 Certificate
53:   document.write("<tr><td colspan=2>X509 Certificate Data</td></tr>")
54:   document.write("<tr><td colspan=2>"+
55:      "<textarea style='font-size:12pt;width:680px;height:
56:      130px' readonly>"+ nodes.item(2).text +
         "</textarea></td></tr>")
57:   document.write("</table><br />");
58: }
59: xml_dom();
60: </script>
61: </body></html>
```

Fig. 10.64 A digital contract with X509 certificate information

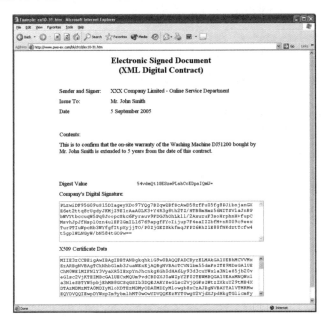

In this page fragment, the information about the X509 certificate is displayed by statements in lines 53–56. First, the certificate data stored in `<X509Data>` element is captured by the notation `nodes.item(2).text` using the parser. This notation is then output to the XHTML text area by the statement in lines 55–56. A screenshot of this example is shown in Figure 10.64.

Although we now have a theory of digital contracts and their implementation, their application on a global scale is in its infancy. Hopefully, you and I will both receive a digital contract over the World Wide Web one day in the near future.

Glossary

active Attack   Attack in which the intention of the attacker is to create or modify information.

Advanced Encryption Standard (AES)   Replacement for the Data Encryption Standard (DES); a conventional block cipher chosen by the National Institute of Standards and Technology (NIST) for general use by the US government.

algorithm   Description of a sequence of operations that can be used to finish a particular task.

American National Standard Code for Information Interchange (ASCII) Eight-bit character set defining alphanumeric characters. For example, the ASCII code for character A is 65. ASCII is widely used to represent English characters on computers.

American National Standards Institute (ANSI)   Founded in 1918; voluntary organization with over 1300 members that creates standards for the computer industry.

ANSI X509   Digital certificate specification developed as part of the X.500 directory specification, and widely used in public-key encryption systems.

ANSI X917   ANSI standard for secret key exchange using the DES algorithm.

Apache   Public domain Web server software developed by a group of volunteers. Free, with sophisticated features and excellent performance. Used to host more than 50% of all Web sites in the world.

Apache md5Crypt password   Password scheme used by Apache server software to perform authentication.

arbitrary precision mathematics (APM)   Set of functions to provide arbitrary high accuracy of mathematical calculations on computers.

asymmetric algorithm   Encryption algorithm that uses different keys for encryption and decryption; most often a public-key algorithm.

asynchronous   Describes communications without a regular time basis, allowing transmission at unequal rates.

attachment   File, such as a word processing document, spreadsheet, graphics or sound, that has been sent along with an email message.

attack   General ways in which an intruder may try to 'break' or penetrate the secrecy of a cipher.

authentication The process of verifying that a particular name really belongs to a particular entity.

authenticity The ability to ensure that the given information was in fact produced by the entity whose name it carries, and that it was not forged or modified.

bandwidth The amount of data that can be transmitted through a medium in a fixed amount of time. For digital devices, usually expressed in bits per second (bps) or bytes per second. For analog devices, expressed in cycles per second, or hertz (Hz).

base64 (or base64 encoding) Method for encoding 8-bit characters using only ASCII-printable (64) characters.

basic HTTP authentication Basic authentication scheme employed by the HTTP. Uses base64 encoding to identify a user.

binary digit (bit) The most basic computation unit used by computers. A single bit can hold only one of two values: 0 or 1. More meaningful values are obtained by combining consecutive bits into larger units.

binary number system (base 2) Number system that uses bits (0 or 1) as digits.

bit rate The rate at which bits are transmitted over a network; usually expressed in number of bits per second.

bitwise AND (&) If bits of both operands are 1s, returns a 1 in each bit position.

bitwise left shift (<<) Shifts first operand a number of bits to the left as specified in the second operand, shifting in zeros from the right.

bitwise NOT (~) Flips the bits in the operand.

bitwise operator Performs mathemtical operations on binary number system (or bits). Some bitwise operators are AND (&), OR (|), XOR (^), left shift (<<) and right shift (>>).

bitwise OR (|) If bits of either operand are 1s, returns a 1 in a bit position.

bitwise XOR (^) If a single operand is a 1, returns a 1 in a bit position.

bitwise zero-fill right shift (>>>) Shifts first operand a number of bits to the right as specified in the second operand, discards displaced bits, and shifts in zeros from the left.

block cipher Cipher that encrypts data in blocks of a fixed size. DES, Blowfish, CAST and AES are block ciphers.

Blowfish cipher Encryption algorithm designed by Bruce Schneier.

Blum-Blum-Shub (BBS) Pseudo-random number algorithm designed by Blum, Blum and Shub.

broadcast Simultaneous transmission of the same data to all nodes connected to a network.

browser–server interaction (or browser–server dialog)   Refers to the dialog and operations between Web server and browser.

browser   *See* Web browser.

brute-force attack   The process of trying to recover a password (or a crypto key) by trying all possibilities or combinations.

buffer   Memory area used for handling input and output.

bypass   Flaw in a security device that allows messages to go around the security mechanisms.

byte   Series of bits of a particular length, usually 8. Computer storage space is measured in bytes.

Caesar code   Encryption scheme originally used by the dictator of ancient Rome.

CAST-128 and CAST-256   CAST-128 is a DES-like cipher using 64-bit blocks and 128-bit keys. CAST–256 is a candidate cipher for the AES standard, based largely on the CAST-128 design.

CAST ciphers   Series of block ciphers (CAST-128 and CAST-256) developed by Carlisle Adams/Stafford Tavares (CAST).

certificate   *See* digital certificate.

certification authority (CA)   Trusted third-party organization or company that issues digital certificates. The CA guarantees that the identity of the party in the certificate is true.

certificate signing request (CSR)   Unsigned certificate for submission to a certification authority (CA), which signs it with the private key of its CA certificate. Once the CSR is signed, it becomes a real certificate.

checksum   Numeric value used to verify the integrity of a block of data.

chosen plaintext attack   Technique for attacking a cipher by feeding it chosen plaintext and watching for patterns in the ciphertext.

cipher   Procedure that transforms data between plaintext and ciphertext. Also the general term for encryption and decryption.

cipher block chaining (CBC)   Block cipher mode that combines the previous block of ciphertext with the current block of plaintext before encrypting it.

cipher feedback (CFB)   Block cipher mode that feeds previously encrypted ciphertext through the block cipher to generate the key that encrypts the next block of ciphertext.

ciphertext   The encrypted data produced by an encryption algorithm or a cipher.

client   Computing entity in a network that seeks service from other entities on the network.

client script Sometimes called client side script. Usually embedded into HTML/XHTML document and run by the Web browser to generate special or dynamic features. ECMAScript is the standard to develop client script.

common gateway interface (CGI) Specification for transferring information between a program on the Web server and a Web client.

confidentiality The ability to ensure that information is not disclosed to people who aren't intended to receive it.

connection Link between two or more computers, processes, applications, devices, networks and so on. Connections may be logical, physical or both.

contract *See* digital contract.

cookie Message from a Web server computer, sent to and stored by your browser on your computer. Sent back to the server each time the browser requests a page from the server.

cracking The process of overcoming a security measure. Cracking a password (or a key) means an attempt to recover the password; cracking a ciphertext means an attempt to recover the corresponding plaintext.

Crypt() password Password scheme used by early UNIX/LINUX systems.

cryptanalysis Process of trying to recover encryption (or crypto) key or plaintext associated with a crypto system.

crypto-attacks Use of scientific methods to crack crypto-systems.

crypto-system Software or hardware systems with cryptographic features.

cryptographically secure random numbers (CSRN) Random number schemes suitable for cryptographic applications.

cryptography General term for encryption and decryption methods for data transmission and protection.

cryptology General term for encryption, decryption, and attacks for data transmission and protection.

cut and paste attack Attack in which an attacker substitutes a portion of ciphertext with another. The goal is for the subsequently decrypted plaintext to cause a particular response so that some knowledge of the key is obtained.

cyclic redundancy check (CRC) Method to check data integrity; often used in data transmission.

Data Encryption Standard (DES) Federal FIPS standard block cipher used by US government and in many commercial systems. However, its key length (56 bits) is not long enough, and it is vulnerable to many brute-force related attacks.

data integrity The assurance that information can be accessed or modified only by authorized people.

decoding   The process of converting the encoded transmitted data back into its original format. The opposite of encoding.

decryption   The process of restoring plaintext from ciphertext. The opposite of encryption.

differential cryptanalysis   Technique to attack a cipher by feeding it with chosen plaintext and looking for patterns in the ciphertext.

Diffie–Hellman (DH) key exchange   Public-key cipher that generates a shared secret between two entities after they publicly share some randomly generated data.

digest HTTP authentication   Authentication scheme employed by the HTTP; uses message digest (MD5) to identify a user.

digital certificate   Electronic document that establishes the identity of an individual or a organization.

digital contract   Electronic document for which both the data integrity and the authenticity can be verified; has the same legal force as a written contract.

digital key   Information that causes a cipher to encrypt or decrypt information in a distinctive way.

digital message   The presentation of text message by digital data.

digital signature   Piece of trusted data or information which demonstrates that the identity of the originator of the file can be authenticated.

digital signature algorithm (DSA)   Public-key method, used primarily for digital signature and authentication.

Digital Signature Standard (DSS)   US government standard specifying the digital signature algorithm (DSA).

domain name   The textual name assigned to a host on the Internet.

e-commerce   Conducting of business on-line; includes, for example, buying and selling products on the Internet.

E-Sign law   Electronic Signatures in Global and National Commerce Act of 2000 in the US; also called the E-Sign Law. Authorizes the use of electronic signatures as a legal substitute for handwritten signatures.

ECMAScript (ECMA262)   Standard scripting language developed by ECMA; based on JavaScript, and supported by all major browsers such as IE, NS and Opera.

electronic codebook (ECB)   Block cipher mode that consists of simply applying the cipher to blocks of data in sequence, one block at a time.

electronic funds transfer (EFT)   Electronic Funds Transfer provides for electronic payments and collections at point of sale. Type of system that takes money straight out of your bank account when you pay for something with your plastic card.

electronic mail (email)   Electronic messages transmitted on a network; a general term for electronic mail or Internet mail.

element   In HTML, refers to the name usually put inside a tag (e.g. < . . >). All elements in XHTML should also have an end tag (e.g. </. . >).

elliptic curve   The set of solutions (x,y) to an equation of the form $y^2 = x^3 + ax + b$, where a and b are constants.

elliptic curve cryptography (ECC)   Encryption and decryption using elliptic curves.

encoding   The process of converting information into the required transmission format.

encryption   The process of transforming a readable document (or plaintext) into unreadable gibberish (or ciphertext).

encryption mode   One of several ways to apply a block cipher to a data stream. Typical modes include ECB, CBC, CFB and OFB.

European Computer Manufacturers Association (ECMA)   ECMA was founded in 1961 and is also known as the European Association for Standardising Information and Communication Systems. Computer standards set by this organization are usually prefixed with 'ECMA' such as ECMAScript or ECMA-262.

export control   Laws and regulations intended to prevent products from being exported when not in a government's interest. Typically, munitions are placed under export control.

Extensible Hyper Text Markup Language (XHTML)   Language similar to HTML with XML syntax; recommended by the W3C authority for creating documents on the World Wide Web.

Extensible Markup Language (XML)   Specification developed by the W3C for Web pages; allows designers to create their own customized elements.

Extensible Style Language Transformation (XSLT)   The language used in XSL style sheets to transform XML documents into other document formats such as HTML or XHTML for display purposes.

Federal Information Processing Standard (FIPS)   Standards published by NIST, with which US government computer systems should comply.

Feistel cipher   Class of iterated block ciphers in which the ciphertext is generated from the plaintext by repeated application of the same transformation, called a round function.

file transfer protocol (FTP)   Internet application and network protocol for transferring files between host computers. There are no protections specified in FTP communications.

finite field   Mathematical structure consisting of a finite set of elements (or numbers) together with two binary operations called addition and multipication.

Firewall   Device installed at the point where network connections enter a site to apply rules that control the type of networking traffic that flows in and out. Most commercial firewalls are built to handle Internet protocols.

Forgery   Data item whose contents mislead the recipient into believing the item and its contents were produced by someone other than the actual author.

Gateway   Networking device that translates protocols of one type of network into those of another.

Gnu Privacy Guard (GnuPG)   Complete implementation of the Open Pretty Good Privacy (OpenPGP) standard.

graphical user interface (GUI)   Program interface that uses the graphics capabilities of the computer to make the program easier to use.

hash   When a mathematical transformation such as one-way encryption is used to convert a message into a fixed string of digits, the fixed string is called a hash or hash value.

hash function   Function that generates a hash value.

hexadecimal   Base 16 number system consisting of 16 unique symbols: 0, 1, 2, 3, 4, 5, 6, 7, 8, 9, A, B, C, D, E and F. For example, hexadecimal F represents 15 in decimal, and FF is 255 in decimal.

hexadecimal number system (base 16)   Number system that uses hexadecimals.

hijacking   Attack in which the attacker takes over a live connection between two entities in order to masquerade as one of the entities.

host   Computer system residing on an network and capable of independently communicating with other systems on the network.

hybrid encryption   Encryption process that combines two or more encryption algorithms.

Hyper Text Markup Language (HTML)   Language originally developed by Tim Berners-Lee and later adopted as a standard to create documents on the Web or World Wide Web.

Hyper Text Transfer Protocol (HTTP)   The underlying protocol defining how messages are formatted and transmitted on the Web, and what actions Web servers and browsers should take in response to various commands.

Hypertext Transport Protocol with SSL Security (HTTPS)   Embedding security features into HTTP protocol.

information security (INFOSEC)   Technical security measures that involve communications security, cryptography, and computer security.

integrity   *See* data integrity.

intellectual property rights (IPR)   General term for property right granted by the government of a country (or countries) to an inventor. For example, the US government can grant the IPR to an inventor 'to exclude others from making, using, offering for sale, or selling the invention throughout the United States or importing the invention into the United States' for a limited time in exchange for public disclosure of the invention when the patent is granted.

International Data Encryption Algorithm (IDEA)   Block cipher developed in Switzerland and used in PGP.

International Standards Organization (ISO)   International organization that published a large number of networking standards (the OSI protocols), most of which are incompatible with the Internet protocols. Protocols originally developed by the CCITT are generally ISO protocols.

Internet   The vast collection of interconnected networks that all use the TCP/IP protocols; sometimes called TCP/IP network.

Internet Engineering Task Force (IETF)   Technical organization that establishes and maintains Internet protocol standards.

Internet Explorer (IE)   Web browser developed by Microsoft for Windows platforms. The most popular browser used on the Web.

Internet Information Services (IIS)   Microsoft's Web server running on Windows platforms; comes bundled with Windows NT, 2000 Professional and XP Professional.

Internet protocol (IP)   Protocol that carries individual packets between hosts, and allows packets to be automatically routed through multiple networks if the destination host isn't on the same network as the originating host.

Internet service provider (ISP)   Company that provides services and access to the Internet.

intranet   Private network, usually within an organization, that uses the Internet protocols but is not connected directly to the global Internet.

IP address (or IP number)   Unique number consisting of four parts separated by dots, e.g. 165.113.223.2. Each part can have values from 0 to 255. For TCP/IP network (or Internet), IP address can be used to uniquely identify a computer on the network.

ISAAC   Cryptographic random number generator; uses Indirection, Shift, Accumulate, Add and Count to generate 32-bit random numbers.

ISAAC stream cipher   Stream cipher using the ISAAC random number generator.

Java   High-level programming language developed by Sun Microsystems. An object-oriented language similar to C++, but simplified to eliminate language features that cause common programming errors. By convention, Java program files end with a .java file extension.

JavaScript   Scripting language developed by Netscape to enable Web authors to design interactive Web pages. JavaScript can embed and interact with HTML/XHTML source code. JavaScript is not Java; they are different.

key-space   The collection of all possible keys for a given cryptosystem.

key   *See* digital key.

key distribution problem   General problem with symmetric-key encryption where the key must be shared or distributed to the person for decryption.

linear congruential generator (LCG)   Uses the linear congruential formula $xi + 1 = (a * xi + c)$ mod m to generate random numbers.

linear feedback shift registers (LFSR)   Hardware design or device to produce random bits using the XOR gate.

LINUX   Implementation of UNIX that runs on PCs and many other platforms; developed mainly by Linus Torvalds. UNIX is freely distributable with open source.

local area network (LAN)   Network of computers and devices that spans a relatively small area. With a LAN many users can share devices.

mail agent   Electronic mail program that helps end users manage messages, for example Microsoft's Outlook Express.

mail client   Front-end application used to compose, send and receive electronic mails (emails).

mail exchanger   System used to relay mail into a network.

man-in-middle attack   Public-key exchange in which the attacker substitutes their own public key for the requested public key.

md5Crypt password   Password scheme used in UNIX BSD to identify users as a replacement of the crypt(). Apache also uses it worldwide in the Web environment.

Message Digest #5 (MD5)   One-way hash function; takes a message and converts it into a fixed string (120-bit) of digits.

Microsoft Outlook Express   Mail client application developed by Microsoft.

Moving Picture Expert Group (MPEG or MPG)   Working group of ISO to set standards for digital audio and video compression. MPEG or MPG compression formats are widely used in compact discs (CDs), video compact discs (VCDs) and digital versatile/video discs (DVDs). By convention, MPEG files usually end with an .mpeg or .mpg file extension.

MPEG layer 3 format (MP3)   One of three coding schemes (layer 1, layer 2 and layer 3) for the compression of audio or sound signals. By removing all signals the human ear doesn't hear, it compresses 10 times more than layer 2.

multimedia   The use of computers to present text, graphics, sound, video, movie and animation in a unifying way. Nearly all PCs are now capable of multimedia features up to a certain level, depending on the power of the computer's video adapter and CPU.

Multipurpose Internet Mail Extensions (MIME)   Specification for formatting non-ASCII messages so that graphics, audio and video can be sent over the Internet.

Munitions   Anything that is useful in warfare. Crypto systems are munitions according to US law; this is the rationale behind export controls on crypto systems.

MySQL Database   Popular structured query language (SQL) database server from MySQL AB. Free, distributable open source software, available on all major platforms including Windows, Solaris, and LINUX.

name resolution   The process of mapping names or nodes to an IP address. The domain name system (DNS) is one system that does this.

National Computer Security Center (NCSC)   US government organization that evaluates computing equipment for high-security applications.

National Institute of Standards and Technology (NIST)   Agency of the US government that establishes national standards.

National Security Agency (NSA)   Agency of the US government responsible for intercepting foreign communications for intelligence reasons and for developing crypto systems to protect US government communications.

Netscape browser (NS)   Web browser developed by Netscape Communication, runs on all major platforms, such as Windows, Macintosh and UNIX/LINUX.

Network News Transfer Protocol (NNTP)   The protocol used to post, distribute, and retrieve USENET messages. The official specification is RFC 977.

network service   Operating system process that operates continuously and unattended to perform a service over a network. TCP/IP network uses several network services to establish communications processes and provide server facilities.

node   For TCP/IP networks, refers to network devices. For Web pages, represents a branch of elements in the structure (tree-structure) of the page.

non-repudiation   Generally refers to the inability to deny having signed a document, transaction or file. The intended receiver cannot deny receiving it.

nonce   Random value sent in a communications protocol exchange; often used to detect replay attacks.

obfuscation   In general, a practice used to intentionally make something more difficult to understand.

octal number system (base 8) Number system that uses 0, 1, 2, 3, 4, 5, 6, 7 as basic digits.

one-way encryption Encryption technique for which decryption is difficult or impossible.

one-time-pad (OTP) Vernam cipher in which one bit of new, purely random key is used for every bit of data being encrypted.

one-time password Password that can be used only once; usually produced by special password-generating software, or by a hardware token.

one-way hash Hash function for which it is extremely difficult to construct two blocks of data that yield exactly the same hash result. Ideally, it should require a brute-force search to find two data blocks that yield the same result.

Open Database Connectivity (ODBC) Standard database access method developed by Microsoft. The goal of ODBC is to make it possible to access data from any database product regardless of manufacturers.

Open Pretty Good Privacy (Open PGP) Encryption standard based on Pretty Good Privacy (PGP), widely used on emails. Defined by the OpenPGP Working Group of the Internet Engineering Task Force (IETF) standard RFC 2440.

Open Source Initiative (OSI) International organization to promote open source software (completely free, distributable software with source code). Some famous products of OSI on the Web are Apache, Perl and sendmail.

Open System Interconnection (OSI) Family of communications protocols and related abstract model (the OSI reference model) developed by the ISO, most of which are incompatible with the Internet protocols.

OpenSSL Collaborative project to develop a robust, commercial-grade, full-featured, and open source toolkit implementing the Secure Sockets Layer (SSL v2/v3) and Transport Layer Security (TLS v1) protocols as well as a full-strength general-purpose cryptography library.

Opera Popular Web browser from Opera Software; small, fast, and available for all major platforms including Windows, Solaris and LINUX.

output feedback (OFB) Block cipher mode in which the cipher is used to generate the key stream. Also called autokey mode.

packet In TCP/IP networks, term referring to the data passing between the Internet layer and the data link layer. Also a generic term used to refer to data transferred through a network.

passive attack Attack in which data is observed but not modified. This is the type of attack performed by 'peeping'.

password Secret data item used to authenticate an entity. Passwords are often words that an individual is supposed to memorize; the system authenticates the person on the assumption that the password is known only by the person it belongs to.

password sniffing   Attack in which someone examines data traffic that includes secret passwords in order to recover the passwords, presumably to use them later in masquerades.

permutation cipher   Using re-ordering (i.e. permutation) of elements to perform encryption.

personal data assistant (PDA)   Handheld device that combines computing, telephone/fax, Internet and networking features.

Personal Web Server (PWS)   Web server software from Microsoft; used mainly on Windows 9x platforms.

PHP Hypertext Preprocessor (PHP)   Server side, HTML embedded scripting language used to create dynamic Web pages; has built-in support for database applications on the Web. By convention, PHP files end with .php as file extension.

plaintext   Data that has not been encrypted, or data that has been decrypted from ciphertext.

port number   Number carried in Internet transport protocols to identify which service or program is supposed to receive an incoming packet. Certain port numbers are permanently assigned to particular protocols by the IANA. For example, email generally uses port 25 and Web services traditionally use port 80.

Post Office Protocol (POP)   Internet protocol for retrieving email from a server host.

Practical Extraction and Report Language (Perl)   Programming language developed by Larry Wall; especially designed for processing text. Because of its strong text-processing abilities, Perl has become one of the most popular languages for writing CGI scripts. By convention, Perl files end with .pl as file extension.

Pretty Good privacy (PGP)   Method developed by Phil Zimmermann to encrypt or disguise computer information so that it can be securely transmitted over a network.

Privacy Enhanced Mail (PEM)   Email crypto protocol published by the IETF and provided in some commercial products; essentially superseded by PGP, MSP and S/MIME.

private-key (or secret-key)   The digital key to keep secret in a public-key encryption algorithm. See also public-key encryption.

protocol   Rules governing the behaviour or method of operations.

protocol suite   Collection of communications protocols that work together to provide useful services. There are two widely known protocol suites: the Internet protocols and the ISO/OSI protocols.

proxy   Facility that indirectly provides some service. Proxy crypto applies crypto services to network traffic without individual hosts having to support the services themselves. Firewall proxies provide access to Internet services that are on the other side of the firewall while controlling access to services in either direction.

pseudo random number generator (PRNG)   Procedure that generates a sequence of numerical values that appear random. Cryptographic PRNGs strive to generate sequences that are almost impossible to predict. Most PRNGs in commercial software are statistical PRNGs that strive to produce randomly distributed data whose sequence may in fact be somewhat predictable.

public-key-ring   Data structure that stores public-keys.

public-key   Key used in public-key encryption, and distributed publicly. Others can use the public-key to encrypt data that only the associated private-key can decrypt.

public-key cipher   *See* public-key encryption.

Public-Key Cryptography Standard # 12 (PKCS#12)   Standard format for the exchange of private data. Simplifies the process of transferring certificates and related private-keys from one machine to another in a secure manner.

Public-Key Cryptography Standards (PKCS)   Standards published by RSA Data Security that describe how to use public key crypto in a reliable, secure and interoperable fashion.

public-key encryption   Encryption technique using two digital keys: a public-key known to everyone and a private-key or secret-key to keep secret. When John wants to send a secure message to Mary, he uses Mary's public key to encrypt the message. Only Mary, or the owner of the corresponding private-key, can decrypt the message.

public-key infrastructure (PKI)   System of digital certificates, certification authorities and other registration authorities that verify and authenticate the validity of each party involved in an Internet transaction.

random number   Number whose value cannot be predicted. Truly random numbers are often generated by physical events that are believed to occur randomly.

replay attack   Attack that attempts to trick the system by retransmitting a legitimate message. Some protocols include anti-replay mechanisms to detect and reject such attacks.

Request For Comments (RFC)   Publications from the Internet Engineering Task Force (IETF) that detail the Internet's standards.

reusable password   Password that can be used over and over again, as opposed to a one-time password. Most passwords used today are reusable passwords.

rewrite attack   Attack that modifies an encrypted message's contents without decrypting it first.

Rijndael algorithm   Rijndael encryption is the winner of the AES competition and officially called AES.

Rivest Cipher #4 (RC4)   Stream cipher developed by Ron Rivest and used in many commercial products.

Rivest Cipher #6 (RC6)   Symmetric-key block cipher developed by Ron Rivest as a candidate for the AES competition.

Rivest, Shamir, Adelman (RSA)   Public key crypto system that can encrypt or decrypt data and also apply or verify a digital signature.

router   Device that connects LANs into the Internet and routes traffic between them.

RSA algorithm   Widely used public-key encryption scheme developed by Rivest, Shamir and Adelman (RSA).

RSA digital signature   Use of the RSA algorithm for digital signature.

script   Similar to a macro or batch file; a list of commands or simple functions that can be executed without user interaction. Scripts are popular on the Web to create dynamic features. *See also* client script and server script.

secret-key   *See* private-key.

secret-key ring   Data structure for storing secret-keys (or private-keys).

secure electronic transfer (SET)   Standard used by major credit companies to set up secure credit card transactions on the Internet. SET allows your credit card number go direct to the credit card company without being seen by the merchant.

secure email   Use of encryption to maintain the security of email messages.

Secure Hash Algorithm #1 (SHA-1)   Also known as FIPS 180-1; produces a 160-bit digest from a message with a maximum size of 264 bits.

secure hash algorithm (SHA)   Family of algorithms to produce hash values for security purposes.

Secure Multipart Internet Message Extensions (S/MIME)   Proposed protocol for embedding crypto-protected messages in Internet email.

secure site   Web site with SSL security; can usually be accessed by the HTTPS protocol.

Security Socket Layers (SSL)   Protocol developed by Netscape to set up public-key cryptography-type connection on the Web. SSL allows a Web browser to locate and display a Web page in secure mode. The Web browser and server, in this case, are performing encryption/decryption using public-key technologies online.

seed   Random data value used when generating a random sequence of data values with a PRNG.

server   Computer or device on a network that manages network resources. Usually, servers are set up on a network to provide services to clients. *See also* file server, database server and web server.

server script   Script to be run by server. Most server scripts are CGI script, used to generate HTML/XHTML documents and return to browser. Perl, ASP and PHP are languages that can be used to write server scripts.

session key   Crypto key intended to encrypt data for a limited period of time, typically only for a single communications session between a pair of entities. Once the session is over, the key will be discarded and a new one established when a new session takes place. Also called a data key.

shuffle technique   Process that randomizes a given set of data; comparable to shuffling a deck of playing cards.

Simple Mail Transfer Protocol (SMTP)   Protocol for sending Email messages between servers. Most email systems that send mail over the Internet use SMTP to send messages from one server to another.

snake oil   Derogatory term applied to a product whose developers describe it with misleading, inconsistent, or incorrect technical statements.

sniffing   Attack that collects information from network messages by making copies of their contents. Password sniffing is the most widely publicized example.

Software-optimised Encryption Algorithm #2 (SEAL2)   Stream cipher designed by Rogaway and Coppersmith.

stream cipher   Cipher that operates on a continuous data stream instead of processing a block of data at a time.

substitution cipher   Encryption using symbolic substitution.

symmetric-key encryption   Encryption algorithm that uses the same key for encrypting and decrypting. Symmetric-key algorithm is also called secret-key algorithm.

synchronous   Describes the transfer of data between two devices on a network at a timed rate (as opposed to asynchronous).

TCP/IP network   Network using TCP and IP protocols. TCP protocol guarantees data transmission; IP protocol deals with packets and address. TCP/IP networks are generally called the Internet.

traffic   General term used to describe the amount of data on a network.

Transmission Control Protocol (TCP)   One of the main protocols in TCP/IP networks. Enables two hosts to establish a connection and exchange data. TCP guarantees delivery of data and also guarantees that packets will be delivered in the same order in which they were sent. Data will be re-transmitted if necessary.

Transport Layer Security (TLS)   An extension of SSL; based on Netscape's SSL 3.0.

transposition cipher   Special permutation cipher in which the permutation is simply the exchange of two elements.

Triple Date Encryption Standard (Tri-DES or 3DES)   Cipher that applies the DES cipher three times with either two or three different DES keys.

trojan horse   Program with secret functions; surreptitiously accesses information without the operator's knowledge, usually to circumvent security protections.

Twofish   Encryption algorithm designed by Bruce Schneier as a candidate for the AES competition.

unconditionally secure cipher   Encryption that cannot be decrypted by brute-force attack.

Unicode   Universal character encoding, maintained by the Unicode Consortium (http://www.unicode.org/). An encoding standard for processing, storage and interchange of text data in any language in all modern software and information technology protocols.

uniform resource identifier (URI)   Generic term for all types of global name and address that refer to objects on the Web. The uniform resource locator (URL) is one kind of URI.

uniform resource locator (URL)   Global address of documents and other resources on the Web. For example, http://www.pws-ex.com/ex01-01.htm and ftp://www.pws-ex.com/ex01-01.htm are two URLs to identify the same file on the Web.

UNIX   Operating system written by Ken Thompson of Bell Labs and used for mainframes and minicomputers. Now available on personal computers (PCs).

user agent   Device that interprets HTML or other Web documents. The most commonly used User Agents are Web browsers on computer screens.

VENONA   US military project to crypto-analyze Soviet one-time-pad ciphertext from the 1940s.

Vernam cipher   Cipher developed for encrypting teletype traffic by computing the exclusive-or (XOR) of the data bits and the key bits. This is a common approach for constructing stream ciphers.

virus   Small program that attaches itself to a legitimate program. When the legitimate program runs, the virus copies itself onto other legitimate programs in a form of reproduction.

Web Community of Internet servers that support HTML/XHTML formatted documents. The documents or Web pages support a feature that links to other documents, as well as graphics, audio, and video files.

Web browser Software application used to locate and display Web pages on the Internet.

Web client Computer or device running a Web browser to request network resources.

Web page Document on the Web. Every Web page is identified by a unique address called a uniform resource locator (URL).

Web server Machine running Web server software such as Apache or IIS, assigned an IP address, and connected to the Internet so that it can provide documents on the Web. Sometimes called a host computer.

Web site Web server with a global unique URL.

Web site address The IP address (such as 165.181.109.11) of the host computer, or the name (such as www.pws-ex.com) that can be translated into an IP address.

wide area network (WAN) Network that connects host computers and sites across a wide geographical area.

work factor The amount of work an attacker must perform to overcome security measures.

World Wide Web (WWW or Web) *See* Web.

World Wide Web Consortium (W3C) An international consortium of companies to set standards on the Web; founded by Tim Berners-Lee in 1994.

worm Computer program that copies itself into other host computers across a network. In 1988 the Internet Worm infected several thousand hosts.

XML digital contract Represents a digital contract with XML pages (*see also* digital contract).

XML encryption and decryption Performing encryption or decryption and representing the results as XML pages.

XML Security Library (XMLSEC) Collection of C functions or libraries to provide encryption and digital signature including signing and verifying functionalities for XML pages conforming to the W3C recommendations.

Index

ciphers 76
  binary additive stream 308
  computationally secure 76
  conditionally secure 76–7
  Feistel ciphers 224, 391
  one-way 77, 308
  public-key 77
  self-synchronising stream 308–9
  substitution 78
  transposition 79
  unconditionally secure 76
  see also block ciphers; stream ciphers;
    symmetric-key ciphers
ciphertext 76, 146
clearsigned documents in GnuPG 673–4
click-through agreements 749
clients 8–9
Common Gateway Interface (CGI)
    507–10
  and preprocessors 510–16
    in Perl 511–13
    in PHP 513–16
  server storage for 527–46
computationally secure ciphers 76
conditionally secure ciphers 76–7
confidentiality in cryptography 4
contracts *see* digital contracts
cookies, and security 498–505
Coppersmith, D. 226, 374
`crypt()` authentication scheme 82–3
Crypt() in one-way encryption 171–3
  implementation of 173–6
crypto-analysis 78, 80
crypto-attacks 77–8
cryptographically secure pseudo-random bit
    generator (CSPRBG) 341
  big numbers, implementation on
    343–50
  blum-blum-shub CSPRBG 343
  quadratic residue CSPRBG 343
  randomness tests 341–2
cryptography: objectives 4
cryptology
  definition 75–8
  overview 75–81

CSPRBG (cryptographically secure
    pseudo-random bit generator) 341–3
'cut and join' attack 81

Daemen, Joan 443
Data Encryption Standard (DES) 81, 82
  and AES 442–3
  and brute-force attacks 115–17
  decryption in 169–71
  and one-way functions 147
    bit selection tables 151
    encrypting plaintext 150
    expansion tables 151
    iteration formula 150–5
    permuted choice tables 148
    shift tables 148–9
    step-by-step scheme 147–55
    16 subkeys for 148–9
  optimization of 233–55
    and block effect 260–7, 268
    double DES 267–71
    Meet-in-the-Middle attacks 267–71
    optimized encryption/decryption
      247–51
    optimized page 256–60
    permutation sequences for table lookup
      240–7
    process 233–4
    subkeys, seting up and scheduling
      251–5
    Table P and S boxes in 234–40
  single scheme 156–76
    on 64-bits of data 160–9
    decryption 169–71
    sub-keys 156–60
    table lookup techniques 156–60
data integrity 4
  in ElGamal public-key algorithm 598–600
  in public-key encryption 569–71
database
  Apache, basic authentication with 95–100
  DBM files, authentication using 95–100
  MySQL, password accounts
    new, adding 557–62
    updating and changing 562–7

documents, signing in GnuPG 670–5
  in binary form 671–3
  clearsigned 673–4
  detached signatures 674–5
double DES 267–71
  scheme 270

'E-sign' law (USA) 748
ECMAScript (European Computer
      Manufacturers Association) 18–19
  bitwise operators in 40
  and one-way encryption 158–60
Electronic codebook (ECB) cipher mode 227
  in CAST-128 algorithm 301–3
ElGamal, Taher 584
ElGamal public-key algorithm 584–605
  data integrity 598–600
  digital signatures 598–600
    implementation 600–5
    verification 604–5
  encryption/decryption with APM 586–90
  example 584–6
  implementation 590–8
ElGamal subordinate keys 662
elliptic curves 633–54
  adding points on 635–6, 638–43
  definition 633–6
  elliptic curve cryptography (ECC) 636–8
    encryption/decryption 649–54
    public and secret keys, generating 637,
      643–8
  scalar multiplication on 635–6, 643–8
emails
  in GnuPG
    encrypted emails 719–31
    using Perl 710–16
    signing 704–9
    using SMTP 716–19
  Perl, encrypted emails in 719–26
  in PHP 726–31
embedded preprocessors 510
encryption 2, 76
  in AES 445–8
    optimization of 459–71
    with RSA 626–32

in ARC4 353–61
with bitwise operators 41–6
in Blowfish 393–4, 406
  web page for 398–405
in CAST-128
  algorithm for 283
  with CCB 302, 304
  with ECB 302–3
  operation modes 298–305
  tools 292–305
in ECC 649–54
ElGamal public-key algorithm
  with APM 586–90
  example 584–6
  implementation 590–8
on elliptic curves 638, 648–54
using GnuPG 668–70
in ISAAC 366–73
OFB mode 310–13
one-way 83
  in single scheme DES 171–3
in OpenSSL 766–73
page of one-time pad 320–7
on PkZip and WinZip 64–6
in RC6 421–3
  web page for 424–31, 434
in RSA 147, 607
  with AES 626–32
  message encryption 614–20
for Web Page protection 478–82
  generating 483–6
in WinPT 691–9
  in clipboard 693–7
  in current window 697–9
  using file manager 691–3
in XML 832–9
XOR 54–6
  bitwise 58
  implementation 56–64
  see also Advanced Encryption Standard;
      Data Encryption Standard
Entrust 225
expansion tables in DES 151
Extensible Hypertext Mark-up Language
      (XHTML) 14–16

Internet Explorer 5
  brute-force key-space scheme 120, 125, 130
  digest passwords on 113–14
  importing certificates into 784–92
  password authentication 90–1
  password displays 86
Internet Information Service (IIS) 8
ISAAC (indirection, shift, accumulate, add and count) 361–6
  implementations 366–73
iteration formula in DES 150–5
iterative functions in CAST-128 283–4

JavaScript 18
Javascript Chaos Engine 488–9
Jenkins, Robert 362

Karn, Phil 251
Katz, Phil 64
Kelsey, John 443
Kerchkoff's principle 76
key-code 115
key distribution 224
  and public-key encryption 568–9
key length 116, 224–5, 260
key schedule in CAST-128 284–5
key sizes in CAST-128 285–6
key-space 116
  of brute-force attacks 117–20
key stream in stream ciphers 307, 308
  in RC4 352
  in SEAL2 376
keys 76
known plaintext attack methods 72, 74
Knudsen, Lars 443
Koblitz, Neal 633
Kocher, Paul 407

Lai, X. 225
licencing Web Pages 492–8
linear congruent algorithms in RNG 336–41
  in PRNG 336
linear feedback shift register (LFSR) 334–6

LINUX systems
  CGI technology on 508–9
  MySQL on 547
  and OpenSSL
    installing 756–8
    integrating with Apache 797–802
  password files 105
  user authentication in 87–9
little-endian machines 392
long-run tests in FIPS 140 342
lookup tables
  in AES 454–8
  in DES 240–7
Lucifer algorithm 82

magic numbers of RC6 435–41
Man-in-the Middle (MITM) attacks 78
MARS 443
Martin, I. 353, 355
Massey, J. 225
mathematics
  arbitrary precision mathematics (APM) 575–9
  used by AES 443–5
Mauborgne, J. 314
MD5 see message digest (MD)
Meet-in-the-Middle attacks 267–71
message digest (MD) 103, 178
  applications 193–208
    checksum and document signatures 193–5
    md5Crypt password algorithm 197–200
    passwords, UNIX and Apache 201–8
    viruses and alteration, protection against 195–7
  128-bit algorithm (MD5) 178–81, 627
    defining data and functions 179–80
    message processing 180–1
    padding bits and length 178–9
    passwords
      algorithm for 197–200
      brute-force attack on 138–45
      computing string 199
      formatting string 200
      input/output 198

message digest (MD) (*continued*)
    and one-way functions 147
    for UNIX and Apache 201–8
    utility, building 189–92
    web implementation 181–9
  in OpenSSL, generating 763–6
  and SHA 209
message processing in MD 180–1
messages, numerical representation of 31–4
Microsoft Script Encoder 487
Microsoft Windows 547
  password files 105
Miller, K. 338, 340
Miller, Victor 633
Mod_SSL
  integrating OpenSSL with Apache 797–802
    configuring 801
    SSL-aware Apache 801–2
mono-bit tests in FIPS 140 341
Moor's law 78
Morris, Robert 171
Multiple Internet Mail Extension (MIME)
  format 732–6
    of attachments 733–4
    of binary files 734–6
    of email 732–3
multiplication modulo 572
Multipurpose Internet Mail Extension
    (MIME) 11
MySQL
  driver configuration 555
  encrypted password table in 547–51
  installation 552–3
  new password accounts
    adding to database 557–62
    handling 547–67
    updating and changing 562–7
  user authentication using 551–7

National Institute of Standards and
    Technology (NIST) 82, 209
National Security Agency (NSA) 209
Netscape 7 5
  brute-force key-space scheme 120, 125, 130
  password authentication 91

network security 1–3
no-collision hash functions 177
non-embedded preprocessors 510
non-repudiation 4
  in public-key encryption 569–71
nonce 103, 110–11
NOT operator 40
number systems on Web 17–19
numerical representation of messages
    31–4

Obfuscation 487–90
one-time pad 64, 314–33
  and brute-force attacks 314–15
  encryption/decryption of page 320–7
  generating 316–20
  probabilities in 314
  pseudo-random number generator in
    316
  random number generator in 316–20
  web applications 328–33
one-way ciphers 77, 308
one-way encryption 83
  in single scheme DES 171–3
one-way functions 146–55
  in DES 147
    16 subkeys for 148–9
    bit selection tables 151
    encrypting plaintext 150
    expansion tables 151
    iteration formula 150–5
    permuted choice tables 148
    shift tables 148–9
    step-by-step scheme 147–55
  and hash functions 177–8
  and passwords 146–7
one-way hash functions 177–8
Open Database Connectivity (ODBC)
    551–7
  driver for 553
  installation 553
Open Pretty Good Privacy (OpenPGP) 571,
    584
  description of 655–6
  standardization of 656

Perl (*continued*)
  passwords
    new accounts 540–2
    user authentication using 533–6
    verifying in 519–24
  preprocessor in 511–13
  secure attachments using 736–43
  secure email with GnuPG 710–12
    encrypted emails 719–26
    sending 712–16
  user authentication using password files
    533–6
permutation encryption 79
permutation sequences in DES 240–7
permuted choice tables in DES 148
PHP 181, 506
  in CGI 510–16
  database configuration 555–6
  emailing with 726–7
  encrypted emails with 727–31
  file access using 530–3
    modes 532
  passwords
    new accounts 542–6
    user authentication using 536–9
    verifying in 524–6
  preprocessor in 513–16
  secure attachments using 743–7
  user authentication using 551
pi, in Blowfish 390
  generating any digit of 411–20
PKCS#12 certificate format 782–4
PkZip
  encryption/decryption on 64–74
  implementation 66–74
  password window 65
  as stream cipher 225, 306
poker test in FIPS 140 341
position updating attack 126–31
'Pretty Good Privacy' (PGP) 225, 282, 571
  description of 655–6
  and US export law 656–7
prime factorization attacks 608–9
prime numbers 146–7

private networks 1
pseudo-random number generator (PRNG) 308
  in ISAAC 361–6
  linear congruent algorithms in 336
  in one-time pads 316
  in RC4 351
pseudo-random sequences 69
public-key ciphers 77
public-key encryption
  data integrity in 569–71
  in Diffie–Hellman key exchange 577
  in elliptic curve cryptography 637
  elliptic curves in 633–54
    adding points on 635–6, 638–43
    definition 633–6
  in GnuPG
    exporting 664–5
    generating and handling 660–4
    importing 665–8
    in WinPT 682–7
  and key distribution 568–9
  in RSA 606–7, 608–14
  security with 568–71
public-key information 607

quadratic residue CSPRBG 343
quotient and remainder attack 121–6

radio buttons, using 41–5
random hash functions 177
random number generator (RNG) 307
  in one-time pads 316–20
  techniques 334–50
    big numbers, implementation on 343–50
    linear congruent algorithms 336–41
    linear feedback shift register 334–6
    randomness tests 341–3
    shuffle algorithm 340–1
raw key 272
RC4
  algorithm 226, 351–3
    implementation of 353–61
    as stream cipher 307–8
  encrypting scheme 491–2

server technologies 506–26
  introduction to 506–10
  and passwords 516–26
    passing to servers 516–19
    verifying in Perl 519–24
    verifying in PHP 524–6
  and preprocessors 510–16
servers 8–9
  dialogs 9–12
  storage and security 527–46
Shamir, A. 353, 355, 606
shared key encryption in Diffie–Hellman key
    exchange 579
shift operators 40
shift register in RNG 335
shift tables in DES 148–9
shuffle algorithm in RNG 340–1
signatures *see* digital signatures
signing certificates 749–51
  signing with OpenSSL 779–82
signing documents
  in GnuPG 670–5
    in binary form 671–3
    clearsigned 673–4
    detached signatures 674–5
signing of emails 704–9
Simple Mail Transfer Protocol (SMTP) 712
  sending email with 716–19
small devices, block ciphers in 390–1
software-optimized encryption algorithm
    (SEAL2) 374–89
  utility, building 386–9
  web implementation 378–86
Software-optimized Encryption Standard
    (SEAL) 226
Solaris 547
SP-boxes 234–40, 247–8
SSL-aware Apache 801–2
state table in RC4 351, 362
stream ciphers 224–6, 306–13
  using block ciphers in 308–10
  characteristics of 306–8
  cipher feedback mode in 308–9
  output feedback mode as 310–13
strong cryptography 4

Structured Query Language (SQL) 547
subBytes table in RC6 447, 450
subkeys
  in AES 452–3
  for Blowfish 396–7, 411
  for DES 148–9
    setting up and scheduling 251–5
    and table lookup techniques 156–60
substitution ciphers 78
substitution-permutation network in
    Blowfish 391
symbolic substitution encryption 78
symmetric-key ciphers 77
  introduction to 224–6
  operation modes 227–32
symmetric-key encryption 54
  in GnuPG 670
synchronising stream ciphers 308
  implementation 311–13
  OFB mode as 310

Table E in DES 247
tables
  lookup
    in AES 454–8
    in DES 240–7
  in MySQL 549–50
Tavares, Stafford 225, 282
Thompson, Ken 171
Transport Socket Layer (TSL) 752
transposition ciphers 79
Tri-DES procedure 155
Tri-DES scheme 232
Triple Data Encryption Standard (Tri-DES)
    225, 226
  CSPRBG in 342
  implementation of 271–6
    with one key 275
  utility, building 276–81
Twofish 226, 443

unconditionally secure ciphers 76
Unicode 24–31
  and ASCII 25
  characters 25–6

X509 certificate format 782–4
XML
    contracts 842–8
    encryption/decryption 832–9
    introduction to 818–21
    and OpenSSL 830–2
    using parser 827–30
    security library 830–2
    signatures 839–42
    using XSLT 821–30

XML Style Sheet Language Transformation
    (XSLT) 821–30
XOR encryption/decryption 54–6
    bitwise decryption 59–61
    bitwise encryption 58
    implementation on Web 56–64
XOR operator 40

Young, Eric 234, 243

Zimmermann, Philip 656–7